UNDERSTANDING TORTS

John L. Diamond

University of California,
Hastings College of the Law

Lawrence C. Levine

University of the Pacific,
McGeorge School of Law

M. Stuart Madden

James D. Hopkins Professor
Pace University School of Law

LEGAL TEXT SERIES

1996

MATTHEW BENDER

(Matthew Bender & Co., Inc.) (Pub.582)

QUESTIONS ABOUT THIS PUBLICATION?

For questions about the **Editorial Content** or reprint permission, please call:

Mark Wasserman, J.D. .... (800) 924-0651 (ext. 270)
Outside the United States and Canada please call .... (212) 967-7707

For assistance with shipments, billing or other customer service matters, please call:

Customer Services Department at .... (800) 533-1646
Outside the United States and Canada, please call .... (518) 487-3000
Fax number .... (518) 487-3584

LIBRARY OF CONGRESS CATALOGING IN PUBLICATION DATA

Diamond, John L.
Understanding Torts / John L. Diamond, Lawrence C. Levine, M. Stuart Madden.
p. cm. — (Legal text series)
Includes index.
ISBN 0-8205-2486-7 (softcover)
1. Torts—United States. I. Levine, Lawrence C. II. Madden, M. Stuart, 1948- . III. Title. IV. Series.
KF1250.D5 1996
346.7303—dc20
[347.3063]
96-21224
CIP

MATTHEW BENDER

MATTHEW BENDER & CO., INC.
Editorial Offices
11 Penn Plaza, New York, NY 10001-2006 (212) 967-7707
2101 Webster St., Oakland, CA 94612-3027 (510) 446-7100

JLD: With love to my wife, Lucia, my son, Danny, and to my parents, Rhoda and Monroe Thomas Diamond

LCL: With love to my parents, Lois and Gerald Levine

MSM: To Mary-Anne, for her love and support, and to Christopher and Michael, and for my brother Michael

PREFACE

This book examines the common law of torts. A tort is a civil wrong beyond a breach of contract for which the law provides redress.[1] These tortious wrongs can take various forms, such as personal injury or death, harm to property, or interference with other protectable interests such as the right to be free from unwarranted invasions of privacy. Although state and federal statutes define some facets of tort law, by and large contemporary tort law remains defined by judicial decisions. Tort law, then, provides an excellent vehicle for viewing the dynamic nature of the common law, and for observing how a given body of law, with its often complex rules, has evolved into what it is today.

Writing first and foremost for law students, we have endeavored to provide a readable and concise treatise without oversimplifying the rules or the policy considerations that affect those rules. We examine the key topics covered in virtually any Torts course—intentional torts and privileges, negligence, strict liability, and products liability. We also explore other important areas—damages, joint and several liabili ty, nuisance, economic torts, misuse of legal process, defamation and privacy.[2] Where appropriate, we cover contemporary developments in the law of torts, such as current efforts to redefine the scope of strict products liability and the modern treatment of intentional infliction of emotional distress. We have provided primary and secondary authority to support our textual analyses without overburdening the reader with excessive footnotes.

Central to the study of tort law is the fundamental question of the purposes to be served by the imposition of liability on wrongdoers (tortfeasors). The contours of the tort system reflect broad policy concerns and often conflicting goals on a larger societal basis. The system is pervasive and raises the threshold issue of how the legal system should compensate, if at all, those who suffer injury at the hands of another. A cornerstone of the debate involves the extent to which tort liability should rest on fault, as opposed to strict liability. Resolution of this central issue depends upon one's perspective of the goal of tort liability. For example, the tort system could rely primarily on notions of corrective justice, seeking to right a wrong perpetrated on a specific individual. Alternatively, a utilitarian approach could be adopted instead that would seek to effect the greatest good for society as a whole. Or economic efficiency could serve as the driving force of the tort system. All these models, and more, are represented in American tort law and we have presented them as appropriate in the text. Our goal in so doing has not been to resolve the

1 The law of torts focuses on private rights of redress. The aggrieved party sues in tort to recover damages for the harm caused her by the defendant. Contrast this to the criminal law where a State, through government-employed prosecutors, pursues the action and exacts the punishment.

2 Because of space limitations, we have not undertaken discussion of alternative approaches to liability for accidents, such as workers' compensation or no-fault insurance.

debate about the proper justifications for the tort system, but to illuminate the divergent, and often complex, policy issues confronting courts and legislatures as they seek to fine tune, or even substantially alter, the tort system.

We have organized this treatise in a traditional format that is consistent with the way Torts is taught in most American law schools. We begin with an examination of intentional torts and privileges and turn next to negligence. Later chapters consider areas of strict liability, and other torts such as nuisance, misrepresentation, and defamation. The one organizational change that is not necessarily typical is that we have placed several topics, such as causation and defenses, after the chapters dealing with types of liability.

At times, we have had occasion to refer to Restatements of the law. Because most references are to the Restatement (Second) of Torts, we have adopted the simpler appellation "Restatement" for those references.

Tort law has been undergoing unprecedented scrutiny in the last decade. Within the legal community and in the public at large, there has been a growing sense that the civil litigation system generally, and personal injury law specifically, merit retooling and even wholesale restructuring. As the Twenty-first Century approaches, we will probably witness substantial changes in the law of torts. As we write, movements to limit punitive damages and to substitute various types of no-fault compensation systems for tort liability are alive and well. In addition to helping readers understand the existing torts system, this text provides the basis from which an evaluation of the current torts system can be made with an eye toward understanding future developments.

ACKNOWLEDGMENTS

Each of us has many people to thank for making this book a reality. Each of us is grateful to Clark Kimball, our editor, and the editorial, composition and production staffs at Matthew Bender for their faith, assistance and patience.

Professor Diamond expresses appreciation for the outstanding research and other assistance provided by Anthony P. Canini, Steven J. Dow, Geoff S. Long, Amy B. Lovell, Vincent Moyer, Martin L. Pitha, Barbara A. Topchov, Lucia M. Walters, and Linda Weir. He would also like to express gratitude for the continuing insights provided by his colleagues in torts at the University of California, Hastings College of the Law: Professors Margreth Barrett, Marsha N. Cohen, David J. Jung, David I. Levine, Leo J. O'Brien, Naomi Roht-Arriaza, Joseph Modeste Sweeney, and Francis R. Walsh. In addition, Professor Diamond expresses heartfelt appreciation to his tort students who share the adventure of torts with him and teach him so much along the way.

Professor Levine is indebted to his colleague and friend, Julie Davies, for her extraordinarily generous and helpful assistance with this project. Outstanding research assistance was provided by McGeorge law students: Linda Yackzan Mills, John Bachman, and James McGuire, while invaluable secretarial assistance was supplied by Pauline Rodriguez. McGeorge School of Law provided much-appreciated financial support for this project. Most importantly, Professor Levine expresses his enormous gratitude to his students for teaching him so much.

Professor Madden extends his appreciation to the research and financial support of Pace University School of Law. Special thanks are due to Dean Richard L. Ottinger, Professor and Law Librarian Nicholas Triffin, and his able research assistants Kimberly L. Weston and Matthew N. Ross.

We welcome your suggestions, thoughts, comments and criticisms. While this was a collaborative effort with each of us working on the entire book, to facilitate feedback, note that Chapters 1, 2, 11-15, 19, 20 and 22 were the primary responsibility of John Diamond, Chapters 3-10 and Chapter 21 were Lawrence Levine's primary responsibility, and Stuart Madden was primarily responsible for Chapters 16-18.

John L. Diamond
Lawrence C. Levine
M. Stuart Madden

TABLE OF CONTENTS

PART A. INTENTIONAL TORTS AND PRIVILEGES

Page

Chapter 1. INTENTIONAL INTERFERENCES WITH PERSONS AND PROPERTY

Page

Chapter 2. PRIVILEGES TO INTENTIONAL TORTS

Page

PART B. NEGLIGENCE

Chapter 3. THE NEGLIGENCE CONCEPT AND THE REASONABLE PERSON STANDARD OF CARE

Chapter 4. THE DETERMINATION OF UNREASONABLENESS: BREACH OF DUTY, CUSTOM AND THE ROLE OF THE JURY

Chapter 5. PROOF OF BREACH

Page

Chapter 6. STATUTORY STANDARDS OF CARE — "NEGLIGENCE PER SE"

Chapter 7. PROFESSIONAL NEGLIGENCE

Chapter 8. DUTY IN NEGLIGENCE CASES

Page

Chapter 9. LAND OCCUPIER DUTY

Chapter 10. DUTY LIMITED BY KIND OF HARM

PART C. GENERAL CONCEPTS

Chapter 11. CAUSE-IN-FACT

Page

Chapter 12. PROXIMATE OR LEGAL CAUSE

Chapter 13. JOINT & SEVERAL LIABILITY

Chapter 14. DAMAGES

Chapter 15. DEFENSES

Page

PART D. LIABILITY WITHOUT FAULT AND PRODUCTS LIABILITY

Chapter 16. STRICT LIABILITY

Page

CHAPTER 17. PRODUCTS LIABILITY

Page

PART E. OTHER TORTS

Chapter 18. NUISANCE

Page

Chapter 19. ECONOMIC TORTS

Page

Chapter 22. INVASION OF PRIVACY

CHAPTER 1

INTENTIONAL INTERFERENCES WITH PERSONS AND PROPERTY

SYNOPSIS

§ 1.01 INTENT

[A] *Overview and Definition*

Intentional torts share the requirement that the defendant intentionally commit the elements that define the tort.[1] Intent is a term of art. Most contemporary courts adhere to the Restatement definition, which defines intent to mean either that the defendant desires the result *or* knows to a substantial certainty that it will occur.[2] The definition is in the alternative and is subjective. The defendant must, in her mind, exhibit desire or substantial certainty. The fact that a reasonable person would have been substantially certain is not dispositive, but only evidentiary in determining whether the defendant actually had the requisite mental state.

[B] *Intent as "Desire"*

Intent is satisfied if the defendant desires the consequences of her acts. This becomes legally relevant if those desired consequences constitute a tort.[3] For example, if A desires to pick up a concrete block and then inadvertently drops it on B's foot, A has not desired to cause harmful or offensive contact on B, and therefore is not liable for intentional battery.[4] The injury is unintentional, and any potential liability depends on proving negligence. In many instances, A will not confess to having desired consequences resulting in a tort. In those cases, the finder of fact must consider whether circumstantial evidence justifies concluding that A desired the tort. For example, if A loads a gun and then shoots directly at B, the court will almost inevitably conclude that A desired to cause B consequences which constitute battery. However, the test is subjective, meaning that the court must conclude that A in her own mind did in fact desire consequences constituting the tort.

[C] *Intent as "Substantial Certainty"*

Intent is usually also satisfied when the defendant is substantially certain that her acts will cause the elements of the tort to occur. If A blows up a stagecoach, knowing B is on the coach, A has intentionally injured B, even if A had no desire to injure B.[5] The substantial certainty test is

---

[1] *See generally* David J. Jung & David I. Levine, *Whence Knowledge Intent? Whither Knowledge Intent?*, 20 U.C. Davis L. Rev. 551 (1987); Richard A. Posner, ECONOMIC ANALYSIS OF LAW § 6.15 (4th Ed. 1992); William L. Prosser, *Transferred Intent*, 45 Tex. L. Rev. 650 (1967).

[2] Restatement § 8A.

[3] *See* Lambertson v. United States, 528 F.2d 441 (2d Cir. 1976) (intent to cause contact constituted a battery and not negligence).

[4] *See* § 1.02, *infra*, for definition of battery.

[5] *Cf.* Garratt v. Dailey, 279 P.2d 1091 (Wash. 1955), where the court remanded to the trial court the issue of whether a five-year-old boy was substantially certain the victim would fall while attempting to sit on a chair the boy had moved.

subjective. The defendant must actually in her own mind know the results that constitute the tort will occur.

Substantial certainty should not be confused with reckless conduct. The defendant is reckless when she takes a substantial, unreasonable risk that the elements of the tort will occur, such as when A drives at a very excessive speed, risking a collision. Intentional conduct requires a showing that the actor either desires or *knows* with substantial certainty the tortious result will occur as a result of her conduct.

[D] *Transferred Intent*

Historically, the transferred intent doctrine has been applied to five intentional torts.[6] The five torts are battery, assault, false imprisonment, trespass to chattel, and trespass to land. Under transferred intent, if the defendant intends any of these five torts, but her acts, instead or in addition, result in any of the other five intentional torts, the defendant is liable, even though she did not intend the other tort. For example, if A intends to assault B, but accidentally commits battery against B or another party C, A is liable for the battery.[7] As the example illustrates, not only does the intent to commit one tort satisfy the intent requirement for the other tort, but the intent to commit a tort against one victim can transfer to any other victim.[8]

The transferred intent rule may have emerged because these five torts were historically associated with a single action for trespass. The concept of trespass was not limited to the contemporary meaning of trespass to land, but embodied many types of direct injuries. It is important, consequently, to recognize that courts have applied the concept only to these five intentional torts.[9]

The Restatement does not adopt transferred intent generally. It does accept, however, transferred intent between battery and assault. The Restatement allows the intent to commit a battery or assault to satisfy the requisite intent required under the definitions for both torts.[10]

Transferred intent can be criticized for blurring the concept of intent. The intent to injure property is very different from the intent to injure a person, and yet the doctrine permits the intent requirement of one to satisfy the intent requirement of the other. The concept of transferred intent also can

---

[6] *See* William L. Prosser, *Transferred Intent*, 45 Tex. L. Rev. 650 (1967).

[7] *See* Etcher v. Blitch, 381 So. 2d 1119 (Fla. Ct. App. 1979), where defendant intended to frighten the plaintiff by shooting at him, but the bullet, in fact, struck the plaintiff.

[8] *See* Talmage v. Smith, 59 N.W. 656 (Mich. 1894). *See also* Manning v. Grimsley, 643 F.2d 20 (1st Cir. 1981), where a professional baseball player threw a ball into the crowd intending to hit a heckler, but instead struck another spectator.

[9] Transferred intent is not applicable even to other similar torts. For example, although conversion is very similar to trespass to chattel, transferred intent doesn't apply to conversion. *See* § 1.05[C], *infra*.

[10] *See* Restatement §§ 13, 21.

run counter to notions of proximate cause which, in negligence, generally impose liability only for foreseeable risks.[11] On the other hand, the intentional tortfeasor is arguably more deserving to bear the risk of a different kind of tortious injury than is an innocent victim.

[E] *The Mistake Doctrine*

Under the mistake doctrine, if a defendant intends to do acts which would constitute a tort, it is no defense that the defendant mistakes, even reasonably, the identity of the property or person he acts upon or believes incorrectly there is a privilege. If, for example, A shoots B's dog, reasonably believing it is a wolf, A is liable to B, assuming B has not wrongfully induced the mistake.[12] Similarly, if A enters B's land, believing reasonably it is A's land, A is liable to B for trespass to land.[13] So long as the defendant intends to enter the property, the fact that she mistook the identity of the property or other circumstances is irrelevant.

Courts have applied the mistake doctrine to a variety of intentional torts.[14] Nevertheless, in many instances actors benefit from specific privileges,[15] such as self-defense,[16] which protect the defendant from liability for reasonable mistakes, notwithstanding the mistake doctrine.

Is the mistake doctrine appropriate? While a principle applied to intentional torts, it effectively imposes strict liability on a defendant who interferes with another's property or person by mistaking the object's identity or other circumstances that would justify interference. From a moral perspective, the defendant may not be at fault. From a deterrent perspective, the mistake doctrine, by not exonerating reasonable mistakes, can excessively discourage reasonable risks by a potential defendant. On the other hand, in the context of property loss, the defendant might gain an unjust enrichment if she, for example, mistakenly consumes A's corn without having to compensate A. This may justify the use of the doctrine in the context of injury to or loss of property.

[F] *Insanity and Infancy*

Unlike in criminal law, neither insanity nor infancy are defenses for intentional torts.[17] However, intent is subjective and requires that the

---

11 For a discussion of proximate cause in the context of intentional torts, see § 12.01, *infra*.

12 *See* Ranson v. Kitner, 31 Ill. App. 241 (1889).

13 *See* Perry v. Jefferies, 39 S.E. 515 (S.C. 1901), where defendant was held liable for removing trees from the plaintiff's own land although defendant believed the land to be his own.

14 The Restatement specifically endorses the mistake doctrine in § 164 for trespass to land and in § 244 for trespass to chattel and conversion.

15 *See* Chapter 2, *infra*.

16 *See* § 2.02, *infra*.

17 *See* Curran, *Tort Liability of the Mentally Ill and Mentally Deficient*, 21 Ohio St. L.J. 52 (1960). *See also* McGuire v. Almy, 8 N.E.2d 760 (Mass. 1937) (insane person intended

defendant actually desires or be substantially certain the elements of the tort will occur. Consequently, if the defendant is extremely mentally impaired or very young, she may not actually possess the requisite intent. For example, if A, a one-year-old, pulls the trigger of a gun, she may intend to pull the trigger, but not intend a battery and for that reason not be liable. The child or the insane person need not, however, appreciate the significance or wrongness of their act. If a child knows an adult will fall when he pulls a chair from under her, he intends wrongful contact and consequently a battery, without the need to prove the child intended serious harm.[18]

From a moral perspective, it would appear questionable to impose liability on individuals too immature or mentally impaired to know right from wrong. On the other hand, the law of torts is not criminal law and does not condemn, but only shifts the economic burdens of loss. Should the victim bear the loss when the insane or juvenile defendant has assets to pay for the loss inflicted by their conduct? From an accident avoidance perspective, one can argue that liability encourages those responsible for preserving the insane or juvenile's assets to control the risks presented by such defendants. Such arguments, however, ignore the proposition that the guardians themselves may, in many instances, be personally liable for their negligent failure to adequately supervise juveniles or the insane.

§ 1.02 BATTERY

[A] *Overview and Definition*

Battery[19] occurs when the defendant's acts intentionally cause harmful or offensive contact with the victim's person.[20] Battery in tort law, unlike criminal law, is exclusively an intentional tort. Accidental contact, in contrast, must be analyzed under negligence or strict liability.

Battery has historically compensated not only harmful contact but also offensive contact. Hence, the tort from its earliest origin in English common law has recognized the validity of compensating psychological as well as physical injury. Indeed, by grouping offensive and harmful contact together as one tort, the tort declines to delineate what many even today would argue are at least two distinct kinds of wrongs.

---

harmful contact). For a discussion of the impact of insanity and infancy on negligence, see §§ 3.04 and 3.05.

[18] *See supra* note 5.

[19] *See generally* Charles E. Carpenter, *Intentional Invasion of Interest of Personality*, 13 Or. L. Rev. 227 (1934); Osborne M. Reynolds, Jr., *Tortious Battery: Is "I Didn't Mean Any Harm" Relevant?*, 37 Okla. L. Rev. 717 (1984).

[20] *See* Restatement §§ 13, 16, and 18.

[B] *Intent Requirement*

While battery requires intent, the prevailing tort definition does not require an intent to harm. It is only necessary that the defendant intend to cause either harmful or offensive contact. As the ancient case of *Cole v. Turner*[21] held, "the least touching of another in anger is battery." Once the defendant intends and accomplishes the offensive or harmful touching, she is responsible for harm caused by the battery even if minimal or no physical harm was actually intended. Consequently, where a school boy playfully but without privilege slightly kicks a classmate without intending harm, he is responsible for the unexpected serious illness which resulted.[22] Furthermore, where a physician performs a medical procedure without the patient's consent, thereby constituting a battery, regardless of her good intentions, she is responsible for all consequential harm even if the procedure was performed competently.[23]

The preceding illustrations demonstrate how, once the defendant has engaged in even a mere technical battery against the plaintiff, the risk of unforeseen harm arising from the battery is borne by the defendant.[24] Consequently, the defendant can be liable for far greater damages than she may have intended. Since battery is one of five intentional torts between which there is transferred intent,[25] the risk of unforeseen liability can be extended much further. If, for example, A intends to deface B's book (trespass to chattel) by throwing ink at it, but in the attempt inadvertently misses and hits either B or bystander C in the eye causing a serious injury, A is liable for the unintended battery against B or C.

[C] *Harmful or Offensive Contact*

Battery encompasses either harmful or offensive contact. As such, the tort compensates for psychological affronts where even trivial physical

---

[21] 90 Eng. Rep. 958 (Nisi Prius 1704).

[22] Vosburg v. Putney, 50 N.W. 403 (Wis. 1891). The touching must, however, be unlawful. In *Vosburg*, the kick was not in the context of athletic play, but during class period. *See* James A. Henderson, Jr., *Why Vosburg Comes First?*, 1992 Wis. L. Rev. 853. *See also* Lambertson v. United States, 528 F.2d 441 (2d Cir. 1976), where unconsented horseplay resulted in the victim being impaled on a meathook.

[23] *See* Mohr v. Williams, 104 N.W. 12 (Minn. 1905), where a physician operated on the patient's left ear when consent was only given for operating on the right ear. For a discussion contrasting unconsented medical procedures constituting battery with negligent informed consent, *see infra* § 7.03.

[24] Implicit in this liability, but generally not discussed by courts in the context of intentional torts, is when, if ever, rules requiring proximate causation limit liability, particularly for unexpected consequences. *See infra* § 12.01.

[25] The transferred intent doctrine historically transferred intent between battery, assault, false imprisonment, trespass to land, and trespass to chattel. The Restatement adopts transferred intent between battery and assault by defining the requisite intent for the two torts to include either the intent to commit a battery or assault. *See* Restatement §§ 13, 21. *See supra* § 1.01[D].

contact has occurred. The offensive contact need not even physically touch the body. In *Fisher v. Carrousel Motor Hotel, Inc.*,[26] plaintiff recovered for the aggressive and demeaning grabbing of a plate the plaintiff was holding.[27] The cause of action in battery clearly protects not only injurious physical intrusions, but personal autonomy as well.

There is no requirement that the victim be conscious of either the contact or its harmful or offensive nature at the time of the intrusion. Consequently, if A, without consent or privilege, kisses B while she is asleep, A is still liable for battery.[28] Where A imposes an offensive or harmful contact on B, motive is irrelevant. So long as society defines the contact as harmful or offensive, A is liable for battery.[29]

Suppose A, unlike an ordinary person, would be offended by a friendly pat on the back. If B innocently pats A's back, the requisite intent to cause offensive or harmful contact is missing and there should be no liability even if A does find the contact offensive. Suppose, however, B continues to pat A in a context that most people would not find offensive, but A does. Should B's knowledge of A's hypersensitivity to contact constitute a battery? The Restatement, in a caveat, declines to decide the question, and judicial authority is sparse and ambiguous.[30] If A's hypersensitivity would result in physical injury, the tort of battery would more likely provide protection. Where only psychological injury is claimed, perhaps the courts should look to the feasibility of acquiescing to the victim's demands. Was the contact difficult to avoid in a crowded elevator or merely gratuitous?

[D] *Causation*

The defendant's voluntary action must be the direct or indirect legal cause of the harmful or offensive contact.[31] However, defendant need not herself actually contact the victim. For example, if A intentionally hits B with a rock, A has committed battery.

---

[26] 424 S.W.2d 627 (Tex. 1967).

[27] The court concluded that "the intentional snatching of an object from one's hand is as clearly an offensive invasion of his person as would be an actual contact with the body." Fisher v. Carrousel Motor Hotel, Inc., 424 S.W.2d 627, 629 (Tex. 1967). The plaintiff, a black male, was an engineer for the National Aeronautics and Space Agency who had been invited to a business luncheon and was then denied service on account of his race.

[28] *See also* Doe v. Johnson, 817 F. Supp. 1382 (W.D. Mich. 1993), where the victim's consent to sexual intercourse did not preclude liability for battery where the defendant knowingly did not disclose risk of transmission of AIDS virus. In contrast, assault and, generally, false imprisonment require a victim's contemporaneous awareness of tort. *See infra* §§ 1.03[B][2] and 1.04[E], respectively.

[29] *See* Clayton v. New Dreamland Roller Skating Rink, Inc., 82 A.2d 458 (N.J. Super. Ct. App. Div. 1951), where the defendant's employees, over the victim's objections, attempted with the best of intentions to treat an arm injury.

[30] Restatement § 19.

[31] *See infra* §§ 11.01 and 12.01.

[E] *Policy Rationale*

Protection from unlawful contact readily appears a basic right worthy of recognition in tort law. Morally such affronts are difficult to justify. From a deterrent perspective, legal redress discourages wrongful contact and violent retaliation. The historic willingness of courts to compensate for merely offensive contacts represents an extremely early acknowledgment that psychological injury is worthy of compensation. Contemporary observers of tort law may be wary of extending compensation, however small, to trivial contacts. On the other hand, where a plaintiff's interest in vindication is sufficiently significant to justify the transactional costs of a lawsuit, the risk of alternative extralegal remedies may justify the tort remedy. For example, if A spits on B, the opportunity to sue for battery may discourage a more violent retaliation for B's psychological injury.

§ 1.03 ASSAULT

[A] *Overview*

The ancient tort of assault represents the still controversial recognition that pure psychological injury should be compensable.[32] The historic case of *I de S et Ux v. W de S*[33] allowed the husband (the wife had no legal standing) to recover from the defendant who wielded an axe at the plaintiff's wife. The court concluded that even though the wife was not physically touched, the attack had caused her harm, the fear of imminent physical injury. Given its groundbreaking foray into the concept of purely emotional injury, it is understandable that the tort of assault is construed very narrowly. Subsequent to this early recognition of a cause of action in assault, a variety of other torts now allow compensation for emotional harm. One question for contemporary students of the law is whether, and to what degree, the fetters on assault should be lifted. Alternatively, perhaps the development of tort compensation for psychological harm only demonstrates the risks of allowing any monetary redress for emotional harm.

[B] *Definition*

Assault occurs when the defendant's acts intentionally cause the victim's reasonable apprehension of immediate harmful or offensive contact. The Restatement, unlike many courts, deletes the requirement that apprehension be "reasonable."[34] The tort definition must be contrasted with the traditional criminal common law definition of assault. Under the criminal law, assault is an attempted battery. Under the tort definition, only *apprehension* of immediate contact must be established. Furthermore, an actual attempt to

[32] *See generally* Lawrence Vold, *The Legal Allocation of Risk in Assault, Battery and Imprisonment — The Prima Facie Case*, 17 Neb. L. Rev. 149 (1938).

[33] Year Book, Liben Assisarum, fol. 99, pl. 60 (1348).

[34] Restatement § 21 (*see infra* discussion § 1.04).

commit battery, while always a criminal assault, would not constitute a tortious assault unless the victim suffered apprehension of immediate contact. Thus, a perpetrator swinging a bat at the head of one who was looking the other way would be vulnerable to a charge of criminal assault, but not the tort of assault.

[1] Intent Requirement

Assault is an intentional tort. The defendant must desire or be substantially certain that her action will cause the apprehension of immediate harmful or offensive contact. The accidental creation of such apprehension is not assault, but may constitute the much more recently created tort of negligent infliction of emotional distress.[35] If A suffers fright because B is running carelessly toward A, there is no assault. If, on the other hand, A insists on shooting an arrow above B and A knows with a substantial certainty it will cause apprehension to B, A is liable for assault even if A does not desire to cause apprehension. The defendant's motive is irrelevant, provided she either desired or knowingly created apprehension.

Under the transferred intent doctrine, the intent to commit any of the four other intentional torts of battery, false imprisonment, trespass to chattel and trespass to land satisfies the requisite intent for assault.[36] Consequently, if A intends a battery against B, but instead assaults B or C, A is liable for assault.[37]

[2] Apprehension

The victim must *perceive* that harmful or offensive contact is about to happen to him. If the victim is attacked from behind or while asleep,[38] there is no apprehension prior to contact and consequently no assault. Although B may be upset at discovering, after the fact, that a rock nearly hit him, there is no assault.[39] Indeed, even if B is hit, while battery exists, assault does not without the requisite advance apprehension of contact. Apprehension can be created, however, without the actual attempt to cause contact. For example, if the defendant uses an unloaded gun but intentionally leads the victim to believe the gun *is* loaded, assault occurs if the defendant fires at the victim, even though the defendant had neither the intent nor the ability

---

[35] *See infra* § 10.01.

[36] *See supra* § 1.01[D]. The Restatement adopts transferred intent between battery and assault by defining the requisite intent for the two torts to include the intent to commit either a battery or assault. *See* Restatement §§ 13, 21.

[37] *See* Alteiri v. Colasso, 362 A.2d 798 (Conn. 1975).

[38] Consider McCraney v. Flanagan, 267 S.E.2d 404 (N.C. Ct. App. 1980), where the court dismissed the alleged assault because the victim, who was drunk, was not conscious at the time of the alleged assault. Note that recollection of the assault is not required if other proof establishes contemporaneous apprehension.

[39] *See* Restatement § 22. *See also* State v. Barry, 124 P. 775 (Mont. 1912), where the plaintiff was not aware of a gun pointed at him until after the threat had passed.

to shoot the victim. The intent to cause apprehension of imminent contact suffices to create the assault.[40]

To create the victim's apprehension, the defendant must have, however, the apparent (if not actual) ability to cause imminent harmful or offensive contact. One illustration is *Western Union Telegraph Co. v. Hill*,[41] in which the court held it was a question of fact for the jury whether the manager of a telegraph office was liable for assault when he attempted to touch plaintiff's wife and offered "to love and pet her"[42] while still behind a counter that divided him from the victim.

[3] Imminent Harmful or Offensive Contact

For assault to be actionable the victim's apprehension must be of *imminent* harmful or offensive contact. In *Cucinotti v. Ortmann*,[43] the court rejected attempts by the plaintiff to assert a claim for assault since the plaintiff failed to claim in his pleading that the defendant did anything more than verbally threaten to strike him with blackjacks. The court affirmed the traditional rule that words alone are insufficient to establish assault since the lack of an overt act in furtherance of the assault failed to establish the imminence of the attack. The Restatement argues against rigid acceptance of the traditional rule, and concludes that verbal statements can on occasion imply sufficient imminency.[44] Under the Restatement view, for example, A's announcement that B is instantly to be shot, although only verbal, can create imminent apprehension.

The Restatement does not challenge, however, the basic assault requirement that the victim perceive *imminent* harmful or offensive contact. Consequently, if A, with a perfect record of successfully carrying out his threat, promises to beat up B in 30 minutes, B cannot seek compensation for assault, at least until nearly 30 minutes has expired, and under traditional doctrine only after an overt act toward contact by A has commenced.[45]

The apprehension can be of either imminent harmful or offensive contact. Consequently, apprehension that A will throw a water balloon on B, or will spit on B, can, if perceived as sufficiently imminent, constitute assault even when the threatened contact is only offensive and not harmful. Such applications of assault emphasizes the tort's ability to compensate a purely psychological affront to the victim.

---

[40] *See* Allen v. Hannaford, 244 P. 700 (Wash. 1926), where the defendant pointed what he knew to be an unloaded gun at the victim, who thought gun was loaded.

[41] 150 So. 709 (Ala. Ct. App. 1933).

[42] *Id.* at 710.

[43] 159 A.2d 216 (Pa. 1960).

[44] *See* Restatement § 31.

[45] *See* Dicken v. Puryear, 276 S.E.2d 325 (N.C. 1981), where the court did not find the defendant liable for assault for a threat to kill the victim in the future if the victim didn't leave the state.

[4] "Reasonable" Apprehension

Many judicial recitations of the elements of assault require the victim to suffer "reasonable" apprehension. The Restatement rejects this requirement.[46] If A knows B believes, unreasonably, that a pencil is a gun and A pushes on the eraser as if to shoot B, causing B apprehension of imminent harm, the Restatement would characterize A's conduct as assault. Because A has intentionally created apprehension by exploiting B's unreasonable beliefs or gullibility, the Restatement argues that intent is still satisfied and A's intentional exploitation of B's gullibility should be compensable. The argument is most persuasive when A's intent to cause imminent apprehension is "purposeful" intent. The Restatement also characterizes substantial certainty to cause a result as intent.[47] Consequently, the Restatement's definition of assault could include the situation where A, knowing B is unreasonably intimidated by A's appearance, proceeds to enter the elevator where A is standing. The Restatement definition was, undoubtedly, not intended to encompass such a situation where A is privileged to act.

[5] Fear versus Apprehension

The Restatement and several court decisions distinguish between "fear" and "apprehension."[48] The requisite apprehension of imminent contact need not produce fear in the victim. The apprehension simply acknowledges the victim's awareness that imminent harmful or offensive contact will occur unless the victim takes effective evasive action. Consequently if A, within hitting range, strikes out at B, even though B is confident she can move to avoid A's contact, B has still suffered an assault. B's superior strength or evasive techniques do not immunize A from liability for the attack, provided B apprehends imminent contact would occur in the absence of evasive action. Furthermore, even apprehension of an offensive, but non-harmful contact, can constitute assault, even though the mere offensiveness of the imminent contact would not induce fear.

[6] Conditional Assault

An assault made conditional on the victim's noncompliance with an unlawful demand still constitutes an assault, even if the victim is confident no assault will actually occur if the victim complies with the unlawful request.[49] If A brandishes a club toward B, but offers not to strike B if he hands over his wallet, A has assaulted B. Even though B may not actually apprehend contact so long as B is prepared to submit to A's demands, courts have traditionally found A liable for assault. While an overt act by the

[46] *See* Restatement § 27.

[47] *See supra* § 1.01.

[48] *See* Restatement § 24 cmt. b; Coleman v. Employment Security Dep't, 607 P.2d 1231 (Wash. Ct. App. 1980).

[49] *See* Keefe v. State, 19 Ark. 190 (1857); Restatement § 30.

defendant is required, such decisions do reflect an early willingness of courts to expand assault beyond the strictest requirement of actual apprehension of imminent contact.

On the other hand, if A effectively assures B that his overt menacing act will not imminently consummate in harmful or offensive contact regardless of B's actions, no assault exists. For example, if A announces that but for the presence of a police officer, A would hit B with the stick he is brandishing above B, there is no assault.[50]

[7] Source of the Contact

It is not necessary that the defendant be the perceived source of the threatened harmful or offensive contact. If A persuades B that a stick A has positioned next to B is actually a snake about to strike B, A has created apprehension of imminent harmful contact and is liable for assault.[51]

[C] *Justifications for the Tort*

[1] Moral Justifications

From a moral perspective, assault reflects a wrongful affront to the victim. On the other hand, by requiring advance apprehension of contact, it arguably is under-inclusive. An attack from behind is just, if not more, reprehensible and yet excluded from the tort definition of assault. While any attempted battery constitutes criminal assault, the tort definition of assault excludes compensation for the distress derived from a subsequent awareness that a battery was attempted. This is in contrast to the tort of battery, which allows compensation for both harmful and merely offensive contact even when the victim was not cognizant of the contact at the time. It is also possible to argue that assault is over-inclusive from a moral perspective. The act of creating apprehension of merely offensive contact, even when no contact at all is intended, constitutes tortious assault. Such behavior appears far less morally offensive than an actual attempt to seriously harm a victim, which is excluded from tortious assault if the victim was not cognizant of the attack.

[2] Compensation Rationale

From a compensation perspective, assault does introduce the concept that purely psychological injury constitutes compensable harm when it is intentionally inflicted. By excluding as compensable psychological distress prompted by future threats or awareness of a past attack, the tort is extremely restrictive in what kind of psychological stress it will allow to be compensated. While arguably perception of imminent contact reflects a special kind

---

[50] *See* Tuberville v. Savage, 86 Eng. Rep. 684, 1 Mod. Rep. 3 (1669), where the defendant stated, "If it were not assize [tax] time, I would not take such language from you."

[51] *See supra* § 1.03[B][3].

of psychological injury more worthy of compensation, it is hard to justify the inclusion of mental distress prompted by imminent offensive but not harmful contact, while excluding mental distress caused by threats of nonimminent but very harmful contact. On the other hand, the strict time frame does provide a bright line dividing compensable and noncompensable distress. Furthermore, as detailed in § 1.06, *infra*, the newer tort of intentional infliction of mental distress does allow severe mental distress in other categories to be compensated, mitigating the exclusionary impact of limiting recovery to apprehension of imminent contact under assault.

[3] Deterrence Rationale

The tort of assault can deter violent retaliatory responses to an unlawful attack. The tort provides a legal redress to the victim when apprehension of imminent attack allows a legitimate privilege of self-defense. Nonimmediate threats or attacks that the victim does not perceive in advance neither constitute assault nor justify self-defense.[52] In short, the tort of assault correlates with the victim's privilege of self-defense. Arguably the tort discourages wrongful retaliation to an assault by providing monetary compensation which could be offset by the victim's own tortious behavior if he responded excessively to the initial attack. Such deterrence, however, depends on a potential wrongdoer's awareness that legal liability will ensue.

The tort definition of assault does not compensate, and therefore does not act to deter, a surreptitious attack in which the victim does not apprehend imminent contact. A successful attack, however, would make the aggressor liable for battery. Consequently, the assault tort, while not by itself a deterrent to many forms of initial attacks, does arguably work to encourage the victims of attacks to refrain from behavior in excess of that justified by self-defense.

§ 1.04 FALSE IMPRISONMENT

[A] *Overview and Definition*

In false imprisonment, the defendant unlawfully acts to intentionally cause confinement or restraint of the victim within a bounded area.[53] Accidental confinement is not included and must be addressed under negligence or strict liability. It is generally held that the victim must be aware of the confinement at the time of the restraint.[54] False imprisonment compensates for psychological, physical and economic injury occasioned by the imprisonment. A recurring issue for courts is the often factually based distinction between wrongfully coerced confinement from confinement that is lawfully encouraged or persuaded.

---

[52] For a discussion of the privilege of self-defense, *see* § 2.02, *infra*.

[53] *See generally* William L. Prosser, *False Imprisonment: Consciousness of Confinement*, 55 Colum. L. Rev. 847 (1955); *see also* Restatement §§ 35-45A.

[54] *But see* Restatement § 42, discussed § 1.04[E], *infra*.

[B] *Bounded Area*

The victim must be confined within an area bounded in all directions. It is not false imprisonment if the victim is free to proceed in any direction, even though she is prevented from going in the direction she wants.[55] The bounded area can be, however, a large area, even an entire city.[56] A vehicle, although moving, can still constitute a bounded area.[57] Reasonable means of escape precludes liability for false imprisonment. The escape is not reasonable if it requires the victim to be heroic, endure excessive embarrassment or discomfort, or if the victim is unaware of the means of escape.[58]

[C] *Means of Confinement or Restraint*

For false imprisonment to exist, the victim must be confined or restrained. The confinement may be accomplished by (1) physical barriers; (2) force or threat of immediate force against the victim, the victim's family or others in her immediate presence, or the victim's property; (3) omission where the defendant has a legal duty to act; or (4) improper assertion of legal authority.

[1] Physical Barrier

If physical barriers are utilized to restrain the victim, the barriers to constitute false imprisonment must surround the victim in all directions so that no reasonable means of escape exists.[59]

[2] Force or Threat of Immediate Force

Force or threat of immediate force can also be utilized to restrain the victim. The force may be directed at the victim, her family, companions or property. Consequently, if A wrongfully grabs B's coat and B refuses to leave without her coat, A is liable to B for false imprisonment. Although B could have left without her coat, the restraint that results from not abandoning her property constitutes imprisonment.[60] On the other hand,

---

[55] *See* Bird v. Jones, 115 Eng. Rept. 668 (1845), where the court held it was not false imprisonment when part of a public highway was closed for a boat race, and the victim could not pass through but was allowed to leave.

[56] *See* Allen v. Fromme, 126 N.Y.S. 520 (1910). *Cf.* Albright v. Oliver, 975 F.2d 343 (7th Cir. 1992), indicating an entire state may be a bounded area.

[57] *See* Sindle v. New York City Transit Authority, 307 N.E.2d 245 (N.Y. 1973), acknowledging the failure of a school bus driver to release a student at a stop could constitute false imprisonment, but holding that imprisonment in this case was justified to protect persons and property; *see also* Cieplinski v. Severn, 168 N.E. 722 (Mass. 1929).

[58] *See* Talcott v. National Exhibition Co., 128 N.Y.S. 1059 (1911), where the plaintiff was found reasonably unaware of a means of escape in a baseball stadium.

[59] *See* Whittaker v. Sandford, 85 A. 399 (Me. 1912), where the victim was detained on a yacht surrounded by water without access to rowboat. *See also* Restatement § 36, indicating that unreasonable means of escape includes exposure of individual, material harm to clothes, or danger of harm to another.

[60] *See* Fischer v. Famous-Barr Co., 646 S.W.2d 819 (Mo. Ct. App. 1982); *but see* Marcano v. Northwestern Chrysler-Plymouth Sales, Inc., 550 F. Supp. 595 (N.D. Ill. 1982).

if A threatens B with serious injury on the following day, if B leaves the premises, A is not liable for false imprisonment, even if B remains on the premise, since no immediate force has been threatened. Presumably, in the latter instance the victim is at liberty to leave and seek protection from the threat. Furthermore, the use of threats of economic retaliation or termination of employment to coerce a victim to remain also do not constitute false imprisonment.

The tort of false imprisonment recognizes the coercive restraint of immediate force, even when only applied to personal property, but fails to recognize highly coercive but non-immediate threats. Contemporary critics may conclude that more judicial flexibility in finding coercion is warranted. Indeed, some contemporary cases, while ostensibly based on marginal immediate physical force, appear to be influenced by the accompanying economic coercion.[61] On the other hand, the more courts depart from requiring obvious force to find false imprisonment, the more difficult it becomes to distinguish voluntary from coerced submissions. Indeed, many decisions already grapple with the subtle factual distinction between voluntary compliance with a request to stay and submission to implied threats of immediate force.[62]

[3] Omissions

False imprisonment can also result from a defendant's omission when the defendant had a legal duty to act. If A invites B out to his boat and promises to bring A ashore when requested, B's failure to do so constitutes false imprisonment.[63] Since there is no general duty to act, the plaintiff must establish that the defendant, in the specific context, does have an obligation to act.[64]

[4] Improper Assertion of Legal Authority (False Arrest)

The improper assertion of legal authority can unlawfully restrain a victim. This form of false imprisonment constitutes false arrest. The victim must submit to the arrest for it to constitute imprisonment. The arrest is improper if the actor imposing confinement is not privileged under the

---

[61] *See* Dupler v. Seubert, 230 N.W.2d 626 (Wis. 1975) (finding physical threats were utilized to restrain employee).

[62] *See* Lopez v. Winchell's Donut House, 466 N.E.2d 1309 (Ill. Ct. App. 1984), where a cashier was held to have merely complied with moral pressure when she submitted to go to a back room for an interrogation by her supervisor regarding a possible theft. *See also* Hardy v. LaBelle's Distributing Co., 661 P.2d 35 (Mont. 1983). *Cf.* Peterson v. Sorlien, 299 N.W.2d 123 (Minn. 1980), where the parents of an adult child were held to have right to place certain limits on adult child's liberty during "deprogramming" from cult faith so long as plaintiff assents at some point to the action.

[63] *See* Whittaker v. Sandford, 85 A. 399 (Me. 1912).

[64] *See infra* § 8.02.

circumstances.[65] The applicable privileges vary for police officers and private citizens.[66] For example, if A fraudulently induces B into wrongfully believing A is a police officer and B submits to detention under circumstances where only a police officer is privileged to detain, A is liable for false arrest.[67]

[D] *Contrast With Malicious Prosecution and Abuse of Process*

False imprisonment compensates for unlawful confinement. Confinement that is privileged[68] is not unlawful. False arrest is a form of false imprisonment where the confinement is accomplished through the unlawful assertion of legal authority. Where an arrest is privileged and therefore conforms to all requisite legal requirements to justify arrest, the possibility of liability for false arrest is precluded. An arrest pursuant to lawful procedures, and therefore not false imprisonment, if motivated by bad faith and satisfying other important elements, may constitute malicious prosecution.[69] The improper use of certain compulsory processes such as subpoenas, despite conforming to legal requirements, and therefore not false imprisonment, may be tortious as an abuse of process.[70]

[E] *Consciousness of Confinement*

False imprisonment requires that the victim be conscious of the confinement at the time of imprisonment.[71] The Restatement modifies this

---

65 *See* Enright v. Groves, 560 P.2d 851 (Colo. Ct. App. 1977), where the victim was wrongfully arrested for failure to produce a driver's license while walking a dog.

66 In general, under the common law, arrests pursuant to an apparently valid warrant are privileged. A police officer is privileged to arrest for a felony without a warrant when she reasonably suspects the other is guilty. A private citizen is only privileged when she reasonably suspects the individual arrested committed a felony *and* a felony in fact has taken place. This allows the private citizen a privilege to make a reasonable mistake in arresting the wrong person *only* if the crime actually occurred. Both police officers and private citizens are privileged to arrest for misdemeanors constituting breaches of the peace occurring in their presence. *See* Restatement §§ 116, 119, 121, 122.

67 *See* Restatement § 41.

68 *See infra* Chapter 2 and *supra* note 66.

69 *See infra* § 20.02.

70 *See infra* § 20.05; Consider Maniaci v. Marquette University, 184 N.W.2d 168 (Wis. 1971), where the court reversed liability on a claim of false imprisonment, but held that the plaintiff alleged a proper case for abuse of process. Plaintiff, a student at Marquette University, was restrained from leaving campus by the university dean and others through wrongful use of temporary civil commitment procedures designed to determine whether the student's mental condition required imposing detention. The university officials knew the student's mental condition did not justify civil commitment, but used the procedure to temporarily detain the student until her father could be notified of her intent to withdraw from the university. The court held that the university's compliance with legal procedures precluded plaintiff's claim of false imprisonment, but that the defendant's misuse of procedure allowed liability for abuse of process.

71 *See* Parvi v. City of Kingston, 362 N.E.2d 960 (N.Y. 1977), where the court held that partial intoxication during confinement and lack of recollection of confinement does not

requirement and would find liability for false imprisonment, even when the victim is not aware of the confinement, if the victim is harmed by the confinement.[72] Thus, under the Restatement view, if A, an infant, is locked in a car trunk and suffers injury, B is liable for false imprisonment, even if A is unaware of the confinement. The general requirement of consciousness emphasizes that false imprisonment is a tort protecting a psychological perception of autonomy and not simply the denial of personal autonomy.

[F] *No Minimum Time*

False imprisonment covers even minimal lengths of detention. Thus if A is detained by B for one minute, B is liable for false imprisonment. Obviously, however, the amount of the compensation awarded for false imprisonment will reflect the length of the detention.

[G] *Transferred Intent*

False imprisonment is one of five intentional torts[73] where intent transfers. If A intends an assault against B and either B or C is unintentionally imprisoned, A is liable for false imprisonment.

[H] *Policy Issues*

From a moral perspective, the tort of false imprisonment appropriately responds to a deprivation of individual liberty. Arguably problematic is the general requirement that the victim must be contemporaneously conscious of the restraint. Nevertheless, unknowingly being subject to restraint appears a less serious affront to the individual's autonomy.[74]

Perhaps the most difficult issue false imprisonment raises is attempting to delineate what kinds of restraints are wrongful. Traditional doctrine includes immediate force against personal chattels as a method of restraining victims who declined to leave their chattels, but excludes threats of non-immediate future violence to accomplish restraint of movement. Similarly, intense economic pressure does not constitute a method for restraint. Arguably, while such pressures are less immediate, courts should be prepared to include broader categories of wrongful coercion as potentially constituting the tort, despite the factual difficulty such inclusion might pose.

---

preclude a finding that victim was sufficiently conscious of confinement to sustain claim for false imprisonment.

[72] Restatement § 42.

[73] The others include battery, assault, trespass to land and trespass to chattel. *See supra* § 1.01[D].

[74] The Restatement's waiver of the requirement that the plaintiff be conscious of the restraint, when an injury occurs, addresses concerns that the requirement of consciousness will preclude compensation when there is a cognizable loss.

§ 1.05 TRESPASS TO CHATTEL AND CONVERS

[A] *Overview*

Trespass to chattel and conversion are two separate intentional torts that protect personal property from wrongful interference.[75] The two torts, which overlap in part, are derived from different historical origins. In many, but not all, instances, both torts may be applicable.

Not all interference with personal property is tortious. For trespass to chattel there must be actual damage to the property, significant deprivation of use, or dispossession. Unlike trespass to land, which awards nominal damages for technical trespass, minor intermeddling of personal property is not tortious. Conversion exists only when the damage or other interference with the personal property is sufficiently serious to justify a forced sale to the defendant. The defendant is liable for the entire market value of the chattel and not simply a smaller repair or rental cost. Consequently, conversion requires more serious interference with the chattel than might satisfy the minimal threshold for trespass to chattel. Adequate interference with property to constitute conversion does not preclude, however, liability under trespass to chattel. In such instances, the torts overlap.

[B] *Definition of Trespass to Chattel*

Trespass to chattel is the intentional interference with the right of possession of personal property. The defendant's acts must intentionally damage the chattel, deprive the possessor of its use for a substantial period of time, or totally dispossess the chattel from the victim.[76]

[1] Bad Faith Not Required

Trespass to chattel does not require that the defendant act in bad faith or intend to interfere with the rights of others. It is sufficient that the actor intends to damage or possess a chattel which in fact is properly possessed by another. In the classic case of *Ranson v. Kitner*,[77] the defendant killed the plaintiff's dog but argued that the "dog had a striking resemblance to a wolf,"[78] which the defendant could have legally hunted. The court held good faith was not a defense. So long as the defendant intended to kill the particular animal, the requisite intent is satisfied, and even a reasonable mistake as to identity or ownership, unless wrongfully induced by the victim, cannot exonerate the defendant from liability. *Ranson* is illustrative

---

[75] *See, generally,* William L. Prosser, *The Nature of Conversion*, 42 Cornell L. Q. 168 (1957); John R. Faust, Jr., *Distinction Between Conversion and Trespass to Chattel*, 37 Or. L. Rev. 256 (1958); Jeff C. Dodd, *Rights in Information: Conversion and Misappropriate Causes of Action in Intellectual Property Cases*, 32 Hous. L. Rev. 459 (1995).

[76] *See* Restatement §§ 217, 218.

[77] 31 Ill. App. 241 (1888).

[78] *Id.* at 242.

of the "mistake doctrine"[79] which applies to both trespass to chattel and conversion. In such instances, once the defendant merely intends to act upon a chattel, the concept of "intent" approaches strict liability.

[2] Actual Damage, Substantial Deprivation, or Dispossession Required

Unlike trespass to land,[80] trivial interference with another's personal chattels is not actionable in tort. If A knows that B does not want anyone touching his automobile, but A touches it anyway, there is no trespass to chattel in the absence of actual damage to the automobile. While it could be argued that torts should vindicate any intentional interference with personal property, the prevailing law does not allow such recovery, as would be granted for similar interference with real property.[81] In an era of extensive litigation, it appears unlikely such an extension would appeal to courts.

Depriving the possessor of the use of his chattel also constitutes trespass to chattel, provided there is significant deprivation and not mere momentary interference. For example, if A without privilege uses B's suitcase for one week, the conduct can constitute trespass to chattel. By contrast, an unauthorized three minutes use of the luggage would ordinarily not constitute the tort (unless the three minutes were critical) since there is no measurable deprivation.

Trespass to chattel also exists if the tortfeasor totally dispossesses the victim of his chattel, as by stealing or otherwise wrongfully asserting dominion and control over the property. Such dispossession is sufficient interference to constitute the tort even if the chattel is quickly recovered from the perpetrator. In such instances, the tortfeasor has more than used the chattel, but challenged the victim's right of possession to the property. Liability can be imposed in such instances, even when the defendant, as discussed above in § 1.05[B][1], acts in a good faith but incorrect belief the chattel is his/her own.

The Restatement would also include as trespass to chattel interference with a chattel which results in injury to the possessor or injury to a person or thing in which the possessor has a legally protected interest.[82] Consequently, if A without privilege touches B's dog, causing the dog to bite B, A is liable for the injury to B.

---

[79] *See supra* § 1.01 [E].

[80] *See* § 18.02, *infra*.

[81] *See* Glidden v. Szybiak, 63 A.2d 233 (N.H. 1949), holding that pulling a dog's ears did not harm the dog and therefore did not constitute a trespass to chattel.

[82] Restatement § 218.

[3] Transferred Intent

Historically, the doctrine of transferred intent has been applied to trespass to chattel (unlike conversion). Under the doctrine, intent for any of four other torts (battery, assault, trespass to land, or false imprisonment) can be substituted to satisfy the requisite intent for trespass to chattel.[83] If A intends to hit B with ink and misses, but hits B's or C's book, A is liable for the damage to the book under trespass to chattel. Even if the book is destroyed, conversion would not exist since the book's destruction was not intentional and transferred intent is not applicable to conversion.

[C] *Definition of Conversion*

The Restatement defines conversion as "an intentional exercise of dominion and control over a chattel which so seriously interferes with the right of another to control it that the actor may justly be required to pay the other the full value of the chattel."[84] It is derived from the action of trover which originally addressed the recovery of lost property. While conversion is no longer restricted to lost property, courts still generally limit protection to tangible property unless the intangible property has distinct scientific, literary or artistic value.[85]

[1] Serious Interference

Only very serious harm to the property or other serious interference with the right of control constitutes conversion. Damage or interference which is less serious may still constitute trespass to chattel. The Restatement has identified six factors in determining the seriousness of the interference:

(a) the extent and duration of the actor's exercise of dominion or control;

(b) the actor's intent to assert a right in fact inconsistent with the other's right of control;

(c) the actor's good faith;

(d) the extent and duration of the resulting interference with the other's right of control;

(e) the harm done to the chattel;

---

[83] *See supra* § 1.01[D].

[84] Restatement § 222A.

[85] *See* Pearson v. Dodd, 410 F.2d 701 (D.C. Cir. 1969), where receiving, copying, and returning the private files taken by third parties from the office of a United States Senator was held not to constitute conversion. In Moore v. Regents of the University of California, 793 P.2d 479 (Cal. 1990), the California Supreme Court held that a patient's cells, which were extracted by a physician and utilized to manufacture a patented cell line, were not subject to conversion because the patient did not retain ownership of the cells following their removal.

(f) the inconvenience and expense caused to the other.[86]

Applying these factors, there is a general agreement that if A intentionally destroys B's chattel, A is liable for conversion. If A intentionally caused minor damage to B's chattel, A would not be liable for conversion but would be liable for trespass to chattel. If A attempts to steal B's chattel, but is caught within minutes, A is liable for conversion because of the weight placed on his bad faith. If A mistakenly takes B's chattel, but returns it within minutes after realizing her error, A is not liable for conversion. If, however, A mistakenly takes B's chattel and then accidentally loses or destroys it, A's intentional taking, although in good faith, constitutes conversion since the deprivation is permanent.

Purchasing stolen property, even if the purchaser was acting in good faith and was not aware the seller did not have title, constitutes conversion by both the seller and innocent buyer. Both A's and B's acts seriously interfere with the ownership of the rightful owner.

§ 1.06 INTENTIONAL INFLICTION OF MENTAL DISTRESS

[A] *Overview*

The tort of intentional infliction of mental or emotional distress is relatively new, but has now gained general recognition in the latter half of this century.[87] Unlike most traditional intentional torts, the elements of intentional infliction of mental distress are far less precise. While this allows for a flexible individual approach to determination of liability, it also introduces greater uncertainty and has on some occasions collided with First Amendment values.

[B] *History*

While there exists some older authority in support of independent liability for mental distress,[88] general recognition of the tort was roughly commensurate with its endorsement by the First Restatement in 1934.[89] Indeed, the

[86] Restatement § 222A.

[87] *See generally* Daniel Gilvelber, *The Right to Minimum Social Decency and the Limits of Evenhandedness: Intentional Infliction of Emotional Distress by Outrageous Conduct*, 82 Colum. L. Rev. 42 (1982); Calvert Magruder, *Mental and Emotional Disturbance in the Law of Torts*, 49 Harv. L. Rev. 1033 (1936); William L. Prosser, *Intentional Infliction of Mental Suffering: A New Tort*, 37 Mich. L. Rev. 874 (1939). Intentional infliction of emotional distress should be contrasted with the subsequent judicial acceptance of liability for negligent infliction of emotional distress, *see infra* § 10.01.

[88] *See* Wilkinson v. Downton, 2 Q.B. 57 (1897), where the defendant falsely told the plaintiff that the plaintiff's husband had been seriously injured in an accident and instructed her to retrieve him. The plaintiff, whose resulting serious shock led to physical injury, was held to warrant compensation by the court. *See also* Bouillon v. Laclede Gaslight Co., 129 S.W. 401 (Mo. Ct. App. 1910), where the victim suffered a miscarriage when a gas company employee allegedly instigated an argument in front of victim.

[89] First Restatement § 46.

First Restatement only recognized the tort when the severe distress caused physical injury in the victim. Such intentional infliction of mental distress was deemed tortious by the First Restatement only because such extreme and outrageous conduct manifested negligence toward the physical health of the victim since it was foreseeable the victim would suffer physically from his distress.[90] Numerous cases allowing recovery by patrons for gross insults from common carriers and innkeepers, without proof the victim suffered severe distress, were viewed as a special exception.[91]

In 1947 the Restatement was amended to recognize the tort without requiring physical manifestation, a position subsequently adopted by a majority of American states for intentional infliction of emotional distress.[92] In an influential decision, the California Supreme Court endorsed the 1947 Restatement amendment in *State Rubbish Collectors Ass'n v. Siliznoff.*[93] The recognition of intentional infliction of emotional distress in *Siliznoff* allowed plaintiff to recover for threats against himself, his property and business. In that case, the plaintiff, a garbage collector, did not comply with the association's division of customers and was subjected to an array of threatening behaviors by association representatives. The court held that liability could not be based on assault[94] since the threats of personal injury were not immediate. Rather than expand assault and other traditional torts to cover future threats of violence, the court embraced the new tort. Contemporary scholars can still debate whether this potentially massive expansion in potential liability is warranted.

[C] *Definition*

Intentional infliction of mental distress exists when the defendant, by extreme and outrageous conduct, intentionally or recklessly causes the victim severe mental distress. Most states no longer require that the victim suffer physical manifestations of the mental distress.

[1] Extreme and Outrageous Conduct

The Restatement defines extreme and outrageous conduct as behavior which is "beyond all possible bounds of decency and to be regarded as atrocious, and utterly intolerable in a civilized community."[95] While there is no objective standard, mere rudeness or callous offensiveness is insufficient. The vulnerability of the victim and the relationship of the defendant to the victim can be critical. Cruelness toward a young child or a very ill

---

90 *Id.*, cmt. c. For an excellent historical review, see State Rubbish Collectors Ass'n v. Siliznoff, 240 P.2d 282 (Cal. 1952).

91 *See* First Restatement § 48 cmt. c; *see also infra* § 1.06[E].

92 *See* First Restatement § 46 as amended (1947); *see also* Restatement § 46.

93 240 P.2d 282 (Cal. 1952).

94 *See* § 1.03[B][2], *supra.*

95 Restatement § 46 cmt. d.

patient is more likely to be perceived as outrageous than would be comparable conduct directed towards a healthy adult.[96] The presence of a superior-subordinate relationship will also be taken into account. Accordingly, continuous mocking by an employer toward her employee or a principal to his student is more likely to be characterized as outrageous than taunting among equals.[97] Knowledge of the victim's particular hypersensitivity can make otherwise non-outrageous conduct sufficiently culpable.[98]

[a] Sexual Harassment and Racial Epithets

Courts have hesitated in extending the tort of intentional infliction of emotional distress to situations involving sexual and racial harassment, based on the theory that many instances of harassment are comprised of language that might be objectionable or morally repugnant, but nevertheless fail to meet the higher standard of "extreme and outrageous conduct."[99] This undoubtedly reflects an historical societal tolerance of sexual and racial harassment which should change as society and courts become more sensitive to the extreme repugnancy of such behavior.

Isolated propositions or attempts at seduction have, traditionally, not been actionable.[100] Nor, usually, has liability been imposed in the past based solely on racial slurs.[101] However, courts have been more likely to recognize liability where a pattern of harassment is constant and ongoing.[102] Additionally, corporations have been held liable for failing to respond to harassment perpetrated by employees, particularly those in supervisorial roles.[103] Most situations where liability has been imposed for

---

[96] *Consider, e.g.*, Alabama Fuel and Iron Co. v. Baladoni, 73 So. 205 (Ala. Ct. App. 1916), where liability was imposed when the defendant, who was aware that the plaintiff was pregnant, intentionally shot the plaintiff's pet dog, to which she was greatly attached, in her presence. The plaintiff suffered a miscarriage as a result of the mental anguish.

[97] *Cf.* Harris v. Jones, 380 A.2d 611 (Md. App. 1977), where a General Motors supervisor regularly mocked an employee's stuttering and nervousness. The court found that the supervisor's conduct was extreme and outrageous, but found insufficient evidence that such conduct caused plaintiff to suffer extreme distress.

[98] *Consider, e.g.*, Nickerson v. Hodges, 84 So. 37 (La. 1920), where the plaintiff was obsessed with finding a buried pot of gold purportedly located on land near her property. The plaintiff's neighbors, as an April Fools' Day joke, buried an iron pot filled with earth and stones where she would find it with a note instructing her to open it in front of a large crowd. Plaintiff suffered great distress, and the court awarded her heirs recovery. *Consider also* George v. Jordan Marsh Co., 268 N.E.2d 915 (Mass. 1971), where the plaintiff suffered a first heart attack attributed to the defendant's harassment intended to induce her to pay her son's debt. After the first heart attack and after being advised to stop bothering the victim, the defendant continued the harassment which led to a second heart attack. The court recognized potential liability.

[99] *See* Restatement § 46 cmt. d.

[100] *See* Reed v. Maley, 74 S.W. 1079 (Ky. 1903).

[101] *But see, e.g.*, Wiggs v. Courshon, 355 F. Supp. 206 (S.D. Fla. 1973).

[102] *See* Hogan v. Forsyth Country Club Co., 340 S.E.2d 116 (N.C. Ct. App. 1986).

[103] *See, e.g.*, Ford v. Revlon, Inc., 734 P.2d 580 (Ariz. 1987).

racial or sexual harassment involve a combination of speech and conduct.[104] The trend towards recognizing liability should be viewed in the context of the evolution and various interpretations given to the phrase "extreme and outrageous conduct."[105]

[b] Constitutional Limits

In *Hustler Magazine v. Falwell*,[106] the United States Supreme Court held unconstitutional the determination that a parody "advertisement" in *Hustler* magazine could result in liability under intentional infliction of emotional distress. The mock advertisement, while clearly satirical, suggested Jerry Falwell, a nationally known religious and political leader of the Moral Majority, had his first sexual encounter with his mother in an outhouse. The majority held that a public figure could not recover without proving such statements were made with *New York Times* malice, i.e., with "knowledge or reckless disregard toward the truth or falsity" of the assertion.[107] As the parody was never asserted to be truthful, and as it would not reasonably be interpreted as truthful by an ordinary reader, the Court found there could be no liability.

Since *New York Times* malice is required to be proved by public figures in media defamation, the Supreme Court concluded that public figure plaintiffs should not be allowed to use intentional infliction of emotional distress as an alternative tort to evade First Amendment protections afforded defendants in defamation cases. Consequently, verbal disparagement to public figures, which are not asserted as factual, would appear, however extreme and outrageous, to be protected under the First Amendment. Public figures may presumably recover for other types of outrageous conduct under the tort. Moreover, the Supreme Court did not suggest that private plaintiffs would also be precluded from seeking redress in a similar context if the publisher is not asserting fact. While the *New York Times* standard would not apply to private plaintiffs, a lesser standard requiring proof of negligence toward the truth is applied in defamation cases involving private plaintiffs in public controversies.[108] By analogy, this lesser standard could be held applicable. On the other hand, the social value of satirizing private

---

104 *See* Jean C. Love, ***Discriminatory Speech and the Tort of Intentional Infliction of Emotional Distress***, 47 Wash. & Lee L. Rev. 123 (1990).

105 *Consider* Wilson v. Bellamy, 414 S.E.2d 347 (N.C. Ct. App. 1992), where the defendants were found not liable for intentional infliction of emotional distress in taking advantage of a female student's intoxication and impaired consciousness by kissing and fondling her. The defendants were, however, found liable for sexual battery. Notwithstanding the decision, contemporary courts should be increasingly ready to characterize such conduct as extreme and outrageous.

106 485 U.S. 46 (1988).

107 *See* New York Times Co. v. Sullivan, 376 U.S. 254 (1964). *See infra* § 21.03.

108 Gertz v. Robert Welch, Inc., 418 U.S. 323 (1974). *See infra* § 21.03[C].

individuals appears much less compelling. At present there are no indications courts are prepared to limit a private victim's remedy under intentional infliction of emotional distress.

[2] Intent or Recklessness to Cause Severe Mental Distress

For recovery under intentional infliction of emotional distress, the plaintiff must prove that the defendant intended to cause severe emotional distress or acted with reckless disregard as to whether the victim would suffer severe distress. Although characterized as an "intentional" tort, recklessness, in addition to intent, generally suffices for liability.[109] The inclusion of recklessness, which is endorsed by the Restatement[110] and derived from early precedent,[111] includes liability for defendant's behavior when she acts with a deliberate disregard of a high degree of probability that severe mental distress will result even when that was not the defendant's intention. The intentional (and reckless) tort must be distinguished from negligent infliction of mental distress, which evolved later.[112]

[3] Severe Mental Distress

Intentional infliction of mental distress requires proof both that the defendant intended or recklessly imposed the risk of severe mental distress and that the victim actually suffered severe mental distress. Mild distress will not suffice. Initially, physical manifestations of severe mental distress were required, but most jurisdictions no longer require physical manifestations for the intentional tort.[113] Physical manifestations can range from heart attacks to serious stomach disorders attributed to stress and shock. While physical manifestations were the original justification for compensating for intentional infliction of mental distress,[114] the requirement evolved as an ostensible mechanism for authenticating distress and discouraging fraudulent claims. The trend away from the requirement reflects recognition that the authenticity of severe distress can best be documented by the outrageousness of the wrongdoer's conduct, and that a prerequisite of often unconfirmable physical manifestations, such as stomach trouble, is more prone to fraudulent claims.

---

[109] This is in contrast to most intentional torts where recklessness will not suffice. *See* § 1.01[C].

[110] Restatement § 46 cmt. i.

[111] *See, e.g.*, Boyle v. Chandler, 138 A. 273 (Del. 1927), where a dead body was buried recklessly.

[112] *See infra* § 10.01.

[113] *See supra* § 1.06[B]; *but see infra* Negligent Infliction of Mental Distress, § 10.01, where most states, in contrast, require physical manifestation.

[114] *See supra* § 1.06[B].

[D] *Third-Party Recovery*

Intentional infliction of mental distress is not one of the five historic intentional torts that transfers intent between these torts and between victims.[115] However, since intent is defined to be either desire or substantial certainty,[116] if A beats up B, knowing that B's son C is present, A may be substantially certain, and therefore intend, that C will suffer severe mental distress, even if A had no specific desire to cause C mental distress.[117] Indeed, since recklessness can suffice for intentional infliction of mental distress, the defendant needs only to act with a deliberate disregard of a high degree of risk that his conduct would cause severe distress to a third party.

Courts, however, appear concerned that this encompassing definition of intent and recklessness may cover too many individuals in the context of intentional infliction of emotional distress. Consequently, courts have usually awarded a third-party victim recovery only if, in addition to proving the elements of the tort, she is (1) a close relative of the primary victim; (2) present at the scene of the outrageous conduct against the primary victim; and (3) the defendant knows the close relative is present. The Restatement is somewhat less restrictive, requiring only that a primary victim's immediate family members be present and can prove the elements of the tort. Non-relatives who satisfy the elements of the tort can also recover under the Restatement if they are present and suffer physical manifestation of severe distress.[118] The Restatement's more permissive requirements have not received general explicit judicial acceptance. On the other hand, the more commonly stated requirement that the defendant knows that the third party is present appears to be anomalous in the large minority of jurisdictions which allow bystander recovery for negligent infliction of mental distress where the close relative is present and witnesses the accident. Such jurisdictions do not in negligence cases require the defendant to know the bystander is present, and presumably would not so require for the intentional tort.[119]

Indeed, the argument for restricting bystander recovery in the intentional tort has weaknesses. The defendant, having engaged in outrageous conduct,

---

[115] *See supra* § 1.01.

[116] *See supra* § 1.01.

[117] *See* Taylor v. Vallelunga, 339 P.2d 910 (Cal. Ct. App. 1959), where a daughter suffered distress from observing attack on her father.

[118] Restatement § 46 cmt. l; such restrictions on bystanders are applicable only when they are in fact third parties and not primary victims. For example, attacking a husband out of a desire to inflict pain on his wife would make the wife a primary victim. The defendant's action was directed toward the wife. Consequently, the wife could recover without being present.

[119] *See infra* § 10.01[C].

is highly culpable. Intentional torts are commonly not insurable. Consequently, there is no general imposition on the insured community. On the other hand, the reverberations of distress suffered by relatives and friends can be great, imposing enormous liability. Less persuasive for the restrictions is the rationale that the defendant will only be "substantially certain" to cause severe distress to bystander relatives who are in fact present and witness the outrageous conduct. As long as the defendant knows of the existence of the close relatives, distress for seriously harming a relative would appear certain or at least be encompassed by recklessness, which also suffices for the tort.

[E] *Exception for Innkeepers, Common Carriers, and Other Public Utilities*

Innkeepers, common carriers, and other public utilities (such as a telegraph company) are liable for intentional gross insults which cause patrons to suffer mental distress.[120] The requirement that the defendant behave in an extreme and outrageous manner to impose liability for intentional infliction of emotional distress is waived. The plaintiff, to benefit from this lower threshold of liability, must be a patron of the defendant, although there is no requirement that, for example, a ticket be purchased by the patron prior to the tort's occurrence. If A, a bus driver, tells B, a pedestrian crossing the street in front of the bus, that he is an odoriferous, fat slob, A is not liable unless A's knowledge of B's special hypersensitivity or other unusual circumstances makes the conduct extreme and outrageous and the victim suffers severe emotional distress. If A makes the same remark to C, a passenger preparing to board the bus, A is liable under the special exception without the need to prove extreme and outrageous circumstances or that the victim suffered severe distress.

While the exception for innkeepers, common carriers and other public utilities is supported by venerable precedent,[121] the original rationale for the exception is debatable. Common carriers have traditionally owed passengers an exceptionally high duty of care, and perhaps this heightened liability is reflected in the exception. As well, historically carriers and inns have been monopolies with out-of-town travellers circumstantially compelled to use their services. Furthermore, others have argued that the traditional exception is explained by a class attitude toward the typical common carrier employee. While some courts have extended the exception to other commercial establishments, the questionable contemporary justifications for the special rule have resulted in most courts acknowledging the exceptions, but not extending them.[122]

---

[120] *See* Restatement § 48.

[121] *See, e.g.*, Jones v. Atlantic Coast Line Railroad Co., 94 S.E. 490 (S.C. 1917).

[122] *See* Slocum v. Food Fair Stores of Florida, 100 So. 2d 396 (Fla. 1958), where the court held, without deciding whether to generally adopt tort of intentional infliction of mental

[F] *Policy Rationales*

The tort of intentional infliction of mental distress can be criticized for being too vague. While this allows individual flexibility, it also adds uncertainty as to when the tort applies. Arguably, more specific torts could be crafted for special needs in its place with less danger of chilling legitimate First Amendment speech or other non-tortuous activity. On the other hand, the requisite requirement of outrageousness limits the tort's application and allows it to address wrongdoings that more specific torts would not anticipate. The tort gives distinct recognition to the concept that mental injury is compensable. While this can be criticized, in part because it is difficult to place monetary value on such losses, it must be acknowledged that the tort is not breaking new ground in compensating mental injury. Historic torts, like assault and battery, attempt to compensate such losses and unlike intentional infliction of mental distress do not limit recovery to severe mental distress. On the other hand, intentional infliction of mental distress is much broader in its application and its boundaries await individual jury interpretation of its limits.

---

distress, that special liability for public utilities did not apply to a grocery store. A grocery clerk told a customer, "You stink to me," allegedly causing the victim a heart attack aggravated from pre-existing heart condition. *Id.* at 397. There was no allegation defendant knew about the pre-existing condition. See *supra* § 1.06[C][1].

CHAPTER 2

PRIVILEGES TO INTENTIONAL TORTS

SYNOPSIS

This chapter considers privileges applicable to intentional torts. While the plaintiff has the burden of proving the elements of the tort, the defendant has the burden of proving a privilege.

§ 2.01 CONSENT

[A] *Overview*

Consent is a defense to intentional tort liability. If the asserted victim gives permission, what would otherwise be tortious is instead privileged. Consent is, however, more complex than it first might appear. Consent can be express and can be implied. Even when the consent is expressed, factors can arise that can invalidate the consent. Alternatively, other factors may compel courts to recognize consent despite the victim's lack of a subjective intent to grant consent.

[B] *Express and Implied Manifestations of Consent*

Consent is, in general, a valid defense when it is objectively manifested.[1] Assume A says "yes," to B's request to come on A's land. B has the defense of consent to trespass, even if A secretly means "no" when he says "yes." It is the objective manifestation of consent which a potential defendant can rely on to assert privilege for what would otherwise be a tort. On the other hand, if B knew A means "no" when he says "yes," B's actual knowledge that A does not really consent negates the defense.

An individual can convey consent expressly in words or through pictorial gestures. Alternatively, an individual can imply consent. Consent is implied when, under the circumstances, the conduct of the individual reasonably conveys consent. In *O'Brien v. Cunard S.S. Co.*,[2] the plaintiff, a steamship passenger, joined a line of people, not knowing that persons in the line were to obtain an inoculation. Despite the fact that the plaintiff did not intend to consent to the inoculation, the court held that her actions objectively manifested implied consent. Similarly, if A gives B a friendly greeting every time B walks across her property, A's lack of objection implies consent

---

[1] *See* Francis H. Bohlen, *Consent as Affecting Civil Liability for Breaches of the Peace*, 24 Colum. L. Rev. 819 (1924); Restatement § 892.

[2] 28 N.E. 266 (Mass. 1891).

to such intrusions. In the absence of contrary expressions by the individual, consent can also be implied by community custom. If, for example, it is customary to allow an individual to walk on private property to ring the front door bell, A's consent can be assumed unless she objectively communicates her objection to the custom, as by posting a sign.

[C] *Consent by Law*

Consent can also be implied by law. Generally courts recognize by law consent to emergency medical treatment by health professionals when a victim is unconscious and unable to provide consent. Such implied consent can be negated, however, such as when an adult wears a bracelet which expresses objection to medical treatment in an emergency, perhaps on religious grounds.[3] The policy of legally implying consent, in the absence of specific evidence to the contrary, serves a utilitarian purpose of presuming what most in society would want in an emergency.

[D] *Invalidating Manifestations of Consent*

[1] Incapacity

Both express and implied manifestations can be held invalid. An individual can be held to lack capacity to consent. A child, depending on her age, may consent to certain things, such as giving permission for someone to borrow a toy. On the other hand, the child's legal guardian must consent before the child undergoes elective surgery. The rights of adolescents to consent without parental permission is the source of significant legal and social controversy, most notably in the context of legal abortions.

An individual without sufficient mental capacity due to insanity or retardation may not legally consent. Such a general statement leaves unanswered the degree of incapacity required to invalidate consent, which like infancy undoubtedly varies with the activity in question. When, for example, is the right of the mentally impaired to engage in sexual intercourse invalidated by an inability to consent, thereby making the partner liable for battery?

Incapacity can also be the result of drug ingestion (including alcohol).[4] A, knowing B is drunk, may not accept as a gift B's car based on consent. While there exists limited judicial considerations of the issue, it would appear that, at least in most instances, incapacity that is not known or should

---

[3] *Cf.* In re Osborne, 294 A.2d 372 (D.C. Ct. App. 1972), where the plaintiff's hospital bed writings indicated that the patient would regard a transfusion under any circumstances as violative of his religious beliefs.

[4] *See* Bailey v. Belinfante, 218 S.E.2d 289 (Ga. Ct. App. 1975), where the patient claimed that he was not conscious when asked by dentist, immediately prior to surgery, for his signature on a consent form to extract the remainder of his teeth. The court held existence of consent was a jury question.

not be reasonably known by the potential defendant should not invalidate a defense of consent.

[2] Action Beyond Scope of Consent

Consent is also invalidated if the action goes beyond the consent manifested. A consent to play football does not constitute a consent that the opposing team can bite an opponent's arm or gouge an opponent's eyes while tackling,[5] as such conduct is not accepted in either the rules or the custom of the game. What constitutes the dimensions of the consent can often be a difficult issue of fact.

Since medical treatment requires consent, the determination of the effective actual consent is critical in this context. A physician may engage in medical procedures that go beyond what the patient intended to authorize. A medical procedure without consent[6] constitutes a battery and would subject the physician to liability for any injury involved, regardless of whether the procedure was performed competently. Determining the limits of the patient's consent often poses a difficult factual issue. Consider *Mohr v. Williams,*[7] where the physician received consent to perform surgery of the right ear. While the patient was anesthetized under surgery, the physician discovered that the left ear was in need of an operation. The physician performed the operation and was held liable. But in *Kennedy v. Parrott,*[8] a physician's decision to puncture cysts discovered on ovaries during an appendix operation was held reasonable to avoid an additional operation.

[3] Fraud

Consent is invalid if it is induced by fraud that misrepresents an essential aspect of the interaction. For example, fraud negates the consent if A asks B to eat pizza without informing B the pizza contains rat poison.[9] However, fraud to a collateral matter does not negate the consent. For example, misstating the brand name would not negate the consent under normal circumstances.

In the medical context, the failure of a physician to inform the patient about the risks of medical treatment before procuring the patient's consent

[5] *See* Hackbart v. Cincinnati Bengals, Inc., 601 F.2d 516, 520 (10th Cir. 1979), *cert. denied,* 444 U.S. 931 (1979), where the court stated, while choosing not to decide, that it was "highly questionable" whether professional football player consented to be hit by opponent after play had stopped merely by playing in the game.

[6] These cases must be distinguished from instances where the physician procures consent, but the patient is inadequately informed of the risks. *See* § 2.01 [D][3] and § 7.03, *infra.*

[7] 104 N.W. 12 (Minn. 1905).

[8] 90 S.E.2d 754 (N.C. 1956).

[9] *See* Kathleen K. v. Robert B., 198 Cal. Rptr. 273 (Cal. Ct. App. 1984), where a fraudulent failure to disclose a sexually transmitted disease was held to negate consent to sexual intercourse.

is most often treated as an issue of negligence under medical malpractice. The consent is negated only if a reasonable physician would have informed the patient.[10]

[4] Duress

Consent procured under physical threat is invalid. However, as a general rule, economic pressure, while coercive, does not negate consent. Given situational pressures, much consent is to some degree not totally voluntary. In very extreme instances, situational duress can negate consent. If A, under a duty to help B summon help to escape from a stalled elevator, demands B's car before notifying authorities that B is trapped, B's consent is coerced and not a defense.

[5] Illegality

Should the courts recognize consent to acts which are criminal in that jurisdiction? The traditional majority rule holds that a person *cannot* consent to a criminal act; the consent is always invalid. Consequently, if A and B are engaged in an illegal boxing match, the participants' consent, which would otherwise prevent liability for battery, is invalidated.[11] The winner of the fight loses the tort action. By contrast, some courts have rejected this position to a large extent. Taking the minority position, the Restatement, for example, holds that a person can consent to a criminal act for purposes of tort liability.[12] The consent is still valid except where the criminal law is specifically designed to protect members of the victim's class. Consequently, even under the Restatement minority position, a criminal law making it illegal for a juvenile to engage in prize-fighting would negate the consent in tort law and enable the victim to sue in tort.

§ 2.02 SELF-DEFENSE

[A] *Overview and Definition*

Self-defense, both in tort and criminal law, constitutes a defense which can justify and therefore negate intentional tort liable. In essence, reasonable force can be used where one reasonably believes that such force is necessary to protect oneself from immediate harm. The defense is both objective and subjective. The defendant must sincerely believe the force is necessary for protection, but in addition must act reasonably. Sincere but unreasonable actions are not privileged.

[B] *The Threat Must be Immediate*

Self-defense must be in response to an immediate threat of harm.[13] If A is in the process of hitting B, B can use reasonable force to protect

[10] *See infra* § 7.03.

[11] *See* Hart v. Geysel, 294 P. 570 (Wash. 1930).

[12] Restatement §§ 60, 61.

[13] Restatement § 63.

himself. The threat must be immediate; a preemptive strike is not justified under common-law rules. Under traditional rationale, permitting preventive strikes would accelerate violence in instances where the use of force, despite ominous signs, could otherwise be avoided. It would also greatly enlarge the zone of possible misinterpretation of the other's intention.

On the other hand, some contemporary commentary and limited statutory formulations support varying degrees of modification of the immediacy requirement. If A is confined in a cell with B, who announces he will use his superior strength to attack A later that night, must A forsake a preemptive strike?[14] Some criminal statutes do relax immediacy to include harm threatened during the "present occasion."[15] Particularly in the context of spousal abuse, where it is argued that the victim of the abuse is effectively entrapped in the relationship, some commentators have argued that the abuse victim's attack on the other spouse should be justified as an extended concept of self-defense. There has been, however, little judicial acceptance of this position.[16]

It is clear that retaliation is not a basis for justification under self-defense.[17] If A hits B and retreats, B cannot hit A to retaliate. The cessation of hostility by A must, however, be effectively conveyed to B, or B may reasonably believe self-defense is still justified. If the initial aggressor does effectively convey retreat and the initial victim attacks, the initial aggressor is now justified in exercising self-defense.

[C] *The Victim's Response Must be Reasonable*

Self-defense is only justified if the individual reasonably believes that force is necessary to avoid an unlawful attack.[18] Even if the belief proved reasonable, the individual must also sincerely believe self-defense is necessary. The belief need not be correct, however. If A reasonably and sincerely believes B is imminently going to attack, A is justified in using force in self-defense even if the perception of B's attack is wrong and an innocent B is injured or even killed. A is not liable in this instance.

Force intended to inflict death or serious bodily injury is only justified if the individual reasonably believes she would suffer serious bodily injury or death from the attack. A cannot intentionally inflict serious bodily injury or death to prevent non-serious bodily injury even if that is the only way

---

[14] *See* State v. Schroeder, 261 N.W.2d 759 (Neb. 1978) (court in criminal context held preemptive attack in prison cell unlawful).

[15] *See* Model Penal Code § 3.04.

[16] *See generally* David L. Faigman, Note, *The Battered Woman Syndrome and Self-Defense: A Legal and Empirical Dissent*, 72 Va. L. Rev. 619 (1986). *See also* Holly Maguigan, *Battered Women and Self-Defense: Myths and Misconceptions in Current Reform Proposals*, 140 U. Pa. L. Rev. 379 (1991).

[17] *See* Drabek v. Sabley, 142 N.W.2d 798 (Wis. 1966).

[18] *See* Restatement §§ 63-65.

to prevent non-serious bodily injury. If A is about to kick B, B cannot shoot A even if this is the only way to avoid being kicked. The threat of serious bodily injury does not, however, constitute the infliction of serious bodily injury. Consequently, the threat to shoot may be deemed reasonable when actually firing the gun would not.[19]

[D] *The Obligation to Retreat From Deadly Force*

There is general agreement that there is no obligation to retreat from force *not* threatening death or serious bodily injury. For example, assume A is facing an attack from B that will not involve serious bodily injury. Even if A knew that she could safely retreat from B's attack, A need not retreat even if A recognizes that her failure to retreat will require her to respond to B's attack with comparable force in the exercise of self-defense.

There is disagreement among jurisdictions whether retreat is required where self-defense would require the use of force intended to inflict serious bodily injury or death. The majority position does not require retreat, assuming the threatened individual has the legal right to be present or to proceed. Under the majority rationale, the right and dignity of the individual can be defended with deadly force.

The minority position, endorsed by the Restatement,[20] requires retreat where serious bodily injury or death would otherwise be required in self-defense. The minority position does not, however, require retreat from the victim's dwelling unless, according to the Restatement, the assailant also lives in the dwelling. Furthermore, retreat is not required if the victim neither correctly nor reasonably believes such a retreat could be safely accomplished. The Restatement and the minority positions prefer that the victim suffer some loss of personal rights rather than inflict, even on the wrongdoer, death or serious bodily injury if retreat would safely avoid such violence.

§ 2.03 DEFENSE OF OTHERS

[A] *Overview*

A person can use reasonable force to protect a third person from immediate unlawful physical harm. The prevailing rule does not limit the right of protection to family or household members. An individual can interfere on behalf of a stranger.

[B] *Limited Privilege Rule*

Some courts adhere to the rule that the privilege to use force in defense of a third person exists only when the person being defended was privileged to use force. The intervener must stand in the "shoes of the person" being

---

[19] *See* Restatement § 70.

[20] Restatement § 65 cmt. g.

protected. Consequently, only when the person being defended has the right of self-defense can the intervener claim a privilege. Under this rule, if A reasonably believes B is being unlawfully attacked by C and D and uses reasonable force against C and D to protect B, A is liable if it turns out B was knowingly resisting a lawful arrest by undercover agents. Since B did not have the privilege of self-defense, A's behavior, however reasonable, is not privileged.[21]

[C] *Restatement Rule*

Other courts have concluded there is a privilege to use reasonable force to protect a third party whenever the actor reasonably believes a third party is entitled to exercise self-defense. Under this rule, endorsed by the Restatement, if A reasonably believes B is being unlawfully attacked by C and D, A's use of reasonable force is privileged even if B in fact is the wrongdoer with no privilege of self-defense.[22]

[D] *Competing Policy Considerations*

The Restatement rule appears justified from a moral perspective. A Good Samaritan acting reasonably to defend a third party has behaved without fault and perhaps heroically. A reasonable mistake from this perspective should not lead to liability. From a utilitarian, accident avoidance perspective, the issue is more clouded. Arguably, intervention by a Good Samaritan should be encouraged. The Good Samaritan may be available to help when police or other professionals are not on the scene. On the other hand, the risk of stranger intervention is high since there is an inherent risk the force will be misdirected against an innocent party instead of a wrongdoer. There is ample documentation that even professional police intervention will occasionally direct force against an innocent party in error. Should an untrained citizen, where the risk of misdirected force is even higher, be encouraged to intervene with force or to solicit instead professional assistance?

§ 2.04 DEFENSE AND RECOVERY OF PROPERTY

[A] *Overview*

An individual is privileged to use reasonable force to prevent a tort against her real or personal property. However, unlike self-defense, a reasonable mistake will not excuse force that is directed against an innocent party.

[B] *Reasonable Force*

Only reasonable force can be exercised in protection of property.[23] Force

[21] *See* Robinson v. City of Decatur, 29 So. 2d 429 (Ala. Ct. App. 1947).

[22] Restatement § 76.

[23] *See* M'Ilvoy v. Cockran, 2 A.K. Marsh 271 (Ky. 1820); Brown v. Martinez, 361 P.2d 152 (N.M. 1961). *See* Restatement § 77.

intended to inflict death or serious bodily injury is never reasonable to protect just mere property. If A's only method of preventing B from stealing his money is to shoot B, A must refrain from exercising such force in defense of property and allow the property to be stolen. One is, however, privileged to exercise deadly force if it is reasonably believed necessary in self-defense or defense of others from deadly force. Consequently, if A defends her property from B and concurrently must exercise self-defense, deadly force may be justified under self-defense, but not defense of property.

Even slight force is unreasonable in defense of property if it is excessive. Consequently, if a verbal request would suffice, A may not push B off his property before requesting B to leave. The level of force utilized to protect property is privileged provided it appeared reasonable. Subsequent recognition that the force used exceeded what was necessary does not negate the privilege. If A reasonably believes B is ignoring her request to leave her property, A may push B off the property, even if A later learned B would have left with an additional verbal request.

[C] *Force Against a Privileged Party*

A reasonable mistake that an individual is not privileged to intrude or use property is not an excuse, unless the victim intentionally or negligently causes the actor to believe the intrusion is unprivileged. A's use of force to evict B off her property, when in fact B is privileged to be on her property, eliminates the defense even though A's mistake was reasonable. If, however, A's eviction of B is based on self-defense and not merely defense of property, a reasonable mistake defense would be allowed.

[D] *Defense of Habitation*

The Supreme Court has recognized that there is no stronger area of privacy than the "unambiguous physical dimensions of an individual's home."[24] The common law has traditionally protected the dwelling more vigorously than more ordinary property. Remarkably, the Restatement would authorize the use of deadly force when needed to prevent any breaking and entry into a dwelling and leaves open, in a caveat, whether deadly force could be used to prevent similar intrusion in other buildings as well under certain circumstances.[25]

The far better and more current view is that the use of deadly force or force likely to cause serious bodily harm is not justified unless the intruder threatens the occupants' safety, by committing or intending to commit a dangerous felony on the property.[26] Additionally, the homeowner may not

---

[24] Payton v. New York, 445 U.S. 573, 589 (1980).

[25] Restatement § 143 and caveat.

[26] *See, e.g.*, Morrison v. State, 371 S.W.2d 441 (Tenn. 1963). Note that while burglary is often characterized as a dangerous felony, it includes, under the common law, mere

eject a non-threatening trespasser or invited guest when doing so would subject that person to serious physical harm.[27]

[E] *Mechanical Devices*

The use of mechanical devices intended to inflict serious injury or death to protect property is severely discouraged by the courts. Such force, even when inflicted personally by an individual defending her property, would be unlawful, unless another privilege, such as the right of self-defense against deadly force, was implicated. Similarly, mechanical infliction of deadly force, such as by the use of spring guns, is not privileged unless such force would be justified if the actor were himself inflicting the harm.[28] Indeed, there is increasing authority, including the Model Penal Code in the criminal context, which holds that mechanical devices which are intended to inflict death or serious bodily injury are never justifiable.[29] This latter position reflects the public policy concern that such devices are too hazardous to the innocent and lack the potential to provide the requisite warning to a dangerous intruder and thereby insure that deadly force was necessary.

Barbed wire fences and similar deterrents to enter land unlawfully are not generally perceived as intended to inflict death or serious bodily injury. Unlike spring guns, they are visible and less likely to cause serious injury.

---

entering of a dwelling at night to commit any felony. Modern statutes also frequently extend the definition of burglary to include the entry of a store during business hours with the intent to commit even petty larceny. Entry with the intent to commit larceny should not, in the absence of a threat of death or serious bodily injury, justify the use of deadly force. *See* Tennessee v. Garner, 471 U.S. 1 (1985), where the Supreme Court held that the police use of deadly force to stop a fleeing fifteen-year-old who was characterized as a burglar was unconstitutional despite the traditional common law rule allowing the use of deadly force to halt a fleeing felon.

[27] *See* Depue v. Flatau, 111 N.W. 1 (Minn. 1907), where defendant had removed an ill dinner guest from the house during a blizzard, put the guest back into the guest's sleigh, and wrapped the reins around the guest's hands. The plaintiff was held liable for damages caused by the frostbite to the guest as a result. *But see* Tucker v. Burt, 115 N.W. 722 (Mich. 1908), where the ejection of an invited guest was permitted because the guest had a communicable illness.

[28] *See* Katko v. Briney, 183 N.W.2d 657, 659 (Iowa 1971), where the court held that a spring gun was justified only "when the trespasser was committing a felony of violence or a felony punishable by death, or where the trespasser was endangering human life by his act." In *Katko*, the trespasser was intruding into an uninhabited farm structure with the intent to commit larceny. If it had been a dwelling at nighttime, the felony of burglary would have existed under the common law. Modern statutes have extended burglary to non-dwellings. While historically some courts have justified deadly force to prevent burglary, the modern and better view is to limit deadly force to acts endangering human life. *See* Tennessee v. Garner, *supra* note 26 and accompanying text. *See also* Restatement § 85, which provides a privilege to use mechanical devices intending death or serious bodily injury only when actor, were he present, in fact would be so privileged.

[29] *See* Model Penal Code § 3.06(5). *See also Bishop v. State*, 356 S.E.2d 503 (Ga. 1987).

Consequently, in most instances, injury to a trespasser would be unintended. Whether liability ensues depends on whether the method of protecting the property under the circumstances was negligent.

[F] *Recovery of Personal Property*

An individual may use reasonable force to recover property when in "hot pursuit" of the wrongdoer.[30] The requirement of hot pursuit adds to the likelihood that the self-help of the victim will be directed at the actual wrongdoer. In addition, there is the strong argument that if the victim forgoes force and awaits police assistance, the wrongdoer and the victim's chattel will be much harder to locate.

The individual acts at her peril, however. If force is directed at an innocent party, against whom the privilege does not apply, the actor is liable even if the mistake was reasonable, so long as the mistake was not knowingly induced by the victim. This is consistent with the general unwillingness of courts to allow even a reasonable error directed against an innocent party when only property is being protected.

Many states have adopted a merchant's privilege which allows stores to use reasonable force to detain a person for reasonable periods to investigate possible theft.[31] The detention must be within or near the immediate parameters of the store. The merchant's privilege generally allows reasonable mistake, so an innocent customer cannot recover against the store, provided the store acted reasonably. In no event would force intended to inflict death or serious bodily injury be reasonable even if such force was the only method capable of recovering the property.

§ 2.05 NECESSITY

[A] *Overview and Definition*

Necessity is a defense which allows the defendant to interfere with the property interests of an innocent party in order to avoid a greater injury.[32] The defendant is justified in her behavior because the action minimizes the

---

[30] *See* Hodgeden v. Hubbard, 18 Vt. 594 (1846); Kirby v. Foster, 22 A. 1111 (R.I. 1891). Restatement §§ 101-04. The Restatement endorses the privilege against an actor who has tortiously taken the chattel from the victim's possession without claim of right or under claim of right but by force, duress, or fraud or who tortiously takes the chattel from the victim's possession and is about to tortiously remove it from the victim's premises or who has received custody of the chattel and refused to surrender it, or is about to remove it from the victim's premises. The privilege also applies against an actor who knowingly induces the other to believe the privilege exists or has been given the chattel by a tortfeasor and knows or should know that the tortfeasor obtained the chattel in the above manner. *See* Restatement § 101.

[31] *See* Bonkowski v. Arlan's Department Store, 162 N.W.2d 347 (Mich. Ct. App. 1968).

[32] *See* Francis H. Bohlen, *Incomplete Privilege to Inflict Intentional Invasions of Interests of Property and Personalty*, 39 Harv. L. Rev. 307 (1926).

overall loss. The defense is divided into two categories: public and private necessity.

Public necessity exists when the defendant appropriates or injures a private property interest to protect the community. Private necessity exists when the individual appropriates or injures a private property interest to protect a private interest valued greater than the appropriated or injured property. Public necessity is a complete defense, but private necessity is an incomplete defense: the defendant is privileged to interfere with another's property, but *is* liable for the damage. An unresolved issue is whether necessity should justify intentional injury or even death. There is sparse, but famous, authority that justifies intentionally killing one life to save a multitude.[33]

[B] *Private Necessity*

In private necessity, an individual has the privilege to interfere with the property right of another to avoid a greater harm, but must compensate the plaintiff for the interference.[34] This incomplete privilege can benefit the actor if another wrongly uses force to prevent the actor from entering his land or using or injuring his chattel. In *Ploof v. Putnam*,[35] a sudden storm arose, forcing the plaintiff to moor his boat on defendant's dock. The landowner's servant loosened the boat, causing the plaintiff's family and boat to be injured. The plaintiff and his family, under private necessity, were entitled to use the landowner's dock to avoid the greater harm of personal injury to themselves and more severe property damage to their boat. Consequently, the landowner was liable for his servant's wrongful use of force to expel the plaintiff and his family.

Under the particular facts of *Ploof*, the servant's actions constituted excessive force in defense of property, since forcing the family into the storm constituted deadly force which is unjustified to protect mere property. The privilege of necessity would have been critical, however, if the servant's action had been directed at the boat alone without the family in it.[36] The boat owner was privileged to use or damage an innocent party's property to avoid a greater property loss, although the party whose property was appropriated must be compensated.

Should a private party be able to appropriate property of another to protect greater property interests? From a utilitarian perspective, society gains since the greater property loss is avoided. Fairness is accomplished by requiring compensation. Query whether such justification is satisfactory for highly

---

[33] *See* United States v. Holmes, 26 F. Cas. 360 (C.C.E.D. Pa. 1842) (No. 15,383). *See* § 2.05[D], *infra*.

[34] Restatement §§ 197, 263.

[35] 71 A. 188 (Vt. 1908).

[36] *See* Vincent v. Lake Erie Transp. Co., 124 N.W. 221 (Minn. 1910).

personal property such as the diversion of water to destroy a less expensive dwelling to avoid destroying a more expensive one. Theoretically, private necessity would appear to justify such action.[37]

[C] *Public Necessity*

Public necessity allows the appropriation or injury of an innocent party's property to avoid more substantial public harm.[38] In *Surocco v. Geary*,[39] plaintiff's house was blown up to create a fire line with the intent to save more of San Francisco from destruction by fire. The destruction precluded the house's owner from saving possessions from the house even if the fire reached the house later. Unlike private necessity, there is no liability for inflicting private loss to protect the public. There is no clear line where the cumulative private interests to be saved reaches the level of a public need, but massive catastrophes, such as the historic San Francisco fire of 1849, obviously qualify.

Why should the innocent party not be compensated, particularly since there is compensation in private necessity? On the one hand, an individual should not be deterred by potential liability from acting for the public good. On the other hand, from a moral perspective, the rule appears arguably inconsistent with constitutional restraints limiting government appropriation without due compensation. While emergency exigencies can be distinguished technically from more deliberate eminent domain, there is still a strong argument to be made that the government should compensate rather than having a private individual bear the full burden.

[D] *Intentional Injury and Killing*

There is only sparse authority supporting the use of necessity to inflict personal injury on an innocent party. In a renowned criminal case, the crew threw male passengers out of a lifeboat to save the remainder.[40] Dictum concluded that if a fair lottery had been used, the killing of some to save more would be justified. There appears little reason from an injury

---

37 Consider, that while private necessity requires compensation for an injury even when the defendant was acting *reasonably*, given the circumstances, to inflict the injury, the intentional imposition of *only* a substantial *risk* of injury which results in injury (strict liability aside) requires that the risk be *unreasonable* and thus negligent to require compensation. *See infra* § 4.02.

38 Restatement §§ 196 and 262. *See also* United States v. Caltex, Inc., 344 U.S. 149 (1952), where the United States Army's destruction of an oil company's property was found privileged to prevent the capture of the equipment by advancing Japanese forces.

39 3 Cal. 69 (1853).

40 United States v. Holmes, 26 F. Cas. 360 (C.C.E.D. Pa. 1842) (No. 15,383); *see also* Regina v. Dudley & Stephens, 14 Q.B.D. 273 (1884), where three adult seamen killed and ate a 17-year-old youth in an effort to survive a period during which they were stranded on a lifeboat. Two of the seamen, who carried out the killing, were sentenced to death, but the punishment was later commuted by the Crown to six months' imprisonment.

avoidance perspective not to extend necessity where personal injury or even death must be inflicted to avoid greater public harm.[41]

---

[41] The Restatement takes no position, but the Model Penal Code argues necessity should be a defense in criminal law even when it requires intentional killing. *See* Model Penal Code § 3.03.

CHAPTER 3

THE NEGLIGENCE CONCEPT AND THE REASONABLE PERSON STANDARD OF CARE

SYNOPSIS

§ 3.01 OVERVIEW

The tort of negligence now lies at the heart of tort liability. Yet liability for negligence, as distinct from intentional tort liability or strict tort liability, is of relatively recent origin.

To recover for negligence, the plaintiff must establish each of the following elements by a preponderance of the evidence (that is, by more than 50%) to establish a prima facie case:

<u>Duty</u> — a legally recognized relationship between the parties

Standard of Care	—	the required level of expected conduct
Breach of Duty	—	failure to meet the standard of care
Cause-in-Fact	—	plaintiff's harm must have the required nexus to the defendant's breach of duty
Proximate Cause	—	there are no policy reasons to relieve the defendant of liability
Damages	—	the plaintiff suffered a cognizable injury

Although the above elements are a variation of the classic formulation of the required parts of the negligence tort, there are other ways to visualize its components. Often "standard of care" is not treated as a separate element, but is encompassed as part of the breach or duty element. The standard of care element receives separate treatment in this Chapter. There is significant overlap among the elements. Yet, as a starting point, it is useful to try to keep each element analytically separate.

This Chapter begins with a brief look at the development of the tort of negligence. It then develops the central standard of care in negligence cases, that of the reasonably prudent person. The Chapter then discusses the standard of care applied to children. This is followed by a consideration of whether there are degrees of negligence. Later chapters look at other standards of care in the law of negligence as well as the other negligence elements.

§ 3.02 HISTORICAL DEVELOPMENT

At the expense of some oversimplification, pre-negligence tort liability was based on a rather rigid writ system. To recover, the plaintiff had to establish the provisions of the appropriate writ. The two writs most relevant to tort liability were "trespass" and "trespass on the case" (or "case"). Over time, the writ of trespass encompassed direct and immediate harms. Liability was strict. Plaintiffs who suffered indirect harms were required to prove some fault on the part of the defendant to recover. Case was the proper writ for fault-based liability and, thus, became the precursor to negligence.

Around the mid-1800s, the negligence principle began to assert itself in the United States. Under negligence theory, *fault* played the key role. Without proof of fault, the plaintiff could not recover, even for direct and immediate harm.[1] Many contend that it was not coincidental that the development of the fault principle coincided with industrialization. By requiring those injured by industrial development to prove fault, as opposed to direct harm under the trespass writ, defendants were much more likely to avoid liability.[2] Thus, negligence, as a form of fault-based liability,

[1] Brown v. Kendall, 60 Mass. (6 Cush.) 292 (Mass. 1850), is widely credited with firmly establishing the negligence principle in the United States. In *Brown*, Justice Shaw also made clear that the burden of proving D's fault rested with the plaintiff.

[2] Charles O. Gregory, *Trespass to Negligence to Absolute Liability*, 37 Va. L. Rev. 359, 368 (1951) (adoption of fault-based liability was out of a "desire to make risk-creating

became established and continues to be the central basis for liability in most tort cases.

§ 3.03 THE STANDARD OF CARE

Although the "standard of care" is not traditionally listed as one of the elements of a negligence cause of action, it is a central concept in the law of negligence. In fact, negligence liability only flows where the defendant's conduct has fallen below the relevant standard of care.[3]

Most simply put, the standard of care is the level of conduct demanded of a person so as to avoid liability for negligence. Failure to meet this standard is characterized as breach of duty. For example, in most cases the standard of care requires the defendant to act as would a reasonably prudent person under the same or similar circumstances. Failure to act reasonably, then, constitutes the defendant's breach of duty. This section examines the most common standard of care — that of the reasonable person.

§ 3.04 THE REASONABLE PERSON[4]

The most common standard of care in negligence law commands the defendant to act as would a reasonably prudent person in the same or similar circumstances.[5] If the defendant does so, she is protected from negligence liability. Failure to do so constitutes unreasonable conduct and, hence, breach of duty.

Early in this century, much debate occurred about the proper manner to measure fault for negligence liability. The key controversy was whether the standard should be a subjective one that takes into account each defendant's abilities, such as mental acuity,[6] or whether the standard should

---

enterprise less hazardous to investors and entrepreneurs"). *But see* Gary T. Schwartz, *Tort Law and the Economy in Nineteenth Century America: A Reinterpretation*, 90 Yale L.J. 1717 (1981) (contending that negligence law was well-established in nineteenth century America).

[3] The element of breach of duty is intertwined with the standard of care because breach is established by the defendant's failure to meet the relevant standard of care. The standard of care is also closely connected to the duty concept as the standard of care is the measure of the duty owed.

[4] *See generally* Edward Green, *The Reasonable Man: Legal Fiction or Psychosocial Reality?*, 2 L. & Soc. Rev. 241 (1968); Fleming James, Jr., *The Qualities of the Reasonable Man in Negligence Cases*, 16 Mo. L. Rev. 1 (1951); Osborne M. Reynolds, Jr., *The Reasonable Man of Negligence Law: A Health Report on the "Odious Creature,"* 23 Okla. L. Rev. 410 (1970); David E. Seidelson, *Reasonable Expectations and Subjective Standards in Negligence Law: The Minor, the Mentally Impaired, and the Mentally Incompetent*, 50 Geo. Wash. L. Rev. 17 (1981); Jacobus tenBroek, *The Right to Live in the World: The Disabled in the Law of Torts*, 54 Cal. L. Rev. 841 (1966).

[5] This standard has been variously characterized as the standard of "a reasonable person," "a person of ordinary prudence," "a reasonable and prudent person," and "a reasonable man of ordinary prudence." Throughout this Chapter, "reasonable person" is used most frequently.

[6] Under a subjective standard the defendant's mental state, as opposed to her conduct, is the relevant focus. Thus, under that approach, a defendant could exculpate herself from

be an objective one that compares the defendant's conduct to an external standard. In the seminal case presenting this conflict, hay piled by the defendant on his land near the plaintiff's home caught fire and destroyed the plaintiff's home. Plaintiff alleged that the fire and the harm to plaintiff's home were probable. The court rejected defendant's contention that he should not be deemed negligent if he "had acted honestly and bona fide to the best of his own judgment." Instead of employing the subjective focus advocated by the defendant, the court adopted an objective standard requiring the defendant to use such "caution as a man of ordinary prudence would observe."[7] The objective approach has prevailed and, accordingly, the determination of breach of duty in most negligence cases requires finding that the defendant failed to act as a reasonable person would act in the same or similar circumstances. This objective standard looks at the defendant's conduct, comparing it to the external standard of a reasonable person.

What justifies the use of an objective standard in the negligence context? Adherents of the objective standard raise several points. First, there is concern that a truly subjective standard would be too difficult to employ. There are infinite gradations of ability and intellect, and measuring these differences would be virtually impossible.[8] Further, there is a compensation rationale, positing that those who are the most likely to cause harm should pay those they injure.[9] Finally, there is a fairness concern that members of a community should be able to expect a certain level of behavior from those around them.[10] As one advocate for the objective standard explained:

---

negligence liability by showing that she lacked awareness that her conduct was risky because of subnormal intelligence.

[7] Vaughan v. Menlove, 132 Eng. Rep. 490 (1837) ("Instead, therefore, of saying that the liability for negligence should be co-extensive with the judgment of each individual, which would be as variable as the length of the foot of each individual, we ought rather to adhere to the rule which requires in all cases a regard to caution such as a man of ordinary prudence would observe.").

[8] *See, e.g.*, O.W. Holmes, Jr., THE COMMON LAW (1881) ("[T]he impossibility of nicely measuring a man's powers and limitations is far clearer than that of ascertaining his knowledge of law.").

[9] Some of those who recognize the compensation goal of the objective standard point out that the use of an objective standard to evaluate the *plaintiff's* conduct (for purposes of analyzing the defense of contributory negligence) is unwarranted. They propose instead a dual standard, by which the plaintiff's fault is judged by a subjective standard while the defendant's behavior is evaluated by an objective standard. *See, e.g.*, Fleming James, Jr. and John J. Dickinson, *Accident Proneness and Accident Law*, 63 Harv. L. Rev. 769, 782-791 (1950).

[10] Osborne M. Reynolds, Jr., *The Reasonable Man of Negligence Law: A Health Report on the "Odious Creature,"* 23 Okla. L. Rev. 410, 426-427 (1970). Professor Reynolds defends the objective standard as follows: "[T]he reasonableness standard suffices by meeting the test of holding everyone to the socially acceptable minimum while still being flexible enough to allow great variation in conduct. Such a standard allows for change as ideas of acceptability shift. . . . The present rule allows judge and juror to bring to bear on the

> [W]hen men live in society, a certain average of conduct, a sacrifice of individual peculiarities going beyond a certain point, is necessary to the general welfare. If, for instance, a man is born hasty and awkward, is always having accidents and hurting himself or his neighbors, no doubt his congenital defects will be allowed for in the courts of Heaven, but his slips are no less troublesome to his neighbors than if they sprang from guilty neglect. His neighbors accordingly require him, at his proper peril, to come up to their standard, and the courts which they establish decline to take his personal equation into account.[11]

Thus, the law imposes on each person an obligation to conform to the objective reasonableness standard.

Critics of the objective standard note the anomaly of proclaiming persons at fault (that is, negligent) for failing to meet some standard that they are simply unable to meet. For example, if D is born with unusually slow reflexes, should D be at fault when she fails to hit her brakes quickly enough to avoid harm to P because so-called reasonable persons, who had the good fortune to have been born with faster reflexes, would have reacted more quickly? There is, then, an undercurrent of potential unfairness in this objective standard.

The objective standard has become well-settled in negligence law. The debate centers around the extent to which there is flexibility in this standard.

The adoption of the objective standard has an enormous impact on the evidence that a jury is permitted to consider in its evaluation of the defendant's conduct. For the most part, only evidence relevant to the general characteristics of this reasonable person are admitted for jury consideration.

[A] *The Characteristics of the Reasonable Person*

It is challenging to define the qualities of the reasonable person that a jury is expected to use as its guidepost in determining the reasonableness of the defendant's conduct. To a large measure the standard is constantly being redefined by each jury as it determines such things as the appropriate level of knowledge or skill expected of members of the community. The reasonable person possesses those attributes that a jury decides represent the community norms, and the expected qualities of the reasonable person are not necessarily what is the average or even what most do in the community.[12] Employing something akin to the common parental

---

question of liability their ideas of what is average, typical, ethical, and moral in society, while not limiting the standard to any one of these sub-points."

[11] O. W. Holmes, Jr., THE COMMON LAW (1881). In the following paragraph, Holmes continues: "The law considers, in other words, what would be blameworthy in the average man, the man of ordinary intelligence and prudence, and determines liability by that. If we fall below the level in those gifts, it is our misfortune; so much as that we must act at our peril. . . ." *Id.*

[12] What is customary, however, can have a great influence on the jury's determination of breach of duty. *See infra* § 4.03.

admonition of "Do as I say, not as I do," the jury determines what the expected level of conduct in the community should be.[13]

In order for the jury to decide whether the defendant's conduct is unreasonable under the circumstances presented in the case, the judge instructs the jury to compare the defendant's conduct to that of a reasonable person. Based on this broad instruction, the jury considers the attributes of the reasonable person as the jurors see them. There are some important parameters, however. The reasonable person is entirely a concoction of the common law, a wholly mythical creation. The reasonable person is no real person nor any member of the jury.[14] Further, while the reasonable person's qualities are those the jury determines are the expected attributes of those in the community, the reasonable person cannot be expected to be infallible. Instead, the reasonable person should possess the weaknesses and frailties acknowledged in others in the community.[15]

In addition, there are certain things that the reasonable person is expected to know such as that fire burns and loaded firearms are potentially dangerous.[16] Thus, the defendant's claimed ignorance of a well-known hazard, such as the danger posed by immersing an electrical appliance in water, is irrelevant to the defendant's liability under the objective standard. Further, the reasonable person is usually expected to notice that which is evident, open, and apparent, and a defendant can be liable for not seeing what reasonably should have been noticed. Accordingly, D's contentions that he neither knew his car tire was badly in need of repair nor realized that driving on a worn tire posed risks of harm to others are irrelevant because failure to know these facts is unreasonable.[17] In addition, because

---

[13] Thus, the jury can, and probably often does, set a rather exacting standard of reasonableness. Although the jury is instructed not to evaluate the defendant's actions through hindsight, it is likely that the temptation to do so is great where the jury is presented with a case involving injury caused by the defendant.

[14] Indeed, it may be reversible error to instruct the jury that its members should put themselves in the position of the defendant in determining reasonableness. Freeman v. Adams, 218 P. 600 (Cal. 1923).

[15] *See* Andre Tunc, *Fault: A Common Name for Different Misdeeds*, 49 Tul. L. Rev. 279, 280 (1975) (Error "is a departure which is occasionally unavoidable for every reasonable man or even the most cautious one. . . . Error is merely the consequence of human nature. It is statistically unavoidable. . . .").

[16] Restatement § 290, which provides that the actor "is required to know the qualities and habits of human beings and animals and the qualities, characteristics, and capacities of things and forces in so far as they are matters of common knowledge at the time and in the community. . . ." Comment e continues this point: "As a reasonable man, the actor is required to possess such scientific knowledge as is common among laymen at the time and in the community. Thus, he is required to know the ordinary operation of well-known natural laws."

[17] Delair v. McAdoo, 188 A. 181, 184 (Pa. 1936) ("Any ordinary individual, whether a car owner or not, knows that when a tire is worn through to the fabric, its further use is dangerous and it should be removed. . . . All drivers must be held to a knowledge of

the objective standard assumes that the reasonable person possesses the general experience of the community, the driver would be unable to show that, as a new driver, he was ignorant of the danger of worn tires. Finally, because this objective standard is a community standard, it is the knowledge and understanding generally held by members of the community that is relevant. That D comes from another area with different common community knowledge does not matter; she is expected to rise to the level of the community that she is in.[18]

[B] *Flexibility in the Reasonable Person Standard*

Although an objective standard is usually employed in negligence cases, there is debate about how objective this so-called objective standard should be. Using the standard of the reasonable person under the same or similar circumstances, flexibility can be added through the "circumstances" part of the analysis. However, if all of the defendant's specific qualities are permitted to be considered by the jury, there is no longer an objective standard. Ultimately, in most jurisdictions, a jury will be permitted to consider the physical conditions of the defendant and that the defendant was acting under emergency conditions. Most other characteristics, such as mental conditions or inexperience, are not taken into account.

[1] Emergency

Nearly all states permit the jury to consider in its determination of the defendant's reasonableness evidence that the defendant was acting under emergency conditions. Because the standard of care includes the circumstances under which the defendant was acting, it takes into account that the defendant acted during an emergency. In other words, the defendant is held to a standard of a reasonable person under those emergency circumstances. Some courts refer to this as the "emergency doctrine."

The fact that the defendant was acting in an emergency does not necessarily exculpate the defendant from liability. A jury in determining the reasonableness of the defendant's conduct must decide whether in light of the emergency the defendant acted with due care. For example, D is waiting in his car in a line at the drive-up teller window. Suddenly, the car in front of D begins to back up. Without signaling, D immediately puts

---

these facts. An owner or operator cannot escape simply because he says he does not know. He must know. . . . The law requires drivers and owners of motor vehicles to know the condition of those parts which are likely to become dangerous where the flaws or faults would be disclosed by a reasonable inspection.").

[18] So, for example, if D has never been out of Manhattan before her first foray into Wyoming, her claimed lack of knowledge about the traits of mules will not be relevant to a determination of her liability. *Cf.* Tolin v. Terrell, 117 S.W. 290 (Ky. 1909) ("[I]t is a matter of common knowledge and common experience that there is no telling when or under what circumstances a mule will or will not kick."). *See* William L. Prosser and W. Page Keeton, TORTS, § 32, at 184 (West 5th ed. 1984).

his car into reverse and backs up into P's car behind him, causing property damage. The jury is entitled to consider the fact that D was acting in an emergency situation, but could conclude that the reasonable person in that predicament would have employed greater care than did the defendant.[19] The defendant acting in a predicament is not expected to employ the same level of judgment and reflection as would a reasonable person not in an emergency.[20] Thus, where the defendant makes an error in judgment there will be no negligence liability provided that reasonable persons in that position could make a similar mistake.[21]

The standard of care does not change in cases where the defendant asserts she was acting in an emergency context. The relevance of the emergency goes to the jury's determination of breach of duty. Upon request from the defendant, many courts will give the jury a specific instruction on the role of emergency, although it can be argued that such an instruction is unnecessary as repetitious of the general instruction asking the jury to consider if the defendant acted as would a reasonable person in similar circumstances.[22]

The "emergency doctrine" is unavailable where the defendant's tortious conduct contributed to the creation of the emergency. Thus, if D is speeding and suddenly finds herself confronted with the choice of hitting a child or

---

[19] Wilson v. Sibert, 535 P.2d 1034 (Alaska 1975) (finding that the lower court was correct in refusing to grant P's motion for a directed verdict on D's liability because it was for the jury to evaluate D's conduct in light of the emergency).

[20] As Judge Cardozo noted about those acting in an emergency: "Errors in judgment, however, would not count against him, if they resulted from the excitement and confusion of the moment. . . . The reason that was exacted of him was not the reason of the morrow. It was the reason fitted and proportioned to the time and the event." Wagner v. International Ry. Co., 133 N.E. 437, 438 (N.Y. 1921).

[21] This point is made in a case known more because of its author's flowery verbiage than for any profound legal point. In Cordas v. Peerless Transp. Co., 27 N.Y.S.2d 198 (1941), D, a taxi driver, was confronted by a gun-wielding thief who jumped into D's cab, threatening D's life. The plaintiffs were injured when the taxi ran into them after D abruptly jumped out of his moving cab with the gunman still inside. Justice Carlin noted: "If under normal circumstances an act is done which might be considered negligent, it does not follow as a corollary that a similar act is negligent if performed by a person acting under an emergency, not of his own making, in which he suddenly is faced with a patent danger with a moment left to adopt a means of extrication." He continued: "The chauffeur–the ordinary man in this case–acted in a split second in a most harrowing experience. To call him negligent would be to brand him coward; the court does not do so in spite of what those swaggering heroes, 'whose valor plucks dead lions by the beard,' may bluster to the contrary." *Id.* at 202.

[22] Some courts have come to that conclusion and do not permit an instruction on emergency. *See, e.g.,* Simonson v. White, 713 P.2d 983 (Mont. 1986) ("The instruction adds nothing to the law of negligence and serves only to leave an impression in the minds of the jurors that a driver is somehow excused from the ordinary standard of care."). Most jurisdictions, however, continue to permit an instruction on emergency. For a sample jury instruction regarding emergency, see Wilson v. Sibert, 535 P.2d 1034, 1039 n.11 (Alaska 1975).

P's car and opts for the latter, D will not be able to have the jury instructed to consider the emergency context in which D had to act.

Finally, there are contexts in which a defendant can be negligent for failing to anticipate an emergency. Many business establishments are expected to anticipate the possibility of fire; operators of public pools should anticipate drownings; and drivers should be on the lookout for unexpected hazards.[23] Failure to take those precautions that would be taken by a reasonable person will lead to negligence liability.

[2] Physical Conditions

As a general principle, because they are easily measured and perceived as tangible, the defendant's own physical qualities may be taken into account by the jury in the breach determination. Thus, the jury may consider such things as the defendant's height, loss of a limb, or deafness in deciding whether the defendant acted reasonably, and the standard of care will reflect the actor's physical condition.[24] Negligence law does not command that the blind see and the deaf hear.[25] For example, D, blind since birth, is walking down the street and collides into and injures P. In P's action against D for negligence, the jury will evaluate D's conduct, comparing her to a reasonable blind person under the same or similar circumstances.

As with emergency, just because the party's physical condition is taken into account does not mean that she will be exonerated. The jury will be asked to decide if a reasonable person with the same condition would have behaved like the defendant. Thus, in the above hypothetical, a jury could still find D negligent if it concludes that a reasonable blind person would have taken greater precautions. Sometimes the physical condition of the party requires the use of greater care; sometimes it bars the party from an activity entirely, such as a blind person from driving.

To some degree, intoxication can be viewed as a physical condition. Because the reasonable person is viewed as sober, the voluntarily

---

[23] Fowler V. Harper, et al., THE LAW OF TORTS, § 16.11, at 490 ("To an extent that varies tremendously with the circumstances, we will all be held to expect the unexpected.").

[24] The Restatement provides: "If the actor is ill or otherwise physically disabled, the standard of conduct to which he must conform to avoid being negligent is that of a reasonable man under like disability." Restatement § 283C. Contrast this situation to those where the party is acting entirely involuntarily. There is no tort liability where the defendant is rendered unconscious with no warning of impending danger or unreasonable conduct putting her in that state. *See, e.g.*, Hammontree v. Jenner, 97 Cal. Rptr. 739 (Cal. Ct. App. 1971) (no negligence where D has epileptic seizure).

[25] But it does require that the slow-reflexed be quicker and the insane be sane. This latter point is explored in the next subsection. Is the different treatment for physical conditions justified?

intoxicated defendant will be required to perform as well as a sober person, not as well as a reasonable person at that level of intoxication.[26]

[3] Mental Conditions

Most courts have treated mental conditions entirely differently from physical conditions, making the former wholly irrelevant for purposes of negligence liability. In most jurisdictions, the insane are to be held to a standard of sanity, because the reasonable person is deemed sane. Similarly, people with cognitive disabilities are held to a level of normal intelligence.[27] Several justifications have been offered for this seemingly harsh rule: that mental disability is too hard to measure, that it is easily feigned, that an innocent plaintiff should be compensated, and that imposing liability will make guardians take greater care of those who are mentally disabled.[28]

There has been substantial criticism of the rule that refuses to take a person's mental condition into account in determining the reasonableness of the conduct.[29] It has been viewed as unfair and outmoded in light of greater modern understanding of mental illness. Despite mounting criticism, as a practical matter, there have been few cases challenging the traditional rule. At least one court, however, has signalled a willingness to move away from a purely objective test in insanity cases. In *Breunig v. American Family Ins. Co.*, the plaintiff motorist was injured by an insane driver, who saw a white light on the back of the car preceding her, followed it believing God had taken hold of her steering wheel, and stepped on the gas in order to fly "because Batman does it." Breaking with the traditional approach, the Wisconsin Supreme Court determined that the typical rule that "insanity

---

[26] Restatement § 283C cmt d ("A drunken man may still act in all respects as reasonably as one who is sober; and if he does, he is not negligent. If, however, his conduct is not that of a reasonable man who is sober, his voluntary intoxication does not excuse him from liability."). Involuntary intoxication, as where a person drinks from a punch bowl which is spiked or suffers an unexpected reaction to medication, is typically treated as a physical ailment.

[27] Restatement § 283B provides: "Unless the actor is a child, his insanity or other mental deficiency does not relieve the actor from liability for conduct which does not conform to the standard of a reasonable man under like circumstances." Comment c, after noting that insanity is not taken into account, continues: "As to mental deficiency falling short of insanity, as in the case of stupidity, lack of intelligence, excitability, or proneness to accident, no allowance is made, and the actor is held to the standard of conduct of a reasonable man who is not mentally deficient, even though it is in fact beyond his capacity to conform to it."

[28] *See id.*

[29] *See* James W. Ellis, *Tort Responsibility of Mentally Disabled Persons*, 1981 Am. B. Found. Res. J. 1079; David E. Seidelson, *Reasonable Expectations and Subjective Standards in Negligence Law: The Minor, the Mentally Impaired and the Mentally Incompetent*, 50 Geo. Wash. L. Rev. 17 (1981); Daniel W. Shuman, *Therapeutic Jurisprudence and Tort Law: A Limited Subjective Standard of Care*, 46 SMU L. Rev. 409 (1992). *But see* Stephanie I. Splane, Note, *Tort Liability of the Mentally Ill in Negligence Actions*, 93 Yale L.J. 153 (1983) (supporting holding the mentally disabled to a reasonableness standard).

is no defense is too broad when it is applied to a negligence case where the driver is suddenly overcome without forewarning by a mental disability or disorder which incapacitates him from conforming his conduct to the standards of a reasonable man under like circumstances."[30] The court ultimately upheld the jury verdict for the plaintiff, however, finding that the jury could have found that the insane driver had notice of prior insane delusions.

While *Breunig* is a step away from the traditional rule, it represents a small and confusing step. If a person is so mentally disabled that she is unable to conform herself to the requirements of the law, or even to understand what she is doing, why should the suddenness of the onset of the delusion determine liability?[31]

It may be time to reconsider the traditional rule that excludes mental condition from consideration. This approach toward people with mental disabilities may no longer be justified in light of the many other areas of negligence law where there has been a move toward recognizing the validity of mental upset, and a move away from the belief that permitting recovery for mental distress is unworkable because it is too hard to measure or too easily feigned,[32] two of the justifications for the traditional rule.[33]

Some jurisdictions, in fact, now employ a dual standard that uses the objective standard for the mentally disabled when they are defendants, but a more flexible standard taking mental condition into account when they are plaintiffs and the issue is their contributory negligence.[34] The justification is that this approach furthers the compensation goal of torts. To the extent that courts have concluded that it is workable to take mental disabilities into account, use of a dual standard calls into question the claims of some that mental conditions are too hard to measure or too easily feigned.

Finally, the distinction between the physical and the mental is becoming unworkable as science increasingly discovers physical causes of mental

---

[30] Breunig v. American Family Ins. Co., 173 N.W.2d 619, 624 (Wis. 1970).

[31] The *Breunig* court analogized the sudden mental lapse to an unforeseeable sudden lapse of consciousness, such as that brought on by a sudden heart attack, and argued for similar treatment. Perhaps the *Breunig* requirement that the incident be without warning or otherwise unforeseeable is an effort toward a fairer balance between true fault and compensation, and recognizes that caretakers will have less incentive to control where there is a lack of foreseeability.

[32] *See infra* § 10.01.

[33] *See, e.g.*, Cowan v. Doering, 545 A.2d 159 (N.J. 1988) ("The modern trend appears to favor the use of a capacity-based standard for the contributory negligence of mentally disturbed plaintiffs.").

[34] *See, e.g.*, Mochen v. State of New York, 352 N.Y.S.2d 290 (N.Y. App. Div. 1974).

disabilities. Times may have changed enough that mental conditions may soon be treated like physical conditions.[35]

On the other hand, if mental disabilities were taken into account it might be hard to formulate a workable standard. What would be the appropriate standard of care? As a practical matter, would this be a move to an entirely subjective focus?

[4] The Effect of Superior Abilities, Skill or Knowledge

A particularly challenging issue involves the treatment of defendants (who are not "professionals"[36]) with greater than average skills and abilities. To what degree should extraordinary qualities affect the reasonable person standard of care? The answer is that *the standard of care* will not be changed although the defendant's special skills may affect the jury's breach determination. For example, D, a trucker with decades of driving experience, hits P. Although P contends in his negligence action against D that D should be held to a standard higher than that of the reasonable person because of D's special driving skill and experience, a court would hold D to the standard of a reasonable person under the same or similar circumstances.[37] Yet, D's special skills are not irrelevant. The defendant's special talents are relevant to the jury's determination of breach of duty. One court, in permitting a jury to consider the defendant's particular experience with and knowledge about certain machinery, explained:

> The standard of the reasonable man requires only a minimum of attention, perception, memory, knowledge, intelligence, and judgment in order to recognize the existence of the risk. If the actor has in fact more than the minimum of these qualities, he is required to exercise the superior qualities that he has in a manner reasonable under the circumstances.[38]

---

[35] Indeed, even as strong a proponent of the objective standard as Oliver Wendell Holmes, Jr. assumed that mental illness would be accounted for in the negligence determination. In his famous piece justifying the objective standard, he noted: "Insanity is a more difficult matter to deal with [than physical disabilities], and no general rule can be laid down about it. There is no doubt that in many cases a man may be insane, and yet perfectly capable of taking the precautions, and of being influenced by the motives, which the circumstances demand. But if insanity of a pronounced type exists, manifestly incapacitating the sufferer from complying with the rule which he has broken, good sense would require it to be admitted as an excuse." O.W. Holmes, Jr., THE COMMON LAW (1881).

[36] Professionals, those with specialized knowledge due to postgraduate education, are usually afforded a different standard of care that relies on custom. This topic is dealt with in depth in Chapter 7 *infra*.

[37] Fredericks v. Castora, 360 A.2d 696 (Pa. Super. Ct. 197 6) ("To begin to vary the standard according to the driver's experience would render the application of any reasonably uniform standard impossible.").

[38] Hill v. Sparks, 546 S.W. 2d 473, 476 (Mo. Ct. App. 1976). The Restatement is in accord. *See* Restatement § 298 cmt. d.

To a large measure, then, the reasonable person standard sets the minimum of community expectations, and those able to provide more are expected to do so.

Taking the defendant's special qualities into account conflicts with the objective focus employed in the reasonable person standard of care. One effort to reconcile this apparent conflict notes that the reasonable person is expected to use all the knowledge and skills she possesses, and, thus, consideration of the defendant's special qualities is consistent with the objective standard. While not entirely satisfactory, it is hard to imagine a jury's ignoring a defendant's special talents in determining that party's reasonableness.

[C] *Gender Bias in the Reasonable Person Standard*

Initially, the general standard of care in negligence cases used a "reasonable man" as its focus. Although this standard was supposedly gender neutral, "it is not a neutral, generic term, but one that has always been latent with gender bias."[39] As Professor Leslie Bender, a prominent feminist torts scholar, noted: " 'Man' was used in the generic sense to mean person or human being. But man is not generic except to other men."[40] Most courts and scholars have come to acknowledge the blatant sexism of a "reasonable man" standard that pretended to encompass the experiences of women.

Most courts have replaced the "reasonable man" with a "reasonable person," believing that this word change manages to remedy the male bias of the standard and the exclusion of women from the standard. Many feminist scholars disagree. Professor Bender claims that the word change simply means the reasonable person becomes interpreted by a standard which is "almost exclusively from the perspective of a male judge, lawyer, or law professor, or even a female lawyer trained to be 'the same as' a male lawyer."[41] Much feminist scholarship has gone to great lengths to explain the differences between the perceptions and experiences of men and

[39] Ronald K.L. Collins, *Language, History and the Legal Process: A Profile of the "Reasonable Man,"* 8 Rut.-Cam. L.J. 311, 312 (1977). In this article, Professor Collins explains that the traditional common law view virtually robbed women of any separate legal status, thus omitting them from consideration.

[40] Leslie Bender, *A Lawyer's Primer on Feminist Theory and Tort*, 38 J. Legal Educ. 3, 22 (1988). Professor Finley also establishes that the reasonable man standard excluded women. Lucinda M. Finley, *A Break in the Silence: Including Women's Issues in a Torts Course*, 1 Yale J.L. & Feminism 41, 58-59 (1989).

[41] Leslie Bender, *A Lawyer's Primer on Feminist Theory and Tort*, 38 J. Legal Educ. 3, 23 (1988). Again, Professor Finley adds support for the proposition that the linguistic change has been largely cosmetic. Lucinda M. Finley, *A Break in the Silence: Including Women's Issues in a Torts Course*, 1 Yale J.L. & Feminism 41, 60-62 (1989).

women.[42] These differences get lost in a generic reasonable person standard.

If the "reasonable person" standard is inadequate because it excludes women, is there a better standard to use in its place? This topic has engendered debate, and the answer has been elusive.[43] An obvious possibility is a "reasonable woman" standard because, by its terms, it cannot be criticized as excluding women.[44] Yet, a "reasonable woman standard" raises its own host of problems. As Professor Finley explains:

> [S]ubstituting a reasonable woman standard to judge the conduct of women, but not going further to question the inclusiveness of the norms informing the reasonable person standard, implies that women's experiences and reactions are something for women only, rather than normal human responses. . . . A reasonable woman standard may also create the perception that the law allows "special" treatment for women that it lets them off the hook with regard to expected normal, human (that is, "male") behavior. . . . Rather than create a special standard for women, and thereby uphold the notion that women are something abnormal, we must constantly question and challenge the inclusiveness of the model underlying the assessment of a reasonable person.[45]

Another concern is the workability of a reasonable woman standard. Because of the predominance of men as attorneys and judges, will appropriate substance be given to a standard focusing on women?[46] These concerns, along with worries about harmful stereotyping, have led to cries of caution before the wholesale advocacy of a reasonable woman standard.[47]

---

[42] This viewpoint is often called "difference feminism," because it embraces an approach that highlights the distinctions between the genders. "Sameness feminists" look for common ground between the sexes and, thus, would be more supportive of a "reasonable person" standard that is appropriately inclusive. Naomi R. Cahn, *The Looseness of Legal Language: The Reasonable Woman Standard in Theory and Practice*, 77 Cornell L. Rev. 1398, 1411-1415 (1992).

[43] *See generally* Naomi R. Cahn, *The Looseness of Legal Language: The Reasonable Woman Standard in Theory and Practice*, 77 Cornell L. Rev. 1398 (1992).

[44] Some courts, in the context of Title VII-based sexual harassment litigation, have employed a reasonable woman standard. *See, e.g.*, Ellison v. Brady, 924 F.2d 872 (9th Cir. 1991).

[45] Lucinda M. Finley, *A Break in the Silence: Including Women's Issues in a Torts Course*, 1 Yale J.L. & Feminism 41, 64 (1989).

[46] Ultimately, just like is done with a reasonable person standard, in most cases a jury would be charged with deciding what a reasonable woman would do under similar circumstances.

[47] Naomi R. Cahn, *The Looseness of Legal Language: The Reasonable Woman Standard in Theory and Practice*, 77 Cornell L. Rev. 1398, 1415 (1992) ("[T]he reasonable woman standard is problematic. Not only does it remind us of earlier stereotypes of women as more pure and moral than men, but it also reduces women's experiences by attempting to capture the essential, relegating 'other' experiences to the margins of acceptance.").

Ultimately, the debate about the proper standard will continue, with some advocating a gender-inclusive standard and others arguing for a standard that focuses on the unique experiences of women. It is not just the person underlying the standard that is being examined, but also what is meant by the concept of "reasonableness." In law, language matters, and the outcome of this debate will have a profound impact on the development of tort law.[48]

§ 3.05 THE CHILD STANDARD OF CARE[49]

American courts long ago determined that children should not be held to the reasonable (adult) person standard of care. Special treatment of children primarily arose out of recognition of their inability to possess and use the judgment expected of adults.[50] Most jurisdictions hold children to a variation of a standard that compares their conduct to other children of the same age, experience, and intelligence under like circumstances.[51] This

---

[48] Professor Bender advocates a different focus for the negligence standard, away from "reason and caution" to a focus on "care and concern." She asks: "What would happen if we understood the 'reasonableness' of the standard of care to mean 'responsibility' and the 'standard of care' to mean the 'standard of caring' or 'consideration of another's safety and interest'?" She adds: "We could convert the present standard of care . . . to a standard of conscious care and concern of a responsible neighbor or social acquaintance for another under the same or similar circumstances." Leslie Bender, *A Lawyer's Primer on Feminist Theory and Tort*, 38 J. Legal Educ. 3, 31 (1988).

There are other biases potentially relevant to the reasonable person standard as well. For example, an individual's cultural perspective could affect the circumstances by which reasonableness is judged. Courts may have the opportunity to consider the effect of cultural values on the reasonableness standard in light of an increasingly multicultural society.

[49] *See generally* Oscar S. Gray, *The Standard of Care for Children Revisited*, 45 Mo. L. Rev. 597 (1980); Harry Shulman, *The Standard of Care Required of Children*, 37 Yale L.J. 618 (1927).

[50] The Restatement notes that this special standard for children "arises out of the public interest in their welfare and protection, together with the fact that there is a wide basis for community experience upon which it is possible, as a practical matter, to determine what is to be expected of them." Restatement § 283A cmt. b. It also recognizes that those who deal with children anticipate that the children will not use the care and judgment of adults. Although the special treatment of children is well-settled, one scholar argued that child defendants should be held to the adult standard because compensation for the plaintiff, as a practical matter, comes either from insurance or from an adult. If the child is the plaintiff and the issue is the plaintiff's possible contributory negligence, the child standard would be employed. *See* Fleming James, Jr., *Accident Liability Reconsidered: The Impact of Liability Insurance*, 57 Yale L.J. 549 (1948).

[51] This is the Restatement formulation. *See* Restatement § 283A. Another variation requires a child "to exercise the same care that a reasonably careful child of the same age, intelligence, maturity, training and experience would exercise under the same or similar circumstances." Robinson v. Lindsay, 598 P.2d 392, 393 (Wash. 1979). A few jurisdictions still adhere to the much-criticized common law approach that holds that children under seven are conclusively presumed incapable of negligence, while those between seven and fourteen are rebuttably presumed to be incapable of negligence. Children over fourteen are rebuttably presumed capable of negligence. *See, e.g.*, Dunn v. Teti, 421 A.2d 782 (Pa. Super. Ct. 1980). Some jurisdictions following the majority approach still will find a very young child incapable of negligence. *See* Ellis v. D'Angelo, 253 P.2d 675 (Cal. 1953).

is very different from the standard of care used for adults. While it is objective in that it compares the child to an external standard of other children, it is far more subjective than the adult reasonable person standard as it allows the jury to consider the child's specific qualities such as experience and intelligence. Thus, a jury would be permitted to consider that a child had subnormal intelligence, or never had been out of her small town. The jury could still find that the child's conduct was unreasonable in light of her estimated capacity.[52]

[A] *Adult Activities*

Many jurisdictions have concluded that children should not be entitled to special treatment when they are engaged in certain types of activities. Instead, these children are required to meet the wholly objective reasonable person standard used for adults. A few courts have applied the adult standard where the child was engaged in an inherently dangerous activity, such as snowmobiling.[53] Most have used the adult standard when the child is engaged in a so-called adult activity.[54] Typically, either approach will get to the same result and most cases where a child is held to the adult standard involve children driving motorized vehicles, such as cars and motorcycles. Other activities, such as hunting, are more debatable and the test used may determine the result.[55]

Some courts that have elected to hold child defendants to an adult standard for adult activities do not do so for child plaintiffs. These jurisdictions have concluded that the compensation goal is best served by adopting such a dual standard.[56]

§ 3.06 DEGREES OF NEGLIGENCE

Courts and legislatures sometimes talk in terms of degrees of negligence. For example, it is at times stated that common carriers owe the hig hest duty of care toward their passengers or that, in some contexts because of

[52] Courts have been reluctant to extend special treatment to those on the other end of the spectrum, the elderly, although a special standard for the elderly has some advocates. *See, e.g.*, Charles V. Barrett, Note, *Negligence and the Elderly: A Proposal for a Relaxed Standard of Care*, 17 J. Marshall L. Rev. 873 (1984).

[53] *See, e.g.*, Robinson v. Lindsay, 598 P.2d 392 (Wash. 1979) (13-year-old snowmobiling defendant should be held to adult standard of care because it is an inherently dangerous activity).

[54] *See, e.g.*, Dellwo v. Pearson, 107 N.W.2d 859 (Minn. 1961) (12-year-old defendant driving motor boat held to adult standard because this is adult activity).

[55] Many of the courts utilizing the adult activity standard have determined that children who are hunting are to be held to the child standard of care because hunting is not necessarily an adult activity. Jurisdictions using the standard of inherent dangerousness typically hold a hunting child to an adult standard of care, however.

[56] For a discussion of the tension between the statutory standard of care and the standard of care for children, *see infra* § 6.05.

the great danger involved, the defendant owes the highest duty of care to the plaintiff. The notion of highest degrees of care, though not uncommon, makes little sense. Such language cannot be justified in light of a standard of care requiring the defendant to act as a reasonable person under the same or similar circumstances. A defendant is negligent because of the failure to exercise reasonable care, and the amount of due care required of a defendant will vary with the circumstances. The standard of care, however, does not change.[57] For example, suppose that D assembles a roller coaster at a traveling carnival. If P is injured and sues D for negligent assembly, it does not make sense to claim that D owes more than a duty of reasonable care. However, because of the enormous gravity of the harm involved with the ride, for D to exercise reasonable care, D must take great precautions to ensure maximum possible safety. The standard remains static, commanding reasonableness.

---

[57] As one court explains: "The measure of duty of a negligence-charged defendant is . . .'reasonable care *appropriate to the circumstances of the case*, a standard of negligence which allows the fact finder to determine tha t some factual circumstances reasonably require greater or lesser diligence than do other circumstances in order to constitute reasonable due care.' " Felgner v. Anderson, 133 N.W.2d 136, 140 (Mich. 1965) (emphasis in original).

CHAPTER 4

THE DETERMINATION OF UNREASONABLENESS: BREACH OF DUTY, CUSTOM AND THE ROLE OF THE JURY

SYNOPSIS

§ 4.01 OVERVIEW

The standard of care is the measure of the duty owed by the defendant to the plaintiff. Breach of duty is the defendant's failure to meet that standard. In most negligence cases, the standard required of the defendant is that of a reasonable person under the same or similar circumstances. Breach of duty, then, is the defendant's failure to act as a reasonable person would have under the same or similar circumstances. More simply, breach is unreasonable conduct by the defendant.

The jury is charged with the task of deciding whether the defendant has breached a duty. This Chapter considers how the jury carries out this responsibility and what evidence is relevant to this undertaking.

This Chapter also looks at the role custom evidence plays in the jury's determination of whether the defendant has acted unreasonably. Both the effect of the defendant's deviation from custom and compliance with custom are explored.

§ 4.02 THE RISK CALCULUS[1]

All conduct involves some risk creation. Negligence[2] is not established just by showing that the defendant engaged in the risk-creating conduct that led to the plaintiff's injury. One may create risks and even cause harm without negligence liability as long as the conduct is reasonable. Negligence liability is only imposed where the defendant engages in *unreasonable* risk creation, that is where the defendant creates risks that a reasonable person would not. Further, this determination of unreasonableness considers the risks that should have been foreseen at the time of the defendant's conduct, not through hindsight after the harm occurred.

There are various justifications for placing legal responsibility only on those at fault, and for not holding liable those who cause harm through non-negligent conduct. One rationalization is that the greatest good comes from providing the greatest freedom of activity. As Oliver Wendell Holmes noted: "to redistribute losses simply on the ground that they resulted from the defendant's act" would offend our "sense of justice."[3] Another explanation is that a fault-based system is economically justified. As Judge Posner explained: "[T]he dominant function of the fault system is to generate rules of liability that if followed will bring about, at least approximately, the efficient — the cost-justified — level of accidents and safety."[4] Thus, both fairness and efficiency support premising liability on fault.

A fundamental issue is how unreasonableness is to be assessed. Although there are various ways that unreasonableness could be measured,[5] the approach that has garnered the greatest support is that posited by Judge Learned Hand. He explained:

> The degree of care demanded of a person by an occasion is the resultant of three factors: the likelihood that his conduct will injure others, taken

[1] *See generally* Fleming James, Jr., *Nature of Negligence*, 3 Utah L. Rev. 275 (1953); Richard A. Posner, *A Theory of Negligence*, 1 J. Legal Stud. 29 (1972).

[2] "Negligence" has two distinct meanings. The term may refer to the tort itself, for which the plaintiff must establish each of the elements (duty, breach of duty, cause-in-fact, proximate cause and damages). It may also be used as shorthand for the breach of duty element. This section focuses on this second usage.

[3] O. W. Holmes, Jr., THE COMMON LAW (1881).

[4] Richard A. Posner, *A Theory of Negligence*, 1 J. Legal Stud. 29, 33 (1972).

[5] *See, e.g.*, Adams v. Bullock, 125 N.E. 93 (N.Y. 1919) (court, finding no breach as a matter of law, looked at burden and probability only) and Bolton v. Stone, 1 All E.R. 1078 (1951) (Lord Reid, concurring, looked only at probability and magnitude, noting that burden should be irrelevant); Restatement §§ 291-293 (Magnitude of Risk and Utility of Conduct).

> with the seriousness of the injury if it happens, and balanced against the interest which he must sacrifice to avoid the risk.[6]

Judge Hand later, in the famous case of *United States v. Carroll Towing Co.*, reconfigured his approach, denominating the likelihood of injury as "probability," the seriousness of the injury as "injury," and the interest sacrificed as "burden." He then proceeded to put this into an algebraic formula: "[I]f the probability be called P; the injury, L; and the burden, B; liability depends upon whether B is less than L multiplied by P: i.e., whether B < PL."[7] In other words, under the formula, D will have acted unreasonably where the burden of avoiding the harm is less than the probability of that harm occurring multiplied by the likely seriousness of the harm if it does occur.

The *Carroll Towing* decision exemplifies how the formula works. Judge Hand used the formula to affirm a finding of contributory negligence by the plaintiff's bargee (leading to a reduction of P's damages under admiralty law principles). Judge Hand reasoned that the probability of a barge getting loose and causing harm due to a bargee's absence was substantial in light of the high level of activity in the harbor, that magnitude of the loss was significant because the harbor was crowded with other vessels, and that the burden of avoidance was minor given that the events occurred during what should have been the working hours of the plaintiff's bargee.

The formula was intended to be flexible. Judge Hand acknowledged that a firm rule defining reasonableness would rarely exist because the formula would be necessarily affected by the surrounding facts.[8] Had the harbor been slow or virtually empty, or had the incident occurred late at night, the determination about the bargee's breach might have been different.

The plaintiff and the defendant often will have different views of probability, magnitude, and burden. It is ultimately for the trier of fact to undertake the balancing of these factors in order to assess the reasonableness of the defendant's conduct. Because the standard of care is that of the reasonable person, that is the vantage point from which the balancing is done. The proper focus, then, is on how a reasonable person would balance the probability of harm and its magnitude against the burden of avoidance at the time of the act in issue.

---

[6] Conway v. O'Brien, 111 F.2d 611, 612 (2d Cir. 1940).

[7] United States v. Carroll Towing Co., 159 F.2d 169, 173 (2d Cir. 1947).

[8] *Id.* at 173. Hand explained: "[T]here is no general rule to determine when the absence of a bargee or other attendant will make the owner of the barge liable for injuries to other vessels if she breaks away from her moorings. . . . It becomes apparent why there can be no such general rule, when we consider the grounds for such a liability. Since there are occasions when every vessel will break from her moorings, and since, if she does, she becomes a menace to those about her, the owner's duty, as in other similar situations, to provide against resulting injuries is a function of three variables: (1) the probability that she will break away; (2) the gravity of the resulting injury, if she does; (3) the burden of adequate precautions."

[A] *Probability*

The first factor looks at probability, the likelihood of harm. Virtually any action creates some potential risk of harm. The probability factor seeks to measure the likelihood of the harm-causing occurrence taking place.[9] Probability is different from "foreseeability" in that probability measures *how* foreseeable the harm-causing event is.

Although probability must be considered in relation to magnitude and burden, where there is a minuscule likelihood of harm it is doubtful that the defendant breached a duty. For example, D is sued for negligence for leaving a golf club in his backyard. His 11-year-old son picked it up, swung at a stone, and hit the plaintiff in the head with the club. Was D unreasonable? Under these facts, one court upheld the dismissal of the action against the defendant father by simply noting: "It would hardly be good sense to hold that this golf club is so obviously and intrinsically dangerous that it is negligence to leave it lying on the ground in the yard."[10] The court suggested, in essence, that the probability of harm from the defendant's act of leaving the golf club in the backyard was so tiny that there was no breach as a matter of law.[11]

[B] *Magnitude of the Loss*

The magnitude of the loss looks at the likely harm flowing from the injury-causing event when it occurs. The proper focus is neither the most severe possible harm nor the least severe; rather, it is what a reasonable person would foresee as the *likely* harm. In *Carroll Towing*, the issue regarding magnitude of the loss was the likely harm that would flow from a barge getting loose. The likely harm was significant because of the numerous ships in the harbor.

The proper focus is on the likely harm, not the actual harm that occurred. There are situations where far less or far greater harm than that which would be typically expected occurs. It would be odd to decide that conduct was not unreasonable just because the plaintiff fortuitously suffered minor harm, or to find conduct negligent just because the plaintiff suffered great harm.[12]

Because the Hand factors are relative, the more serious the potential injury, the smaller the probability of harm needed for liability.[13] So, if the

---

[9] In *Carroll Towing*, this was the likelihood that a boat would get loose and cause harm.

[10] Lubitz v. Wells, 113 A.2d 147 (Conn. Super. Ct. 1955).

[11] Although the court did not analyze the other factors, the limited magnitude of the harm and the substantial burden involved in keeping anything that could be used to harm another locked away buttress the court's finding of the lack of unreasonable conduct. Had the defendant left a gun out rather than a golf club, the result would have been different.

[12] The harm that the plaintiff actually suffers is highly relevant, however, as the defendant will pay damages based on the actual injury inflicted. This is wholly distinct from the determination of whether the defendant's conduct was unreasonable.

[13] And, as will be discussed immediately below, the more serious the potential injury, the greater the amount of caution required of a defendant.

defendant's conduct creates a risk of enormous harm (such as death), the fact that there is little likelihood of the harm-causing event coming about (that is, a small probability) will not preclude a finding of breach of duty. For example, in light of the likely magnitude of the loss, D would be unreasonable for hitting a pedestrian while backing her car out of her driveway even if she shows that it is very unlikely that, at the exact moment she was backing out of the driveway, a pedestrian would be passing by.[14]

[C] *Burden of Avoidance*

A determination of unreasonableness requires that the product of probability and magnitude be balanced against the burden of avoidance. The burden element is multi-faceted. An analysis of burden, which Hand also referred to as "the value of the interest to be sacrificed," requires consideration of such things as the costs associated with avoiding the harm, alternatives and their feasibility, the inconvenience to those involved and the extent to which society values the relevant activity.

A reasonable defendant need not take all possible measures to avoid all possible risk. Virtually all activity creates some risk of harm to others, and to avoid all risk of injury arising from a given activity, the entire activity would have to be prohibited. If the goal were to avoid all injuries caused by automobiles, for example, driving would have to be banned. But this is not done because of the great value attached to the activity. Similarly, if a defendant to avoid negligence liability would have to stop running a trolley line because of the lack of a cost-effective way to make the activity safer, negligence would not be found because of the great social value of the undertaking.[15]

Liability is typically imposed only upon a finding of reasonable means to make an activity safer.[16] For example, while the value of railroads and

---

[14] As one court explained: "Danger consists in the risk of harm, as well as the likelihood of it, and a danger calling for anticipation need not be of more probable occurrence than less. If there is some probability of harm sufficiently serious that ordinary men would take precautions to avoid it, then failure to do so is negligence. That the danger will more probably than otherwise not be encountered on a particular occasion does not dispense with the exercise of care. . . . The test is not of the balance of probabilities, but of the existence of some probability of sufficient moment to induce action to avoid it on the part of a reasonable mind." Tullgren v. Amoskeag Mfg. Co., 133 A. 4 (N.H. 1926).

[15] *See, e.g.*, Adams v. Bullock, 125 N.E. 93 (N.Y. 1919), in which Judge Cardozo, for the majority, found that the defendant trolley line could not be unreasonable because to avoid the harm suffered by the plaintiff it would have to "have abandoned the overhead system, and put the wires underground." *Id.* at 94.

[16] In rare instances, the fault system is rejected, and liability is imposed even where there are no cost-justified ways to make the activity safer. Much of the justification for strict liability is premised on the determination that in some limited contexts we want to permit compensation of a party injured even where the defendant's conduct was reasonable. *See infra* Chapter 16.

the dangerous machinery needed by them to function properly is clear, courts have imposed negligence liability for failing to use available and inexpensive devices to prevent probable harm.[17] And, because technology changes over time, conduct that was not negligent at one point may become unreasonable once reasonable means to lessen the danger become available.[18]

The toll that existing alternatives would exact on the undertaking is relevant to deciding the burden. Thus, where the cost of an available safety device is so large that its use would bankrupt most in the industry, a finding of an excessive burden would be likely. To be distinguished, however, is the situation where the individual defendant asserts that an available safety device is unduly burdensome due to the defendant's own precarious financial situation. Because negligence law uses an objective standard, the defendant's own circumstances are irrelevant.

The burden a jury will likely expect a defendant to absorb is relative to probability and magnitude. The greater the risks of serious danger, the more onerous the burden that a jury will find a reasonable person is expected to accept.

[D] *Value of the Hand Formula*

As a practical matter, the jury does not expressly consider the factors identified by Judge Hand. The trial judge typically instructs the jurors to determine the reasonableness of the defendant's conduct, without any real direction as to how they are to accomplish this task.[19]

Yet, the Hand factors — probability, magnitude, and burden — reflect the kinds of things that a jury grapples with in determining reasonableness. Because the determination of fault is necessarily fluid and fact sensitive,

---

[17] For example, a railroad may be liable for failing to use locks to prevent children from being harmed when playing on its turntable. *See, e.g.*, Chicago, B. & Q. R. Co. v. Krayenbuhl, 91 N.W. 880 (Neb. 1902). The court there explained: "The business of life is better carried forward by the use of dangerous machinery; hence the public good demands its use, although occasionally such a use results in loss of life or limb. It does so because the danger is insignificant, when weighed against the benefits resulting from the use of such machinery, and for the same reason demands its reasonable, most effective, and unrestricted use, up to the point the benefits resulting from such use no longer outweigh the danger to be anticipated from it. At that point the public good demands restrictions." *Id.* at 882-83.

[18] For example, a court refused to permit a jury to find a municipality liable when the plaintiffs suffered injuries when their car broke through what the plaintiffs claimed to be inadequate guard rails because to do so, under the facts of the case, would be excessively burdensome. Davison v. Snohomish County, 270 P. 422 (Wash. 1928). Four decades later the court permitted a similar case to get to the jury because of possible advances in engineering. Bartlett v. Northern Pacific Railway Co., 447 P.2d 735 (Wash. 1968).

[19] *See* Stephen G. Gilles, *The Invisible Hand Formula*, 80 Va. L. Rev. 1015 (1994), in which the author explores the relationship of the Hand formula and the "reasonably prudent person" standard, ultimately advocating that the jury be instructed to use the Hand formula for its breach analysis.

the jury needs to engage in the kind of balancing and weighing made explicit in the Hand formula. In addition, the attorneys when arguing the case to the jury surely raise points, such as the ease of avoiding the harm, that fit into a Hand-type analysis. Further, the Hand factors often are expressly used by judges reviewing jury verdicts.

There is debate about the degree to which the Hand formula provides a basis for an economic analysis of negligence law. Judge Posner, one of the key players in the "Law and Economics" movement, asserted that "Hand was adumbrating, perhaps unwittingly, an economic meaning to negligence." Posner advanced that the Hand formula provides that negligence arises when the cost of the accident exceeds the costs of the precautionary measures.[20] Is the Hand test, then, a means "to structure incentives to minimize primary accident costs?"[21]

Hand himself did not intend for his approach to be viewed as an economic formula. While Hand resorted to algebra to express the negligence concept, he had earlier expressed the view that his approach could not be subjected to quantification. He explained that the factors "are practically not susceptible of any quantitative estimate. . . . For this reason a solution always involves some preference, or choice between incommensurables, and it is consigned to a jury because their decision is thought most likely to accord to commonly accepted standards, real or fancied."[22] Indeed, in *Carroll Towing*, Hand's analysis went far beyond consideration of the replacement cost for another bargee. Rather, Hand acknowledged that the barge could not become the bargee's prison, recognizing that the concept of burden encompasses intangible interests such as freedom of movement.

Even where efforts to quantify are made, the Hand formula does not serve effectively where the defendant's liability is premised on inadvertence, as opposed to the defendant's election to forgo available alternatives that

[20] Richard A. Posner, *A Theory of Negligence*, 1 J. Legal Stud. 29, 32-33 (1972). Posner explained: "Discounting (multiplying) the cost of an accident if it occurs by the probability of occurrence yields a measure of the economic benefit to be anticipated from incurring the costs necessary to prevent the accident. The cost of prevention is what Hand meant by the burden of taking precautions against the accident. . . . If the cost of safety measures or of curtailment — whichever cost is lower — exceeds the benefit in accident avoidance to be gained by incurring that cost, society would be better off, in economic terms, to forgo accident prevention. . . . If, on the other hand, the benefits in accident avoidance exceed the cost of prevention, society is better off if those costs are incurred and the accident averted, and so in this case the enterprise is made liable, in the expectation that self-interest will lead it to adopt the precaution in order to avoid a greater cost in tort judgments." *See also* McCarty v. Pheasant Run, Inc., 826 F.2d 1554, 1557 (7th Cir. 1987) (Posner, J.: "The [Hand] formula translates into economic terms the conventional legal test for negligence. . . . Unreasonable conduct is merely the failure to take precautions that would generate greater benefits in avoiding accidents than the precautions would cost."

[21] David W. Barnes and Lynn A. Stout, THE ECONOMIC ANALYSIS OF TORT LAW, at 35 (West Pub. Co. 1992).

[22] Conway v. O'Brien, 111 F.2d 611, 612 (2d Cir. 1940).

would have made the activity safer.[23] For example, consider a case where D, a mechanic repairing a cash register near where P is standing, kneels to continue with his repair efforts. P falls over D's outstretched leg and sues him for negligence. Was D unreasonable for failing to warn P that he changed position? What is the burden of such a seemingly minor act as giving a warning? The answer is that it is gigantic, taking into account the enormous infringement on one's freedom of movement if a warning need be given every time there is a change of position.[24]

Even if the Hand formula cannot be, or should not be, quantified, it still plays a useful role in the analysis of negligence. The formula provides an analytical structure which can make some sense out of the amorphous "reasonableness" concept.

§ 4.03 THE ROLE OF CUSTOM[25]

This section examines custom, evidence that may be relevant to a jury's determination of breach of duty. Custom typically refers to a well-defined and consistent way of performing a certain activity, often among a particular trade or industry. In many cases evidence of custom is raised by one of the parties. The plaintiff may try to assert the defendant's deviation from custom as evidence of lack of due care. Conversely, the defendant may try to avoid liability by showing compliance with custom. Custom evidence does not exist in a vacuum. Rather, it relates to the Hand factors of probability and burden.

[A] *Deviation from Custom*

P is injured when she is cut by glass that shattered when she fell against her shower door. P sues her landlord for negligence, contending that the landlord acted unreasonably by using glass that shatters in a shower door. In her effort to prove this, P seeks to enter evidence that most landlords use shatterproof glass for shower doors.[26] Is this evidence admissible? If so, what is its effect on P's negligence action?

The rules regarding the admissibility of evidence showing D's deviation from custom are quite well-settled. If P can persuade the jury that there is a *well-established custom* — that is, a practice widespread enough that either D knew of it or should have known of it — the jury may consider D's deviation from custom in its determination of breach of duty. Evidence of D's deviation from custom is often powerful evidence of breach, though

[23] Mark F. Grady, *Why Are People Negligent? Technology, Nondurable Precautions, and the Medical Malpractice Explosion*, 82 Nw. U. L. Rev. 293 (1988).

[24] Greene v. Sibley, Lindsay & Curr Co., 177 N.E. 416 (N.Y. 1931).

[25] *See generally* Fleming James, Jr. & David K. Sigerson, *Particularizing Standards of Conduct in Negligence Trials*, 5 Vand. L. Rev. 697 (1952); Clarence Morris, *Custom and Negligence*, 42 Colum. L. Rev. 1147 (1942).

[26] *See* Trimarco v. Klein, 436 N.E.2d 502 (N.Y. 1982).

its impact ultimately depends on the unique facts of each case and on how a jury elects to assess the facts. Thus, custom evidence does not itself establish breach of duty. Further, the standard of care is unchanged; D continues to be held to the requirement of acting as a reasonable person under the same or similar circumstances. The evidence of deviation from custom may suggest that D failed to do so.[27]

Custom evidence does not derive its impact as evidence of breach in a vacuum. It directly relates to the consideration of the risk calculus.[28] First, the existence of a custom suggests some degree of probability of the harm. The custom must have developed in response to an industry's perception of the potential risks of a particular activity. Accordingly, for the evidence of D's deviation from custom to affect the breach determination properly, P must show that the harm the custom developed to avoid is the same as that suffered by P. Thus, returning to the shatterproof shower door, P must show that the reason most landlords use shatterproof glass in shower doors is to avoid cuts to tenants.[29]

The second way in which evidence of D's deviation from a relevant and well-established custom affects the jury's evaluation of breach is that the existence of the custom suggests that for D to have acted as do most others would not have been too burdensome. D's claim that using shatterproof glass is generally too difficult or expensive is much less persuasive in light of a custom to the contrary.[30]

[B] *Compliance with Custom*

What impact does D's compliance with custom have on D's negligence liability? If D shows that virtually no other landlords use shatterproof glass in shower enclosures, does D escape liability?

As the mirror image of "deviation from custom," evidence of D's compliance with custom is usually admissible as evidence of D's lack of breach. Again, it does not alter the standard of care to which D is held. Nor does it conclusively establish D's lack of unreasonableness. A jury,

---

27 Herein lies the most fundamental distinction between ordinary negligence cases and professional negligence cases. Professional negligence cases treat custom entirely differently from other negligence cases. *See infra* Chapter 7.

28 That is, "the Hand formula." *See supra* § 4.02.

29 The task is not always this easy. For example, P is injured when her hand gets cut on coarse rope she is pulling. P introduces evidence that most use a smooth rope in this situation. This alone would not be relevant evidence, unless P could also show that smooth rope was used out of safety concerns, rather than because it was stronger or easier to grasp. *See* Levine v. Russell Blaine Co., 7 N.E.2d 673 (N.Y. 1937).

30 Under the objective standard used in negligence law, D's claim that compliance with custom would be too expensive or too difficult for D itself is not relevant. The D's own specific situation is immaterial. This differs from D's contention that performing as P suggests would negatively impact most in the industry or trade. This latter evidence is relevant to D's lack of breach of duty.

if it elects to do so, may find D's compliance with custom suggestive of a high burden of avoidance or low probability of harm.

Because evidence of D's compliance with custom does not establish D's due care, the jury is free to find "customary negligence" on D's part, determining that the entire custom itself is unreasonable. Thus, a jury could well conclude that the custom of refraining from the use of shatterproof glass is itself unreasonable.[31] In fact, some customary practices may be so unreasonable that a judge will refuse to admit them, as where D tries to show her excessive speed was consistent with the norm of the community.

§ 4.04 THE JURY ROLE

In addition to the critical issue of *how* unreasonableness is determined looms the related issue of *by whom* it is determined. While it is now well-settled that the jury decides whether the defendant acted unreasonably, thereby breaching her duty, this result has not been without exception or controversy. On one hand, the determination that the decision-making resides with the jury seems wholly appropriate, flowing logically from the adoption of an objective standard. Who better to decide whether the defendant acted as would a reasonable person than members of the defendant's community? On the other hand, leaving the question of reasonableness to a jury invites differing results in similar cases, which in turn leads to concerns about the arbitrariness of the tort system and the erosion of public confidence.

Even though the rule is that the jury decides the reasonableness issue, this principle is not absolute. Sometimes a judge makes the ultimate call. Most often this arises in the context of a directed verdict, or judgment notwithstanding the verdict, in which a judge concludes that, based on the evidence put forth by the plaintiff, no reasonable jury could find that the defendant was unreasonable.[32] But the finding of no breach as a matter of law is rare. If reasonable minds can disagree, the decision is left to the jury.

The judge's infrequently used right to intervene and take the breach of duty issue from the jury does not eliminate the concern about uncertain

[31] This was Judge Hand's point in the famous case of T.J. Hooper, 60 F.2d 737, 740 (2d Cir.), *cert. denied*, 287 U.S. 662 (1932), in which he stated: "[I]n most cases reasonable prudence is in fact common prudence; but strictly it is never its measure; a whole calling may have unduly lagged in the adoption of new and available devices. It never may set its own tests, however persuasive be its usages. Courts must in the end say what is required; there are precautions so imperative that even their universal disregard will not excuse their omission."

[32] *See, e.g.*, Adams v. Bullock, 125 N.E. 93 (N.Y. 1919), in which Judge Cardozo wrote for the court that no reasonable jury could find the defendant's failure to insulate, bury, or reconfigure its trolley line wires to constitute unreasonable conduct. A judge may also conclude that the plaintiff's evidence so strongly shows breach that no reasonable jury can find the defendant acted reasonably.

and arbitrary results. Judges disagree about the proper amount of deference owed to the jury. Thus, as is true when a jury decides the breach issue, judges may interpret cases with similar facts differently—some judges sending the case to the jury for resolution and others deciding the breach issue as a matter of law. Worries about inconsistent results led to an intense debate centering on whether an approach could be fashioned that would lend greater predictability to the breach determination. A school of thought, exemplified by the writings of Justice Holmes, sought to do just that by advocating fixed standards of reasonableness set by the court whenever possible. Adherents to this viewpoint reasoned that this approach would reduce the possibility of arbitrary results, thus giving greater predictability and coherence to negligence law. This tack was taken in *Baltimore & Ohio Railroad Co. v. Goodman,*[33] in which Justice Holmes held that whenever people cross railroad tracks with an obstructed view, they are negligent unless they stop and get out of their vehicle to ensure that it is safe to cross. As Justice Holmes put it, though the question of breach generally is left to the jury, when the appropriate "standard [of conduct] is clear it should be laid down once and for all by the Courts."

Holmes' approach dramatically limited the role of the jury in the determination of breach.[34] In *Goodman*, Holmes was not simply acknowledging a judge's power to keep the breach issue from a jury where reasonable minds necessarily agreed about the proper result. Nor was he saying that, on the evidence before the court, in that particular case, any reasonable jury would find that the plaintiff failed to use due care. Instead, Holmes laid out a specific, fixed rule as to what due care required — mandating that a person with an obstructed view of railroad tracks had to exit the vehicle.

This "fixed standard of reasonableness" approach was short-lived. In *Pokora v. Wabash Railway Co.,*[35] a case with facts similar to *Goodman*, Justice Holmes' replacement on the Supreme Court, Justice Cardozo, rejected the Holmes approach. For a unanimous Court, Cardozo urged "caution in framing standards of behavior that amount to rules of law." The Court noted that rules of law lack the flexibility to take into account unusual situations and, indeed, could lead to irrational results, observing as an example that leaving one's car to observe obstructed railroad tracks could create more risk, not less. Further, completely identical fact patterns rarely arise in negligence cases. The concerns expressed by Justice Cardozo have

[33] 275 U.S. 66 (1927).

[34] Prior to *Goodman*, Holmes had expressed the willingness to keep a relatively tight rein on the jury. *See* O. W. Holmes, Jr., THE COMMON LAW, at 123-24, in which he advocated an increasingly strong role for the judge in determining the reasonableness of conduct.

[35] 292 U.S. 98 (1934).

generally carried the day, and it is now quite rare for a court to set a fixed standard of reasonableness.[36]

---

[36] But do not assume that this never happens. For example, most jurisdictions proclaim that an owner of a baseball field is not negligent as long as the most dangerous areas at a baseball park are screened.

CHAPTER 5

PROOF OF BREACH

SYNOPSIS

§ 5.01 OVERVIEW[1]

As a general matter, the plaintiff has the burden to prove each element of a negligence cause of action — duty, breach, cause-in-fact, proximate cause, and damages — by a preponderance of the evidence. If the plaintiff fails to carry this burden, the case must necessarily be decided for the defendant.

This chapter looks at the issues that arise in the context of proof of the breach of duty element in negligence cases. Regarding breach, it is incumbent upon the plaintiff to put on enough evidence so that a jury can find that more likely than not the defendant failed to act reasonably. To

[1] *See generally* Fleming James, Jr., *Proof of the Breach in Negligence Cases (Including Res Ipsa Loquitur)*, 37 Va. L. Rev. 179 (1951); Clarence Morris, *Proof of Negligence*, 47 Nw. U. L. Rev. 817 (1953).

accomplish this, the plaintiff must put on evidence that enables a reasonable jury to determine without pure speculation that the defendant failed to use due care. The happening of an accident is never enough by itself to permit a jury to find that a defendant behaved unreasonably; something more is always required. For example, if P introduces evidence that D was driving and heard a thump, which turned out to be P, who was badly injured by D's car, there is inadequate evidence from which a jury could reasonably conclude that D failed to use due care.[2]

The analysis of proof of breach begins with a brief look at the two key kinds of evidence used to prove breach of duty: direct and circumstantial. The focus then turns to a consideration of a context raising particularly challenging proof issues, the role of constructive notice in slip and fall cases. Finally, this Chapter explores the special form of circumstantial evidence known as res ipsa loquitur.

§ 5.02 KINDS OF EVIDENCE

There are two key forms of evidence that a plaintiff can use in attempting to establish negligence by the defendant: direct and circumstantial. Direct evidence is evidence that comes from personal knowledge or observation, such as from an eyewitness or by videotape. There is no need to draw any inferences from direct evidence. The only issues are credibility and reliability. Thus, if P is suing D for her injuries, claiming that D was speeding, X's eyewitness testimony that she observed D driving very fast is a form of direct evidence. The impact of this direct evidence will depend on the jury's determination of X's credibility based on X's demeanor and other similar factors. As a practical matter, direct evidence is rather rare in negligence cases.

Circumstantial evidence is the most common form of evidence used by plaintiffs to establish the defendant's unreasonable conduct. Circumstantial evidence is proof that requires the drawing of an inference from other facts to have probative value. Circumstantial evidence can be very powerful evidence, however.[3] For example, in the above hypothetical with the

---

[2] *See* Gift v. Palmer, 141 A.2d 408 (Pa. 1958). In *Gift*, the court determined that there was no evidence from which a jury could find breach of duty on the part of the defendant driver who hit the three-year-old plaintiff, Robert Gift. After noting that the "mere happening of an accident is not evidence of negligence," the court explained: "In the instant case there was no eye witness to the accident; there was no evidence of the speed of defendant's automobile; there was no evidence where Robert Gift was just prior to the accident; there was no evidence where he was at the time of the accident, when he bumped into the front fender of defendant's car; there was no evidence of facts or circumstances showing as the only reasonable conclusion that defendant could have seen Robert was in a place of danger and was likely to run into or be struck by his automobile and that defendant could have, by the exercise of reasonable care, stopped his automobile in time to avoid the accident." *Id.* at 409, 410.

[3] Dog prints in fresh snow, for example, permit the inference that a dog has passed by recently.

allegedly speeding car, P's evidence of long skid marks could permit the trier of fact to infer that the car was going quickly. From that, the jury could decide that the driver was acting unreasonably. Some circumstantial evidence is weak and will not be admitted because it would require the jury to speculate rather than to draw a reasonable inference.

In many cases, a plaintiff relies on circumstantial evidence to persuade the jury that the defendant engaged in unreasonable conduct. As long as the jury can draw a reasonable inference (as opposed to speculate) the circumstantial evidence will be admitted. Such is the case with evidence of the length of skid marks, for example. In some contexts, however, special rules regarding circumstantial evidence apply. One of these is the setting of slip and fall cases, examined in the next section, where courts have established particularized proof requirements for plaintiffs relying on circumstantial evidence.

§ 5.03 SLIP AND FALL CASES AND THE ROLE OF CONSTRUCTIVE NOTICE

Where a plaintiff slips and falls on the defendant's property, the plaintiff must show more than the fact that she fell and was injured. Because negligence is her cause of action, she must show by a preponderance of the evidence that the defendant failed to exercise reasonable care. Most courts require the plaintiff to show that the condition on which she slipped existed long enough so that the defendant should have discovered it and should have remedied it. For example, D slips on a banana peel that was lying on the floor in the produce aisle while shopping in D's store and sues D for negligence. If that is all the evidence she puts on, her case will not get to a jury.[4] In order to permit a jury to infer reasonably that the banana peel was there long enough so that the defendant should have discovered it and picked it up, she must put on evidence about the condition of the peel, such as that it was gritty, smashed, blackened or flattened.[5] The jury

[4] *See* Goddard v. Boston & M. R. Co., 60 N.E. 486 (Mass. 1901), in which the plaintiff sued for injuries he suffered from falling on a banana skin lying on the floor of defendant's railroad platform. The full text of the opinion disposing of the plaintiff's case provides: "The banana skin upon which the plaintiff stepped and which caused him to slip may have been dropped within a minute by one of the persons who was leaving the train. It is unnecessary to go further to decide the case." *Id.* at 486. *See also* Gordon v. American Museum of Natural History, 492 N.E.2d 774 (N.Y. 1986) (plaintiff has not put on enough evidence from which a jury could have found fault where he testified that he fell on "a piece of white, waxy paper"). In these cases, the dangerous condition was created by an unidentified third party. Where the plaintiff's allegation is that the defendant or its employees caused the dangerous condition by their unreasonable conduct, no special proof problem arises.

[5] *See* Anjou v. Boston Elevated Railway Co., 94 N.E. 386 (Mass. 1911), in which a plaintiff who fell on a banana peel on the defendant's railroad platform was entitled to get to a jury because of testimony such as the banana peel was "flattened down, and black in color." The court noted: "The inference might have been drawn from the appearance and condition of the banana peel that it had been upon the platform a considerable period of time, in such

is not required to draw any particular inference from the evidence, but the evidence that permits an inference of constructive notice by the defendant enables the plaintiff to have her case withstand pre-trial motions and motions for a directed verdict,[6] thereby getting the case to the jury.

Some jurisdictions permit the plaintiff to try to make a case without proof of actual or constructive notice on the part of the defendant. These courts recognize a "mode of operation" basis for liability by which the plaintiff bases the defendant's liability on the methods used by the defendant to run the business. The plaintiff seeks to show that the way the business is operated creates foreseeable risks of harm, such that the defendant's notice (actual or constructive) of a specific danger is rendered irrelevant.[7]

§ 5.04 RES IPSA LOQUITUR[8]

Res ipsa loquitur,[9] an important and somewhat complicated form of circumstantial evidence, may be relevant to a plaintiff's efforts to establish the defendant's unreasonable conduct. Like any circumstantial evidence, res ipsa loquitur evidence permits the drawing of an inference. But there is a key difference between res ipsa loquitur and other circumstantial evidence. With other forms of circumstantial evidence, the jury draws an inference that when combined with other evidence permits the jury to find that the defendant failed to use due care. Where res ipsa loquitur applies, a jury may infer that the defendant acted unreasonably without any other proof.

---

position that it would have been seen and removed by the employees of the defendant if they had been reasonably careful in performing their duty." *Id.* at 386. *See also* Negri v. Stop and Shop, Inc., 480 N.E.2d 740 (N.Y. 1985) (plaintiff, who fell while shopping in D's store, can get to jury based on testimony that baby food on which she slipped was "dirty and messy").

[6] Commonly, where the probative value of the plaintiff's evidence is subject to challenge, the defendant will move for a directed verdict after the plaintiff has put on her case. In so doing, the defendant is contending that there is not enough evidence presented by the plaintiff that a jury could reasonably find for the plaintiff. As to the element of breach of duty, the defendant is asserting that there is not enough evidence for the jury to find that the defendant probably acted unreasonably.

[7] *See, e.g.*, Jasko v. F.W. Woolworth Co., 494 P.2d 839 (Colo. 1972) (plaintiff injured on slice of pizza on terrazzo floor near pizza counter in defendant's store may have case heard by jury due to allegations that operating methods of the proprietor "are such that dangerous conditions are continuous or easily foreseeable"). *See also* Chiara v. Fry's Fast Food Stores, 733 P.2d 283 (Ariz. 1987) (plaintiff slipping on creme rinse on defendant's floor states case if defendant could "reasonably anticipate that creme rinse would be spilled on a regular basis" and failed to take reasonable precautions).

[8] *See generally* Mark F. Grady, *Res Ipsa Loquitur and Compliance Error*, 142 U. Pa. L. Rev. 887 (1994); Louis L. Jaffe, *Res Ipsa Loquitur Vindicated*, 1 Buff. L. Rev. 1 (1951); William L. Prosser, *The Procedural Effect of Res Ipsa Loquitur*, 20 Minn. L. Rev. 241 (1936); David E. Seidleson, *Res Ipsa Loquitur—The Big Umbrella*, 25 Duq. L. Rev. 387 (1987).

[9] Res ipsa loquitur means "the thing speaks for itself." Unfortunately, it doesn't always speak clearly.

In a negligence case, typically the plaintiff specifies what the d allegedly did unreasonably (such as drove too fast or failed to wa a defective step). Res ipsa loquitur is most important and has its greatest impact in cases where the plaintiff is unable to make specific allegations about what the defendant did wrong.[10] The heart of res ipsa loquitur is that from the happening of the accident, the plaintiff seeks to establish 1) that the harm-causing event was probably due to negligence, and 2) that the defendant was probably the culpable party. This is a shorthand version of the traditional conditions required for the application of res ipsa loquitur: "an accident that normally does not happen without negligence; exclusive control of the instrumentality by the defendant; and absence of voluntary action or contribution by the plaintiff."[11] In order for the plaintiff to have the benefit of res ipsa loquitur, she must convince the jury that each of these factors more likely than not exists. If the plaintiff fails to establish by a preponderance of the evidence any of the res ipsa loquitur elements, she will be denied the benefit of the doctrine and probably will be unable to get her case to the jury.[12]

[A] *Byrne v. Boadle*

The case of *Byrne v. Boadle*,[13] in which the plaintiff was seriously injured when a barrel of flour fell on him, is credited with adding "res ipsa loquitur"

---

[10] As Professor James explains: res ipsa loquitur "is probably more often invoked in practice in run of the mill occurrences where the facts of the occurrence before the courts are meager. A chain, a cable, or a hook breaks, a structure collapses, a boiler explodes, plaster falls, a foreign substance is found in canned, baked, or bottled food, a water main bursts, and as a result plaintiff is injured. It is here the doctrine is most sorely needed. . . ." Fleming James, Jr., *Proof the of Breach in Negligence Cases (Including Res Ipsa Loquitur)*, 37 Va. L. Rev. 179, 200-201 (1951). Yet, an increasing number of jurisdictions permit a plaintiff to assert res ipsa loquitur even though she introduces specific evidence of the defendant's unreasonable conduct. *See, e.g.*, Widmyer v. Southeast Skyways, Inc., 584 P.2d 1 (Alaska 1978).

[11] Widmyer v. Southeast Skyways, Inc., 584 P.2d 1, 13 (Alaska 1978). Many states follow this traditional approach. The Restatement has a somewhat different formulation: "It may be inferred that harm suffered by the plaintiff is caused by negligence of the defendant when (a) the event is of a kind which ordinarily does not occur in the absence of negligence; (b) other responsible causes, including the conduct of the plaintiff and third persons, are sufficiently eliminated by the evidence; and (c) the indicated negligence is within the scope of the defendant's duty to the plaintiff." Restatement § 328D. Some jurisdictions have adopted the Restatement approach. *See, e.g.*, Valley Properties Limited Partnership v. Steadman's Hardware, Inc., 824 P.2d 250, 254 (Mont. 1992).

[12] *See* Holmes v. Gamble, 655 P.2d 405, 408-09 (Colo. 1982) ("For the case to be submitted to the jury on a theory of *res ipsa loquitur*, the circumstantial evidence of these three elements must be such that it is more likely that the event was caused by negligence than that it was not. Where the probabilities are at best evenly balanced between negligence and its absence, it becomes the duty of the court to direct a verdict for the defendant."). In rare situations, all three elements can be established as a matter of law. *See, e.g.*, Newing v. Cheatham, 540 P.2d 33 (Cal. 1975).

[13] 2 H. & C. 722, 159 Eng. Rep. 299 (Exch. 1863).

to the legal lexicon. In *Byrne*, neither the plaintiff nor any of the witnesses testified as to anything done by the defendant that could have led to the barrel falling. The defendant's lawyer had persuaded the trial judge to dismiss the action based on his argument that the plaintiff could not state a case because of the lack of any proof that the defendant was the responsible party and any evidence of an unreasonable act by the defendant. On appeal by the plaintiff to the Exchequer Court, the defendant's attorney was reiterating these points when Chief Baron Pollock interrupted to opine, "There are certain cases of which it may be said res ipsa loquitur, and this seems one of them." In rendering the court's decision for the plaintiff, Pollock explained: "A barrel could not roll out of a warehouse without some negligence, and to say that a plaintiff who is injured by it must call witnesses from the warehouse to prove negligence seems to me preposterous." Since *Byrne*, courts and commentators have refined the doctrine and its proof requirements.

Although there is language to the contrary in *Byrne*, even when res ipsa loquitur is applied, more than just the happening of an accident is required for the plaintiff to prove the defendant's breach of duty. The harm-causing event has to be tied to the defendant, and the event must be one that generally does not occur absent negligence.

[B] *Probably Negligence*

In order to get the benefit of res ipsa loquitur, a plaintiff must persuade a jury that more likely than not the harm-causing event does not occur in the absence of negligence. The plaintiff does not have to eliminate all other possible causes for the harm, nor does the fact that the defendant raises possible non-negligent causes defeat plaintiff's effort to invoke res ipsa loquitur. The key is that a reasonable jury must be able to find the likely cause was negligence. In some cases, such as where two trains collide on the same track, bottles explode or rodents are cooked into food, it is quite evident that negligence probably was the reason for the mishap. In other cases, such as the typical slip and fall case or where a person falls down stairs, negligence cannot be deemed the likely cause. In many cases there is room to debate whether negligence is the likely cause and the jury is charged with making that determination.

Aviation cases provide an example of the evolution of the "probably negligence" prong of res ipsa loquitur. During the early stages of air travel, plaintiffs bringing negligence cases could not rely on res ipsa loquitur because courts were unwilling to find that the likely cause of an air mishap was negligence. Since the 1950s, due to technological advances made by the industry as well as increased experience with and understanding of air travel, courts have found that airplane crashes are probably the result of negligence.[14] As in other cases in which the plaintiff establishes res ipsa

[14] Some courts permit the inference of negligence only when the flight occurs during good weather. Others apply it regardless of the weather. *See, e.g.*, Widmyer v. Southeast

loquitur, even where the defendant airline puts on evidence of its reasonable care, a jury may still find negligence on the part of the airline relying on the inference created by res ipsa loquitur.[15]

Medical malpractice cases often raise particular proof challenges for plaintiffs.[16] In some cases, such as where the results of the defendant's lack of due care are glaring, as where an instrument is left inside a patient, res ipsa loquitur is frequently used by medical malpractice plaintiffs. In more complicated cases, a plaintiff may need expert testimony to assist her in showing that the harm she suffered was likely the result of negligence. Where an inherent risk comes to pass after a medical procedure, however, its occurrence alone, regardless of how unlikely it is, will never support the use of res ipsa loquitur. The result provides no indication of probable negligence.[17]

[C] *Probably the Defendant*

Even if a plaintiff is able to show that the harm-causing occurrence was likely the cause of negligence, she cannot prevail until she ties the unreasonable conduct to the defendant. She must do both to get the benefit of res ipsa loquitur.

Under the traditional formulation of the elements of res ipsa loquitur, the plaintiff had to establish that the defendant likely had "exclusive control" over the harm-causing instrumentality. Taken literally, this posed a substantial hurdle for the plaintiff. For example, if P sits on D's bar stool and the stool collapses under her, a narrow interpretation of "exclusive control" would lead a court to deny her the use of res ipsa loquitur because the stool was under her control as well as that of other patrons.[18]

Even those jurisdictions that continue to adhere to the traditional res ipsa loquitur elements have liberalized the exclusive control element, however. It is usually enough for a plaintiff to get to a jury on res ipsa loquitur if she can provide evidence showing that others were probably not the responsible party and that the defendant probably was. For example, where

---

Skyways, Inc., 584 P.2d 1, 14 (Alaska 1978) (permitting res ipsa loquitur in air crash occurring in bad weather and noting that the "general safety record of air travel and the present state of air technology compel us to conclude that air crashes do not normally occur absent negligence, even in inclement weather.").

15 *See* Cox v. Northwest Airlines, Inc., 379 F.2d 893 (7th Cir. 1967) (court upheld a jury finding of negligence on the part of the defendant airline via res ipsa loquitur even though the defendant put on ample evidence of its due care).

16 *See infra* § 7.02[B].

17 *Id.* For example, if there is a 2% chance of internal bleeding following an appendectomy, the fact that the plaintiff bleeds after an appendectomy cannot alone support the invocation of res ipsa loquitur.

18 *See, e.g.*, Kilgore v. Shepard Co., 158 A.2d 720 (R.I. 1932) (plaintiff, injured when defendant's chair on which she sat collapsed, denied use of res ipsa loquitur because defendant not in exclusive control).

P is injured by an exploding soda bottle and sues the bottler, she may prevail on res ipsa loquitur by showing evidence that neither the manufacturer, the retailer, nor the consumer was probably the responsible party.[19] Indeed, the plaintiff need not eliminate all other possibly culpable parties; she must provide enough evidence from which a rational jury could conclude that the defendant probably was the responsible party.

Other jurisdictions have followed the lead of the Restatement and have made it clear that the plaintiff need only establish a likely nexus between the defendant and the harm-causing instrumentality. The Restatement states forthrightly that "exclusive control is not essential to a res ipsa loquitur case."[20] The key is that the plaintiff establish that the defendant is probably the responsible party, and exclusive control, while helpful, is not a prerequisite.

The traditional res ipsa loquitur formulation has required the plaintiff to show that she did not contribute to her harm. The rationale behind this factor is to provide further support for the required showing that the defendant is the culpable party.[21] Most jurisdictions recognize that this element has lost much of its importance either because of the advent of comparative fault or because the focus is encompassed within the showing that the defendant has probable control.

Notwithstanding this liberalization of the control element, this factor may still provide an insurmountable hurdle to the plaintiff's effort to establish res ipsa loquitur. Thus, in a case where P slips on a banana peel in D's store, res ipsa loquitur will not apply because P will be unable to show D's control (or responsibility) for the banana peel.[22] Similarly, res ipsa loquitur was properly denied a plaintiff pedestrian who sued a hotel when hit by a chair thrown from a hotel room's window because of the lack of control by the hotel over the harm-causing instrumentality.[23]

---

[19] *See, e.g.*, Escola v. Coca Cola Bottling Co., 150 P.2d 436 (Cal. 1944). Or the evidence can point to the retailer as the likely culpable party. *See* Giant Food, Inc. v. Washington Coca-Cola Bottling Co., 332 A.2d 1 (Md. Ct. App. 1975) (plaintiff's evidence supported jury inference that the bottle exploded due to the retailer's negligence).

[20] Restatement § 328D cmt. g.

[21] Indeed, the Restatement requires that the plaintiff show that she was not a responsible cause of the harm as part of establishing the defendant's control. Restatement § 328D cmt. i.

[22] As discussed *supra*, P will have to show D had actual or constructive notice of the dangerous condition to get to a jury.

[23] Larson v. St. Francis Hotel 188 P.2d 513, 515 (Cal. Ct. App. 1948) ("A hotel does not have exclusive control, either actual or potential, of its furniture. Guests have, at least, partial control. . . . To keep guests and visitors from throwing furniture out windows would require a guard to be placed in every room in the hotel, and no one would contend that there is any rule of law requiring a hotel to do that."). The outcome would likely be the same even under the liberalized Restatement approach because there would be no realistic way for the defendant to exercise control. *Compare* Restatement § 328D cmt g (A defendant "may be responsible where he is under a duty to control the conduct of a third person, as in the case of a host whose guests throw objects from his windows.").

[D] *The Outer Reaches of Res Ipsa Loquitur — Ybarra v. Spangard*

In a negligence case, the plaintiff must typically specify what was the unreasonable conduct and who is the responsible party. While res ipsa loquitur may relieve the plaintiff of the obligation to designate the improper conduct, it does not relieve her of the obligation to specify the identity of the allegedly culpable party. Thus, if P is hit on the head with a flower pot while walking past an apartment building, P may not successfully sue all the tenants in that building who have windows facing the street. Because the plaintiff has the burden of proof, it is deemed unfair to let her cast a wide net and force the defendants to exculpate themselves or pay her damages.

Yet, in one controversial case, the California Supreme Court seemed to come close to permitting the plaintiff to do this. In *Ybarra v. Spangard*, the plaintiff's shoulder was injured while he was unconscious and undergoing an appendectomy. Plaintiff sued all those who might have been responsible for his injury, admitting that he knew neither how he was harmed nor by whom. The defendants supported their motion for a nonsuit on two grounds:

> (1) that where there are several defendants, and there is a division of responsibility in the use of an instrumentality causing the injury, and the injury might have resulted from the separate act of either one of two or more persons, the rule of res ipsa loquitur cannot be invoked against any one of them; and (2) that where there are several instrumentalities, and no showing is made as to which caused the injury or as to the particular defendant in control of it, the doctrine cannot apply.[24]

The court was unpersuaded by the defendant's arguments, however, and permitted the plaintiff to rely on res ipsa loquitur, acknowledging that this would have the effect of calling on all of the defendants who had control over the plaintiff's "body or the instrumentalities which might have caused the injuries . . . to meet the inference of negligence by giving an explanation of their conduct."[25] The court was particularly influenced by the fact that the plaintiff's inability to put on specific evidence was because the

---

[24] Ybarra v. Spangard, 154 P.2d 687, 688-689 (Cal. 1944).

[25] *Id.* at 691. The plaintiff did have expert testimony that suggested that the probable cause of this injury was the negligence of someone. Further, the court warned that if the res ipsa loquitur doctrine would have precluded the plaintiff's recovery, the court would have still found a basis to rule for the plaintiff by opting for the imposition of strict liability on the defendants. *Id.* at 689. The relationship of res ipsa loquitur to strict liability has been raised in other contexts. For example, Justice Traynor, in advocating the adoption of strict liability for defective products, noted that the result was quite similar, and more intellectually honest, than the strained interpretation of res ipsa loquitur used in the majority opinion. Escola v. Coca Cola Bottling Co., 150 P.2d 436, 441 (Cal. 1944) (Traynor, J. concurring) *See infra* Chapter 17.

defendants had rendered him unconscious and that, in the medical context, the defendants were acting as a team. The court also was aware of the value of res ipsa loquitur as a means of "smoking out" evidence from the defendants.[26]

The facts of *Ybarra* create a compelling case for judicial creativity: an unconscious patient, probable negligence, an unwillingness on the part of anyone to come forward to claim responsibility or to blame another, perhaps due to a tradition of refusal to testify against other medical professionals, and solvent, well-insured defendants. Some courts and commentators have followed and agreed with the result.[27] Others have been highly critical of the decision.[28] Even in those jurisdictions following *Ybarra*, it is unlikely that the case will be extended much beyond its facts.

[E] *The Effect and Value of Res Ipsa Loquitur*

The plaintiff has the burden of proving that the defendant breached a duty and in most jurisdictions the plaintiff's invocation of res ipsa loquitur does not change this. In the majority of states, upon proof of res ipsa loquitur by the plaintiff, a jury may elect to infer that the defendant was unreasonable if it so chooses.[29] This permissible inference is often extremely important to the plaintiff's case. In many cases, if the plaintiff was unable to prove the res ipsa loquitur requirements, the case would never have gotten to a jury. With res ipsa loquitur, the case gets to a jury and the jury decides whether the defendant was more likely than not at fault.

Thus, a defendant has not automatically lost on the issue of breach of duty once a jury finds the res ipsa loquitur elements have been proven. The defendant's evidence of her reasonable conduct may be persuasive enough

---

[26] The efforts to get the defendants to come forward were unsuccessful with each defendant proclaiming her or his freedom from fault. Ultimately, the trial judge found them all jointly liable.

[27] *See, e.g.*, Beaudoin v. Watertown Memorial Hosp., 145 N.W.2d 166, 169 (Wis. 1966) (court acknowledges similarity to facts of *Ybarra*, supporting similar result). *See also* E. Wayne Thode, *The Unconscious Patient: Who Should Bear the Risk of Unexplained Injuries to a Healthy Part of His Body?*, 1969 Utah L. Rev. 1 (supporting the result in *Ybarra*).

[28] *See, e.g.*, Barrett v. Emanuel Hospital, 669 P.2d 835 (Or. Ct. App. 1983). *See also* Warren A. Seavey, Comment: *Res Ipsa Loquitur: Tabula in Naufragio*, 63 Harv. L. Rev. 643, 648 (1950) ("It is not equitable to impose liability upon all the members of the group where it is evident that the harm was not the result of group action and that most of the members of the group were innocent of wrongdoing.").

[29] While this is the approach in most jurisdictions, there are two other possible effects of res ipsa loquitur: "it raises a *presumption* of negligence which requires the jury to find negligence if defendant does not produce evidence sufficient to rebut the presumption" or it "not only raises such a presumption but also *shifts the ultimate burden of proof* to defendant and requires him to prove by a preponderance of all the evidence that the injury was not caused by his negligence." Sullivan v. Crabtree, 258 S.W.2d 782, 785 (Tenn. Ct. App. 1953) (emphasis in original).

for a jury to conclude that the defendant was probably not at fault.[30] But often the defendant's efforts to show due care through the precautions taken create something of a dilemma for her because a jury can interpret the occurrence of the harm-causing event notwithstanding those precautions to suggest negligence on the part of the defendant.[31]

[F] *The Role of the Defendant's Superior Knowledge*

A powerful rationale for res ipsa loquitur has been that it forces a defendant who has the most understanding of how the harm-causing event came about to come forward with that information.[32] Indeed, some commentators contend that res ipsa loquitur only should be applied in situations where the defendant possesses greater knowledge about how the harm occurred.[33]

Although the defendant's superior knowledge is a compelling reason for res ipsa loquitur, most courts and the Restatement do not require that the defendant have greater access to the facts than the plaintiff for the doctrine to apply.[34] Indeed, most jurisdictions permit a plaintiff to attempt to prove the defendant's unreasonable conduct with evidence of specific wrongdoing as well as through the use of res ipsa loquitur.[35]

---

30 The defendant's other avenue of defense is to try to defeat res ipsa loquitur by showing either that the harm-causing event does happen just as often absent negligence or by showing lack of control over the harm-causing instrumentality. If the defendant succeeds, res ipsa loquitur cannot apply and the case will probably be dismissed for lack of proof by the plaintiff.

31 As Professor James explains: "[T]he less effective his precautions to prevent the occurrence the more apt they are to appear negligent; the more effective the precautions testified to, the less likely they are to have been taken in this case since the accident *did happen.* Indeed the showing of a foolproof system of precautions *demonstrates* negligence unless it succeeds in convincing the trier that no such occurrence ever proceeded from defendant." Fleming James, Jr., *Proof of the Breach in Negligence Cases (Including Res Ipsa Loquitur)*, 37 Va. L. Rev. 179, 227 (1951) (emphasis in original).

32 In both *Byrne* and in *Ybarra*, the courts recognized this "smoking out" function of res ipsa loquitur.

33 *See, e.g.*, Charles E. Carpenter, *The Doctrine of Res Ipsa Loquitur in California*, 10 S. Cal. L. Rev. 166 (1937) (contending that a condition for the application of res ipsa loquitur is "that knowledge of the causes of the injury must appear more accessible to the defendant than to the plaintiff").

34 Restatement § 328D cmt. k. *See also* Newing v. Cheatham, 540 P.2d 33 (Cal. 1975) (even though all those with knowledge of how the accident occurred were killed in the plane crash at issue, the court found res ipsa loquitur to apply as a matter of law).

35 *See, e.g.*, Mobil Chemical Co. v. Bell, 517 S.W.2d 245, 254 (Tex. 1974) ("[P]laintiff does not necessarily lose the right to rely on the *res ipsa* doctrine by pleading specific acts of negligence. . . . [I]f the plaintiff's pleading gives fair notice that he is not relying solely on specific acts but instead intends to also rely on any other negligent acts reasonably inferable from the circumstances of the accident, his proof is not limited to the specific acts alleged."). *But see* Malloy v. Commonwealth Highland Theatres, Inc., 375 N.W.2d 631, 637 (S.D. 1985) ("When there is direct evidence concerning the cause of the incident and all the facts and circumstances surrounding it, the res ipsa loquitur rule is inapplicable.").

Under modern approaches to discovery in civil cases, it is questionable whether there is much need for the "smoking out" function of res ipsa loquitur. Further, there is criticism that the liberal use of res ipsa loquitur takes away any incentive for the plaintiff to make every effort to try to discern how the harm-causing event came about. In fact, some courts will deny the plaintiff the right to use res ipsa loquitur if it appears that she could have conducted an investigation into the cause of the accident and failed to do so.[36]

---

[36] *See, e.g.*, McDonald v. Smitty's Super Value, Inc., 757 P.2d 120, 125 (Ariz. Ct. App. 1988) ("Invocation of res ipsa loquitur is no substitute for reasonable investigation and discovery. The doctrine may benefit a plaintiff unable directly to prove negligence; it does not relieve a plaintiff too uninquisitive to undertake available proof.").

CHAPTER 6

STATUTORY STANDARDS OF CARE—"NEGLIGENCE PER SE"

SYNOPSIS

§ 6.01 OVERVIEW[1]

D, driving at night without headlights, collides with P. The accident occurs in a jurisdiction with a variety of traffic laws, including one requiring the use of headlights at night.[2] What is the effect of D's violation of this

[1] *See, e.g.*, Fleming James, Jr., *Statutory Standards and Negligence in Accident Cases*, 11 La. L. Rev. 95 (1950); Clarence Morris, *The Relation of Criminal Statutes to Tort Liability*, 46 Harv. L. Rev. 453 (1932); Clarence Morris, *The Role of Criminal Statutes in Negligence Actions*, 49 Colum. L. Rev. 21 (1949).

[2] This is a simplified version of the situation in Martin v. Herzog, 126 N.E. 814 (N.Y. 1920), in which the effect of the *plaintiff's* failure to use lights after dusk was the issue.

statute? Clearly, D is criminally liable for violating this traffic law and will probably have to pay a fine to the State. But what relevance does D's violation of the traffic law have in a negligence action brought by P against D? This is the focus of this section.

State legislatures can regulate tort law as long as the statutes they enact are constitutional. Thus, if a state's legislature enacted a statute stating that "any person driving after dusk without headlights who gets in an accident shall be found to have acted unreasonably," any court in that state would be compelled to find that D failed to exercise reasonable care. Statutes designed to affect negligence law are rare, however.[3]

Such *civil* enactments that *must* be used in a negligence determination are sometimes confused with the "negligence-per-se" doctrine. This doctrine provides that in certain situations a criminal statute (or administrative regulation or municipal ordinance)[4] *may* be used to set the standard of care in a negligence case. These statutes make no mention of civil liability but, rather, impose fines or even imprisonment as punishment for those violating their dictates. Confusion about the negligence-per-se concept is not surprising since, at first blush, it seems odd that legal provisions passed with no express intention to influence tort actions are used nevertheless as the standard of care in negligence cases.

There are several rationales for the negligence-per-se doctrine. Some courts have justified the approach by concluding that, because the reasonable person is law-abiding, one who violates a criminal law is thus per se unreasonable.[5] More persuasively, many courts and commentators explain the negligence-per-se approach as a justifiable judicial decision to adopt the determination of a representative body which, through a deliberative process, defined what constitutes appropriate conduct in a specific context. Accordingly, under this view, a specific legislative standard should replace the more general reasonable person standard.

---

[3] Though infrequent compared to criminal statutes, statutes focusing on tort actions do exist. For example, some states have statutorily immunized certain providers of alcohol from liability when a third party is injured by a drunken patron. *See infra* § 8.02[B][1] [b]. Similarly, a state legislature decides who may recover in wrongful death actions and in many jurisdictions determines the impact a plaintiff's fault will have on that plaintiff's recovery. Ultimately, the legislature can enact tort-related measures as long as they pass constitutional muster.

[4] Because most of the cases deal with criminal statutes, they are the primary focus in this section. But other regulatory provisions, such as administrative regulations and municipal ordinances, may be equally relevant.

[5] As will be discussed, this thinking is somewhat flawed if no account is given for why a person broke the law.

§ 6.02 FACTORS USED FOR DETERMINING THE PROPRIETY OF ADOPTING A STATUTE AS THE STANDARD OF CARE

Not every criminal statute becomes the standard of care in a negligence case. A *judge* must first examine the statute to determine if it is the sort of legislative pronouncement appropriate to set the standard of care in a negligence case. In other words, the statute must provide the sort of specific guidance that justifies its use by a civil court. For example, a judge would not adopt as the standard of care a criminal law requiring drivers to "use care and prudence" when operating a car, because this statute lacks specificity and adds nothing to the usual reasonably prudent person standard of care.

Even where a statute is generally appropriate because it is specific in focus, the judge nonetheless may decline to use the statute as the standard of care. The judge must examine the statute in order to determine two more things: whether the statute was designed to protect against the type of harm suffered by the plaintiff, and whether the class of persons designed to be protected by the statute includes the plaintiff.[6] This determination is wholly for the judge to make and often is no easy task, investing the judge with great discretion.[7]

[A] *Type of Harm*

Determining the type of harm against which a statute was designed to protect can be quite simple or very difficult. It is uncomplicated where the statutory purpose can be easily discerned from the language of the statute or from its clear legislative history. For example, in one famous case, the plaintiff sued for property lost when his livestock washed overboard while being transported on the defendant's ship. In his negligence action, the plaintiff tried to get the court to use as the standard of care a provision of a Contagious Diseases Act that required animals on ships be kept in pens. The judge refused to use the terms of the Act in place of the usual reasonable person standard of care because, as its name suggested, the purpose of the Act's requirement that animals be kept in pens was to prevent the transmission of disease, not to prevent their drowning.[8]

Often the statutory purpose is not readily discernible from the statute's language or legislative history. Sometimes even without clear language or express legislative history, a court can easily discern the statutory purpose. For example, a judge would likely conclude that a statute requiring the use

---

[6] *See* Restatement § 286.

[7] As Justice Traynor noted: "The decision as to what the civil standard should be still rests with the court, and the standard formulated by a legislative body in a police regulation or criminal statute becomes the standard to determine civil liability only because the court accepts it." Clinkscales v. Carver, 136 P.2d 777, 778 (Cal. 1943).

[8] Gorris v. Scott, L.R. 9 Ex. 125 (Eng. 1874).

of headlights after dusk is designed to prevent nighttime automobile accidents. Yet, in many situations the statutory purpose is not this straightforward.

"Key-in-the-ignition" statutes are prime examples of ambiguity regarding statutory purpose. These criminal statutes impose fines on drivers who fail to remove their keys from vehicle ignitions. Judges have taken widely divergent views regarding the type of harm against which these statutes are designed to protect. Some find the purpose is to deter theft in order to help reserve police resources, while others find the purpose is to protect the public from personal injury and property damage caused by the operation of a stolen car.[9]

[B] *Plaintiff in Protected Class*

In addition to finding the type of harm suffered by P was contemplated by the statute, a judge must also determine that the plaintiff falls in the class intended to be protected by the statute. Often this is easy, as where legislation is passed to promote worker safety, and the person injured by the statutory violation is a non-employee. Sometimes, however, the scope of the protected class is uncertain. For example, returning to the "key-in-the-ignition" statutes, what if D is being sued by P, a mental patient who, finding D's car with the keys in the ignition, takes the car for a joy ride and injures *himself*? Even if a court were to find a safety purpose behind the statute, would such a statute be interpreted to protect an unauthorized user of the vehicle?[10] Where neither the face of the statute nor the legislative history provides clues to the determination of the proper protected class, the judge has enormous leeway.

[C] *Licensing Statutes*

D is driving *using all due care* when she hits P's car. If P can show that D was driving without a valid license, as required by law, can she prevail based on D's statutory violation in her negligence action against D? Should the law requiring a valid driver's license become the standard of care and should the failure to have a valid license establish breach of duty? Most courts would refuse to invoke the negligence-per-se doctrine in this context, requiring P to prove D's lack of due care. The rationale for the refusal of the majority of courts to use licensing statutes as the standard of care is that, because the purpose of licensing statutes is to protect

---

[9] *See* Ney v. Yellow Cab Co., 117 N.E.2d 74 (Ill. 1954) (majority found statute applied when third party was injured by a thief driving a stolen car, but a dissenter argued that the type of harm was limited to harm caused by "mere negligent or inadvertent starting of the automobile and an ensuing uncontrolled movement thereof").

[10] *See* Rushink v. Gerstheimer, 440 N.Y.S.2d 738 (N.Y. App. Div. 1981) (majority refused recovery, finding P to fall outside the protected class, with other judges finding protected class to include all members of the public who could be foreseeably harmed by unauthorized vehicle users).

the public from those lacking requisite skill, the plaintiff should have to prove the defendant's lack of ability in order to recover. This rationale is not entirely satisfactory, but courts are wary of an overly harsh result, as where an unlicensed person using all the skill of a doctor in good standing fails to cure someone and is found negligent per se for practicing medicine without a license.[11]

§ 6.03 EFFECTS OF NON-ADOPTION AND OF ADOPTION OF STATUTE

[A] *Effects of Non-adoption of a Statute*

The judge's determination that the proffered statute should not be adopted as the standard of care (because it was not designed to protect this plaintiff, was not designed to protect against this type of harm, or because it is otherwise inappropriate) does not foreclose P's recovery for negligence. Upon the judge's refusal to use the statute as the standard of care, the case proceeds under the usual "reasonably prudent person" standard of care. P may still prevail upon proof that D failed to act reasonably.[12]

[B] *Effects of Adoption of the Statute and Statutory Violation*

What is the effect of a judge's determination that the statute is designed to protect the plaintiff from the harm that occurred? In an overwhelming majority of jurisdictions, the statute replaces the usual reasonably prudent person standard of care. As an example, return to the headlight statute beginning this Chapter. Because it is intended to protect motorists (thus, proper class of plaintiff) from personal injury and property damage (thus, proper type of harm), the standard of care to which the P will be held in that case is to use headlights after dusk, rather than to act as a reasonably prudent person. Breach of duty — the failure to meet the standard of care — is shown by proof that D failed to use headlights after dusk.

Where a statute sets the standard of care, the jury role is quite limited. Rather than having to grapple with whether D used reasonable care, all the jury needs to find is that the statute was violated. Many times this is not even contested. Because under this approach, breach of duty is the violation of the statute, most jurisdictions call this "negligence per se."

---

[11] Though the negligence-per-se doctrine can come close to imposing liability without fault in some situations, using the lack of a license may simply go too far for most courts. *See* Brown v. Shyne, 151 N.E. 197 (N.Y. 1926) (chiropractor who undertook to perform a treatment only to be performed by doctors not negligent per se for violation of licensing statute).

[12] Indeed, in some instances, the statute that was rejected as the standard of care may be admissible to show lack of due care by the defendant. For example, if a non-employee is trying to use a worker safety regulation, the regulation may be generally relevant to show lack of reasonableness by the defendant although the regulation will not set the standard of care as P is not in the protected class.

The plaintiff does not automatically recover upon a finding of breach of the statutory standard of care. She must still establish the other elements of a negligence cause of action: cause-in-fact, proximate cause and damages. Thus, even if the headlight statute becomes the standard of care and the jury finds that D breached a duty by failing to use headlights after dusk, P, to recover, must prove no injury would have likely occurred if D had been using headlights.[13]

A small minority of jurisdictions do not follow the negligence-per-se approach. In these jurisdictions, the relevant statute is simply admitted for the jury's consideration in determining whether D used reasonable care. The statute has no effect on the relevant standard of care; its only relevance is as a factor in the jury's analysis of the reasonableness of D's conduct.

§ 6.04 THE ROLE OF EXCUSE

A related issue is the extent to which D should be permitted to show some excuse for the violation. What if, in the initial hypothetical, D's headlights had just gone out due to a malfunction through no fault of D? Or what if D, in order to avoid hitting a child who suddenly ran into the street, swerves into the lane of oncoming traffic, colliding with P's car? Should P prevail upon a showing D violated a statute requiring a driver to stay in her own lane, or should consideration be given to the reasons that D violated the law?

Early in the development of the negligence-per-se doctrine, some courts took a very literal view of the dictates of the approach and refused to consider D's excuses. This led to rather harsh and illogical results. If no excuses were permitted, the driver who, in violation of statute, swerved into the wrong lane to miss a child would be liable to the other driver because of the statutory violation.

Modern courts have recognized excused statutory violations.[14] In certain instances, all jurisdictions excuse a party's violation of statute. Acceptable excuses include: a sudden emergency that is not of the actor's making; compliance would involve greater danger than violation; the actor neither knows nor should know of the occasion for diligence; the actor has some incapacity rendering the violation reasonable; or, after reasonable efforts

[13] In other words, P must show that D's statutory violation was the *cause-in-fact* of P's damages. *See infra* Chapter 11.

[14] In order to avoid the harsh result of an unexcused statutory violation, some courts engaged in some creativity. For example, in one case, P was walking with his back to oncoming traffic, in violation of a statute requiring pedestrians to walk facing oncoming traffic. D asserted that P should be barred from recovery because he was contributorily negligent per se for violating the statute. The court disagreed and noted that under the circumstances it would have been more dangerous for P to comply with the statute than to violate it. To get to this end the court creatively characterized the statute at issue as "a rule of the road" to which violation is not negligence per se. Tedla v. Ellman, 19 N.E.2d 987 (N.Y. 1939).

to comply, the party is unable to do so.[15] In most states, a judge makes an initial determination that the proffered excuse is appropriate and the jury resolves any factual disputes. If there is an excused violation, the statute no longer affects the outcome. In practical effect, the finding of an excused violation frequently exculpates the defendant from liability because the excuse shows the reasonableness of the defendant's conduct.

§ 6.05 NEGLIGENCE PER SE AND CHILDREN

There is an inherent conflict between the standard of care usually applied to children, which compares them to other children of the same age, experience and intelligence, and the statutory standard that is a product of the negligence-per-se doctrine. The child standard of care provides greater flexibility than the reasonable person standard of care, recognizing the need to account for a child's immaturity of judgment and inability to appreciate dangers. On the other hand, the negligence-per-se doctrine seeks to provide a more rigid standard of care. Thus, if 14-year-old D injures P because D was riding a bicycle without a headlight as required by municipal ordinance, which standard of care should apply in P's negligence action against D, the child standard of care or that set by the municipal ordinance? Most jurisdictions have concluded that the child standard of care should apply in such a case, though the statutory violation could be relevant evidence of breach if a jury finds that a reasonable child of the same age, maturity, intelligence and experience of the defendant would not have violated the statute under the circumstances.[16]

§ 6.06 COMPLIANCE WITH STATUTE

D's violation of a relevant statute can go far toward establishing breach under the negligence-per-se doctrine. Does the converse apply? Should D's *compliance* with a relevant statute, regulation or ordinance establish due care? Assume D is walking facing heavy traffic, as commanded by statute. P, in order to avoid hitting D, swerves and hits a pole, denting his car. P contends that D acted unreasonably by facing heavy traffic, contending the reasonable person would have walked on the other side where there was much less traffic. Is D exonerated because she was complying with the statute?

The rule is well-settled that compliance with a statute is merely relevant evidence of reasonableness. Compliance does not establish due care. The statute sets a minimum standard which at times the reasonable person should

---

[15] *See* Restatement § 288A. There are a few types of statutes, such as child labor laws, for which no excuse will be permitted. *Id.* at cmt. c. These are quite rare.

[16] *See, e.g.*, Bauman v. Crawford, 704 P.2d 1181 (Wash. 1985); Gottschalk v. Rudes, 315 S.W.2d 361 (Tex. Civ. App. 1958). In most states, if the child is engaged in an adult activity, the child standard of care no longer applies and negligence per se will become central to the case.

exceed. Thus, if D, due to heavy rain pulls her car off the road and puts on her flashers as required by statute, she may still be liable to P, who was injured by colliding into D's car, if a jury concludes that a reasonable person would have taken additional precautions under the circumstances.

The rule that compliance is merely evidence of due care has been criticized, especially in the context of compliance with governmental standards and administrative regulations. Some contend that compliance with a specific regulation of an expert governmental agency should establish due care.[17] Notwithstanding this criticism, a drug manufacturer who places a warning on its product in compliance with governmental requirements may still be found negligent if a jury concludes that a reasonable company would have exceeded the governmental mandate.

§ 6.07 CRITICISMS OF THE NEGLIGENCE-PER-SE DOCTRINE

The negligence-per-se doctrine has been widely accepted for over half a century. In most jurisdictions, the language of a relevant statute becomes the standard of care and its unexcused violation is breach. Though well-settled, there is certainly room to question the propriety of placing so much weight on laws that were enacted without any indication of an intent to affect negligence law.

The negligence-per-se doctrine has been criticized. One key criticism arises from the widely divergent impact the violation of a criminal statute has in a criminal prosecution from that in a tort case. Violation of most of the criminal statutes used in negligence-per-se cases leads to the imposition of a modest fine in the criminal context. Because of the slight penalty and the enormous administrative burden required by considering all possible defenses, these offenses are often strict liability in nature, thus disposing of the State's requirement to show a bad intent. In the negligence-per-se context, however, the impact of violation can be enormous as the defendant is liable for all the harm proximately caused by the statutory violation.[18] Further, this result can be achieved without providing the sort of safeguards (such as an elevated burden of proof) provided in criminal cases.

Additionally, the negligence-per-se doctrine greatly constricts the jury's traditional role of determining breach and often invests the trial judge with broad discretion. To the extent that judge-made standards of care have been

[17] *See, e.g.*, Peter Huber, *Safety and the Second Best: The Hazards of Public Risk Management in the Courts*, 85 Colum. L. Rev. 277 (1985). This issue often arises in the area of products liability, particularly in the context of the debate about preemption. *See infra* Chapter 17.

[18] Of course, most jurisdictions increasingly consider whether there is an excused violation. To the extent that broad excuses are permitted, is the justification for the doctrine diminished? Are limits on flexbility justified by the doctrine's ability to provide greater certainty than the usual reasonable person standard?

rejected, should judges have wide discretion to impose legislative standards?[19] Finally, is the doctrine an inappropriate encroachment upon the domain of the legislature? If the legislature elects to do so, it surely may impose civil liability. When it does not elect to do so, should a court presume such an intent nevertheless?

---

[19] *See supra* § 4.04. Of course, the situations are not id entical as the judge in the negligence-per-se context is taking direction from a legislative or administrative body.

CHAPTER 7

PROFESSIONAL NEGLIGENCE

SYNOPSIS

§ 7.01 OVERVIEW

In most negligence cases, the defendant's liability results from a failure to act as a reasonably prudent person. As part of the evaluation of the defendant's reasonableness, the jury may consider several factors, including the defendant's compliance with or deviation from custom. The custom evidence is not determinative; it is simply evidence for the jury to consider in its determination of breach of duty.[1]

These general rules do not apply in the context of professional negligence. Because of the specialized skill and training needed to be a doctor, lawyer,

[1] *See supra* § 4.03.

accountant, architect, or engineer, courts defer to the expertise of the profession to determine the appropriate standard of care.[2] In the professional negligence context, custom plays a central and determinative role — the defendant's compliance with the custom of the profession insulates the defendant from negligence liability. Custom, then, establishes the standard of care.[3] In addition, because of the complexity of the issues involved, expert witnesses are usually necessary for the plaintiff to establish the standard of care and to help determine if the defendant deviated from that standard.

Because most of the focus in the discussion of professional negligence is on medical malpractice, this Chapter begins with an analysis of that topic. The medical malpractice discussion first examines traditional medical malpractice and then turns to liability for failure to obtain informed consent. The medical malpractice analysis is followed by an examination of legal malpractice. It should be kept in mind that the general principles that apply to medical and legal malpractice apply to other professions as well.

§ 7.02 MEDICAL MALPRACTICE[4]

A physician will be held to the professional standard of care when acting in a professional capacity.[5] Medical malpractice actions typically arise from a patient's allegation of negligent diagnosis or treatment. In order to prevail, the patient must show that the physician fell below the applicable standard of care, thereby causing the patient's injury. The standard of care to which physicians are held is set by the custom of their profession. The physician must possess and use the knowledge and skill common to members of the

---

[2] The professional standard of care applies only where there is specialized skill and training, and, often, post-graduate education. While the Restatement intends that the professional standard of care apply to "those in the practice of a skilled trade," which includes vocations such as electricians, pilots and plumbers (Rest. § 299A), many courts have restricted the standard of care to "professionals," such as lawyers, doctors and architects. Under this interpretation, extra skill derived from experience will not lead to the application of the professional standard of care. For example, a truck driver, even if specially trained to drive big rigs, will not be held to the professional standard of care but will, instead, be held to that of a reasonable person. *See supra* § 3.04[B][4]. There may be some elitism at work in the determination of which "professions" are afforded the professional standard of care, and which are not.

[3] Contrast this approach with the tack taken in most negligence cases where custom does not set the standard of care, but, rather, serves only as evidence of the defendant's unreasonable conduct. *See supra* § 4.03.

[4] *See generally* David W. Louisell and Harold Williams, MEDICAL MALPRACTICE (1994); Joseph H. King, Jr., *In Search of a Standard of Care for the Medical Profession: The "Accepted Practice" Formula,* 28 Vand. L. Rev. 1213 (1975); Allan H. McCoid, *The Care Required of Medical Practitioners,* 12 Vand. L. Rev. 549 (1959).

[5] When a physician is engaged in conduct that does not require the use of her specialized skills, such as driving a car, she is held to the usual reasonable person standard of care.

profession in good standing. This standard demands of the physician minimal competence.[6]

Although courts occasionally refer to the professional standard in medical malpractice cases as the "reasonable doctor" standard of care, this terminology is misleading. Were a "reasonable doctor" standard to apply, it would permit the jury to balance factors such as burden, magnitude and probability in order to determine if the defendant breached a duty owed to the plaintiff. This approach is not used in medical malpractice cases and, thus, a reference to a "reasonable doctor" is an imprecise manner of stating the appropriate standard of care. In the medical malpractice context, the standard of care is set by custom, and the determination of breach of duty arises from the defendant doctor's failure to act with the minimal competence exercised by other doctors in good standing. Put another way, liability flows from the physician's failure to conform to the profession's customary practice and, unlike the typical negligence case, the jury has no discretion to find that the standard practice is unreasonable.

It is not always correct to view the standard of care expected of professionals as a "higher standard." In most cases, the conduct demanded of a physician exceeds that of a reasonable person, but not always. For example, if the well-settled custom of ophthalmologists is to test only those over 40 years old for glaucoma, notwithstanding a tiny burden to test those under 40, a patient who is under 40 years old suing for medical malpractice because of her ophthalmologist's failure to test her for glaucoma has no case. This is so even if the custom itself could be deemed unreasonable.[7]

[A] *Alternative Approaches to the Practice of Medicine*

Often there is more than one accepted way to practice medicine. As long as one of the accepted approaches is followed, a doctor is protected from malpractice liability. Thus, if Dr. X treats P's ailment in one manner, that other doctors might treat it differently is irrelevant provided Dr. X's approach is a "reputable" or "respectable" one. Further, the relative merits

[6] Rest. § 299A cmt. e ("[T]he standard of skill and knowledge required . . . is that which is commonly possessed by members of that profession or trade in good standing. It is not that of the most highly skilled, nor is it that of the average member of the profession or trade, since those who have less than median or average skill may still be competent and qualified.").

[7] *But see* Helling v. Carey, 519 P.2d 981 (Wash. 1974). In *Helling*, the Washington Supreme Court took the unusual step of refusing to treat the plaintiff's malpractice action based on the defendant ophthalmologist's failure to test her for glaucoma as one in which the custom of the profession determines liability. Rather than using the professional custom as the standard of care, the court engaged in a Hand balancing test to reach the conclusion that the defendant's failure to test the plaintiff was unreasonable as a matter of law. Because the court refused to defer to the professional custom, *Helling* is an anomaly. The Washington Legislature responded quickly by enacting a statute making it clear that professional custom is to be used as the standard of care in medical malpractice cases.

of each approach are irrelevant provided there is an established custom supporting the method employed.

Sometimes what constitutes an acceptable method is debatable. Permitting judges or juries to make this determination seems odd in light of the justification for a professional negligence standard in the medical malpractice context in the first place — that judges and juries are not equipped to determine how medicine should be practiced and, thus, must defer to the expertise of the profession. Allowing judges and juries to decide what constitutes a reputable way of practicing medicine appears to ignore this concern. Further, a requirement that the physician's approach be deemed acceptable may discourage new and alternative treatments. If doctors were subjected to liability for *any* harm until the alternative method became accepted enough to be "respectable and reputable," fear of liability could cause the practice of medicine to stagnate.[8]

[B] *Proof Issues in Medical Malpractice*

To establish a claim for medical malpractice, the plaintiff must show more than an unwanted result. The physician's failure to cure, for example, cannot itself serve to establish liability, because a physician does not generally promise positive results. Nor does the fact that a rare complication materializes establish lack of due care by the defendant. For example, Dr. D performs an appendectomy on P. Assume that in five percent of non-negligently performed appendectomies infection ensues, requiring further surgery. The fact that the patient gets a post-operative infection requiring additional surgery does not suggest lack of due care by the defendant.[9] Nor would res ipsa loquitur be of use to the plaintiff because the development of an inherent risk, albeit a slight one, cannot alone suggest negligence.

[1] Expert Witnesses

Because of the technical nature of most medical malpractice cases, a plaintiff typically will need qualified expert witnesses to help establish the appropriate standard of care and the defendant's breach of duty. The expert must delineate the relevant medical custom. The expert's testimony that she personally would have behaved differently from the defendant is not the relevant focus. The issue is the custom of other doctors in the relevant medical community. For example, P sues D, claiming that D was negligent for failing to X-ray P in order to diagnose and treat P's ankle pain. P's

---

[8] At a minimum, the physician would be well-advised to inform her patient about the experimental nature of the treatment, the alternatives and the risks involved. *See infra* § 7.03[B].

[9] *See* Cobbs v. Grant, 502 P.2d 1 (Cal. 1972), in which the particularly unlucky plaintiff was unable to establish lack of due care by the surgeon-defendant based on evidence that slight, but inherent risks, materialized on several occasions. As was the case in *Cobbs*, there may be an alternative basis for liability based on the physician's nondisclosure of these inherent risks. *See infra* § 7.03[B].

expert, Dr. X, testifies that she would have immediately done an X-ray in light of P's complaints. A directed verdict for D would be proper because there is no evidence presented by P that the custom of the profession was to X-ray the ankle in light of P's complaints.[10]

The plaintiff's expert must be familiar with the custom applicable to the defendant's practice. The expert need not practice exactly the same type of medicine as the defendant to testify, although the expert must have familiarity with the custom applicable to the defendant's practice. For example, an orthopedic surgeon cannot testify about the alleged malpractice of a podiatrist absent a showing that the surgeon is familiar with the custom applicable to podiatrists or that the custom for podiatrists is the same as that for orthopedic surgeons.[11] Absent such a foundation for the offered testimony, the expert's evidence would be inadmissible.

The admissibility of expert testimony also depends upon the community in which the defendant practices medicine. The relevant professional custom may differ depending on whether it is drawn from a local, statewide or national practice. There have been significant jurisdictional splits on this topic with states electing to hold physicians to the standard practice of their community, of similar communities, of their state, or even of the nation. Thus, the propriety of expert testimony depends on the geographic area used in the jurisdiction.

Because of concerns about holding rural doctors to standards they could not meet, initially physicians were only required to adhere to the customary standard of the community in which they practiced. Restricting expert testimony to the professional standards employed in the same community as the defendant's often prevented plaintiffs from getting to trial. Plaintiffs frequently could not find a doctor willing to testify against the defendant due to fear of ostracism by other doctors in the community or concern about insurance policy cancellation.

Because of these concerns, the locality standard has been expanded in most instances to one permitting testimony from an expert familiar with the practice in the "same or similar locality" as that of the defendant. As the Restatement explains in supporting the expansion to a "same or similar locality" test:

> The standard is not, however, that of the particular locality. If there are only three physicians in a small town, and all three are highly incompetent, they cannot be permitted to set a standard of utter inferiority for a fourth who comes to town. The standard is rather that of persons

---

[10] Boyce v. Brown, 77 P.2d 455 (Ariz. 1938). *See also* Walski v. Tiesenga, 381 N.E.2d 279 (Ill. 1978) (expert's testimony about his personally preferred approach does not establish the generally accepted medical standard).

[11] Melville v. Southward, 791 P.2d 383 (Colo. 1990).

engaged in a similar practice in similar localities, considering geographical location, size, and the character of the community in general.[12]

This "same or similar locality" standard protects defendants from being required to practice in a manner of which they are incapable due to geographic limitations, while expanding the potential pool of experts. It does, however, generate debate about what constitutes a "similar" locality, and can be criticized on the ground that it perpetuates substandard medical practice if the custom in similar localities is also inadequate.[13]

The degree to which varying geographical standards are needed today is debatable. The practice of medicine is far more standardized. Medical education, too, is more uniform. Further, advances in communication and the increasing availability of medical literature all suggest that localized, or even state, standards no longer are necessary.[14] Indeed, where medical specialists, such as obstetricians or radiologists, are involved, there has been a strong trend toward using a national standard.[15]

There has been some concern that a national standard of care fails to account adequately for differences in resources available to rural and urban doctors. Yet, even under a national standard, a physician would not be liable for failing to employ a procedure requiring the use of unavailable equipment since the focus requires consideration of the surrounding circumstances.[16]

Even where there is no debate about the qualifications of the proposed expert, challenges arise. In most medical malpractice cases, both parties introduce testimony from appropriately qualified experts. These experts often disagree and there are often varying opinions about the proper custom.

---

[12] Rest. § 299A cmt. g.

[13] Morrison v. MacNamara, 407 A.2d 555 (D.C. 1979). *See also* Vergara v. Doan, 593 N.E.2d 185 (Ind. 1992) (rejecting the same or similar locality approach because it "permits a lower standard of care to be exercised in smaller communities because other similar communities are likely to have the same level of care," because it requires the expenditure of money and time to debate what is a similar community and because the "disparity between small town and urban medicine continues to lessen with advances in communication, transportation, and education").

[14] In Vergara v. Doan, 593 N.E.2d 185 (Ind. 1992), the Indiana Supreme Court rejected the "same or similar locality rule," adopting instead a national standard of care. The standard proposed states that "a physician must exercise that degree of care, skill and proficiency exercised by reasonably careful, skillful, and prudent practitioners in the same class to which he belongs, acting under the same or similar circumstances."

[15] While most of the development regarding the geographical standard to be applied has been the result of court decisions, some state legislatures have made the determination. *See, e.g.*, Henning v. Thomas, 366 S.E.2d 109 (Va. 1988), interpreting a Virginia statute mandating that all physicians practicing in that state, including specialists, would be held to a statewide standard. The court held that out-of-state experts were permitted to testify, provided they were familiar with the Virginia standard.

[16] There could be liability for the failure to refer the patient to a place where more sophisticated testing was available if the custom was to do so.

The trier-of-fact then has the difficult task of deciding which expert testimony to believe and which to discount.

[2] The Common Knowledge Exception and Res Ipsa Loquitur

Experts are not always required in medical malpractice cases. There are situations where the negligence of the physician is so egregious that laypersons may determine breach themselves. Examples of such cases — said to fall within the "common knowledge" of laypersons — include operating on the wrong organ, leaving foreign objects (such as sponges) inside the patient, and amputating the wrong limb. These contexts are often amenable to proof by res ipsa loquitur. Also, sometimes these cases fall outside malpractice entirely because they do not involve the use of special medical training and skill.

Res ipsa loquitur also may be used in malpractice cases that do not fall within the "common knowledge" exception. In these cases, the plaintiff will usually need expert testimony to help establish that the harm she suffered does not ordinarily occur in the absence of the lack of due care.[17]

§ 7.03 INFORMED CONSENT[18]

A second basis for medical malpractice liability is predicated upon a physician's failure to provide information to the patient. The defendant doctor is not being sued for failure to diagnose a condition, prescribing the wrong treatment, or for negligently performing a medical procedure. Rather, liability arises from the defendant's failure to obtain the plaintiff's informed consent.

[A] *Battery*

Initially, informed consent actions gave rise to an intentional tort action for battery.[19] Although most informed consent cases now are based on negligence, there are still situations where a battery action is appropriate. For example, where a physician performs a substantially different procedure from that to which the plaintiff-patient agreed or where the doctor significantly exceeds the scope of the plaintiff-patient's consent,[20] a battery action will be the likely cause of action.

---

[17] *See, e.g.*, Morgan v. Children's Hospital, 480 N.E.2d 464, 466 (Ohio 1985). *See also* the discussion of Ybarra v. Spangard, 154 P.2d 687 (Cal. 1944), *supra* § 5.04[D].

[18] *See generally* Mark Fajfar, *An Economic Analysis of Informed Consent to Medical Care,* 80 Geo. L.J. 1941 (1992); Jay Katz, *Informed Consent—A Fairy Tale? Law's Vision,* 39 U. Pitt. L. Rev. 137 (1977); Marjorie M. Schultz, *From Informed Consent to Patient Choice: A New Protected Interest,* 95 Yale L.J. 219 (1985); Alan J. Weisbard, *Informed Consent: The Law's Uneasy Compromise With Ethical Theory,* 65 Neb. L. Rev. 749 (1986).

[19] *See supra* § 1.02.

[20] *See, e.g.*, Mohr v. Williams, 104 N.W. 12 (Minn. 1905) (battery action appropriate where physician operated on plaintiff's left ear, although plaintiff consented to operation

The determination of whether an informed consent action is based in battery or in negligence has important repercussions. A battery action often has a shorter statute of limitations than negligence, elevates the possibility that the physician will be liable for punitive damages, and usually renders the defendant's medical malpractice coverage inapplicable. Further, the proof requirements are entirely different. A final distinction is that a plaintiff may recover in battery without proof of actual harm while negligence requires the plaintiff to prove injury as part of the prima facie case.

[B] *Negligence*

Most informed consent cases in a majority of jurisdictions are now based in negligence. The typical negligence-based informed consent case occurs where an undisclosed complication with a medical procedure or treatment arises.[21] The action is premised on patients getting enough information about the risks of a proposed treatment or procedure that they are able to make an intelligent decision about their medical care. Although there is agreement about the general purpose of informed consent, there is dispute about the appropriate standard of care in an informed consent action. Many jurisdictions treat a negligence-based informed consent claim as a species of medical malpractice, using the professional standard of care set by custom (the "physician rule"). Other states have determined that the particular interests involved mandate that informed consent cases be treated as distinct from typical medical malpractice actions, leading to the adoption of a rule requiring the disclosure of all material information (the "patient rule").[22]

[1] The Physician Rule

Under the physician rule, informed consent cases are treated like other medical malpractice actions. Accordingly, custom sets the standard of care, and expert testimony is required to establish this custom. In informed consent cases, where liability is based on the physician's nondisclosure of a risk of a given procedure or treatment, a plaintiff must show that the customary practice of doctors in good standing in the relevant community is to disclose that risk. Absent this proof, the plaintiff cannot prevail. Thus, if P sues Dr. D because Dr. D did not inform P that there was an inherent 5% risk of hearing loss from the proposed ear surgery, P cannot recover in a jurisdiction following the physician rule absent expert testimony

---

on right ear). *See also* Cobbs v. Grant, 502 P.2d 1, 7 (Cal. 1972) (listing examples of battery cases in the medical context).

[21] As Professor Schultz explains: "Discomfort with treating doctors under a doctrine aimed at antisocial conduct has prompted most jurisdictions to limit the battery action to those relatively unusual situations where a medical procedure has been carried out without any consent, rather than where the consent has merely been insufficiently informed." Schultz, *supra* note 18, at 226.

[22] Many jurisdictions now have statutes that determine the standard to be used in an informed consent case.

showing that the relevant professional custom is to divulge the risk of hearing loss.[23] This approach allows the medical community itself to determine what risks should be divulged.

[2] The Patient Rule

During the late 1960s and early 1970s, courts increasingly recognized personal autonomy rights and deemed them worthy of legal protection. Criticism of the professional rule mounted with courts and commentators noting that investing physicians with the decision of what a patient was entitled to be told was paternalistic and ignored the patient's right to make important medical decisions. In the seminal case eschewing the professional rule, the court noted that "respect for the patient's right of self-determination on particular therapy demands a standard set by law for physicians rather than one which physicians may or may not impose upon themselves."[24]

Many jurisdictions have replaced the "professional rule" with a "patient rule," under which a physician is obligated to disclose to a patient all material risks involved in a given procedure or treatment. Under a disclosure rule based on a patient's reasonable disclosure expectations, the more certain standard of the professional rule mandating customary disclosures is replaced with a more ambiguous standard of "materiality." How is a physician to determine what is material? This avowedly imprecise standard is premised on the notion that patients should be told of risks that would likely affect their medical decisions.[25]

Although the standard is imprecise, there is agreement on the core principles. Materiality will depend on the gravity and probability of the potential harm. Any real risk of death, for example, would likely be material; a modest risk of infection probably would not.[26] Thus, for a physician to

---

[23] *See* Eccleston v. Chait, 492 N.W.2d 860 (Neb. 1992), in which the defendant doctor told the plaintiff patient several risks of the proposed ear surgery but failed to divulge a 5% risk of hearing loss. The defendant admitted that he normally tells patients undergoing this procedure of the 5% risk of hearing loss. However, because expert testimony at trial established that physicians in the state customarily did not disclose the 5% risk of hearing loss, the court held that it was irrelevant that the defendant doctor typically did disclose this risk, and upheld a defendant's verdict based on the physician rule.

[24] Canterbury v. Spence, 464 F.2d 772, 784 (D.C. Cir. 1972). *See also* Cobbs v. Grant, 502 P.2d 1, 9 (Cal. 1972) ("[A] person of adult years and in sound mind has the right, in the exercise of control over his own body, to determine whether or not to submit to lawful medical treatment.").

[25] *See* Scott v. Bradford, 606 P.2d 554, 558 (Okla. 1979) ("There is no bright line separating the material from the immaterial; it is a question of fact. A risk is material if it would be likely to affect [a] patient's decision."). *See also* Harnish v. Children's Hospital Medical Center, 439 N.E.2d 240, 243 (Mass. 1982) ("Materiality may be said to be the significance a reasonable person, in what the physician knows or should know is his patient's position, would attach to the disclosed risk or risks in deciding whether to submit or not to submit to surgery or treatment.").

[26] As the California Supreme Court explained: "First, the patient's interest in information does not extend to a lengthy polysyllabic discourse on all possible complications. A mini-

meet the standard of care in a case governed by the patient rule, the doctor must divulge, at a minimum, material risks involved with the treatment and recuperation, as well as the alternatives available and their attendant material risks. Significantly, under the patient rule, the plaintiff can prevail without expert testimony, because lay persons are able to determine what is material.

Courts have differed about whether the test for materiality is an objective or subjective one. A subjective test focuses on whether the risk is material to the plaintiff, while an objective test turns on risks material to a reasonable person. In most cases, there would be little difference in effect between these approaches. The objective test would ensure that a physician would not be liable for failing to disclose a risk that is only material to the patient due to some undisclosed idiosyncracy, such as an unusually intense fear of needles. The objective test could be unduly restrictive, however. Patients should have the ability to make something material by informing the physician of its particular importance to them. Some courts that have adopted the patient rule have confused the proper focus of materiality with other elements of the cause of action.[27]

Even where the plaintiff can establish nondisclosure of a material risk, the plaintiff has an additional hurdle: proof of causation. The plaintiff must show that had she been properly informed she would not have undergone the procedure that caused injury. In many cases, this is extremely difficult. The trier of fact will likely be suspicious of a plaintiff who contends that, even though she was suffering from high fever and great pain that would not respond to medication, she would not have agreed to a diagnostic test that had a one in 100,000 chance of causing kidney failure.[28]

Regarding proof of causation, many courts have opted for an objective standard while others use the subjective causation standard typically employed in negligence cases. Those courts that use an objective standard for causation require the plaintiff to show that a reasonable person in her situation would not have undergone the procedure if she had been told of

---

course in medical science is not required; the patient is concerned with the risk of death or bodily harm, and problems of recuperation. Second, there is no physician's duty to discuss the relatively minor risks inherent in common procedures, when it is common knowledge that such risks inherent in the procedure are of very low incidence." Cobbs v. Grant, 502 P.2d 1, 11 (Cal. 1972). In *Cobbs*, the court also required that physicians divulge customarily disclosed risks if these are not already covered by the materiality test.

[27] *See, e.g.*, Pauscher v. Iowa Methodist Medical Center, 408 N.W.2d 355 (Iowa 1987) (holding that a 1 in a 100,000 risk of *death* is not material as a matter of law). As will be discussed shortly, the better focus would have been on whether the plaintiff could establish the requisite causation. With *Paucher*, *compare* Reyes v. Wyeth Laboratories, 498 F.2d.1264 (5th Cir. 1974) (holding that a few in a million chance of polio from the live polio vaccine should have been disclosed).

[28] *See id.*, in which a 1 in a 100,000 risk of death was not disclosed. As noted in the previous footnote, the *Pauscher* court relied solely on the lack of materiality.

the risk.[29] An objective test, however, is at odds with the very rationale underlying the patient rule. One court persuasively argued that the objective approach of causation

> severely limits the protection granted an injured patient. To the extent the plaintiff, given an adequate disclosure, would have declined the proposed treatment, and a reasonable person in similar circumstances would have consented, a patient's right of self-determination is *irrevocably lost.*[30]

Even under a subjective test of causation it is unlikely that a jury will believe a plaintiff's claim that she would have opted to forgo the treatment absent some credible explanation.

Even in jurisdictions employing the "patient rule," there are recognized exceptions to the obligation to disclose material risks. A physician will not be liable where the nondisclosure of a material risk was justified due to an emergency or where the patient requests that the doctor not inform her. Many states also recognize a therapeutic privilege under which a physician may justify nondisclosure upon proof that "complete and candid disclosure might have a detrimental effect on the physical or psychological well-being of the patient."[31] If permitted at all, such a privilege should be narrowly construed, because it creates the risk that the patient's right to make her own decisions — the very justification for the patient rule in the first place — will be severely undermined.

In summary, for a plaintiff to prevail under the patient rule approach to informed consent, she must show 1) a nondisclosure of a material fact by the defendant; 2) that had there been proper disclosure she would have rejected the proposed treatment (thus, establishing cause-in-fact); and 3) that the undisclosed adverse consequences did occur. If the plaintiff proves these elements, the defendant may then try to prove that the nondisclosure was justified.

[C] *Extensions of the Informed Consent Doctrine*

Some courts have expanded the informed consent obligation to require disclosure of risks of forgoing a medical procedure or treatment. For example, suppose that P consulted Dr. D regarding a medical condition. Dr. D suggested to P that he have his prostate checked. Being squeamish about such things, P declines. A year later, P is diagnosed with incurable prostate cancer. P sues Dr. D claiming the lack of informed consent because Dr. D did not tell P of the risks of *refusing* to undergo the proposed procedure. Should this situation fall within the informed consent doctrine

---

29 *See, e.g.*, Cobbs v. Grant 502 P.2d 1 (Cal. 1972); Canterbury v. Spence, 464 F.2d 772 (D.C. Cir. 1972).

30 Scott v. Bradford, 606 P.2d 554, 559 (Okla. 1979) (emphasis in original).

31 Pauscher v. Iowa Methodist Medical Center, 408 N.W.2d 355, 360 (Iowa 1987).

or should the doctrine be limited to cases where the doctor has in fact performed an operation or treatment on the plaintiff?[32] If such an action is permitted, causation remains a substantial hurdle as the plaintiff must show that he would have undergone the procedure if he had been told of the risks of *failing* to do so.[33]

§ 7.04 ATTORNEY MALPRACTICE[34]

Most of the medical malpractice rules also apply to attorney malpractice. Accordingly, the relationship (here, attorney-client) establishes duty,[35] the custom of the profession sets the standard of care,[36] and breach of duty is shown by the attorney's failure to meet that standard of care. Further, unless the alleged attorney malpractice is glaringly apparent, the plaintiff can only prevail with expert testimony regarding both the standard of care and breach.

What conduct may give rise to a malpractice action? Clearly, a malpractice action does not follow just because the client got an unfavorable result. In fact, because the practice of law requires an attorney to make various tactical decisions, malpractice liability will not arise from a mere mistake in strategy. Some courts have gone so far as to say that lawyers are not liable for mere errors of judgment provided that they use their best efforts.[37] This seems overly deferential. Where the attorney performs below the minimum acceptable standard established by the custom of the profession — where she acts in a manner evidencing the lack of knowledge or skill ordinarily possessed by other attorneys in good standing — malpractice liability may logically follow notwithstanding the attorney's belief that she made her "best efforts." Thus, if an attorney advises a client improperly

---

[32] *See, e.g.*, Truman v. Thomas, 611 P.2d 902 (Cal. 1980) (physician liable for failing to disclose risk of declining pap smear).

[33] How far should the informed consent doctrine be expanded? For example, should a physician have to divulge that she has a financial interest in the proposed test, as where she has an interest in a laboratory? *See* Moore v. Regents of the University of California, 793 P.2d 479 (Cal. 1990) (a patient may recover for lack of informed consent if a physician, attempting to garner consent for a medical procedure, fails to disclose research or economic interests in that procedure unrelated to the patient's health).

[34] *See generally* William H. Fortune and Dulaney O'Roark, *Risk Management for Lawyers,* 45 S.C. L. Rev. 617 (1994); Ronald E. Mallen and Jeffrey M. Smith, LEGAL MALPRACTICE (3rd ed. 1989); *Symposium, Legal Malpractice,* 17 Mem. St. U. L. Rev. 465 (1987).

[35] In rare instances, an attorney may owe a duty to a nonclient. *See infra* § 10.04[D].

[36] As one court explained the standard of care, an attorney "is required to exercise the knowledge, skill, and ability ordinarily possessed and exercised by members of the legal profession in similar circumstances." Keister v. Talbott, 391 S.E.2d 895, 898 (W. Va. 1990).

[37] *See, e.g.*, Hodges v. Carter, 80 S.E.2d 144, 146 (N.C. 1954) ("An attorney who acts in good faith and in an honest belief that his advice and acts are well founded and in the best interest of his client is not answerable for a mere error in judgment . . . .").

because of an erroneous understanding of the law, she has breached her duty if others in good standing would have discerned the correct law.[38]

As in the medical malpractice context, expert witnesses are usually required to assist the plaintiff establish both the standard of care and the attorney defendant's breach of duty. To what extent should geographical considerations affect the propriety of this expert testimony? Is a local, state or national standard appropriate? Because admission to the practice of law virtually always requires passage of a statewide bar exam, a statewide standard seems most appropriate. On the other hand, the practice of law may have become standardized enough throughout the country that a national standard is justified?[39] Where an attorney holds herself out as a specialist (as in federal taxation or patent law), it is particularly likely that she will be held to a national standard.

In legal malpractice cases, the causation element often poses a substantial hurdle. Beyond establishing the attorney's negligence, the legal malpractice plaintiff must show by a preponderance of the evidence that if it had not been for that attorney's negligence she would have prevailed in the underlying action. For example, if D, an attorney representing P in a legal action against X, fails to file the complaint within the statute of limitations, there is a clear breach of professional custom.[40] In order to prevail in a malpractice action against D, P must show that she probably would have prevailed in her action against X had D filed the complaint in a timely manner. In essence, the legal malpractice action requires the resolution of two conflicts: the initial lawsuit and the malpractice action — in essence, a trial within a trial.[41]

---

[38] *See, e.g.*, Smith v. Lewis, 530 P.2d 589, 595 (Cal. 1975), in which the court explained: "[A]n attorney does not ordinarily guarantee the soundness of his opinions and, accordingly, is not liable for every mistake he may make in his practice. He is expected, however, to possess knowledge of those plain and elementary principles of law which are commonly known by well-informed attorneys, and to discover those additional rules of law which, although not commonly known, may readily be found by standard research techniques."

[39] *See* Russo v. Griffin, 510 A.2d 436 (Vt. 1986), in which the court rejected the "locality" standard that had been previously in place. The majority used a statewide standard, while the dissent advocated a national standard.

[40] This is such an evident breach that expert testimony might be unnecessary for the plaintiff to prevail.

[41] *See* Donald G. Weiland, *Another Early Chapter: Attorney Malpractice and the Trial Within a Trial: Time for a Change,* 19 J. Mar. L. & Com. 275 (1986).

CHAPTER 8

DUTY IN NEGLIGENCE CASES

SYNOPSIS

(Matthew Bender & Co., Inc.) (Pub.582)

§ 8.01 OVERVIEW

The element of duty establishes that there is a legally recognized relationship between the defendant and the plaintiff that obligates the defendant to act (or to refrain from acting) in a certain manner toward the plaintiff.[1] Duty, then, can be viewed as a legal obligation owed by the defendant to the plaintiff.

Whether a duty exists is largely a policy-based determination. Indeed, the repercussions of finding or declining to find a duty are so profound that it is left to a judge to make the determination. The judge evaluates the policy arguments for and against finding a duty, ultimately determining whether the law will recognize a claim by the plaintiff against the defendant.[2] To accomplish this task, a judge often balances such factors as: the foreseeability of the harm to the plaintiff; the degree of certainty that the plaintiff suffered injury; the closeness of the connection between the defendant's conduct and the injury suffered; the moral blame attached to the defendant's conduct; the policy of preventing future harm; the burden to the defendant and the consequences to the community of imposing a duty to exercise care with resulting liability for breach; and the availability, cost and prevalence of insurance for the risk involved.[3]

In most cases it is clear that the defendant owes the plaintiff a duty. Usually there is no room for a duty debate because there is no compelling policy concern suggesting duty should not be recognized. The duty concept has been expanding to the point that now one engaged in risk-creating conduct generally owes a duty to avoid causing foreseeable personal injuries to foreseeable plaintiffs.[4] For example, where D is speeding in his car and physically injures P, another motorist, courts concur that P may sue D for negligence. In short, there is no question that D owes a legal duty to P.

---

[1] *See* Restatement § 4 ("The word 'duty'. . . denote[s] the fact that the actor is required to conduct himself in a particular manner. . . .").

[2] Procedurally, duty issues are often dealt with early in the trial process, with the defendant moving to dismiss the plaintiff's complaint for failure to state an action. In essence, the defendant contends that even if everything the plaintiff claims is true, the law will not recognize the claim.

[3] Rowland v. Christian, 443 P.2d 561, 564 (Cal. 1968). These *Rowland* factors have been used frequently by California judges confronted with challenging duty questions. Other jurisdictions have borrowed these factors or use similar ones.

[4] The foreseeable plaintiff issue is discussed *infra* § 8.04 and in Chapter 12, in the context of the famous case of Palsgraf v. Long Island R.R. Co.

As early as 1883, courts proposed a broad general duty of care. In Heaven v. Pender, 11 Q.B.D. 503 (1883), one judge suggested that "whenever one person is by circumstances placed in such a position with regard to another that every one of ordinary sense who did think would at once recognize that if he did not use ordinary care and skill in his own conduct with regard to those circumstances he would cause danger of injury to the person or property of the other, a duty arises to use ordinary care and skill to avoid such danger." As this chapter and subsequent duty chapters will show, the generalized duty standard of Heaven v. Pender oversimplifies the issue of when a duty is owed.

This Chapter and the two subsequent Chapters examine those areas of negligence law where duty is not a given. In some situations — because of forceful policy concerns — courts have either refused to find a duty or have limited substantially the scope of any duty owed.

This Chapter begins by looking at the restrictions on duty in the context of "nonfeasance." Generally, negligence law only has imposed liability on those whose affirmative conduct led to the plaintiff's harm. Where the plaintiff's harm is caused by the defendant's failure to intervene — called nonfeasance — no duty has been found. This Chapter examines this no-duty rule and its numerous exceptions. Several other areas where limitations on duty are common, such as governmental duty, are then considered. In these contexts, other policy-based concerns have led courts to restrict duty.

The next Chapter studies the special duty limitations that have traditionally shielded land possessors from lawsuits by persons injured on their property. The limited duty rules governing this area are complex and heavily influenced by the historical context in which they developed. The duty discussion ends by examining limitations due to the type of harm suffered by the plaintiff. Chapter 10 analyzes those areas where courts have typically circumscribed duty because of the kind of harm the plaintiff suffered, namely negligently inflicted emotional distress, pure economic loss, wrongful death and loss of consortium, and wrongful conception, birth, and life.

§ 8.02 NONFEASANCE

The starting point for a duty analysis in some areas of negligence law is the well-established distinction between misfeasance, for which a duty is typically found, and nonfeasance, for which it usually is not. Professor Francis H. Bohlen explained long ago the difference well:

> There is no distinction more deeply rooted in the common law and more fundamental than that between misfeasance and nonfeasance, between active misconduct working positive injury to others and passive inaction, a failure to take positive steps to benefit others, or to protect them from harm not created by any wrongful act of the defendant. . . . In the case of active misfeasance the victim is positively worse off as a result of the wrongful act. In cases of passive inaction plaintiff is in reality no worse off at all. His situation is unchanged; he is merely deprived of a protection which, had it been afforded him, would have benefited him.[5]

It is not always easy to distinguish between misfeasance and nonfeasance. Consider the case where the defendant cajoled the decedent to jump into deep water, refusing to rescue him after realizing that he was about to drown. Although the court characterized this as a case of nonfeasance on the part of the defendant,[6] it could also be seen as involving affirmative

[5] Francis H. Bohlen, *The Moral Duty to Aid Others as a Basis of Tort Liability,* 56 U. Pa. L. Rev. 217, 219-220 (1908).

[6] Yania v. Bigan, 155 A.2d 343, (Pa. 1959). The defendant was not liable for failing to rescue a person he cajoled into jumping into a trench filled with water, and then let drown.

conduct by the defendant leading to the harm. Similarly, many other contexts such as the failure to make promised repairs, to arrest a drunken driver, or to inspect equipment can be portrayed as either inaction or an affirmative act that creates an unreasonable risk of harm to others. This distinction can be critical because a plaintiff's ability to recover damages often turns on whether the court characterizes the defendant's conduct as misfeasance or nonfeasance. To reiterate, in general, an actor is liable for affirmative acts that create an unreasonable risk of harm, but not for nonfeasance.

The analysis is further complicated by the concept of negligent *omissions*, which are just a species of misfeasance. Misfeasance often consists of affirmative acts of misconduct — doing something that a reasonable person would not do — such as firing a gun in the center of town. Misfeasance can also be shown by a negligent omission — failing to do something that a reasonable person would do while engaged in other activity — such as not paying attention while driving. Either risk-creating affirmative acts or risk-creating omissions generally give rise to a duty.

Efforts must be made to differentiate between misfeasance, whether based on an act or omission, and nonfeasance. Where a plaintiff asserts that the defendant should be liable for nonfeasance, the plaintiff is claiming that the defendant should have intervened in order to prevent harm to the plaintiff. Because of the failure of the defendant to intervene, the plaintiff suffers injury. Unlike omissions and acts constituting misfeasance, a defendant who is sued based on his nonfeasance has not created the risks that ultimately injure the plaintiff; rather, the defendant has failed to prevent harm caused by some other source from occurring. Accordingly, a defendant generally does not owe a duty in the nonfeasance context.

In some instances, however, courts will impose liability for nonfeasance. The most common situations involve (1) a special relationship, (2) an undertaking to act, or (3) where the defendant caused the plaintiff to rely on a gratuitous promise.

Typically nonfeasance-based actions arise where the plaintiff contends that the defendant should have intervened to rescue the plaintiff, or where the claim is that the defendant should have prevented harm to the plaintiff by controlling a third party or by taking measures to protect the plaintiff from injury.

[A] *Duty to Rescue*[7]

D, an Olympic gold medalist swimmer, is sunbathing on a deserted beach. D spots a person nearby who is screaming for help and is clearly drowning. D continues to work on her sun tan. These facts somehow become known, and the parents of the person who drowned bring a wrongful death action against D, claiming correctly that D easily could have rescued their child. Can they prevail?

The clear general rule remains that a person does not have a duty to aid another. Courts consistently have refused to require a stranger to render assistance, even when faced with seemingly egregious examples of nonfeasance,[8] and even where the person could have rendered aid with little risk or effort. Because this result appears to many as outrageous and immoral, few topics have generated more scholarship and classroom debate as students and commentators wrestle with why the Olympic swimmer can ignore a drowning child or a passerby can disregard a baby in front of an oncoming train.

A number of reasons are given for the law's no-duty-to-rescue rule. First and foremost, the rule is seen as the embodiment of the value placed on individualism in American society.[9] Not surprisingly, those societies that value community over the individual, which include many countries throughout the world, impose rescue obligations on its citizenry.

Other forceful justifications for the no-duty-to-rescue rule exist. Because rescue is the morally right thing to do, some argue it cheapens rescue if it is required.[10] Some oppose an obligation to rescue because of the lack

---

[7] Few topics have generated more scholarly commentary. *See generally, e.g.*, John Adler, *Relying on the Reasonableness of Strangers: Some Observations About the Current State of Common Law Affirmative Duties to Aid or Protect Others,* 1991 Wis. L. Rev. 867; Francis H. Bohlen, *The Moral Duty to Aid Others as a Basis of Tort Liability,* 56 U. Pa. L. Rev. 217 (1908); Richard A. Epstein, *A Theory of Strict Liability,* 2 J. Legal Stud. 151 (1973); William M. Landes & Richard A. Posner, Salvors, *Finders, Good Samaritans and Other Rescuers: An Economic Study of Law and Altruism,* 7 J. Legal Stud. 83 (1978); Ernest J. Weinrib, *The Case for a Duty to Rescue,* 90 Yale L.J. 247 (1980); James A. Henderson, Jr., *Process Constraints in Tort,* 67 Cornell L. Rev. 901 (1982); Saul Levmore, *Waiting for Rescue: An Essay on the Evolution and Incentive Structure on the Law of Affirmative Obligations,* 72 Va. L. Rev. 879 (1986); Christopher H. Schroeder, *Two Methods for Evaluating Duty to Rescue Proposals,* 49 Law & Contemp. Probs. 181 (1986).

[8] *See, e.g.*, Handiboe v. McCarthy, 151 S.E.2d 905 (Ga. 1966) (Defendant had no duty when minor child falls into defendant's pool while playing with defendant's child). The Restatement is in accord with the no-duty-to-rescue rule as well. *See* Restatement § 314.

[9] As Professor Bohlen noted, the no-duty rule "is founded on that attitude of extreme individualism so typical of anglo-saxon legal thought." Francis H. Bohlen, *The Moral Duty to Aid Others as a Basis of Tort Liability,* 56 U. Pa. L. Rev. 217, 220 (1908).

[10] Courts have consistently said they will not enforce a "moral obligation." They feel that the legal system is not the proper forum to deal with these cases. As one judge wrote: "For withholding relief from the suffering, for failure to respond to the calls of worthy charity, or for faltering in the bestowment of brotherly love on the unfortunate, penalties are found

of a causal connection between the defendant's conduct and plaintiff's peril.[11] Other explanations for the rule include the belief that courts should focus on deterring people from doing wrong, rather than attempting to force them to do good; concern about the complicated liability question should a number of people fail to render aid; the difficulty of determining whether someone callously decided not to act or froze in an emergency, perhaps out of a genuine but misplaced fear; and more generalized concerns about the legal system's inability to deal with a rule imposing liability for the failure to rescue.[12]

Compelling arguments for a duty to rescue have been made as well.[13] Commentators who advocate abandoning the no-duty rule cite a number of justifications beyond the potential saving of lives: the belief that the law should reflect and shape society's moral values; the value of the savings accrued in a cost-benefit formula from encouragement of rescues with small societal and personal sacrifice that avert enormous potential losses; encouragement for the timid to get involved because it would be the law-abiding thing to do; and simplification of a judicial system that has become bogged down in many complicated exceptions to the duty-to-aid cases. Further, American feminist torts scholars point to this no-duty rule as evidence of a male bias in the law, and of a lack of caring in the current tort system. As one commentator explained:

> The "no duty" rule is a consequence of a legal system devoid of care and responsiveness to the safety of others. We certainly could create a

---

not in the laws of men, but in that higher law, the violation of which is condemned by the voice of conscience, whose sentence of punishment for the recreant act is swift and sure." Union Pacific Railroad Co. v. Cappier, 72 P. 281, 282 (Kan. 1903) (finding that, since the railroad had no legal duty to care for a trespasser who had limbs severed by a train, it was not negligent for delays getting help for the accident victim).

[11] Richard A. Epstein, *A Theory of Strict Liability*, 2 J. Legal Stud. 151 (1973). Professor Epstein is correct that there is no causation in these cases to the extent that there is no causation in *any* nonfeasance case. The very essence of nonfeasance is that liability is premised on the defendant's failure to intervene rather than on the defendant's risk-creating behavior. The reason for the defendant's need to rescue comes about from a source independent of the defendant. But causation can be proven in a nonfeasance case. Indeed, it must be. For the plaintiff to prevail, she must show that had the defendant intervened, the plaintiff probably would not have been injured (or would not have been as badly injured). In the sunbathing, medal-winning swimmer hypothetical, if a duty to rescue were imposed on D, P could only prevail upon proof that had D rescued her she would have suffered less harm.

[12] James A. Henderson, Jr., *Process Constraints in Tort*, 67 Cornell L. Rev. 901 (1982) ("Courts have refused to impose a general duty to rescue largely because it would be unmanageable as a guide to either primary or adjudicative behavior.").

[13] Since early in this century, the argument has been made that the law should impose liability on those who fail to rescue when they could do so "with little or no inconvenience" to themselves. James Barr Ames, *Law and Morals*, 22 Harv. L. Rev. 97, 113 (1908). *See also* Wallace M. Randolph, *The Duty to Act: A Proposed Rule*, 44 Neb. L. Rev. 499 (1965); Ernest J. Weinrib, *The Case for a Duty to Rescue*, 90 Yale L.J. 247 (1980).

duty to aid generated from a legal recognition of our interconnectedness, an elevated sense of the importance of physical health and safety, a rejection of the act/omission dualism, and a strong legal value placed on care and concern for others rather than on economic efficiency or individual liberty.[14]

There are a substantial number of exceptions to the no-duty-to-rescue rule. Indeed, because of judicial discomfort with the rule, courts have been rather creative in crafting exceptions. It is likely that jurisdictions will continue to expand the exceptions as the opportunity arises. Today, there are several contexts in which courts regularly impose liability for failing to render aid. The duty can be found if the defendant created the peril, had a "special relationship" with the plaintiff, undertook or volunteered to act, or had a contractual obligation to act. Also, it can be imposed by statute.[15]

[1] Creating the Peril

A well-established exception to the no-duty-to-rescue rule applies when the need for rescue arises because of the defendant's negligence. Thus, if D negligently swerves too close to P's car forcing P off the road and down an embankment, D has a duty to P to make reasonable rescue efforts.[16]

One of the fastest developing exceptions to the common law rule extends this rescue obligation to a person whose *fault-free* conduct gives rise to the need to rescue. At common law, if D was passing P on a narrow road with all due care, and P, to avoid D, swerved too sharply, lost control and went down an embankment, D would have no obligation to rescue P because D was not at fault. An increasing number of courts have imposed a rescue obligation on D because D's conduct, though innocent, gave rise to the need for rescue.[17] Indeed, there is movement toward imposing rescue obligations on those who are connected in any way to the need for rescue.

---

[14] Leslie Bender, *A Lawyer's Primer on Feminist Theory and Tort*, 38 J. of Legal Ed. 3, 36 (1988).

[15] A few states, such as Vermont and Minnesota, have enacted legislation criminalizing a person's failure to rescue in certain situations. The violation of these statutes leads to the imposition of a small fine, but may give rise to civil liability as well.

[16] This applies even when D's negligence is less direct, as where D negligently knocks over a telephone pole which blocks a street. D must make reasonable efforts to prevent harm to those who might be potentially injured. *See* Restatement § 321.

[17] This position is supported by Restatement § 322. This rescue obligation applies even if P's own negligence contributed to the event giving rise to the need for rescue. For a case in which the court adopts Restatement § 322, no doubt due to its particularly moving fact pattern, see South v. National Railroad Passenger Corp., 290 N.W.2d 819 (N.D. 1980). In *South*, an employee of the defendant railroad, which collided with the plaintiff's pickup truck possibly through no fault of the railroad, refused to protect the plaintiff from the cold because he did not want to get blood on his new jacket.

[2] Special Relationships

Courts have imposed a duty to rescue when justified by a "special relationship" between the parties. Historically, these special relationships were narrowly construed, applying only where the plaintiff clearly entrusted his safety to the defendant. Thus, in the context of a common carrier-passenger, innkeeper-guest and ship captain-seaman, courts found a special relationship such that the former had to act to rescue the latter. These special relationships have expanded to the point that they likely include employer-employee, school-student, and business-customer relationships, among others. While the Restatement proceeds cautiously in defining special relationships, it does note that the "law appears, however, to be working slowly toward a recognition of the duty to aid or protect in any relation of dependence or of mutual dependence."[18]

There has been some judicial creativity in defining special relationships. In one case, *Farwell v. Keaton,*[19] for example, the court found that companions on a social venture had an understanding that one would come to the aid of the other if necessary. This is quite a departure from traditional special relationships.

[3] Undertaking to Act and Reliance

While people generally have no obligation to intervene, once they do, a duty arises.[20] Many gratuitous acts, such as a passerby's vow to get medical attention or an employer's pre-employment physical for a prospective employee, may result in the creation of a duty.

There are different views about the extent of the obligation. Under the traditional view, once a person undertakes to rescue, he must not leave the victim in a worse position. Under the more modern view, the rescuer is obligated to act reasonably once he has begun to act. This is a distinction of substance. Returning to the medal-winning swimmer sun tanning on the

---

[18] Restatement § 314A cmt. b. Yet, the Restatement even leaves open the possibility that spouses do not stand in a special relationship requiring one spouse to come to the aid of the other. It is likely, however, that most jurisdictions would elect to impose a duty in the spousal context.

[19] 240 N.W.2d 217 (Mich. 1976). In *Farwell*, the defendant and the deceased went out drinking. They got into a fight with some other people. The defendant got away and the decedent was badly injured. The defendant came back for the decedent, drove him around, and left him passed out in a car parked in the decedent's grandparents' driveway. Because a duty could be found on a much more secure basis (undertaking to act discussed immediately *infra*), the court's broad interpretation of special relationship was unnecessary and particularly startling.

[20] *See, e.g.*, Parvi v. City of Kingston, 362 N.E.2d 960 (N.Y. 1977), in which the defendant police picked up the intoxicated plaintiff and drove him to a park near a highway. The police left and, soon thereafter, the plaintiff wandered onto the highway and was struck by a car. The court held that, while the police may have had no obligation to take the plaintiff into custody, once they did so, this undertaking to act created a duty.

deserted beach, assume that she spots the drowning person, swims out to him, pulls him halfway toward the shore and then abandons him. She returns to the beach. Is she now liable? Under the view that she is liable only if she left the plaintiff in a worse position, she would not be.[21] Under the reasonableness approach, liability is likely because there seems to be no reason for D to have stopped her rescue effort.

Which approach is most sensible? On one hand, because there is no obligation to rescue in the first place, imposing liability on D where she has not made things worse seems illogical. On the other hand, though, there is something unseemly about permitting a person to terminate a rescue when it could easily be completed. If the reasonableness approach is employed, people could be dissuaded from undertaking rescue efforts because it entails a substantial obligation. Virtually all jurisdictions, however, protect potential liability through Good Samaritan statutes which insulate rescuers from liability for negligence.[22]

A duty will be found where the defendant's unfinished rescue efforts have dissuaded others from helping, or where the defendant has prevented others from assisting.[23] Again, courts have been creative about what constitutes interference. For example, one court, expressing great hostility toward the general no-duty rule, found the defendant bar-owner owed a duty where a Good Samaritan, seeking to aid the victim injured at another establishment nearby, was denied use of the defendant's telephone. The court labelled its holding as "a logical extension of Restatement section 327 which imposes liability for negligent interference with a third person who the defendant knows is attempting to render necessary aid."[24]

Because of discomfort with the no-duty rules, courts have been quick to find that a defendant has undertaken to act. In one case, the defendant's employee permitted the plaintiff to make a phone call. This was viewed as enough to constitute an undertaking to act, creating a tort duty.[25]

---

[21] If others failed to come to P's aid because of D's initial rescue efforts, P was left in a worse position. Because the beach was deserted, however, there is no basis to claim that her initial rescue efforts dissuaded others from coming to the swimmer's aid.

[22] Tort law creates a subtle incentive for rescue by deeming all rescue efforts as per se foreseeable. Thus, where the need for rescue arises due to D's culpable conduct, a rescuer injured effecting a rescue would have a negligence action against D. *See infra* Chapter 12.

[23] A defendant can be liable for either intentionally or negligently preventing rescue. Restatement §§ 326 and 327. *See* Maldonado v. Southern Pac. Transp. Co., 629 P.2d 1001 (Ariz. Ct. App. 1981).

[24] Soldano v. O'Daniels, 190 Cal. Rptr. 310 (Cal. Ct. App. 1983). In justifying its expansion of the exceptions to the no-duty-to-rescue rule, the court explained: "The creative and regenerative power of the law has been strong enough to break chains imposed by outmoded former decisions. What the courts have power to create, they also have power to modify, reject and re-create in response to the needs of a dynamic society." *Id.* at 318.

[25] In O'Neill v. Montefiore Hosp., 202 N.Y.S. 2d 436 (N.Y. App. Div. 1960), plaintiff and her husband entered defendant hospital's emergency room because of the husband's

Closely related to the undertaking to act concept, is that of reliance. Courts have found a duty where the defendant caused the plaintiff to rely on promised aid. For example, in one case, a railroad was liable to a motorist who, after learning to count on a railway watchman giving warnings of approaching trains, got hit when the watchman failed to give a warning.[26]

[4] Contract

Occasionally, a rescue obligation arises from contract. Accordingly, a lifeguard or baby-sitter is generally required to rescue. There is debate about the extent to which a defendant's gratuitous promise, without more, gives rise to a duty. As noted above, a promise creating reliance may give rise to a tort duty. Yet, some courts, relying on *Thorne v. Deas*[27] and its progeny, have refused to permit plaintiffs to recover damages where they were injured by the defendant's gratuitous promise to render aid or to provide a service. Other courts have abandoned this strict rule, particularly where the plaintiff suffers personal injury as opposed to pure economic loss.

[5] Conclusion

It is unlikely that there will be any serious strides toward overturning the no-duty-to-rescue rule. Instead, courts will find more and more exceptions, such as by broadening the definition of "special relationship." Meanwhile, debate about the propriety of a rescue obligation will surely continue, focusing on the tension between interests in individual autonomy and social responsibility so much a part of American culture.

[B] *Duty to Control and to Protect*[28]

A person typically is not legally obligated to control the conduct of another or to take steps to protect another from harm. Thus, if D is drinking at a bar and is approached by X, a stranger, who tells D that she is about to leave the bar and shoot P, D has no legal obligation to warn P of this imminent harm even if D could do so easily. Similarly, if D sees P about to enter an alley that D knows is the site of frequent muggings, D has no

---

chest pains. Because they belonged to a plan not accepted at that hospital, they were referred elsewhere. Before leaving, the wife requested and received permission to use the receptionist's phone to call their doctor. Soon thereafter plaintiff's husband died of a heart attack.

[26] Erie R. Co. v. Stewart, 40 F.2d 855 (6th Cir. 1930). A key issue becomes whether the defendant can ever stop providing the warning without potential liability. Once reliance is created, how can it be terminated?

[27] 4 Johns. R. 84 (N.Y. 1809). In *Thorne*, the defendant had promised the plaintiff that he would procure insurance for the ship of which they were co-owners. The defendant failed to do so and, when the ship was lost at sea, the plaintiff incurred an enormous loss. The court permitted recovery neither on contract nor tort grounds. The Restatement expressly takes no position on this issue of whether a promise without more can give rise to a tort duty. *See* Restatement § § 323, 324A.

[28] *See generally* Fowler V. Harper and Posey M. Kime, *The Duty to Control the Conduct of Another,* 43 Yale L.J. 886 (1934).

obligation to try to prevent P from doing so. In neither instance does the law obligate D to make any effort to intervene for P's benefit.

The distinction between cases raising a duty to control issue and those involving the duty to protect can be quite blurry. Often they are treated together, and exceptions to both arise from special relationships — a special relationship *either* between the defendant and the person threatening harm or between the defendant and the person threatened with harm.[29] In the duty to control context the primary focus is generally on whether the relationship between the defendant and the third party inflicting harm to the plaintiff is one giving rise to an obligation to control on the part of the defendant. In the duty to protect context the focus is on whether the relationship between the plaintiff and the defendant is such that the defendant is obligated to take affirmative steps to protect the plaintiff.

[1] Duty to Control

While generally a person has no obligation to control another person's conduct to prevent harm to a third person, exceptions arise where there is a special relationship. The relationships giving rise to a duty to control require some relationship between the defendant and the third party, combined with knowledge (actual or constructive) of the need for control. The clearest examples arise where the defendant takes custody of dangerous persons such as certain criminals or mental patients and negligently permits them to escape. The special relationships giving rise to a duty to control extend beyond these custodial arrangements, however. For example, a child's parents are liable when their child attacks another child if they permit the child to play unsupervised with other children once they are aware (or should have been aware) of their child's tendency to assault other children.[30] Other relationships giving rise to a duty to control include a master and a servant, and a possessor of a chattel or land and a person using the land or chattel in the defendant's presence and with the defendant's permission.[31]

There can be substantial debate about which relationships give rise to a duty to control. The determination requires consideration of the basis for such an obligation as well as the public policy reasons for and against

---

[29] Restatement § 315.

[30] *See* Linder v. Bidner, 270 N.Y.S.2d 427 (N.Y. Sup. Ct., 1966). The court explained: "It has uniformly been held that a parent who knows of the dangerous propensities of his child is bound to use reasonable care to control the child so as to prevent the indulgence in those propensities." *Id.* at 430. *See also* Restatement § 316. In this and similar cases, liability is being imposed on the defendant parents for their own unreasonable conduct in failing to control their child. They are not being held vicariously liable for their child's own tortious conduct. Absent a statute, parents are not vicariously liable for the torts of their children. Many jurisdictions have such statutes imposing vicarious liability up to some specified monetary threshold, however.

[31] Restatement §§ 317–318.

imposing a duty. The relationships that trigger a duty to control are not automatically the same as those creating a duty to rescue. For there to be a duty to control, the defendant must be in a position to exercise control over the third party for the protection of the plaintiff. For example, one spouse likely has an obligation to make reasonable efforts to aid the other spouse. But whether one spouse has a duty to control the other is more uncertain. For example, assume that D knows her husband is a pedophile. She knows that she is going to be leaving town for a business trip and that some of the neighborhood children will likely come over to use the swimming pool. Does she have a duty to warn the neighbors with children about her husband?[32]

The determination of whether a duty should be found may depend on whether the conduct is characterized as misfeasance by the defendant or as the defendant's failure to control the conduct of another. For example, in *Pulka v. Edelman,*[33] the plaintiff pedestrian was injured by a car leaving the defendant's parking garage. The majority refused to find a duty, noting that the defendant did not have a duty to control its patrons as they exited the structure. The dissenters viewed the plaintiff's claim as one asserting actionable misfeasance arising from the negligent operation of the garage.[34]

[a] Tarasoff v. Regents of University of California

Perhaps the most famous duty-to-control case is *Tarasoff v. Regents of University of California,*[35] in which the plaintiffs asserted that the defendant therapist had a duty to warn them or their daughter of threats made by the psychotherapist's patient. In *Tarasoff,* the California Supreme Court held that a psychotherapist has an obligation to take reasonable steps to protect a third party where the therapist knows or, based on professional standards, should know that the therapist's patient presents a serious risk of physical harm to the third party.

The court reached its result through analogizing to common law cases imposing liability on a physician who misdiagnoses a communicable disease to the detriment of those coming into contact with the patient, and by relying

---

[32] *Compare* Pamela L. v. Farmer, 169 Cal. Rptr. 282 (Cal. Ct. App. 1980) (finding a duty to warn) *with* Rozycki v. Peley, 489 A.2d 1272 (N.J. Super. L. 1984) (finding no duty in light of importance of preserving spousal confidentiality).

[33] 358 N.E.2d 1019 (N.Y. 1976).

[34] By finding no duty, the case is over. If, as the dissenters contended, this was a case of misfeasance where duty would be evident, the jury would have to decide breach of duty.

[35] 551 P.2d 334 (Cal. 1976). The *Tarasoff* decision has generated considerable comment. *See, e.g.*, Elizabeth M. Crocker, *Judicial Expansion of the Tarasoff Doctrine: Doctors' Dilemma,* 13 J. Psychiatry & L. 83 (1985); Alan A. Stone, *The Tarasoff Decisions: Suing Psychotherapists to Safeguard Society,* 90 Harv. L. Rev. 358 (1976) (highly critical of the decision); Leslie B. Small, Comment, *Psychotherapists' Duty to Warn: Ten Years After Tarasoff,* 15 Golden Gate U. L. Rev. 271 (1985).

upon the Restatement's duty-to-control provisions.[36] The court acknowledged the difficulty psychotherapists have with determining the validity of patients' threats to harm others, and the importance of the confidentiality of the psychotherapist-patient relationship, but found that greater policy concerns supported the imposition of a duty. The court buttressed its holding by pointing out other existing exceptions to the patient-psychotherapist privilege, such as a California Evidence Code provision enabling a therapist to testify about patient communications where it is necessary to prevent threatened harm.

The *Tarasoff* decision is controversial for several reasons. First, the court's reliance upon the Restatement may be something of a stretch because the patient was being seen on an outpatient basis, making the degree of control exercised by the defendant questionable. Second, the confidentiality of the therapist-patient relationship is surely compromised by the decision.[37] Third, the scope of the decision is unclear. Does the defendant have an obligation to disclose generalized threats or only specific ones, only threats of serious physical harm or lesser threats?

Jurisdictions have overwhelmingly adopted the *Tarasoff* rationale with differences in its application. In some jurisdictions, the duty to warn extends only to "readily identifiable victims,"[38] while in others all foreseeable victims must be warned. If X tells her therapist that she intends to shoot some unidentified person at that evening's football game, in those jurisdictions using the "readily identifiable" standard, no warning appears necessary. But in those using a foreseeability standard, the defendant would have to take reasonable steps to prevent harm to those attending the football game. Some jurisdictions do not apply *Tarasoff* to threats of property damage.[39] Some jurisdictions have clarified the reach of the *Tarasoff*-type duty statutorily.[40]

---

[36] In *Tarasoff*, the defendant in fact requested the campus police to detain the patient. They released him after a short time, and two months later he committed the killing. The court declined to find the campus police had a duty because, unlike the therapist, they had no special relationship with the patient-killer.

[37] Indeed, the therapist may even have an informed consent responsibility to disclose the obligation to warn if threats are made. *See supra* § 7.03.

[38] For example, in Thompson v. County of Alameda, 614 P.2d 728 (Cal. 1980), the court refused to impose a duty to warn where officials released a juvenile offender to his mother even though he threatened to kill an unidentified neighborhood child. Within 24 hours of release, the juvenile killed a child in the neighborhood. The majority noted an obligation to warn in such a situation would be detrimental to the rehabilitative process, limiting the reach of *Tarasoff* to specifically identified victims.

[39] *Compare* Bellah v. Greenson, 146 Cal. Rptr. 535 (Cal. Ct. App. 1978) (declining to apply *Tarasoff* where the harm is self-inflicted or "mere property damage.") *with* Peck v. Counseling Service of Addison County, Inc., 499 A.2d 422 (Vt. 1985) (therapist had duty to notify plaintiff that his son, seeing the defendant on an outpatient basis, had threatened to burn down the plaintiff's barn).

[40] *See, e.g.*, Cal. Civ. Code § 43.92, limiting reach of *Tarasoff* to "a serious threat of physical violence against a reasonably identifiable victim or victims."

Questions about the reach of *Tarasoff* remain. For example, would a similar obligation arise if an attorney's client made specific threats of harm toward a third party? Surely an attorney is less equipped to determine the seriousness of the threat than a therapist, but, if the lawyer believes the threat to be serious, does this justify breaching a client confidence? Another post-*Tarasoff* issue is the degree to which a physician has the obligation to notify third parties upon discovering a patient has a sexually transmissible disease, such as AIDS. Absent legislation or judicial guidance, the physician runs the risk of liability to the patient for breach of the confidential relationship, and to certain third parties for failing to warn. A judge must evaluate and consider thorny ethical and public policy concerns.[41]

[b] *Suppliers of Liquor*

X is served alcoholic drinks by D until X becomes intoxicated. En route home, X, due to intoxication, injures P. P certainly has a tort action against X. Does she have an action against D? Should it matter whether D is in the business of selling liquor or is a social host? At common law, neither sellers of liquor nor social hosts were liable to those injured by those to whom they served alcohol. Courts viewed the inebriated driver, not the supplier of the liquor, as the sole proximate cause of the harm.

Starting in the late 1970s, courts began to reconsider this common law view. Several imposed liability on commercial suppliers of liquor.[42] A few went further and determined that a social host could be liable to a third party injured by a drunken guest. These decisions are controversial and raise complex policy issues. On one hand, there is increasing concern about the carnage created by drunk drivers and a recognition that the imposition of tort liability on the suppliers of alcohol could have an impact on this enormous problem. For example, the New Jersey Supreme Court, after noting the enormous toll taken by alcohol-related accidents, decided in favor of social host liability.[43] Most courts, however, have refused to impose

[41] With regard to AIDS, a judge must balance the importance of assurances of confidentiality in light of potentially discriminatory behavior by others and the desire to have people elect to get tested against the deadly nature of the disease. *See* Donald H.J. Hermann and Rosalind D. Gagliano, *AIDS, Therapeutic Confidentiality, and Warning Third Parties*, 48 Md. L. Rev. 55 (1989).

[42] Some jurisdictions have enacted "dram shop acts" that impose liability on commercial establishments who serve visibly intoxicated patrons. Many states limit liability to situations where a minor is served.

[43] Kelly v. Gwinnell, 476 A.2d 1219 (N.J. 1984). The bold step taken by this court was tempered somewhat by the rather narrow holding which imposed liability only in cases where "a host provides liquor directly to a social guest and continues to do so even beyond the point at which the host knows the guest is intoxicated, and does this knowing that the guest will shortly thereafter be operating a motor vehicle . . . ." *Id.* at 1230. The *Kelly* court does not decide how to deal with a party where guests serve themselves, or the case where the defendant host herself is intoxicated.

liability on social hosts out of concerns that the imposition of liability on the supplier of liquor minimizes the responsibility of the drunk driver, interferes with well-established social customs, and creates a standard difficult to apply.[44]

These cases are viewed as duty to control cases because the plaintiff is asserting that the defendant should have stepped in to prevent the drunken third party from driving. But there is a potential analogy to negligent entrustment,[45] which is a species of misfeasance, in that the defendant is providing the third party with the material that renders her unfit to drive. The defendant is not a wholly disinterested party and there is a relationship of some sort between the defendant and the third party (bar-patron, social host-guest). Where the defendant knows the third party is too intoxicated to drive but is not responsible at all for the third party's inebriation, a duty to prevent the third party from driving is unlikely even if there is some sort of special relationship. Where, however, the defendant, who did not supply alcohol to the plainitff, has taken steps that facilitate an obviously drunk person's driving, liability may be imposed.[46]

[c] *Negligent Entrustment*

A related topic is liability for negligent entrustment. Although closely related to the duty to control context, negligent entrustment cases involve misfeasance by the defendant. The defendant's liability is premised on supplying a potentially dangerous instrumentality (such as a car or gun) to a person the defendant knows or should know is not fit to handle it. Thus, where D gives P, D's nine-year old neighbor, a loaded gun to play with, and P injures herself when the gun goes off accidently, P may successfully sue D for negligent entrustment. Similarly, D would be liable if D lent X, who D knew to be intoxicated, D's car, which X drove, causing P's injuries.

---

[44] In most of those jurisdictions in which the courts have found social host liability, legislative response has been swift either to limit the reach of the opinion (as was done to the *Kelly* decision in New Jersey), or to overrule it entirely (as was done in California). *See, e.g.*, Cal. Civ. Code § 1714 (c) ("No social host who furnishes alcoholic beverages to any person shall be held legally accountable for damages by such person, or for injury to the person or property of, or death of, any third person, resulting from the consumption of such beverages.").

[45] *See infra* § 8.02[B][1][c].

[46] *See, e.g.*, Otis Engineering Corp. v. Clark, 668 S.W.2d 307 (Tex. 1983), in which the badly divided court found a duty owing from the employer to the injured plaintiff where the employer knew the employee was drunk, escorted him to his car and sent him home during his shift. It is unclear how much more than knowledge of the third party's drunkenness is needed before liability can be imposed. Should a gas station that sells gasoline to a motorist known to be drunk be liable to persons injured by that driver? Someone who jump starts the third party's car? On this point, *see* Leppke v. Segura, 632 P.2d 1057 (Colo. Ct. App. 1981) (imposing a duty on a person who jump started an inebriant's car). *See also* McGee v. Chalfant, 806 P.2d 980 (Kan. 1991) (no duty to injured third party by one transporting drunk person to his car).

Does negligent entrustment provide a basis for imposing social host liability on those who provide a guest alcohol? In *Kelly v. Gwinnel*, the court analogized to negligent entrustment cases stating that "[i]f, by lending a car to a drunk, a host becomes liable to third parties injured by the drunken driver's negligence the same liability should extend to a host who furnishes liquor to a visibly drunken guest who he knows will thereafter drive away."[47] An analogy to negligent entrustment, however, while compelling, is not complete. Courts have typically required a closer connection between the defendant's negligent act and the harm, and have limited negligent entrustment cases to situations where the defendant has the right to control the instrumentality causing the plaintiff's harm.

There has been some extension of the negligent entrustment notion, however. For example, some courts have imposed liability on those who provide money to one they know to be unfit to purchase a potentially dangerous chattel.[48]

[2] Duty to Protect[49]

P, a patron of D, is assaulted in D's parking lot. She sues D for negligence, claiming that D provided inadequate security. Does D owe P a duty? Is the analysis easier if D is a landlord and P is her tenant?

As a general principle, there is no obligation to protect another from harm. Where, however, the defendant and plaintiff stand in a relationship in which the latter has ceded the ability for self-protection, the former has a duty to make reasonable efforts to protect the latter. The clearest situations involve a jailor-prisoner or innkeeper-guest. However, the obligation to make reasonable efforts to protect another from harm by a third party encompasses other relationships too, such as parent-child, school-student, hospital-patient, common carrier-passenger, and employer-employee.[50]

A duty to protect may arise too where the defendant undertakes to protect the plaintiff and the plaintiff relies on that protection. For example, a court

---

[47] Kelly v. Gwinnel, 476 A.2d 1219, 1224-1225 (N.J. 1984).

[48] *See* McKenna v. Straughan, 222 Cal. Rptr. 462 (Cal. Ct. App. 1986) (parents liable for giving daughter funds to purchase car knowing of her long history of alcohol-related problems) and Vince v. Wilson, 561 A.2d 103 (Vt. 1989) (D potentially liable for providing funds for grandnephew to purchase car knowing grandnephew had no license, had failed the driver's test several times, and was a drug and alcohol abuser).

[49] *See generally* Michael J. Bazyler, *The Duty to Provide Adequate Protection: Landowners' Liability for Failure to Protect Patrons From Criminal Attack,* 21 Ariz. L. Rev. 727 (1979) (advocates placing duty on commercial landowners to protect patrons from criminal attack); Olin L. Browder, *The Taming of a Duty—The Tort Liability of Landlords,* 81 Mich. L. Rev. 99 (1982); Miriam J. Haines, *Landlords or Tenants: Who Bears the Costs of Crime?,* 2 Cardozo L. Rev. 299 (1981) (landlords should make reasonable efforts to protect tenants from criminal acts on their premises).

[50] *See, e.g.,* Fazzolari v. Portland School Dist. No. 1J, 734 P.2d 1326 (Ore. 1987) (the relationship of a high school to its students is one requiring the school to make reasonable efforts to protect students from third-party criminal assaults).

imposed a duty to protect where the defendant grandparents had assured the plaintiff father that they would supervise their grandchildren's visit with their mentally unstable mother. The children were left alone with the mother, who shot them to death.[51]

[a] *Landlord Duty to Protect*

Absent a traditional special relationship, or the undertaking to protect and reliance, the extent to which a duty to protect applies in other contexts is more debatable. In the well-known case of *Kline v. 1500 Massachusetts Ave. Apartment Corp.*,[52] the plaintiff asserted that her landlord had a duty to protect her from third-party criminal assaults in the common hallway of the apartment complex. She claimed that the duty arose from the landlord-tenant relationship, prior criminal acts in the building, and a reduction in security. The court acknowledged the reluctance of courts to find a duty in this context, listing as the reasons for a no-duty rule:

> judicial reluctance to tamper with the traditional common law concept of the landlord-tenant relationship; the notion that the act of a third person in committing an intentional tort or crime is a superseding cause of the harm to another resulting therefrom; the oftentimes difficult problem of determining foreseeability of criminal acts; the vagueness of the standard which the landlord must meet; the economic consequences of the imposition of the duty; and conflict with the public policy allocating the duty of protecting citizens from criminal acts to the government rather than the private sector.[53]

Nevertheless, the court imposed a duty, analogizing to the innkeeper-guest relationship and noting that the defendant had created reliance in the plaintiff by providing better security when she had moved into the building, and that the landlord was the only party equipped to deal with third-party threats in common areas.

Several questions arise from *Kline*. For example, would the landlord owe a duty to a non-tenant, such as a friend of Mrs. Kline's who has come for a visit? In such a case there would be the same degree of foreseeability, but would there be reliance or relationship? Further, would a duty extend beyond common areas and to criminal activity taking place in the tenant's own unit?

Even where the court finds a duty to protect, the plaintiff has not established liability. The plaintiff must show the other remaining elements of the negligence cause of action. For example, the plaintiff still must show

---

51 Crowley v. Spivey, 329 S.E.2d 774 (S.C. Ct. App. 1985).

52 439 F.2d 477 (D.C. Cir. 1970). The trial court had dismissed the case finding no duty on the part of a landlord to protect tenants from foreseeable criminal assaults in common areas of the building.

53 *Id.* at 481.

breach of duty — unreasonable security efforts by the defendant — to prevail. Also, the plaintiff has to establish causation in these cases, which can at times be a challenge as the plaintiff must show that, had the defendant provided better security, she would not have been hurt.[54]

[b] *Business Duty to Protect*

A common scenario involves criminal assaults on patrons of a business. Jurisdictions differ on how to treat these cases.[55] The business-patron relationship is rarely enough to itself establish a duty. More is required in order to establish duty in the context of a third-party assault; courts typically require a high degree of foreseeability to establish a duty. How high is subject to some debate. Some courts require that the plaintiff show evidence of "prior, similar incidents" before a duty to protect can be found.[56] Courts imposing this requirement do so out of concerns of crushing liability on businesses, difficulties in crafting a workable standard, and a recognition that crime-fighting is a government function. Many courts have criticized the requirement of prior, similar incidents, however, advocating a "totality of the circumstances" standard of foreseeability instead.[57] This standard would not permit a defendant who had notice of foreseeable criminal activity to escape liability to a person assaulted for the first time by claiming the lack of prior, similar criminal activity, and would allow more cases to go to a jury.

---

[54] Proximate cause, however, is rarely a hurdle even though these cases involve intervening criminal conduct because the very risk created by the defendant's breach is a criminal assault. *See infra* Chapter 12. *See also* Restatement § 314A cmt. d (The duty to protect the other extends to risks arising from the defendant's own conduct, from the condition of the defendant's land or chattels, and to forces of nature, animals, or from "acts of third parties, whether they be innocent, negligent, intentional, or even criminal.").

[55] *Compare* Butler v. Acme Markets, Inc. 445 A.2d 1141 (N.J. 1982) (defendant owed duty to customer attacked in parking lot) *with* Errico v. Southland Corp., 509 N.W.2d 585 (Minn. Ct. App. 1993) (no duty owed to patron assaulted in defendant's parking lot). The *Errico* result was particularly surprising because the state's high court just a few years earlier had found a duty owing by a parking garage to a patron raped in the garage even though there had been no prior serious crimes in the garage. Erickson v. Curtis Investment Co., 447 N.W.2d 165 (Minn. 1989). The *Errico* court distinguished *Erickson* based on the special opportunities for criminal activity posed by parking structures.

[56] *See, e.g.*, Savannah College of Art and Design, Inc. v. Roe, 409 S.E.2d 848 (Ga. 1991) (no duty owed by college to student raped in dorm in high-crime area because of no prior rape in dorm). The California Supreme Court, without saying so directly, has changed course recently to require proof of prior, similar crimes in virtually all third-party criminal-act cases. *See* Ann M. v. Pacific Plaza Shopping Center, 863 P.2d 207 (Cal. 1993).

[57] *See, e.g.*, Sharp v. W.H. Moore, Inc., 796 P.2d 506 (Idaho 1990), in which the court rejected the prior-similar-incidents rule by explaining: "Reduced to its essence, the 'prior similar incidents' requirement translates into the familiar but fallacious saying in negligence law that every dog gets one free bite before its owner can be held to be negligent for failing to control the dog. That license which is refused to a dog's owner should be withheld from a building's owner and the owner's agents as well. There is no 'one free rape' rule in Idaho." *Id.* at 510.

The extent to which a duty to protect will be found outside the traditional areas will continue to be a source of debate. As criminal activity generally becomes more widespread, efforts to sue for lack of protection will surely increase. Is it right that a duty standard here will depend on the prevalence of criminal activity in an area, so that apartments and stores in "high crime" areas will be subject to liability while those in more tranquil areas will not? If these expenses are passed on as a cost of doing business, items will be more expensive in those neighborhoods where criminal activity is prevalent. A related question is whether businesses should be required to make their patrons safer on the premises than they are in the surrounding community.[58] Where there are foreseeable risks of criminal harm to patrons, the defendants are best situated to make efforts to protect them from danger. Further, the standard merely insists on reasonable efforts, not a guarantee of safety.[59]

[c] *Police Duty to Protect and the Public Duty Doctrine*

Special duty issues often arise when the plaintiff seeks to recover from a government entity such as a police department, school district, or public transit authority. Initially, governmental liability was rare due to widespread recognition of governmental immunity. While governmental immunity still exists, it has shrunk dramatically.[60] In negligence actions against government actors, the element of duty is now often used to limit the scope of governmental liability. Under the public duty doctrine, a government actor performing improperly is not usually liable to individuals harmed by the misperformance, because any duty owed is limited to the public at large rather than to any specific individual.

[i] Police Duty

Police departments are typically not liable for failing to protect individual citizens. In one influential case, no duty was found owing to a plaintiff who had called the police on several occasions because her former boyfriend had threatened her with serious physical harm. The police did not come to her aid and the plaintiff suffered severe injuries when acid was thrown

---

58 *See* Williams v. Cunningham Drug Stores, 418 N.W.2d 381 (Mich. 1988), in which the court, in refusing to find a duty where the plaintiff was injured during an armed robbery of the defendant store, noted: "To require defendant to provide armed, visible security guards to protect invitees from criminal acts in a place of business open to the general public would require defendant to provide a safer environment on his premises than his invitees would encounter in the community at large." *Id.* at 384. *But see* Taco Bell, Inc. v. Lannon, 744 P.2d 43 (Colo. 1987), in which the court found a duty owed to the plaintiff injured during a robbery of the defendant restaurant, stating that it was for the jury to decide if the defendant took reasonable precautions to protect its patrons.

59 When courts wish to find a duty owing in these criminal assault cases, they generally speak in terms of a duty "to take reasonable protective measures." When courts seek to justify the denial of a duty, they often characterize a plaintiff's claim more narrowly, as, for example, a duty "to provide security guards."

60 *See infra* 15.05[E].

in her face by an assailant hired by her former boyfriend. In justifying the denial of a duty to an admittedly foreseeable plaintiff, the New York high court explained:

> The amount of protection that may be provided is limited by the resources of the community and by a considered legislative-executive decision as to how those resources may be deployed. For the courts to proclaim a new and general duty of protection in the law of tort, even to those who may be the particular seekers of protection based on specific hazards, could and would inevitably determine how the limited police resources of the community should be allocated and without predictable limits.[61]

Most jurisdictions have adhered to this no-duty rule.[62]

In order for there to be a duty to protect in a police case, then, the plaintiff must establish far more than just the general relationship of the police to the public. Most courts have limited a finding of duty to situations where the defendant police undertook to act and created reliance,[63] enlisted the aid of the plaintiff,[64] or increased the risk of harm to the plaintiff.[65]

Because of discomfort with this no-duty rule, there has been some judicial creativity here. For example, the New York high court later circumvented its *Riss* decision and found a duty owing by the police to a child who was badly injured by her father, against whom a protective order had been issued because of his history of violence toward his ex-wife. In distinguishing *Riss*, the court relied on the existence of the protective order, on the assailant's known history of violence, and on the fact that the police officers whom

---

[61] Riss v. City of New York, 240 N.E.2d 860, 861 (N.Y. 1968). The dissenting judge reduced the logic of the holding to a view that, because the police owe a general duty to everybody, they owe it to nobody. *Id.* at 862 (J. Keating dissenting). Two side notes about the *Riss* case are that the jilted suitor who orchestrated the attack on the plaintiff was an attorney, and that after he was released from prison he and the plaintiff married.

[62] A few jurisdictions have eschewed the majority rule, preferring an obligation for the police to use reasonable care to protect the citizenry. *See, e.g.*, Austin v. City of Scottsdale, 684 P.2d 151 (Ariz. 1984).

[63] *See, e.g.*, Morgan v. County of Yuba, 41 Cal. Rptr. 508 (Cal. Ct. App. 1964), in which the police promised to inform the plaintiff's wife when a prisoner was to be released and failed to do so, and the plaintiff's wife was killed. *See also* Florence v. Goldberg, 375 N.E.2d 763 (N.Y. 1978), in which a duty was found because the police had voluntarily assumed an obligation to supervise a school crossing and failed to do so without notice to those using the school crossing.

[64] *See, e.g.*, Schuster v. City of New York, 154 N.E.2d 534 (N.Y. 1958), in which a duty was found to protect a person threatened with harm after responding to police requests for help with apprehending a criminal. *See also* Wallace v. City of Los Angeles, 16 Cal. Rptr.2d 113 (Cal. Ct. App. 1993), in which the court found a duty owing to a witness in an upcoming criminal trial who had requested protection from the police after they asked her to help them and implied there was no danger in doing so.

[65] *See, e.g.*, McCorkle v. City of Los Angeles, 449 P.2d 453 (Cal. 1969), in which the investigating police officer directed the plaintiff into the middle of an intersection where the plaintiff was hit by another car.

the victim's mother contacted kept assuring her that action would be taken at some appropriate point.[66] Further, in some instances, courts have imposed a duty on the police based on constitutional grounds. For example, one court held that a police policy of treating domestic violence claims as a low priority violated the plaintiff's equal protection rights.[67] Thus, litigants find it worthwhile to explore federal civil rights laws as well as common law tort principles in some circumstances.[68]

[ii] The Public Duty Doctrine in Other Contexts

The public duty doctrine has been applied to limit duty in contexts other than that of the police. For example, many jurisdictions will not permit an individual harmed by a fire department's unreasonable failure to respond to recover against the municipal fire department.[69] Concerns about the judicial branch violating principles of separation of powers by dictating policy to the executive and legislative branches of government, and an understanding of the delicacy of decisions affecting the allocation of limited resources have even led most courts to use great caution in cases where the defendant is a government entity. Some courts have gone so far as to refuse to find a duty owing from a government-run common carrier sued for its failure to protect passengers from third-party harm[70] or to permit

---

66 Sorichetti v. City of New York, 482 N.E.2d 70 (N.Y. 1985). New York has remained quite restrictive in permitting actions against the police, however. For example, in Kircher v. City of Jamestown, 543 N.E.2d 443 (N.Y. 1989), the court refused to find a duty owing where a police officer assured a Good Samaritan that the officer would report information given about the plaintiff's abduction because there was no reliance by the plaintiff on the defendant police officer's promise.

67 Thurman v. City of Torrington, 595 F. Supp. 1521 (D. Conn. 1984). The U.S. Supreme Court, however, has held that the Due Process Clause cannot be used as a basis for imposing a duty to protect. DeShaney v. Winnebago County Dep't. of Social Services, 489 U.S. 189 (1989). Because the victim/plaintiff in these police duty cases is usually female, the traditional no-duty rule has profoundly affected women. *See* Lucinda M. Finley, *A Break in the Silence: Including Women's Issues in a Torts Course,* 1 Yale J.L. & Feminism, 41, 71-72 (1989).

68 Plaintiffs have particularly relied on 42 U.S.C. § 1983 and Title VII.

69 *See, e.g.,* Cyran v. Town of Ware, 597 N.E.2d 1352 (Mass. 1992). In holding that there can be no cause of action for negligent firefighting, the court explained: "Society would not favor, and public policy does not support, a rule which would expose a municipality to liability for damages every time its fire department does not, in a plaintiff's view, fight a fire satisfactorily. In busy urban areas such exposure could be limitless . . . ." *Id.* at 1354. *But see* Williams v. City of Tuscumbia, 426 So. 2d 824, 825 (Ala. 1983), in which the court rejected the public duty doctrine, explaining: "Tuscumbia contends that a duty imposed upon a municipal fire department is owed to the general public — not to an individual. Does this mean that the whole town has to be on fire before the fire department responds to a call?"

70 *See* Weiner v. Metropolitan Transportation Authority, 433 N.E.2d 124 (N.Y. 1982) (even though a duty would be found against a nongovernmental common carrier, concerns about resource allocation merit different treatment for a government-run common carrier). *But see* Lopez v. Southern California Rapid Transit District, 710 P. 2d 907 (Cal. 1985) (public transit system will be treated like nongovernmental common carriers).

the questioning of a school district's decision about where to place school bus stops.[71]

The public duty doctrine has been much criticized as an attempt to resurrect governmental immunity in contexts where it ostensibly has been abolished. It has also been seen as unfairly placing the burden of loss on the few innocent victims of government error, and as creating a disincentive for government to use care in carrying out its functions.[72]

§ 8.03 THE LIMITS OF THE MISFEASANCE/NONFEASANCE DISTINCTION

The determination of whether a duty exists is fundamentally a policy-based decision. The misfeasance/ nonfeasance distinction is not the "be all and end all" of duty analysis. Rather, there are cases where the classification of the conduct in issue is secondary to policy concerns. One example is the famous case of *H.R. Moch Co., Inc.v. Rensselaer Water Co.*,[73] in which the plaintiff suffered property damage because the defendant water company, who had contracted with the city to supply water to the city's fire hydrants, failed to do so. Judge Cardozo, writing for the unanimous court, refused to find a duty owing under these facts by classifying the defendant's breach as nonfeasance, "the denial of a benefit," rather than the "commission of a wrong."[74] The court ignored the reason for the defendant's failure to provide adequate water (for example, was it because an employee of the water works failed to open a valve?), and ignored the possibility of the plaintiff's reliance. The decision sought to limit the scope of the defendant's liability, possibly out of the recognition that water, as a necessity, must be kept affordable. Indeed, the *Moch* rationale has been followed in cases of obvious misfeasance, such as in *Strauss v. Belle Realty*,[75] where the defendant electric company's gross negligence led to a blackout. There, the New York high court refused to find a duty owing from the power company to a person physically injured in the common area of his apartment building due to the power failure because of concerns about excessive liability.[76]

[71] *See* Pratt v. Robinson, 349 N.E.2d 849 (N.Y. 1976) ("[T]he existence of such a duty at common law would be inconsistent with the discretionary nature of the functions of planning and allocation of resources placed in the legislative branch of government.").

[72] Stewart v. Schmieder, 386 So. 2d 1351 (La. 1980) (finding a duty owed by the city to persons injured by the negligent issuance of building permits).

[73] 159 N.E. 896 (N.Y. 1928).

[74] *Id.* at 899.

[75] 482 N.E.2d 34 (N.Y. 1985).

[76] In reaching its decision, the court relied heavily on cases involving pure economic loss, though the case before them involved personal injury. No doubt the court's protective posture was due to the defendant's status as a utility, suggesting, along with *Moch*, the likelihood of a narrowly defined duty in these types of cases. Some jurisdictions would not be so protective of the defendant utility.

§ 8.04 THE FORESEEABLE PLAINTIFF REQUIREMENT

Absent some other basis for limiting the scope of duty, the defendant owes a duty to foreseeable victims for foreseeable harm. Consequently, even if the defendant breaches the requisite standard of conduct and causes injury to a plaintiff, no liability will ensue if the plaintiff falls outside some zone of foreseeability. Thus, in order to establish a duty, the plaintiff must show that defendant's negligence created foreseeable risks of harm to persons in her position.

The concept that the scope of duty is limited to a foreseeable plaintiff arises out of one of the most famous cases in American law, *Palsgraf v. Long Island Railroad Co.*[77] In that case, the plaintiff, Helen Palsgraf, was standing on the defendant's railroad platform waiting for a train when she was injured by an explosion that caused a nearby scale to fall on her. The explosion was caused when a railroad guard dislodged a passenger's package while attempting to help the passenger board a moving train. The package, only 15 inches long and covered by a newspaper, contained fireworks which caused the explosion that knocked the scale onto Mrs. Palsgraf.

The New York trial and intermediate courts upheld a jury verdict of $6,000 for the plaintiff against the railroad. The New York Court of Appeals, by one vote, reversed the lower courts, finding that no legal duty was owed by the defendant to Mrs. Palsgraf. In his majority opinion, Chief Judge Cardozo interpreted the element of duty as a relational concept. He explained:

> The conduct of the defendant's guard, if a wrong in its relation to the holder of the package, was not a wrong in its relation to the plaintiff, standing far away. Relatively to her it was not negligence at all. Nothing in the situation gave notice that the falling package had in it the potency of peril to persons thus removed. Negligence is not actionable unless it involves the invasion of a legally protected interest, the violation of a right. "Proof of negligence in the air, so to speak, will not do". . . .[78]

Because Mrs. Palsgraf was not a foreseeable victim of the railroad's apparent negligent handling of the package, Cardozo determined that the jury verdict had to be reversed. Mrs. Palsgraf was nowhere near the package and there was no reason for the guards to believe the package contained fireworks or other explosives. Consequently, she was outside any "zone of risk," the area in which she could have foreseeably been harmed by the negligent handling of the package. Therefore, she was owed no duty.[79]

---

[77] Palsgraf v. Long Island Railroad Co., 162 N.E. 99 (N.Y. 1928). *See generally* William L. Prosser, *Palsgraf Revisited,* 52 Mich. L. Rev. 1 (1953).

[78] *Palsgraf,* 162 N.E. at 99.

[79] Under the majority's approach to the case, it appears that Mrs. Palsgraf would have had to be standing near enough to the package that it could have fallen on her in order

Judge Andrews, writing for the dissenting judges, rejected the majority's proposition that a duty is owed only to foreseeable victims, viewing a duty as owing to anyone injured by another's unreasonable conduct. Judge Andrews contended that where the "act itself is wrongful," "[i]t is a wrong not only to those who happen to be within the radius of danger, but to all who might have been there — a wrong to the public at large." He continued:

> It may well be that there is no such thing as negligence in the abstract. "Proof of negligence in the air, so to speak, will not do." In an empty world negligence would not exist. It does involve a relationship between man and his fellows, but not merely a relationship between man and those whom he might reasonably expect his act would injure . . . .
>
> The proposition is this: Every one owes to the world at large the duty of refraining from those acts that may unreasonably threaten the safety of others. Such an act occurs. Not only is he wronged to whom harm might reasonably be expected to result, but he also who is in fact injured, even if he be outside what would generally be thought the danger zone. There needs be duty due the one complaining, but this is not a duty to a particular individual because as to him harm might be expected. Harm to some one being the natural result of the act, not only that one alone, but all those in fact injured may complain. We have never, I think, held otherwise . . . .[80]

Duty, then, according to Andrews did not serve as a limit on liability. He recognized the need for some restriction on the scope of liability, however. Andrews viewed proximate cause as the element that serves as the ultimate brake on the scope of liability.[81]

Why has the *Palsgraf* case commanded so much fame and analysis? While both the majority and dissent continue to be cited regularly, neither seems to represent accurately the state of modern tort law. The case remains important, however, for the debate it raises about how to place limitations on the scope of liability. It raises the continuing tension between the element of duty on the one hand, and proximate cause on the other. While the concept of duty had developed as a mechanism for limiting liability in specific contexts, Cardozo's decision articulated a generalized theory of duty based on the foreseeability of the plaintiff. "Duty" in addition to

---

to be in the "duty zone." Of course, if she had been that close, or nearly that close, the court may have approached the case differently.

80 *Palsgraf,* 162 N.E. at 104 (Andrews, J. dissenting).

81 At the time of the *Palsgraf* decision, proximate cause extended to all "directly traceable" consequences per the *Polemis* rule. Cardozo acknowledged that proximate cause did not provide much of a limit on the scope of liability and, thus, looked instead to the duty element as a basis to restrict the breadth of duty. Andrews advocated a limitation through proximate cause where "because of convenience, of public policy, of a rough sense of justice, the law arbitrarily declines to trace a series of events beyond a certain point." *Id.* at 103 (Andrews J., dissenting). *See infra* § 12.03[D].

proximate cause emerged as a general mechanism to limit liability in all cases based on foreseeability. Furthermore, duty, unlike proximate cause, is a question of law and, thus, within the province of the court and not that of the jury.

Whether *Palsgraf* was decided correctly remains subject to debate.[82] Critics point out that Mrs. Palsgraf, as a prospective passenger, clearly was owed a duty of care by the railroad. Alternatively, Mrs. Palsgraf's location next to a railroad scale which could be dislodged easily perhaps itself placed her in a foreseeable zone of risk. More fundamentally, critics as prominent as Dean William Prosser,[83] Reporter for the Second Restatement, and Dean Leon Green[84] have questioned whether a general formula based on foreseeability could set appropriate limits on the liability of culpable defendants. Despite such criticism, foreseeability has become a fundamental, although certainly not the sole, tenet in both duty and proximate cause analysis.

§ 8.05 CONCLUSION

Where the duty element is in issue, there is room for considerable reflection and policy analysis. The duty determination profoundly affects the scope of negligence liability. Indeed, courts often employ the duty element as a way to restrict the scope of liability. The duty question is influenced by numerous public policy factors: fairness, accident prevention, cost spreading, concerns about excessive burdens, separation of powers, allocation of public resources, and economic development. Certain policy rationales dominate particular areas of the law, and the good lawyer tailors the policy discussion to the particular duty problem at issue.

For some wrongs, there simply is no tort remedy. Either because of the kind of harm the plaintiff suffered or because of other policy concerns, sometimes no tort recovery is permitted. Where there are compelling public policy reasons to limit duty, the fact that the defendant could readily foresee harm to the plaintiff will not be enough to justify the imposition of liability.[85]

The determination of duty is not mathematical or even precise; it extends past a determination of whether the case is one of misfeasance or nonfeasance. Rather, the duty decision is the result of the balancing of various

---

[82] *See generally* Robert E. Keeton, *A Palsgraf Anecdote*, 56 Tex. L. Rev. 513 (1978).

[83] William L. Prosser, *Palsgraf Revisited,* 52 Mich. L. Rev. 1 (1953).

[84] Leon Green, *Foreseeability in Negligence Law,* 61 Colum. L. Rev. 1401 (1961).

[85] As one court explained: "The decision to impose a duty turns in part upon the probability or foreseeability that a defendant's negligent conduct will result in harm to the plaintiff, but also upon the desirability in terms of social policy of the extension of such a duty." Laflin v. Estate of Mills, 368 N.E.2d 522, 526 (Ill. 1977). *See also* Leong v. Takasaki, 520 P.2d 758, 764 (Haw. 1974) (Duty decisions entail "the sum total of those considerations of policy which led the law to say that the particular plaintiff is entitled to protection" from the risk created or the injury sustained.).

competing interests. In many instances, duty determinations reflect a judge's view of society's paramount interests at a specific time. Thus, the duty determination is a dynamic and evolving concept. For example, early in this century tort law permitted a woman (or her father) to sue a man who lured her into sexual relations for the tort of seduction.[86] In the second half of this century, concern about privacy rights became paramount and courts refused to intervene in the realm of private sexual relations. More recently, there has been heightened concern about sexually transmitted diseases and courts have increasingly permitted a legal action by one who contracted a sexually transmitted disease from another. As society changes, the negligence duties will change along with it.

---

[86] *See generally* Jane E. Larson, *Women Understand So Little, They Call My Good Nature "Deceit": A Feminist Rethinking of Seduction,* 93 Colum. L. Rev. 374 (1993).

CHAPTER 9

LAND OCCUPIER DUTY

SYNOPSIS

§ 9.01 OVERVIEW

One of the most complex areas of duty involves the responsibility of land possessors[1] to persons injured on their land. Under the common law approach, the measure of the duty owed depends on the status of the person entering the land — whether the entrant is a "trespasser," a "licensee," or an "invitee." The *status* of the person entering the land determines the standard of care owed by the land occupier. Because these standards of care vary significantly, the status of the injured person is critical to the

[1] The limited duty rules discussed in this chapter apply to those in *possession* of the land. Thus, a person in physical possession of the land (such as a tenant), even though not the owner of the land, will be able to assert the common law duty limitations. Thus, though the terms land owner and land occupier are often used interchangeably, the latter is more accurate. *See* Restatement § 328E.

determination of whether that person may recover for injuries. Some jurisdictions have rejected the status approach to liability, using a generalized duty of ordinary care instead. This Chapter also looks at the duty owed by land possessors to those outside the property, and ends with a brief discussion of the landlord-tenant relationship.

Grasping the relevant law in this area is particularly challenging for several reasons. First, there has been little uniformity among the states in determining the measure of the duty owed to certain persons coming onto the land. Further, because of the harshness of the traditional status-based rules, courts have created a variety of often-complicated exceptions. The parameters of these exceptions vary by jurisdiction. Additionally, the standard may vary depending upon whether the focus is on the defendant's conduct, natural conditions on the land, or artificial conditions on the land. Finally, in a strong minority of jurisdictions, the common law status approach has been replaced with a generalized duty of reasonable care.

To understand this area fully, it is important to identify the reasons that gave rise to the common law status approach to landowner duty, and the justifications for the exceptions that courts have created. Further, two prominent policy issues are raised here: whether the common law approach remains justified and the effects on the legal system of replacing it with a generalized duty standard.

§ 9.02 THE COMMON LAW STATUS APPROACH[2]

The common law approach to landowner liability measures the duty owed by a land occupier to persons entering the property by the status of the entrant. This status-based approach came into existence for a variety of reasons. Some scholars have posited the special duty rules here as a species of the nonfeasance/misfeasance distinction;[3] the landowner's failure to take precautions to protect those coming onto the land is not actionable because it constitutes nonfeasance.[4] A more persuasive explanation for the common law rules that limited land-occupier duty arises from the importance placed on the ownership, possession, and use of land in the seventeenth and eighteenth centuries. Because of the value attached to private land ownership, the law developed in a way that was highly protective of these interests.

Some duty is owed to all entrants upon the land, but the *extent* of that duty varies greatly based on the entrant's status. Thus, it is critical to determine the status of the person entering the land. In many instances there is room to debate what designation is appropriate. What follows is a

[2] *See generally* Fleming James, Jr., *Tort Liability of Occupiers of Land: Duties Owed to Licensees and Invitees,* 63 Yale L.J. 605 (1954).

[3] *See supra* § 8.02.

[4] *See, e.g.,* Laurence H. Eldredge, *Tort Liability to Trespassers,* 12 Temple L.Q. 32 (1937).

summary of the state of the law under this majority common law approach. A later subsection looks at the effects of a generalized standard.

[A] *Trespassers*[5]

A "trespasser" is one who enters or remains on the property in the possession of another without the permission (express or implied) of the land occupier. Trespassers need not have any "bad" intent to fall into this category; indeed, they may not even know that they are trespassing.[6] The key is the absence of the land occupier's permission to enter the land or the absence of any privilege for the land entrant to be there.

The duty owed to trespassers was (and in many ways remains) extremely limited. Requiring landowners to maintain their property or to conduct themselves in any special way in order to protect trespassers was contrary to the notion that the land occupier should have virtually unfettered use of the property. The trespasser took the property as it existed upon entry onto the land, including its concealed artificial or natural dangers. The land occupier had no legal obligation to discover, remedy, or even warn a trespasser of such dangers. Accordingly, the only obligation initially imposed on land possessors was to refrain from wilfully harming the trespasser.[7] This meant, for example, that the defendant was barred from shooting a person who was trespassing on the property.

Courts expanded the duty owed to trespassers to include requiring warnings about "traps." At the outset, the concept of "traps" was narrowly defined, precluding a land occupier from purposely creating hidden dangers designed to seriously injure trespassers (such as setting spring guns).[8] Dangerous conditions not aimed at inflicting harm to a trespasser did not constitute "traps." More recently, courts have engaged in some creativity, adopting a broader interpretation of "trap."

Jurisdictions adhering to the common law status approach have eased the harshness of the original common law rule as applied to trespassers by adopting relaxed rules for known or frequent trespassers and special treatment of some child trespassers.

[1] Frequent or Known Trespassers

In most common law jurisdictions, the traditional rule has been altered in the case of known or frequent trespassers. Where a land occupier actually

---

[5] *See generally* Graham Hughes, *Duties to Trespassers: A Comparative Survey and Revaluation,* 68 Yale L.J. 633 (1959); Fleming James, Jr., *Tort Liability of Occupiers of Land: Duties Owed to Trespassers,* 63 Yale L.J. 144 (1953).

[6] *See infra* Chapter 18.

[7] Even to this narrow rule, exceptions existed. For example, a land possessor could use reasonable force to eject a trespasser who failed to heed an oral warning. *See supra* § 2.04.

[8] This is consistent with the common law rules regarding defense of property discussed *supra* § 2.04.

is aware of the presence of a trespasser and knows that the trespasser is approaching a non-evident artificial (human made) condition, the land occupier is obligated to warn the trespasser if there is danger of serious bodily harm or death.[9]

Even where there is neither a specific trespasser identified nor a trap, the defendant land occupier may owe a greater duty than that laid out in the traditional duty rule. If the land occupier is on notice of frequent trespassing, or has reason to know[10] of such, as by the existence of a well-worn path, an obligation to warn of hidden dangers known to the land possessor and risking serious injury or death may be imposed.[11] No warning need be given of conditions on the land that a trespasser would be expected to discover or which are inherent in the use of the land.

Further, the land occupier who knows of a trespasser's presence must use reasonable care for the protection of the trespasser in carrying on activities.[12] Obviously, the land possessor need not take any precautions where there is no basis to know about the presence of trespassers.[13]

[2] Child Trespassers[14]

Without a relaxation of the traditional rules for children, most trespassing children would be barred from recovery. For example, assume that D owned unfenced property next to an elementary school, and that children frequently used D's property as a short cut. D built a pool on the property and used it to store toxic chemicals. One hot day, eight-year-old P cut across D's property on the way to school, spotted the pool and jumped in to cool off. Nothing indicated the pool's dangerous nature, and P, poisoned by the water, suffered serious injuries. Under the traditional common law approach, P's

---

[9] The Restatement supports this position in § 337. It is hard to justify a different treatment for natural conditions, although perhaps the distinction was created to avoid burdening the absentee landowner or those owning vast, undeveloped tracts.

[10] "Has reason to know" differs from "should have known" in that the latter could suggest an obligation on the part of the defendant to search for clues of trespassers while "has reason to know" suggests that the clear evidence of trespassing exists and that it should be obvious to the defendant land occupier. Restatement § 12.

[11] Restatement §§ 336-337.

[12] Restatement § 336. Ultimately, for activities, unlike for conditions on the land, there is no limitation on the duty owed. The land possessor owes invitees, licensees and known trespassers a duty of reasonable care when carrying on an activity.

[13] The Restatement proposes a sliding scale, with the amount of evidence of a trespasser's presence being inversely proportional to the dangerousness of the activity. For example, as the potential gravity of harm increases, the amount of evidence needed regarding the presence of a trespasser decreases. Restatement § 336.

[14] *See generally* Leon Green, *Landholders' Responsibility to Children,* 27 Tex. L. Rev. 1 (1948); William Prosser, *Trespassing Children,* 47 Cal. L. Rev. 427 (1959).

action against D would be dismissed because, as a trespasser, D only was legally obligated to avoid wilful and wanton misconduct.[15]

The rules barring recovery for most injured trespassing children caused discomfort for the courts, especially where the harm to the child could have been avoided with little effort by the defendant. By the 1870s, cases began broadening the land possessor's duty to trespassing children in limited situations. This special treatment was known first as the "turntable doctrine" because the cases involved young children injured on railroad turntables.[16] This approach became better known as the "attractive nuisance doctrine," recognizing that the harm-causing device lured the child onto the defendant's property.

The attractive nuisance doctrine was widely accepted and became refined by a particularly influential Restatement section adopted in many jurisdictions. Under the child trespasser doctrine of the Restatement a child trespasser will be owed a duty of ordinary care if a judge balances several factors and finds that they support providing the plaintiff special treatment. The effect is a dramatic one — the land possessor, who at common law would otherwise only be obligated to avoid wilful and wanton conduct toward the child trespasser,[17] now is required to exercise reasonable care. Restatement section 339 provides:

> A possessor of land is subject to liability for physical harm to children trespassing thereon caused by an artificial condition upon the land if
>
> (a) the place where the condition exists is one upon which the possessor knows or has reason to know that children are likely to trespass, and
>
> (b) the condition is one of which the possessor knows or has reason to know and which he realizes or should realize will involve an unreasonable risk of death or serious bodily harm to such children, and
>
> (c) the children because of their youth do not discover the condition or realize the risk involved in intermeddling with it or in coming within the area made dangerous by it, and
>
> (d) the utility to the possessor of maintaining the condition and the burden of eliminating the danger are slight as compared with the risk to children involved, and

---

15 The hypothetical is based on United Zinc & Chemical Co. v. Britt, 258 U.S. 268 (1922) (finding no duty owing from the defendant to the child plaintiff because child not enticed onto property by harm-causing condition).

16 *See, e.g.*, Chicago, B. & Q.R. Co. v. Krayenbuhl, 91 N.W. 880 (Neb.1902) (railroad could be liable to child injured on its turntable because harm could be avoided by minor actions on the part of defendant).

17 Even under the more generous Restatement view expressed in § 337, the land possessor would only have to *warn* about a known artificial danger. The child trespasser doctrine may require the land possessor to do more than warn.

(e) the possessor fails to exercise reasonable care to eliminate the danger or otherwise to protect the children.[18]

Several points need be made about the Restatement's child trespasser doctrine. First, no longer does the condition injuring the child have to lure the child onto the property. Thus, "child trespasser doctrine" is a more descriptive title than the "attractive nuisance doctrine." Second, the doctrine is quite narrow. It does not apply to cases where the trespassing child is harmed by a natural condition on the defendant's property.[19] Thus, if a child is harmed by caves on the property, or by an avalanche, or by a lake, the doctrine provides no redress. Nor does the doctrine apply where the condition harming the child is one that a child of the plaintiff's age should appreciate. Thus, the doctrine often does not apply where a child is harmed by such things as moving machinery, heights, water or fire, because most children would be expected to appreciate the dangers posed by these things.[20] Additionally, there is no special treatment unless the defendant had clear evidence that a child might come into contact with the harm-causing artificial condition; that a reasonable person would have known is not enough. Further, and critically, the doctrine will not apply if avoiding the harm would pose a great burden on the defendant, although the greater the risk of harm the more precautions the defendant must take.[21]

[B] *Licensees*

The most perplexing status of the common law categories is the licensee. A licensee is someone who enters the land with the express or implied consent of the land possessor, as is the case with social guests or those visiting for their own personal business (such as a door-to-door salesperson prior to the land occupier agreeing to transact business).[22] The licensee

[18] Restatement § 339.

[19] The Restatement expresses no opinion regarding whether the child trespasser doctrine should apply to natural conditions. Restatement § 339 *caveat.* By the terms of § 339, it does not.

[20] *See* Holland v. Baltimore & Ohio Railroad Co., 431 A.2d 597 (D.C. App. 1981) (nine-year-old injured by moving freight train denied use of child trespasser doctrine because he was old enough to understand danger). While most jurisdictions do not have an absolute age limit for the doctrine, the older the child, the less likely that she will be the found entitled to special treatment.

[21] As the Restatement summarizes: "A particular condition is, therefore, regarded as not involving unreasonable risk to trespassing children unless it involves a grave risk to them which could be obviated without any serious interference with the possessor's legitimate use of his land." Restatement § 339 cmt. n.

[22] One court put it this way: "A licensee is a person who is neither a customer, nor a servant, nor a trespasser, and does not stand in any contractual relation with the owner of the premises, and who is permitted expressly or impliedly to go thereon merely for his own interest, convenience or gratification." Chatham v. Larkins, 216 S.E.2d 677, 679 (Ga. App. 1975).

takes the property in the condition in which the land possessor uses it. The land possessor has no obligation to make affirmative efforts to make the property safe for the licensee. Generally, the only obligation owed to the licensee is to warn the licensee of concealed artificial or natural dangers on the property *known* to the land possessor.[23] Unlike the known or anticipated trespasser, the danger may be natural or artificial and it need not pose risks of serious injury or death. The land possessor, however, may assume that the licensee will be reasonably attentive to the surroundings, and will notice readily apparent dangers; warnings need only be given about hidden dangers known to the land possessor. There is no obligation that the land possessor take steps to inspect the property to discover potential dangers. In sum, a land possessor may be liable to a licensee injured by a condition on the property where the land possessor knows of a dangerous condition on the property, fails to make the condition safe or to warn the licensee about the risk involved, and the licensee does not know about the danger nor would be expected to discover the dangerous condition.[24]

As with known trespassers, a different standard is used where the plaintiff is harmed by the defendant's activity, as opposed to a condition on the land. Where the presence of a licensee is known or should be known to the defendant, most jurisdictions require land possessors to use reasonable care in carrying out activities on the property and will hold them liable to a licensee injured by the land possessors' failure to do so.[25] Consequently, there is no limited duty for activities as opposed to conditions.

[C] Invitees

An invitee, like a licensee, comes onto the land with the express or implied consent of the occupier. For invitee status more is needed, however. There are two primary types of invitees: business invitees and public invitees. Business invitees are on the premises for the potential financial benefit of the land occupier.[26] Public invitees are on land held open to the

---

[23] The Restatement views the licensee as choosing to enter the defendant's land and, once electing to do so, accepting risks thereon. But, in order to make a reasoned decision to accept those risks, the licensee is entitled to be informed of those dangers that are not readily apparent and that are known to the land possessor. *See* Restatement § 341. The Restatement explains: "A licensee's privilege to enter is a gift, and the licensee, as the recipient thereof, is entitled to expect nothing more than a disclosure of the conditions which he will meet if he acts upon the license and enters, in so far as those conditions are known to the giver of the privilege." Restatement § 342 cmt. d.

[24] The exception for child trespassers, discussed *supra* § 9.02[A][2], also applies to child licensees if it enhances the duty owed by the land occupier.

[25] *See, e.g.*, Bowers v. Ottenad, 729 P.2d 1103 (Kan. 1986) (host who burned social guest with coffee held to standard of reasonable care).

[26] *See* Restatement § 332 ("A business visitor is a person . . . on land for a purpose directly or indirectly connected with business dealings with the possessor of the land.").

public at large.[27] Thus, customers, business guests and museum patrons are invitees.

As to invitees, land possessors must use reasonable care in maintaining the premises and in their activities. This often entails taking affirmative steps to discover dangers on the property, which is not required of the land possessor when dealing with a licensee. If the land possessor knows *or should know* of a danger on the property, she must either remedy it or warn the land entrant of its existence where the risk is not known or obvious. Where the danger can be eliminated with little effort or poses sufficiently grave harm, a warning about the danger may be inadequate.[28]

The obligation of the land possessor to an invitee then is one of reasonable care. The land possessor is not an insurer of the entrant's safety, however, and will not be liable unless the plaintiff establishes that the defendant land possessor failed to act as a reasonable person would in that situation. The use of the land and the relationship of the parties will affect the degree of care expected of the land possessor.[29] For example, a mall owner might be expected to ensure no moisture collects in the walkways, while the owner of an outdoor park would not be.

[D] Determining Status

The determination of the plaintiff's status can be challenging and has a profound impact on the plaintiff's ability to recover. For example, in one case, in which the plaintiff motorcyclist was injured when he hit some holes while riding on the defendant's property, there was enough factual dispute that the jury could have found the plaintiff to be an invitee, a licensee, or even a trespasser.[30] In another case, the plaintiff was injured in the parking

---

[27] *See id.* ("A public invitee is . . . on land as a member of the public for a purpose for which the land is held open to the public."). The land possessor must induce and desire others to enter the property; mere acquiescence is not enough. Restatement § 332 cmt. d. *See also* Parker v. Hult Lumber & Plywood Co., 488 P.2d 454, 457 (Or. 1971), in which the court explained that a person is a public invitee "if the occupier, expressly or impliedly, has led such person to believe that the premises were intended to be used by visitors for the purpose which the plaintiff is pursuing and that such use was not only acquiesced in by the occupier but was in accordance with the intention or design with which the place was adopted and prepared."

[28] Wilk v. Georges, 514 P.2d 877 (Or. 1973) (warning about potentially slippery wooden planks not enough if the reasonable action would have been to take measures to make planks less slippery).

[29] As the Restatement explains: "One who enters a private residence even for purposes connected to the owner's business, is entitled to expect only such preparation as a reasonably prudent householder makes for the reception of such visitors. On the other hand, one entering a store, theater, office building, or hotel, is entitled to expect that his host will make far greater preparations to secure the safety of his patrons than a householder will make for his social or even business visitors." Restatement § 343 cmt. e.

[30] Basso v. Miller, 352 N.E.2d 868 (N.Y. 1976) (the court ultimately rejected status-based distinctions).

lot of a bar which he frequently patronized. On the day of the accident, he had gone to the bar to use the telephone. The court reversed a jury verdict for the plaintiff, holding that he was merely a licensee and, thus, unable to recover under the undisputed facts of the case.[31] Where there are disputed facts affecting the plaintiff's status, the jury ultimately decides the appropriate classification. For example, in a case in which a social guest ventured out onto an unlit and unfinished deck to her detriment, the court concluded that it was for the jury to decide whether a reasonable person in the plaintiff's position could reasonably believe that she had an implied invitation from the defendant hosts to go out onto the deck.[32]

A plaintiff's status can change. For example, if P is injured while shopping at D's grocery store, there is little doubt that she is an invitee. She remains an invitee when she is injured in a back storeroom, to which she was directed in order to ask the manager about ordering a certain product. If her purpose in venturing to the back of the store, however, was to find the non-public bathroom that she has been given special permission to use, she may have become a licensee while in that area.[33] If D, once in the back room, enters the store owner's private living quarters attached to the store, she is likely to be deemed a trespasser there.

Courts have particularly struggled with the proper classification for public employees injured by a condition on a land possessor's property while acting in their professional capacity. A professional rescuer, such as a firefighter, is hard to classify because

> [h]e is not a trespasser, for he enters pursuant to public right. Although it is frequently said he is a licensee rather than an invitee, it has been correctly observed that he falls within neither category, for his entry does not depend upon permission or invitation of the owner or occupier, nor may they deny him admittance . . . . The question is ultimately one of public policy, and the answer must be distilled from the relevant factors involved upon an inquiry into what is fair and just.[34]

Most jurisdictions have chosen to classify a professional rescuer as a licensee. A professional rescuer's ability to recover is further restricted in most jurisdictions due to the "firefighter's rule," which bars the rescuer's recovery for most injuries against a person whose negligence created the

---

[31] Adams v. Ferraro, 339 N.Y.S.2d 554 (N.Y. App. Div. 1973). The court suggested, however, if there had been proof that availability of the phone could somehow further an interest of the land possessor, such as a potential business stimulus, the result could have been different. New York subsequently rejected these status-based distinctions.

[32] Fitch v. Adler, 627 P.2d 36 (Or. Ct. App. 1981).

[33] *Compare* Campbell v. Weathers, 111 P.2d 72 (Kan. 1941) (P, who is a regular customer of D could be invitee in area of toilet often used by customers, though not per se public toilet) *with* Whelan v. Van Natta, 382 S.W.2d 205 (Ky. 1964) (customer injured in back room while searching for boxes is licensee).

[34] Krauth v. Geller, 157 A.2d 129, 130 (N.J. 1960).

emergency to which the professional rescuer is responding. Under this rule, a rescuer harmed by smoke inhalation fighting a fire caused by a homeowner's negligent act of smoking in bed would have no legal recourse against the homeowner.[35] Yet, the "firefighter's rule" does not prohibit recovery for negligence occurring after the rescuer reaches the scene or for undisclosed and unanticipated dangerous conditions on the property.[36] As a licensee, most jurisdictions require the land possessor to warn the professional rescuer of concealed dangers. Most states treat public employees on the property for non-emergency situations differently. Such persons as building inspectors, mail carriers and meter readers are commonly characterized as invitees, even where the land possessor neither consents to their presence nor derives a financial benefit from the visit. They regularly maintain the business interest of the land possessor, however.

§ 9.03 THE UNITARY STANDARD[37]

Dissatisfaction with the complexity of the common law status approach began to mount and by the 1950s a growing number of commentators contended that the common law approach had outlived its usefulness. During the second half of that decade two developments took place that pointed toward a likely move away from the status approach. First, in 1957, England, where the status approach was born, eliminated the distinction between invitees and licensees by statute. Second, in 1959, the United States Supreme Court refused to employ the status distinctions in admiralty cases, noting:

> The distinctions which the common law draws between licensee and invitee were inherited from a culture deeply rooted to the land, a culture which traced many of its standards to a heritage of feudalism. In an effort to do justice in an industrialized urban society, with its complex economic

---

[35] *See infra* § 15.04[C]. Courts have cited a number of reasons explaining why an injured public rescuer cannot recover from the person whose negligence caused the emergency: the employee assumed the risk; imposing liability would dissuade the public from seeking help; liability would be excessive; and the public is already paying through taxes supporting workers' compensation benefits to the injured rescuer. *See generally* Boyer v. Anchor Disposal, 638 A.2d 135 (N.J. 1994).

[36] Boyer v. Anchor Disposal, 638 A.2d 135, 139 (N.J. 1994) ("When the firefighter is hurt as a result of exposure to risks of injury that are neither inevitably involved in firefighting nor unavoidable in the sense that the officer could not have fulfilled firematic duties without traversing the area in question, the values of the doctrine are not implicated."). *See, e.g.*, Lipson v. Superior Court, 644 P.2d 822 (Cal. 1982) (land occupier potentially liable for failing to warn firefighters of toxic chemicals stored on the property).

[37] *See generally* Carl S. Hawkins, *Premises Liability After Repudiation of the Status Categories: Allocation of Judge and Jury Functions*, 1981 Utah L. Rev. 15; Kerrie Restieri-Heslin, Note, *The Common Law Categories of Trespasser, Licensee and Invitee That Govern a Landowner's Duty in a Premises Liability Action Are Replaced By a Single Standard to Exercise Reasonable Care Against Foreseeable Harms—Hopkins v. Fox & Lazo Realtors*, 24 Seton L. Rev. 2227 (1994).

> and individual relationships, modern common-law courts have found it necessary to formulate increasingly subtle verbal refinements to create subclassifications among the traditional common-law categories, and to delineate fine gradations in the standards of care which the landowner owes to each. Yet even within a single jurisdiction, the classification and subclassifications bred by the common law have produced confusion and conflict. As new distinctions have been spawned, older ones have become obscured. Through this semantic morass the common law has moved, unevenly and with hesitation, towards "imposing on owners and occupiers a single duty of reasonable care under all circumstances."[38]

Despite growing agreement with the rationale of the opinion, it was over a decade before any jurisdiction followed the Supreme Court's lead.

California was the first state to replace the status approach to land possessor liability with a generalized reasonable person standard. In *Rowland v. Christian*,[39] the plaintiff cut his hand on a broken faucet handle while on the defendant's property for a social call. He sued his host, who was aware of the broken handle (she had reported it to her landlord) and who provided him no warning about it. Summary judgment was granted for the defendant due to the plaintiff's status as a licensee.[40] The California Supreme Court rejected the common-law status approach, noting that it was no longer justified in "modern society." The court went on to declare:

> A man's life or limb does not become less worthy of protection by the law nor a loss less worthy of compensation under the law because he has come upon the land of another without permission or with permission but without a business purpose. Reasonable people do not ordinarily vary their conduct depending upon such matters, and to focus upon the status of the injured party as a trespasser, licensee, or invitee in order to determine the question whether the landowner has a duty of care, is contrary to our modern social mores and humanitarian values. The common law rules obscure rather than illuminate the proper considerations which should govern determination of the question of duty.[41]

Under *Rowland*, the measure of the duty owed to persons coming onto the land was one of reasonableness regardless of the land entrant's status.

---

[38] Kermarec v. Compagnie Generale Transatlantique, 358 U.S. 625, 630-31 (1959).

[39] 443 P.2d 561 (Cal. 1968).

[40] Interestingly, under these facts in many status-based jurisdictions, the plaintiff could have prevailed because the defendant failed to warn about a known concealed risk. It seems that California treated licensees much like trespassers, requiring the land possessor to avoid wilful and wanton acts or to warn of traps. A far less dramatic resolution of the case, then, would have entailed an expansion of the duty owed to a licensee to comport with that used in many other jurisdictions.

[41] *Rowland*, 443 P.2d at 568.

Rowland proved influential. A significant number of jurisdictions followed the decision during the following decade[42] to the point that currently a substantial minority of jurisdictions no longer rely on the status approach. The movement toward a unitary standard slowed markedly, however, with a number of jurisdictions reaffirming allegiance to the common law approach.[43] Those courts choosing to adhere to the common law have offered various justifications for so doing: juries will be imbued with excessive discretion due to the lack of guidance provided them under a unitary standard; the status categories have provided stability and predictability; a more gradual change is more appropriate; and any rejection of the long-standing common-law approach should come from the legislature, not the courts. Some jurisdictions have elected to take a middle approach of merging the licensee and invitee categories while retaining the trespasser classification.

The most controversial aspect of the unitary standard is the inclusion of trespassers. Yet, there are at least two strong reasons for permitting trespassers to benefit from the reasonableness standard. First, failing to do so will retain much of the complexity of the common law approach, such as the child trespasser doctrine[44] and the debate about traps, which is what led in large measure to the rejection of the status approach in the first instance. Second, there is a recognition that the defendant's unreasonable conduct created foreseeable risks of harm to land entrants, and it is only by fortuity that the person injured was on the property without permission. For example, assume that D negligently maintained her front steps. P, a magazine salesperson climbing the steps to try to sell magazines to D despite D's "No Soliciting" sign, suffers severe injuries due to D's unreasonable failure to maintain her front steps. Though a trespasser, should she be barred from recovery? The dangerous condition of the steps could have injured just as easily a social guest or even a business visitor. D, then, was just as unreasonable regardless of the status of the person injured. Yet, there

[42] *See, e.g.*, Basso v. Miller, 352 N.E.2d 868 (N.Y. 1976) (motorcycle rider injured when his motorcycle hit holes in road on defendant's property owed a duty of reasonable care regardless of status).

[43] *See, e.g.*, Younce v. Ferguson, 724 P. 2d 991 (Wash. 1986) (reaffirming commitment to a status-based approach and classifying person paying $4 to attend a kegger at friend's house as licensee). *See also* Gerchberg v. Loney, 576 P.2d 593, 597-98 (Kan. 1978), in which the court explained: "The traditional classifications were worked out and the exceptions were spelled out with much thought, sweat and even tears by generations of Kansas legal scholars who have gone before us. Should this body of law be discarded completely in favor of a free hand by a lay jury? We feel at this time there is too much value in our premises law with respect to rights of possessors of premises to warrant its abandonment."

[44] Because the effect of the child trespasser doctrine is to elevate the plaintiff's protection beyond that owed to an ordinary trespasser, where a unitary standard is adopted for all land entrants, the child trespasser doctrine is no longer needed.

has been discomfort with permitting trespassers to recover, especially where the trespasser has criminal mischief in mind.[45]

There is debate about the ultimate impact on the resolution of cases between the common-law approach and that of the generalized reasonableness standard. The latter unitary standard surely permits more cases to get to the jury than the status approach. Under the status approach, where there is no factual dispute and the plaintiff is a licensee or trespasser, the trial judge is often able to resolve the dispute. Under the unitary standard, as long as reasonable minds can find some unreasonable conduct by the defendant (breach), the case goes to the jury. Some, asserting a general sympathy of juries to plaintiffs, contend that this results in more awards for plaintiffs. While at least one persuasive article showed that ultimately the results under the status approach and the unitary standard are similar,[46] an impact of the general reasonableness standard on the litigation process is undeniable. The case is less likely to be disposed of by pretrial motion under the unitary standard because the status of the plaintiff cannot itself prevent the case from proceeding. For example, returning to the negligently maintained front steps example, at common law a trespasser injured by that condition would rarely ever be able to withstand a pretrial disposition of the case in the land possessor's favor, while under the unitary standard the case would proceed to trial. Thus, at a minimum, the cost of litigating is affected by which standard is used.

§ 9.04 LAND POSSESSOR DUTY TO THOSE OUTSIDE THE LAND

The developments in the law regarding the land possessor's duty to those outside the land have paralleled to a large degree those regarding the duty owed to those entering the land. The common law imposed a very restrictive duty, for which some exceptions developed. Some jurisdictions have rejected the common law approach, using instead an obligation of reasonable care.

The common law rule provides that a land possessor owes no duty to those outside the land for natural conditions on the land, even where the land possessor realizes that the condition creates a significant risk of serious harm.[47] Where harm is occasioned by an artificial condition or the land possessor's activity, however, a duty is recognized.

---

[45] Some jurisdictions that have adopted the unitary standard have enacted statutes barring certain criminals from recovering against land possessors. *See, e.g.*, Cal. Civ. Code § 847 (injured plaintiff barred from recovery if convicted of committing or attempting to commit certain felonies).

[46] Carl S. Hawkins, *Premises Liability After Repudiation of the Status Categories: Allocation of Judge and Jury Functions,* 1981 Utah L. Rev. 15.

[47] Restatement § 363(1).

An exception to the no-duty-for-natural-conditions rule is generally recognized regarding trees in urban areas so that a land possessor is required to exercise care to see that trees on the property do not pose unreasonable risks to those outside the land.[48] Some jurisdictions have expanded this to cover rural areas as well.[49]

Some jurisdictions have rejected the no-duty rule regarding natural conditions and have replaced it with a generalized duty of reasonable care. For example, in one case, P, a downhill landowner whose house was damaged by a landslide from D's uphill property, was permitted to establish a duty even though the parties agreed that the landslide was a natural condition. The court weighed various duty factors and concluded that a general duty of reasonable care should be owed by land possessors to those outside the land even for harm occasioned by natural conditions.[50]

§ 9.05 LANDLORD-TENANT RELATIONS[51]

Initially the law of property governed the landlord-tenant relationship and, because the lease was viewed as a complete conveyance of the property investing full control in the tenant during the duration of the leasehold, no tort duty was owed by the lessor to the lessee. Over time, all jurisdictions have come to recognize some exceptions to this no-duty rule. In some contexts the landlord now owes a duty to the tenant and even to the tenant's guests.

Jurisdictions have come to recognize some or all of the following exceptions to the rule fully insulating a landlord from tort liability so that liability is imposed for defects in common areas, negligent repairs, undisclosed dangerous conditions known to the lessor, the lessor's covenant to repair, premises leased for admission to the public, and a condition dangerous to persons outside the leased premises.[52] As to liability for common areas such as hallways, common stairways and lobbies, holding the lessor liable for defects is not really inconsistent with even the narrowest view of landlord liability because the landlord never ceded control of these areas. The landlord's liability extends beyond the tenant here to those who

[48] Restatement § 363(2).

[49] *See generally* Taylor v. Olsen, 578 P.2d 779 (Or. 1978) (while land possessor has a duty of reasonable care regarding the condition of trees on her property regardless of whether area is urban, suburban or rural, directed verdict was proper where plaintiff failed to put on enough evidence for a jury to find unreasonable conduct by D).

[50] Sprecher v. Adamson Companies, 636 P.2d 1121 (Cal. 1981).

[51] *See generally* Olin L. Browder, *The Taming of a Duty—the Tort Liability of Landlords,* 81 Mich. L. Rev. 99 (1982); Michael J. Davis and Phillip E. DeLaTorre, *A Fresh Look at Premises Liability as Affected by the Warranty of Habitability,* 59 Wash. L. Rev. 141 (1984); Jean C. Love, *Landlord's Liability for Defective Premises: Caveat Lessee, Negligence, or Strict Liability?,* 1975 Wis. L. Rev. 19. The topic of a landlord's duty to protect tenants from criminal assaults is dealt with *supra* § 8.02[B][2][a].

[52] Borders v. Roseberry, 532 P.2d 1366 (Kan. 1975).

are foreseeably on the property. Regarding negligent repairs, where a landlord, even without an obligation to do so, elects to repair, the landlord can be liable to those foreseeably injured by the landlord's negligent repairs.[53] Under a third exception, it is well-settled that a landlord is liable for failing to disclose known concealed defects on the property. Some jurisdictions apply broader liability, holding the landlord liable where the landlord should have known of the defect. A more controversial exception involves situations where the landlord covenants to keep the premises in good repair. Initially courts viewed the landlord's failure to repair as a breach of contract, restricting the plaintiff to a contract recovery. Most courts now permit the tenant, and other foreseeable plaintiffs, to bring a negligence action based on the landlord's failure to repair pursuant to the contractual promise to do so.

Most jurisdictions have required a plaintiff to fall within one of the recognized exceptions in order to establish a tort duty owing from the landlord. Some jurisdictions, however, often relying on property law developments recognizing an implied warranty of habitability, have expanded landlord liability significantly. In a case that began a movement toward imposing a general duty of reasonable care on landlords, a child visiting the tenants fell to her death due to an inadequate railing on an outdoor stairway. The stairway was part of the leased property and none of the recognized exceptions applied to establish a duty on the part of the landlord. Nonetheless, the New Hampshire Supreme Court eschewed the common law rule and replaced it with a duty requiring the landlord to exercise reasonable care in the maintenance of the leased premises.[54] The imposition of this reasonableness standard may be particularly compelling in jurisdictions that have abandoned the status approach to land possessor liability to land entrants.[55]

---

[53] In many jurisdictions, once the tenant knows of the landlord's negligent repairs, the landlord is no longer liable. *See, e.g.*, Borders v. Roseberry, 532 P.2d 1366 (Kan. 1975) (even if the lessor negligently failed to repair roof and should have put on gutters, landlord not liable because the tenant was aware of the condition).

[54] Sargent v. Ross, 308 A.2d 528 (N.H. 1973).

[55] *See* Pagelsdorf v. Safeco Ins. Co. of America, 284 N.W.2d 55, 60 (Wis. 1979) ("Having recognized that modern social conditions no longer support special exceptions for land occupiers, it is but a short step to hold that there is no remaining basis for a general rule of nonliability for landlords."). The court also buttressed its decision to use a general reasonableness standard by the jurisdiction's recognition of an implied warranty of habitability noting that "[i]t would be anomalous indeed to require a landlord to keep his premises in good repair as an implied condition of the lease, yet immunize him from liability for injuries resulting from his failure to do so." *Id.*

CHAPTER **10**

DUTY LIMITED BY KIND OF HARM

SYNOPSIS

---

§ 10.01 NEGLIGENT INFLICTION OF EMOTIONAL DISTRESS

[A] *Overview*[1]

Historically, tort law provided compensation for a victim's mental distress only when it followed physical injury. Recovery for this emotional upset was parasitic to the plaintiff's claim for physical harm.[2] Just as intentional infliction of mental distress is now an independent tort, negligently inflicted mental distress is currently also recognized as a basis for recovery.

The road to recognition of emotional distress as a free-standing compensable harm has been a bumpy one. Because of a general skepticism of emotional distress as an injury, and a fear that permitting emotional distress recovery will lead to fraudulent claims, much judicial effort has gone toward constraining this cause of action. Courts have been concerned about the possibility of potentially limitless claims flowing from a single negligent act as well.[3] The debate about the proper parameters of the cause of action continues, and significant jurisdictional differences remain.

Traditionally, as a prerequisite to recovery for mental distress, the defendant's negligence must have caused some form of physical *impact* on

---

[1] There are few topics that have attracted so much scholarly attention. *See generally, e.g.*, Peter A. Bell, *The Bell Tolls: Toward Full Tort Recovery for Psychic Injury*, 36 U. Fla. L. Rev. 333 (1984); Julie A. Davies, *Direct Actions for Emotional Harm: Is Compromise Possible?*, 67 Wash. L. Rev. 1 (1992); John L. Diamond, *Dillon v. Legg Revisited: Toward a Unified Theory of Compensating Bystanders and Relatives for Intangible Injuries*, 35 Hastings L.J. 477 (1984); Richard N. Pearson, *Liability for Negligently Inflicted Psychic Harm: A Response to Professor Bell*, 36 U. Fla. L. Rev. 413 (1984).

[2] These damages are generally called "pain and suffering," and permit recovery for the physical pain and emotional suffering that follow from wrongfully inflicted physical harm. *See infra* Chapter 14.

[3] *See, e.g.*, Payton v. Abbott Laboratories, 437 N.E.2d 171, 179 (Mass. 1982).

the plaintiff's person. Most states today only require that the plaintiff have been at risk of physical impact, sometimes referred to as being within the "zone of impact" or the "zone of danger." Most states also require that the victim's mental distress be sufficiently severe to cause physical symptoms of the distress.

Some jurisdictions have flirted with a much broader recovery for pure emotional distress — dispensing with a requirement of physical manifestations and broadly defining the class of proper plaintiffs. But even in these states, restrictions on a broad right of recovery are being recognized increasingly.

A separate development has been the gradual recognition of *bystander* recovery for negligently inflicted emotional distress. In these situations, the plaintiff is seeking to recover for her emotional distress suffered from the defendant's physical injury to someone else. For example, a parent may seek compensation from a driver whose negligence killed or seriously injured her child. This controversial legal action, like that for direct emotional harm,[4] has spawned jurisdictional splits.

A majority of states allow a bystander to recover only if the bystander is also within the zone of physical risk. A significant minority of states now allow recovery for bystanders who are not in risk of physical impact if they (1) are physically near the accident; (2) have contemporaneous sensory perception of the accident; and (3) are closely related to the victim. Most of the states following this approach also continue to require that the bystander-plaintiff suffer some physical manifestation of her distress. Some court decisions have dispensed with requiring one or more of these factors. Significant policy debate and litigation focus on fashioning a rule that permits recovery by highly foreseeable plaintiffs without leading to crushing liability for a single negligent act.

[B] *Direct Actions*[5]

[1] The Impact Rule

Very few states, if any, retain the once generally held requirement that the victim must suffer physical contact by the defendant's negligence to recover successfully for mental distress, known as the "impact rule." This impact requirement is derived from the historic limitations on recovery for pain and suffering except when parasitic to a physical injury. This traditional

---

[4] "*Direct actions*" are those actions where the plaintiff sues for emotional harm occasioned by the defendant's tortious conduct directed toward the plaintiff. To be contrasted are "*bystander*" actions, where the gravamen of the action is emotional harm suffered by the plaintiff as a result of physical harm caused by the defendant to someone other than the plaintiff.

[5] For an analysis of direct actions, see Julie A. Davies, *Direct Actions for Emotional Harm: Is Compromise Possible?*, 67 Wash. L. Rev. 1 (1992).

perspective reflects an unwillingness to recognize as a compensable event an injury consisting only of mental distress. Courts continue today to treat pain and suffering accompanying a physical injury very differently from mental distress alone, even if the distress causes physical symptoms.

Because the line between negligence causing a personal injury and mere physical impact to the plaintiff was difficult to draw, courts allowed mental distress recovery so long as the plaintiff experienced any impact. The impact need not itself cause physical injury.[6] Further, "impact" was defined broadly. For example, courts have found a slight electric shock and even x-rays to be a sufficient "impact" to permit a plaintiff to proceed with an action for negligently caused emotional harm.

The few jurisdictions that continue to require impact on the plaintiff reason that the rule still reflects the clearest and most logical line for determining when mental distress should be compensated. The vast majority of jurisdictions, however, have abandoned the impact requirement, reasoning that its artificiality creates an incentive for overly creative pleading and excessive litigation as plaintiffs try to fashion new exceptions to the impact requirement.[7] These jurisdictions employ other means to circumscribe the scope of recovery for emotional distress.

[2] Risk of Impact Rule — The Zone of Danger

A clear majority of American states allow recovery for mental distress if the plaintiff was at risk of physical impact and suffered a physical manifestation of the distress. This so-called "zone of danger" or "target zone" requirement allows the plaintiff to recover for mental distress caused by *near misses*. The rule reflects an evolution of the impact rule prompted by cases like the unfortunate pedestrian who was denied recovery when she was nearly hit by a run-away team of horses.[8] The majority rule continues to require *physical manifestations* of the mental distress. Classically this physical ailment was characterized as fright, although the term is no longer required. While a heart attack or miscarriage are clearly

[6] For example, the victim who had a circus horse relieve itself on him was allowed to recover for his distress without proving the excretion's impact caused any significant personal injury. Christy Brothers Circus v. Turnage, 144 S.E. 680 (Ga. App. 1928).

[7] As one court noted: "The ultimate result is that the honest claimant is penalized for his reluctance to fashion the facts within the framework of the exceptions." Battalla v. State of New York, 176 N.E.2d 729, 731 (N.Y. 1961). *See also* Daley v. LaCroix, 179 N.W.2d 390, 395 (Mich. 1970) (abolishing "impact" requirement due to "changed circumstances relating to the factual and scientific information available . . . .").

[8] Mitchell v. Rochester Ry. Co., 45 N.E. 354 (N.Y. 1896). The plaintiff's complaint was dismissed due to the lack of impact even though her fear of being trampled by the on-coming horses resulted in a miscarriage.

adequate, such severe physical manifestations are not required, and assertions of stomach trouble have sufficed.[9]

[3] Special Cases

In limited situations, courts have been willing to relax the limitations on recovery for negligently inflicted emotional distress. For example, a plaintiff can readily recover for mental distress occasioned by the negligent handling of a close relative's corpse, or the erroneous notification of a close relative's death, situations lacking either impact or threat of physical danger to the plaintiff. Nonetheless, since the authenticity and severity of such distress are rarely questioned, recovery is permitted. Further, in these situations, physical manifestations are generally not required.

Although courts have been generally reluctant to permit a plaintiff to recover for emotional harm occasioned by negligent harm to chattel,[10] some courts have allowed recovery if plaintiff's chattel is of particular sentimental value (e.g., an heirloom), and if the defendant should have foreseen such distress.

[4] Broadest Direct Recovery

A few jurisdictions have moved toward permitting a broader recovery for negligently inflicted emotional distress, employing general notions of foreseeability. In the place of restrictions such as impact or presence in the danger zone, these states permit recovery for mental distress to all foreseeable plaintiffs.[11]

For example, in *Molien v. Kaiser Foundation Hospitals*,[12] the California Supreme Court came close to endorsing potential recovery for all "direct" victims of negligently inflicted mental distress. In *Molien*, the plaintiff's

---

[9] What constitutes a "physical manifestation" is debatable. *Compare* Olson v. Connerly, 445 N.W.2d 706, 712 (Wis. Ct. App. 1989) ("panic attacks" including extreme abdominal pain sufficient physical injury) *with* Robbins v. Kass, 516 N.E.2d 1023, 1027 (Ill. App. 1987) (crying, sleeplessness, increased migraine headaches and upset feelings do not constitute sufficient physical symptoms to warrant recovery).

[10] *See, e.g.*, Van Patten v. Buyce, 326 N.Y.S.2d 197 (N.Y. App. Div. 1971) (no recovery for mental distress resulting from concern for damaged property, including wedding gifts). *See also* Roman v. Carroll, 621 P.2d 307 (Ariz. App.1980) (summary judgment for defendant proper where plaintiff suing for emotional distress suffered from watching "defendants' St. Bernard dismember her poodle" while plaintiff was walking poodle near plaintiff's home because "damages are not recoverable for negligent infliction of emotional distress from witnessing injury to property.") *But see* Campbell v. Animal Quarantine Station, 632 P.2d 1066 (Haw. 1981) (plaintiffs permitted to recover for emotional distress where their nine-year-old boxer died of heat prostration because the defendants negligently put the dog in a van with no ventilation).

[11] *See, e.g.*, Rodrigues v. State, 472 P.2d 509 (Haw. 1970) (permitting recovery for emotional distress from witnessing negligently inflicted harm to the plaintiff's home).

[12] 616 P.2d 813 (Cal. 1980).

wife was erroneously diagnosed as suffering from syphilis, and the physician told the spouse that plaintiff, himself, should be tested. In sustaining liability, the court indicated that direct victims should be compensated for reasonably foreseeable mental distress.[13]

California subsequently limited its broad interpretation of "direct" victims. In *Marlene F. v. Affiliated Psychiatric Medical Clinic*,[14] the California Supreme Court identifies foreseeability as a threshold requirement, but predicates recovery for emotional distress on more: a significant pre-existing relationship between the plaintiff and defendant, assumption of duty by the defendant, or a legally imposed duty. Liability in *Marlene F.*, itself, was imposed because the plaintiff's mother had a professional relationship with the therapist who had molested her son. *Marlene F.* has significantly limited the scope of the duty owed in the context of direct emotional distress.[15]

[5] Recovery for Fear of Future Physical Harm

A particularly challenging issue receiving increasing attention is whether emotional distress damages should be recovered for the fear of *future* physical harm.[16] The problem often arises in the toxic tort or defective product context. Recent cases range from pollution of drinking water to potentially defective heart valves. For example, if D negligently contaminates P's drinking water with a known carcinogen, may P recover emotional

---

[13] In addition to showing foreseeability, the plaintiff must have suffered "serious emotional distress" which the court found where "a reasonable man, normally constituted, would be unable to adequately cope with the mental distress engendered by the circumstances of the case." This requirement was to prevent recovery for trivial emotional injury. *Id.* at 819-820.

The *Molien* court also abolished the requirement of physical manifestations as a prerequisite to recovery for emotional distress, reasoning that the requirement "is underinclusive because it mechanically denies court access to claims that may well be valid and could be proved if the plaintiffs were permitted to go to trial." *Molien,* 616 P.2d at 820. *See also* St. Elizabeth Hospital v. Garrard, 730 S.W.2d 649 (Tex. 1987) (Texas Supreme Court holds proof of physical injury is no longer required to recover for negligent infliction of mental anguish). *But see* Garrett v. City of New Berlin, 362 N.W.2d 137, 144 (Wis. 1985) (refusing to abolish "requirement that in negligence actions emotional distress must be manifested by physical injury . . . in order to avoid flooding the courts with fraudulent or trivial claims").

[14] 770 P.2d 278 (Cal. 1989).

[15] *See, e.g.*, Schwarz v. Regents of University of California, 276 Cal. Rptr. 470 (Cal. App. 1990) (father, not involved in treatment, denied recovery for emotional distress he suffered from psychiatrist's negligent treatment of his son).

[16] This issue also raises challenging causation and damages issues. *See infra* Chapter 11. The problem arises most often in the context of toxic or environmental torts where the plaintiff is seeking damages for the mental anguish she is experiencing due to fear of contracting a disease in the future, often termed "cancerphobia." *See* Gerald W. Boston and M. Stuart Madden, LAW OF ENVIRONMENTAL AND TOXIC TORTS 191–204 (West 1994).

distress damages based on the fear of contracting cancer in the future? This issue, and others like it, have generated much litigation. Courts have reached varying results.[17] Most are wary of permitting recovery due to the difficulty of measuring damages, potentially crushing liability, and serious proof problems such as the possibility of multiple causes.

[6] Conclusion

While negligently inflicted mental distress could be claimed in a variety of contexts, it appears no state is prepared to permit recovery on a showing of foreseeability alone.[18] Courts will continue to struggle in an effort to define the appropriate boundaries of a direct action for negligently inflicted emotional distress.

[B] *Bystander Actions*

If direct actions for emotional distress have led to debate and confusion among the courts, recovery for emotional distress suffered from the defendant's negligently inflicted harm to another has been even more controversial.[19] While it is clearly foreseeable that, for example, a parent would suffer emotional distress when her child is killed by a negligent driver, courts have attempted to permit recovery for the most worthy plaintiffs without unduly burdening the negligent defendants, who are already liable to the victim for their actions.[20] Courts have asserted various

---

[17] *Compare* Potter v. Firestone Tire and Rubber Co., 863 P.2d 795 (Cal. 1993) (concluding that, absent present physical injury, recovery of damages for fear of cancer in a negligence action is limited to cases where the plaintiff proves that it is probable that the plaintiff will develop cancer in the future due to the toxic exposure) *with* Hagerty v. L & L Marine Services, Inc. 788 F.2d 315 (5th Cir. 1986) (holding that plaintiff is entitled to recover damages for serious mental distress arising from fear of developing cancer where the fear is reasonable and causally related to the defendant's negligence.).

[18] Hawaii has limited its broad "foreseeability" test. Although the Hawaii Supreme Court suggested that recovery for emotional distress is permissible by all foreseeable plaintiffs (Rodrigues v. State, 472 P.2d 509 (Haw. 1970)), ultimately the court felt compelled to deny recovery as "too remote" to a grandfather living in California who suffered a fatal heart attack when informed by telephone that his daughter and granddaughter had been killed due to the defendant's negligent driving. Kelley v. Kokua Sales and Supply, Ltd., 532 P.2d 673 (Haw. 1975).

[19] Indeed, some jurisdictions severely restrict bystander recovery for negligently inflicted emotional distress. *See, e.g.*, Saechao v. Matsakoun, 717 P.2d 165 (Or. App.1986) (bystander recovery limited to those suffering impact). Until relatively recently, New York also refused to permit any bystander recovery noting that, though there are "cogent reasons for extending liability in favor of victims of shock resulting from injury to others, there appears to be no rational way to limit the scope of liability." Tobin v. Grossman, 249 N.E.2d 419, 424 (N.Y. 1969). New York ultimately decided to permit bystander recovery in Bovsun v. Sanperi, 461 N.E.2d 843 (N.Y. 1984).

[20] Most jurisdictions view a bystander action as a *derivative* action, as opposed to an independent action. In order for a bystander-plaintiff to recover for the emotional injury, the underlying victim must first be able to establish her own recovery. Only then can the

tests in an attempt to strike this delicate balance, each being met with charges of arbitrary line-drawing. The debate will continue about the proper balance of bystander recovery for negligently inflicted emotional distress.

[1] Zone of Danger

Courts have used the near-impact rule not only to compensate victims in a "direct" action who suffer distress from a near collision, but also to compensate a bystander for distress that may be a product of fear for one's own safety and distress over the safety of another. Thus, if P witnesses a close relative's injury or death caused by D's negligence, P can seemingly recover for both her own mental distress suffered by the near miss and for the emotional trauma of witnessing a serious injury to a close relative, provided P is also in the physical zone of danger. Under the zone-of-danger rule, the plaintiff can recover for emotional harm suffered from witnessing negligently inflicted harm causing death or serious injury to another (generally a close relative) when she is in a position to fear for her own safety.

Some courts justify recovery only on the basis of the plaintiff's fright for her own safety, while a large number allow recovery regardless of whether plaintiff's mental distress is attributable to fright over one's own safety or distress over the accident of another.[21] The theoretical distinction is often blurred because there is no viable way to distinguish between the injury occasioned by fear for the plaintiff's own safety and the emotional trauma resulting from witnessing harm to another. Ultimately this distinction can be ignored because the mental distress is an "indivisible" injury, and,

---

bystander plaintiff seek to establish a duty owing to her. Further, as a derivative action, the victim's negligence would affect the bystander plaintiff's recovery. For example, if Mom sues for her emotional harm suffered from witnessing D negligently running over Mom's child, V, Mom would only be able to assert a claim if V could establish an action against D. Further, in a comparative fault jurisdiction, fault on V's part would lead to a reduction of Mom's recovery. In a jurisdiction still recognizing contributory negligence as a complete bar to recovery, Mom would be precluded from any recovery. Any negligence on Mom's part will affect her recovery as well. *See infra* Chapter 15.

[21] Herein lies one of the key criticisms of the zone-of-danger rule in the bystander context. It is often impossible to tell whether the basis for the plaintiff's emotional trauma is the plaintiff's own fear of injury, the upset of witnessing another being injured, or some combination of the two. *See, e.g.*, Niederman v. Brodsky, 261 A.2d 84 (Pa. 1970). ***But see*** Bovsun v. Sanperi, 461 N.E.2d 843, 848 n.10 (N.Y. 1984) (explaining that permitting bystander recovery under the "zone-of-danger principle . . . will obviate the practical difficulties that juries otherwise have to face in seeking to separate the emotional distress suffered by a plaintiff attributable to his own physical injuries or fear thereof from the plaintiff's emotional distress in consequence of observing an injured or dying family member.") It is arguable that a bystander action under the zone-of-danger test adds relatively little: in the zone-of-danger context, the plaintiff already is likely to have her own direct action due to the "near miss," and the recovery for emotional upset from witnessing harm to another is just an additional element of damage. This additional element, however, can be quite substantial.

under traditional joint liability principles,[22] the defendant must pay for the entire injury, even if a large portion is attributable to the plaintiff's distress over another's injury.

[2] Dillon v. Legg: Minority Rule

A large minority of states have extended potential recovery to bystanders of an accident who were not at risk themselves, thus failing to fit into the majority zone of danger rule. These courts reason that the zone-of-danger test is unacceptably arbitrary. For example, under the zone-of-danger test, a father witnessing, from across the street, a negligently driven car seriously injure his child would be denied recovery. If he were standing close enough to his child that he himself feared for his own safety (or at least could have been injured by the negligently driven car), he would recover. *The Dillon v. Legg*[23] decision in California, which led the movement away from the zone-of-danger test, articulated three factors for a judge to consider in determining whether to establish a duty to the plaintiff:

(1) whether plaintiff was located near the scene of the accident

(2) whether the shock resulted from a direct emotional impact upon plaintiff from the sensory and contemporaneous observance of the accident

(3) whether plaintiff and the victim were closely related

In addition, most states adopting the *Dillon v. Legg* rule require a physical manifestation of the distress.[24]

Dillon v. Legg and decisions following it claim that foreseeability is the true test of defining whether a duty is owed to a bystander plaintiff. Proponents of this approach argue that the three articulated factors are predictive of whether it is foreseeable that the plaintiff, as a bystander, would suffer significant emotional distress. These "factors" themselves, however, have become subject to claims of arbitrariness. For example, cases soon were decided in which the bystander plaintiff did not actually witness the accident, but arrived seconds later. Courts differed about what constituted "sensory and contemporaneous observation."[25] In another setting, a

---

[22] *See infra* Chapter 13.

[23] 441 P.2d 912 (Cal. 1968).

[24] California, itself, subsequently abolished the physical manifestation requirement in the bystander context. Hedlund v. Superior Court, 669 P.2d 41 (Cal. 1983).

[25] *Compare, e.g.*, Nazaroff v. Superior Court, 145 Cal. Rptr. 657 (Cal. Ct. App. 1978), in which recovery was permitted when the plaintiff heard her child's scream from next door and hurried to the scene of his near drowning, *with* Hathaway v. Superior Court, 169 Cal. Rptr. 435 (Cal. Ct. App. 1980), in which no duty was found owing the plaintiff who rushed to the scene in time to see her child still suffering the effect of being electrocuted by a defective water cooler. Some courts permit recovery to a close family relative whose emotional injury "follows closely on the heels of the accident . . . ." Ferriter v. Daniel O'Connell's Sons, Inc., 413 N.E.2d 690, 697 (Mass. 1980). Further, is it enough to witness

plaintiff who has witnessed the injury-causing event may be denied recovery because she only later appreciated its tragic significance.[26] Another issue concerns the type of relationship between the bystander plaintiff and the victim which will allow for recovery. While close family relatives are the most logical and most acceptable plaintiffs, there are many gray areas here. For example, are stepchildren to be treated as other children? What about witnessing the negligently caused death of a longtime best friend? Should cohabitants engaged in a long-term relationship be provided the same legal rights to recover as legally married couples?[27]

In the area of bystander actions, courts have shied away from permitting recovery founded on foreseeability alone. It is certainly foreseeable that a parent will suffer great emotional harm upon learning of the death of a child regardless of the immediacy of the information and regardless of the physical location of the parent. Nevertheless, although courts disagree about the proper scope of recovery, there is a general concern that liability to bystanders flowing from a negligent act will create liability disproportionate to the defendant's fault. This concern has prompted some courts to discourage expansive findings of foreseeability. Indeed, there has been some recent movement toward narrowing bystander recovery even on the limited *Dillon* approach.[28] It has also been recognized that a family unit may already have been substantially compensated for the accident through the primary victim's personal injury action, wrongful death actions, or potential loss of consortium actions. On the other hand, the bystander's particular injury may be significant and not otherwise compensated.

---

the harm to a close relative on a television? For example, could Christy McAuliffe's husband recover for his emotional distress suffered from witnessing the explosion of the Challenger Space Shuttle against a party whose negligence led to the disaster? Is his injury different if he were present at the site or watching on television?

[26] *See, e.g.*, Mobaldi v. Regents of the University of California, 127 Cal. Rptr. 720 (Cal. Ct. App. 1976) (mother not permitted to recover though witnessing negligently administered injection to child because no awareness of the harm-causing effects at the time of the injection).

[27] Regarding this last point, *compare* Elden v. Sheldon, 758 P.2d 582 (Cal. 1988) (refusing to permit unmarried cohabitants involved in a stable and significant relationship the right to bystander recovery for negligently inflicted emotional distress) *with* Dunphy v. Gregor, 642 A.2d 372 (N.J. 1994) (cohabitants proving a stable and significant relationship may recover for bystander emotional distress).

[28] The *Dillon* duty "guidelines" were narrowed and transformed into requirements in Thing v. La Chusa, 771 P.2d 814 (Cal. 1989). In *Thing*, the majority held: "[A] plaintiff may recover damages for emotional distress caused by observing the negligently inflicted injury of a third person if, but only if, said plaintiff: (1) is closely related to the injury victim; (2) is present at the scene of the injury producing event at the time it occurs and is then aware that it is causing injury to the victim; and (3) as a result suffers serious emotional distress — a reaction beyond that which would be anticipated in a disinterested witness and which is not an abnormal response to the circumstances." *Id.* at 829-830.

[3] Restatement Position

The Restatement (Second) of Torts endorses liability in § 436 if the plaintiff's mental distress results from the risk of impact, or "shock or fright at harm or peril to a member of his immediate family occurring in his presence," and the plaintiff is in the zone of danger. In requiring the plaintiff to be within the zone of danger, the Restatement is generally consistent with the majority approach. A caveat to Restatement § 313 suggests the possibility of further expansion, but comment h warns that further expansion of liability may sufficiently risk uncertainty as to the genuineness or seriousness of the emotional disturbance to justify a denial of liability.

Restatement § 436A requires that the plaintiff suffer "bodily harm or other compensable damage." Three reasons for this requirement are cited: (1) injury without physical manifestation is normally trivial and temporary; (2) there is an absence of a guarantee of genuineness; (3) the risk of fraudulent claims is reduced.

[4] Policy Considerations

Several significant policy perspectives influence the debate on potential expansion of negligently inflicted mental distress. From an accident-avoidance perspective, failure to allow recovery for injuries caused by negligence fails to deter culpable behavior. Further, as general tort principles favor placing the burden of accident cost on the actor responsible for the injury, denial of recovery fails to shift the cost of mental distress to the culpable defendant. To a large extent this is part of the broader debate as to the appropriate extent intangible losses should be compensated by the tort system. Since most states only recognize negligently inflicted mental distress when manifested by physical injury, depending on the degree and nature of the physical injury, at least some portion of the injury is more than an intangible loss. This again argues for compensating mental distress in a manner similar to negligently inflicted physical loss.

In addition, to the extent the tort system is viewed as a compensation system, the limits on recovery leave the injured victim uncompensated.[29] While some of the loss may not have a clear economic cost, serious mental distress with physical manifestations often results in economic loss. Furthermore, when pain and suffering is parasitic to physical injury, tort law traditionally compensates for non-economic loss associated with mental pain.

The potentially large liability for imposing mental distress loss on defendants argues, on the other hand, for limitations on recovery. While reasonable foreseeability is an effective limit on physical loss, it is a far less effective limit on liability for mental distress. Consequently, without

---

[29] Peter A. Bell, *The Bell Tolls: Toward Full Tort Recovery for Psychic Injury*, 36 U. Fla. L. Rev. 333 (1984).

special limits, reasonably foreseeable mental distress imposes a large burden of liability on defendants and ultimately the insured community. This increases the costs of legitimate and productive industries prone to unavoidable instances of negligence.

From a fairness perspective, the culpable defendant should compensate an injured victim. In the context of negligently inflicted mental distress, however, the amount of liability caused by the defendant may disproportionately exceed the defendant's culpability. In many instances, the defendant is already liable to at least one party for the full extent of that party's injuries.

Finally, the risk of fraudulent claims is perceived by some courts as particularly dangerous in the mental distress context. Nevertheless, there are factual contexts so compelling as to avoid any real question that the plaintiff suffered distress. Further, our understanding of mental trauma has grown considerably over the last few decades to the point that psychic injury should not raise the suspicions that it had when mental harm was less understood.

For the bystander plaintiff, in addition to the above policy considerations, there are arguments that the tort of negligently inflicted mental distress must be viewed in the context of other potential tort recovery for the family unit. Wrongful death, the primary victim's personal injury claim, survival actions, and loss of consortium may coexist as vehicles for recovery.[30] On the other hand, none of those other torts address the specific loss of bystander mental distress.

Because of the many areas of tension arising in the emotional distress arena, it is certain that the debate about the proper parameters for recovery will continue to rage for years to come.

§ 10.02 WRONGFUL CONCEPTION, WRONGFUL BIRTH AND WRONGFUL LIFE[31]

[A] *Overview*

This Chapter continues to look at limitations on duty based on the type of harm suffered by the plaintiff. In this section the debate centers on whether any recovery should be allowed, and, if so, the proper measure

[30] John L. Diamond, *Dillon v. Legg Revisited: Toward a Unified Theory of Compensating Bystanders and Relatives for Intangible Injuries,* 35 Hastings L.J. 477 (1984).

[31] *See generally* James Bopp, Jr. et al., *The "Rights" and "Wrongs" of Wrongful Birth and Wrongful Life: A Jurisprudential Analysis of Birth Related Torts,* 27 Duq. L. Rev. 461 (1989); Michael B. Kelly, *The Rightful Position in "Wrongful Life" Actions,* 42 Hastings L.J. 505 (1991); Philip G. Peters, Jr., *Rethinking Wrongful Life: Bridging The Boundary Between Tort and Family Law,* 67 Tul. L. Rev. 397 (1992); Thomas D. Rogers, *Wrongful Life and Wrongful Birth: Medical Malpractice in Genetic Counseling and Prenatal Testing,* 33 S.C. L. Rev. 713 (1982); *Special Project, Legal Rights and Issues Surrounding Conception, Pregnancy, and Birth,* 39 Vand. L. Rev. 597 (1986).

of damages. Duty, in this context, is often restricted by the kind of damages permitted.

The cases in this area pose a special challenge because of the thorny philosophical and moral issues that they often raise.[32] In essence, the plaintiffs in these cases contend that the birth of a child is a compensable harm. These cases typically arise in the medical malpractice context, such as when a physician fails to disclose the possibility that a certain sterilization procedure will not be successful or when a doctor fails to diagnose a condition in a parent or fetus that leads to the birth of an unhealthy child.[33]

It is important to begin by explaining what is *not* at issue in the cases explored in this section. If a defendant's negligence injures an otherwise healthy fetus, upon birth the infant may pursue a tort action against the defendant.[34] While at an earlier time these cases were thought to raise a duty hurdle, it is now quite settled that the defendant owes a duty to the fetus once the child is born alive.[35]

In the cases discussed in this section, the defendant's negligence has not rendered a healthy child unhealthy. Had there been no fault, the child would not have been born at all. This notion of life as "harm" has caused courts great discomfort and has made the cases arising in this area particularly controversial.

The terminology courts and commentators use in this area varies. Most categorize the claims as we do here: the parents' action for the negligently caused birth of a *healthy* child is a "wrongful conception" (or "wrongful pregnancy") claim; the parents' claim for damages due to the negligently caused birth of an *unhealthy* child is a "wrongful birth" claim; and the

---

[32] For an argument that many of the problems posed are due to the use of male norms to interpret an area that has its greatest impact on females, see Shelley A. Ryan, *Wrongful Birth: False Representations of Women's Reproductive Lives,* 78 Minn. L. Rev. 857 (1994).

[33] These cases, of course, can arise outside of the medical malpractice context, as when the action is brought against a pharmacist for negligently filling a prescription for contraceptives or when the action is based on a defective product leading to the birth of a child (e.g., a defective condom).

[34] When a defendant negligently *kills* a fetus, the challenging issue of whether there is a basis for a wrongful death action brought on behalf of the viable but unborn fetus arises. *See, e.g.,* Endresz v. Friedberg, 248 N.E.2d 901 (N.Y. 1969). Jurisdictions have reached different results, with determinations often depending on whether the jurisdiction's wrongful death statute considers a fetus a "person."

[35] There remain potential duty (or proximate cause) issues if a substantial amount of time has elapsed between the negligent act and the injury to the plaintiff, as where the defendant negligently injures a woman who years later gives birth to a child born in an unhealthy condition due to the defendant's earlier negligence. *Compare* Renslow v. Mennonite Hospital, 367 N.E.2d 1250 (Il. 1977) (permitting an action by the child notwithstanding the passage of over eight years from the defendant's negligent act and the birth of the plaintiff) *with* Albala v. City of New York, 429 N.E.2d 786 (N.Y. 1981) (refusing to find a duty where the defendant's negligence occurred four years before the birth of the plaintiff).

child's own legal claim is one for "wrongful life." Each of these will be examined in turn.

[B] *Wrongful Conception*

Paul and Paula, for financial reasons, decide not to have a second child. Paul consults Dr. D and decides to undergo a vasectomy. Dr. D. performs the procedure negligently, and Paula becomes pregnant, giving birth to a healthy child. Have Paul and Paula suffered a compensable injury — the conception and birth of a second child — for which they may recover damages from Dr. D? If so, what elements of damage may be appropriately recoverable?

Virtually all courts confronted with a "wrongful conception" claim have permitted some recovery, recognizing that the defendant's breach of the standard of care has led to foreseeable harm. While there is agreement about permitting *some* recovery, courts have taken widely divergent views as to the allowable elements of that recovery.

Some elements of the plaintiffs' damages are recoverable without much controversy. Damages directly associated with the pregnancy and birth are universally compensable. These include the costs and the pain and suffering associated with the failed procedure, as well as any subsequent corrective procedure; the costs and the pain and suffering associated with the unwanted pregnancy and the birth; the wife/mother's lost wages; and the husband/father's loss of consortium.

The key controversy in wrongful conception cases is whether the parents may recover the cost of raising the child to majority. Most courts have rejected this damage claim for varying reasons. Some courts simply deny recovery by finding that the birth of a child cannot be a compensable harm. Others rely on the "emotional bastard" theory which posits that the child will one day suffer emotional harm upon learning that his parents sued upon his birth and that he is being supported by a stranger forced to do so by judicial decree. Ultimately, the courts that refuse to permit such recovery do so because of their belief that permitting an award of child-rearing expenses debases both the child and the family.

These rationales for denying an award of child-rearing expenses have been the object of considerable criticism. As one court explained:

> The suit is for costs of raising the child, not to rid themselves of an unwanted child . . . . The love, affection, and emotional support any child needs they are prepared to give. But the love, affection, and emotional support they are prepared to give do not bring with them the economic means that are also necessary to feed, clothe, educate and otherwise raise the child.[36]

[36] Marciniak v. Lundborg, 450 N.W.2d 243, 246 (Wis. 1990).

A few courts have applied a motivational analysis in determining whether to allow recovery of child-bearing expenses. These courts permit the claim if the parents sought to avoid pregnancy for financial reasons, but deny it if the plaintiffs' motivation was concern for the mother's health or fear of possible genetic defects.[37] This distinction seems sensible because in the wrongful conception context there has been a successful delivery of a healthy child. A harder case arises when a wrongful conception claim is brought by a couple who elected to take steps to forgo pregnancy, despite the means to raise a child. What effect, if any, should a motivational test play here? Because to a large measure the plaintiffs' injury is the deprivation of procreative choice, their financial status should not affect the recoverable damages. But a pure motivational test could force courts to inject themselves into this typically private domain.

Some courts require an offset based on the "benefit rule" embodied in the Restatement.[38] These courts ask the jury to reduce the damage award by the emotional gains of having a healthy child. Requiring the jury to measure and offset emotional benefits of having a healthy child, albeit an unwanted one, poses a substantial challenge.

Some courts and commentators have, accordingly, criticized a benefits offset as unworkable and inappropriate. Surely, any justification for a benefits offset depends on the interests being compared. For example, to the extent that the plaintiffs are seeking to recover *economic* losses, the setoff for *emotional* benefits is illogical (though required by some courts). While an offset of economic losses and economic gains is more sensible, there would rarely be any basis for such a setoff in light of the insignificant economic benefits conferred on the plaintiffs by the birth of a child. If a setoff makes sense at all, it is between the emotional distress the plaintiffs claim from having an unwanted child and the emotional benefits conferred by having a healthy child. Even if limited to this context, the benefits setoff poses substantial valuation problems.[39]

Another damages principle that defendants have asserted in wrongful conception cases (as well as in wrongful birth cases) is the requirement that a plaintiff mitigate damages.[40] Defendants have contended that the

[37] *See, e.g.*, Burke v. Rivo, 551 N.E.2d 1 (Mass. 1990).

[38] Restatement § 920 provides: "When the defendant's tortious conduct has caused harm to the plaintiff or to his property and in so doing has conferred a special benefit to the interest of the plaintiff that was harmed, the value of the benefit conferred is considered in mitigation of damages, to the extent that this is equitable."

[39] Of course, some challenging damages calculations are commonplace in the law of torts, as when a jury tries to measure pain and suffering. *See infra* § 14.03[E]. Is the task in the wrongful conception context that much harder?

[40] Restatement § 918 prohibits a plaintiff from recovering "damages for any harm that . . . could have [been] avoided by the use of reasonable effort or expenditure after the commission of the tort."

plaintiffs' failure to terminate the unwanted pregnancy or to put the child up for adoption constitutes a failure to mitigate damages. Courts, however, have been generally unwilling, in light of the highly personal nature of the decision involved, to permit jury consideration of the impact of the plaintiffs' decision to go to term and to keep the child.

The debate about the proper parameters of a wrongful conception action continues. There has been some modest movement recently toward permitting a broader damage recovery in these cases. They have generally been seen as raising less controversy than the wrongful birth and wrongful life actions.[41]

[C] *Wrongful Birth*

Pam, two months pregnant, consults Dr. D who negligently fails to diagnose her as having German measles. Pam gives birth to Parker, who is born with multiple serious birth defects caused by his mother's German measles. Pam sues Dr. D. Has Pam suffered a compensable injury and, if so, what is the proper measure of damages?

Wrongful birth actions typically arise when, due to negligent genetic counseling or a misdiagnosis about the condition of a fetus, an infant is born with a severe medical disability. In these cases, the plaintiffs are not suing due to an unwanted pregnancy, as in the wrongful conception context; rather, they are suing because of the loss of their ability to make an informed decision about whether to procreate, or whether to carry a potentially impaired child to term. This latter aspect — that the injury to the plaintiff was depriving her of the chance to terminate a pregnancy — has made wrongful birth cases particularly controversial. In many instances, as in the hypothetical with Pam and the child born with multiple birth defects, the plaintiff must be prepared to show by a preponderance of the evidence that "but for" the defendant's negligent failure to diagnose the condition giving rise to the birth defect, the plaintiff would have learned of the potential danger and would have elected to terminate the pregnancy. Since the U.S. Supreme Court's decision in *Roe v. Wade*, conferring a constitutionally protected right on a woman to terminate a pregnancy, courts have been increasingly willing to permit some damage recovery in these wrongful birth cases. Again the major debate centers around what damages should be recoverable.

Many of the damage issues discussed in the wrongful conception subsection apply here too, though a central difference is that the wrongful birth plaintiff does not claim that the child was unwanted. Accordingly,

---

[41] *See* James Bopp, Jr. et al., *The "Rights" and "Wrongs" of Wrongful Birth and Wrongful Life: A Jurisprudential Analysis of Birth Related Torts*, 27 Duq. L. Rev. 461 (1989), in which the authors favor a very restrictive interpretation of wrongful life and wrongful birth claims, while finding wrongful conception actions falling within well-established categories of negligence liability.

an award of child-rearing expenses is not justifiable in the wrongful birth context. Most jurisdictions have permitted the wrongful birth plaintiff to recover extraordinary expenses associated with the birth defect.[42] Some have also permitted recovery of emotional distress damages.[43]

The "benefit rule" may apply in the wrongful birth context. Some courts require the jury to reduce the plaintiff's damage recovery by the emotional benefits of having the child. The jury may deem these benefits substantial or minor depending on the condition of the child.

[D] *Wrongful Life*

Where the infant, Parker, was born with severe defects due to Dr. D's misdiagnosis of his mother's condition, the parents may have a wrongful birth claim. Should Parker, the infant born with multiple defects, have his own legal recourse against Dr. D?

Without doubt the wrongful life context has generated the most controversy and the greatest amount of judicial caution. Jurisdictions have largely refused to recognize the claim. A central reason for the rejection of a wrongful life claim is the difficulty calculating damages. Courts have found it impossible to apply conventional tort damage principles, by which the injured plaintiff is to be returned to a pre-injury state, in the wrongful birth context because the wrongful life plaintiff's pre-injury state would have been *nonexistence*.[44] The difficulty of measuring this harm and the judicial determination that life is always preferable to nonexistence have led most courts to reject the wrongful life claim.

A few courts have permitted limited wrongful life recovery.[45] These jurisdictions have decided that the infant-plaintiff may recover the extraordinary expenses associated with the impairment if these are not recovered

---

[42] Such recovery extends to the time of the child's majority if the parent will no longer incur those expenses. Further, it may be limited by the life expectancy of the parent.

[43] The New Jersey experience with wrongful birth is intriguing. First, in 1967, the New Jersey Supreme Court rejected any recovery for wrongful birth. Over a decade later the court revisited the issue and permitted an action, limiting the plaintiffs' recovery to *emotional distress* damages. Then, two years later, the New Jersey Supreme Court decided that the wrongful birth plaintiff could also recover the extraordinary expenses needed to raise the child in light of the child's special condition. *See* Procanik v. Cillo, 478 A.2d 755 (N.J. 1984). Emotional distress recovery in the wrongful birth context remains rare, however. *See, e.g.*, Smith v. Cote, 513 A.2d 341 (N.H. 1986) (limiting wrongful birth recovery to pecuniary losses suffered by the parents).

[44] *See, e.g.*, Gleitman v. Cosgrove, 227 A.2d 689, 692 (N.J. 1967) ("The infant plaintiff would have us measure the difference between his life with defects against the utter void of nonexistence, but it is impossible to make such a determination."). *See also* Smith v. Cote, 513 A.2d 341 (N.H. 1986) (rejecting a wrongful life action, noting that courts "have no business in declaring that among the living are people who should never have been born.").

[45] *See* Procanik v. Cillo, 478 A.2d 755 (N.J.1984); Turpin v. Sortini, 643 P.2d 954 (Cal. 1982).

by the parents in their wrongful birth action. This situation appears where the infant is born with a condition that will not substantially affect her life expectancy because the parents' claim is limited by their life expectancy. Although two appellate courts had at one time permitted the wrongful life plaintiff to recover for pain and suffering attributable to her condition,[46] no jurisdiction currently permits the recovery of these general damages in wrongful life claims. Permitting special damages, which are readily ascertainable, does not require the courts to grapple with the philosophical problems raised by an award of general damages in the wrongful life context.

[E] *Conclusion*

The debate about the propriety and scope of wrongful conception, wrongful birth and wrongful life cases will continue and, possibly, intensify as public discussion of abortion and euthanasia continues. Where should the boundaries be set? Should usual tort principles be applied here as they would to other personal injury cases, thus permitting a broad recovery by the plaintiff?[47] Would this lead to liability on a negligent tortfeasor that exceeds that imposed in other personal injury actions? Do wrongful life and wrongful birth cases thrust courts into a metaphysical debate for which the judicial system is ill-suited?

§ 10.03 LOSS OF CONSORTIUM, WRONGFUL DEATH AND SURVIVAL

[A] *Overview*

A single tortious act often has consequences for more than the person directly harmed. There are often repercussions to members of the family unit. The next sub-sections look at two kinds of compensable harm to certain family members arising from tortiously inflicted injury to another: loss of consortium and wrongful death. Another sub-section then considers a topic closely related to wrongful death, so-called survival actions.

Loss of consortium and wrongful death are most appropriately viewed as a *type* of injury. They are not torts themselves; rather, they are kinds of harm to members of the family unit. Loss of consortium and wrongful death damages may be recovered outside the negligence context, such as with intentional torts and strict liability. Because loss of consortium and

[46] *See, e.g.*, Curlender v. Bio-Science Laboratories, 165 Cal. Rptr. 477 (Cal. App. 1980) (permitting a wrongful life plaintiff to recover pain and suffering damages and pecuniary damages arising from the plaintiff's impaired condition).

[47] At least one scholar has advocated this position. In so doing, he suggests that, in denying broad recovery for wrongful life, "all courts treat the issue on a rather superficial level, exploring neither the tort policies the action would serve nor the legal doctrines upon which they rely." Michael B. Kelly, *The Rightful Position in "Wrongful Life" Actions*, 42 Hastings L.J. 505, 589 (1991).

wrongful death are generally taught in the context of negligence, we have included these topics in the discussion of duty limited by the type of harm. As a duty issue, the debate focuses on *who* should be permitted to recover, as well as *what* should be recoverable.

[B] *Loss of Consortium*[48]

Driving carelessly, D seriously injures T. Clearly, T will recover for his injuries in his negligence action against D. If T is married to P, does *P* have a compensable injury arising from the negligently inflicted serious physical harm to her husband? Nearly all jurisdictions permit such a claim, usually calling it an action for "loss of consortium."[49]

The scope of and the rationale for recovery have changed significantly over time. Common law permitted a very limited recovery for loss of consortium. Initially, recovery was granted to a husband who lost his wife's services due to a defendant's tortious conduct under the rationale that the wife was the husband's servant.[50] The concept of "consortium" gradually expanded to permit recovery for more than the economic loss of the wife's household services, permitting the husband to recoup intangibles such as loss of companionship, comfort, and sexual services.

States not only broadened *what* could be recovered under the consortium label, but also *who* could recover. Most significantly, they expanded the scope of recovery by permitting a wife to recover for loss of consortium when her husband was tortiously injured.[51] Virtually all states now permit either spouse to recover for loss of consortium, and recovery is largely for such intangible harms as loss of companionship, affection, and society.

Of course, recovery for loss of consortium is not automatic. The party seeking recovery for loss of consortium must prove her loss — that the

---

[48] *See generally* Jean C. Love, *Tortious Interference with the Parent-Child Relationship: Loss of an Injured Person's Society and Companionship,* 51 Ind. L.J. 590 (1976); Michael A. Mogill, *And Justice for Some: Assessing the Need to Recognize the Child's Action for Loss of Parental Consortium,* 24 Ariz. St. L.J. 1321 (1992).

[49] The following subsection looks at the legal rights arising from the tortiously caused *death* of a close family member — the so-called wrongful death action. In the loss of consortium context, the defendant has caused *serious injury* to the victim, not death. While this serious injury tends to be physical harm, consortium recovery can arise where the defendant has tortiously inflicted emotional harm on the initial victim.

[50] The wife was viewed as an "asset" of the husband worthy of protection from tortious interference by others. The injury was, thus, treated like any other tortious harm to any servant of the plaintiff.

[51] The District of Columbia became the first jurisdiction to permit a wife to recover for loss of her husband's consortium. Hitaffer v. Argonne Co., 183 F.2d 811 (D.C. Cir. 1950). Remarkably, the expansion of consortium recovery to wives developed gradually only over the last quarter century. For the basis for debate, see Millington v. Southeastern Elevator Co., 239 N.E.2d 897 (N.Y. 1968), in which the New York high court by a 4-3 vote permitted a wife to recover for loss of consortium. Some courts have held that denying a wife a consortium action would be unconstitutional.

tortious harm to her spouse has led to an impairment of what was a fulfilling and strong relationship.[52] Further, the conduct of the initially injured party may affect consortium recovery because most jurisdictions view the consortium action as derivative — arising out of the underlying negligence action.

The current debate involves the extent to which a consortium action should expand beyond spouses. Assume T, the hypothetical accident victim, has three young children. Should his children recover for loss of parental consortium? Or, if T's child is tortiously injured, should T be able to recover for loss of consortium? Finally, if T and P are not legally married, but cohabiting, should P be able to recover her loss of consortium as if legally married to T?

Courts have been very reluctant to expand consortium rights beyond spouses, fearing excessive liability and potential double recovery. Some courts, in order to restrict consortium recovery to spouses, have characterized the essential harm in consortium actions as loss of sexual services.[53]

Expanding consortium rights certainly expands a defendant's potential liability, often substantially. For example, several minor children may seek recovery for loss of consortium if such a right is permitted, while only one other person is compensated in the context of spousal consortium. Permitting a parent an action for loss of a child's consortium does not pose such a broad expansion of liability, however. The fear of double recovery, while legitimate, is a rather unpersuasive excuse for restricting recovery to spouses because the spouse context itself raises substantial concerns about potential collusion or double recovery.[54]

There has been some recent movement toward expanding consortium recovery to include parents and children. As is the case with most line-drawing, charges of arbitrariness are invited in jurisdictions restricting the consortium action to spouses. Critics note that limiting recovery based on "foreseeability" cannot be a valid basis for the limitation to spouses because when a family member is seriously injured, a child or parent will suffer loss of companionship along with a spouse. Courts expanding consortium rights have noted the inconsistency of permitting a spousal action while

---

[52] *See* 2 Dan B. Dobbs, LAW OF REMEDIES, § 8.1(5), at 402 (2d ed. 1993) (noting the propriety of evidence showing such things as "reduced sexual companionship," the inability to "engage in sports or social activities as they did before," and evidence of new negative personality traits caused by the injury).

[53] *See* Borer v. American Airlines, 563 P.2d 858 (Cal. 1977) (denying an action to the victim's nine children) and Baxter v. Superior Court, 563 P.2d 871 (Cal. 1977) (denying a parent's right to recover for loss of consortium).

[54] This is particularly true where the party seeking consortium damages has an emotional distress claim as well.

denying an action by parents or children,[55] especially in light of the fact that parents and children are permitted to recover for wrongful death.[56]

Cohabitants, including "significant others" and "life companions," have been refused consortium rights, with courts expressing concerns about expansive liability, fraudulent claims and a purported state interest in marriage.[57]

Loss of consortium presents several challenges. Can a workable and consistent standard for consortium recovery be found? Would a solution be to broaden the class of those who may recover while constricting damage recovery? Should consortium recovery be abolished entirely because it has wandered so far from its initial common-law roots? Is there a modern justification for consortium recovery such that a tortfeasor who does not have to pay these damages escapes from paying fully for all the harm caused?

[C] *Wrongful Death*[58]

Returning to the hypothetical that began the discussion of loss of consortium,[59] assume that T *died* as a result of D's negligence. What legal recourse, if any, is available to T's wife and minor children in this instance? By *statute*, all jurisdictions permit them an action against D for the negligently inflicted wrongful death of T. As with loss of consortium, the principal issues deal with *who* may properly recover for wrongful death and *what* may properly be recovered.

Common law did not permit family members an action against someone who tortiously killed another family member. And because the victim died (as opposed to being just seriously injured), there was no basis for a loss of consortium action by the victim's spouse. Finally, at common law, no action vested in the victim's heirs to recover for the harm they suffered due to the tortiously caused death of the victim.[60] Thus, it was D's good

---

[55] *See, e.g.*, Ferriter v. Daniel O'Connell's Sons, 413 N.E.2d 690 (Mass. 1980) (the first state high court to recognize consortium recovery beyond spouses).

[56] Wrongful death recovery, however, tends to be limited to pecuniary losses. *See infra* § [C].

[57] *See, e.g.*, Elden v. Sheldon, 758 P.2d 582 (Cal. 1988). This prohibition applies regardless of evidence of a "stable and significant" relationship and where the option of marriage is unavailable. For example, in *Elden*, the majority's refusal to permit a consortium action absent a legal marriage has the effect of prohibiting recovery by those in gay or lesbian relationships due to a state bar against same gender marriage.

[58] *See generally* 1 Stuart M. Speiser et al., RECOVERY FOR WRONGFUL DEATH AND INJURY (3d ed. 1992); Wex S. Malone, *The Genesis of Wrongful Death,* 17 Stan. L. Rev. 1043 (1965).

[59] *See supra* § [B].

[60] Justification for the common law view that the death of a human being could not be complained of as a tortious injury is hard to find. Justice Harlan suggested that the explanation for this "legal anomaly" was that, at the time the rule arose, any intentional or negligent

fortune when her tortious conduct led to the victim's death, because the victim's action died with the victim.

The anomaly created by the common law rejection of wrongful death actions was changed in 1846 by Parliament's adoption of Lord Campbell's Act. This Act had enormous influence in the United States, and now every state has enacted some sort of wrongful death statute. The parameters of these laws vary.

[1] Who May Recover

Under any wrongful death statute, the plaintiff is suing for loss suffered due to the tortiously inflicted death of a close relative. A key issue becomes who is a "close relative" for wrongful death recovery purposes. Because wrongful death is purely statutory, an action may be brought only by those permitted to do so pursuant to the jurisdiction's wrongful death statute. A surviving spouse, parents and children are typically permitted to bring an action. Some statutes exclude other possible dependents such as siblings or stepchildren who have not been legally adopted.[61]

[2] Recoverable Damages

Initially nearly all wrongful death statutes limited wrongful death recovery to *pecuniary* losses. The wrongful death plaintiff could only recover those relatively concrete monetary losses that the plaintiff would have received from the deceased. Strictly interpreting the limitation to pecuniary losses led to minimal recovery for the death of the elderly, the young and those not working outside the home.[62]

Today, most jurisdictions permit designated dependents to recover lost support and other benefits arising from the tortious death.[63] Even working within the pecuniary damage limitation, plaintiffs have been able increasingly to recover the replacement value of the services provided by the decedent. Some jurisdictions have expanded the scope of recoverable damages to include loss of consortium-type damages such as loss of companionship and affection. Some states have accomplished this by pretending that these are pecuniary losses. Others have been more forthright,

---

killing was a felony that led to death and property forfeiture, leaving no assets to compensate the victim's heirs. Moragne v. States Marine Lines, Inc., 398 U.S. 375, 382 (1970).

[61] The ability of a state's wrongful death statute to exclude classes of potential beneficiaries can be limited by constitutional concerns, such as the denial of equal protection. But this is rare.

[62] *See* Jane Goodman et al., *Money, Sex, and Death: Gender Bias in Wrongful Death Damage Awards,* 25 Law & Soc'y Rev. 263 (1991).

[63] This is often called the "loss-to-the survivor" approach, because the focus is on the dependent/plaintiff's loss. Several jurisdictions use a different approach — the "loss-to-the-estate" approach — which requires a determination of the deceased's likely lifetime earnings less the amount the decedent would have spent on herself. Here, the inheritance interest is protected. *See* 2 Dan B. Dobbs, LAW OF REMEDIES, § 8.3, at 421.

permitting recovery while acknowledging the non-pecuniary nature of consortium-type damages. The clear majority of jurisdictions disallow recovery in a wrongful death action for the plaintiff's grief, sorrow and upset arising from the tortiously inflicted death.

[3] Proof Problems

Wrongful death recovery is never automatic, even by one clearly permitted to bring the action under a wrongful death statute. The plaintiff must prove with some degree of certainty the losses suffered from the tortious death. Calculating these damages is not easy and is sometimes extraordinarily challenging.

How is the loss to be proved? The plaintiff must establish the relevant time period for support, typically the lesser of the decedent's life expectancy before death and that of the beneficiary. The focus is on the value of the support that would have been provided the plaintiff as well as the value of lost services. Clearly, all of the deceased's lost wages would not be recoverable since not all of the wages would go to the plaintiff. Because the focus is on the loss to the plaintiff, the plaintiff's own economic state is only relevant as it relates to the amount of support likely to go to the plaintiff. The relationship of the plaintiff and decedent is highly relevant to this calculation, as is the character of the decedent (his propensity toward generosity or stinginess, for example). Delving into such matters can make discovery something of a soap opera, especially where relations were strained between the plaintiff and the decedent.

The death of a minor child has presented special challenges. It is extremely difficult to predict what pecuniary benefits would have accrued to the surviving heirs had the child lived. The decedent's parents may try to claim that their child would have grown up to be a highly paid corporate executive, a movie star, a professional athlete, or an attorney who would have provided generous monetary parental support. Yet, the jury cannot base damages on pure speculation. Plaintiffs need to provide factual support for claim of damages. The educational level of the plaintiffs, the career paths of other family members, and similar considerations are admissible in the plaintiffs' effort to establish damages.

In those jurisdictions that limit wrongful death awards to pecuniary damages, recovery by the plaintiff parents is limited to the pecuniary value of the parents' loss. Further, any such award must take into account the amount of money the parents would have had to spend to feed, clothe and educate the deceased child. Under this approach to damages, it could be argued that if the pecuniary damages limitation is strictly followed, the defendant's negligence has spared the parents significant expense.[64] Some

---

[64] *See* Selders v. Armentrout, 207 N.W.2d 686, 688-689 (Neb. 1973), in which the court noted: "To limit damages for the death of a child to the monetary value of the services

jurisdictions have avoided this result by giving a broad reading to "pecuniary" in this context,[65] while others have moved beyond the pecuniary damage limitation and permit recovery of loss of consortium-type damages.

[4] Defenses

The effect of the wrongful death plaintiff's negligence or that of the decedent may affect wrongful death recovery. Assume that P, X's mother, is suing D for the wrongful death of X. Assume, too, that a jury finds that P was at fault for not supervising X more closely. What effect, if any, does this have on P's wrongful death recovery? As the wrongful death plaintiff, P's own fault affects her recovery, either wholly barring it or, depending on the jurisdiction, reducing it in proportion to her fault.[66]

The situation can get even more complicated. Assume that X, the deceased child, contributed to his own death. Should this affect P's recovery? Because wrongful death actions seek compensation for the loss to the family unit, it might seem at first blush that the decedent's conduct is unrelated to the wrongful death heir's recovery. But such is not the case in most states. In the majority of jurisdictions, the action is treated as *derivative* of the decedent's tort action, and the deceased's fault affects the wrongful death heir's recovery. Thus, in contributory negligence jurisdictions, the wrongful death plaintiff's action is barred, while in comparative fault states recovery is reduced by the deceased's percentage of fault.[67] Accordingly, if a jury found X to have negligently contributed to his death, his mother's wrongful death action would either be barred or her recovery reduced, depending on the jurisdiction, even if she was without fault herself.

[D] *Survival Actions*

Survival actions need to be distinguished from recovery for wrongful death. Although survival actions, like wrongful death actions, are created by statute, they serve a very different function. A survival action is the continuation of the *decedent's* action against the tortfeasor.[68] As such it

---

which the next of kin could reasonably have expected to receive during his minority less the reasonable expense of maintaining and educating him stamps almost all modern children as worthless in the eyes of the law. In fact, if the rule was literally followed, the average child would have a negative worth."

[65] In Green v. Bittner, 424 A.2d 210 (N.J. 1980), the jury took the pecuniary damage limitation quite literally and returned a verdict of no damages to the parents in the case of a high school student's death. The court remanded, stating pecuniary damages for such things as loss of the child's companionship as the parents age, as well as the pecuniary value of the lost advice and guidance the child would have provided to her parents, should have been awarded in the wrongful death action.

[66] *See infra* Chapter 15.

[67] *See infra* Chapter 15.

[68] At common law most tort actions ended when either party died. As noted in the wrongful death discussion, this led to the anomalous situation where the defendant was often pleased by the passing of the plaintiff. Statutes have changed this unseemly result and now neither the death of the defendant nor the plaintiff terminates most tort actions.

does not give rise to new legal claims; it simply continues a pre-existing one. The action is brought by the administrator, executor or personal representative of the decedent's estate. As the continuation of the decedent's action, the representative can, in most jurisdictions, recover any damages that the decedent would have recovered if she had lived. Some jurisdictions limit what can be recovered in a survival action, such as by barring recovery of decedent's pain and suffering or by prohibiting punitive damages under the view that such damages only confer a windfall on the heirs. Any defenses that could have been asserted against the decedent if she had lived can be raised against the person bringing the survival action.

Where the defendant's tortious conduct leads to the instantaneous death of the plaintiff, there is no survival action available to the defendant's estate. Thus, even after the adoption of survival statutes, there remains a benefit to the defendant when her tortious conduct results in the immediate death of the plaintiff.

In most cases, however, the decedent suffered damages prior to her death and, thus, there is a basis for a survival action. The tortious conduct need not lead to the victim's death for there to be a survival action. The tortiously caused pre-death injuries are the basis for the survival claim, and they may be wholly independent from a subsequent death. For example, D negligently injures P's car and P, who is 90 years old. P sues D, but dies of natural causes unrelated to the accident before the trial. Under a survival statute, P's action against D will continue.[69] There is no basis for a wrongful death action here, however.

Virtually all jurisdictions permit both survival actions and wrongful death actions by statute. Where the tortious conduct contributes to the victim's death, often both actions are brought simultaneously. The survival action typically permits the estate to recover the decedent's medical expenses, lost wages and, perhaps, her pain and suffering.[70] The post-death losses are recoverable in the wrongful death action by the appropriate statutory heirs for the losses they suffer from the tortiously caused death.

---

[69] Similarly, if D dies before trial, her estate remains liable to P for the negligently inflicted harm per the survival statute.

[70] The survival action can be passed by the decedent's will to whomever the testator selects. It need not be limited to statutory heirs, as is the case in wrongful death actions.

§ 10.04 NEGLIGENTLY INFLICTED ECONOMIC LOSS[71]

[A] *Overview*

The final section about duty limited by the type of harm looks at negligently inflicted pure economic loss. Here the defendant's unreasonable conduct has caused neither physical injury nor property damage; the plaintiff's sole harm is economic. The overwhelming majority of jurisdictions refuse to find a duty in these cases.

It is important to understand the focus of this section: the degree to which a plaintiff should be able to recover for negligently inflicted pure economic injury. Where a defendant's negligence causes physical injury from which the plaintiff suffers economic loss (such as lost wages) or causes property damage from which flows economic harm (such as lost profits), there is no duty debate about recovery for economic loss. Economic loss following tortiously caused personal injury or property damage is parasitic and, thus, readily recoverable.[72]

After an examination of economic loss in general, this section turns to a context which has given rise to substantial litigation in the economic loss context: accountant malpractice. Courts have developed several different approaches to determine when an accountant should be liable in negligence to non-clients. As will be discussed, the problem posed in the accountant setting also arises in other contexts, such as where an attorney negligently drafts a will to the detriment of an intended beneficiary.

[B] *Pure Economic Loss*

D negligently maneuvers a ship. The ship crashes into a bridge, damaging the bridge badly enough that it has to be closed for months. The collision causes D's ship to spill much of its cargo, a powerful pesticide, into the water.

The impact of D's negligence is far-reaching. The city-owned bridge stands in disrepair. Hundreds of motorists, caught in traffic jams caused by the bridge closure, lose hours of work. Others have greatly extended commutes. Businesses near the bridge suffer lost profits not only from being forced to evacuate the day of the collision, but into the future as access

---

[71] *See generally* Richard Abel, *Should Tort Law Protect Property Against Accidental Loss?*, 23 San Diego L. Rev. 79 (1986); James M. Dente, *Negligence Liability to All Foreseeable Parties for Pure Economic Harm: The Final Assault Upon the Citadel*, 21 Wake Forest L. Rev. 587 (1986); Fleming James, Jr., *Limitations on Liability for Economic Loss Caused by Negligence: A Pragmatic Appraisal*, 25 Vand. L. Rev. 43 (1972); Ann O'Brien, *Limited Recovery Rule as a Dam: Preventing a Flood of Litigation for Negligent Infliction of Pure Economic Loss*, 31 Ariz. L. Rev. 959 (1989); Robert L. Rabin, *Tort Recovery for Negligently Inflicted Economic Loss: A Reassessment*, 37 Stan. L. Rev. 1513 (1985).

[72] To this extent, economic loss parallels emotional distress, as the latter is readily recoverable when flowing from negligently inflicted personal injury. *See supra* § 10.01.

to them is impaired due to the closed bridge. Soon business is so poor in the affected area that workers are laid off. D's cargo badly pollutes the waterway. Neither commercial nor recreational fishing can occur for several years. Some other ships in the area suffer body damage from the pesticide, requiring that they be taken out of commission for repair. Which, if any, of these potential plaintiffs should be permitted to recover in a negligence action against D?

Under the general rule, there may be no negligence recovery by those suffering purely economic losses. Thus, the businesses losing profits, the workers losing their jobs, and the delayed drivers losing business deals are all barred from recovery because there is no legally recognized duty owed by D. Conversely, those suffering some property damage, no matter how minor — the ship owners and the bridge owner — may recover their economic losses flowing from the property damage caused by D.

The rule that bars recovery for negligently inflicted pure economic loss has been amazingly durable.[73] While courts eliminated contractual privity in defining tort duties in negligence cases[74] and expanded the scope of recovery for emotional distress,[75] there has been little movement away from the rule that there is no duty to avoid inflicting pure economic loss.[76] What has justified this no-duty rule? Why are plaintiffs who would clearly recover for personal injury or property damage left uncompensated when their loss is purely economic? Are there any workable alternatives?

Courts have suggested several reasons to justify the no-duty rule. Some are more compelling than others. The most persuasive justification for the no-duty rule arises from a concern about potential liability out of proportion to fault. Where a defendant has committed an intentional or wilful act, courts expand the scope of liability even in the context of pure economic loss. Where the defendant has been merely unreasonable, however, courts hesitate to impose liability of potentially enormous magnitude on the defendant. As the bridge hypothetical illustrates, the specter of crushing liability can be a genuine policy concern in the economic loss context.

---

[73] This no-duty rule dates back to English cases from the 1800s. It was solidified in the United States by Justice Holmes' majority opinion in Robins Dry Dock & Repair v. Flint, 275 U.S. 303 (1927).

[74] *See, e.g.*, MacPherson v. Buick, 111 N.E. 1050 (N.Y. 1916), in which Judge Cardozo permitted negligence recovery for personal injury by a person not in privity of contract with the defendant. *See infra* § 17.01[C].

[75] All jurisdictions currently recognize a duty to avoid negligent infliction of pure emotional harm, although the requirements for establishing this duty differ widely. *See supra* § 10.01.

[76] One court explained that the property damage requirement has "stood against a sea of change in the tort law. Retention of this conspicuous bright-line rule . . . is a strong testament both to the rule's utility and to the absence of a more 'conceptually pure' substitute." Louisiana ex rel. Guste v. M/V Testbank, 752 F.2d 1019, 1023 (5th Cir. 1985).

Courts have proffered other justifications for the no-duty rule as well. These include a lack of deterrence flowing from the imposition of liability due to the unpredictable nature of the harm and the notion that it is preferable for plaintiffs to self-insure to protect themselves from the limited losses they suffer than to require the defendant to insure against potentially vast damage claims. Further, there is a benefit to litigants and to the tort system to have clearly defined, bright-line rules. Finally, a few courts have articulated concerns about the difficulty in measuring damages.[77]

The no-duty result has not gone without criticism. Those who favor a relaxation of the no-duty rule contend that there would be greater fairness (*i.e.,* as between the innocent plaintiff and the negligent defendant, the latter should bear the losses inflicted); fewer accidents, as tort liability would deter carelessness; and more simplicity, because duty in the economic loss context would be treated like it is in most other areas of negligence law.

Critics of the no-duty rule are surely correct in pointing out the apparent capriciousness of a system that permits full recovery where there has been a minor amount of property damage yet denies any recovery where there has been foreseeable economic loss. For example, a business that suffered a small amount of smoke damage due to the defendant's negligence can recover its lost profits while a neighboring business, spared smoke damage but experiencing an identical amount of lost business due to the defendant's negligence, will recover nothing. One commentator explained:

> A rule which permits compensation only for physical harm and economic losses which accompany it will inevitably be capricious in operation, showering its benefits along the path of physical causation and withholding them elsewhere. Thus, when the power supply of a number of businesses is interrupted, only those sustaining physical damage will be permitted to recover economic losses, even if all suffer the same total loss. Perhaps more important, the nonliability rule frequently does not achieve a broad distribution of losses. In some cases, the economic consequences of a negligent act are largely borne, not by the whole community, but by a few businesses or individuals. These injured parties may be incapable of absorbing or passing on their losses, causing further economic and social dislocation. While it is undesirable to place a crushing burden of liability on a negligent defendant, it is worse to leave such a burden on a few non-negligent plaintiffs.[78]

---

[77] This rationale, however, rings particularly hollow. Though admittedly economic losses, such as lost profits, can be challenging to appraise, they surely pose less demands than emotional harm damages, including pain and suffering, that are readily recoverable as parasitic to physical injury.

[78] *See* Recent Cases, *Torts—Interference With Business or Occupation—Commercial Fishermen Can Recover Profits Lost as a Result of Negligently Caused Oil Spill—Union Oil Co. v. Oppen,* 88 Harv. L. Rev. 444, 450 (1974).

Even advocates of a broadened duty in the context of pure economic loss recognize the need to put limits on the potential scope of recovery. Other tort doctrines, such as proximate cause and damage rules are suggested as methods of keeping liability limited to its proper scope. Even the element of duty itself can be reconfigured to permit a broader, though not excessive, recovery. The challenge is to design a rule that permits recovery for particularly meritorious claims while barring recovery for others.

A few jurisdictions have tried to meet the challenge by limiting duty to "particularly foreseeable" plaintiffs. One court, for example, found a duty owing to an airline that suffered substantial economic loss when it was forced to shut down. The defendant's negligence caused a fire that created a danger to all within the airline's terminal. The court, in permitting the airline to recover its lost profits and other economic losses, found the plaintiff to be part of "an identifiable class of plaintiffs," making them "particularly foreseeable."[79] The court rejected recovery by other foreseeable plaintiffs, such as passengers who, because of cancelled flights, lost business deals. According to the court, a duty is owed only to members of an "identifiable class of plaintiffs . . . [that is] particularly foreseeable in terms of the type of persons or entities comprising the class, the certainty or predictability of their presence, the approximate numbers of those in the class, as well as the type of economic expectations disrupted."[80]

Even this expanded duty is subject to claims of arbitrariness, ambiguity and unpredictability. How are the merely foreseeable plaintiffs, who are to be denied recovery, to be distinguished from the particularly foreseeable plaintiffs, who will be permitted to pursue a negligence action? For example, in the ship collision hypothetical, which of the plaintiffs, if any, would be "particularly foreseeable?" The businesses near the bridge? The businesses that depend on the bridge for customers? There has been little movement toward this "particularly foreseeable" standard.[81]

---

[79] People Express Airlines, Inc. v. Consolidated Rail Corp., 495 A.2d 107 (N.J. 1985). The defendant had created an emergency response plan showing that, in the case of fire, the plaintiff airline's terminal would need to be evacuated.

[80] *Id.* at 116.

[81] Perhaps the most permissive recovery for negligently caused pure economic loss can be found in the controversial case of J'Aire Corp. v. Gregory, 598 P.2d 60 (Cal. 1979). In *J'Aire,* the plaintiff was the owner of an airport restaurant that had to be closed while the defendant contractor renovated the airport's heating and air conditioning system. Due to an unreasonable delay by the defendant, plaintiff's restaurant had to remain closed longer than anticipated, resulting in substantial lost profits. The California Supreme Court, recognizing the plaintiff's claim for "negligent interference with prospective economic advantage," permitted the plaintiff to proceed against the defendant contractor despite the lack of contractual privity. This decision has not been widely followed and has been criticized. *See* Gary Schwartz, *Economic Loss in American Tort Law: The Examples of J'Aire and of Products Liability,* 23 San Diego L. Rev. 37 (1986).

[C] *Liability of Negligent Information Suppliers*[82]

Much of the litigation in the economic loss arena has arisen in the context of negligent information suppliers. Where an accountant, auditor, or other supplier of information is negligent, the typical injury is economic. Notwithstanding strict limits on duty in the economic loss context generally, courts have recognized an exception where the plaintiff and defendant have a special relationship. Often this is evidenced by contract, as where a company hires an accountant to review its books. There is no question that the accountant owes a duty to the hiring party. If the accountant fails to conform to professional custom,[83] he is liable in negligence to the injured plaintiff, even though the plaintiff's harm is solely economic.

The controversy in this economic loss context is the degree to which *third parties* harmed by the defendant's negligence are owed a duty. Assume that Company X hires accounting firm D to conduct an audit so that Company X can attract investors. P, relying on D's audit showing the secure financial status of Company X, invests in Company X. Because of D's negligence, the audit report is wrong. Company X is not solvent, notwithstanding the contrary showing in the audit report. Instead, Company X is in such precarious financial shape that it declares bankruptcy shortly after P's investment. P seeks to recover her large financial loss from D. To what extent, if any, should P, who was not in privity of contract with D, have a valid claim? This scenario, and others closely related to it,[84] have spawned much litigation, commentary and debate.

All courts recognize that duty in this context may extend beyond privity of contract. Yet there is great divergence beyond this point. Some courts enlarge duty beyond privity only minimally, while others support a far more expansive duty. Most courts have selected among three primary approaches: the narrowest, which extends a duty only to those who are virtually in privity with the defendant ("quasi-privity"); the middle approach, which extends a duty to those the defendant intended to influence; and the broadest, which extends a duty to those who could be foreseeably injured. As one court summarized:

---

[82] *See generally* Mark F. Boveri and Brent E. Marshall, *The Enlarging Scope of Auditors' Liability to Relying Third Parties,* 59 Notre Dame L. Rev. 281 (1983); Thomas L. Gossman, *The Fallacy of Expanding Accountants' Liability,* 1988 Colum. Bus. L. Rev. 213; John A. Siliciano, *Negligent Accounting and the Limits of Instrumental Tort Reform,* 86 Mich. L. Rev. 1929 (1988); Howard B. Weiner, *Common Law Liability of the Certified Public Accountant for Negligent Misrepresentation,* 20 San Diego L. Rev. 233 (1983).

[83] In these cases, the defendant (accountant, attorney, etc.) is usually held to a professional standard of care, which insulates the defendant from negligence liability as long as the defendant conforms to the custom of the profession. *See supra* Chapter 7.

[84] Though most of the cases involve audit reports, the principles that are discussed in this section apply to other professional information suppliers as well, such as architects, engineers, title insurers, weighers and, even to a large measure, attorneys.

The traditional rule is that the auditor's duty is owed only to those with whom he is in privity or to those who are known beneficiaries at the time of the auditor's undertaking. This rule is commonly attributed to an opinion by Chief Judge Cardozo in *Ultramares* . . . . A second rule has been expressed in Section 552 of the Restatement (Second) of Torts. Under the Restatement, liability is extended to a known and intended class of beneficiaries . . . . A third rule is that the auditor's duty is owed to those whom the auditor should reasonably foresee as recipients from the company of the financial statements for authorized business purposes.[85]

Each of these approaches will now be explored.

[1] Quasi-Privity

The high court of New York, in two famous opinions authored by Judge Cardozo, formulated the quasi-privity approach still used by many jurisdictions today. The first case, *Glanzer v. Shepard*,[86] illustrates when a third party may recover, and the second, *Ultramares v. Touche*,[87] exemplifies when a third party may not.

In *Glanzer*, a bean seller contracted with the weigher-defendant to weigh and certify a shipment of beans for sale to the buyer-plaintiff. The defendant-weigher made arrangements with the buyer-plaintiff to weigh the beans on the pier prior to delivery and, though paid by the bean seller, the defendant supplied a copy of the weight certificate directly to the buyer. When it was later discovered that the beans weighed less than certified due to the defendant's negligence, the New York high court permitted recovery by the purchaser because, although not in contractual privity with the defendant, "the end and aim of the transaction" was for the plaintiff's benefit.

Less than a decade later, the *Glanzer* extension of duty beyond privity was narrowly construed in *Ultramares*. In *Ultramares*, the accountant-defendant supplied 32 copies of an inaccurate audit report to its client. The defendant knew that the audit report was to be distributed to creditors, investors and suppliers, although the specific identities of those receiving the information were unknown to the defendant. Recovery for negligence was not allowed in part because the audit could have been used for numerous different transactions, and the court was concerned about crushing liability. The court explained: "If liability for negligence exists, a thoughtless slip or blunder, the failure to detect theft or forgery beneath the cover

---

[85] Rosenblum v. Adler, 461 A.2d 138, 142 (N.J. 1983). In *Rosenblum*, the New Jersey Supreme Court adopted the broad "foreseeability" rule. Another, more recent case, which provides a thorough analysis of the three approaches is Bily v. Arthur Young & Co., 834 P.2d 745 (Cal. 1992), in which the California Supreme Court opted for the Restatement approach. Even within the three principal categories there remain jurisdictional distinctions.

[86] 135 N.E. 275 (N.Y. 1922).

[87] 174 N.E. 441 (N.Y. 1931).

of deceptive entries, may expose accountants to a liability in an indeterminate amount for an indeterminate time to an indeterminate class." The court distinguished *Glanzer* by noting that in *Glanzer* the "bond [between the plaintiff and defendant] was so close as to approach that of privity," while in *Ultramares*, the audit was primarily for the client's benefit and "only incidentally or collaterally" for investors like the plaintiff.

New York and other jurisdictions have adhered to this narrow quasi-privity approach.[88] In the 1980s, as some jurisdictions moved to the Restatement approach and as a few adopted the foreseeability standard, the New York high court reaffirmed its allegiance to the quasi-privity approach.[89]

[2] *Restatement Section 552*

The Restatement has broadened the scope of duty in the jurisdictions that have adopted it. Restatement § 552 proposes an extension of liability to a limited group of persons for whose guidance the defendant intended to supply the information. This is an enlargement of the quasi-privity rule because it no longer demands that the plaintiff be specifically identified to the defendant. The Restatement rule only requires that the plaintiff be a member of a limited group to which the accountant-defendant knows the client plans to give the audit report in an effort to have influence. Further, liability for negligent misrepresentations is limited to the transactions the accountant "intends, or knows that the recipient intends, to influence, or to a substantially similar transaction."[90] In addition to the many jurisdictions that have moved from the restrictive quasi-privity approach by adopting the Restatement approach, at least one has moved from the broader foreseeability approach to the middle ground of the Restatement.[91]

---

[88] A few courts have broadened the *Glanzer* "end and aim" evaluation of the transaction slightly to include situations where supplying information to a third party was "one of the ends and aims" of the audit. John A. Siliciano, *Negligent Accounting and the Limits of Instrumental Tort Reform,* 86 Mich. L. Rev. 1929, 1938 (1988).

[89] In Credit Alliance Corp. v. Arthur Anderson & Co., 483 N.E.2d 110 (N.Y. 1985), the court determined: "Before accountants may be held liable in negligence to noncontractual parties who rely to their detriment on inaccurate financial reports, certain prerequisites must be satisfied: (1) the accountant must have been aware that the financial reports were to be used for a particular purpose or purposes; (2) in the furtherance of which a known party or parties was intended to rely; and (3) there must have been some conduct on the part of the accountants linking them to that party or parties, which evinces the accountants' understanding of that party or parties' reliance." *Id.* at 118. The third prong, the linkage requirement, may have created a standard even more restrictive than that laid out in *Ultramares*, and has been widely criticized.

[90] Restatement § 552 cmt. j.

[91] *See, e.g.*, Bily v. Arthur Young & Co., 834 P.2d 745 (Cal. 1992). Relying on the Restatement approach, the court recommended a jury instruction imposing liability on negligent information suppliers when they know with "substantial certainty that plaintiff, or the particular class of persons to which plaintiff belongs, will rely on the representation in the

[3] *Foreseeability Approach*

During the early 1980s, a few jurisdictions considered extending duty in the accounting malpractice arena to all foreseeable plaintiffs.[92] New Jersey became the first jurisdiction to move in this direction, finding a duty owing from an accountant to "foreseeable users who receive the audited statements from the business entity for a proper business purpose to influence a business decision of the user."[93] In other words, to establish a duty, the plaintiff must have received the audit directly from the accountant's client for a legitimate business purpose, and the client must have intended the audit to influence the plaintiff. The foreseeability standard expands upon the Restatement approach because the Restatement confines an auditor's duty to "foreseen plaintiffs" as opposed to those who are foreseeable.[94]

[4] Debating Which Approach is Best

An intense debate has raged on which approach is most appropriate, permitting an airing of the advantages and disadvantages of each. The debate has largely centered on the merits of the foreseeability standard versus some more limited duty.

Those favoring the foreseeability test contend that "the reasons advanced in support of the *Ultramares* and Restatement position provide no persuasive rationale for treating accountants differently from any other potential defendants whose negligence causes injury."[95] A foreseeability approach treats duty in the economic harm context as it is treated in most other negligence cases. More importantly, advocates of foreseeability contend that this approach will spur greater accuracy in audits, particularly in light of

---

course of the transactions. If others become aware of the representations and act upon it, there is no liability even though defendant should reasonably have foreseen such a possibility." *Id.* at 773.

[92] A law review article by a California appellate court justice that advocated a foreseeability approach was quite influential. The author argued for the foreseeability-based approach, noting that it is "the same economically sound standard applied to negligence liability in virtually ever other context." Howard B. Weiner, *Common Law Liability of the Certified Public Accountant for Negligent Misrepresentation,* 20 San Diego L. Rev. 233, 259 (1983).

[93] Rosenblum v. Adler, 461 A.2d 138, 153 (N.J. 1983). The court broadened the scope of duty in this case even though the plaintiff could have recovered under the Restatement approach, and perhaps even under the quasi-privity approach. *See also* Citizens State Bank v. Timm, Schimidt & Co., 335 N.W.2d 361 (Wis. 1983) (adopting foreseeability approach unless enumerated public policy factors militate against liability).

[94] Even the New Jersey approach falls short of a true foreseeability standard as it restricts recovery to those who receive the audit directly from the company for a proper business purpose and to cases where the company disseminated the information in order to influence the plaintiff.

[95] Howard B. Weiner, *Common Law Liability of the Certified Public Accountant for Negligent Misrepresentation,* 20 San Diego L. Rev. 233, 259 (1983).

the conflicting demands on accountants. As one proponent of the foreseeability approach explained:

> What clients of auditing services want above all is not a careful audit but an unqualified opinion to satisfy investors, lenders, and others concerned with the clients' financial health . . . . The accountant is thus caught between client pressure to produce an unqualified opinion and the moral and ethical obligation to maintain high standards of care and thoroughness. It is vital that accountants resolve the conflict in favor of careful auditing . . . . Holding negligent accountants liable to those who reasonably and foreseeably rely to their detriment on defective audit reports compensates innocent victims, encourages greater care in the performance of audits, reinforces the independence of accountants from their clients, and avoids the misallocation of capital resources, all to the benefit of the accounting profession, those who rely on its services, and the public at large.[96]

Advocates of the foreseeability standard have also noted that accountants are best positioned to spread the costs of any negligence for which they are found liable through malpractice insurance, and that they are already protected more than most other defendants in light of the professional negligence standard of care used in these cases. Additionally, the argument continues, the plaintiffs' burden in an accounting malpractice action is significant in light of their obligation to prove justifiable and detrimental reliance on the defendants' negligently prepared report. Finally, some commentators have suggested that the strict limits on accountant liability are no longer justified in light of the modern role of auditors, which is principally that of providing financial statements for the use and benefit of outside businesses or lenders.[97]

---

[96] Bily v. Arthur Young, 834 P.2d 745, 781-83 (Cal.1992) (Kennard, J., dissenting). Justice Kennard added that defendants could avoid liability by placing disclaimers in their opinions, though they do not like to do so because it reduces the value of the audit. She explained that they should "not be permitted to have it both ways: they should not profit from the value produced by anticipated third party reliance and yet escape all responsibility when their negligence results in injury to relying third parties." *Id.* at 786. In addition, the high court of New Jersey justified its adoption of a foreseeability approach because of its belief that such a standard would encourage accountants "to exercise greater care leading to greater diligence in conducting audits." Rosenblum v. Adler, 461 A.2d 138, 152 (N.J. 1983).

[97] *See, e.g.*, Howard B. Weiner, *Common Law Liability of the Certified Public Accountant for Negligent Misrepresentation*, 20 San Diego L. Rev. 233, 250 (1983), in which the author states: "At an earlier time the primary responsibility of an auditor was to the owner of a business to report on the operation of that business and to detect fraud and embezzlement by the company's employees. However, as businesses needed capital beyond what the owners could supply, auditors were called upon to provide the lending and investing public with independent opinions on how fairly financial statements had been made . . . . Today, the audit of public companies is largely for the benefit of third party users."

Despite the persuasiveness of many of the pro-foreseeability arguments, there has been little movement toward a foreseeability standard. The predominant justification for special limits on the scope of duty for information suppliers arises from concern about excessive liability out of proportion to fault. There are a large number of persons who may come into contact with the defendants' reports and rely on them. More critically, because of the very nature of the defendants' product — financial information in the form of reports — there is an inability of the defendant to limit effectively its dissemination. Further, some commentators doubt that increasing the scope of liability would lead to greater care on the part of accountants. There are already competitive forces at work pressuring the defendant to perform well. Additionally, the nature of an audit requires the defendant to rely heavily on information provided by the client. Limited recovery also encourages plaintiffs, who are often sophisticated investors, to contract for their own audits before making investments, and forces investors to diversify their investments. Finally, some writers have noted an existing accountant malpractice insurance crisis that "threatens the existence of small and large accounting firms."[98] The California Supreme Court justified its rejection of the foreseeability rule that had been used in California for the previous six years as follows:

> [A] foreseeability rule applied in this context inevitably produces large numbers of expensive and complex lawsuits of questionable merit as scores of investors and lenders seek to recoup business losses. In view of the prospects of vast if not limitless liability for the "thoughtless slip or blunder," the availability of other efficient means of self-protection for a generally sophisticated class of plaintiffs, and the dubious benefits of a broad rule of liability, we opt for a more circumscribed approach.[99]

Most jurisdictions have rejected the foreseeability approach for some of these reasons. They have largely opted for the middle ground represented by the Restatement, viewing the quasi-privity test as too restrictive.[100]

[D] *Attorney Liability*

The debate about how far a duty should extend has also arisen in the context of legal malpractice.[101] As with accountants, courts have struggled to decide when an attorney's tort duty should extend to a nonclient. Courts have been even more reticent in the attorney context to expand a duty beyond privity of contract — that is, to any persons other than those who

---

[98] Thomas L. Gossman, *The Fallacy of Expanding Accountants' Liability*, 1988 Colum. Bus. L. Rev. 213, 214-15.

[99] Bily v. Arthur Young, 834 P.2d. at 767.

[100] *Id.* at 767. The California Supreme Court opted for the Restatement approach, explaining: "In so doing, we seek to deter careless audit reporting while avoiding the spectre of a level of liability that is morally and economically excessive."

[101] *See supra* § 7.04.

engaged the attorney as their counsel. In most jurisdictions the rule remains that "absent fraud or other bad faith an attorney is not liable for negligent conduct to nonclient third parties."[102] In other words, there is no duty owed to a nonclient to avoid negligently inflicted economic harm.

Some jurisdictions have permitted a limited expansion of the duty beyond clients in certain particularly compelling circumstances. Where an attorney understood that the client's intent was to benefit a third party, in some contexts that third party is permitted to sue for legal malpractice. This situation often arises in the context of wills, where an intended beneficiary is deprived of receiving that which the deceased testator intended because of the negligence of an attorney or notary.[103] The logic behind this limited exception to the rule restricting liability to clients is that if a strict privity requirement were used, there would be no one to bring an action against the negligent attorney because the person who contracted with the attorney is dead.

Beyond the will context, courts have proceeded cautiously, rarely extending duty to those not in privity. For example, if an attorney negligently prepares an opinion letter for a client, few jurisdictions would permit a legal claim by someone who foreseeably relies on the opinion letter. Much of the reluctance to expand a duty to third parties has been out of concern over the impact such liability could have on the attorney-client relationship. As the California Supreme Court noted:

> To make an attorney liable for negligent confidential advice not only to the client who enters into a transaction in reliance upon the advice but also to the other parties to the transaction with whom the client deals at arm's length would inject undesirable self-protective reservations into the attorney's counseling role . . . . The attorney's preoccupation or concern with the possibility of claims based on mere negligence . . . by any with whom his client might deal "would prevent him from devoting his entire energies to his clients' interests."[104]

A related rationale for a narrowly defined duty is that if a third party seeks to validate information, she can hire her own attorney, with whom she will be in privity.[105]

---

[102] Douglas A. Cifu, *Expanding Legal Malpractice to Nonclient Third Parties—At What Cost?*, 23 Colum. J. L. & Soc. Probs. 115 (1989).

[103] *See* Biakanja v. Irving, 320 P.2d 16 (Cal. 1958), in which an intended will beneficiary was permitted a negligence action against a notary public who failed to properly validate a will. The court provided several factors for a court to consider in determining whether a duty should extend beyond those in privity.

[104] Goodman v. Kennedy, 556 P.2d 737, 743 (Cal. 1976) (citations omitted). This concern is a longstanding one. *See* Savings Bank v. Ward, 100 U.S. 195, 200 (1879) ("[T]he obligation of the attorney is to his client and not to a third party . . .").

[105] Although this was raised as a justification for a narrow duty in the accountant context, it is far more persuasive in the attorney context. As a practical matter, a third party cannot

---

usually conduct his own audit of a company's finances and, thus, must to some extent rely on the reputation and skill of the accountant hired by the company. There is usually no impediment (other than cost, of course) to a person hiring her own attorney to determine, for example, whether there are any encumbrances on property she is considering purchasing.

CHAPTER 11

CAUSE-IN-FACT

SYNOPSIS

§ 11.01 OVERVIEW

It is generally accepted that tort liability is dependant on proof that the defendant's culpable conduct or activity was the actual cause of the plaintiff's injury.[1] The traditional and still prevalent way of characterizing this prerequisite to recovery is to require that the plaintiff prove by a preponderance of evidence that "more likely than not" the defendant's conduct was a "but for" cause of the plaintiff's injury.

However, there are increasing instances where courts may not rigorously require proof of a "but for" cause. These generally involve multiple defendants or professional misconduct in contexts where requiring definite proof would effectively immunize culpable defendants because of the difficulty of proving causation.

[1] *See generally* Wex S. Malone, *Ruminations in Cause-In-Fact*, 9 Stan. L. Rev. 60 (1956); Richard W. Wright, *Causation in Tort Law*, 73 Cal. L. Rev. 1735 (1985).

The "but for" test of causation has been supplemented and in some instances replaced by an alternative "substantial factor" test for causation. Even where "but for" remains the primary basis for determining actual causation, versions of the "substantial factor" test are used where redundant causes of a plaintiff's injury would otherwise preclude recovery under the traditional "but for" test.[2] The substantial factor test is also increasingly being utilized by courts in other instances, such as certain medical malpractice cases, where traditional "but for" causation would otherwise result in no liability.[3]

The difficulty of scientific proof of causation in environmental, medical, toxic, and product liability cases has generated vigorous and continuing debate concerning the proper method for requiring or dispensing with proof of causation.[4] Nevertheless, the notion that the defendant's conduct must not only be culpable but have a causal connection with the plaintiff's injury remains a strongly held tenet in any analysis of tort liability.

§ 11.02 "BUT FOR" ANALYSIS

The traditional and still dominant test for actual causation is the "but for" test. For the defendant to be held liable, the plaintiff must establish that but for the defendant's culpable conduct or activity the plaintiff would not have been injured.[5] For example, if A negligently fails to keep a life preserver aboard her ship and B, a passenger, would have been saved but for the absence of the life preserver, then A's negligence is a "but for" cause of B's drowning. If, however, B would have drowned or been consumed by a shark despite A's culpable conduct in not keeping a life preserver aboard, then A's negligence is not a "but for" cause.

There is a degree of artificial abstraction in the concept of "but for" causation.[6] If A is speeding and hits B, A can argue that she would have hit B even if she had been travelling at a lawful speed. Under conventional accepted causation analysis, A's negligence is not a "but for" cause if the outcome would have been the same even if A had not been negligent. On

---

[2] Actual causation is supplemented by the additional requirement that the defendant's conduct be a "proximate" or "legal" cause. The requirements for finding proximate or legal cause are discussed in Chapter 12, *infra*.

[3] *See* § 11.04[C], § 11.04[E], *infra*.

[4] *See, e.g.*, Robert L. Rabin, *Environmental Liability and the Tort System*, 24 Hous. L. Rev. 27 (1987); David Rosenburg, *The Causal Connection in Mass Exposure Cases: A Public Law Vision of the Tort System*, 97 Harv. L. Rev. 851 (1984).

[5] While the Restatement does not utilize the term "but for," it also generally requires proof that the harm would not "have been sustained even if the actor had not been negligent." *See* Restatement § 432(1).

[6] In effect "but for" analysis determines causation based on what hypothetically would occur in the absence of the defendant's negligence. *See generally* E. Wayne Thode, *The Indefensible Use of the Hypothetical Case to Determine Cause in Fact*, 46 Tex. L. Rev. 423 (1968).

the other hand, one could argue that it was the speed with which A was travelling that placed A in the position on the road where she collided with B, warranting a conclusion that A's excessive speed was the cause. Courts, however, have almost invariably rejected this analysis and relied on the conventional approach to find the speed inconsequential.

As a general rule, the plaintiff has the burden of proving "but for" causation.[7] As in civil law generally, the plaintiff must prove causation by a preponderance of the evidence. Consequently, the plaintiff must prove that more likely than not the defendant was a "but for" cause of her injury.

It is quite possible to have more than one "but for" cause for an injury.[8] For example, if A is a passenger on a bus, the bus driver may negligently fail to observe a railroad crossing. In addition, the railroad crossing guard may negligently fail to stop the bus.[9] Furthermore, the train engineer may negligently fail to see the bus. In this instance, the bus driver, the crossing guard, and the train engineer are all "but for" causes of the passenger's injury, assuming any of the three could have avoided the accident by acting reasonably. Thus, while the substantial factor test is often used in the context of multiple causes, there are certain contexts involving multiple causes appropriately resolved by the "but for" test.

§ 11.03 SUBSTANTIAL FACTOR TEST

The substantial factor test is used by many courts as a supplement to the "but for" test when redundant multiple causes would preclude liability under the "but for" analysis.[10] If A starts a fire on the left side of B's house and C starts a fire on the right side, and both fires merge concurrently and destroy B's house, then neither fire is the "but for" cause of the destruction.[11] In the absence of either fire, B's house would have been destroyed at the same time by the remaining fire. Because both causes are redundant, neither is a "but for" cause, a result that potentially precludes the plaintiff's recovery against either defendant. In order to avoid this inequitable result,

---

[7] *See* Wilder v. Eberhart, 977 F.2d 673 (1st Cir. 1992).

[8] *See, e.g.*, Hill v. Edmonds, 270 N.Y.S.2d 1020 (N.Y. App. Div. 1966), where a truck driver left his tractor truck parked without lights in the middle of the road and it was hit by a negligent motorist. The court held that where separate acts of negligence combine to directly produce a single injury each tortfeasor is responsible for the entire result.

[9] *See* Washington & Georgetown R.R. Co. v. Hickey, 166 U.S. 521 (1897).

[10] The substantial factor test was originally proposed by Jeremiah Smith, *Legal Cause in Actions of Tort*, 25 Harv. L. Rev. 102 (1911). *See generally* Robert J. Peaslee, *Multiple Causation and Damage*, 47 Harv. L. Rev. 1127 (1934), and Charles E. Carpenter, *Concurrent Causation*, 83 U. Pa. L. Rev. 941 (1935).

[11] *See* Anderson v. Minneapolis, St. P. & S. St. M. Railroad Co., 179 N.W. 45 (Minn. 1920). *See also* Corey v. Havener, 65 N.E. 69 (Mass. 1902), where two defendants independently operating motorcycles simultaneously rode by a horse, frightening the horse and injuring the plaintiff. Because each motorcycle was deemed sufficient to frighten the horse, both defendants were found substantial factors of plaintiff's harm.

many courts, including those that adhere to the "but for" test, utilize a "substantial factor" test which simply requires that the defendant materially contributed to the plaintiff's injury.[12]

Rather than alternatively instructing the jury on "but for" or "substantial factor," depending on whether there may be redundant causes, the Restatement and some jurisdictions utilize a substantial factor test to convey to the jury the requirement of both actual and "legal"[13] causation in all cases.[14] Nevertheless, the Restatement still requires that, except in redundant cause cases, "but for" should effectively be established.[15]

What constitutes a "substantial factor" is vague, and some commentators have criticized it as an unintelligible "formulation, which can scarcely be called a test."[16] Critics argue it conveys, unlike "but for," little precise meaning. The language may, however, be increasingly appealing to courts who are finding other instances beyond redundant causes, such as some medical malpractice cases, where policy concerns justify relaxing the "but for" requirement.[17] The substantial factor test has also been advanced as a mechanism arguably tightening causation requirements by eliminating liability for insignificant contributions to causation, as, for example, a

---

[12] Some commentators have argued that if both redundant causes are the result of the actions of culpable defendants, the defendants should be liable, but if one cause out of two is natural it is inappropriate to relax "but for" requirements and find a single defendant liable. *See* Robert J. Peaslee, *Multiple Causation and Damage*, 47 Harv. L. Rev. 1127 (1934). The Restatement rejects this argument and expressly applies the substantial factor test for simultaneous causes even if one or more are natural. *See* Restatement § 432(2). Query, what should be the result if defendant A burns plaintiff's house just prior to a natural fire's inevitable destruction of the house. Should the substantial factor test make A fully liable as the test would if the causes were simultaneous under principles of joint and several liability (*see* Chapter 13, *infra*), or should A be responsible only for the reduced market value of the house in anticipation of its inevitable natural destruction, which conventional "but for" analysis would appear to dictate? *See* Dillon v. Twin State Gas & Electric Co., 163 A. 111 (N.H. 1932), where utility company's liability for electrocution of boy already falling from bridge was limited to value of pain if incremental life expectation was negligible due to inevitable fatal injury from imminent impact.

[13] *See* Chapter 12, *infra*, for a discussion of legal or proximate cause.

[14] *See* Restatement §§ 431-33. *See also* Mitchell v. Gonzales, 819 P.2d 872 (Cal. 1991), where the California Supreme Court replaced a "but for" causation requirement with a "substantial factor" jury instruction.

[15] Restatement § 432. *See* note 5, *supra*.

[16] *See* Prosser & Keeton, THE LAW OF TORTS (5th ed. & supp.) at 267-69, arguing against use of substantial factor test. Such criticism ignores the utility of a criterion for establishing actual causation which enables the court to escape a single formula standard and instead more broadly evaluates the policy nuances presented by the case. *See* § 11.04[E], *infra*.

[17] *See* Herskovitz v. Group Health Coop. of Puget Sound, 664 P.2d 474 (Wash. 1983), discussed at § 11.04[C], *infra*, where plaintiff was allowed recovery under substantial factor test against physician who significantly reduced victim's chances of survival even when plaintiff failed to prove malpractice was "but for" cause of patient's death.

person who throws a match into a forest fire. It is questionable, however, that such immaterial contributions would satisfy "but for" causation in any event.[18]

§ 11.04 PROOF PROBLEMS IN CAUSE-IN-FACT

[A] *Shifting the Burden of Proving Causation*

There are rare instances when courts will shift the burden of proof by requiring defendants to prove they were not the actual cause. In *Summers v. Tice*,[19] two hunters negligently fired while the plaintiff stood in the line of fire. A shotgun pellet hit the plaintiff's eye, but it was impossible to establish which hunter had fired the pellet. Under a standard "but for" analysis, the plaintiff would be unable to prove more likely than not that either of the defendants was the cause of the injury. However, neither defendant was innocent — each having breached a duty of care to the plaintiff — and the cause of the injury was necessarily the responsibility of one of them.

In order to solve this dilemma, the *Summers v. Tice* court shifted the burden of proof to require the defendants to prove they were not the cause of the injury. If the defendants were unable to exculpate themselves, as was the case in *Summers*, both defendants would be found liable as joint tortfeasors.[20] It is important to emphasize that in *Summers* the plaintiff had the obligation to establish that both defendants had breached a duty of care. Only the burden of proof regarding causation was shifted. Neither defendant was innocent, although only one caused the injury.

The principle of *Summers v. Tice* has been adopted by the Restatement,[21] and is generally accepted where a small number of defendants have engaged in substantially simultaneous culpable conduct imposing similar risks on the victim. Courts have also required that all such wrongdoers be joined as defendants.[22]

Occasionally, jurisdictions have shifted the burden in other contexts as well. In *Haft v. Lone Palm Hotel*,[23] the court shifted the burden of proof for causation when the plaintiff, a relative of a drowned father and child, was able to prove non-compliance with a California safety statute requiring

---

[18] *Cf.* Challis Irrigation Co. v. State, 689 P.2d 230 (Idaho 1984) (exacerbating flood conditions).

[19] 199 P.2d 1 (Cal. 1948).

[20] *See infra* § 13.02.

[21] Restatement § 433B.

[22] *See* Restatement § 433B cmts. e, g, and h.

[23] 478 P.2d 465 (Cal. 1970). *See also* Smith v. Americania Motor Lodge, 113 Cal. Rptr. 771 (Cal. Ct. App. 1974), where the burden didn't shift for two drowned boys because they had negligently entered a pool with a posted "no lifeguard on duty" warning, which satisfied the safety statute.

that "lifeguard service shall be provided or signs shall be erected clearly indicating that such service is not provided" at the site of the drownings. The court justified the shift because the statute was violated and because this violation made it difficult for the plaintiff to prove the cause of the drownings.

From a moral perspective, the shifting of the burden appears appropriate in cases like *Summers* and *Haft* because the plaintiff has already established fault for each of the defendants. Accident avoidance goals are enhanced by the inability of defendants to escape liability in contexts where proving actual causation may ordinarily be impossible. The plaintiff is thus compensated by those bearing behavioral, if not causal, responsibility for the accident.

[B] *Market Share Liability*

Some influential jurisdictions have extended and modified the principle of *Summers v. Tice*[24] to create a theory based on market share liability. This theory pertains to suppliers of defective products where the plaintiff cannot prove which brand of the product she used.[25] In *Sindell v. Abbott Laboratories,*[26] daughters of women who had used the drug diethylstilbestrol ("DES") to limit the chance of miscarriage developed various reproductive diseases, including ovarian cancer, years later. The diseases could be attributed to the drug, but in many instances the plaintiff could not establish which brand of DES their mother used. The court held that once the plaintiff had established culpability, in the sense that the manufacturers had made and marketed a drug dangerous for the use proscribed, the defendant manufacturer had the burden of proving it was not a supplier of the DES the plaintiff's mother ingested.[27]

If a defendant manufacturer was unable to disprove causation, that manufacturer would be liable for its percentage of the DES market at the

---

[24] *See supra* § 11.04 [A].

[25] *See generally* Glen O. Robinson, *Multiple Causation in Tort Law: Reflection on the DES Cases,* 68 Va. L. Rev. 713 (1982).

[26] 607 P.2d 924 (Cal. 1980), *cert. denied,* 449 U.S. 912 (1980).

[27] The *Sindell* court rejected liability based on Summers v. Tice (*see* § 11.04[A], *supra*) and observed that, unlike in *Summers*, not all the defendants were joined. The court also found there was no "concert of action" among the defendants. *See* § 13.02[A], *supra*. The *Sindell* court also rejected a novel theory of "enterprise liability" that had been suggested in Hall v. E.I. du Pont de Nemours & Co., 345 F. Supp. 353 (E.D.N.Y. 1972). In *Hall*, six blasting cap manufacturers, virtually the entire blasting cap industry in the United States, were found to have adhered through their trade association to an industry-wide standard for the manufacture and design of the caps. Since the defendants jointly controlled the risk, each blasting cap company would have the burden of proving that it did not manufacture the blasting caps which caused the injuries. The *Sindell* court concluded the *Hall* approach was inapplicable to the DES industry, with its 200 manufacturers. In addition, in the DES cases there was no allegation that standards had been delegated to a trade association.

time of the mother's exposure to the product. Thus, under the "market share" approach, each defendant pays the damages its culpable conduct has inflicted proportional to its share of the market. For example, if drug company A markets 15 percent of the DES drug and drug company B markets 10 percent, drug company A will pay each plaintiff 15 percent of her damages and drug company B will pay each plaintiff 10 percent of her damages. Under *Sindell*, the plaintiffs are required to join as defendants enough drug companies so that a substantial share of the market is represented in the proceedings. Consequently, the liability of each drug company will cumulatively compensate each victim for most of her damages, even though the victim cannot establish which of the defendants provided the drugs which caused her injury.[28] Plaintiffs under this approach are able to recover when ordinary rules of causation would preclude recovery because the identity of the manufacturer which inflicted the harm in any individual case cannot be established.[29]

Significant variations exist among the jurisdictions relaxing causation requirements in DES cases. While California and New York utilize a national market share, Florida attempts to ascertain the local market shares where the plaintiffs reside.[30] Furthermore, unlike in *Sindell*, the New York court in *Hymowitz v. Eli Lilly & Co.*[31] precluded the defendant manufacturers from proving they could not have supplied the drug to a particular plaintiff. The New York court concluded that:

> [B]ecause liability here is based on the overall risk produced, and not causation in a single case, there should be no exculpation of a defendant who, although a member of the market producing DES for pregnancy use, appears not to have caused a particular plaintiff's injury. It is merely

---

28 Subsequent to *Sindell*, the California Supreme Court held that plaintiffs should remain uncompensated for any missing market share caused by defendants who are absent from the litigation. In other words, liability is several only. *See* Brown v. Superior Court, 751 P.2d 470 (Cal. 1988). Given that each defendant is only liable for the percentage of damage reflected by its market share, the rationale for the requirement that plaintiff must join enough defendants in the litigation to constitute a substantial share of the market represented appears questionable.

29 The jurisdictions which have adopted a market share theory as it relates to DES include California, Florida, New York, and Washington. Wisconsin and Michigan (by applying Summers v. Tice) have also relaxed causation requirements in DES cases. *See* note 33, *infra*. *See also* Hymowitz v. Eli Lilly & Co., 539 N.E.2d 1069 (N.Y. 1989), where the court discussed the various jurisdictional permutations of market share liability.

30 *See* Conley v. Boyle Drug Co., 570 So. 2d 275 (Fla. 1990), indicating that the market should be as narrowly defined as possible in order to better insulate defendants who did not market DES in the area where the plaintiff purchased it. *Conley* also held that a plaintiff must show due diligence in attempting to find the specific source of the DES before being allowed to bring a suit based on a market share theory. Other courts have concluded that determining local market share is not practical. *See* Hymowitz v. Eli Lilly & Co., 539 N.E.2d 1069 (N.Y. 1989).

31 539 N.E.2d 1069 (N.Y. 1989).

a windfall for a producer to escape liability solely because it manufactured a more identifiable pill, or sold only to certain drugstores.[32]

The New York opinion illustrates how market share liability is an attempt to impose equitable overall social responsibility rather than imposing liability based on the dominant tort notion that a particular defendant has caused a particular plaintiff harm.[33]

Some states have expressly rejected plaintiffs' efforts to relax causation requirements in DES cases.[34] Furthermore, most courts have been disinclined to extend the market share theory to products other than DES.[35] For example, California rejected market theory liability for the manufacturers of Salk polio vaccine. In *Sheffield v. Eli Lilly & Co.*,[36] the court noted that the hazards posed by the vaccine were not uniform among manufacturers since "the injuries did not result from the use of a drug generally defective when used for the purpose it was marketed, but because some manufacturer made and distributed a defective product."[37] In addition, the court noted the shorter lapse in time period between exposure to the vaccine and injury and the public policy of encouraging vaccinations.

From a moral perspective, market share theory can impose liability reasonably proportional to the manufacturer's responsibility for injuries. Deterrence is served by imposing liability on culpable defendants even when evidence would often preclude correlating individual manufacturers with individual victims of the product. Nevertheless, the system of market share liability remains a challenge to traditional tort notions of culpability based on causation and appears to remain a rare exception to ordinary tort causation prerequisites to recovery.

[C] *Medical Uncertainty Cases*

Should a plaintiff ever be permitted to recover for malpractice even when the plaintiff cannot prove the malpractice more likely than not caused the

---

[32] *Id.* at 1078.

[33] Two states have also relaxed causation requirements in DES cases, but have not imposed liability based entirely on the DES manufacturers' market shares. Wisconsin has utilized an apportioned liability system based on an assessment of risk each manufacturer has imposed on the plaintiff, where market share is only one factor in that risk assessment. *See* Collins v. Eli Lilly & Co., 342 N.W.2d 37 (Wis. 1984). Michigan has utilized an approach similar to Summers v. Tice, where each manufacturer is jointly severally liable rather than basing liability on market share. *See* Abel v. Eli Lilly & Co., 343 N.W.2d 164 (Mich. 1984).

[34] *See, e.g.*, Zafft v. Eli Lilly & Co., 676 S.W.2d 241 (Mo. 1984); Mulcahy v. Eli Lilly & Co., 386 N.W.2d 67 (Iowa 1986).

[35] *See, e.g.*, Lee v. Baxter Healthcare Corp., 721 F. Supp. 89 (D. Md. 1989) (lead paint); Shackil v. Ledeile Laboratories, 561 A.2d 511 (N.J. 1989) (diphtheria-pertussis-tetanus vaccine). Hawaii, however, accepted market share liability for a blood clotting protein in Smith v. Cutter Biological, Inc., 823 P.2d 717 (Hawaii 1991).

[36] 192 Cal. Rptr. 870 (Cal. Ct. App. 1983).

[37] *Id.* at 877.

plaintiff's death? In *Herskovitz v. Group Health Cooperative of Puget Sound,*[38] the court allowed a plaintiff to recover for wrongful death against a physician whose malpractice significantly reduced the patient's chance of survival, despite evidence indicating that the patient would have most likely died had the defendant not been negligent. It was undisputed that the patient had less than a fifty percent chance of surviving at all times, irrespective of any malpractice. However, the defendant's negligence caused a 14% reduction in the patient's chance of survival, from 39% to 25%.[39] The court held that the "reduction of chance of survival" in this case was sufficient evidence to allow the jury to determine whether the increased risk to the patient was a "substantial factor" in causing death. In effect, *Herskovitz* relaxed causation requirements by not requiring proof that the malpractice was a "but for" cause of premature death.[40] The approach reflects an additional application of the substantial factor test to satisfy actual causation.[41] While courts using this approach can award full wrongful death damages, some may give the fact-finder discretion to reduce full recovery. *Herskovitz* is ambiguous on this point.[42]

An alternative approach endorsed by some courts is to recognize a new cause of action for "loss of opportunity to survive." Under this approach but for causation is not relaxed, but instead loss of a *substantial* chance is perceived as a cognizable damage for which the victim may be compensated.[43] If, for example, physician A's malpractice reduces patient B's chance of survival 14% as in *Herskovitz,* this lost opportunity could be compensated and would be valued as an appropriate percentage of a wrongful death claim.[44]

---

[38] 664 P.2d 474 (Wash. 1983).

[39] *Id.* at 479.

[40] *See also, e.g.,* Daniels v. Hadley Memorial Hospital, 566 F.2d 749 (D.C. Cir. 1977); Kallenberg v. Beth Israel Hospital, 357 N.Y.S.2d 508 (N.Y. App. 1974).

[41] *See* § 11.03, *supra.*

[42] In *Herskovitz,* the court noted that full compensation for wrongful death need not be provided but then immediately followed the statement by reciting limits on recovery that applied to all wrongful death actions. *See* 664 P.2d at 479.

[43] *See* Falcon v. Memorial Hospital, 462 N.W.2d 44 (Mich. 1990). In *Falcon,* the decedent's chance to survive would have risen from zero to 37.5% had the treating physician provided her the proper care. The physician negligently failed to do so, however, and the court awarded the plaintiff 37.5% of wrongful death damages on the theory that the decedent had lost a "substantial" opportunity for survival.

[44] Under the loss of opportunity approach, plaintiff receives a percentage compensation for wrongful death as discussed in the text. This has been applied by some courts to the benefit of plaintiffs who could not establish that medical malpractice made a difference since the patient probably would have died at the same time anyway. One issue this approach raises is whether a plaintiff who can prove the physician's malpractice reduced from 55% to 45% a deceased patient's chance of survival should be fully compensated for the patient's death since traditional "but for" causation has been proven, or compensated for only the percentage reduction in chance of survival caused by the malpractice.

The desirability of such decisions is that they hold medical professionals accountable in situations where a patient presents herself with a chance of survival of 50% or less. Under traditional causation requirements, even blatant malpractice leading to a patient's death would not be subject to liability in tort unless it appears that with proper care the plaintiff had a better than fifty percent chance of survival. Other states, however, refuse to impose liability unless traditional "but for" causation is established. In those jurisdictions the malpractice must have been proven to have adversely affected the patient's survival.[45]

[D] *Statistical Evidence of Causation*

Courts are grappling in a variety of contexts whether purely statistical evidence should be the basis of proving causation or whether more than probability should be required. If A and B both drive by a mailbox, should the fact that A drove by the mailbox twice be sufficient to prove that, more likely than not, A was the cause if the mailbox is later found to have been struck by a car?

Courts usually appear more comfortable with some anecdotal evidence of liability in addition to pure probability.[46] Commentators have also noted the difficulty in showing a causal connection based on pure statistical probability in toxic tort cases:

> [The plaintiff] must prove that the substance for which the defendant is responsible can cause his injury or disease, that the defendant and not someone else was the source of the substance, and that he was in fact exposed to the substance in a way that caused his disease . . . . In many cases, however, meeting the traditional burden of proof as to each of these elements is no minor accomplishment . . . . [T]he data necessary to support the probabilistic measures of causation that could serve as surrogates for causal responsibility will rarely be available.[47]

Courts, in most situations, therefore seek further proof of causation, including manifestations of diseases which are particular to the product. This additional data can help to establish that the defendant was more likely than not the "but for" cause of the plaintiff's disease. In the absence of

---

[45] *See, e.g.*, Fennell v. Southern Maryland Hospital Center, Inc., 580 A.2d 206 (Md. 1990), where plaintiff was denied all recovery after showing that defendants' negligence precluded a 40% chance of recovery.

[46] "The use of statistics in trials is subject to criticism as being unreliable, misleading, easily manipulated, and confusing to a jury." Fennell v. Southern Maryland Hospital Center, Inc., 580 A.2d 206, 213 (Md. 1990). *But see, e.g.*, Stubbs v. City of Rochester, 124 N.E. 137 (N.Y. 1919), where plaintiff's use of statistical evidence was held to justify submission of the case to a jury because it was sufficient to support an inference of contaminated water causing the alleged illness. *See generally* Saul Levmore, *Probabilistic Recoveries, Restitution, and Recurring Wrongs*, 19 J. Legal Stud. 69 (1990).

[47] Kenneth S. Abraham, *Individual Action and Collective Responsibility: The Dilemma of Mass Tort Reform*, 73 Va. L. Rev. 845, 860, 867-68 (1987).

meeting this burden, most courts today would not find liability. This raises the issue of whether it would be appropriate to impose partial liability on defendants based on the statistical possibility that the defendant's culpable activity caused the plaintiff's disease in environmental toxic tort cases,[48] just as some jurisdictions imposed market share liability for product manufacturers in the DES cases.[49]

[E] *Future Developments*

An extended consideration of actual cause-in-fact suggests that it is far from a value-free analysis[50] of cause and effect even before it is supplemented and modified by theories of "proximate" or "legal" causation.[51] In cases as diverse as DES liability, hunting and swimming accidents, and medical malpractice, courts have been willing to adjust or waive traditional proof of actual causation. In most other cases, including toxic environmental liability cases, courts have routinely declined to accommodate alternatives in the burden of proving causation.

Perhaps actual causation should ultimately be viewed more generally not as a necessary prerequisite, but as merely one factor to consider in whether to find proximate or legal cause and impose liability. The increasing popularity of using the substantial factor test, which by its vagueness allows courts the opportunity to ignore the requirement of "but for" causation, may provide an important vehicle for movement in this direction. In the interim, however, actual causation remains a fundamental and in most cases a well-established requirement for imposing tort liability against culpable actors in our society.

---

[48] *See* Jackson v. Johns-Manville Sales Corp., 781 F.2d 394 (5th Cir. 1986), where the plaintiff was allowed to recover damages for a greater than 50% chance of becoming afflicted with cancer as a result of asbestos exposure. Significantly, the plaintiff had already been diagnosed with asbestosis, a factor the court explicitly considered in its decision.

[49] *See* § 11.04[B], *supra*. Plaintiffs have also sought recovery for mental distress associated with exposure to toxins even without proof that they have thus far suffered physical injury from the exposure, thereby avoiding some difficult causation burdens. *See* § 10.04, *supra*.

[50] *See generally* Symposium, *Causation in Law of Torts*, 63 Chi.-Kent L. Rev. 397 (1987).

[51] *See* Chapter 12, *infra*.

CHAPTER 12

PROXIMATE OR LEGAL CAUSE

SYNOPSIS

§ 12.01 OVERVIEW

The plaintiff must prove the defendant's culpable conduct is the proximate cause of the plaintiff's injuries. "Proximate" or "legal" cause[1] modifies and adds to the requirement that the defendant's culpable conduct be the actual cause of the plaintiff's injury. Even when the plaintiff establishes actual cause, courts will preclude recovery when the causal relationship between the defendant's conduct and the plaintiff's injury is too attenuated, remote, or freakish to justify imposing responsibility on the defendant. Famous court decisions and numerous scholarly articles have attempted to

[1] The Restatement has substituted the term "legal cause" for "proximate cause." Restatement § 431.

articulate the point at which the "proximate" cause requirement excuses tortious conduct that has caused injury.[2] Contemporary analysis generally recognizes that the application of the proximate cause requirement is ultimately a policy question rather than the precise mechanical application of rules.[3] To a large extent the issue of proximate cause is a factual question for the jury, although like any jury question, courts can hold as a matter of law that no reasonable jury could differ from the court's finding. It is those extreme cases of judicial imposition on jury discretion that have spawned some of the classic court opinions which attempt to define the rules and rationales of proximate cause.

Proximate cause rarely becomes a factor in intentional tort cases because those cases do not ordinarily test the limits of what should constitute legal responsibility. Authority is sparse as to when, if ever, proximate cause will preclude liability for intentional torts. In light of the greater culpability inherent in intentional wrongdoing, courts appear, at the very least, ready to stretch to find liability.[4]

Although different rules of proximate cause exist, the prevailing rule requires that the plaintiff's injury be a foreseeable consequence that the defendant should reasonably have anticipated. Ultimately, proximate cause addresses the fundamental tort issue of when it is appropriate to shift a plaintiff's loss to a culpable party who inflicted the loss.

§ 12.02 THE PROBLEM PROXIMATE CAUSE ADDRESSES

There is a general judicial consensus that it is insufficient for a plaintiff merely to establish that a defendant has breached a duty to the plaintiff and was the "cause in fact" of an injury. Courts also require proof that the defendant was the "proximate" or "legal"[5] cause, in order to establish a defendant's legal responsibility for an injury. Assume A negligently manufactures and sells to B a defective contraceptive pill which fails to prevent the birth of Child X. Child X grows up and conceives Child Y, who grows up and conceives Child Z. Child Z at the age of 16 negligently

---

[2] *See generally* Leon Green, *The Rationale of Proximate Cause* (1927); Arthur L. Goodhart, *The Unforeseeable Consequences of a Negligent Act*, 39 Yale L.J. 532 (1930); Charles O. Gregory, *Proximate Cause in Negligence — A Retreat from "Rationalization"*, 6 U. Chi. L. Rev. 36 (1938). *See also* H. L. A. Hart and T. Honore, CAUSATION IN THE LAW (2d ed. 1985).

[3] *See generally* Steven Shavell, *Analysis of Causation and the Scope of Liability in the Law of Torts*, 9 J. Legal Stud. 463 (1980); Aaron D. Twerski, *Informed Decision Making and the Law of Torts: The Myth of Justiciable Causation*, 1988 U. Ill. L. Rev. 607 (1989).

[4] *See* Derosier v. New England Telephone & Telegraph Co., 130 A. 145, 152 (N.H. 1925), observing that "[F]or an intended injury the law is astute to discover even very remote causation." This approach is consistent with the use of transferred intent for some intentional torts. *See* § 1.01[D], *supra*.

[5] *See supra* note 1.

causes an automobile accident injuring C. A's initial negligence in manufacturing a defective contraceptive is an actual "but for" cause of C's injury, since Z would not have been alive otherwise. However, A would not be held liable for the accident because, in part, A was too remote a cause and therefore not a proximate cause of the accident.

A variety of factors influence the policy issues which confront courts in attempting to determine whether proximate cause is established. These factors include but are not limited to foreseeability of injury, intervening actors, acts of God, and general social and economic policy goals. Indeed, some old decisions based proximate cause on purely spatial factors.[6]

From a moral perspective, the courts must look at who most fairly should bear the loss. In the defective contraceptive example, the automobile accident seems far beyond the limits of the manufacturer's causal responsibility. From a perspective concerned with distribution of loss and adequate compensation to the victim, it appears impractical to ask the contraceptive manufacturer to incorporate within its pricing mechanism something so remote as an automobile accident many years later. The difficulty of anticipating such a remote event makes it highly impractical to efficiently obtain or realistically price insurance for such losses.[7] From an accident avoidance perspective, damages imposed upon the defendant should be proportional to the risk, in order to avoid the over-deterrence of social and economically productive activity.[8] The confluence of these factors has tended to support increasing use of foreseeability tests as the measure for establishing proximate cause.[9] Nevertheless, a number of different tests and factors still exist.

§ 12.03 PROXIMATE CAUSE TESTS

[A] *Foreseeability Test — Definition*

The leading test for proximate cause focuses on whether the defendant should have reasonably foreseen, as a risk of her conduct, the general consequences or type of harm suffered by the plaintiff.[10] While the result

---

[6] *See* Ryan v. New York Central R.R. Co., 35 N.Y. 210 (1866), where the court held that although the defendant negligently caused a fire, he was only responsible for the first building to burn.

[7] *See* Allen E. Smith, *The Miscegenetic Union of Liability Insurance and the Tort Process in Personal Injury Claims System*, 54 Cornell L. Rev. 645 (1969).

[8] Over-deterrence would result in higher costs for operation of business via higher insurance rates, causing overall higher market costs of affected goods sold and a lower level of market efficiency.

[9] *See* § 12.04, *infra*.

[10] *See, e.g.*, Mauney v. Gulf Refining Co., 9 So. 2d 780 (Miss. 1942). *See also* Petition of Kinsman Transit Co., 338 F.2d 708 (2nd Cir. 1964), where Judge Friendly for the majority ruled proximate cause was satisfied when "the damages resulted from the same physical forces whose existence required the exercise of greater care than was displayed and were

or type of harm must be reasonably foreseeable, the extent and the precise manner in which the harm occurs need not be foreseeable.[11]

Even if the result is foreseeable, the defendant is relieved from liability if there is a *superseding* intervening force. An intervening force is a new force which joins with the defendant's conduct to cause the plaintiff's injury. An intervening force can be human, animal, mechanical, or natural, such as a wind shift. It is considered intervening because it has occurred sequentially in time *after* the defendant's conduct. An intervening force does not necessarily bar the plaintiff from establishing proximate cause under the foreseeable type of harm test. If the intervening force is characterized as *superseding*, proximate cause is not established even though the type of harm is foreseeable. An intervening force is generally characterized as superseding only when its occurrence appears extraordinary under the circumstances. In essence then, the foreseeable harm test requires (1) a reasonably foreseeable result or type of harm, *and* (2) no *superseding* intervening force.

[1] The *Wagon Mound* Cases and the Requirement of Reasonably Foreseeable Consequences[12]

The foreseeability test gained prominence with the publication of the *Wagon Mound* cases issued by the Privy Counsel in Great Britain, the ultimate judicial court of appeal for Commonwealth countries, including at that time Australia where the accident occurred. In *Wagon Mound No. 1*,[13] the plaintiff's dock was burned as a result of oil negligently spilled by the defendant's ship. This oil joined with the hot molten metal that was released into the water by the plaintiff's employees while they were soldering the dock. The *Wagon Mound* court articulated the principle that "liability (culpability) depends on the reasonable foreseeability of the consequent damages."[14] Relying on the trial court's somewhat questionable

---

of the same general sort that was expectable, unforeseeability of the exact developments and of the extent of the loss will not limit liability." *Id.* at 726. In *Kinsman*, defendant's improperly moored ship escaped from its moorings, crashing into a properly moored ship and causing both ships to crash into a drawbridge which, because of negligence, could not be raised in time, thereby creating a wreckage that, with ice, effectively dammed the river. The defendants were held liable for flooding which injured the property of upstream landowners. *See* Kinsman II, note 58, *infra*.

[11] *See, e.g.*, Derdiarian v. Felix Contracting Corp., 414 N.E.2d 666 (N.Y. 1980); *see also* Restatement § 435(1).

[12] *Wagon Mound No. 1* (Overseas Tankship (U.K.), Ltd., v. Morts Dock & Engineering Co., Ltd.), [1961] A.C. 388; "Wagon Mound No. 2" (Overseas Tankship (U.K.), Ltd. v. Miller Steamship Co.), [1967] 1 A.C. 617.

[13] [1961] A.C. 388. Palsgraf v. Long Island R.R., 162 N.E. 99 (N.Y. 1928), had earlier endorsed the use of foreseeability to limit liability in the context of duty. *See* § 8.04, *supra*, for a discussion of Chief Justice Cardozo's decision in *Palsgraf*. *See also* § 12.03[D], *infra*, for a discussion of Justice Andrew's dissent.

[14] *Id.*

findings that the defendant could not reasonably have been expected to know that the spilled oil was capable of being set on fire on the water, the appellate court ruled for the defendant since the consequence was not reasonably foreseeable.[15]

In a subsequent and somewhat contradictory decision, *Wagon Mound No. 2*,[16] the owner of another ship destroyed in the fire sued the same defendant for the negligent discharge of oil. This plaintiff argued that the resulting fire was a foreseeable risk from the oil spill, and the court accepted the claim.[17] *Wagon Mound No. 2* acknowledged the ambiguity of the words "foreseeable" and "reasonably foreseeable" and sought to define the terms. The court emphasized that, while the risk of fire was relatively remote, the foreseeability required need not be great when the risk, if manifested, would be significant and there were no justification to incur the risk. The court concluded that "[i]f it is clear that the reasonable man would have realized or foreseen or prevented the risk, then it must follow the appellant is liable."[18]

Most courts today require a finding of reasonable foreseeability, but as the *Wagon Mound* cases demonstrate, what constitutes reasonable foreseeability is not always an easy or uncontentious issue. In *Bigbee v. Pacific Telephone & Telegraph Co.*,[19] the California Supreme Court observed that "foreseeability is not to be measured by what is more probable than not, but includes whatever is likely enough in the setting of modern life that a reasonably thoughtful [person] would take account of it in guiding practical conduct."[20]

[2] Type of Harm Versus Manner and Extent

As noted above, while the consequence or type of harm must be reasonably foreseeable, the precise manner in which it occurs and the extent of the harm need not be foreseeable.[21] If A negligently keeps a lighted

---

15 The factual conclusion may not have been totally consistent with actual scientific foreseeability concerning the flammability of oil in water. Presumably, the plaintiff never argued that the fire was foreseeable to avoid a successful contributory negligence defense. Plaintiff's employees had resumed the soldering which ignited the hot molten metal after observing the spilled oil in the water. If the fire was foreseeable, the plaintiff's employees would have been contributorily negligent to resume the soldering. Since *Wagon Mound No. 1* introduced the requirement for foreseeability to proximate cause, the plaintiff presumably did not anticipate that it would be necessary to prove foreseeability to establish proximate cause.

16 *Wagon Mound No. 2* [1967] 1 A.C. 617.

17 The plaintiff ship owner, unlike the plaintiff dock owner in *Wagon Mound No. 1*, would not have been concerned with a possible contributory negligence claim.

18 *Id.*

19 665 P.2d 947 (Cal. 1983).

20 *Id.* at 952.

21 *See* Derdiarian v. Felix Contracting Corp., 414 N.E.2d 666 (N.Y. 1980) (a negligent motorist was foreseeable, but the exact manner of his negligence was not); Bigbee v. Pacific

flame next to a gas outlet, an explosion is a foreseeable type of harm. That a rat's fur might became ignited by the flame[22] and that the rat might then approach the gas outlet, causing an explosion, are, for example, facts that need not be foreseeable under the rule that the exact scenario or manner of the occurrence does not have to be foreseeable.[23] Similarly, so long as the type of harm or general consequence is reasonably foreseeable, the extent of the harm need not be. Consequently, a claim based upon a fire that unforeseeably expands to cover a larger area would not be precluded under the foreseeability test.[24]

[3] Superseding Intervening Forces

The foreseeability test is limited by the additional requirement that there be no superseding intervening force. As indicated above in § 12.03[A], intervening forces are new forces which join with the defendant's negligence to injure the plaintiff. Highly improbable and extraordinary intervening forces are generally found superseding and preclude liability.[25]

Some courts have characterized intervening forces as dependent or independent. A dependent intervening force is stimulated by the defendant's negligence,[26] while an independent intervening force is not. For example, if A knocks B into the water, C's effort to rescue B by navigating toward B is stimulated by A's earlier negligence and consequently is a dependent intervening force. If D, waterskiing, inadvertently collides into B, D's actions were not stimulated by A's actions, and would be characterized as

---

Telephone & Telegraph Co., 665 P.2d 947 (Cal. 1983) (a negligent motorist hitting a nearby telephone booth was foreseeable but not the precise manner in which such an accident would occur).

[22] *See, e.g.*, United Novelty Co. v. Daniels, 42 So. 2d 395 (Miss. 1949), where an employee was cleaning a machine with gasoline when a rat escaped and ran into a open flame gas furnace. The rat then returned to the machine in flames, causing the machine to explode. The employer was found liable because the proximity of the gasoline and flame made the type of harm, namely an explosion, foreseeable despite the odd manner by which the flame and gas came in contact.

[23] Attorneys can be expected to manipulate the distinction between type and manner, using broader categories to support a finding of proximate cause for plaintiffs and narrower interpretations on behalf of the defendant.

[24] The majority position in *Palsgraf, see supra* § 8.04, requires that plaintiffs be foreseeable. Consequently, the element of duty may effectively limit liability when unforeseeable plaintiffs are damaged. While proximate cause under the foreseeability test limits the types of damages the defendant is liable for, duty may restrict to which plaintiff(s) the defendant is liable. The requirement of foreseeability is used in several basic elements of negligence, including duty, proximate cause, and establishing a breach.

[25] "If the intervening act is extraordinary under the circumstances, not foreseeable in normal course of events or independent of or far removed from the defendant's conduct, it may well be a superseding act which breaks the causal nexus . . . ." Derdiarian v. Felix Contracting Corp., 414 N.E.2d 666, 670 (N.Y. 1980). *See also* Hairston v. Alexander Tank and Equipment Co., 311 S.E.2d 559 (N.C. 1984).

[26] *See* Restatement § 441 cmt. c.

an independent intervening force. While dependent intervening forces are less likely to be extraordinarily unforeseeable, the terminological distinction by itself is generally nondeterminative. Ultimately, the characterization of the term "superseding" ordinarily depends on how improbable the intervening force is.

If A drops gasoline carelessly at a service station, fire is a foreseeable type of harm.[27] If B then carelessly drops a match that ignites the dropped gasoline, B is an intervening force, but not a superseding intervening force, since such negligence is not extraordinary or highly improbable in this context. If B intentionally drops the match, the criminal act of arson is more likely to be characterized as superseding.[28] However, it would be incorrect to generalize that negligent acts are not superseding while intentional acts are superseding.[29] The location of the tort and frequency of crimes, like arson, may impact on the determination of how extraordinary an intervening force is perceived.

Acts of nature, such as storms, may be superseding, but if the storm should have been anticipated (even if it is extraordinarily strong), then the storm is nevertheless foreseeable and hence not superseding. For example, in *Johnson v. Kosmos Portland Cement Co.*,[30] the court upheld liability when lightning struck a barge where the defendant had negligently permitted gas to collect. The court observed that "[l]ightning is, at least at the time and place here involved, no extraordinary manifestation of natural force."[31] It is likely that courts are less quick to characterize an act of nature as superseding than a culpable human force where responsibility may appear to have shifted to another person.[32]

How unforeseeable must an intervening force be to be characterized as superseding? Courts have described superseding intervening forces as "so highly improbable and extraordinary an occurrence . . . as to bear no reasonable connection to the harm threatened."[33] Ultimately the concept

---

27 *See, e.g.*, Teasdale v. Beacon Oil Co., 164 N.E. 612 (Mass. 1929).

28 *See, e.g.*, Watson v. Kentucky & Indiana Bridge & R.R. Co., 126 S.W. 146 (Ky. 1910), holding malicious igniting superseding.

29 In the context of suicide, courts having increasingly found that intentional self-killing is not necessarily superseding when the victim is sufficiently disturbed to be unaware of his acts or suffers irresistible impulse. *See,e.g.*, Fuller v. Preis, 322 N.E.2d 263 (N.Y. 1974).

30 64 F.2d 193 (6th Cir. 1933).

31 *Id.* at 196.

32 The *Kosmos* court further noted that "the operation of natural forces do not constitute such (intervening) agency, unless of such exceptional violence, so extraordinary, that human prudence would not have foreseen or provided against them." 64 F.2d at 196 n.2. The Restatement would not find a natural force superseding unless "(a) the operation of the force of nature is extraordinary and (b) the harm resulting from it is a kind different from that the likelihood of which made the actor's conduct negligent." Restatement § 451.

33 Hairston v. Alexander Tank and Equipment Co., 311 S.E.2d 559, 567 (N.C. 1984).

of superseding intervening forces is an exception to the basic approach of the foreseeability test where the consequences must be foreseen but not the manner in which the event happened. An intervening force that is merely unlikely is not ordinarily superseding provided it existed as a reasonably possible contingency.[34] Automobile accidents and medical malpractice have been held, for example, not to be superseding although the odds of them occurring may be slight.[35] The tortfeasor who placed the victim in a situation where he was exposed to such risks must quite often share responsibility for the victim's aggravated harm. On the other hand, very extreme malpractice, as amputating the wrong leg, would ordinarily be so highly improbable as to likely be characterized as a superseding intervening force.

It is also important to remember that proximate cause is ordinarily a question of fact based on the specifics of individual cases. Ultimately notions of justice impact on whether proximate cause and therefore liability will be imposed on the defendant. While the intervening intentional wrongdoing of a third party may, under the circumstances, be foreseeable and not superseding, the relative culpability of an intervening force will inevitably influence, particularly in a close case, the decision to characterize an intervening force as superseding.[36] Indeed, occasionally, other factors such as an extended lapse of time will prompt a court to conclude that an intervening force has become superseding.[37] What is characterized as superseding in the end constitutes a determination that the earlier tort-feasor, although still an actual cause of a foreseeable consequence, should nevertheless be relieved of any further responsibility.

[B] *"Egg-shell" Plaintiff Personal Injury Rule*[38]

While foreseeability of consequences is generally required to find liability, courts make an exception and do not require that the type of

---

[34] Such contingencies include risk creation. *See, e.g.*, O'Malley v. Laurel Line Bus Co., 166 A. 868 (Pa. 1933), where defendant was held liable after obstructing sidewalk, forcing the plaintiff to walk in the street where he was hit by a negligently driven automobile.

[35] *See* Pridham v. Cash & Carry Building Center, Inc., 359 A.2d 193 (N.H. 1976), where plaintiff's decedent suffered serious injury as a result of defendant's negligence, then died when the driver of the ambulance suffered a heart attack and drove into a tree while driving him to the hospital. The initial tortfeasor was held liable. *See also* Lucas v. City of Juneau, 127 F. Supp. 730 (D. Alaska 1955), where the original defendant was held liable for injuries sustained by the plaintiff while being moved by hospital employees 18 days after the initial injury.

[36] *See* Restatement § 442(c).

[37] *See, e.g.*, Goar v. Village of Stephen, 196 N.W. 171 (Minn. 1923), where the court held that municipal corporation's failure for more than 17 months to inspect and discover construction defect in electrical plant operated by municipality precludes original defect from being a proximate cause of victim's electrical burns.

[38] Also known as the "thin skull" rule, the concept purportedly originated in Dulieu v. White, 2 K.B. 669 (1901).

personal injury suffered by a victim be foreseeable. Courts have consistently held that the defendant takes the plaintiff as he finds him.[39] Assume A tortiously bumps B in the head, and that such a bump would ordinarily only cause a minor injury. B, however, has an egg-shell-like head and the bump results in a catastrophic brain injury. A's bad luck at bumping the one individual vulnerable enough to suffer serious injury or death does not protect A from liability. In some sense, this could be viewed as an extension of the foreseeability test, which does not require the *extent* of the injury to be foreseeable, only the *type*. Personal injury could be characterized as one foreseeable type of harm, whether a sprained ankle or a heart attack. Nevertheless, courts have forthrightly found proximate cause without attempting to categorize all personal injuries as one kind of harm.[40] Once any personal injury is foreseeable, the particular type need not be foreseeable.

More controversial is whether psychological sensitivity should also be covered under the egg-shell plaintiff rule. Some courts have so held, such as when a minor automobile accident resulted in the plaintiff's suffering a severe psychological breakdown.[41]

It must be recognized, however, that in measuring damages for personal injury, the life expectancy and prospective health of the plaintiff are taken into account. Therefore, a medically vulnerable plaintiff would have a poor general prognosis for ill health or death taken into account in assessing the plaintiff's damages.[42]

---

[39] "[A]ll courts are agreed that the defendant is liable for the wholly unexpected breaking . . . ." Warren A. Seavey, *Mr. Justice Cardozo and the Law of Torts*, 39 Colum. L. Rev. 20, 32-33 (1939).

[40] *See* Keegan v. Minneapolis & St. Louis R.R. Co., 78 N.W. 965, 965 (Minn. 1899), where a sprained ankle injury caused death from endocarditis (heart inflammation). The victim's injury occurred when he stepped off a train into a hole in the station's platform. The railroad's negligence in not adequately maintaining the railroad platform was held a proximate cause of death. The court observed that "the fact that [railroad] could not have reasonably anticipated the particular result which followed, viz. that the injury might produce rheumatism, causing death, is also immaterial." *See also* Clark v. Associated Retail Credit Men of Wash., D.C., 105 F.2d 62 (D.C. Cir. 1939). "Neither is it an excuse [for intentional injuring] that an injured man's skull was thin or his constitution sensitive and that the means by which defendant . . . injured him would not have injured a normal man." Lee v. Reagan, 267 S.E.2d 909 (N.C. App. 1980), where the court noted North Carolina's recognition of the "special sensitivity" or "thin skull" rule.

[41] Steinhauser v. Hertz Corp., 421 F.2d 1169 (2d Cir. 1970), where court held that 14-year-old girl with a predisposition to schizophrenia may recover when slight automobile accident causing no bodily injuries was precipitating factor in causing her to suffer schizophrenia. *See* Malcom v. Broadhurst, 3 All E. R. 508 (Q. B. Div'l Ct. 1970), stating no difference in principle between an egg-shell skull and an egg-shell psyche.

[42] *See infra* § 14.03[B]. *See also* McCahill v. New York Transp. Co., 94 N.E. 616 (N.Y. 1911), where the decedent was an alcoholic and his relative was awarded damages. Although not allowed as a defense, the fact that the decedent might have died as a result of his alcoholism was noted as an important element in determining damages.

It is thought-provoking that the egg-shell plaintiff's personal injury rule of proximate cause should remain so accepted despite the increasing dominance of the foreseeability test. While as noted above, one can attempt to reconcile the two approaches through agile manipulations of what constitutes a single type of harm, ultimately personal injuries are receiving special treatment. For those seeking the single rationale for proximate cause, the disparity between foreseeability and the personal injury rule is a salient reminder that the values inherent in determining liability through proximate cause vary in the contexts of different kinds of harms.[43]

[C] *The Direct Causation Test*

What courts described as "direct" has undoubtedly evolved from a simple characterization to a more precise formula. Today, a direct cause is generally understood to preclude any intervening force.[44] Consequently, if any new force, whether human, mechanical, or natural, joins the defendant's action to cause the injury, the defendant is not deemed to be the direct cause.[45]

While once very widely accepted,[46] it is questionable whether the direct test has any viability in contemporary law.[47] Under the direct test the plaintiff is not concerned with establishing the foreseeability of the consequences, but must instead prove the absence of *any* intervening forces. This is in contrast with the foreseeable type of harm test, where the existence of intervening forces do not preclude liability so long as the type of injury is foreseeable and the intervening force is not classified as *superseding*.

The classic English case, *In re Polemis, Furness, Wilty and Co.*,[48] illustrates a fact pattern where the plaintiff could establish proximate cause under the direct test, but not the foreseeable type of harm test. In *Polemis*, servants of the defendant who leased a yacht dropped a plank, creating a spark that caused petrol fumes to ignite and the ship to explode. The explosion was deemed unforeseeable, but the defendant's servants' actions were the direct cause of the explosion because no intervening force existed. The defendant in *Polemis* failed to persuade the court to replace the then

---

[43] By comparison, note the comparative distinctions in limited duty rules based on type of harm. *See* Chapter 10, *supra*.

[44] *See supra* § 12.03[A][3].

[45] *But see* E.T. and H.K. Ide v. Boston & Maine R.R. Co., 74 A. 401 (Vt. 1909), where defendants were held liable under the direct test despite a sudden wind shift. What constitutes a new intervening force is subject to verbal manipulation.

[46] *See, e.g.*, Christianson v. Chicago, St. Paul, Minneapolis & Omaha R.R. Co., 69 N.W. 640 (Minn. 1896).

[47] The direct test is now more likely ignored or rejected: "[S]ubstituting 'direct' for 'reasonably foreseeable' leads to a conclusion . . . illogical and unjust." Overseas Tankship (U.K.) Ltd. v. Morts Dock & Engineering Co. (Wagon Mound I), [1961] A.C. 338. *See also* Arthur L. Goodheart, *The Brief Life Story of the Direct Consequence Rule in English Tort Law*, 53 Va. L. Rev. 857 (1967).

[48] 3 K.B. 560 (1921).

dominant direct test with a foreseeability test, a development which occurred later in the *Wagon Mound* cases[49] and other decisions.[50]

Ultimately the demise of the direct test can be explained by the admonition of a court which adhered to it. Reprimanding the trial court's venture into a foreseeability test for proximate cause, the appellate court explained that proper (direct test) proximate cause is "a rule of physics and not a criterion of negligence."[51] Since proximate cause is ultimately a question of when negligence liability should be imposed, it is not surprising that the happenstance of whether a new force has intervened should not satisfactorily provide a general theory for finding proximate cause.

This is not to conclude that direct causation is theoretically irrelevant to the determination of proximate cause, but only that by itself it is clearly inadequate. Some scholars conclude that the "egg-shell" plaintiff's personal injury rule[52] is a surviving manifestation of liability based on direct causation.[53] Once the victim is impacted, foreseeability becomes irrelevant. Furthermore, the relevance of intervening forces, albeit only when they are labeled "superseding," remains an integral component of the foreseeability test for proximate cause.

[D] *"Practical Politics" and "Rough Sense of Justice" Test*

In a famous dissent to Chief Justice Cardozo's opinion in the renowned *Palsgraf v. Long Island R.R.* decision,[54] Justice Andrews considered the appropriate tests for proximate cause. Ultimately he concluded that proximate cause is a question of public policy, fairness and justice, which cannot be reduced to any mechanical formula:

> What we do mean by the word "proximate" is, that because of convenience, of public policy, of a rough sense of justice, the law arbitrarily declines to trace a series of events beyond a certain point. This is not logic. It is practical politics . . . .
>
> It is all a question of expediency. There are no fixed rules to govern our judgment. There are simply matters of which we may take account. We have in a somewhat different connection spoken of "the stream of events." . . .
>
> There are some hints that may help us. The proximate cause, involved as it may be with many other causes, must be, at the least, something

---

49 *See supra* § 12.03[A][1].

50 *See, e.g.*, Mauney v. Gulf Refining Co., 9 So. 2d 780 (Miss. 1942). *See also* Leon Green, *Foreseeability in Negligence Law*, 61 Colum. L. Rev. 1401 (1961).

51 Collier v. Citizens Coach Co., 330 S.W.2d 74, 76 (Ark. 1959).

52 *See* § 12.03[B], *supra*.

53 *See* Robert Keeton, LEGAL CAUSE IN THE LAW OF TORTS (1963).

54 162 N.E. 99 (N.Y. 1928); *see infra* § 8.04, for full discussion of *Palsgraf* in the context of duty.

without which the event would not happen. The court must ask itself whether there was a natural and continuous sequence between cause and effect. Was the one a substantial factor in producing the other? Was there a direct connection between them, without too many intervening causes? Is the effect of cause on result not too attenuated? Is the cause likely, in the usual judgment of mankind, to produce the result? Or, by the exercise of prudent foresight, could the result have been foreseen? Is the result too remote from the cause, and here we consider remoteness in time and space . . . .[55]

In analyzing the mix of factors that should inform the court in making its public policy decision on whether to find proximate cause, Justice Andrews explains how foreseeability should be considered: "The foresight of which the court speaks assumes prevision."[56] Consequently, Justice Andrews' approach would analyze foreseeability not from the defendant's perspective before the accident, but from the perspective of what would appear to be the "natural results of a negligent act [looking] back to the catastrophe," a technique embraced by the Restatement.[57] In the context of the *Palsgraf* case, the question for Justice Andrews would not be whether the railroad conductor should have foreseen knocking a passenger's innocuous appearing package would cause an explosion, but whether knowing in advance the package contained explosives, the consequence would be foreseeable.

On occasion, courts have explicitly quoted Justice Andrews' assertion that proximate cause is a matter of public policy and justice and not logic to justify rulings on proximate cause that could not be explained consistently with its application of other standards, such as the foreseeability test.[58]

[E] *Restatement Test*

The Restatement utilizes the term "legal" rather than "proximate" cause. Restatement § 431 defines an actor's negligent conduct to be a legal cause if "(a) his conduct is a substantial factor in bringing about the harm, and (b) there is no rule of law relieving the actor from liability because of the manner in which his negligence has resulted in harm." The Restatement utilizes the substantial factor requirement to encompass both actual cause-in-fact[59] and causation in "the popular sense, in which there always lurks

[55] *Palsgraf,* 162 N.E. at 103–04.

[56] *Id.* at 105.

[57] *See* § 12.03[E], *infra.*

[58] *See* Kinsman Transit Co. v. City of Buffalo ("Kinsman II"), 388 F.2d 821 (2d Cir. 1968), where Judge Kaufman, citing Justice Andrews' opinion, held an earlier decision that awarded damages to riparian property owners for flooding caused by a barge crashing into a bridge did not require awarding damages to owners of ships delayed by the same accident. The court could have, but did not, rely on a limited duty for economic loss. *See* § 10.04, *supra.*

[59] *See* Chapter 11, *supra.*

the idea of responsibility."[60] Section 433 lists considerations important in determining whether conduct is a substantial factor:

(a) the number of other factors which contribute in producing the harm and the extent of the effect which they have in producing it;

(b) whether the actor's conduct has created a force or series of forces which are in continuous and active operation up to the time of the harm, or has created a situation harmless unless acted upon by other forces for which the actor is not responsible;

(c) lapse of time.

Once the tortfeasor's conduct is established as a substantial factor for the plaintiff's injury, the Restatement in § 435 indicates that liability will not be restricted merely because the actor could not foresee the extent or the manner in which the harm occurred. The defendant will not be held the legal cause of the harm under § 433, however, if "looking back from the harm to the actor's negligent conduct, it appears to the court highly extraordinary that it should have brought about the harm."

Restatement § 442 defines considerations important in determining whether an intervening force is superseding and thereby relieves the defendant from liability, even when the defendant's conduct is a substantial factor in causing the plaintiff's injury. The factors are to be considered in the disjunctive, i.e., it is not necessary that the force introduced satisfy all, or even most, of the factors to be considered a superseding cause:

(a) the fact that its intervention brings about harm different in kind from that which would otherwise have resulted from the actor's negligence;

(b) the fact that its operation or the consequences thereof appear after the event to be extraordinary rather than normal in view of the circumstances existing at the time of its operation;

(c) the fact that the intervening force is operating independently of any situation created by the actor's negligence, or, on the other hand, is or is not a normal result of such a situation;

(d) the fact that the operation of the intervening force is due to a third person's act or to his failure to act;

(e) the fact that the intervening force is due to an act of a third person which is wrongful toward the other and as such subjects the third person to liability to him;

(f) the degree of culpability of a wrongful act of a third person which sets the intervening force in motion.[61]

---

[60] *See* Restatement § 431 cmt. a.

[61] Restatement § 442. Specific provisions of the Restatement indicate that the intervening negligence of a third party will not be superseding when it would not be regarded as

The Restatement approach borrows substantial elements from Justice Andrews' dissent in *Palsgraf*, which considers proximate cause in the light of "prevision" of what subsequently occurred.[62] While the Restatement's principle of legal cause may be consistent with many decisions, the articulated comprehensive theory itself, unlike many provisions of the Restatement, has failed to gain general acceptance. Instead of accepting a proximate cause theory based on what is, in hindsight, viewed as extraordinary, courts are embracing the general notion that consequences should be reasonably foreseeable.

§ 12.04 THE POLICY OBJECTIVES ADDRESSED BY PROXIMATE CAUSE

The increasing dominance of the foreseeability test can be explained by its effectiveness in advancing several tort law objectives. Limits based on foreseeability appear proportionate to the culpability of the defendant and in this sense consistent with notions of corrective justice. Foreseeability allows for appropriate insurance or other techniques for distributing losses and for efficient compensation.[63] It also deters negligent conduct proportionate to the risks that should be foreseen and, conversely, does not overdeter socially useful conduct.[64]

Foreseeability is less dominant in resolving the proximate cause issue in personal injury than injury to property cases, although one could argue that all personal injuries can be characterized as a single, foreseeable type of injury.[65] Although foreseeability of the extent of the injury is not required

---

"extraordinary that the third person had so acted" (*see* Restatement § 447 (b)), or when the intervening tortious or criminal acts were done under an "opportunity afforded by" the defendant when she should have realized the likelihood a third person would commit the tort or crime (*see* Restatement §§ 447, 448). The Restatement also, consistent with the eggshell plaintiff rule (*see* § 12.03 [B], *supra*), imposes liability on a negligent actor when the victim's harm is increased because of the other's unforeseeable physical condition. *See* Restatement § 461.

[62] *Palsgraf*, 162 N.E. at 105: "I think . . . the foresight of which the court speaks assumes prevision." *See supra* § 12.03[D].

[63] *See generally* Kenneth S. Abraham, DISTRIBUTING RISK — INSURANCE, LEGAL THEORY, AND PUBLIC POLICY (1986).

[64] Foreseeability is an efficient mechanism for encouraging the rational conduct of actors. If a risk is foreseeable its likelihood of occurrence can ideally be determined, thereby allowing rational actors to insure against a contingency or consciously assume the risk of its occurrence. Furthermore, because the foreseeability standard is based upon what a reasonable person should have foreseen it deters defendants from failing to look into the probable consequences of their actions.

In the alternative, if a contingency is not foreseeable then imposing liability can provide no deterrent effect and may hamper continuing development of goods and services. This can result in problems of over-deterrence.

For further analysis, see generally H. L. A. Hart and T. Honore, CAUSATION IN THE LAW (2d ed. 1985).

[65] *See* § 12.03[B], *supra*.

under proximate cause analysis, liability for the extent of injury is often limited by the concept of duty.[66]

It is tempting to define a comprehensive approach to proximate cause and, ultimately, liability. While foreseeability has been, since *Palsgraf*,[67] an accepted component of the duty as well as proximate cause analysis, there is an increasing proliferation and reshuffling of limited duties which modify foreseeability in the duty element of negligence. In short, a review of current concepts of duty[68] reveals that there is no overarching, comprehensive theory of duty. The decision to impose liability is too multifaceted. The more relative coherency of proximate cause theory can therefore be misleading.

Ultimately the foreseeability test, as noted above, can provide a large cover for courts to inject a variety of values in deciding whether a culpable defendant who caused in fact an injury should nevertheless be found not to be a proximate cause and thereby escape liability. Foreseeability allows for a large degree of malleability, particularly in how courts delineate between the type of harm, which must be foreseeable, and the precise manner of injury, which need not be foreseeable. This enables a court to exercise discretion without always requiring its acknowledgement of other policy factors that may influence its decision. To the extent proximate cause ever in practice becomes inhospitable to multifaceted analysis of whether to impose liability on a defendant, duty or some other element of negligence will inevitably pick up the slack.

---

[66] *See infra* § 8.04.

[67] 162 N.E. 99 (N.Y. 1928). For a discussion of foreseeability in the context of duty, see § 8.04, *supra*.

[68] *See* Chapters 8, 9, 10, *supra*.

CHAPTER 13

JOINT AND SEVERAL LIABILITY

SYNOPSIS

§ 13.01 OVERVIEW AND DEFINITION

Joint tortfeasors are two or more individuals who either (1) act in concert to commit a tort, (2) act independently but cause a single indivisible tortious injury, or (3) share responsibility for a tort because of vicarious liability. Under traditional common law, each such tortfeasor is "jointly and severally" liable for the plaintiff's total damages.[1] This means that each individual is fully liable to the plaintiff for the entire damage award. If the plaintiff is unable to collect a co-tortfeasor's portion of the liability, the tortfeasor(s)

[1] *See generally* William L. Prosser, *Joint Torts and Several Liability*, 25 Cal. L. Rev. 413 (1937); Lewis A. Kornhauser and Richard L. Revesz, *Multidefendant Settlements Under Joint and Several Liability: The Problem of Insolvency*, 23 J. Legal Stud. 517 (1994). The term "several" indicates multiple defendants and "joint" indicates shared responsibility for total liability.

from whom the plaintiff can collect are responsible for the other tortfeasor's(s') share. The result is that a "deep pocket" defendant, who is partly responsible for the plaintiff's injury, may be required to pay all, or a disproportionate share, of the damages. In many states, relatively recent reform statutes have limited or amended joint and several liability for joint tortfeasors in different ways.[2]

The method by which such tortfeasors must share responsibility for the damages remains an intensely controversial area of contemporary tort law.[3] While this controversy may at first appear highly technical, the resolutions of these issues hold enormous implications for the functioning of tort law.

§ 13.02 JOINT TORTFEASORS

As indicated above, joint tortfeasors are individuals who either act in concert to commit a tort, act independently to cause a single indivisible tortious injury, or share responsibility for a tort because of vicarious responsibility.

[A] *Acting in Concert*

A person acts in concert to commit a tort with another when she aids or encourages another in committing the tort.[4] Acting in concert is the tort equivalent of being a criminal accessory or co-conspirator. If an individual intentionally aids or encourages another to commit a tort, he is as liable as the individual who actually committed the physical acts of the tort. For example, if A, a passenger in B's car, urges B to speed, then A is acting in concert with B's negligent driving, and both are joint tortfeasors responsible for any resulting accident.[5] There is no requirement that A's

---

[2] *See* Aaron D. Twerski, *The Joint Tortfeasor Legislative Revolt: A Rational Response to the Critics*, 22 U.C. Davis L. Rev. 1125 (1989). *See also* U.S. Attorney General, Tort Policy Working Group, *Report of the Tort Policy Working Group on the Causes, Extent, and Policy Implications of the Current Crisis in Insurance Availability and Affordability* (1986). Reform statutes are often the result of rancor regarding suits where municipal or state governments are named as defendants. *See, e.g.*, Cal. Civ. Code § 1431 (West 1995) (joint and several liability for economic damages, but several and not joint liability (each defendant only responsible for her proportional share) for non-economic loss); Ariz. Rev. Stat. Ann. § 12-2506 (West 1995) (abolishing joint and several liability except in specific contexts such as toxic tort cases).

[3] *See* Richard W. Wright, *Allocating Liability Among Multiple Responsible Causes: A Principled Defense of Joint and Several Liability for Actual Harm and Risk Exposure*, 21 U.C. Davis. L. Rev. 1141 (1988). *Compare* Aaron D. Twerski, *The Joint Tortfeasor Legislative Revolt: A Rational Response to the Critics*, 22 U.C. Davis L. Rev. 1125 (1989). *See also* Lewis A. Kornhauser and Richard L. Revesz, *Multidefendant Settlements Under Joint and Several Liability: The Problem of Insolvency*, 23 J. Legal Stud. 517 (1994).

[4] Restatement § 876.

[5] *See* Bierczynski v. Rogers, 239 A.2d 218 (Del. Super. Ct. 1968), where the defendants, racing two automobiles at high rates of speed, were found to have shared a common plan with reckless disregard to the consequences.

encouragement or assistance be the "but for" cause of the accident.[6] It is sufficient that the encouragement or aid be a factor that had some impact on B's action, even if ultimately B would have acted the same way regardless.[7]

[B] *Independent Acts Causing a Single Indivisible Injury*

Two or more individuals who act independently but whose acts cause a single indivisible tortious injury are also joint tortfeasors. If A is driving negligently in her car, and B is driving negligently in her car, and they both collide, causing injury to C, A and B are joint tortfeasors responsible for C's injury. This is so as long as C's entire injury is attributable to the collision and cannot in fact be separately allocated to A or B.[8] Here, neither A nor B aided or encouraged the other to commit a tort, but their independent actions caused the plaintiff a single indivisible injury.[9]

[C] *Vicarious Liability*

A defendant may be jointly liable for the actions of another through vicarious liability.[10] The most frequent example is a situation where employers are held liable under a theory of respondeat superior[11] for the actions of employees within the scope of their employment. Thus, employers who have neither acted nor intended the action may be liable for their employees' negligence. A great deal of litigation in this area has focused on when employee activities are "within the scope of employment" in the factual context of specific cases.[12]

Employers cannot insulate themselves from liability by simply enacting safety procedures or even by taking all possible precautions, because despite

[6] Nor is there any requirement that the agreement be express; a tacit understanding is all that is necessary. *See* Restatement § 876 cmt. a.

[7] An individual who does something innocently that inadvertently furthers another's tortious conduct is not deemed "acting in concert." Restatement § 876 cmt. c. *See, e.g.*, Day v. Walton, 281 S.W.2d 685 (Tenn. 1955).

[8] If, on the other hand, it can be determined that A injured C's foot and B injured C's hand, the injuries are divisible and can be individually allocated to the appropriate defendant.

[9] *See* Coney v. J.L.G. Industries, Inc., 454 N.E.2d 197 (Ill. 1983), where both an aerial platform manufacturer and the plaintiff's employer were held jointly and severally liable for the plaintiff's fall. *See also* Bartlett v. New Mexico Welding Supply, Inc., 646 P.2d 579 (N.M. Ct. App. 1982), where plaintiff's car was simultaneously struck by two automobiles.

[10] *See* Restatement §§ 416-429.

[11] ". . . which simply means 'let the employer answer.' " Fruit v. Schreiner, 502 P.2d 133, 138 (Alaska 1972).

[12] The "coming and going" rule generally excludes imposing liability on employers for ordinary commuting by employees unless special risks are created. *See, e.g.*, Ducey v. Argo Sales Co., 602 P.2d 755 (Cal. 1979). *But see, e.g.*, Fruit v. Schreiner, 502 P.2d 133 (Alaska 1972), where an insurance salesman attending an overnight convention trip was within the scope of his employment when found driving negligently at 2:00 A.M.

such precautions they are ultimately responsible for the acts of their employees within the scope of employment.[13] However, employers are generally not liable for the torts of independent contractors,[14] with exceptions for public policy reasons in situations involving non-delegable duties[15] and inherently dangerous activities.[16] Courts have held that those who hire an independent contractor may also be held liable if they closely supervise the contractor's day-to-day activities.[17] Similarly, partners and those participating in temporary joint enterprises are vicariously liable for torts committed by each other when acting in furtherance of the partnership or enterprise.[18]

Historically, the common law did not impose vicarious liability upon parents for torts committed by their children. However, many states have enacted statutes imposing limited liability in situations where children intentionally harm others or their property.[19] In a similar vein, automobile owners are not liable for the negligence of a permitted user under the

[13] Vicarious liability is also applicable to intentional torts when the employee's acts are reasonably connected with the employment. *See, e.g.*, Jefferson v. Rose Oil Co., 232 So. 2d 895 (La. Ct. App. 1970), where the employer was held liable because its employee, a gas station attendant, shot a customer while attempting to collect payment.

[14] *See* Restatement § 409. *See, e.g.*, Leaf River Forest Products, Inc. v. Harrison, 392 So. 2d 1138 (Miss. 1981). As observed in Murrell v. Goertz, 597 P.2d 1223, 1225 (Okla. Ct. App. 1979): "The line between an independent contractor and a servant is not clearly drawn. An independent contractor is one who engaged to perform a certain service for another according to his own methods and manner, free from control and direction of his employer in all matters connected with the performance of the service except as to the result thereof."

[15] *See* Restatement § 424. Such "non-delegable" duties may be created by statute, the common law, or contract. *See, e.g.*, Johnson v. Salem Title Co., 425 P.2d 519 (Or. 1967), where the plaintiff sued an architect, landowner, building contractor, and masonry contractor for injuries resulting from a gust of wind which toppled masonry. The architect was found to have a non-delegable duty to meet building code specifications and found liable because the code specifications encompassed the negligent construction which had caused the masonry's collapse.

[16] *See* Restatement § 423. *See, e.g.*, Western Stock Center, Inc. v. Sevit, Inc., 578 P.2d 1045 (Colo. 1978). *See, e.g.*, Community Gas Co. v. Williams, 73 S.E.2d 119 (Ga. Ct. App. 1952), where a gas company was held liable for the negligent work of the independent contractor it had hired to unload propane gas because propane gas is an inherently dangerous substance.

[17] *See, e.g.*, Murrell v. Goertz, 597 P.2d 1223 (Okla. Ct. App. 1979).

[18] Restatement (Second) of Agency § 14A. *See, e.g.*, Royal Bank and Trust Co. v. Weintraub, Gold, and Alper, 497 N.E.2d 289 (N.Y. 1986), where a law partnership was held liable for the actions of a partner deemed to be acting within the partnership's authority.

[19] *See, e.g.*, Cal. Civ. Code § 1714.1 (West 1995). Some jurisdictions have extended this, adopting "strict vicarious liability" for *any* of the child's harmful acts, even where the child is deemed below the age necessary to be culpable for negligence. *See* Turner v. Bucher, 308 So. 2d 270 (La. 1975). Parents may also be personally liable for negligent supervision of their children.

common law, but statutes in many states impose responsibility for limited maximum amounts.[20]

[D] *"Joint and Several" Liability*

Under the traditional common law, joint tortfeasors are "jointly and severally" liable for the plaintiff's total damages. The "several" indicates more than one tortfeasor. The "joint" indicates each of the "several" tortfeasors is fully liable for the entire damage. Just as joint tenants are each liable to a landlord for an entire month's rent, joint tortfeasors are each liable to a plaintiff for an entire damage award. The plaintiff cannot seek multiple damage payments, but may look to any of the tortfeasors for the entire amount.[21]

§ 13.03 SPECIAL PROBLEMS AFTER COMPARATIVE FAULT

[A] *Allocations of Liability Among Joint Tortfeasors*

When all joint tortfeasors are required and able to pay, how are the shares of the liability to be allocated? Traditionally, each liable defendant paid a pro rata share of the damages based on the number of joint tortfeasors. If there were two tortfeasors, they each paid one-half; if there were three, each paid one-third. This traditional approach, however, has been replaced in recent years in many states by a system of comparative allocations of responsibility among joint tortfeasors. Most states have adopted comparative negligence, and many of these have extended the concept to include comparative allocation of responsibility among multiple tortfeasors as well as between the plaintiff(s) and defendant(s).

Under a comparative approach, instead of dividing liability by the number of joint tortfeasors, liability is divided by the proportion of responsibility each tortfeasor bears to the plaintiff. For example, the fact-finder may decide that defendant A should pay 60% of the damages, defendant B 30%, and defendant C 10%.

In the absence of a reform statute, this comparative allocation does not necessarily alter joint liability. If defendant A is unable to pay his 60% share, defendants B and C would still pay A's share, usually in proportion to their own relative liability.

---

[20] *See, e.g.*, Cal. Veh. Code § 17151 (West 1995), which imposes maximum liability on the owner of "$15,000 for the death of or injury to one person in any one accident and, subject to the limit as to one person, is limited to the amount of $30,000 for the death of or injury to more than any one person in any one accident and is limited to the amount of $5,000 for damage to property of others in any one accident" for the negligent actions of any person using the owner's vehicle with the owner's express or implied permission.

Owners may be negligent for entrusting their car to an incompetent driver. *See, e.g.*, Jackson v. Hertz Corp., 590 So. 2d 929 (Fla. Ct. App. 1991).

[21] *See* Restatement § § 433A, 875. As discussed *infra* in § 13.02[D], numerous reform statutes have limited or altered joint and several liability.

Jurisdictions disagree as to whether a negligent plaintiff, in a comparative negligence jurisdiction, should also share responsibility for a defaulting tortfeasor's portion of the damages. Some states, under a strict interpretation of joint and several liability, require the solvent defendants to make the plaintiff whole by paying the defaulting tortfeasor's share.[22] Many others, however, would make the plaintiff absorb some of the defaulting tortfeasor's share based on the plaintiff's percentage of comparative fault. In such an instance, the plaintiff would not only have her damages deducted by her percentage of comparative fault, but an additional deduction would be made for her relative share of the defaulting tortfeasor's portion.

[B] *Impact of Settlement on Percentage Shares*

It is critical to distinguish between settlements which act as satisfactions from those executed as releases. A satisfaction results in receipt of full compensation for an injury and extinguishes the claim against all potential tortfeasors. In contrast, a release is a surrender of the plaintiff's claim against only one or more of the tortfeasors. The plaintiff still preserves his right to seek compensation from other tortfeasors for their remaining liability for the injury.

Historically, the release of one tortfeasor under the "unity of release" rule constituted a release of all tortfeasors.[23] Plaintiffs could avoid inadvertently releasing non-settling tortfeasors from liability for the claim by drafting "covenants not to sue" in lieu of a "release." The far better and now majority approach is to construe a release to affect only the named party.[24] The remaining tortfeasors still remain liable.

How do settlements releasing one or more tortfeasors impact on the liability of the remaining tortfeasors? Such settlements obviously precede the court's determination of each tortfeasor's relative liability. Jurisdictions have generally opted for one of two approaches.

The first approach allows the settling defendant's payment to be deducted from the final total damages owed to the plaintiff.[25] This results in the remaining joint tortfeasors paying the full damage amount actually awarded minus the settling defendant's payment, even if that increases the percentage of the damages for which the remaining defendants were originally liable. For example, assume the jury awards $10,000 in damages and determines

---

[22] *See, e.g.*, American Motorcycle Ass'n v. Superior Ct., 578 P.2d 899 (Cal. 1978). In June 1986, however, the voters of California passed Proposition 51 which retained traditional joint and several liability for economic damages but adopted several liability for noneconomic damages such as mental distress; therefore, a defendant is only liable for noneconomic damages up to the percentage amount for which the defendant is found responsible.

[23] Bundt v. Embro, 265 N.Y.S.2d 872 (1965).

[24] *See* McMillen v. Klingensmith, 467 S.W.2d 193 (Tex. 1971).

[25] *See, e.g.*, Md. Code Ann. art. 50, § 19 (1994).

defendant A is 70% at fault and B is 30% at fault.[26] If neither of the defendants had settled and both were solvent, A would pay $7,000; B would pay $3,000.[27] If, however, A settles for $1,000, B must pay $9,000 ($10,000 -$1,000), in effect 90% of the judgment. Jurisdictions utilizing this approach generally require a "good faith" hearing to confirm that the settlement is not a conspiracy by the plaintiff and the settling defendant to make another defendant pay an excessive share.[28] Nevertheless, given the uncertainty over whether there is liability, the amount of damages the fact-finder might award, and the comparative fault of the plaintiff and defendants, a great deal of discretion must be allowed for the attorneys to fashion a settlement. This approach encourages settlements by allowing a plaintiff to accept a low offer, and thus immediate compensation, while maintaining a right to full recovery from non-settling defendants.[29] It also puts obvious pressure on defendants to settle rather than remain liable for the settling defendant's remaining equitable share under joint and several liability.[30]

A second approach has the settling defendant's percentage of fault, as determined by the fact-finder, deducted from the damages awarded the plaintiff regardless of the actual payment by the settling defendant to the plaintiff.[31] In this case, the plaintiff risks losing part of his ultimate recovery if he accepts too small a payment from a settling defendant. For example, defendant A settles for $1,000, and defendant B goes to trial. The fact-finder determines the damages owed to the plaintiff are $10,000, and concludes A is 60% responsible while B is 40% responsible. Under this second approach, A's 60% is deducted so B only owes his forty percent, or $4,000. The plaintiff, by accepting $1,000 from A in the pre-verdict settlement, loses $5,000 from the awarded recovery. Instead of receiving 60% of $10,000 or $6,000 from A, he receives $1,000. Here, in contrast to the first approach, the risk of a low settlement is allocated to the plaintiff. This protects the uninvolved non-settling defendant while still allowing room for mutually beneficial settlement agreements.[32]

---

[26] Where comparative principles are not used, each party would be liable for his pro rata share based on the number of defendants, in this instance 50%.

[27] The example assumes the plaintiff is not at fault.

[28] *See* Florrie Young Roberts, *The "Good Faith" Settlement: An Accommodation of Competing Goals*, 17 Loy. L. Rev. 841 (1984); 1955 Uniform Act § 4; Restatement § 886A cmt. m(2).

[29] It is of course possible the settling defendant will overpay, decreasing the other defendants' shares.

[30] *See* American Motorcycle Ass'n v. Superior Ct. of Los Angeles County, 578 P.2d 899 (Cal. 1978), adopting this approach and Justice Clark's spirited dissent.

[31] *See, e.g.*, Chattin v. Cape May Greene, Inc., 524 A.2d 841 (N.J. 1987).

[32] This approach is now endorsed by the Uniform Comparative Fault Act. An older third approach noted as a third alternative by the Restatement would require a settling defendant to contribute to remaining defendants if it was determined the remaining defendant had been required by a judgment to pay more than his equitable share. This approach clearly removes the incentive for a defendant to settle. The Restatement in a caveat takes no position on the three approaches. *See* Restatement § 866A.

Strategic rivalry between multiple defendants has sometimes prompted private agreements between the plaintiff and a defendant. In what are now referred to as "Mary Carter" agreements,[33] after an early case addressing the issue, a defendant will remain in the litigation despite having (often secretly) agreed to a settlement with the plaintiff which is contingent on the trial's outcome. Ordinarily, the settling defendant's liability will be reduced under the agreement with the plaintiff if the plaintiff is awarded above specified amounts at trial from the other defendants. Consequently, while still a defendant, "Mary Carter" agreements motivate that defendant to act in ways that helps the plaintiff's case. Some courts prohibit such agreements, some permit them, and still others allow them only if they are public and not secret agreements.[34]

[C] *Contribution and Indemnification*

The sections above discuss different approaches for dividing liability among multiple tortfeasors. Suppose the plaintiff fails to name one or more potential tortfeasors as a defendant. Under joint and several liability principles, the tortfeasor sued must still bear full responsibility for the injury to the plaintiff. Initially, courts would not allow a sued defendant to seek a contribution from another tortfeasor for their share of the liability. With the exception of tortfeasors liable for intentional torts, a defendant required to pay the plaintiff more than her share of the damage judgment (under either a pro rata or comparative system) can now seek in most states appropriate contribution from her co-tortfeasor.[35] In contrast, an intentional tortfeasor is generally precluded from seeking contribution on the public policy ground that an intentional wrongdoer should not be accommodated by the courts.[36]

Some states will allow a tortfeasor to seek a contribution only after a court judgment has been reached against her, while most states allow a tortfeasor who has settled a claim for more than her share to also seek contribution. The tortfeasor seeking a contribution must, of course, prove the others liable. Normally, procedural rules allow one defendant in an action to "implead" or file a claim against other potential tortfeasors who have not been named as defendants by the initial plaintiff so that their liability for contribution can be determined in the same proceeding. Alternatively, a tortfeasor can also file a separate action for contribution, provided the statute of limitations has not expired.

---

[33] *See* Booth v. Mary Carter Paint Co., 202 So. 2d 8 (Fla. App. 1967).

[34] *See* Elbaor v. Smith, 845 S.W.2d 240 (Tex. 1992).

[35] Some states use the term comparative indemnification in lieu of comparative contribution. *See, e.g.*, American Motorcycle Ass'n v. Superior Ct., 578 P.2d 899 (Cal. 1978).

[36] *But see* Southern Pacific Transp. Co. v. State of Cal., 171 Cal. Rptr. 187 (Cal. Ct. App. 1981), where the court held that contribution among joint tortfeasors is not barred by willful misconduct.

Generally, a defendant cannot seek a contribution from a tortfeasor who is immune from liability to the plaintiff for the accident. For example, A, a child, may sue B, claiming B's negligent driving injured A while A was playing in the road. B may claim A's parents should share in the liability for the parents' alleged negligence in supervising the child. If the jurisdiction in question immunizes the parents from liability to their child, B can generally not bypass parental immunity by seeking an equitable contribution from A's parents for the injury to A.[37]

Historically, courts have allowed a defendant to seek "indemnification" or total reimbursement from another tortfeasor when the defendant was only technically liable, but the other tortfeasor was far more culpable.[38] The more culpable tortfeasor is sometimes characterized as the "active" as opposed to the "passive" tortfeasor. Such indemnification was allowed by courts prior to the general acceptance of contribution discussed above. Unlike contribution, the defendant's liability is always completely shifted to the other tortfeasor.

Indemnification has been permitted where the defendant is vicariously liable for another's negligence or where a retailer is liable for selling a defective product negligently constructed by the manufacturer. For example, if A sues B (C's employer) after C negligently drives into A, B can seek indemnification or total reimbursement from C. Indemnification is also allowed pursuant to indemnification contracts in which one party may agree to reimburse the other in the event of liability specified in the contract.

In jurisdictions where contribution liability is still based on a pro rata division based on the number of defendants, indemnification allows a more equitable shifting of responsibility to the tortfeasor primarily responsible for the injury.[39] The trend toward comparative contribution has, in many instances, blurred the distinction between the two actions since there is nothing in theory precluding a finding under comparative contribution that one tortfeasor should be fully responsible. Furthermore, where comparative contribution is available, it allows courts flexibility to allocate precisely relative responsibility among tortfeasors rather than simply deciding whether to shift entire responsibility to one tortfeasor. Courts may, for example, find it more equitable to hold a retailer partly responsible for selling a defectively manufactured product under comparative contribution rather than shifting full liability to the negligent manufacturer under indemnification. This has prompted some courts to allow only comparative contribution and not indemnification, except when indemnification is based

---

[37] For a discussion of parent-child immunity, see § 15.05[D], *infra*. Most jurisdictions will also not permit an employee immune from liability because of workers' compensation laws to be impleaded in action brought by an employee.

[38] *See* Tolbert v. Gerber Industry, Inc., 255 N.W.2d 362 (Minn. 1977).

[39] *But see* Vertecs Corp. v. Reichhold Chemicals, Inc., 661 P.2d 619 (Alaska 1983) (eliminating noncontractual indemnification in the context of pro-rata contribution).

on a contract or the party seeking indemnification was only vicariously liable.[40]

[D] *Policy Debate and Reform Statutes*

Since courts started comparing the relative responsibility of defendants, the concept of "joint and several" liability among defendants has been increasingly attacked. Numerous reform statutes have limited or altered joint and several liability rules in many states. For example, in California, joint and several liability is now limited to economic damages.[41] Why should a tortfeasor, who is only responsible for 1% of the damages, have to pay 86% because the other defendant, allocated 85% responsibility, is insolvent?[42] This rule, critics claim, encourages seeking out "deep pocket" defendants, such as government entities, and essentially forcing them to pay all damages when their true liability is nominal.

For example, in *Gehres v. Phoenix*,[43] a tavern served alcohol to an allegedly intoxicated patron, who killed the plaintiff's wife in an automobile collision while attempting to elude Phoenix police during a vehicular chase. The jury determined the drunk driver was 95% at fault, the tavern 3% at fault, and the city 2% at fault. Because the drunk driver was killed in the collision and left no funds in his estate, the tavern and city were liable for all damages.[44] Disproportionate liability situations like this have been further aggravated by some settlement rules.[45]

On the other hand, all of the joint tortfeasors, by definition, acted tortiously and actually and proximately caused the plaintiff's injury. In most cases, under usual "but for" causation analysis, the injury would have been totally avoided if any of the defendants had acted nonculpably. In this sense, the percentage allocation determined by the fact-finder is only a comparative measure of an ideal apportionment among wrongdoers, each of whom, it can be argued, should be fully liable to the plaintiff for all the plaintiff's losses because any one of them could have, by acting non-negligently, protected the plaintiff from any injury.

From a compensation perspective, "joint and several" liability better insures compensation to the plaintiff. Nevertheless, disproportionate liability

---

[40] *See, e.g.*, B&B Auto Supply v. Central Freight Lines, Inc., 603 S.W.2d 814 (Tex. 1980).

[41] Cal. Civ. Code § 1431(West 1995); *see also, e.g.*, Ariz. Rev. Stat. Ann. § 12-2506 (West 1995) (abolishing joint and several liability except in certain specified contexts such as toxic tort cases).

[42] *See* Walt Disney World Co. v. Wood, 515 So. 2d 198 (Fla. 1987), where, on appeal, Disney was found to be one percent at fault and was forced to pay eighty-six percent of the damage award.

[43] 753 P.2d 174 (Ariz. 1987).

[44] The Arizona legislature abolished most joint and several liability shortly thereafter. *See* note 41, *supra*.

[45] *See supra* § 13.03[B].

for this compensation may fall on the "deep pocket" defendants. This arguably creates an incentive for a "deep pocket" defendant to take precautions, but disproportionate liability may result in excessive precautions or termination of certain services. For example, a city providing docking facilities for recreational boaters may cease offering such services rather than face total liability for injuries caused mostly by the negligence of nonsolvent defendants.

Finally, the moral appeal of joint and several liability may have been more compelling prior to replacement of contributory negligence with comparative negligence in most states. Under contributory negligence systems, a successful plaintiff could not recover unless he was, at least in theory, an entirely innocent victim of others' wrongdoing. When the plaintiff is comparatively negligent, he too bears responsibility for his injury since he could have avoided the accident by acting reasonably. Consequently, it seems less morally compelling that a culpable plaintiff should necessarily be fully compensated by deep pocket tortfeasors with limited relative responsibility for the accident.

CHAPTER 14

DAMAGES

SYNOPSIS

§ 14.01 OVERVIEW[1]

Damages[2] in torts constitute the "money awarded to the person injured by the tort of another."[3] Tort damages include nominal damages, compensatory damages, and punitive damages.

[1] Limited duties address the issue of compensation for mental distress, loss of consortium, wrongful conception, wrongful birth, wrongful life, pure economic loss, and permissible types of damages recoverable under wrongful death. *See supra* Chapter 10.

[2] *See generally* Dan B. Dobbs, LAW OF REMEDIES: DAMAGES, EQUITY, RESTITUTION (2d ed. 1993); Marilyn K. Minzer et al., DAMAGES IN TORT ACTIONS (1982).

[3] *See* Restatement § 902.

Nominal damages are a symbolic award (often one dollar) given to the plaintiff when liability for a tort is established but no actual harm occurred or is proven with sufficient certainty.[4] The nominal damage award indicates that the defendant committed the tort and may serve to clarify or vindicate the rights of the plaintiff. For example, the award of nominal damages in trespass can be useful in establishing judicial recognition of property boundaries.[5] Some torts, such as negligence, require proof of actual harm to be actionable. In such torts nominal damages are never awarded.

Compensatory damages are typically defined as damages "awarded to a person as compensation, indemnity, or restitution for harm sustained by him."[6] Compensatory damages are awarded for both pecuniary and non-pecuniary losses. In the context of property damages, pecuniary injury constitutes the diminished market value of damaged property, appropriate replacement value, or rental value to compensate for unauthorized use. Pecuniary compensatory damages for personal injury includes compensation for the victim's medical expenses, lost wages or diminished earning capacity, and other economic expenses incurred because of the injury. Compensatory damages are also available for non-pecuniary losses, such as pain and suffering and other variations of mental distress.

Tort law also provides for punitive damages to punish and deter particularly egregious conduct.[7] Punitive damages are discretionary and awarded when a tort is committed with malice. Traditionally, and still most often, punitive damages, when awarded, go entirely to the plaintiff. In some jurisdictions, however, the state receives a portion of the punitive damages.[8] Punitive damages have prompted constitutional challenges, thus far unsuccessful, by those who claim such awards are inappropriately duplicative of criminal law and lack procedural safeguards inherent in criminal prosecutions.

While substantive tort theory has not traditionally dwelled upon damages, concern over tort damages has more recently attracted the attention of legislatures, courts and the public at large. Some reform statutes, particularly in the context of medical malpractice where insurance rate increases have been an issue of public concern, have limited compensation,[9] most often for pain and suffering and punitive damages. The extent to which tort law should attempt to provide monetary compensation for pain and suffering,

---

[4] *See* Restatement § 907.

[5] *See* § 18.02, *supra*.

[6] Restatement § 903.

[7] *See* Restatement § 908.

[8] *See, e.g.*, Or. Rev. Stat. § 18.540.

[9] *See, e.g.*, Cal. Civ. Code § 333.2 (limiting noneconomic damages in medical malpractice claims to $250,000); Md. Code Ann., Cts. & Jud. Proc. § 11-108 (1995) ($350,000 limit on all noneconomic damages in personal injury actions).

including mental distress, or impose quasi-criminal punitive damages are continuing controversies facing both the courts and legislatures.

§ 14.02 PROPERTY DAMAGES[10]

Interference with property is compensable in torts and is primarily based upon a conception of value.[11] Permanent deprivation or destruction of property is generally measured by the market value of the property. Ordinarily, market value is measured at the time of the tort, but particularly in the case of commodities with fluctuating value, courts accommodate the plaintiff's real loss by allowing either the highest market value between the tort and trial or the highest market value from the tort until the victim can reasonably replace the property after discovering its loss.[12]

If real or personal property is damaged but not destroyed, courts generally compensate the victim for the diminished market value of the property. Courts will sometimes award the plaintiff the cost of repairs in lieu of the diminished value where such repairs appear reasonable. If the cost of repairs significantly exceeds the loss in value of the property, courts are hesitant to impose repair costs since the victim theoretically could sell the damaged property and, combined with compensation for diminished value, purchase replacement property. Nevertheless, injury to a personal residence or to personal property with sentimental value often qualifies for compensation based on repair costs even when repair costs exceed the loss in value caused by the injury.[13]

When the victim is prevented from using his property, the tortfeasor is liable for the loss of use or rental value of the property.[14] If it is reasonable for the victim to rent substitute property to mitigate losses, the rental cost for appropriate substitute property can be compensated, even if this exceeds the rental value of the victim's property. Discomfort and annoyances caused by interference to real property are also compensable.[15]

When a defendant should have been aware that the possessor attached sentimental value to personal property, courts sometimes award mental distress damages in addition to compensating for the lost market value of the chattel.[16] For ordinary chattels, however, courts have been quite hesitant

[10] *See generally* Dan B. Dobbs, LAW OF REMEDIES: DAMAGES, EQUITY, RESTITUTION (2d ed. 1993).

[11] *See, e.g.*, Restatement § 911.

[12] *See, e.g.*, Galigher v. Jones, 129 U.S. 193 (1889); Schultz v. Commodity Futures Trading Comm'n, 716 F.2d 136 (2nd Cir. 1983).

[13] *See* Restatement § 929; Andersen v. Edwards, 625 P.2d 282 (Alaska 1981).

[14] *See* Miller v. Sears, 636 P.2d 1183 (Alaska 1981).

[15] *See* Restatement § 929.

[16] When the market cost would be inadequate compensation, the value to the owner may be considered. *See, e.g.*, Brown v. Frontier Theatres, Inc., 369 S.W.2d 299, 304 (Tex. 1963) ("The law recognizes that articles of small market value . . . may have special value . . . as heirlooms.").

to award mental distress damages caused by loss or injury to property. Where malice is established, however, punitive damages can be awarded.

§ 14.03 PERSONAL INJURY[17]

Personal injury victims under tort law can be compensated for (1) medical expenses; (2) lost wages or impaired earning capacity; (3) other incidental economic consequences caused by the injury; and (4) pain and suffering.[18]

[A] *Medical Expenses*

An injured plaintiff can be awarded all reasonable medical expenses caused by the tortfeasor. Such expenses include payments for physicians, hospitals, nursing care, physical therapists, and appropriate diagnostic tests. In addition, the plaintiff can recover anticipated medical expenses that are attributable to the defendant. This can pose very difficult issues of proof concerning the victim's future need for medical care and the anticipated cost of such care.[19] Ordinarily the plaintiff must introduce expert medical testimony to support his claims.[20]

[B] *Lost Wages or Diminished Earning Capacity*

The victim in a personal injury tort can recover past and future lost wages or diminished earning capacity. If the plaintiff finds it advantageous, she is entitled to be compensated for wages or lost business earnings during the period the injury has impacted, and in the future is anticipated to impact, negatively on those earnings.[21] If, for example, A is unable to work at all for 6 months and only half-time for another 6 months, the lost income, including any anticipated pay raises, is calculated.

Alternatively, the plaintiff may seek recovery for past and future impaired earning capacity instead of proving lost wages and income. Impaired earning capacity measures the victim's lost potential to earn income because of the injury and is not dependent on proof that the victim had exploited, or would in the future exploit, that capacity. Under this approach, the defendant cannot reduce his liability by arguing the plaintiff would have, for example,

---

[17] *See generally* Dan B. Dobbs, LAW OF REMEDIES: DAMAGES, EQUITY, RESTITUTION (2d ed. 1993); Marilyn K. Minzer et al., DAMAGES IN TORT ACTIONS (1982).

[18] Restatement § 924.

[19] A special area of controversy concerns whether medical expenses will be awarded to monitor potential disease caused by exposure to toxic chemicals or other environmental pollutants. Ultimately, decisions in this area appear to depend on whether a tort has occurred, which in the case of negligence requires a finding of some cognizable damage to the victim. If the plaintiff's only provable damage is mental distress over the increased potential for disease, liability depends on the circumstances required to recognize liability for the negligent infliction of mental distress tort in that jurisdiction. *See* § 10.04, *supra*.

[20] *See* Callaway v. Miller, 163 S.E.2d 336 (Ga. 1968).

[21] Caldwell v. Seaboard Sys. R.R., Inc., 380 S.E.2d 910 (Va. 1989).

chosen to have lived on another family member's income rather than pursuing his own professional career.

This alternative approach can easily deviate from measuring the plaintiff's actual economic loss. Its general acceptance is, nevertheless, justified by commentators since the victim is in fact being compensated for an injury which deprives him of his opportunity to use his time as he so chooses.[22] Courts value the plaintiff's time by prevailing workplace compensation rates, even if the victim might have attached so much greater value to his time that he would have refrained from in essence selling it at the prevailing rates.

Impaired earning capacity requires proof of the victim's specific ability, skills, and aptitude for a career path prior to the injury. Educational attainment and prior employment history where it exists is very relevant to this determination. A cannot claim impaired capacity to be a lawyer when A, prior to the injury, had failed admission into a four-year college.[23]

In the case of infants and youths the courts are forced to rely on limited data such as evidence of intelligence and performance in school, and the careers and achievements of others in the family.[24] Vague professional aspirations without more substantial evidence of likely success is unlikely to persuade courts that impaired earning capacity should be based on a particular profession or career.

Estimates of lost wages or impaired earning capacity must take into account the life expectancy of the victim prior to the injury caused by the tortfeasor and when she would have been expected to retire or reduce work because of advanced age or illness.

[C] *Incidental Economic Consequences*

Incidental economic consequences caused by the personal injury are also recoverable. This would include travel expenses to seek appropriate medical treatment, as well as expenses incurred for housekeeping services because of the victim's incapacity.[25]

[D] *Reduction to "Present Value"*

Damages for medical and other expenses, as well as lost wages or impaired earning capacity, are generally awarded as a lump sum to the victim. Therefore, if, for example, an award for future lost earnings is intended to cover the next twenty years, the actual award must be reduced to take into account that the money is being transferred to the victim in

---

[22] *See* Dan B. Dobbs, LAW OF REMEDIES: DAMAGES, EQUITY, RESTITUTION (2d. ed. 1993) at § 8.1(2).

[23] *See* Waldorf v. Shuta, 896 F.2d 723 (3d Cir. 1990).

[24] *See* Roussel v. Berryhill, 444 So. 2d 1286 (La. Ct. App. 1984).

[25] *See, e.g.*, Grubbs v. United States, 581 F. Supp. 536 (N.D. Ind. 1984).

advance. This reduction to "present value" reflects that the victim is in large part receiving compensation for losses he has not yet incurred. The reduction in the lump sum award must reflect the interest the plaintiff can earn on the advance transfer of money for future losses in income. This calculation requires, in theory, predicting what the future interest rates or other investment value of the money will be over the future period intended to be compensated. It also, on the other hand, requires taking into account that future inflation can reduce the value of the lump sum. An award in 1996 dollars for lost wages and medical expenses should reflect that comparable wages and expenses will likely increase due to inflation in subsequent years.[26]

Compensation for personal injury torts are not subject to federal income tax.[27] Consequently, to the extent personal injury damages award for lost wages (which would have been taxable), the plaintiff arguably is being excessively compensated. Nevertheless, most courts do not allow the jury to consider the potential tax free windfall to the plaintiff when calculating damages. Courts consider the plaintiff's personal potential tax liability too speculative to attempt to include in calculating damages. This is in striking contrast to elaborate efforts to account for future inflation and interest rates.

[E] *Pain and Suffering*

Courts allow plaintiffs in personal injury cases to recover for pain and suffering proximately caused by a tortfeasor. Pain and suffering is broadly defined to include mental distress over an injury and any disfigurement. It also includes compensation for loss of enjoyment of activities the injury precludes the victim from pursuing. Distress over the inability to play a favorite sport would consequently be compensated. The victim can also be compensated for distress over any reduction in life expectancy or concern over illnesses that the victim is at reasonable risk of incurring due to the physical injuries he or she actually suffered.[28]

---

[26] Courts use different approaches to account for the investment value of advanced payments and the countervailing likelihood of inflation. One approach asks the fact-finder to calculate compensation based on an estimate of future inflation and then to reduce this amount to its present value by calculating the extra investment value of receiving payment in advance. Courts assume rates based on a conservative, safe investment policy. Other courts as a matter of law assume that inflation will cancel out the investment benefit of advance payment and instruct the fact-finder to ignore both factors in their calculations. A third approach assumes that the actual market interest rate for money includes two components, the real rate of return or interest and an additional interest which simply compensates the investor for anticipated inflation. Courts using this approach compensate for inflation by estimating what is perceived to be the real rate of return in discounting the lump sum to present value. *See* Jones & Laughlin Steel Corp. v. Pfeifer, 462 U.S. 523 (1983).

[27] *See* Robert J. Henry, *Torts and Taxes, Taxes and Torts: The Taxation of Personal Injury Recoveries*, 23 Hous. L. Rev. 701 (1986).

[28] *See* Ferrara v. Galluchio, 152 N.E.2d 249 (N.Y. 1958). *See* § 10.01, *supra*. *See* Dan B. Dobbs, LAW OF REMEDIES: DAMAGES, EQUITY, RESTITUTION (2d ed. 1993); Marilyn K. Minzer et al., DAMAGES IN TORT ACTIONS (1982).

Most courts, as noted above, treat loss of enjoyment of life, including distress caused by reduced life expectancy, as components of the compensation for the victim's pain and suffering. Consequently, if the victim is unconscious, he usually cannot recover for loss of enjoyment because he is not aware of, and consequently not distressed by, these losses.[29] Pain and suffering compensation is therefore highly dependent on proof that the victim is or was during his life conscious of his injuries and the negative implications of those injuries.

How does the jury value pain and suffering? How much is pain worth?[30] In arguing how to value pain and suffering, plaintiffs' attorneys are usually allowed to ask the jury to measure the loss on a per diem basis and then to multiply by the appropriate number of days.[31] Courts do not, however, allow plaintiffs to make so-called "Golden Rule" arguments asking the jury members to consider how much payment they would require to exchange places with the victim.[32]

Unlike economic loss, pain and suffering, and other forms of mental distress, have no obvious monetary equivalent. Most courts acknowledge the imprecision of pain and suffering awards by not requiring a reduction to present value.[33] This valuation problem has generated controversy over the desirability of compensating for pain and suffering at all.[34]

On one hand, not to compensate mental distress is to ignore a very real loss, despite the inadequacy of monetary compensation in making the victim whole. Furthermore, from an accident avoidance perspective, if no damages were awarded for pain and suffering, a potential tortfeasor lacks appropriate

---

[29] *See* McDougald v. Garber, 536 N.E.2d 372 (N.Y. 1989). *But see* Kirk v. Washington State University, 746 P.2d 285 (Wash. 1987).

[30] *See* Sullivan v. Old Colony Street Ry., 83 N.E. 1091, 1092 (Mass. 1908), where the court stated "the rule of damages is a practical instrumentality for the administration of justice. Its objective is to afford the equivalent in money for the actual loss excused by the wrong of another." *Compare* Zibbell v. Southern Pacific Co., 116 P. 513, 520 (Cal. 1911), stating "[n]o rational being would change places with the injured man for an amount of gold that would fill the room of the court, yet no lawyer would contend that such is the legal measure of damages."

[31] *See* Beagle v. Vasold, 417 P.2d 673 (Cal. 1966). Some courts argue that per diem awards imply a precision in measurement for pain and suffering that does not exist. *See, e.g.*, Reid v. Baumgardner, 232 S.E.2d 778 (Va. 1977).

[32] Liosi v. Vaccaro, 315 N.Y.S.2d 225 (1970).

[33] *See* § 14.03[D], *supra.*

[34] *See* Louis L. Jaffe, *Damages for Personal Injury: The Impact of Insurance*, 18 Law & Contemp. Probs. 219 (1953), criticizing the rule compensating plaintiffs for pain and suffering. *See also* Cornelius J. Peck, *Compensation for Pain: A Reappraisal in Light of New Medical Evidence*, 72 Mich. L. Rev. 1355 (1974). *But see* Kwasny v. United States, 823 F.2d 194, 197 (7th Cir. 1987), where Judge Posner expressed disagreement with those who believe pain and suffering are not real costs, stating "[i]f they were not recoverable in damages, the cost of negligence would be less to the tortfeasors and there would be more negligence, more accidents, more pain and suffering, and hence higher social costs."

deterrence to avoid imposing such intangible harm on victims. Imposing liability for such intangible losses compels a potential defendant to recognize that culpable conduct can result in costs that encompass more than merely compensating for the victim's economic injury.

On the other hand, to a certain extent monetary recovery will never fully compensate for such intangible injuries. In addition, the cost of a corporate defendant's damages is generally passed on to consumers, increasing the expenses to all consumers. For example, the cost of medical care is increased by the cost of compensation for pain and suffering caused by malpractice. This has prompted some state legislation imposing a maximum recovery for pain and suffering.[35] The debate on pain and suffering is further complicated by the realization that intangible loss recoveries are often utilized to pay contingency fees to attorneys.[36] If no intangible injuries were compensated, the contingency fee would reduce available funds to compensate the victim for his actual economic losses.

§ 14.04 MITIGATION OR THE DOCTRINE OF AVOIDABLE CONSEQUENCES

Injured victims have a responsibility to act reasonably to limit or "mitigate" losses incurred.[37] For example, if A suffers personal injury as a result of B's negligence, A is expected to seek appropriate medical care to avoid more serious consequences from the injury.[38] If a plaintiff fails to act reasonably to mitigate injuries, the defendant will not be held liable for incremental losses that otherwise could have been avoided.

Failure to mitigate should be distinguished from a plaintiff's contributory or comparative negligence which contributed to causing the accident responsible for the injury.[39] The unreasonable failure to wear a motorcycle helmet or seat belt is sometimes characterized as a lapse in "anticipatory mitigation." The lack of a helmet doesn't contribute to an accident occurring but increases the likelihood incremental damages will result if an accident occurs. Nevertheless, many courts in comparative negligence jurisdictions allow such failures in reasonable anticipatory mitigations to be absorbed into comparative negligence. This allows the finder of fact discretion to

---

[35] *See, e.g.*, Cal. Civ. Code § 3333.2 (limiting non-economic damages to $250,000 in malpractice actions).

[36] Contingency fee arrangements are a method by which a lawyer is compensated by receiving a percentage of a plaintiff's recovery.

[37] *See, e.g.*, Zimmerman v. Ausland, 513 P.2d 1167 (Or. 1973). *See also* Marilyn K. Minzer et al., DAMAGES IN TORT ACTIONS (1982).

[38] *See* Restatement § 918. Given the personal nature of medical treatment, courts tend to allow victims some degree of discretion in determining appropriate medical treatment. Controversy remains over whether a court should excuse a victim from responsibility to mitigate when religious convictions prevent the victim from seeking medical treatment.

[39] *See* § 15.02[C].

allocate what is perceived as a fair portion of the damage attributable to a failure of anticipatory mitigation to the plaintiff.

§ 14.05 PUNITIVE DAMAGES[40]

[A] *Overview and Constitutionality*

In addition to compensatory damages, courts in most states award punitive damages against defendants who act with malice. Malice is generally defined to constitute ill will, hatred, or reckless disregard to the victim's rights.[41] Punitive damages are intended to provide both retribution for the defendant's wrongful conduct and to deter such conduct in the future;[42] consequently, it is appropriate for punitive damages to be adjusted to reflect the wealth of the defendant.[43] Therefore, where punitive damages are sought, it is considered relevant for the discovery process to include inquiries about the defendant's net worth.[44] Generally, however, courts also compare potential punitive damages with the compensatory damages and have been hesitant to allow punitive damages which are greatly in excess of actual losses.

Nevertheless, in *TXO Production Corp. v. Alliance Resources Corp.*[45] the Supreme Court, in a plurality opinion, upheld as satisfying constitutional substantive due process requirements, punitive damages that were over five hundred times the amount of the compensatory damages awarded. The Court concluded that punitive damages should take into account not only the injury actually suffered but "the potential harm that might result from the

---

[40] *See generally* Clarence Morris, *Punitive Damages in Tort Cases*, 44 Harv. L. Rev. 1173 (1931); David L. Walther and Thomas A. Plein, *Punitive Damages—A Critical Analysis: Kink v. Combs*, 49 Marq. L. Rev. 369 (1965); James B. Sales and Kenneth B. Cole, Jr., *Punitive Damages: A Relic That Has Outlived Its Origins*, 37 Vand. L. Rev. 1117 (1984); Marilyn K. Minzer et al., DAMAGES IN TORT ACTIONS (1982).

[41] Restatement § 908 states that punitive damages may be awarded where conduct is "outrageous, because of the defendant's evil motive or his reckless indifference to the rights of others." *See, e.g.*, Conn. Gen. Stat. § 52-240b (1995), and La. Civ. Code Ann. §§ 2315.3, 2315.4 (West 1995).

[42] *See, e.g.*, Cal. Civ. Code § 3294 (West 1995), where the plaintiff is allowed to recover "damages for the sake of example and by way of punishing the defendant," in addition to actual damages, in cases where the defendant acts with malice.

[43] *See* Joab, Inc. v. Thrall, 245 So. 2d 291 (Fla. Ct. App. 1971), where the defendants were equally culpable but different punitive damage awards were upheld on the basis of their disparity in wealth. *See generally* Kenneth S. Abraham and John C. Jefferies, Jr., *Punitive Damages and the Rule of Law: The Role of the Defendant's Wealth*, 18 J. Legal Stud. 415 (1989); Dorsey D. Ellis, Jr., *Fairness and Efficiency in the Law of Punitive Damages*, 56 S. Cal. L. Rev. 1 (1982).

[44] *See, e.g.*, Phelan v. Beswick, 326 P.2d 1034 (Or. 1958). For a discussion of various methods with which states procedurally protect defendants' financial privacy in specific instances, see Stephen E. Woodbury, *Limiting Discovery of a Defendant's Wealth When Punitive Damages are Alleged*, 23 Duq. L. Rev. 349 (1985).

[45] 509 U.S. 443 (1993).

defendant's conduct." The Court in *TXO Production Corp.* noted that the potential harm to the victim 'if the scheme had worked in evading royalty payments for oil production' was much greater than the actual damages incurred by the plaintiff. This justified the large punitive damage award.

Punitive damages have withstood other constitutional attack. Courts have rejected arguments that punitive damages constitute double jeopardy even though the defendant may also be subject to punishment under criminal law.[46] Additionally, in *Browning Ferris Industries v. Kelco Disposal, Inc.*, the Supreme Court held the Eighth Amendment and its provision prohibiting excessive fines was inapplicable to punitive damages awarded in civil trials.[47]

In *Pacific Mutual Life Insurance Co. v. Haslip*[48] the Supreme Court ruled that constitutional requirements for procedural due process were satisfied when the jury was instructed to award punitive damages based on "the character and the degree of wrong as shown by the evidence and necessity of preventing similar wrong." The defendant's contention that the jury was given inadequate guidance and excessive discretion was rejected since the trial court had identified the dual purposes of punitive damages to be retribution and deterrence, and explained that imposition of punitive damages was optional.

The Supreme Court also held in *Haslip* that Alabama's post-trial procedures adequately scrutinized punitive damage awards in determining whether they were excessive or inadequate by judicial consideration of seven factors that had been articulated by the Alabama judiciary:

> (a) whether there is a reasonable relationship between the punitive damages award and the harm likely to result from the defendant's conduct as well as the harm that actually has occurred; (b) the degree of reprehensibility of the defendant's conduct, the duration of that conduct, the defendant's awareness, any concealment, and the existence and frequency of similar past conduct; (c) the profitability to the defendant of the wrongful conduct and the desirability of removing that profit and of having the defendant also sustain a loss; (d) the "financial position" of the defendant; (e) all the costs of litigation; (f) the imposition of criminal sanctions on the defendant for its conduct, these to be taken in mitigation; and (g) the existence of other civil awards against the defendant for the same conduct, these also to be taken in mitigation.[49]

---

[46] *See* Wittman v. Gilson, 520 N.E.2d 514 (N.Y. 1988); United States v. Halper, 490 U.S. 435 (1989).

[47] 492 U.S. 257 (1989). *See also* Silkwood v. Kerr-McGee Corp., 464 U.S. 238 (1984), where the Supreme Court held federal atomic energy regulations did not preempt tort punitive damage remedies for victims who suffered injuries from exposure to radiation in a nuclear plant.

[48] 499 U.S. 1 (1991).

[49] *Id.* at 21-22.

[B] Policy Arguments For and Against Punitive Damages

The imposition of punitive damages remains highly controversial. Those opposed to punitive damages argue that it is duplicative of criminal punishment without the safeguards provided by criminal procedures, including the more rigorous burden of proof.[50]

The size of punitive damage awards which, as indicated above, can take into account the wealth of the defendant, is also criticized by some as excessive and too vulnerable to the jury's emotion. In addition, the danger exists that large punitive damage awards in one action may diminish the defendant's resources to adequately compensate victims in subsequent litigation. This has led many state legislatures to adopt caps on punitive damage awards, either by maximum amounts,[51] ratios between punitive and compensatory damages,[52] or some combination of both.[53]

Justifications for the imposition of punitive damages often focus on its role in deterring tortious conduct. The plaintiff is, in one sense, rewarded by punitive damages for her efforts to litigate against a defendant who acted with malice. This reward has long been viewed by defenders of punitive damages as providing added stimulus for private attorneys and clients to file tort actions against malicious wrongdoing.[54] Additionally, punitive damages, particularly because they can be adjusted to reflect the wealth of the defendant, can have a greater deterrent impact than statutorily prescribed fines.[55] Ultimately, the issue of punitive damages continues to

---

[50] *See* James E. Duffy, Jr., *Punitive Damages: A Doctrine Which Should Be Abolished, reprinted in* DEFENSE RESEARCH INSTITUTE: THE CASE AGAINST PUNITIVE DAMAGES 14 (Donald J. Hirsch & James Pouros, eds., 1969). *See also* Dan B. Dobbs, *Ending Punishment in "Punitive" Damages: Deterrence-Measured Remedies*, 40 Ala. L. Rev. 831 (1989).

[51] *See, e.g.*, Va. Code § 8.01-38.1 (Michie 1994), which limits punitive damages to a maximum of $350,000.

[52] *See, e.g.*, Conn. Gen. Stat. § 52-240b (1995), which limits punitive damage awards in products liability cases to two times the amount of compensatory ("actual") damages.

[53] *See, e.g.*, Tex. Civ. Prac. & Rem. Code Ann. § 41.007 (West 1995), which limits punitive damages to the higher of $200,000 or four times the amount of compensatory damages. Note Utah's sliding scale, judicially created in Crookston v. Fire Insurance Exchange, 817 P.2d 789 (Utah 1991), which limits punitive damages to three times the amount of compensatory damages if such damages are under $100,000, then gradually lowers the ratio as compensatory damage amounts increase.

[54] *See* Clarence Morris, *Punitive Damages in Tort Cases*, 44 Harv. L. Rev. 1173 (1931).

[55] For example, continued lawsuits eventually led to the abandonment of the "Dalkon Shield" contraceptive by manufacturer A.H. Robins. *See, e.g.*, Tetuan v. A.H. Robins Co., 738 P.2d 1210 (Kan. 1987), and Palmer v. A.H. Robins Co., 684 P.2d 187 (Colo. 1984), upholding punitive damage awards of $7.5 million and $6.2 million, respectively. Note, that in cases involving the Ford Pinto automobile, internal documents revealed that the manufacturer performed cost-benefit studies which anticipated the number of lawsuits, and the costs to settle each, stemming from the injuries caused by design defect. *See, e.g.*, Grimshaw v. Ford Motor Co., 174 Cal. Rptr. 348 (Cal. Ct. App. 1981).

reflect a tension between differing perspectives, that of torts as merely a compensation system for loss versus a quasi-criminal system punishing and deterring wrongdoing.

[C] *Insurance Liability for Punitive Damages*

Jurisdictions are divided over whether to allow insurance coverage for liability for punitive damages.[56] Some states as a matter of public policy prohibit insurance coverage on the basis that such coverage effectively allows the wrongdoer to escape a judicially imposed punishment. Other courts conclude that potential defendants should be free to contract for protection from punitive damages especially since such damages can be imposed for tortious conduct which may not be intentional. Whether punitive damages is insurable can be a double-edged sword, since a plaintiff may find some defendants, left without insurance, unable to pay a punitive damage award.

[D] *Respondeat Superior and Punitive Damages*

The Restatement indicates that punitive damages may be levied against an employer or "other principal" because of an act by that party's agent if:

(a) the principal or a managerial agent authorized the doing and the manner of the act, or

(b) the agent was unfit and the principal or a managerial agent was reckless in employing or retaining him, or

(c) the agent was employed in a managerial capacity and was acting in the scope of employment, or

(d) the principal or a managerial agent of the principal ratified or approved the act.[57]

The Restatement view has been adopted in many states.[58] A substantial number of jurisdictions, however, allow punitive damages whenever an employee was within the course of her employment when the tortious act

[56] *See* Northwestern Nat'l Casualty Co. v. McNulty, 307 F.2d 432, 442 (5th Cir. 1962), where the court found that the defendant, a particularly reckless driver, should not have been allowed to receive "a windfall at the expense of purchasers of insurance, transferring his responsibility for punitive damages to the very people . . . to whom he is a menace." *But see* Price v. Hartford Accident and Indemnity Co., 502 P.2d 522 (Ariz. 1972), where the court allowed punitive damages to be insured. The court concluded public policy should not invalidate an obligation which the insurance company assumed for payment in a contract. The court also noted that criminal sanctions were also potentially applicable and that defendant's future insurance premium would likely be increased.

[57] Restatement § 909.

[58] *See, e.g.*, Purvis v. Prattco, Inc., 595 S.W.2d 103 (Tex. 1980).

occurred without reference to the culpability of the employer or managerial staff.[59] The constitutionality of this approach has been sustained.[60]

§ 14.06 COLLATERAL SOURCE RULE[61]

Under traditional common law doctrine, the plaintiff's recovery against the defendant is not affected by compensation the plaintiff received for the loss from other sources.[62] Such collateral sources for recovery are not disclosed to the jury under the collateral source rule.[63]

The rule is best demonstrated through an example. If A negligently injures B in an automobile accident, B can sue A for medical costs, lost wages, and property damages. In fact, such medical costs may be covered to a significant extent by B's health insurance. B may also have disability insurance to cover lost wages and automobile insurance to cover the damage to his car. Despite the fact that B may recover compensatory damages in this instance, B's carrying of insurance is prudent since medical expenses and disability can be incurred in many natural contexts where B would not have other remedies. B did not purchase insurance in order to limit the liability of a tortfeasor who injures him. A's liability is thus not affected under the collateral source rule by B's insurance coverage.

The collateral source rule does not displace insurance contracts allowing insurance companies to arrange that, in the event of a tortious injury resulting in a compensatory and punitive damage payout to the insured, the insured's right to recovery of such damages shifts to the insurance company to the extent of policy coverage. These types of insurer-insured agreements are called subrogation clauses.[64]

---

59 *See* Stroud v. Denny's Restaurant, Inc., 532 P.2d 790 (Or. 1975).

60 *See* Pacific Mutual Life Insurance Co. v. Haslip, 499 U.S. 1 (1991).

61 *See* John G. Fleming, *The Collateral Source Rule and Loss Allocation in Tort Law*, 54 Cal. L. Rev. 1478 (1966), and American Law Institute, *Reporter's Study on Enterprise Liability for Personal Injury*, 2, at 161-182 (Paul C. Weiler ed. 1991), criticizing the rule.

62 *See* Restatement § 920A and Restatement § 920A cmt. d.

63 *See* Helfend v. Southern California Rapid Transit District, 465 P.2d 61 (Cal. 1970), where the court held that the collateral source rule applies to government defendants as well as private defendants, and thus the transit district was not allowed to show that the plaintiff's medical costs had already been compensated by his insurer. "To permit the defendant to tell the jury that the plaintiff has been recompensed by a collateral source for his medical costs might irretrievably upset the complex, delicate, and somewhat indefinable calculations which result in the normal jury verdict." Id. at 68.

64 Plaintiffs may attempt to circumvent subrogation clauses. In Smith v. Marzolf, 375 N.E.2d 995 (Ill. Ct. App. 1978), the plaintiff was injured by the defendant's negligence and was insured for up to $50,000 of his medical costs and lost wages. The plaintiff sued the defendant, and the plaintiff's wife added a claim for loss of consortium. The parties settled, allocating $10,000 to the plaintiff's claim and $65,000 to his wife's claim. The insurance company, which had already paid $17,000 to the plaintiff and was likely to be obligated to pay the full $50,000, objected to these settlement terms. It did so out of concern that the plaintiff's relatively small recovery, compared to his wife's derivative claim, would allow

Numerous reform statutes, most notably in the context of medical malpractice, now reject the collateral source rule and allow the jury to consider such insurance payouts and deduct them from the defendant's liability. Some reform statutes explicitly state that the award is to be reduced by the amount of the collateral source's contribution.[65] Other statutes allow collateral source admissibility without indicating what role such evidence should play in the jury's deliberations.[66] In the context of medical malpractice, these reforms are intended to reduce hospitals' and physicians' insurance rates. They may result, however, in increases to the patient's insurance rates because the victim's own health insurance is unable to recoup payment for expenses incurred as a result of the malpractice. In some, but not all, instances, statutory reforms rejecting the collateral source rule have been held unconstitutional.[67]

---

him to evade the subrogation clause of his insurance policy. The court disallowed the ultimate settlement as an attempt by the insured to avoid his obligations to his insurer. *Id.* at 998.

[65] *See, e.g.*, N.Y. Civ. Prac. L. & R. § 4545(c) (West 1995).

[66] *See, e.g.*, Cal. Civ. Code § 3333.1 (West 1995).

[67] *See, e.g.*, Farley v. Engelken, 740 P.2d 1058 (Kan. 1987), ruling abolition of collateral source rule in medical cases discriminated against victims of medical malpractice.

CHAPTER 15

DEFENSES

SYNOPSIS

---

§ 15.01 OVERVIEW

Traditionally, there were only two defenses[1] to negligence: contributory negligence and assumption of risk.[2] Both constituted complete defenses and completely barred the plaintiff from recovery. In all but a handful of states,[3] contributory negligence has been converted by statute or judicial ruling into comparative negligence.[4] Unlike contributory negligence, comparative negligence need not be a complete bar to the plaintiff's recovery, but acts only as partial bar resulting in a percentage deduction from otherwise recoverable damages.

In the rush to convert contributory negligence to comparative negligence, the status of assumption of risk was often left unresolved. The current trend is to merge implied assumption of risk[5] into comparative negligence. Some

---

[1] It is important to distinguish a failure of a plaintiff to prove an element of negligence, such as proximate cause, from a defense to negligence. While either of the two would free the defendant from liability, defendants must affirmatively prove a defense and persuasively establish its application to the facts only after a plaintiff has established a prima facie case for each of the elements of negligence.

[2] *See generally* Wex S. Malone, *The Formative Era of Contributory Negligence*, 41 Ill. L. Rev. 151 (1946); Fleming James, Jr., *Contributory Negligence*, 62 Yale L.J. 691 (1953). *See also* Emlin McClain, *Contractual Limitation on Liability for Negligence*, 28 Harv. L. Rev. 550 (1915); John H. Mansfield, *Informed Choice in the Law of Torts*, 22 La. L. Rev. 17 (1961); Richard A. Posner, *A Theory of Negligence*, 1 J. Legal Stud. 29 (1972); John L. Diamond, *Assumption of Risk After Comparative Negligence: Integrating Contract Theory into Tort Doctrine*, 52 Ohio St. L.J. 717 (1991).

[3] By 1994, 46 states had adopted some form of a comparative negligence scheme. All but 12 of these jurisdictions did so by some legislatively developed statutory scheme. *See generally* Victor E. Schwartz, COMPARATIVE NEGLIGENCE (3d ed. 1994).

[4] Comparative negligence is also often referred to as comparative fault.

[5] Implied assumption of risk occurs when a plaintiff's assumption of risk is implied by her conduct.

states retain assumption of risk as a complete defense, sc types of implied assumption of risk into comparative neg parts as a complete defense, and others have abolished completely.[6]

The decision of most states to adopt comparative negligence has broad implications for the tort of negligence, as even plaintiffs partially responsible for their own harm are now able to recover. This raises serious issues concerning the equitable apportionment of damages between parties, all of whom (including the plaintiff) could have prevented the harm by behaving in a non-negligent manner.

Traditionally, assumption of risk, but not contributory negligence, was a defense to strict liability.[7] Where assumption of risk and contributory negligence are both absorbed into comparative negligence, some jurisdictions are allowing comparative negligence (whether based on contributory negligence or assumption of risk) to be a partial defense.[8]

In addition to the defenses of contributory negligence, comparative negligence and assumption of risk, immunities protect some defendants from tort liability. An immunity is not dependent on the behavior of the plaintiff or the defendant but is granted because of the status of who the defendant is. Historically, charities and the government and its officials enjoyed tort immunity. In addition, spouses were historically immune from suits by the other spouse, and parents and their children were immune from tort suits brought against each other. As discussed below, the trend has been to limit or eliminate many of these immunities.

§ 15.02 CONTRIBUTORY NEGLIGENCE

[A] *Definition*

The Restatement articulates the accepted definition of contributory negligence:

> Conduct on the part of the plaintiff which falls below the standard of conduct to which he should conform for his own protection, and which is a legally contributing cause cooperating with the negligence of the defendant in bringing about the plaintiff's harm.[9]

The standard is objective. The plaintiff, just as the defendant, is compared to a hypothetical person. Ordinarily, this is the reasonable adult, but as with defendants, this is adjusted for children and professionals, if applicable. Consequently, the child plaintiff is only compared to the hypothetical child

---

[6] *See generally* John L. Diamond, *Assumption of Risk After Comparative Negligence: Integrating Contract Theory into Tort Doctrine*, 52 Ohio St. L.J. 717 (1991).

[7] See Chapter 16, *infra*.

[8] *See* Daley v. General Motors Corporation, 575 P.2d 1162 (Cal. 1978).

[9] Restatement § 463.

of like age, intelligence and experience.[10] Indeed, the use of the alternative hypothetical standards are most accepted in the context of contributory negligence. The impulse to be more forgiving to a plaintiff appears intuitively more appealing than allowing defendants to insulate themselves from liability by retreating to a less demanding standard of conduct. While the Restatement does not make any dispensation for a mentally deficient or insane plaintiff,[11] a number of court decisions have made allowances.[12] Such adjustments may be less compelling in the context of comparative negligence where finding the plaintiff at fault would not necessarily bar recovery.[13]

For plaintiff's conduct to preclude her recovery altogether, her negligence towards her own protection must be a cause-in-fact and a proximate cause of the accident resulting in injury.[14] If A's carelessness in not carrying a flashlight would not have precluded B from hitting her while driving his car negligently, A's own negligence did not contribute to the accident and consequently A is not contributorily negligent. Courts have used the requirement that a plaintiff's negligence be a legal cause of the injury to justify a finding of no contributory negligence and avoid the harshness of totally precluding a plaintiff's recovery, where perhaps causation might have been held satisfied in a comparative negligence system.

The failure of a plaintiff to take reasonable precautions to protect himself in the event of an accident should be distinguished from contributory negligence. For example, A fails to put on her seatbelt while driving and is negligently hit by B's automobile. A's negligence in not wearing a seatbelt is not contributory negligence, since the failure to wear a seatbelt did not legally contribute to the accident which induced A's harm. This is so, even if the plaintiff suffers a greater injury as a result of not wearing the seatbelt.[15]

A's failure to wear a seatbelt or, analogously, a motorcycle helmet, has been characterized as a failure of "anticipatory mitigation." Victims have a responsibility to mitigate their injury. If A hits B, causing B's nose to

---

[10] *See supra* § 3.05.

[11] The Restatement's position for plaintiffs is identical with its position for defendants. *See* § 3.04, *supra.*

[12] *See, e.g.*, Cowan v. Doering, 545 A.2d 159 (N.J. 1988), where the court imposed liability upon doctors and nurses of a hospital, based upon a duty to take into account the known suicidal tendencies of a patient. *See also* Bramlette v. Charter-Medical-Columbia, 393 S.E.2d 914 (S.C. 1990); McNamara v. Honeyman, 546 N.E.2d 139 (Mass. 1989).

[13] *See infra* § 15.03.

[14] *See generally* Dan B. Dobbs, *Accountability and Comparative Fault,* 47 La. L. Rev. 939 (1987). *See* Chapters 11 and 12, *supra.*

[15] *Cf.* Mahoney v. Beatman, 147 A. 762 (Conn. 1929), where a speeding plaintiff was hit by a defendant who negligently crossed into her lane. Here it was obvious the speed was not the accident's cause but did aggravate the plaintiff's injuries.

bleed, B cannot allow it to continue to bleed, but must act reasonably to mitigate the bleeding. A's liability is limited to damages that could not reasonably be mitigated.[16] By analogy, some courts have held B's failure to wear a seatbelt as a failure to mitigate in advance of an injury. Under the anticipatory mitigation approach, A is liable for the increased severity of damages attributable to her failure to wear a seatbelt.[17] She is not contributorily negligent and therefore can recover for the negligence causing the injury which would have been suffered even if she was wearing a seatbelt.[18] The distinction between anticipatory mitigation and contributory negligence is less significant in the context of comparative negligence which is not a complete defense.[19] Consequently, in many jurisdictions, negligent failure to mitigate is simply absorbed into comparative negligence.

Contributory negligence is a defense to negligence but not to intentional torts. If A attempts to punch B, it is not a defense that B was contributorily negligent by not ducking quickly enough. Contributory negligence has also been held not to be a defense to willful, wanton, or reckless conduct.[20] Such conduct, while still a variant of negligence, is so extremely unreasonable that courts have held ordinary contributory negligence cannot be a defense. If A negligently steps off a sidewalk curb and is hit by B, who is driving one hundred miles per hour in a thirty-mile-per-hour speed zone with his eyes closed, A's contributory negligence is not a defense to B's reckless conduct. In comparative negligence jurisdictions,[21] the distinction between recklessness and negligence is immaterial, because the great disparity in unreasonable conduct can be accounted for in the comparative negligence determination.

[B] *Last Clear Chance Doctrine*

The last clear chance doctrine[22] instructs the court to ignore the plaintiff's contr ibutory negligence if the defendant's negligence occurred *after* the p laintiff's contributory negligence. This doctrine has evolved from the

[16] If B's failure to address an injury medically is based on religious principles, B's failure to mitigate could arguably be deemed reasonable under the circumstances.

[17] *See, e.g.*, Spier v. Barker, 323 N.E.2d 164, 167 (N.Y. 1974), where the court stated that "by not fastening his seat belt the plaintiff may, under the circumstances of the particular case, be found to have acted unreasonably and in disregard of his own best interests, and, thus, should not be permitted to recover damages for those injuries which a seat belt would have obviated."

[18] *See* Spier v. Barker, 323 N.E.2d 164 (N.Y. 1974); Law v. Superior Ct., 755 P.2d 1135 (Ariz. 1988); Wemyss v. Coleman, 729 S.W.2d 174 (Ky. 1987); Waterson v. General Motors Corp., 544 A.2d 357 (N.J. 1988).

[19] *See* Curry v. Moser, 454 N.Y.S.2d 311 (1982).

[20] *See, e.g.*, Adkisson v. City of Seattle, 258 P.2d 461, 467 (Wash. 1953).

[21] *See infra* § 15.03.

[22] This doctrine was codified in the Restatement. Restatement §§ 479, 480.

historic case, *Davies v. Mann.*[23] In *Davies*, the plaintiff's donkey was tethered improperly and thus vulnerable to highway traffic. Later that day, the defendant drove his team of horses negligently and ran over the donkey. The defendant argued that the plaintiff was contributorily negligent in improperly tethering the donkey and should have been barred from recovery. The court held that the plaintiff's contributory negligence would not bar recovery since the defendant, had he acted with ordinary care, had the last clear chance to avoid the accident.

The doctrine of last clear chance is based purely on chronology.[24] If the defendant was negligent after the plaintiff, the plaintiff's contributory negligence is ignored and the plaintiff can receive a complete recovery.[25] This doctrine reflects a questionable policy.[26] One judge in *Davies* justified the doctrine by concluding "[w]ere this not so, a man might justify the driving over goods left on a public highway, or even a man lying asleep there, or the purposely running against a carriage going on the wrong side of the road." Such arguments ignore that contributory negligence is not a defense to such intentional torts.

More fundamentally, the doctrine excuses what could be egregious contributory negligence while enforcing slight contributory negligence as a complete bar, simply on the basis of chronology and not the degree of culpability. Nor does the doctrine appear to be consistent with a rationale based on proximate cause doctrine where chronology is not a decisive factor.[27] The doctrine can best be explained as one method for nullifying the impact of contributory negligence, which has increasingly been perceived as unduly harsh to plaintiffs.[28] Consistent with this proposition, many jurisdictions reject the last clear chance doctrine when replacing contributory negligence with comparative negligence.

[C] *Plaintiffs Unable to Exercise Self-Protection*

Restatement section 483 also precludes contributory negligence for a defendant who violates a "statute . . . enacted to protect a class of persons

[23] 10 M&W 546, 152 Eng. Rep. 588 (1842).

[24] *See* Steven Shavell, *Torts in Which the Victim and Injurer Act Sequentially*, 26 J.L. & Econ. 589 (1983); Donald Wittman, *Optimal Pricing of Sequential Inputs: Last Clear Chance, Mitigation of Damages, and Related Doctrines in the Law*, 10 J. Legal Stud. 65 (1981).

[25] States utilizing the last clear chance doctrine have in some instances characterized the last attentive party as possessing the last clear chance even when both parties to an accident would be physically able to avoid the accident.

[26] *See generally* Malcolm M. MacIntyre, *The Rationale of Last Clear Chance*, 53 Harv. L. Rev. 1225 (1940).

[27] *See supra* Chapter 12.

[28] *See* Fleming James, Jr., *Last Clear Chance: A Transitional Doctrine*, 47 Yale L.J. 704 (1938).

from their inability to exercise self-protective care." Such statutes would include child labor laws and the sale of liquor to intoxicated patrons.

§ 15.03 COMPARATIVE NEGLIGENCE

In all but four states, contributory negligence has been replaced by some form of comparative negligence,[29] often called comparative fault. Under comparative negligence, "the conduct on the part of the plaintiff which falls below the standard of conduct which he should conform to for his own protection and which is a legally contributing cause cooperating with the negligence of the defendant in bringing about the plaintiff's harm"[30] is only a partial bar to the plaintiff's recovery. Comparative negligence reduces the plaintiff's recovery by the percentage of her responsibility for the injury attributable to the plaintiff.

[A] *Pure Comparative Negligence*

Pure comparative negligence has been adopted by 12 states.[31] Under this approach, plaintiffs can recover some percentage from liable defendants regardless of the extent of their own negligence.[32] If, for example, plaintiff A is sixty percent responsible for an accident with defendant B, A can still recover forty percent of the damages.

[B] *Modified Comparative Negligence*

Thirty-four states utilize one of three forms of modified comparative negligence. Under the modified system, plaintiffs are allowed a partial recovery just as in pure comparative negligence, until the plaintiff reaches a certain level of culpability for her own accident. Once the plaintiff reaches this level of culpability, the plaintiff is completely barred from any recovery just as in contributory negligence.

[1] The Twenty-One State Approach

Under this modified form of comparative negligence a plaintiff is barred from recovery only when she is *more* negligent (greater than 50% at fault) than the defendant(s).[33] For example, if plaintiff A is 50% responsible for the accident, she can still recover 50% of her damages from the liable defendants.

---

[29] *See generally* Victor E. Schwartz, COMPARATIVE NEGLIGENCE (3d ed. 1994); *Comparative Negligence Symposium*, 23 Mem. St. U. L. Rev. (1992); Uniform Comparative Fault Act, 12 U.L.A. 33 (1981 Supp.).

[30] *See* Restatement § 463. The Restatement adopts contributory negligence, *see supra* § 15.02 [A].

[31] *See* Victor E. Schwartz, COMPARATIVE NEGLIGENCE (3d ed. 1994).

[32] *See, e.g.*, Li v. Yellow Cab Co., 532 P.2d 1226 (Cal. 1975).

[33] *See, e.g.*, Minn. Stat. Ann. § 604.01.

[2] The Twelve-State Approach

Under this form of modified comparative negligence a plaintiff is barred from recovery when she is *equal to or more* negligent (greater than or equal to 50% at fault) than the defendant(s).[34] If plaintiff A is 50% at fault she would be barred from recovery. On the other hand, if A is even slightly less than 50% at fault she can recover the percentage of damages in proportion to the defendant(s) fault. For example, if A was 49.9% responsible then she could still recover 50.1% of her damages.

[3] "Slight" Comparative Negligence

One state, South Dakota, utilizes comparative negligence only when the plaintiff's own negligence is "slight."[35] Otherwise the plaintiff's negligence is a complete bar.

[C] *Determining The Percentage of Fault Attributable to the Plaintiff*

How does the court determine in percentages the relative fault of the plaintiff and the defendant under comparative negligence? The question is one of fact, and in essence the trier of fact simply selects a percentage based on its own appraisal of relative fault. The process of comparative negligence has been described as "a flexible, common sense concept, under which a [trier of fact] properly may consider and evaluate the relative responsibility of various parties for an injury . . . in order to arrive at an 'equitable apportionment or allocation of loss.' "[36]

[D] *Comparison Between Different Systems*

[1] Contributory Negligence Versus Comparative Negligence

From a moral perspective, it can be argued that comparative negligence allows for a more equitable allocation of responsibility for the injuries derived from an accident.[37] Under contributory negligence, at least in theory,[38] a plaintiff's slight contributory negligence completely bars

---

[34] *See, e.g.*, McIntyre v. Balentine, 833 S.W.2d 52 (Tenn. 1992). The distinction between 50% and more than 50% is significant because jurors frequently determine both parties are "equally to blame." The plaintiff's percentage of fault is determined in comparison to the sum of all contributors to the accident, whether in the litigation or not.

[35] *See, e.g.*, Myers v. Quenzer, 110 N.W.2d 840 (S.D. 1961).

[36] Knight v. Jewett, 834 P.2d 696, 700 (Cal. 1992).

[37] *See generally Comparative Negligence Symposium*, 23 Mem. St. U. L. Rev. (1992).

[38] Jury "nullification" could result in a finding of no contributory negligence, at least where the plaintiff's fault was slight and the jury believed a finding of contributory negligence would preclude the plaintiff's recovery. Juries determining some plaintiff culpability may reduce the award accordingly. In such instances, the jury is rejecting the judge's instructions to achieve what they perceive to be justice.

recovery. Furthermore, a plaintiff's contributory negligence may, in one sense, be less culpable than the defendant's negligence since the defendant is exposing others or their property to risk, while the plaintiff is only exposing his own interests to risk.[39] On the other hand, contributory negligence, by precluding the plaintiff's recovery, recognizes that the plaintiff, herself, could have avoided all injury by acting prudently. This reflects the historic concept that the plaintiff should not receive judicial redress without innocence or "clean hands."[40]

From an accident avoidance perspective, comparative negligence encourages all the parties to engage in the most cost efficient behavior to avoid potential mishaps.[41] For example, A is a farmer who plants crops adjacent to a railroad track, and B's train carelessly damages A's crop. If A is contributorily negligent, B needn't compensate A and has no incentive to avoid further injury. Under a comparative negligence scheme, B and A must both act reasonably. This can be particularly useful if B's cost to avoid A's injury is much less than A's cost, which might involve substantially decreased productivity.[42]

From a compensation perspective, comparative negligence allows a negligent plaintiff to receive compensation against negligent defendants. Such compensation is, however, reduced by the relative fault of the plaintiff.

[2] Comparison Between Pure and Modified Systems of Comparative Fault

Under pure comparative negligence, the plaintiff can recover from defendants even if the plaintiff is primarily responsible for the accident. If A carelessly drives his Rolls Royce into B's bicycle, which is parked slightly off the curb in a negligent manner, A may be 90% comparatively negligent. Under the pure system, A can still recover 10% of his damages. Assuming the car sustains $10,000 in damages, A could recover $1,000. In a counter suit for damage to his bicycle, B, as plaintiff against A, would get 90% of his damages. If B's bicycle suffered $1,000 damages, B would recover $900.[43] Critics of the pure system would argue the party primarily

---

[39] Some courts characterize this interest as a duty to oneself. *See, e.g.*, Bartlett v. MacRae, 635 P.2d 666 (Or. Ct. App. 1981), where the court found an obligation to use ordinary care for one's own protection. The plaintiff's carelessness may, however, constitute negligence to others in the same context.

[40] *See* Davis v. Guarnieri, 15 N.E. 350 (Ohio 1887).

[41] *See generally* David Haddock and Christopher Curran, *An Economic Theory of Comparative Negligence*, 14 J. Legal Stud. 49 (1985); Robert D. Cooter and Thomas S. Ulen, *An Economic Case for Comparative Negligence*, 61 N.Y.U. L. Rev. 1067 (1986).

[42] *See* Richard A. Posner, ECONOMIC ANALYSIS OF THE LAW (3d ed. 1986) at 155-57.

[43] A comparable example was detailed in Bradley v. Appalachian Power Co., 256 S.E.2d 879 (W. Va. 1979), prompting the West Virginia Supreme Court to adopt modified instead of pure comparative negligence. *Consider also* Sutton v. Piasecki Trucking Inc., 451 N.E.2d 481 (N.Y. 1983), where the plaintiff ignored a stop sign and was hit by the defendant's vehicle. The defendant pleaded comparative negligence as a defense and the plaintiff was found 99% at fault. A recovery of 1% of the damages was thus allowed.

responsible for the accident should not recover damages from others lesser at fault. Proponents of the pure system can argue that each party absorbs his own equitable portion of his own damages. In the above example, A still absorbs $9,000 and B only absorbs $100 of their respective losses.

As discussed above, the modified system precludes the plaintiff from any recovery in 12 states if she is at least 50%[44] at fault and in 21 other states if she is more than 50% at fault for the accident. The modified system embodies in part the rationale of contributory negligence. While contributory negligence bars the plaintiff recovery whenever she shares responsibility for her injuries, modified comparative negligence bars recovery whenever the plaintiff is primarily responsible for her injuries. If responsibility is viewed as a continuum, arguably it is fairer to allow the trier of fact to appropriate equitable portions of responsibility to the plaintiff and defendants. On the other hand, the modified system instead accepts the notion that a primary wrongdoer should be more properly precluded from any redress from tortfeasors who, even collectively, are less responsible than him for the accident.

§ 15.04 ASSUMPTION OF RISK

[A] *Definition*

Along with contributory negligence, assumption of risk has traditionally existed as a complete defense to negligence.[45] The Restatement defines assumption of risk as follows:

> [A] plaintiff who fully understands a risk of harm to himself or his things caused by the defendant's conduct or by the condition of the defendant's land or chattels, and who nevertheless voluntarily chooses to enter or remain, or to permit his things to enter or remain within the area of that risk, under circumstances that manifest his willingness to accept it, is not entitled to recover . . . .[46]

There are thus three basic elements to assumption of risk. The plaintiff must (1) know a particular risk and (2) voluntarily (3) assume it.

---

[44] This approach has been criticized in Claude R. Sowle and Daniel O. Conkle, *Comparative Negligence Versus the Constitutional Guarantee of Equal Protection: A Hypothetical Decision*, 1979 Duke L.J. 1083.

[45] *See generally* Leon Green, *Assumed Risk as a Defense*, 22 La. L. Rev. 77 (1961); Kenneth W. Simons, *Assumption of Risk and Consent in the Law of Torts: A Theory of Full Preference*, 67 B.U. L. Rev. 213 (1987); John L. Diamond, *Assumption of Risk After Comparative Negligence: Integrating Contract Theory into Tort Doctrine*, 52 Ohio St. L.J. 717 (1991). Assumption of risk emerged from a common law action of a servant against his master. It was initially utilized to protect employers from liability to workers for dangers they knowingly encountered in the workplace. *See* Paul Rosenlund and Paul Killion, *Once a Wicked Sister: The Continuing Role of Assumption of Risk Under Comparative Fault in California*, 20 U.S.F. L. Rev. 225, 226 (1986).

[46] Restatement § 496C.

[1] Knowledge of a Particular Risk

Assumption of risk, unlike contributory negligence, employs a subjective standard. The plaintiff must have actual and conscious knowledge of the particular risk. This is in contrast with contributory or comparative negligence, which involve objective inquiries into what the plaintiff knew or should have known. In order for an assumption of risk defense to be successful, the plaintiff must know of the particular risk, along with its magnitude and implications.[47] If A gets on an amusement park ride after seeing that it is a moving sidewalk which throws riders down, A has assumed the risk of falling from that motion.[48] A has not, however, assumed the risk of hidden spikes that could impale those that fall.

[2] Voluntariness

The plaintiff must voluntarily expose herself or her property to the risk to assume the risk. Voluntariness is an amorphous concept, and courts differ in its characterization. In a renowned case, *Rush v. Commercial Realty Co.*,[49] Mrs. Rush, "having occasion" to use a detached outhouse provided by her landlord, "fell through the floor, or through some sort of trap door therein, descended about nine feet into the accumulation at the bottom, and had to be extricated by use of a ladder."[50] The court held as a matter of the law that despite the fact the plaintiff knew the outhouse floor was in "bad order," she had "no choice, when impelled by the calls of nature" and "was not required to leave the premises."[51]

In *Rush*, the court concluded the plaintiff's encounter with the known risk was "involuntary," thereby precluding the defense of assumption of risk. Not all courts may be as lenient. Clearly the term "involuntary" can encompass an entire range of actions, from truly coerced actions to those

---

[47] Note the resulting ease with which a plaintiff may be able to deny she knew and appreciated the risk. To circumvent this problem, courts have stated that the jury need not take the plaintiff at her word, and may examine her actions in a common sense context. Thus, a jury may choose to disbelieve a plaintiff who rode with an obviously drunk driver but denied knowing of his condition. *See* Harlow v. Connelly, 548 S.W.2d 143 (Ky. Ct. App. 1977). Furthermore, plaintiffs themselves may admit they discussed a risk, an admission which no doubt works to their detriment when the defense has been raised. *See* Kaplan v. Missouri Pacific R. R. Co., 409 So. 2d 298 (La. Ct. App. 1981).

[48] *See, e.g.*, Murphy v. Steeplechase Amusement Co., 166 N.E. 173 (N.Y. 1929); *see also* Woodall v. Wayne Steffner Productions, Inc., 20 Cal. Rptr. 572 (Cal. Ct. App. 1962), where a stunt flyer, the "Human Kite," who "flew" while strapped to a makeshift kite attached to a moving automobile, was injured when an inexperienced driver exceeded a safe speed and the kite plunged to the ground as a result. The court found for the plaintiff, holding that while he *did* assume the risk of falling, he did not assume the risk of being driven by an incompetent driver.

[49] 145 A. 476 (N.J. 1929).

[50] *Id.* at 476.

[51] *Id.*

which would be unreasonably difficult to avoid. The court's sympathy to the plaintiff or empathy for her predicament may influence its interpretation of what is voluntary.

[3] Assuming the Risk

The defense of assumption of risk only applies to the particular risk which the plaintiff has knowingly and voluntarily assumed. In essence, it is analogous to the defense of consent in intentional torts. The plaintiff, by voluntarily exposing herself or her property interests to a risk, is deemed to consent to that risk.

[B] *Classifications of Assumption of Risk*

[1] Express Versus Implied Assumption of Risk

Assumption of risk is generally divided into two types: express and implied. Express assumption of risk exists when, by contract or otherwise, a plaintiff explicitly agrees to accept a risk.[52] Implied assumption of risk exists when the plaintiff's voluntary exposure to risk is derived merely from her behavior, and not from explicit assent.[53] The distinction is important because many jurisdictions, as discussed below, are absorbing implied, but not express assumption of risk into comparative negligence.

[2] Express Assumption of Risk

Express assumption of risk is a complete defense to the specific risks that the plaintiff has agreed to assume. Express assumption of risk can be invalidated in specific instances when it would be contrary to public policy.[54] In *Tunkl v. Regents of University of California*,[55] for example, the court invalidated an express agreement by a patient to assume the risk of medical malpractice by a hospital. Courts will often invalidate agreements where plaintiffs assume the risks of very reckless conduct. Assumption of risk of negligent conduct is less likely to be invalidated except when there is such a gross disparity in bargaining power between the defendant and the plaintiff that the plaintiff has little choice but to assume the risk.[56]

---

[52] *See* Restatement § 496B.

[53] *See* Restatement § 496C. Some jurisdictions take a more expansive view of express assumption of risk. *See* Blackburn v. Dorta, 348 So. 2d 287, 290 (Fla. 1977), where the court characterized as express assumption of risk voluntary participation in a contact sport without an explicit agreement to assume risk. *See also* Arbegast v. Board of Educ., 480 N.E.2d 365 (N.Y. 1985), where an injury to a teacher during a donkey basketball game was held to be expressly assumed because she had been informed of the involved risks.

[54] *See* Restatement § 496B.

[55] 383 P.2d 441 (Cal. 1963).

[56] Examples where the disparity of bargaining power may invalidate express agreement include: employer-employee relationships (*see* Restatement § 496B cmt. f) and public utilities (*see, e.g.*, Oklahoma Natural Gas Co. v. Appel, 266 P.2d 442 (Okla. 1954)).

Conversely, courts are likely to uphold express assumption of risk when the plaintiff's participation is clearly voluntary, such as the decision to engage in risky recreational pursuits.[57]

[3] Implied Assumption of Risk

Implied assumption of risk is, as noted above, implied by the plaintiff's conduct in relation to the risk. Ever since contributory negligence has been predominantly replaced by comparative negligence, jurisdictions have been debating the future application of implied assumption of risk. The debate centers upon whether implied assumption of risk should be maintained as a complete defense, or become a partial defense through absorption into comparative negligence.[58] Most statutes converting contributory negligence into comparative negligence have not addressed the debate.[59]

If a modern trend can be discerned, it is to allow implied assumption of risk to be absorbed into comparative negligence. This consequently allows the jury to treat implied assumption of risk as a partial defense. A true consensus regarding the fate of implied assumption of risk has yet to definitively emerge, and thus three distinct approaches to the defense remain.

[a] Approach One: Assumption of Risk Remains a Complete Defense

Some jurisdictions hold that while comparative negligence should properly supplant contributory negligence, assumption of risk should remain a complete defense.[60] If A negligently fails to notice a defect in the steering wheel of her rental car, her recovery will be reduced by the proportion her conduct causally contributed to the harm. If, however, A voluntarily assumes the risk of a defective steering wheel, these courts argue that this is tantamount to consent and should be a complete defense.[61]

---

[57] *See* Schutkowski v. Carey, 725 P.2d 1057 (Wyo. 1986), where the plaintiff sky-diver was barred from recovery after signing a release. *See also* Cain v. Cleveland Parachute Training Center, 457 N.E.2d 1185 (Ohio 1983), where a parachute student who broke his leg was denied recovery due to assumption of risk by a signed waiver.

[58] *See generally* John W. Wade, *The Place of Assumption of Risk in the Law of Negligence*, 22 La. L. Rev. 5 (1961). Some jurisdictions have apparently abolished implied assumption of risk. *See* Blackburn v. Dorta, 348 So. 2d 287 (Fla. 1977).

[59] *But see* Conn. Gen. Stat. § 52.572h (1975); N.Y. Civ. Prac. L. & R. § 1411 (McKinney 1975); Or. Rev. Stat. § 18.470 (1971), where assumption of risk is treated as contributory negligence. *See also* Note, *Contributory Negligence and Assumption of Risk — The Case for Their Merger*, 56 Minn. L. Rev. 47 (1971).

[60] *See, e.g.*, Kennedy v. Providence Hockey Club, 376 A.2d 329 (R.I. 1977), where the plaintiff was struck in the eye by a puck while attending a hockey game. The fact that the plaintiff had attended 30 to 40 games at the auditorium and had seen pucks strike spectators strengthened the court's decision to maintain assumption of risk as a complete defense.

[61] This example illustrates an important distinction between comparative negligence and assumption of risk. Assumption of risk dictates that the plaintiff must subjectively recognize

[b] Approach Two: Questioning the Reasonableness of the Assumed Risk

Another position argues that implied assumption of risk should be divided into reasonable and unreasonable implied assumptions of risk. Unreasonable implied assumption of risk exists when the plaintiff's decision to assume the risk is unreasonable and therefore overlaps with contributory or comparative negligence. A's decision to go to the movies using a car which she knows to have defective brakes is unreasonable and thus she both assumes the risk and is contributorily negligent. Consequently, her *unreasonable* assumption of risk is absorbed into comparative negligence as a partial rather than a complete defense. In contrast, *reasonable* implied assumption of risk does not overlap with contributory negligence but, counter-intuitively, is held to remain a complete defense.

Under this dichotomy, the *unreasonable* plaintiff who assumes the risk is only partially barred from recovery, while the *reasonable* plaintiff who assumes the risk is completely barred.[62] This result appears paradoxical at first, but is rationalized by the theory that a plaintiff who reasonably assumes the defendant's negligence has been fairly compensated for her risk.[63] Examples would include an expert hired to repair an elevated air conditioning unit in a building with negligently designed access[64] or a firefighter employed to control a negligently started fire.[65]

[c] Approach Three: Absorption of Assumption of Risk into Comparative Negligence

A third approach, probably predictive of the modern trend, allows both reasonable and unreasonable implied assumption of risk to be absorbed into comparative negligence.[66] Once implied assumption of risk is absorbed into

---

and then consent to the risk. *See* Soucy v. Martin, 402 A.2d 1167 (R.I. 1979). Comparative negligence does not require such subjective knowledge on the plaintiff's part.

[62] *See, e.g.,* Duffy v. Midlothian Country Club, 481 N.E.2d 1037 (Ill. Ct. App. 1985); Siglow v. Smart, 539 N.E.2d 636 (Ohio Ct. App. 1987).

[63] *See* Ordway v. Superior Court, 243 Cal. Rptr. 536 (Cal. Ct. App. 1988), where a jockey was injured in a quarter horse race the court held that reasonable implied assumption of risk remains a defense. The defendant wasn't required to take precautions against reasonably assumed risks, but was required to "anticipate the fool" and guard against risks unreasonably taken. *Id.* at 539.

[64] *See* King v. Magnolia Homeowners Ass'n, 253 Cal. Rptr. 140 (Cal. Ct. App. 1988). The California Supreme Court subsequently rejected this position. *See infra* discussion of *Knight v. Jewett.*

[65] While most states do not adhere to a position completely barring plaintiffs who reasonably assume risks, they usually do recognize a special firefighter's immunity precluding firefighters from suing parties for injuries sustained in the course of their duties. *See* § 15.04 [C], *infra*. *See* Benjamin K. Riley, Comment, *The Fireman's Rule: Defining Its Scope Using the Cost-Spreading Rationale*, 71 Cal. L. Rev. 218 (1983).

[66] *See* Kopischke v. First Continental Corp., 610 P.2d 668 (Mont. 1980).

comparative negligence, arguably the plaintiff who reasonably assumed the risk would be unlikely to suffer any deduction from her recovery since her behavior was reasonable. On the other hand, unreasonable assumption of risk, since it reflects fault, would result in an appropriate deduction in recovery under comparative negligence. This has prompted some jurisdictions to conclude implied assumption of risk is superfluous, since deduction from the plaintiff's recovery under comparative negligence would only occur when implied assumption is unreasonable and therefore overlaps contributory negligence. Since contributory negligence is, by itself, already absorbed into comparative negligence, this has led some courts to go further and simply abolish implied assumption of risk as an independent concept.[67] Other courts, however, have concluded that reasonable, as well as unreasonable, implied assumption of risk can be the basis of a deduction from recovery under a comparative negligence system. While the plaintiff's behavior does not reflect fault, such courts conclude the fact-finder may still properly allocate some comparative responsibility to the plaintiff for assuming the risk.[68]

In *Knight v. Jewett*,[69] the California Supreme Court attempted to address a situation where a plaintiff reasonably assumed the risk of another's negligence. The court first distinguished between primary and secondary implied assumption of risk, a terminology advanced by Professor James.[70]

Primary assumption of risk characterizes those cases where the defendant lacks a duty or did not breach a duty to the plaintiff. For example, if A was injured by a baseball while watching a game, A might be said to have assumed the risk by choosing to enter the stadium.[71] In fact, the defendant baseball club owner has not breached a duty to A. Assuming the stadium was reasonably safe,[72] the owner was never negligent and acted reasonably in selling A a ticket to watch the game. Professor James characterized primary assumption of risk as cases where, in effect, no defense was needed because the plaintiff could not establish defendant's breach of a duty to the plaintiff.[73] These situations arise when the defendant is not negligent

---

[67] *Id. See* Blackburn v. Dorta, 348 So. 2d 287 (Fla. 1987). Professor James argued vigorously, but to no avail, against implied assumption of risk during debates formulating the Restatement. *See* Fleming James, Jr., *Assumption of Risk: Unhappy Reincarnation*, 78 Yale L.J. 185 (1968).

[68] *See, e.g.*, Knight v. Jewett, 834 P.2d 696, 707 (Cal. 1992), discussed in text, *infra*.

[69] 834 P.2d 696 (Cal. 1992).

[70] Fleming James, Jr., *Assumption of Risk*, 61 Yale L.J. 141 (1952).

[71] *See* Brown v. San Francisco Baseball Club, Inc., 222 P.2d 19 (Cal. Ct. App. 1950). *See also* Davidoff v. Metropolitan Baseball Club, 463 N.E.2d 1219 (N.Y. 1984).

[72] *See* Neinstein v. Los Angeles Dodgers, Inc., 229 Cal. Rptr. 612 (Cal. Ct. App. 1986), where the court determined that a stadium owner had no duty to protect spectators from the natural hazards of a baseball game.

[73] Professor James's goal was to demonstrate that there was no theoretical need for assumption of risk as a defense. He wrote: "The doctrine deserves no separate existence (except

or a limitation on duty precludes liability, even if the defendant behaved unreasonably.

Secondary implied assumption of risk exists where the defendant has breached a duty to the plaintiff.[74] *Knight* held that all secondary implied assumption of risk (both reasonable and unreasonable) was absorbed into comparative negligence.[75] The court further held, however, that co-participants in certain sports owed only a limited duty to refrain from extreme reckless conduct toward other participants. In *Knight*, the plaintiff participant in a co-ed football game was injured by the defendant, also a participant. The defendant argued implied assumption of risk and sought to have at least reasonable implied assumption of risk characterized as a complete defense. The court rejected the defendant's request and held all implied assumption of risk, whether reasonable or unreasonable, is absorbed into comparative negligence.[76] This would have allowed the plaintiff to recover some portion of her damages if the defendant was held negligent. The court, however, also held that there was a limited duty which required the plaintiff to prove intentional injury or "reckless conduct that is totally outside the range of the ordinary activity involved in the sport"[77] and not merely negligence in order to establish a breach. The court found there was no such recklessness.

In a dubious use of superfluous terminology, the court characterized this newly recognized limited duty as an example of primary assumption of risk.[78] In reality, an affirmative defense of assumption of risk was not needed because there was no breach of a duty of care by the defendant. Thus, no prima facie case of negligence was established. The California Supreme Court was correct, however, to recognize that once assumption of risk is allowed to be comparative, it is essential to recognize that limited

---

for express assumption of risk) and is simply a confusing way of stating certain no duty rules or, where there has been a breach of duty towards the plaintiff, simply one kind of contributory negligence." *Assumption of Risk: Unhappy Reincarnation*, 78 Yale L.J. 185, 190 (1968).

[74] *See* Meistrich v. Casino Area Attractions, Inc., 155 A.2d 90 (N.J. 1959).

[75] In so doing, *Knight* rejected the formulation that a reasonable assumption of risk would bar recovery and an unreasonable assumption of risk would be absorbed into comparative negligence.

[76] In a separate opinion, Justice Mosk called for the elimination of implied assumption of risk as a bar to recovery.

[77] 834 P.2d at 710.

[78] As observed in note 73 and accompanying text, *supra*, Professor James had advanced the use of the term "primary assumption of risk" in academic discussions to demonstrate that these so-called assumption of risk defense cases were utilizing the term assumption of risk as "simply a confusing way of stating certain no duty rules." Indeed, the *Knight* court, while utilizing the term primary assumption of risk, also forthrightly characterized the rule for co-participants in certain active sports as a "limited duty." 834 P.2d at 711, n.7.

duties may still preclude a plaintiff from recovering for ordinary negligence in appropriate contexts.

[C] *The "Firefighter's Rule"*

The general acceptance of the so-called "firefighter's rule," precluding firefighters from suing for injuries sustained fighting negligent fires, suggests that certain professionals should not recover for injuries resulting from negligence that they are compensated to address.[79] Thus, while firefighters and others[80] are reasonably assuming the risk, there are public policy reasons for precluding them from suing negligent individuals who call for assistance. The firefighter's rule is, in essence, a form of assumption of risk and arguably the compensation of such professionals already reflects the ordinary risks of negligently created fires inherent in their job. The rule also addresses concern that victims would be deterred from seeking assistance if liability to firefighters was imposed on negligent behavior which created the emergency. Yet it can also be argued that the firefighter's rule is a vestige of the historic use of assumption of risk to preclude worker recovery for injuries on the job and that the modern trend to absorb assumption of risk into comparative fault argues for not precluding some recovery against culpable defendants.

§ 15.05 IMMUNITIES

[A] *Overview*

An immunity protects a defendant from tort liability. Unlike a defense, it is not dependent on the plaintiff's behavior, but on the defendant's status or relationship to the plaintiff. The drastic decision to exempt a defendant from accountability under tort law must be justified by compelling policy reasons. The general trend has been to diminish the immunities available, although recent distress over the cost of tort litigation has prompted some to rethink whether immunities should play a role in limiting potential tort liability.

[B] *Charitable Immunity*

Historically, charitable organizations were immune from tort liability.[81]

---

[79] "[A] person specifically hired to encounter and combat particular dangers is owed no independent tort duty by those who have created those dangers . . .." Anicet v. Gant, 580 So. 2d 273, 276 (Fla. Ct. App. 1991). *Cf.* Mahoney v. Carus Chemical Co., 510 A.2d 4 (N.J. 1986), noting that the "firefighter's rule" doesn't extend so far as to preclude firefighters from suing arsonists.

[80] *See* Santangelo v. State of New York, 521 N.E.2d 770 (N.Y. 1988), where the common-law "firefighter's rule" was extended to police officers; Nelson v. Hall, 211 Cal. Rptr. 668 (Cal. Ct. App. 1985), where the "firefighter's rule" was extended to a veterinarian bitten by a dog.

[81] *See, e.g.*, McDonald v. Massachusetts Gen. Hosp., 120 Mass. 432 (1876). *See generally* Charles Robert Tremper, *Compensation for Harm from Charitable Activity*, 76 Cornell L. Rev. 401 (1991).

Increasingly, this immunity has been abrogated.[82] The immunity has been justified as a means to protect the important work charities perform for their communities. In addition, the immunity has been defended by arguments that funds donated to a charity are given with the purpose of benefiting a specific cause, and therefore should not be diverted as a result of litigation against a charity's operators. The immunity has also been justified by the theory that beneficiaries of a charity have implicitly waived their right to later sue the charity.

With the prevalence of liability insurance and the business-like operation of large charities, it has become increasingly difficult to justify requiring the victim to suffer the full loss of an injury caused by a charity's tortious conduct. The Restatement[83] and most states have abolished the charitable immunity. Most of the remaining states have only partially retained the immunity. For example, New Jersey prohibits suits brought by beneficiaries of specified charities.[84]

[C] *Spousal Immunity*

Historically, spouses could not sue each other. This immunity was rooted in the common law doctrine regarding the legal identity of spouses. Initially, the wife was considered a mere chattel of the husband and was incorporated into his legal identity.[85] Consequently, the prospect of litigation between the two was inconsistent with a wife's lowly status. More recent decisions have justified the immunity on grounds that such suits would damage marital harmony, risk fraudulent testimony and collusion where liability insurance was involved, or invite frivolous legal complaints over trivial, if heartfelt, disagreements.

The weakness of these recent justifications is quite evident. Tortious conduct and not liability creates disharmony. Insurance fraud can exist in many contexts, and there is little to support the proposition that automobile accident litigation involving a spouse driver and passenger is so fraught with fraud that spouses should be denied remedies. Frivolous lawsuits can occur in many contexts but generally are not used as a defense for denying legitimate recovery. The majority of states have eliminated spousal immunity,[86] and those that have retained it tend to impose limitations upon it.

---

[82] *See e.g.*, Abernathy v. Sisters of St. Mary's, 446 S.W.2d 599 (Mo. 1969); Albritton v. Neighborhood Centers Ass'n for Child Dev., 466 N.E.2d 867, 869 (Ohio 1984).

[83] Restatement § 895E.

[84] N.J.S.A. 2A:53A-7 (West 1994).

[85] For a historical discussion, see Carl Tobias, *Interspousal Tort Immunity in America*, 23 Ga. L. Rev. 359 (1989); Freehe v. Freehe, 500 P.2d 771 (Wash. 1972).

[86] *See, e.g.*, Klein v. Klein, 376 P.2d 70 (Cal. 1962). Restatement § 895F rejects spousal immunity, but states that repudiation of the general immunity does not establish liability for acts or omissions that may be privileged or not tortious because of the marital relationship. In § 395F cmt. h, the Restatement notes that "[T]he intimacy of the family relationship may also involve some relaxation in the application of the concept of reasonable care, particularly in the confines of the home."

The immunity is no longer applied against property or economic torts, and some courts, still generally accepting the immunity, embrace additional exceptions.[87]

[D] *Parent-Child Immunity*

Parent-child immunity precludes tort actions between parents and their non-adult children.[88] The immunity was not recognized in England but was conceived in American decisions.[89] Unlike spousal immunity, which has been eliminated in most states, parent-child immunity still exists in some form in many jurisdictions. The immunity has never been held to bar property or purely economic torts, but does preclude intentional torts such as battery or assault[90] and liability for personal injuries caused by negligence.

While some states have completely abolished parent-child immunity,[91] many others have only partially abrogated it. Some courts have, for example, eliminated the immunity for intentional torts or for liability incurred in automobile accidents or during the operation of a business.[92] Other jurisdictions, while eliminating a general immunity, have in essence created limited duties that allow most tort actions, but preclude allegations of negligent parenting.[93] This creates the need to distinguish between ordinary negligence and what is encompassed by negligent parenting. For example, should a dangerous electrical outlet in a house where children live be characterized as negligent parenting or negligent maintenance of a house?

---

[87] *See, e.g.*, Lusby v. Lusby, 390 A.2d 77 (Md. 1978) (exempting intentional torts like assault).

[88] Non-adult children who have been emancipated from parental control are not subject to the immunity. *See* Restatement § 895G cmt. d.

[89] *See* Hewlett v. George, 9 So. 885 (Miss. 1891), where a mother was found not liable for falsely imprisoning her daughter in a mental asylum. *See also* Small v. Morrison, 118 S.E. 12, 16 (N.C. 1923), extending rule to a case involving negligence by observing "[I]f this restraining doctrine were not announced by any of the writers of the common law, because no such case was ever brought before the courts of England, it was unmistakably and indelibly carved upon the tablets of Mount Sinai."

[90] *See, e.g.*, Smith v. Smith, 141 N.E. 128 (Ind. 1924). *See also* Roller v. Roller, 79 P. 788 (Wash. 1905), barring a daughter's tortious rape claim against her father.

[91] *See, e.g.*, Gibson v. Gibson, 479 P.2d 648 (Cal. 1971).

[92] *See* Felderhoff v. Felderhoff, 473 S.W.2d 928 (Tex. 1971) (discussing various exceptions and adopting exception for injuries incurred operating farm machinery).

[93] *See, e.g.*, Goller v. White, 122 N.W.2d 193 (Wis. 1963). Restatement § 895G indicates that "[A] parent or child is not immune from tort liability to the other solely by reason of that relationship [but that] . . . [r]epudiation of general tort immunity does not establish liability for an act or omission that, because of the parent-child relationship, is otherwise privileged or is not tortious." Restatement § 895G cmt. k explains that the "privilege of parental discipline [and] . . . [t]he intimacies of family life affect the determination of whether conduct is negligent or not."

The persistence of the parent-child immunity can be explained, in part, by a reluctance to have judicial review over what constitutes acceptable parenting. Undoubtedly, there is concern that courts will be insensitive to cultural and individual differences in child rearing. As courts become less inhibited in reviewing domestic family abuse, however, the immunity appears less compelling. Arguably courts can distinguish between different schools of child rearing and negligent parental care. Interestingly, however, other proponents of the immunity note that its abolition can effectively decrease recovery for injured children by allowing defendants to implead negligent parents for lax supervision. For example, a negligent driver who hits a child can claim the parents share responsibility for the injury since they negligently failed to keep the child off the road. The family unit's recovery is thus limited by allocating fault to the parents' negligent supervision.[94]

[E] *Governmental Immunity*

Governmental immunity protects the government from tort liability.[95] Under the common law, the immunities were complete and prevented any tort suits against the government.

The immunity is derived from the English common law's prohibition of suits against the monarch.[96] Many states and the federal government have passed detailed statutes modifying the immunities in specific instances. One general provision normally included allows immunity for discretionary

[94] *See* § 13.03[A], *supra*. Note that allocating responsibility to negligent parents of injured children is not necessarily inequitable.

[95] Government immunity should be distinguished from public official immunity which protects government employees from tort liability incurred in the course of performing their official functions. In general, judges and legislators enjoy absolute immunity from liability. Federal executive government officials are generally also protected by an absolute immunity for discretionary decisions. Protection for state executive officials vary. Some state officials only enjoy qualified privileges where bad motive and other factors can negate protection.

In addition to common law torts, state public officials can be liable for civil rights violations under the Civil Rights Act of 1871 (42 U.S.C.A. § 1983). Federal officials can be held liable for constitutional violations based on an implied course of action derived directly from the Constitution. *See* Bivens v. Six Unknown Named Federal Narcotics Agents, 403 U.S. 388 (1971). Most public officials do not have absolute protection for violating constitutional rights. *See* Wood v. Strickland, 420 U.S. 308 (1975); Harlow v. Fitzgerald, 457 U.S. 800 (1982). Absolute protection is, however, afforded the President in his official actions (Nixon v. Fitzgerald, 457 U.S. 731 (1982)), judges in their judicial function (Forrester v. White, 484 U.S. 219 (1988)), and prosecutors when conducting prosecutions (Imbler v. Pachtman, 424 U.S. 409 (1976)). *See* Chester James Antieau and Milo Meachum, TORT LIABILITY OF GOVERNMENT OFFICERS AND EMPLOYEES (1990).

[96] Governmental immunity has, however, been attacked for a considerable period of time. *See* Edwin M. Borchard, *Governmental Liability in Tort*, 34 Yale L.J. 1 (1924); *see also* Molitor v. Kaneland Community Unit District, 163 N.E.2d 89, 94 (Ill. 1959): "[I]n preserving the sovereign immunity theory, courts have overlooked the fact that the Revolutionary War was fought to abolish the 'divine right of kings' on which the theory is based."

functions but not ministerial acts. Discretionary functions are policy-making decisions. Ministerial acts constitute government conduct which implements or executes policy decisions. Discretionary decisions are not subject to tort liability because they are more properly held accountable through electoral politics. Court review of discretionary decisions would interfere with democratic choices. For example, it would infringe on the separation of government branches for a court to hold that the legislature had acted negligently in choosing to allocate funds to build a new state university campus rather than several new police stations. Generally, ministerial acts, such as maintenance of a government building or automobile, are deemed suitable for tort liability when they are negligently performed. Ministerial decisions and actions are not manifestations of public policy decisions by the electorate.

What is categorized as ministerial or discretionary is subtle and not always consistent. The decision is often influenced by policy concerns since ultimately the courts are choosing whether an immunity should properly protectthe government from liability. For example, in *Tarasoff v. Regents of the University of California*,[97] the court held the state university was not immune for a therapist's failure to warn a potential murder victim of the homicidal intention of his patient. The court concluded that the failure to warn constituted ministerial rather than discretionary conduct under California's governmental immunity statute and, therefore, was not immune.[98]

Beyond the discretionary versus ministerial distinction, the extent to which governmental immunity now applies varies between federal and state government and between jurisdictions. The federal government has specifically retained immunity for certain enumerated intentional torts, including assault, battery, false imprisonment, false arrest, malicious prosecution, libel, slander, misrepresentation, deceit, and interference with contract rights, except in the case of acts or omissions of investigative or law enforcement officers resulting in claims of assault, battery, false imprisonment, false arrest, abuse of process or malicious prosecution.[99] The federal government is also immune from claims based on strict liability.[100] Furthermore, the military enjoys extensive immunity.[101] Other provisions

[97] 551 P.2d 334 (Cal. 1976).

[98] Potential liability also required establishing that the therapist had a duty to act. For a discussion of *Tarasoff* in this context, see § 8.02[B][1][a], *supra*. *See also* United Air Lines v. Wiener, 335 F.2d 379 (9th Cir. 1964), concluding decision to conduct military training flights was discretionary, but the failure to warn commercial airlines about the flights was ministerial.

[99] *See* 28 U.S.C.A. § 2680(h).

[100] See Laird v. Nelms, 406 U.S. 797 (1899).

[101] *See* 28 U.S.C.A. § 2680(j). *See also* Feres v. United States, 340 U.S. 135 (1950). Manufacturers supplying products to the military are also precluded from impleading the military when sued by a member of the military. Stencel Aero Eng'g. Corp. v. United States, 431 U.S. 666 (1977).

provide immunity related to mail delivery[102] and the fiscal operation of the Treasury.[103] Whether such extensive immunity is justified raises serious questions concerning in what other manner government activity can be made accountable and adequate compensation for those injured can be provided.

Many states have now abrogated the common law doctrine of governmental immunity, and most now have comprehensive statutes which govern the tort liability of both state and local governmental agencies. These state torts claims acts, some modeled in part after the Federal Act, typically provide for general governmental liability while recognizing limited immunities for specific acts.

Historically, local governments, such as cities, were perceived as corporations providing both "governmental" and "proprietary" functions. Proprietary functions are not government functions but private corporate activities engaged in by the local government. While governmental functions could be immune, proprietary functions were not. An example of a proprietary function might include providing cable television since a private corporation might also offer such services. Courts have had a great deal of difficulty categorizing governmental versus proprietary functions, and the concept of such a distinction is increasingly in disrepute. Increasingly, state statutes address specifically the liability of local governments without reference to these categories. These statutes often abrogate most immunity for local governments.[104]

---

102 *See* 28 U.S.C.A. (b).

103 *See* 28 U.S.C.A. (i).

104 *See* Restatement § 895C cmt. e. Municipalities have also been held subject to liability for civil rights violations based on 42 U.S.C.A. § 1983, when such violations reflect official policy. *See* Monell v. New York City Department of Social Services, 436 U.S. 658 (1978).

CHAPTER 16

STRICT LIABILITY

SYNOPSIS

§ 16.01 OVERVIEW

The preceding Chapters have shown that a great proportion of tort liability turns upon the answer to the question: "Was defendant at fault?" "Fault-based" tort causes of action — the principal one being negligence —

typically involve the evaluation of whether the defendant acted with due care under the circumstances. Where the hazards created by the actor's conduct are high, the care appropriate to the circumstances will be high. It will still, though, be judged by the standard of due care under the circumstances, and where the actor has employed the care that is due, there will be no negligence liability.

It does not, however, follow, that "due care" will relieve an actor of tort liability for all acts or pursuits. From the earliest common law there have been recognized discrete subsets of conduct for which, should injury or damage occur, the actor will be responsible in damages without regard to due care or fault. In these well-defined categories of conduct, a person will be held liable in damages for injury or loss even if he exercised all possible care to prevent it. For these categories of conduct for which defendant may be liable without regard to due care, it is said that the actor is liable without fault, or strictly liable.

Two categories of strict liability are the subject of this Chapter: (1) strict liability for damage or injury caused by animals owned or possessed by defendant; and (2) strict liability for abnormally dangerous activities — ranging from blasting operations to aerial pesticide spraying — that pose an unavoidable risk of substantial harm to others even where the actor has exercised the utmost care. A third category of strict liability, strict products liability, is discussed in Chapter 17.

Why are these two categories of activity severed from negligence law andassigned to strict liability or liability without fault? Judge Richard Posner,one of the leading legal theoreticians of the last twenty years, raises theproposition in *Indiana Harbor Belt Railroad v. AmericanCyanamid Co.*[1] that one purpose of imposing strict liability for high risk activities is to reduce the frequency with which actors choose to pursue these activities. This reduction in activity levels is not explicitly referenced in the Liability For Abnormally Dangerous Activities provisions of Restatement §§ 519-520, but represents a disincentive to such conduct that may be created by strict liability. In Judge Posner's words:

> One might for example start with [Restatement § 520(c)], inability to eliminate the risk of accident by the exercise of due care. The baseline common law regime of tort liability is negligence. When it is a workable regime, because the hazards of an activity can be avoided by being careful

[1] 916 F.2d 1174 (7th Cir. 1990). For valuable treatments of the policy rationales and bases for strict liability for abnormally dangerous activities, see Francis Hermann Bohlen, *The Rule in Rylands v. Fletcher*, 59 U. Pa. L. Rev. 298 (1911); Fleming James, Jr., *Some Reflections on the Bases of Strict Liability*, 18 La. L. Rev. 293 (1958).

Section 16.03 of this Chapter is developed from an article by Professor Madden, titled *Liability for Abnormally Dangerous Activities*, 10 J. Prod. Liab. 1 (1987), with kind permission from Elsevier Science, Ltd., The Boulevard, Langford Lane, Kidlington OX5 1GB, U.K.

(which is to say, nonnegligent), there is no need to switch to strict liability. Sometimes, however, a particular type of accident cannot be prevented by taking care but can be avoided, or its consequences minimized, by shifting the activity in which the accident occurs to another locale, where the risk or harm of an accident will be less [§ 520(e)], or by reducing the scale of the activity caused by it ((f)). By making the actor strictly liable — by denying him in other words an excuse based on his inability to avoid accidents by being more careful — we give him an incentive, missing in negligence regime, to experiment with methods of preventing accidents that involve not greater exertions of care, assumed to be futile, but instead relocating, changing, or reducing (perhaps to the vanishing point) the activity giving rise to the accident. The greater the risk of an accident ((a)) and the costs of an accident if one occurs ((b)), the more we want the actor to consider the possibility of making accident-reducing activity changes; the stronger, therefore, is the case for strict liability.

Professor George Fletcher suggests a rationale that focusses upon the nonreciprocal nature of the risks to which defendant's conduct exposes plaintiff. If our hypothetical plaintiff is driving down the road, the risk a passing motorist creates for plaintiff is roughly equal to the risk plaintiff poses to the other driver. Thus their risks are conceptually reciprocal and negligence law suffices to mediate liability for any accident costs. If, on the other hand, our motorist passes a blasting site that is part of a highway widening project and the concussion of a blast shatters his rear window, plaintiff's conduct has posed no measurable risk when compared to the risk created by the use of explosives to blast rock near a travelled road. The nonreciprocal nature of the risks, Fletcher argues, commends imposition of strict liability.[2]

Two areas where strict liability has been much employed are for injuries caused by animals and by highly dangerous activities, both of which will be discussed in turn.

§ 16.02 STRICT LIABILITY FOR INJURIES CAUSED BY ANIMALS

[A] *Livestock*

The original common law rule provided for liability without fault for trespassing livestock,[3] which rule retains its validity in numerous eastern states.[4] Apart from the technical harm of the trespass itself, the presumptive

[2] George Fletcher, *Fairness and Utility in Tort Law*, 85 Harv. L. Rev. 537, 547, 551 (1972). The strict liability rationales of Judge Posner, Professor Fletcher and others are discussed in Gerald W. Boston and M. Stuart Madden, ENVIRONMENTAL AND TOXIC TORTS 101-106 (1994)

[3] King v. Blue Mountain Forest Association, 123 A.2d 151 (N.H. 1956) (New Hampshire law); see First Restatement of Torts § 504. See generally Williams, LIABILITY FOR ANIMALS (1939); Note, 34 Iowa L. Rev. 318 (1949).

[4] Id.

harm from such livestock trespasses is that when "these animals intrude upon land they usually do harm by eating the grass, trampling down the crops, scratching or digging up the seeds or otherwise."[5] Dogs and cats are exempted from this rule, on the logic that they are "difficult to restrain and are unlikely to do any substantial harm by their intrusion."[6]

Restatement § 504 imposes strict liability for the possessor of trespassing livestock unless (1) the harm is not a foreseeable one;[7] (2) the trespass by animals being "driven" (herded) along the highway is confined to abutting land; or (3) state common law or statute requires the complaining landowner to have erected a fence.[8] Liability has been found for damage or injury ranging from a trespassing scrub bull's corruption of a pedigreed heifer to a landowner's death at the horns of a trespassing goat.

[B] *Domestic Animals*

Keepers of dogs, cats, horses or other domestic animals are liable for injury caused by the animal only where the possessor knew or should have known of the animal's vicious disposition. A possessor with actual or constructive knowledge of the animal's vicious tendencies will be strictly liable for harm, "and no measure of care in its keeping will excuse him."[9]

In the noteworthy early decision of *Sandy v. Bushey*,[10] the Maine Supreme Court applied a similar standard to the claim of a man who, while attempting to feed his horse, was attacked by another. Overruling defendant's motion to set aside a verdict for plaintiff, the court stated: "[T]he evidence discloses facts which fairly tend to establish that the defendant's horse had exhibited a vicious and ugly disposition at various times prior to the day on which the plaintiff was injured, and notice of the animal's vicious propensities had been brought home to the defendant."[11]

---

[5] First Restatement of Torts § 507 cmt. b.

[6] *Id.* Wild boar, by contrast, are not so decorous as dogs and cats and actually wreak some destruction upon their turf as a result of their method of feeding, which involves "looking for worms and roots that the boar tears up from the ground with its snout." King v. Blue Mountain Forest Ass'n, 123 A.2d 151, 153 (N.H. 1956).

[7] The Restatement Reporters provide Illustration 2 to § 504:

> Without any fault on the part of A, his cow escapes from his land and wanders into B's barn. The timbers supporting the floor of the barn are rotten, and the cow breaks through them. B, entering the barn, falls through the hole and breaks his arm. A is not liable to be for his bodily harm.

[8] *E.g.*, Maguire v. Yanake, 590 P.2d 85, 88 (Idaho 1978), in which the court stated Idaho law as providing no liability for a livestock owner whose animals trespass onto another's property unless the complaining property owner has enclosed his property with a legal fence.

[9] Sandy v. Bushey, 128 A. 513 (Me. 1925) (claim by a plaintiff who was attacked and kicked by defendant's three-year-old colt; stating the requirement — no longer the majority rule — that the animal's hostile disposition be actually known to the owner).

[10] 128 A.2d 513 (Me. 1925).

[11] *Id.*

As a general rule, the possessor of a dog who knows or has reason to know that the animal has a tendency to bite will be strictly liable for bite injuries even though "he has exercised the utmost care to prevent it from doing harm."[12] What level of knowledge of an animal's dangerous propensities will trigger this rule of strict liability? The Restatement Reporters state that it is not necessary that the possessor know that the dog "has previously attacked human beings or other animals[.]" It is sufficient that he know that the dog "has on other occasions exhibited such a tendency to attack . . . as would apprise him of its dangerous character."[13] This standard gives the lie to the saying "Every dog gets one bite," for aggressive behavior short of biting may serve as notice to the owner or possessor, and trigger this strict liability standard.[14]

What if a statute exempts an owner from dog bite liability where the owner posts a conspicuous sign describing the dog's dangerous propensities? In *Noble v. Yorke*,[15] the Florida Supreme Court pierced the statutory immunity where the owner posted the simple "BAD DOG" sign mandated by statute, but temporized in describing the hazard to a visitor.[16]

[C] *Wild Animals*

Many jurisdictions have followed the rule of strict liability for owners or keepers of wild animals that cause harm even though "the possessor has exercised the utmost care[.]" Restatement § 507 (1) & (2) provide that "a possessor of a wild animal is subject to liability to another for harm . . . that results from a dangerous propensity that is characteristic of wild animals of [that] particular class[.]"[17] A strict liability holding was affirmed in *Eyrich v. Earl*,[18] a suit involving a five-year-old child mauled to death by a circus leopard. Explaining the policy choice of strict liability over negligence, the court stated: "[T]he benefits bestowed by a few hours (or perhaps minutes) of entertainment or recreation for those who like this sort of thing hardly justify the possibility, if not the probability, of disasters such

---

[12] Restatement § 509(1).

[13] Restatement § 509 cmt. g.

[14] *E.g.*, Carrow v. Haney, 219 S.W. 710 (Mo. Ct. App. 1920) (rejecting maxim "Every dog is entitled to one bite."). In many jurisdictions a dog bite statute supersedes the common law, and creates the exclusive remedy for dog bite victims. *E.g.*, Fla. Stat. Ann. 767.04, discussed in Noble v. Yorke, 490 So. 2d 29 (Fla. 1986); Wis. Stats. § 174.02 (strict liability).

[15] 490 So. 2d 29 (Fla. 1986).

[16] In the court's words:

> Although the sign posted by the Nobles was in strict compliance with the terms of the statute, the Nobles are not free from liability because, as a matter of law, a dog owner who tells a victim to ignore the "BAD DOG" sign and pretend it does not exist has not provided the genuine, effective and bona fide notice required by the statute.

[17] The keeper of a wild animal "is required to know the dangerous properties normal to the class to which it belongs." Restatement § 507 cmt. c.

[18] 495 A.2d 1375 (N.J. Super. Ct. 1985).

as the one that occurred here. The magnitude of the risk certainly outweighs the social utility. In such a case those who provide the extraordinary risk must share the responsibility."[19]

Other jurisdictions, however, have manifested a reluctance to so extend strict liability unless directed to do so by the legislature, and opt instead for a negligence standard. In some of these decisions, the courts note that many of the decisions imposing strict liability for harm caused by wild animals could have reached the same result by application of negligence doctrine.[20]

Still other states impose no single liability standard to "wild animals" as a class. In *Ollhoff v. Peck*,[21] a Wisconsin court of appeals considered plaintiff's appeal of a claim arising from bites he received when he reached into a nature pond park containing musky, a legendary northern game fish. At trial, the jury applied a negligence standard, and found plaintiff 90% causally responsible for his injuries. Affirming application of a negligence standard, the Wisconsin court noted that the state legislature had only adopted a strict liability rule to cover certain classes of animals, specifically dogs, as well as stallions, bulls, boars, rams and billy goats allowed to run at large. For all other animals, the court held, the proper instruction "does not distinguish between domesticated and wild animals, but rather instructs the jury to hold owners of animals to the appropriate standard of care given the nature of the animal involved."[22]

What are "wild" animals? Restatement § 506 comment a states that the rule of strict liability applies broadly to not only what we commonly call animals, but also to "birds, fish, reptiles and insects."[23] Wolves, coyotes, leopard, snakes, chimpanzees, lions, bears, and monkeys[24] have been held to be wild animals for the purposes of strict liability, while there is authority holding cats, stallions, mules, steers, horses, heifers, bees and parrots to be domestic animals.

---

[19] *Id.*, 495 A.2d at 147, 148.

[20] King v. Blue Mountain Forest Association, 123 A.2d 151, 154 (N.H. 1956) (New Hampshire law).

[21] 503 N.W.2d 323 (Wis. Ct. App. 1993).

[22] *Id.*, 503 N.W.2d 323, 324.

[23] Certain wild "animals," comment a continues, that have become "customarily recognized as devoted to the service of mankind," such as honey bees, should be classified as domestic animals.

[24] However in Pate v. Yeager, 552 S.W.2d 513, 515 (Tex. Civ. Ct. App. 1977), involving a four-year-old girl who was bitten when she placed her hand inside of a monkey's cage, the court held that the jury could have concluded that the monkey was domesticated, in which event the owner would not be liable unless he was negligent, or knew of the primates's inhospitable characteristics.

[D] *Defenses*

What defenses are available to the owner or possessor of a vicious dog, a wild animal, or another aggressive animal? Some courts have held that as the suit is one in strict liability, and thus is not based upon the possessor's negligence, the plaintiff's mere contributory negligence should not bar the claim in those jurisdictions retaining such a rule. One such decision was that of the Texas Supreme Court in *Marshall v. Ranne*,[25] involving a claim brought by a plaintiff who was attacked by defendant's boar-hog. Eliminating defendant's defense of contributory negligence, the court held that defendant had also failed to prove plaintiff's assumption of the risk in dashing from the relative safety of his own home and attempting to reach his car before the hog attacked. In the court's view, plaintiff's unenviable choices of remaining a prisoner in his own home or racing to his automobile did not represent the free and voluntary choice associated with assumption of the risk.[26]

In contrast, courts in other jurisdictions have applied ordinary comparative fault principles to claims arising from injuries by a wild animal, with the effect of reducing plaintiff's award based upon a showing of incautious conduct amounting only to contributory negligence. For example, in *Mills. v. Smith*,[27] a Kansas appeals court heard the appeal of a plaintiff's verdict arising from injuries inflicted by a juvenile African lion on a 21-month-old infant. There the male lion, named Chester, weighing about 100 pounds and kept at defendant's ranch, regularly wrestled playfully with its keeper, and participated in photographic opportunities. Although the parents had been warned by the keeper to keep the children away from the lion, the child darted near Chester, who took the child's head in its jaws, inflicting moderate lacerations. While finding Chester's owner strictly liable, the jury apportioned only 40% of the fault to him, 50% of the fault to the child's mother, and 10% to another adult who was taking a photograph at the time of the mishap. Affirming the trial court's comparative negligence instruction, the appeals court stated: "[W]hether a defendant's fault stems from negligence or commission of an act for which one is strictly liable, his fault must be compared by the jury to that of any other party who may have contributed to the injury."[28]

---

[25] 511 S.W.2d 255, 258 (Tex. 1974).

[26] *See also* Sandy v. Bushey, 128 A.2d 513 (Me. 1925), where the court states: "Something more than slight negligence or want of due care on the part of the injured party must be shown in order to relieve the keeper of a vicious domestic animal known to be such from his liability as an insurer."

[27] 673 P.2d 117 (Kan. Ct. App. 1983).

[28] *Id.*, 673 P.2d at 120-21.

§ 16.03 STRICT LIABILITY FOR ABNORMALLY DANGEROUS ACTIVITIES

[A] *Introduction*

Some activities create such grave risks when accidentally released from the control of the manufacturer, transporter, or user, that responsible parties may be strictly liable — liable without fault — even where they exercised scrupulous care. This doctrine was once described as liability for "ultra-hazardous activities," although the modern definition uses the term "abnormally dangerous."

It is to plaintiff's substantial advantage to have defendant's conduct characterized as "abnormally dangerous." With this designation, plaintiff can prove liability without having to prove defendant's culpable conduct, *i.e.*, defendant will be strictly liable for plaintiff's damages without the need for plaintiff to prove that defendant acted intentionally, recklessly, or negligently. As revealed in the discussion that follows, however, only a small cluster of potentially hazardous activities have been designated "abnormally dangerous."

Plaintiff's burden to show that defendant's activity is "abnormally dangerous" is substantially greater than a simple showing that defendant's pursuits create the possibility of great harm. Rather, plaintiff must show (1) the risk of an abnormally great harm should defendant's safety efforts fail; (2) the virtual impossibility of defendant's elimination of the risk of harm even with the utmost care; and (3) a resultant harm to plaintiff, or plaintiff's property, caused by the very hazards the risk of which led to describing defendant's conduct as "abnormally dangerous" in the first instance.

How does the proof underlaying a claim in unreasonably dangerous activities differ from that for claims in trespass and nuisance? A threshold distinction is that abnormally dangerous activities liability does not depend upon any showing that the defendant intended (subjectively desired or knew to asubstantial certainty of) the result. In contrast, trespass liability requires a showing of defendant's intent, as defined above, and nuisance liability must be predicated upon a showing of conduct that is intentional, negligent, reckless, *or* constitutes an abnormally dangerous activity.

The absence of an intent requirement for abnormally dangerous activities liability aside, in the review of how the abnormally hazardous activities standard has been applied in state and federal court decisions, one sees that the nature of action that will create liability for abnormally dangerous activities, and the nature of activity that will trigger liability in trespass or nuisance, sometimes differ only in degree. Unlike the causes of action in nuisance or trespass, liability for abnormally dangerous activities, under Restatement (Second) of Torts §§ 519–520, requires an extreme hazard.

An additional distinction is that, while plaintiff's protection of an interest in land is a predicate for maintaining an action in trespass and nuisance, there is no corresponding requirement of a proprietary interest for the plaintiff pleading liability without fault for conducting an abnormally dangerous activity.

The doctrine of liability without fault for engaging in abnormally dangerous activities was introduced into the United States in the late Nineteenth Century as a cause of action that was quasi-trespass or nuisance in nature. Originally the rule was intended to provide a remedy for landowners who suffered damage to their property from an activity or condition maintained upon the defendant's land, the hazardous propensities of which the defendant could not eliminate even with the exercise of the utmost care.

At English common law there had long been a remedy for injury to person or property occasioned by the conduct of extremely hazardous activities on the defendant's land. In the seminal decision of *Rylands v. Fletcher*,[29] an adjoining property owner brought an action against defendant millowners who had built and maintained a large reservoir for the collection of water. The reservoir was built near an abandoned mine shaft, which the engineer and contractor responsible for building the reservoir had negligently failed to reinforce properly. The inevitable mishap occurred when the barriers between the reservoir and the mine shaft failed, sending water and debris into the working shafts of an adjoining mine.

Before the Exchequer Chamber, the majority concluded that on these facts, emerging tort doctrine required formulation of a new theory of strict liability for introducing upon one's property a hazardous condition that creates the risk of injury to a neighbor's person or property if it escapes from its property of origin. Blackburn, J., stated the view of the majority: "the true rule of law is that the person who for his own purposes brings on his lands and collects and keeps there anything likely to do mischief if it escapes, must keep it at his peril and if he does not do so, is prima facie answerable for all the damage which is the natural consequence of its escape." On appeal, the House of Lords held that the landowner's activity would give rise to liability without fault only insofar as the conduct would be described as a "non-natural use."

The adoption by United States courts of the liability without fault tenets of *Rylands v. Fletcher* has been practically universal. Impoundment activity of the nature that prompted the decision in *Rylands* has continued to find support in many of the American decisions as creating liability for an abnormally dangerous activity for which a plaintiff, injured in either person or property, may recover, even where the defendant has exercised the utmost

[29] 13 Hurl & C. 774 (1865); L.R. 1 Ex. 265 (1866), L.R. 3 H.L. 330 (1868). *See generally* William Prosser, *Nuisance Without Fault*, 20 Tex. L. Rev. 399 (1942).

degree of care. The modern doctrine has now extended far beyond the original confines to include, to list only a few, findings of strict liability for the injurious consequences of the storage of explosives, fumigation, crop dusting, the storage of flammable liquids, pile driving, and the maintenance of a hazardous waste site.

[B] *Restatement §§ 519–520*

In 1977 the American Law Institute framed its statement of the dominant authority interpreted in the light of a century of development following *Rylands v. Fletcher*. The Restatement provisions are set forth at §§ 519–520, with § 519 stating the general principle for liability, and § 520 providing the several factors proposed as useful in determining what constitutes an abnormally dangerous activity.

Section 519 states that "One who carries on an abnormally dangerous activity is subject to liability for harm to the person, land, or chattels of another resulting from the activity, although he has exercised the utmost care to prevent the harm." The Section concludes with the significant limiting proviso: "This strict liability is limited to the kind of harm, the possibility of which makes the activity abnormally dangerous."

Section 520, in turn, suggests the factors that will aid in the determination of whether a particular activity should properly be considered abnormally dangerous. The factors include an evaluation of (1) the degree of risk of harm to persons or property; (2) the magnitude of that harm; (3) the inevitability of some risk irrespective of precautionary measures that might be taken;[30] (4) the ordinary (or, conversely, unusual) nature of the activity in the community in which it is found;[31] and (5) the activity's value to the community in comparison to the risk of harm created by its presence.[32]

---

[30] The Restatement Reporters cast this criterion as "inability to eliminate the risk by the exercise of reasonable care." The explanatory comment states: "What is referred to here is the unavoidable risk remaining in the activity, even though the actor has taken all reasonable precautions in advance and has exercised all reasonable care in his operation, so that he is not negligent."

The Reporters continue by employing the example of the manufacture of explosives in the city, which activity, the comment states, "may involve a risk of detonation in spite of everything that the manufacturer may reasonably be expected to do; and although he may not be negligent in manufacturing them at all, he is subject to strict liability for an abnormally dangerous activity."

[31] This factor represents the gravamen of subsections (d) and (e) of Restatement § 520, which provide for the consideration of the "extent to which the activity is not a matter of common usage" and also the "inappropriateness of the activity to the place where it is carried on."

[32] Section 520 provides in full:

"In determining whether an activity is abnormally dangerous, the following factors are to be considered:

(a) existence of a high degree of risk of some harm to the person, land, or chattels of others;

Restatement § 520(d) requires consideration of the "extent to which the activity is not a matter of common usage." What is meant by "common usage"? Comment i to § 520 suggests that while the use of the automobile is so commonplace as to make its operation one of common usage, the use of a tank or a vehicle so large as to be difficult to control safely might be abnormally dangerous. In another example in which the difference between common usage and abnormal danger may be one of degree, comment i proposes that water impounded in a large reservoir in an urban environment might be abnormally dangerous, while water collected in a rooftop cistern would not.

The locality of the activity weighs heavily, and, as comment j to § 520 points out, locality inappropriateness can be dispositive. The Reporters there state that the storage of explosives in the middle of the desert, and far from any property of value, might not be considered an abnormally dangerous activity. Other authority, however, has objected sharply to the review of locational appropriateness in reaching determinations of abnormal danger. As stated by the Alaska Supreme Court in *Yukon Equipment Co. v. Fireman's Fund Insurance Co.*:[33]

> The reasons for imposing absolute liability on those who have created a grave risk of harm to others by storing and using explosives are largely independent of considerations of locational appropriateness. We see no reason for making a distinction between the right of a homesteader to recover when his property has been damaged by a blast set off in a remote corner of the state, and the right to compensation of an urban resident whose home is destroyed by an explosion originating in a settled area. In each case the loss is properly to be regarded as the cost of business of storing or using explosives. Every incentive remains to conduct such activities in locations which are as safe as possible, because there the damages resulting from an accident will be kept to a minimum.

Scattered additional authority concurs that particularly in cases of injury covered by explosives, locational appropriateness should have no bearing and liability should be truly strict.[34]

(b) likelihood that the harm that results from it will be great;

(c) inability to eliminate the risk by the exercise of reasonable care;

(d) extent to which the activity is not a matter of common usage;

(e) inappropriateness of the activity to the place where it is carried on; and

(f) extent to which its value to the community is outweighed by its dangerous attributes."

[33] 585 P.2d 1206, 1211 (Alaska 1978).

[34] *E.g.*, Correa v. Curbey, 605 P.2d 458, 460 (Ariz. Ct. App. 1979) ("We note that the Restatement does not impose a per se rule of strict liability for any activity but rather requires an evaluation of each situation in terms of Sec. 520 to determine if the activity is abnormally dangerous. However, we believe that an evaluation of the use of explosives, under any circumstances where harm results, a finding of [strict liability] presumptively follows [.]").

[1] Danger Unavoidable Even With The Exercise of Due Care

In a tort suit alleging an abnormally dangerous activity, a plaintiff must successfully demonstrate more than the high risk posed by defendant's activity, its incongruity with the surrounding commercial or industrial environment, and its capacity for great harm. Liability will not lie unless plaintiff makes the additional showing that the risk involved cannot be eliminated through defendant's exercise of reasonable care. Illustrative is the decision in *Edwards v. Post Transportation Co.*,[35] the suit by an employee against the delivery company that pumped sulfuric acid into the wrong storage tank at the manufacturer's waste treatment facility. The introduction of sulfuric acid into a tank containing a residue of sodium bisulfate and water created toxic gases that overcame and severely injured plaintiff. Turning to plaintiff's allegation of liability for abnormally dangerous activities, the California court agreed that plaintiff's proof satisfied several of the criteria listed by Restatement §§ 519–520. It held, nonetheless, that plaintiff's claim must fail because the evidence showed that the risk of the misadventure resulting in plaintiff's harm could be "eliminated through the exercise of reasonable care." The court noted the testimony of one of plaintiff's expert witnesses, a civil engineer, who testified that "[i]f sulfuric acid is handled in a proper fashion, it is no danger."

The defendant may successfully avoid abnormally dangerous activities liability by showing that the harm was caused by the unforeseeable intervening act of a third party. For example, in *Davis Enterprises v. Gouza*,[36] a suit brought by residents of a housing development against a petroleum pipeline company and a cable company engaged in excavation work for personal injury and property damage arising from the spillage of 50,000 gallons of unleaded gasoline, the court, finding for defendant, stated: "the leak was allegedly caused by the intervening negligence of Tri-State Communications, Inc., and the obligation of Sun Pipe Line Company does not rise to that of an insurer."

[2] Requirement of An activity Under Defendant's Control

The plaintiff's cause of action for abnormally dangerous activities will fail in the absence of a showing that the defendant was directly involved in and in control of the allegedly abnormally dangerous instrumentality. Thus in one suit brought against the manufacturer of toluene di-isocyanate for injuries sustained by a truck driver who inhaled the product when his truck ran over a drum of the product that fell from another truck, liability was denied on the grounds that the manufacturer exercised no control over

[35] 228 Cal. App. 3d 980, 279 Cal. Rptr. 231 (1991) (review denied).

[36] 576 A.2d 999 (Pa. Super. Ct. 1990).

the independent contractor transporting the drums, and had not been involved in authorization of the mode of transportation.[37]

Claimants proceeding against product manufacturers for claims arising from the manufacture and marketing of products claimed to be abnormally dangerous likewise have been denied recovery under this doctrine for want of demonstrating the "activity" requirement of plaintiff's prima facie case. For example, in *Heinrich v. Goodyear Tire and Rubber Co.*,[38] a tire company employee brought an action against a chemical supplier for injuries sustained due to exposure to the chemical. The federal trial court held that the doctrine of liability for abnormally dangerous activities would not lie, stating that "it is apparent that the party to be held liable under such a theory must have at least the right or duty to control, if not actual control over, the activity causing the harm." A similar result was reached in a decision resolving a claim brought by a plant employee who was sprayed by liquified anhydrous ammonia. In that suit, plaintiff proceeded against the plant's former owner, the plant's designer and installer, and the manufacturer of the valve that had malfunctioned. Recovery was denied on the grounds that the named defendants were not operating the plant at the time of the accident.[39]

Many plaintiffs have brought causes of action against product manufacturers, claiming that the sale of allegedly hazardous products that are later involved in plaintiff's injury constitutes an abnormally dangerous activity. In the majority of these cases no liability has been found. For example, in *Cavan v. General Motors Corp.*,[40] the Oregon Supreme Court considered this issue in hearing the plaintiff's allegation that a tractor with allegedly defective brakes and engine produced an "ultrahazardous condition." The court found for defendant, ruling that: "the strict liability rule of *Rylands v. Fletcher* . . . has no applicability in a products case." A like conclusion was reached in another decision in which the claimant requested that the court apply the doctrine of abnormally dangerous activities liability for injuries arising from the administration of an investigational drug.[41]

The issue of whether the manufacture and sale of small concealable handguns represents an abnormally dangerous activity has been litigated vigorously, again with apparent resolution in favor of defendants. *Perkins v. F. I. E. Corp.*,[42] involved two injuries by gunshot, one of them fatal, and both caused by small concealable handguns. The injured claimants, or their representatives, brought individual actions in Louisiana courts. On

---

[37] Hawkins v. Evans Cooperage Co., 766 F.2d 904 (5th Cir. 1985) (Louisiana law).

[38] 532 F. Supp. 1348 (D. Md. 1982).

[39] Cropper v. Rego Distribution Center, Inc., 542 F. Supp. 1142, 1149 (D. Del. 1982).

[40] 571 P.2d 1249 (Or.1977).

[41] Gaston v. Hunter, 588 P.2d 326, 341 (Ariz. Ct. App. 1978).

[42] 762 F.2d 1250 (5th Cir. 1985).

appeal, the *Perkins* court concluded that under Louisiana law, the injured parties' claim under the abnormally dangerous activities doctrine failed for three reasons: (1) the doctrine requires that the activity be one relating to land or to other immovables,[43] (2) the doctrine required that the defendant be engaged directly in the injury-producing activity, and (3) the doctrine was inapplicable where, to be injurious, the activity required the wrongful conduct of a third party.

In *Kelley v. R.G. Industries, Inc.*,[44] the Maryland Court of Appeals reviewed an action arising similarly from the injuries suffered by the innocent victim of an armed assault. Interpreting Restatement §§ 519–520 alone, the court concluded that the abnormally hazardous activities doctrine was not applicable to product manufacturers that were neither the owners nor occupiers of the land on which the ultimately hazardous action or activity took place.

[3] Type of Hazard Contemplated

Subpart (2) of Restatement § 519 limits the applicability of the strict liability remedy therein to "the kind of harm, the possibility of which makes the activity abnormally dangerous." Accordingly, a property owner neighboring a site at which explosives are stored might have a remedy under this provision should there be an accidental explosion that damaged other landowners by debris or by concussion, but would not have a remedy if the damage occurred because a deluge wettened the stored explosives, and the runoff adversely affected the purity of the groundwater. Similarly, and again for example, in a jurisdiction where crop-dusting by small aircraft has been found to represent an abnormally dangerous activity, the risk to be avoided within the meaning of the doctrine is the erroneous, in content or in target, application of pesticides or herbicides. A mishap of such a nature would be within the contemplation of the abnormally dangerous activities remedy, while an accident involving a crash of the aircraft itself would not.

An influential decision evaluating the requirement that liability "should be confined to consequences which lie within the extraordinary risk whose

---

[43] *Id.* at 1267. The court cites Smith v. Formica Corp., 439 So. 2d 1194 (La. Ct. App. 1983), involving the fumes and fire from a contact adhesive, the court ruling: "[w]e do not feel compelled in this case to . . . adopt a rule of law that would impose absolute liability on a consumer products manufacturer . . ."

Note that the attempted application here of strict liability upon a product manufacturer should be distinguished from the imposition of strict products liability under Restatement § 402A. See *infra* § 17.04.

For an analysis of potential strict liability for manufacturers of unreasonably dangerous products, see John L. Diamond, *Eliminating the "Defect" in Design Strict Products Liability Theory*, 34 Hastings L.J. 529 (1983).

[44] 497 A.2d 1143 (Md. 1985).

existence calls for such responsibility" is *Foster v. Preston Mill Co.*,[45] in which it was alleged that the defendant's blasting operation frightened mother minks owned by the plaintiff, causing the minks to kill their kittens. The court observed that the minks' reaction was to "relatively moderate vibration and noise" from a distance of over two miles, and not the hazard ordinarily associated with blasting, such as "direct contact with flying debris, or being directly affected by vibrations of the earth or concussions of the air." The court concluded that as "the risk of causing harm of the kind here experienced"–that is the impact of relatively minor vibration and noise on the nervous disposition of minks–was not the kind of risk that has been considered to make the activity of blasting "ultrahazardous," strict liability should not be applied.

[C] *Application of the Doctrine*

The assignment of responsibility for the type of activity that has been found to be within the compass of the abnormally dangerous activities doctrine is explicitly "an adjustment of conflicting interests, which interests include, without limitation, the interest of the person conducting the activity, the interests of the community in which the activity is conducted in the continuation of that activity, and the interests of the injured claimant in receiving compensation for any injury suffered thereby."[46] Conceding the never wholly-satisfactory nature of applying arbitrary classifications to decisions, review of the decisions forming the body of United States law governing abnormally dangerous activities reveals that they are situated in analytically distinctive subject areas. These subject areas are found to fit the following classification: (1) blasting activity or other use of explosives; (2) dangerous application or dispersal; (3) dangerous storage; (4) dangerous transportation; and (5) dangerous transmission.

[1] Blasting Activity

In the pursuit of blasting, contractors, builders, and excavators have long been liable in trespass for injury or damage caused by rocks or debris thrown from the site of the detonation. Not as quickly settled was the question of whether a claimant injured by a nontrespassory invasion, usually by concussion, could recover from a person conducting blasting on a nearby premises absent a showing of negligence.[47] The New York Court of

---

[45] 268 P.2d 645, 647 (Wash. 1954).

[46] Loe v. Lenhardt, 362 P.2d 312 (Or. 1961). In the context of a case involving the spraying of agricultural chemicals by the defendant, the court in *Loe*, using the example of strict liability for blasting operations, stated: ". . . Basic to the problem is 'an adjustment of conflicting interests', . . . of the right of the blaster, on the one hand, to pursue a lawful occupation, and the right of an owner of land, on the other, to its peaceful enjoyment and possession. Where the damage is sustained by the latter through the nonculpable activities of the former, who should bear the loss the man who caused it or a 'third person', as Judge Hand says, 'who has no relation to the explosion, other than that of injury.' "

[47] *E.g.*, Booth v. Rome, W., & O.T.R.R. Co., 35 N.E. 592 (N.Y. 1893).

Appeals in *Spano v. Perini Corp.*,[48] finding justification for liability without negligence even without physical trespass, offered its succinct expression that imposition of strict liability was not a condemnation of blasting or related risk-laden endeavors. The question, in the words of the court, "was not whether it was lawful or proper to engage in blasting, but who should bear the cost of any resulting damage — the person who engaged in the dangerous activity or the innocent neighbor injured thereby."

In adopting strict liability for blasting operations arising from the defendant's setting off explosives that damaged plaintiff's apartment complex, the court in *Harper v. Regency Development Co.*,[49] states that application of the strict liability burden of proof to abnormally dangerous activities is not so substantial a change in the law as might be thought, for, in that court's view, in neither negligence nor in absolute liability "is the claimant exempt from definite standards of proof both as to culpability and as to proximate cause."

Similarly, but in the particular context of an explosion during the rail transportation of bombs, a California court reflected that the risk distribution rationale for the invocation of strict liability was particularly suited to injury and damage claims arising from the conduct of abnormally dangerous activities, where, in the assessment of the court, the injured parties are almost always completely helpless; their proximity to the accident is completely fortuitous; and the injury is quite frequently "overwhelming misfortune."[50] In such circumstances, that court continued, "risk distribution benefits the socio-economic body in two ways: (1) the adverse impact of any particular misfortune is lessened by spreading its cost over a greater population and over a longer time period, and (2) social and economic resources can be more efficiently allocated when the actual cost of goods and services (including the losses they entail) are reflected in their price to the consumer."

To the decisions finding liability without fault for blasting and explosives activities can be added precedent for applying abnormally dangerous activities liability in mineral exploration. There is authority applying ultra-hazardous activities liability to claims involving the damage to neighboring land by the oil, sand, mud, and rocks that are emitted forcibly in a blowout, as though it were a simple blasting.[51]

---

[48] 250 N.E.2d 31 (N.Y. 1969).

[49] 399 So. 2d 248 (Ala. 1981).

[50] Chavez v. Southern Pacific Transportation Co., 413 F. Supp. 1203, 1209 (E.D. Cal. 1976).

[51] In Green v. General Petroleum Corp., 270 P. 952, 955 (Cal. 1928), the court offered this explanation: "In our judgment, no other legal construction can be placed upon the operations of the appellant in this case than that, by its deliberate act of boring its well, it undertook the burden and the responsibility of controlling and confining whatever force or power it uncovered. Any other construction would permit one owner, under like circumstances, to use the land of another for his own purpose and benefit, without making compensation for such use. We do not conceive that to be the law."

[2] Dangerous Storage

There is no clean line of demarcation as to what potentially hazardous storage activity, and what substances, will be considered suitable for a community, and what, on the other hand, will be considered unusual, and potentially abnormally dangerous. A Maryland case, *Yommer v. McKenzie*,[52] involved a claim brought by a family in a semi-rural community against the owner of gasoline storage tanks, alleging contamination of the household's drinking water. The court found it appropriate to apply the abnormally dangerous activities doctrine, relying in particular upon the locational inappropriateness of the defendant's activities when seen in relation to the community.[53] Conflicting authority is offered in other decisions that conclude that storage of gasoline is not properly considered an abnormally dangerous activity insofar as, with reference to the criteria enumerated in Restatement §§ 519–520, (1) such storage is not "extraordinary, exceptional, or unusual;" (2) there is no reason to believe that the hazard "cannot be eliminated by the exercise of reasonable care;" and (3) there is no reason to believe that the harm to be anticipated should such seepage occur would be "grave."[54]

Impoundment cases descend directly from the activity that first gave rise to the cause of action in *Rylands v. Fletcher*. A clear-eyed expression of the benefit of applying the rule in the modern impoundment context was given by a Florida court in *Cities Service Co. v. State*.[55] This case involved the defendant's maintenance of a settling pond appurtenant to its phosphate rock mine, occasioning damage described by the court as "approximately one billion gallons of phosphate slimes contained therein" escaping into waterways, "thereby killing countless numbers of fish and inflicting other damage." The court called explicitly for the adoption of *Rylands v. Fletcher* in the state, expressing its view that changed residential and industrial patterns in the state required commitment to the risk distribution public policy of abnormally dangerous activities liability:

---

[52] 257 A.2d 138 (Md. 1969).

[53] *Id.* at 141, the court citing the comments to the Restatement provisions, then in draft form, which state: "The thing which stands out from the cases is that the important thing about the activity is not that it is extremely dangerous in itself, but that it is abnormally so in relation to its surroundings. . . . The same is true of the storage of gasoline, or other inflammable liquids, in large quantities. In a populated area this is a matter of strict liability. But in an isolated area it is not."

[54] Hudson v. Peavey Oil Co., 566 P.2d 175, 178 (Or. 1977). *See also* Bagley v. Controlled Environment Corp., 503 A.2d 823 (N.H. 1986), a landowner's action against an adjoining landowner for the release of gasoline stored thereon. The court approved the trial court's dismissal of the liability without fault claim because, in its view, the mishap was of such a nature that it could be eliminated by the exercise of reasonable care or by application of enforcement proceedings for statutory violations.

[55] 312 So. 2d 799 (Fla. Ct. App. 1975).

In early days it was important to encourage persons to use their lands by whatever means were available for the purpose of commercial and industrial development. In a frontier society there was little likelihood that a dangerous use of land could cause damage to one's neighbor. Today our life has become more complex. Many areas are overcrowded, and even the nonnegligent use of one's land can cause extensive damages to a neighbor's property. Though there are still many hazardous activities which are socially desirable, it now seems reasonable that they pay their own way. It is too much to ask an innocent neighbor to bear the burden thrust upon him as a consequence of an abnormal use of the land next door.

Impoundment cases frequently provide instructive deliberations upon the common usage and the appropriateness to the locality inquiries suggested by Restatement § 520 (d) & (e). One such example of this, reaching a conclusion contrary to that of the Florida court in *Cities Service*, can be found in a Texas opinion in which the court, after describing the climate, agriculture, and topography of the locus of events, concludes that "the impounding of water in streamways" represents "an obvious and natural use" in such Texas communities, rendering the observations in *Rylands v. Fletcher* of "no application."[56]

Contrast an action involving the dumping of industrial waste, in which another Texas court, finding strict liability to attach whenever pollutants are intentionally discharged, added:

> We further believe the public policy of this state to be that however laudable an industry may be, its owners or managers are still subject to the rule that its industry or its property cannot be so used as to inflict injury to the property of its neighbors. To allow industry to inflict injury to the property of its neighbors without just compensation amounts to inverse condemnation which is not permitted under our law. We know of no acceptable rule of jurisprudence which permits those engaged in important and desirable enterprises to injure with impunity those who are engaged in enterprises of lesser economic significance. The costs of injuries resulting from pollution must be internalized by industry as a cost of production and borne by consumers or shareholders, or both, and not by the injured individual.[57]

---

[56] Turner v. Big Lake Oil Co., 96 S.W.2d 221, 226 (Tex. 1936), the court explaining: "In Texas we have conditions very different from those which obtain in England. A large portion of Texas is an arid or semi arid region. . . . The country is almost without streams; and without the storage of water from basin constructed for that purpose, or to hold waters pumped from the earth, the great livestock industry of West Texas must perish. . . . [O]bviously the rule announced in Rylands v. Fletcher, predicated upon different conditions, can have no application here."

[57] Atlas Chemical Industries, Inc. v. Anderson, 514 S.W.2d 309, 315 (Tex. Civ. Ct. App. 1974), *judgment aff'd in part, rev'd in part*, 524 S.W.2d 681 (Tex. 1975).

[3] Dangerous Release or Application

One other type of commercial activity to which the abnormally dangerous activities rule of liability has been applied is that involving aerial administration of agricultural chemicals, or crop dusting.[58] A substantial proportion of jurisdictions employ the theory of negligence in crop duster actions. Sound reasons exist, nonetheless, for application of the abnormally dangerous activities doctrine to such accidents. One of the most persuasive of these reasons is that accidents are extremely difficult to avoid even with defendant's exercise of the utmost care.[59] The types of mishap that can occur in the course of administration of agricultural chemicals by aerial means is varied indeed, and can range from the improvident chemical spraying of product intended for the organic market,[60] to killing bees,[61] to killing hogs.[62]

Other decisions have imposed liability without fault for the landbound administration of pesticides.[63] An interesting application of liability without fault for a fireman's inhalation of escaping antimony pentachloride gas is *Langlois v. Allied Chemical Corp.*,[64] with the Louisiana Supreme Court concluding that liability without fault should apply where "[t]he storage of the dangerous gas by Allied was an activity which, even when conducted with the greatest care and prudence, could cause damage to others in the neighborhood. It was an ultra-hazardous activity, and the possible consequences of the gas escaping and causing harm were known or should have been known."

A significant recent enlargement of the abnormally dangerous activities doctrine has been in the context of the release of, or contamination by, radiation. The nuclear reactor is certainly the most visible of the diverse sources of ambient radiation, and the suitability of nuclear reaction for the generation of energy seems uniquely appropriate for application of the doctrine of liability without fault inasmuch as (1) a nuclear accident is

---

[58] *E.g.*, Boroughs v. Joiner, 337 So. 2d 340 (Ala. 1976) (aerial application of insecticides and pesticides implicated in damage to fishpond located nearby properly considered an inherently dangerous activity); Bella v. Aurora Air, Inc., 566 P.2d 489 (Or. 1977) (spraying of 2 4 D by aircraft on mint crop adjacent to wheat field primary target of activity correctly termed abnormally dangerous activity).

[59] One commentary offered this analysis of the reasons that the drift of agricultural chemicals that are administered by aircraft are extremely difficult to control, attributable to three "uncertain and uncontrollable factors: (1) the size of the dust or spray particles; (2) the air disturbances created by [the aircraft]; and (3) natural atmospheric forces." Note, *Crop Dusting*, 6 Stan. L. Rev. 69, 70 75 (1953).

[60] Langan v. Valicopters, Inc., 567 P.2d 218 (Wash. 1977).

[61] S.A. Gerrard Co. v. Fricker, 27 P.2d 678 (Ariz. 1933).

[62] McPherson v. Billington, 399 S.W.2d 186 (Tex. Civ. Ct. App. 1965).

[63] *E.g.*, Luthringer v. Moore, 190 P.2d 1 (Cal. 1948).

[64] 249 So. 2d 133 (La. 1971).

almost unimaginably lethal; (2) no degree of regulation, superintendence, or technical improvement bids fair to eliminate the risk of accident altogether; and (3) it seems unlikely that a nuclear facility will soon be considered a natural use of the land.[65]

In certain radiation contamination settings, the plaintiff has stated a claim that sounds properly in trespass, nuisance, and abnormally dangerous activity. For example, in *Maryland Heights Leasing, Inc. v. Mallinckrodt, Inc.*,[66] adjoining business owners filed a suit against the defendant, the manufacturer of nuclear and radioactive pharmaceuticals, alleging damage to their property from low-level radioactive emissions. The appellate court found that the landowners' evidence that defendant "created a high degree of risk of harm" to the surrounding property that the defendant was unable or unwilling to abate, and that the "harm significantly outweighs the value of the plant and that they have suffered injuries," was sufficient to permit the abnormally dangerous activities claim to proceed, with the claims in trespass and nuisance, to trial.

[4] Dangerous Transportation

The peril associated with the transportation of a substance may add to its hazardous characteristics so as to compel treatment of such transportation as an abnormally dangerous activity. For transportation of such a material to be subject to liability without fault, it is not necessary that the particular substance be considered abnormally dangerous when in a state of rest, or when it is being transported in moderate quantities.

Gasoline, a product of significant, if governable, risk, has been held to warrant ultra-hazardous activity treatment when that risk is multiplied by the collection of the product for the purposes of transportation. This conclusion is compelled, in the view of one court, by its observation that "Gasoline is always dangerous whether kept in large or small quantities because of its volatility, inflammability and explosiveness. But when several thousand gallons of it are allowed to spill across a public highway — that is, if, while in transit as freight, it is not kept impounded — the hazards to third persons are so great as to be almost beyond calculation."[67]

Many jurisdictions recognize judicial or statutory exceptions to liability without fault for the public carriage of hazardous materials. Such jurisdictions preclude imposition of a strict liability standard upon common carriers

[65] *See* Bennett v. Mallinckrodt, Inc., 698 S.W.2d 854, 869 (Mo. Ct. App. 1985).

[66] 706 S.W.2d 218 (Mo. Ct. App. 1985).

[67] Siegler v. Kuhlman, 502 P.2d 1181, 1184 (Wash. 1972), *cert. denied*, 411 U.S. 983 (1973) ("stored in commercial quantities, gasoline has been recognized to be a substance of such dangerous characteristics that it invited a rule of strict liability even where the hazard is contamination to underground water supply and not its more dangerous properties such as its explosiveness and flammability.").

for mishaps involving abnormally dangerous activities, on the rationale that the actor had a right to engage in such activities under applicable law.

Where this policy is adopted, liability is found only where the transporter is negligent.[68] The conflicting view, held by many jurisdictions, provides that where one is engaged in an ultra-hazardous activity, "even when backed by state authority of the state, [h]e must so use his rights as not to conflict with the rights of another in the enjoyment of life or in the possession of property."[69] This view is of course more consistent with the practically universal application of a higher standard of care to the similar, although concededly distinguishable, operations of the public carrier.

[5] Dangerous Transmission

Depending upon the habitat in which they are maintained, some decisions have found that maintenance of high voltage electrical transmission wires constitutes an abnormally dangerous activity within the meaning of Restatement §§ 519–520. The "enormity of the risk," and the typical community's "lack of awareness" of that risk, were the dispositive factors for the Minnesota Supreme Court in favor of imposition of strict liability in deciding an action brought on behalf of a boy who was injured seriously by electricity escaping from an uninsulated high-voltage transmission line as he and his father were trimming trees in their back yard.[70] In another appellate opinion the Utah Supreme Court gives a concise description of the gravity of the risk of high voltage transmission, stating:

> A high tension transmission wire is one of the most dangerous things known to man. Not only is the current deadly, but the danger is hidden away in an innocent looking wire ready at all times to kill or injure anyone who touches it or comes too near to it. For the average citizen there is no way of knowing whether the wire is harmless or lethal until it is too late to do anything about it.[71]

It has been held as well that a cause of action may lay against a power company for its failure to warn operators of small aircraft concerning the risk of ensnarement in electrical wires.[72]

---

[68] Pope v. Edward M. Rude, Carrier Corp., 75 S.E.2d 584 (W. Va. 1953).

[69] McGrath v. Basich Brothers Construction Co., 46 P.2d 981, 983 (Cal. Ct. App. 1935). See discussion in Chavez v. Southern Pacific Transportation Co., 413 F. Supp. 1203, 1209 1212 (E.D. Cal. 1976).

[70] Ferguson v. Northern States Power Co., 239 N.W.2d 190 (Minn. 1976).

[71] Brigham v. Moon Lake Elec. Ass'n, 470 P.2d 393, 395 (Utah 1970). *Contrast* Kent v. Gulf States Utilities Co., 418 So. 2d 493 (La. 1982), declining to apply strict liability to uninsulated power lines.

[72] *See* Mills v. Orcas Power & Light Co., 355 P.2d 781 (Wash. 1960).

[6] Additional Activites

Claims brought by workers who are contaminated while engaging in abnormally dangerous activities have sometimes established strict liability even where the effects of the defendant's activity have left the property. In suits brought by workers who have suffered from toxic exposure, liability without fault has been found, and recovery permitted, where the injured claimant, no longer on the premises of the activity, has been contaminated by substances such as plutonium from a fuel processing plant.[73] There is decisional support too for applicability of the doctrine of liability without fault for abnormally dangerous activities where a third party servicing the vehicle or means of transporting a dangerous substance is contaminated by contact with the material.[74]

The abnormally dangerous activities doctrine has been applied to activities as widely divergent as the use of field fire,[75] the conducting of rocket tests,[76] pile driving,[77] the use by a roofing contractor of a tar kettle that erupted into flames, setting fire to a nearby warehouse,[78] and the sale, in violation of a statute, of model airplane glue to a minor.[79] Courts have declined to apply abnormally dangerous activities liability to claims arising from injuries sustained by plaintiff being struck by locomotive engines while using a popular community shortcut across the tracks,[80] deer hunting, with permission, in thick brush,[81] or slipping on the slippery floor of a pier while unloading a shipment of frozen fish.[82]

---

[73] Silkwood v. Kerr-McGee Corp., 667 F.2d 908, 921 (10th Cir. 1981), *rev'd on other grounds*, 464 U.S. 238 (1984).

[74] *See* Matkovic v. Shell Oil Co., 707 P.2d 2 (Mont. 1985) (claim brought where plaintiff's decedent, a garage employee, was fatally injured by contamination while working on truck for hauling contractor engaged in transporting for disposal water highly contaminated by hydrogen sulfide).

[75] *E.g.*, Koos v. Roth, 652 P.2d 1255 (Or. 1982).

[76] *E.g.*, Smith v. Lockheed Propulsion Co., 56 Cal. Rptr. 128 (Cal. Ct. App. 1967).

[77] Oja & Associates v. Washington Park Towers, Inc., 569 P.2d 1141 (Wash. 1977).

[78] Henderson Bros. Stores, Inc. v. Smiley, 174 Cal. Rptr. 875, 883 (Cal. Ct. App. 1981).

[79] Zerby v. Warren, 210 N.W.2d 58 (Minn. 1973).

[80] Ruiz v. Southern Pacific Transp. Co., 638 P.2d 406, 412 (N.M. Ct. App. 1981).

[81] Mikula v. Duliba, 94 A.D.2d 503, 464 N.Y.S.2d 910, 912, 913 (1983).

[82] Anderson v. Iceland S. S. Co., 585 F.2d 1142 (1st Cir. 1978).

CHAPTER 17

PRODUCTS LIABILITY

SYNOPSIS

---

§ 17.01 WHAT IS PRODUCTS LIABILITY?

[A] *A Contemporary Survey*

"Products liability" refers broadly to the decisional and statutory law permitting money damages from manufacturers and sellers of defective products that injure persons or property. The four principal theories that underlie products liability suits are (1) negligence; (2) breach of one or more warranties; (3) liability without fault or negligence, *i.e.*, strict liability; and (4) misrepresentation.[1]

Products liability analysis is best appreciated by first introducing the four major causes of action (negligence, warranty, strict liability in tort, and misrepresentation), and then applying these causes of action to the types of factual settings most frequently encountered.

The factual situations accounting for practically all claims in products liability are (1) mismanufacture; (2) defective design or formulation; (3) the failure to give adequate warnings or instructions for safe use; and (4) the failure to truthfully represent the quality of a product.

---

[1] Abundant scholarship exists on product liability subject matters. *See generally* David G. Owen, *The Moral Foundations of Product Liability Law: Toward First Principles*, 68 Notre Dame L. Rev. 427 (1993); William C. Powers, Jr., *A Modest Proposal to Abandon Strict Product Liability*, 1991 U. Ill. L. Rev. 639 (1991); Gary T. Schwartz, Forward: *Understanding Products Liability*, 267 Colum. L. Rev 435 (1979); Marshall S. Shapo, *A Representational Theory of Consumer Protection: Doctrine, Function and Legal Liability for Disappointment*, 60 Va. L. Rev. 1109 (1974); James A. Henderson, Jr. and Aaron D. Twerski, *Closing the American Products Liability Frontier: The Rejection of Liability Without Defect*, 66 N.Y.U. L. Rev. 1263 (1991); David A. Fisher, *Products Liability: The Meaning of Defect*, 39 Mo. L. Rev. 339 (1974); Howard Latin, *Good Warnings, Bad Products and Congitive Limitations*, 41 UCLA L. Rev. 1193 (1994); Jerry Phillips, *The Proposed Products Liability Restatement: A Misguided Revision*, 10 Touro L. Rev. 151 (1993).

Sections 17.01–17.04 and 17.06 of this analysis are abridged from *Products Liability (2d)* (West 1988) and *Products Liability (3d)* (to be published). Section 17.05 is derived from an article that first appeared 89 W. Va. L. Rev. 221 (1986). Permission granted by the West Virginia Law Review.

At the outset, it is essential to understand that a single seller dereliction, such as, for example, mismanufacture, may give rise to an injured party's cause of action under several legal theories. For example, if presented with facts suggesting a manufacturer's responsibility for a design defect, one must examine the viability of plaintiff's cause of action in at least three of the available legal theories, *i.e.*, negligence, warranty, strict liability in tort, and misrepresentation.

[1] Negligence

The law of negligence is primarily concerned with compensating persons suffering personal injury or property loss due to another's failure to act with due care under the circumstances. The actor's liability in tort is limited by concepts of reasonable foreseeability.[2]

From the above, the rule for negligence liability for the sale of an unreasonably dangerous product emerges: A product seller is liable in negligence if he acts or fails to act in such a way as to create an unreasonable risk of harm or loss to the user of a product or to another who might foreseeably be injured.

For plaintiff to prevail in negligence there must be harm to her person or property, and proximate cause between the actor's conduct and the harm suffered. Of course a product may pose a risk of injury that is only reasonable, witness the defect-free bicycle that may upon occasion topple its rider. To be distinguished is the unreasonable risk of injury, such as that created by the placement of the fuel tank on an automobile in such a position that a minor rear-end collision may rupture it, creating the risk of explosion and fire.

Where is the line between the reasonable risk and the unreasonable one? Most courts use the formulation of Judge Learned Hand, or a comparable risk-benefit model. The Hand formulation states that an actor's conduct creates an unreasonable risk of harm where the burden of taking measures to avoid the harm would be less than the multiple of the likelihood that the harm will occur times the magnitude of the harm should it occur. In the formula $(B<(P)(L))$, the actor will be considered in breach of his duty when B is less than (P)(L), that is, B (Burden of precautions) is less than P (likelihood, in terms of Probability) times L (magnitude of Liability should the harm occur at all).[3]

Applying this negligence evaluation to the hypothetical sale of an automobile with a gas tank vulnerable to collision rupture, the facts support a finding of manufacturer negligence if one agrees that on the right side of the equation there is a measurable risk that any motor vehicle will be struck from the rear at some time during its useful life, and further that

---

[2] *See* §§ 3.02. 3.03.

[3] United States v. Carroll Towing Co., 159 F.2d 169 (2d Cir. 1947).

the type of injury that might follow from the rupture of a gas tank in a collision (burn injuries or death) is very great. Turning to the left side of the equation, suppose the financial burden to the manufacturer of either using a more sturdy material for the tank, or placing the tank in a more forward position beneath the vehicle, was $200 per car. The claimant would argue that such a cost is certainly moderate, and is, in any event, less than the risk of some harm multiplied by the seriousness of that harm (death or serious bodily harm) should the design not be changed. Accepting these assumptions, a plaintiff should be able to make out a prima facie case that the manufacturer has breached its duty of care.

The plaintiff's negligence products liability claim may be available in virtually any setting against the product seller, including claims for mismanufacture, defective design, and failure to warn. In each instance, a cost-benefit analysis comparable to that used above will be an element of part or all of the requisite negligence analysis.

[2] Breach of Warranty

Unlike negligence, which is a tort claim, breach of warranty is a claim that arises under principles of contract. There are three ways in which the seller may breach its warranty to the purchaser: breach of an express warranty, breach of the implied warranty of merchantability, and breach of the implied warranty of fitness for a particular purpose. In a given factual setting, it is possible for a product to breach one, two, or even all of these warranties.

The *express warranty* is made when the seller makes a material representation as to a product's composition, durability, performance, or safety.[4] The express warranty may be made by any means of communication, from spoken comment to advertisements.

Not every statement from a seller to a buyer creates an express warranty. Where the seller's assurance of qualities in the product pertain to matters equally understandable and observable to the purchaser, the seller's representation is not "material," and instead is "puffing," which will not create an express warranty. Using as examples comments that might accompany the purchase of an automobile, the seller's statement that the vehicle's paint job is "Great" should be considered puffing, and not an express warranty, because (1) the comment pertains to aesthetics, rather than the performance or the durability of the paint, and (2) the comment pertains to appearance, a matter as to which the buyer is as proficient as the seller to judge. Contrast a hypothetical seller's comment that an automobile's tires have "at least two more good years." Absent some indication that the seller's assurance

[4] *E.g.*, Baxter v. Ford Motor Co., 12 P.2d 409 (Wash. 1932), holding that the trial court erred in excluding from evidence Ford's catalogues and other printed matter pertaining its "Triplex Shatter-Proof Glass Windshield," in that these written materials "set forth representations by the manufacturer that the windshield . . . would not fly or shatter."

was patently untrue, *i.e.*, one tire was flat, or that the buyer had a specialized knowledge about tire wear, this comment creates an express warranty.

Prior to the UCC, to preserve a claim in express warranty the buyer might be required to show that she relied specifically upon the express warranty of the seller. The comments to UCC § 2-313 now provide that the buyer's reliance upon an express warranty will be presumed unless the lack of reliance is proved by the seller. This liberalization of the historical reliance requirement is relevant to the buyer who after the injury or loss may only imperfectly recall (1) the assurances the seller made orally; or (2) which of the seller's written assurances the buyer actually read prior to the mishap. The Code creates a presumption that the buyer relied upon the seller's warranty in deciding to purchase the product, and that presumption will only be defeated by the seller's affirmative proof to the contrary.

The *implied warranty of merchantability*, UCC § 2-314, provides that any seller impliedly warrants that the product sold is fit for its ordinary purposes. This warranty, as its name suggests, conveys with the sale of the product irrespective of the seller's statements or comments.

What is the ordinary purpose of a product? A product's ordinary purpose may be distinguishable from the manufacturer's intended purpose for the product; witness the common use of table chairs to service ceiling fixtures. Most courts would characterize such use of a chair as ordinary, even though admittedly not the use intended by the seller. However, a household screw driver would not ordinarily be used to shape marble, and thong sandals would not ordinarily be worn to climb Mt. Whitney. Injuries associated with either of the latter two uses would not be redressable in implied warranty of merchantability.

The *implied warranty of fitness for a particular purpose*, UCC § 2-315, contemplates the buyer's explicit or implicit request that a seller having specialized knowledge recommend a product suitable for the buyer's goal or project. Where the seller knows of the purchaser's special need, and where the buyer completes the purchase in reliance upon the seller's expertise, there arises an implied warranty of fitness for a particular purpose.

This warranty provides a remedy to a buyer who has purchased an otherwise merchantable product (*e.g.*, housepaint) for use in a specialized way (to paint a home subject to extreme climate variations), and has suffered a loss due to the seller's erroneous advice. In contrast, the homeowner's purchase of ordinary exterior paint for a home would not create an implied warranty of fitness for a particular purpose.

[a] Parties

For the express warranty and the implied warranty of merchantability, the defendant must be a commercial seller of such products. Neither an individual's sale of a used VCR, nor a hardware store's presentation of a prize drawing for a sailboat, would create either of these warranties. Distinguish, however, the implied warranty of fitness for a particular purpose, which has no requirement that the seller ordinarily sells such goods.

In warranty, the proper plaintiffs are decided by reference to which Alternative to UCC § 2-318 a jurisdiction has selected. Alternative A confines the class of plaintiffs along the lines of the common law privity requirement, including members of the buyer's household and guests therein. Alternatives B and C are progressively more inclusive and extend the warranty remedy to nonpurchasing users and to unrelated bystanders. Alternative A is the most widely adopted of the three provisions.

In addition to the buyer, UCC § 2-318 Alternative A permits a cause of action to "any natural person who is in the family or household of his buyer, or who is a guest in his home, . . ." Note that the use of the phrase "natural person" precludes a cause of action to a business or corporation. Alternative B similarly confines the cause of action to natural persons, but extends the class of plaintiffs to all natural persons "who may be reasonably expected to use, consume, or be affected by the goods." Under Alternative C, plaintiffs are not limited to natural persons, and therefore organizations and businesses may bring an action in warranty. The language of reasonable foreseeability is identical to that of Alternative B.

[b] Disclaimers and Limitations

One of the most significant distinctions between products liability remedies in tort and in warranty is that the UCC explicitly grants the seller the ability to disclaim or limit the remedies available to the purchaser. The most straightforward rationale for permitting disclaimers in warranty and not in tort is that the warranty remedies, arising in contract, are said to represent the mutual assent of the buying and selling parties.

Where the seller has given an express warranty, a disclaimer of that warranty will not be allowed. The seller may, however, disclaim the implied warranty of merchantability or fitness for a particular purpose. UCC § 2-316 provides that the implied warranty of merchantability may be effectively disclaimed if the disclaimer mentions merchantability and is conspicuous. The implied warranty of fitness for a particular purpose, in turn, may be disclaimed where the disclaiming language is "by a writing and conspicuous." The decisions are in substantial agreement that disclaiming language will be considered conspicuous where it is on the face of the controlling document, where it is distinctively displayed by positioning, background, border, type, or color, and where the typeface of the disclaimer is at least as large or larger than that used in the balance of the document.

Under all circumstances, UCC § 2-316 states that implied warranties may be excluded "by expressions like 'as is', 'with all faults' or other language which in ordinary understanding calls the buyer's attention to the exclusion of warranties and makes plain that there is no implied warranty; . . . ."

Pursuant to UCC § 2-719, a seller may limit remedies available under a warranty, such as, for example, limiting the buyer's remedies to return of the goods and repayment of the purchase price or repair. Courts will sustain such limitations unless they operate to deprive the buyer of the remedy's essential purpose, *i.e.*, to receive a fit product or a return of purchase money. In addition, while UCC § 2-719(3) permits limitation or exclusion of consequential damages, it adds that where the alleged product flaw results in personal injury, limitation of consequential damages for warranties of consumer goods is "prima facie unconscionable."

[3] Strict Liability in Tort

The limitations inherent in the remedies of negligence and warranty liability encouraged creation of a products liability tort remedy that would alleviate some of the privity and evidentiary burdens placed upon plaintiffs. In negligence the most obvious obstacle to plaintiff's recovery is the requirement that plaintiff identify and prove that point in the process of manufacture or sale that the seller's conduct fell below the requisite due care under the circumstances. Such proof typically requires plaintiff to not only attain a familiarity with often very complex manufacturing processes, but to be prepared as well to rebut the defendant's claims that its practices, conforming with the actions of other producers in the same industry, did represent due care. Distinct but equally imposing obstacles to the plaintiff's recovery in warranty take the form of the requirement of timely notice to the seller, privity barriers that vary from state to state, and the seller's ability to limit warranty remedies or disclaim warranties altogether.

In the 1963 decision in *Greenman v. Yuba Power Products, Inc.*,[5] the California Supreme Court seized the occasion to announce a remedy of tort liability without the necessity of proving negligence, that is, strict liability in tort, stating: "A manufacturer is strictly liable in tort when an article he places on the market, knowing that it is to be used without inspection for defects, proves to have a defect that causes injury to a human being."

Prompted by the decision in *Greenman*, in 1965 the authors of the Restatement published § 402A, proposing strict liability in tort for any person "who sells a product in a defective condition unreasonably dangerous to the user or consumer or his property."[6]

As in warranty (except UCC § 2-315), under § 402A the defendant must be a seller of such products in the ordinary course, although a growing number of courts have extended the strict liability cause of action to businesses whose position in the stream of commerce resembles that of a

[5] 59 Cal. 2d 57, 27 Cal. Rptr. 697, 377 P.2d 897 (1963).

[6] *See* further discussion of strict products liability at § 17.04, *infra*.

product seller in terms of expertise and ability to detect and correct hazards. Thus there is authority imposing strict liability upon product lessors, bailors, and even landlords.[7]

Concerning the language "defective condition unreasonably dangerous", most jurisdictions require that the product be in both a defective condition and unreasonably dangerous. Those courts reason that as tort law is primarily concerned with the creation of remedies for conduct and conditions that create an unreasonable risk of injury, a product that is merely defective, but creates no hazard or danger, is the proper concern of warranty law, but not tort. In a minority of jurisdictions, however, including California, courts have decided that the language "unreasonably dangerous" induces juries to adopt a higher burden of proof than would the language "defective condition," and have removed the "unreasonably dangerous" criterion from plaintiff's prima facie case.

Comment i to § 402A suggests a "consumer expectations" standard for what represents an unreasonably dangerous condition, and states that evaluation of what is unreasonably dangerous should be had by reference to whether the article sold is "dangerous to an extent beyond that which would be contemplated by the ordinary consumer who purchases it, with the ordinary knowledge common to the community as to its characteristics." More particularized risk/utility evaluations for what constitutes a design defect have been adopted by most courts, with "consumer expectations" retained as one of several evaluative factors. Risk/utility evaluations will be discussed more fully below in § 17.04[B][3][b].

[4] Misrepresentation

The remedy of strict liability for misrepresentation, stated in Restatement § 402B, was created to afford a tort remedy to any person injured due to reliance on the product seller's misrepresentation of a material fact. In ways similar to the plaintiff's cause of action in breach of express warranty, § 402B nonetheless differs from warranty in its retention of the requirement that plaintiff prove actual, subjective reliance upon the seller's representations. The section differs also from strict products liability under § 402A in that the § 402B misrepresentation remedy does not require that the product be dangerously defective. Under § 402B even the sale of a merchantable product may create a cause of action if the seller's blandishments as to the product's performance or other material qualities, such as safety, are false, and the user is injured in reliance thereon.

The target of § 402B is misrepresentation by advertisement. The section's "to the public" language has been interpreted as excluding from that section a seller's individual comments to, for example, potential purchasers

[7] *E.g.*, Becker v. IRM Corp., 698 P.2d 116 (Cal. 1985) (landlord), *overruled*, Peterson v. Superior Court, 899 P.2d 905 (Cal. 1995).

on the showroom floor. As in express warranty, the representation must be of a material fact, so seller "puffing" should not be considered an actionable misrepresentation under § 402B.

The plaintiff proceeding under § 402B must show that there has been justifiable reliance upon the misrepresentation, and that personal physical injury resulted from that reliance.[8] Comment j thereto states that the remedy will not be available "where the misrepresentation is not known [to the buyer], or there is [buyer] indifference to it, and it does not influence the purchase or subsequent conduct."

[5] Application of Causes of Action to Typical Claims

Pivotal to understanding products liability is the appreciation that in most states, any fact situation may give rise to a claim in negligence, warranty, strict liability in tort, and even misrepresentation liability simultaneously.[9] Thus any product-related claim must be analyzed in terms of not one, but four causes of action. The following are typical products liability factual situations, accompanied by discussion of the amenability of the causes of action to such claims.

The mismanufacture claim arises where one manufactures a product according to an acceptable design or formulation, but something goes wrong in fabrication, quality control, packaging, or delivery of the product that makes it unreasonably dangerous. A soda bottle that leaves the bottler with excessive pressure, a wholesale jar of pharmaceuticals that is shipped with the wrong label to the pharmacist, or the home air conditioner that is mistakenly shipped with an ordinary, rather than a grounded, electrical plug would each represent a mismanufactured product.

Depending upon the facts, a mismanufactured article would create a claim in negligence if the product's flaw created an unreasonable risk of injury or loss to the user, or to another person, one might reasonably foresee would be affected by the product if negligently made.

A mismanufactured product could also create one or more claims in warranty. An express warranty would be breached if a seller had stated, for example, that a mismanufactured home appliance was "safe for all home applications." An implied warranty of merchantability would be breached if the flaw rendered the product not suited for its ordinary purpose. It is improbable that an implied warranty of fitness for a particular purpose would arise in a mismanufacture context. Appropriate plaintiffs in any

---

[8] The § 402B remedy predicate of personal physical injury distinguishes this products liability doctrine from remedies for fraudulent misrepresentation or negligent misrepresentation.

[9] A number of states confine claimants to a single products liability cause of action, or withhold from the jury all but one count. The Restatement (Third) of Torts: Products Liability will encourage this approach. *See* § 17.07, *infra*.

warranty claim will be determined by the language of the Alternative to UCC § 2-318 adopted in the particular jurisdiction.

A strict liability claim is created by the sale of a mismanufactured product where the mismanufacture results in a product unreasonably dangerous to the user or consumer, to their property, or to other persons who could foreseeably be affected.

A product seller has a duty to warn of product risks that, if not the subject of a timely and adequate notice, expose the purchaser, user, or a bystander to an unreasonable risk of harm. The warning, including, where appropriate, instructions for safe use, should be conveyed not only to the purchaser, but also to the user or consumer, unless there are adequate assurances that the purchaser or other third party, such as the employer, will give this information to the user or consumer.

A significant exception to the general seller duty to warn these persons directly, or provide reasonably that they will be warned, arises in the context of prescription drugs and other prescription products, including medical devices, blood and other biological products. Because of the complexity of considerations involved in patient diagnosis and administration of prescription drugs, the courts permit the drug company to satisfy its duty to warn by giving the necessary product, risk, and side effect information to the prescribing physician.[10] This exception is described as the "learned intermediary" rule, with the prescribing physician assuming the role of theinformed intermediary between the manufacturer and the patient. In settingswhere there is no one-to-one physician-patient contact, such as in massimmunizations, many courts have declined to apply the informed intermediaryrule, and have reverted to the primary rule that the manufacturer must conveyan adequate warning directly to the patient.

How does one decide if a warning is adequate to bring to the attention of the user and others the important risks and the ways to avoid those risks? The decisions, read together, instruct that the warning must plainly describe the *Nature* of the risk; its *Severity*; its *Scope*; and the means of *Avoidance*. The emphasized letters together create the acronym NSSA. To illustrate, the Nature of the risk might be conveyed by language like "Radioactive," "Live Electricity," "Poisonous." Severity could be described by language such as "2000 Volts," "Severe Burns if Used Without Protective Clothes," "No Antidote." Scope might be stated by, for example, "Unprotected Exposure Causes Chronic Respiratory Illness." Means of Avoidance could be explained by language like "A Facemask Must Be Worn," or "If Contact

[10] In an analogous vein, warnings of risks to workers who may risk injury at their place of employment may be given to the empoloyer — the immediate vendee of the product — where the employer is in a better position to communicate the warnings to the employees, and where it is reasonable for the seller to place such reliance upon the employer. *See* Werckenthein v. Bucher Petrochemical Co., 618 N.E.2d 902 (Ill. Ct. App. 1993) (warnings to employer-vendee sufficient).

With Skin Or Eyes, Irrigate With Water For 20 Minutes and Seek Medical Attention Immediately."

To integrate understanding of the seller's duty to warn with the causes of action under discussion, again assuming proximate cause of injury:

> A seller who fails to give warnings as to unreasonable and foreseeable risks that accompany the use of or exposure to its products will be liable in negligence for breach of the duty to warn.

The failure to warn of foreseeable risks may also be a breach of the implied warranty of merchantability where that failure makes the product not reasonably safe for use in its intended purpose, that is, unmerchantable. A tire manufacturer's failure to advise that its product must be inflated to a particular pressure for safe use, or a parachute manufacturer's failure to inform a purchaser that the parachute cords must be treated with preservative at regular intervals in order to last for their ordinary life, would constitute breach of the implied warranty of merchantability *and* breach of the tort duties to warn.

Lastly, concerning the implied warranty of fitness for a particular purpose, imagine a sailboat purchaser, having no substantial expertise in ocean sailing, who explains to a seller his goal of participating in an ocean race. Advised as to the suitability of a particular boat for such a task, and in reliance upon the seller's expertise, the buyer makes the purchase. In the ocean race the boat breaks up in the first substantial squall. Upon evidence that the boat was suited only to inland sailing and not ocean racing, the buyer might have a claim in breach of the implied warranty of fitness for a particular purpose. As suggested above, causes of action might also exist for breach of the tort duties to warn, *i.e.*, the seller's failure to advise the buyer: "Only use this boat on inland waterways."

Substantially similar to the cause of action in negligent failure to warn, a seller's failure to warn that leaves a user or bystander unable to protect himself against an unreasonable risk of injury may make the seller strictly liable in tort. Most courts have nevertheless adopted criteria of foreseeability and the state of scientific knowledge in strict liability failure to warn cases, thereby introducing evaluations familiar to the cause of action in negligent failure to warn.

A seller may likewise be liable in negligence, warranty, or strict liability for the defective design or formulation of a product. It is useful to think in terms of "formulation" as well as "design," as a sizeable number of products liability decisions pertain to pharmaceuticals or substances where it is at the formulation stage that the product went awry.

The law of most jurisdiction requires that the plaintiff show that there was a safer design alternative to the challenged design, and that this alternative was both technologically and economically feasible. To establish that the alternative was technologically feasible, the plaintiff must show that technology existing at the time of the sale of the challenged design would have permitted production of the safer, alternative design. The economic feasibility requirement is that the safer alternative could have been produced at a reasonable cost, that is to say, at a cost that would not destroy the commercial viability of the product in the pertinent market.

A seller will be liable in negligent design or formulation for the adoption of a design that subjects the user or others exposed to the product to an unreasonable risk of injury. Judge Hand's approach remains a valuable means of assessing the reasonableness of a risk. Application of the Hand formula would suggest a comparison of the burden of precautionary measures, including the feasibility of those measures or alternative designs, against the multiple of the probability that an injury will be caused by the design used and the magnitude of the loss that may be anticipated should the injury occur at all.

Consider, for example, a motor bike upon which only one person may safely ride, but which is designed with a bench-like extension of the rider's seat that looks invitingly like a passenger's seat. Assuming injury to a passenger who falls from the vehicle, and putting aside for the moment applicable defenses, a Hand analysis of defective design would be, to the right of the equation (B<(P)(L)), that the Probability of injury is substantial (the likelihood of someone falling off while the vehicle is in operation); and magnitude of the Loss should a mishap occur is great (the passenger might fracture his skull or be hit by another vehicle). To the left of the equation the manufacturer's Burden of avoiding the hazard is probably quite small, involving only the elimination of the bench-type shape of the platform behind the driver's seat. Considering only plaintiff's affirmative case, the defendant manufacturer would appear to be prima facie liable in negligence for defective design.

A product design that poses an unreasonable risk of injury or damage to persons or to property should breach the implied warranty of merchantability, as any such *unreasonably* dangerous product would not be fit for its ordinary purpose. Even dangerous products should, by this logic, be only reasonably dangerous. For example, a stick of dynamite used in demolition work should detonate only when intended. It bears reiteration that not every product that is unfit for its intended purpose, and therefore in breach of UCC § 2-314, would be unreasonably dangerous and redressable in tort. A product might simply fail to function, and unless the malfunction puts a person or property other than the product itself at risk, the mishap would give rise only to a breach of warranty.

A design or formulation defect will support a claim in strict liability where the design flaw results in a defective condition unreasonably dangerous to the user or consumer. Comment i to § 402A states that a defect will be considered to create an unreasonably dangerous condition where it is dangerous to an extent "beyond that which would be contemplated by the ordinary consumer who purchases it." An alternative and influential means of evaluating whether a product's flawed condition represents an unreasonable danger was proposed by Dean John Wade and others, and involves a seven-point risk/utility evaluation for "unreasonable danger." This evaluation is presented in § 17.04[B][3][b], *infra*.

[B] *Defenses*

[1] Generally

Prior to the widespread adoption of comparative fault, on plaintiff's count in negligence, defendant could defend with evidence that plaintiff was contributorily negligent, or that plaintiff assumed the risk of injury. A plaintiff is contributorily negligent if she fails to exercise due care to protect herself from an unreasonable risk of harm. The defense of assumption of the risk requires a higher showing, consisting of plaintiff's actual subjective knowledge of the hazard and subsequent voluntary encounter with it.

Similarly, on any of one or more warranty counts, defendant could defend with a showing of assumption of risk, but not on a showing of mere contributory negligence. Putting aside esoteric reasoning for this limitation upon warranty defenses, the most straightforward logic is that plaintiff's warranty claim or claims are strict liability claims, in that there is no necessity of showing the prudence or imprudence of defendant's conduct. Thus, the thinking continues, where negligence is not a requisite of plaintiff's proof, contributory negligence should not be a categorical defense.

In these latter respects, the permissible defenses to plaintiff's count in strict liability are identical to those permitted in warranty. To plaintiff's strict liability claim defendant may defend by showing plaintiff's assumption of risk, but not contributory negligence. The Notes to § 402A explain: "[c]ontributory negligence . . . is not a defense when such negligence consists merely in a failure to discover the defect in the product, or to guard against the possibility of its existence." However, the Notes continue, "negligence which consists in voluntarily and unreasonably proceeding to encounter a known danger, and commonly passes under the name of assumption of risk, is a defense under this Section as in other cases of strict liability." These suggestions by the authors of § 402A mean that where plaintiff's incautious conduct was of a fairly passive nature, such as the failure to discover the defective condition, this behavior will not create a defense to a claim in strict liability. Where, on the other hand, plaintiff's risk-taking is of a more aggravated nature, such as voluntarily, knowingly, and unreasonably confronting the hazard, this assumption of the risk can bar plaintiff's strict liability claim.

Misuse of a substantial and nonforeseeable nature may be a defense against plaintiff's claims in negligence, warranty, and strict liability. Such misuse will itself become the proximate cause of the loss or injury, precluding any claim against the seller. The misuse must be substantial. For example, inflating a tire evaluated for 22 pounds of pressure to 24 pounds should not be a misuse of such a nature that breaks causation. Removing the couplings on a life preserver to achieve greater mobility while fishing would, on the other hand, be more likely to be a misuse of the quality that would break causation. Foreseeable misuse will not bar plaintiff's claim. It has, for example, been held that a young person's use of new tires at high speeds, occasioning a blowout, was foreseeable where the tires were promoted as high performance and marketed to younger drivers.

[2] Comparative Fault

Comparative fault, in either its pure or its modified form, "is now firmly entrenched in American law,"[11] with one variation or another adopted by statute or by decision in a majority of states. Under comparative fault, the trier of fact compares the proportionate contribution the product defect made to the injury with the causal contribution of plaintiff's conduct in apportioning damages.[12]

[C] *Historical Overview*

The birth of products liability can be dated at 1916, the publication of the immensely influential decision of *MacPherson v. Buick Motor Co.*[13] There the New York Court of Appeals held that the manufacturer of any product capable of serious harm if negligently made owed a duty of care in the design, inspection, and fabrication of the product, a duty owed not only to the immediate purchaser but to all persons who might foreseeably be affected by the product. Following *MacPherson*, the doctrine as formed by decisions of the ensuing decades is that a buyer, user, consumer or bystander in proximity to an unreasonably dangerous product, and who is injured in person or in property by its dangerous propensities, may recover in damages from the manufacturer or intermediate seller.[14]

Modern products liability law is the direct descendant of the tort doctrine, at least one century older, that an individual sustaining loss to person or property by another's breach of a duly of care owed to them may recover damages.[15] In addition to negligence-based liability, recovery for

---

[11] Michael Steenson, *Comparative Negligence in Minnesota*, 9 Wm. Mitchell L. Rev. 299, 303 (1983).

[12] Comparative negligence is discussed *supra*, at § 13.03.

[13] 217 N.Y. 382, 111 N.E. 1050 (1916).

[14] *E.g.*, In re Agent Orange, Product Liability Litigation, 597 F. Supp. 740 (E.D.N.Y. 1984).

[15] *Cf.* Brown v. Kendall, 60 Mass. (6 Cush.) 292, 298 (1850), in which the court describes plaintiff's burden of proof for recovery of damages as a showing sufficient to persuade the jury of defendant's "fault, negligence, carelessness, or want of due care."

product-related damages may also be premised upon contract-based principles of warranty. A plaintiff's recovery in warranty may be on the basis of an express warranty, for which plaintiff must show the seller's breach of a material representation of performance, efficacy, or safety. Implied warranties also accompany the sale of a product, and unless expressly disclaimed, each sale of a product by a merchant of such goods carries with it an implied warranty that the product is substantially similar in safety, quality, and performance, to similar products sold generally. In addition, some products may be sold with an implied warranty of fitness for a particular purpose, where the buyer expresses a need for a product for a specific and special application, communicates such requirements to the seller, and relies upon the seller's expertise in the final selection.

The introduction between 1963 and 1965 of strict tort liability in tort for the sale of "defective" products that were "unreasonably dangerous" to the user or consumer radically advanced American products liability jurisprudence. By "strict" it was meant that liability would be found without regard to whether the seller's conduct was cautious or incautious, prudent or negligent. The gravamen of strict liability is the condition of the product, not the conduct of the seller.[16]

The action in intentional tortious misrepresentation may sound in fraud or in deceit, for which plaintiff must prove a false representation of a material fact, the speaker's knowledge of its falsity, an intent that the statement should be relied upon, and the complainant's justifiable reliance upon the statement to his detriment. A seller's false statement of fact, negligently made, upon which the buyer places justifiable reliance to his consequent damage, may subject the seller to a cause of action in negligent misrepresentation. In addition, a seller may incur liability for misrepresentation irrespective of fraud or negligence pursuant to Restatement § 402B.

Underlying every products liability case are three common elements: a defective product, an injury, and a causal relationship between the two. The proof which plaintiff must present may vary according to the theory upon which his claim is based. The defectiveness of the product ordinarily takes one of these three forms: (1) defectiveness in the manufacturing process; (2) defectiveness in design, inspection or testing; or (3) defectiveness in the warning, instructions or labeling.

At the conclusion of the Nineteenth Century, there existed no generally available remedy for the purchaser of the defective or unreasonably dangerous product. In the absence of an express warranty, or fraud, the commercial relationship between the seller and the buyer of a product was

[16] In this respect strict products liability resembles the strict liability applied to possessors of animals and to abnormally dangerous activities, in that for those categories of activity it is the risk created by the activity, and not the presence or absence of due care by the actor, that supports imposition of liability without fault.

governed by a rule of caveat emptor, or "let the buyer beware." Today the products liability plaintiff's lack of privity with the manufacturer or the seller will not preclude a negligence claim, but this was not always the case. As the Nineteenth Century closed, in addition to the impediments posed by the doctrine of caveat emptor, relief for the injured buyer of a defective product was further retarded by the widespread recognition of a privity barrier to a cause of action for the purchaser not in privity.[17]

The privity doctrine owed much to the mid-nineteenth century decision of *Winterbottom v. Wright*,[18] in which the evidence showed the sale by a manufacturer and repairer of stagecoaches to the regional postmaster. Through a defect in either construction or repair, the coach broke down, injuring the driver. Before the Exchequer, judgment was granted for the defendant, on the ground that a plaintiff could not bring an action against a remote seller with whom there was no privity of contract. The rule in *Winterbottom v. Wright* found approval in such American cases as that of the New York Court of Appeals in *Thomas v. Winchester*,[19] in which the court nevertheless approved a cause of action by a plaintiff not in privity where defendant's negligent mislabeling of the poison belladonna as the innocuous extract of dandelion was imminently dangerous to others.

There developed a limited number of exceptions to the privity rule, connected by a logic that privity should not be required where the conduct of the seller was particularly egregious, or, as in *Thomas v. Winchester*, where the nature of the product was unusually dangerous, and the risk of harm created thereby particularly high. Three principal exceptions were stated at the turn of the century in *Huset v. J.I. Case Threshing Machine Co.*,[20] in which the court pronounced the rule that absence of privity would not bar an injured party's action against a remote seller or manufacturer where the injury arose from: (1) "an act of negligence . . . which is imminently dangerous to the life or health of mankind, and which is committed in the preparation or sale of an article intended to preserve, destroy, or affect human life, . . .;" (2) "an owner's act of negligence which causes injury to one who is invited by him to use his defective appliance upon the owner's premises. . .;" (3) "one who sells or delivers an article which he knows to be imminently dangerous to life or limb to another without notice of its qualities . . . ."

In 1916, New York's highest court entered the watershed decision of *MacPherson v. Buick Motor Co.*,[21] a personal injury action brought by the

---

[17] In the products liability context, privity exists where the complainant has had a direct contractual (vendor-vendee) relationship with the defendant. Thus a plaintiff who purchased a dangerously defective product from a retailer would be in privity with the retailer, but not with the product's manufacturer.

[18] 10 M. & W. 109, 152 Eng. Rep. 402 (Ex. 1952).

[19] 6 N.Y. (2 Seld.) 397, 408 (1852).

[20] 120 Fed. 865 (8th Cir. 1903).

[21] 217 N.Y. 382, 111 N.E. 1050 (1916).

purchaser of a new automobile, a wheel on which proved defective, causing both injury to the driver and damage to the automobile. The evidence showed that spokes of the wheel that failed were constructed of defective wood, and further showed that it had been the practice of the defendant manufacturer to purchase the wheels from an outside supplier.

Buick defended upon the ground that plaintiff, who had purchased the automobile from a dealer, had no privity of contract with the manufacturer. Buick also claimed that its supplier, as the final assembler, should be liable for any arguable negligent construction of the defective wheel. Plaintiff offered proof of Buick's lack of due care, including testimony that Buick received the wheels with the spokes already painted, eliminating the possibility of any effective visual inspection for defects, and that Buick undertook no testing of the wheels other than a brief on-the-road test given to all finished vehicles.

The court, per Cardozo, J., reviewed the development of the negligence remedy and announced its conclusion that there was no jurisprudential or policy reason for continuation of the three restrictive exceptions to the privity bar articulated in *Huset*. A growing body of decisional law, including some cases decided by the New York court itself, had by then moved beyond *Huset* by further loosening of limitations on the negligence cause of action to the purchaser not in privity, including decisions permitting plaintiffs to recover even where the products were not imminently dangerous, if the product "was of such a character inherently that, when applied to the purposes for which it was designed, it was liable to become a source of great danger to many people if not carefully and properly constructed." In *MacPherson* the court stated a new and general rule of manufacturer liability in negligence, irrespective of privity: "If the nature of a thing is such that it is reasonably certain to place life and limb in peril when negligently made, then it is a thing of danger. Its nature gives warning of the consequences to be expected. If to the element of danger there is added knowledge that the thing will be used by persons other than the purchaser, and used without new tests, then, irrespective of contract, the manufacturer of this thing of danger is under a duty to make it carefully."

As for the manufacturer's argument that the supplier alone should be liable, the court responded, "We think the defendant was not absolved from a duty of inspection because it brought the wheels from a reputable manufacturer . . . It was not at liberty to put the finished product on the market without subjecting the component parts to ordinary and simple tests."

The *MacPherson* rule creating negligence liability without privity for the manufacturer of a product capable of causing great harm if negligently made, accelerated the adoption of a rule of manufacturer negligence liability, and *MacPherson* is now accepted by all American courts. Products liability decisions following *MacPherson* would deduce that the manufacturer of locomotives is held to a higher standard of care than would be the weaver of fruit baskets, as the risk of harm from a negligently manufactured locomotive is incalculably greater than that created by a defectively fashioned basket. *MacPherson* also established that a manufacturer could be liable in negligence for any defects attributable to negligently constructed component parts, even where the component part was made by a reputable supplier. Lastly, *MacPherson* held that the manufacturer has a duty to subject its finished product, as well as the components of that product, to reasonable tests and inspections.

Each of the rules advanced in *MacPherson*: (1) the injured plaintiff's negligence remedy against the remote manufacturer without regard to privity; (2) the finished product seller's responsibility for the design and manufacturing integrity of component parts; and (3) the manufacturer's duty to conduct reasonable and necessary tests on the product before its introduction into commerce, represents the established majority rule today.

Warranty law did not elude the gravitational pull of *MacPherson*'s elimination of the privity barrier. Over time, the warranty action had worked effectively, provided the plaintiff was the original purchaser of the product and brought his action against his immediate vendor. Before the industrial revolution, manufacturer and purchaser frequently met face to face, and, if a dispute arose, it could be settled between the two. Modern merchandising methods to a large degree eliminated this contact, and it became relatively rare for the manufacturer to have any direct dealing with the ultimate user.

As in the decades preceding *MacPherson*, courts began to craft limited exceptions for categories of deserving claims that would be otherwise barred for lack of privity. The exceptions started with food, the courts rationalizing that the sale of impure food was virtually certain to result in serious illness, and therefore one who was engaged in such a business should be held to an absolute duty. From this beginning, an exception relating to drugs was a logical step. Based upon the same reasoning applied in the food cases, beverages too fell within the same exception. From these evolved the exception for cosmetics,[22] which like food, drugs and beverages, are products intended for intimate bodily use or consumption.

The most influential expression of judicial hostility towards privity and other contractual obstacles to recovery by plaintiffs suffering loss from a seller's marketing of a defective product was the 1960 decision in *Henningsen v. Bloomfield Motors, Inc.*[23] *Henningsen* arose from a husband's purchase of a new Chrysler automobile for the primary use of his wife. Shortly thereafter, Mrs. Henningsen was severely injured in a low-speed accident, probably due to a defect in the steering wheel assembly. However, the force of impact made it impossible to determine causation with certainty.

---

[22] Rogers v. Toni Home Permanent Co., 167 Ohio St. 244, 147 N.E.2d 612 (1958).

[23] 32 N.J. 358, 161 A.2d 69 (1960).

Both the dealer and the manufacturer argued that as there was no privity between them and Mrs. Henningsen, there could be no recovery for breach of warranty from either.

The New Jersey Supreme Court decided that public policy required otherwise, stating as to both defendants, "We are convinced that the cause of justice in this area can be served only by recognizing that [Mrs. Henningsen] is such a person who, in the reasonable contemplation of the parties to the warranty, might be expected to become a user of the automobile. Accordingly, her lack of privity does not stand in the way of the injury suit against the defendant Chrysler. The context in which the problem of privity with respect to the dealer must be considered is much the same."

A buyer's potential remedy in misrepresentation was advanced in 1932 by the Washington Supreme Court in its decision in *Baxter v. Ford Motor Co.*[24] In that action the plaintiff was injured by the shattering of a windshield that the manufacturer's catalogues had represented to be "shatter-proof" and impervious to breakage "under the hardest impact." In the view of the Washington court, where the ordinary consumer "would be unable to discover" a defect in a product "by . . . usual and customary examination," the buyer's disadvantage was comparable to that of "the consumer of a wrongly labeled drug, who has bought the same from a retailer, and who has relied upon the manufacturer's representation that the label correctly set forth the contents of the container." Reversing the trial court's judgment for the manufacturer, the court held that a consumer should have a strict liability cause of action, with no need to show negligence or privity, against a seller that represented its products as possessing "qualities which they, in fact, do not possess . . . ," where the absence of such qualities "is not readily noticeable," and where the customer suffers damages as a consequence.

The next milestone in the development of modern products liability came not in a modification of negligence doctrine but rather in an argument for its replacement. In *Escola v. Coca Cola Bottling Co.*,[25] the California Supreme Court found for plaintiff, a waitress, recovering damages from a soft drink bottling company whose bottle exploded in plaintiff's hand as she transferred it from its case to a refrigerator. Although plaintiff was unable to prove any act of negligence on the part of the bottler, the court affirmed a finding of liability based upon the doctrine of res ipsa loquitur.

Justice Traynor's concurrence argued forcefully that it was time for that court to abandon the legal fictions of res ipsa loquitur, and to adopt "absolute liability" for manufacturers placing products upon the market knowing that the product will be used without inspection, where the product "proves to

[24] 168 Wash. 456, 12 P.2d 409 (1932).

[25] 24 Cal. 2d 453, 150 P.2d 436 (1944).

have a defect that causes injury to human beings." Noting that liability without negligence, in the form of warranty, already governed liability between and among the other parties to most product transactions, such as the retailer to its immediate seller, the fiction of warranty should not be necessary, Justice Traynor concluded, "[i]f the warranty is severed from the contract of sale between the dealer and the consumer and based on the law of torts."

No American court adopted Justice Traynor's proposal in its entirety until 1963, in the California Supreme Court's decision in *Greenman v. Yuba Power Products, Inc.*[26] Plaintiff's action there arose from an injury by a combination power tool manufactured by the defendant. Plaintiff, after having secured an attachment to make the tool useful as a lathe for turning a large piece of wood, was injured when the wood flew out of the machine and struck him in the head. At trial, the evidence showed that separation of "inadequate" set screws used to hold together the parts of the tool had caused the plaintiff's injury. The court announced its readiness to create a remedy in tort in which plaintiff needn't rely upon either warranty or upon a showing of defendant's negligence. Strict liability in tort would make the manufacturer "strictly liable . . . when an article he places on the market, knowing that it is to be used without inspection, proves to have a defect that causes injury to a human being." The purpose of this liability, the court explained, "is to insure that the costs of injuries resulting from defective products are borne by the manufacturers that put such products on the market rather than by the injured persons who are powerless to protect themselves."

Two years after *Greenman*, the American Law Institute published Restatement § 402A, titled, "Special Liability of Seller of Product for Physical Harm to User or Consumer." This strict liability remedy, grounded in tort and requiring no showing of seller negligence, established liability for sale of a product "in a defective condition unreasonably dangerous to the user or consumer or his property. . . ." Restatement § 402A, or variations upon it, has been adopted in a majority of American jurisdictions.

§ 17.02 NEGLIGENCE

[A] *Basis for Liability*

The maker of a product that is to be used by others and that is capable of harm if not carefully made is under a duty to make it with care commensurate with the risk of harm posed. The law contemplates that care appropriate to the risk be applied to the design, formulation, fabrication, testing, and warnings concerning a product. Intermediate and retail sellers are also under certain more confined duties. As it is ordinarily the manufacturer that designs the product, selects its materials, manufactures

[26] 27 Cal. Rptr. 697, 377 P.2d 897 (1962).

it, packages it, and prepares the warnings or instructions that will accompany it into the marketplace, it is appropriate that the law of negligence place the largest measure of its burden upon the party whose actions are of the greatest significance to the safety of the product.

To prove any products liability claim sounding in negligence, be it negligent design or formulation, negligent mismanufacture, or the negligent failure to warn adequately of hazards associated with the use of the product, the plaintiff must show that the seller owed a duty to the plaintiff, and that the seller breached that duty. As is universally true of any claim in negligence, the products liability plaintiff must further show that the seller's breach was the proximate cause of the injury or loss.

The manufacturer of a product is presumed to be an expert in his or her field, a presumption that is fortified where, as is usually the case, the manufacturer is also the creator and designer of the product. The standard of care to which the manufacturer will be held is that of a reasonable man who is an expert in the pertinent field of manufacture. The law will presume his knowledge of the product's intended purposes and end uses.

The negligence evaluation or equation is often conveniently described as balancing the magnitude of the risk of the seller's conduct against the likelihood of injury should the challenged act be taken, the severity of any such injury should it occur, and the social value or utility of the actor's conduct. An influential formulation of the evaluation was offered in a negligence context by Judge Learned Hand in the opinions in *United States v. Carroll Towing Co.*,[27] and *Conway v. O'Brien.*[28] In those two cases, the court stated that the degree of care appropriate to an occasion is calculated by using three factors: the likelihood that the conduct will injure others, multiplied by the seriousness of the risk if it happens, balanced against the burden of taking precautions against the risk.

The Restatement's expression of liability for negligent manufacture may be seen as the deceptively simple requirement that the manufacturer exercise due care under the circumstances. In language that may be traced directly from *MacPherson v. Buick Motor Co.*,[29] Restatement § 395 proposes manufacturer liability for any person "who fails to exercise reasonable care in the manufacture of a chattel which, unless carefully made, he should recognize as involving an unreasonable risk of causing personal harm . . . ." Comments e and f to that section emphasize that care that is "due" is a function of the risk involved should the product be rendered without due care. The comments continue by distinguishing the high level of care appropriate to the manufacture of high speed machinery or high voltage electrical devices, commending meticulous precautions, with the lower care

[27] 159 F.2d 169, 173 (2d Cir. 1947).

[28] 111 F.2d 611, 612 (2d Cir. 1940).

[29] 217 N.Y. 382, 111 N.E. 1050 (1916).

presumably appropriate to the manufacture of an article that, no matter how poorly made, is unlikely to do more than trivial harm to those who use it.

It is no longer required that the chattel be intended to preserve or destroy human life, *i.e.*, prescription drugs or weapons, and it is not necessary that the chattel be "inherently dangerous," thus avoiding the need in most cases of applying a rather nebulous concept to a specific circumstance. The duty of due care extends to the selection of appropriate materials; to the formulation of a method of production which, if followed, will produce a safe article; to the fabrication of the product by every person having a function to perform in that fabrication; to the making of inspections and tests as reasonably necessary; and to the proper packaging of the chattel for the safety of those expected to unpack it.

Where a product is fabricated by two or more manufacturers or assemblers, the duties in negligence for the ultimate production of the defective product may turn upon the expertise of each participant respectively. Thus, in a suit brought against a manufacturer of truck chassis by a worker injured when a beer truck with neither sufficient rear vision nor a back-up buzzer pinned him between the truck and a loading dock, the evidence showed that the chassis manufacturer sold trucks to secondary manufacturers who would then install beer storage units or any of a variety of other units upon the chassis. In such circumstances, the court concluded that the secondary fabricator, and not the chassis manufacturer, would "have the expertise to assess design implication and the ramifications on safety which any design changes might require," precluding imposition of liability on the chassis manufacturer.[30]

Similarly, the manufacturer's duty in negligence may be limited in circumstances that suggest that the purchaser is in a superior position to know of the operational or safety requirements of the particular use to which the product is to be put, and of the modifications to the product best suited to satisfy those requirements. It is on this analysis that the court in *Biss v. Tenneco, Inc.*[31] held that the manufacturer of a loader, purchased by plaintiff's employer for use in logging operations, was not liable in negligence for not providing a roll-over protection structure (ROPS) on each vehicle, the duty falling instead to the purchaser to require such available safety options as are "suited to the job for which the equipment is purchased and used."

Another important limitation upon the manufacturer's liability in negligence is the general rule that the manufacturer will not be liable in negligence where "after the product leaves the possession and control of the manufacturer there is a subsequent modification which substantially

[30] Elliot v. Century Chevrolet Co., 597 S.W.2d 563, 565 (Tex. Civ. Ct. App. 1980).

[31] 64 A.D.2d 204, 409 N.Y.S.2d 874 (1978), *app. denied*, 389 N.E.2d 841 (1979).

alters the product and is the proximate cause of plaintiff's injuries."[32] Moreover, the manufacturer of a product that is built in accordance with the plans or specifications of a third party should not be liable in negligence for injury or damage caused thereby "unless the plans are so obviously dangerous that no reasonable person would follow them."[33]

[B] *Liability as Limited by Foreseeability*

For a manufacturer to be liable in negligence for the sale of a product, the product must have been put to a reasonably foreseeable use, which in some settings may include a reasonably foreseeable misuse. The plaintiff must also be a person who might reasonably be foreseen to use, consume or be affected by the product. These complementary concepts of foreseeability are illustrated in one South Carolina appellate decision involving a defective soda bottle that exploded. Plaintiff was not injured in the explosion, but rather in the subsequent efforts to clean up the mishap. The court found that plaintiff had established the requisite foreseeability of his injury in that the manufacturer of a defective container intended to hold liquid under pressure should foresee that it may fracture and spill, creating a condition that will invite the user or others to clean-up the broken glass. Thus, to the court, plaintiff's injurious fall in cleaning up after the explosion did not break proximate cause.[34]

The manufacturer's status as an expert in the relevant field of products does not require that she foresee beyond what is scientifically or technologically discoverable at the time of manufacture. As a consequence, negligence liability may fail where plaintiff's harm could not be anticipated on the basis of scientific knowledge in existence when the product was introduced into commerce.

Consistent with the above considerations, the manufacturer's design duty in negligence imports not so much the issue of how the product is meant to function but instead the issue of whether the product has been designed with reasonable care to eliminate avoidable dangers. The manufacturer therefore has been held to have a duty of due care in manufacture requiring the anticipation of the environment in which the product will be used and the foreseeable risks associated with use in that setting. It is on this basis that the manufacturer of an aluminum bracket device that connected a boat's chair post to a helmsman's chair, which broke during use in the pilothouse of a commercial shipping vessel, was liable for negligent design and failure

---

[32] Robinson v. Reed-Prentiss Div. of Package Machinery Co., 403 N.E.2d 440 (N.Y. 1980).

[33] Lenherr v. NRM Corp., 504 F. Supp. 165, 174 (D. Kan. 1980), wherein the court continues: "It is logical to absolve a manufacturer from liability for a negligently designed defective product when the manufacturer is not the designer and plaintiff's theory of recovery is negligence. Under those circumstances a manufacturer is liable only if the defect in design is sufficiently obvious to alert a reasonably competent manufacturer to the danger."

[34] Wallace v. Owens-Illinois, Inc., 389 S.E.2d 155 (S.C. Ct. App. 1989).

to test, notwithstanding defendant's argument that the product had not been intended for commercial-nautical use.[35]

It is now the prevailing rule that, in the design of an automobile, the vehicle manufacturer is required to foresee that the vehicle may, in the course of its useful life, be involved in a collision.[36] It is the foreseeability of such collisions, neither intended nor desired, that imposes upon the manufacturer the duty to design an automobile that is reasonably crashworthy. The term "crashworthy" means a choice of design and materials that does not create an unreasonable risk of additional and enhanced injury to vehicle occupants over and above injuries suffered in the initial impact of the collision.[37]

Distinct considerations govern the evaluation of negligence liability where the injurious product was used without mishap for many years prior to plaintiff's injury. Considerations of reasonable foreseeability, as well as causation, underpin the analysis of whether the manufacturer should be held liable in negligence for injuries caused by the ordinary wear and tear to, or the inevitable eventual product failure of, the aging but otherwise nondefective product. The majority rule is that the passage of time in safe use of the product is admissible on the question of the manufacturer's discharge of the duty of safe manufacture, but is not controlling. As expressed by one court in affirming a jury verdict that the breaking after two and one half years of safe use of a skid used in unloading vessels was attributable to negligent fabrication, "[t]he mere passage of time confers no immunity upon a negligent wrongdoer; but it has relevance to the likelihood, depending upon the circumstances of a particular case, that deterioration due to use, perhaps accelerated by misuse, will be mistaken by a jury for a defect due to negligent manufacture or fabrication."[38] The weight of authorityis that prolonged safe use is only one factor to consider in determining whether there was a defect in the product as originally sold.

---

[35] McIsaac v. Didriksen Fishing Corp., 809 F.2d 129 (1st Cir. 1987).

[36] As explained by the court in Larsen v. General Motors Corp., 391 F.2d 495, 502 (8th Cir. 1968): "While automobiles are not made for the purpose of colliding with each other, a frequent and inevitable contingency of normal automobile use will result in collisions and injury-producing impacts. . . . These injuries are readily foreseeable as an incident to the normal and expected use of an automobile."

[37] *See* Huddell v. Levin, 537 F.2d 726, 735 (3d Cir. 1976) ("We take it as beyond peradventure that an automobile manufacturer has some legal obligation to produce a reasonably crashworthy vehicle. The manufacturer is not required to design against bizarre accidents; the manufacturer is not required to produce an accident-proof vehicle. But the manufacturer is required to take reasonable steps within the limitations of cost, technology, and marketability to design and produce a vehicle that will minimize the avoidable danger.") *See also* Reed v. Chrysler Corp., 494 N.W.2d 224 (Iowa 1992) (Jeep CJ-7 rollover accident).

[38] Fredericks v. American Export Lines, 227 F.2d 450, 452 (2d Cir. 1955), *cert. denied*, 350 U.S. 989 (1956). *See* Raymo v. Textron, Inc., 846 F. Supp. 203 (N.D.N.Y. 1994) (in spreader design suit, court approves instruction concerning "long continued use without accident.").

[C] *The Duty of Non-Manufacturing Sellers*

The non-manufacturing seller, ordinarily a retailer or a wholesaler, will only incur negligence liability where it has failed to exercise due care with respect to the marketing or sale of the product. As the non-manufacturing seller does not ordinarily participate in the design of a product, or in the creation of any warnings or instructions that accompany the product, even where a warnings or a design defect is the legal cause of another's harm, plaintiff will not usually be able to show that the non-manufacturing seller breached any duty of care.

Restatement § 401 provides that the non-manufacturing seller does have a duty to warn purchasers of any defects or hazardous propensities of a product that she knows or has reason to know of, and of which the buyer is probably unaware. The section states:

> A seller of a chattel manufactured by a third person who knows or has reason to know that the chattel is, or is likely to be, dangerous . . . is subject to liability for bodily harm caused thereby . . . if he fails to exercise reasonable care to inform them of the danger or otherwise to protect them against it.

Common illustrations of this principle arise where a dangerous product is sold to a minor. Consider *Salvi v. Montgomery Ward & Co.*,[39] an action arising from the injury of the younger brother of the fourteen-year-old purchaser of an air gun, where the injured child lost an eye when the gun discharged as his older brother was cleaning it. Noting the gun manufacturer's own prominent warning cautioning against the sale of an air gun to persons under the age of sixteen specifically because of the risk of eye injury, the court found liability for negligent sale, concluding that: "The harm suffered by [plaintiff] was a reasonably foreseeable result of [defendant's] placing an air gun in the hands of a minor. . . . Accordingly, . . . [defendant] did have a duty to adopt a sales policy which prohibited air guns from being sold to minors such as [plaintiff]."

[D] *Proof of Negligence*

Proof of defect does not, without more, prove negligence, as even the most careful manufacturer may produce a defective product. The injured plaintiff, therefore, is faced with the requirement that he prove both a standard of care in an industry or business, and the departure from that standard.

[1] The Accident Itself

The occurrence of the accident itself does not, standing alone, make out plaintiff's prima facie case in negligence. Importantly, however, a plaintiff's circumstantial proof of not only the occurrence of the accident itself, but

[39] 489 N.E.2d 394 (Ill. Ct. App. 1986).

also of like evidence tending to negate the possibility of mistake, misuse, or contrivance, will move plaintiff's case measurably towards satisfaction of its prima facie burden. Illustrative is the treatment in *Cohen v. Allendale Coca-Cola Bottling Co.*,[40] a negligence and implied warranty action brought by plaintiff claiming injury sustained when he discovered an insect in a soft drink bottled by defendant. There was no direct evidence that the foreign matter was in the bottle at the time it left the possession of defendant. Nevertheless, the court affirmed the trial court's conclusion that plaintiff's showing that: (1) the insect was noticed shortly after purchase of the drink; (2) the insect was found at the bottom of the bottle, suggesting it had been there for some time; and (3) there were no ambient insects that might have competed with plaintiff for the drink, together constituted sufficient circumstantial evidence to support the jury's finding of negligence.

[2] Other Accidents or Claims

Evidence of other accidents occurring either before or after plaintiff's loss may be admissible to prove negligent manufacture if (1) the product involved in the other accidents was materially indistinguishable from the product implicated in plaintiff's injury, and (2) the circumstances of the other accidents, including the nature of the use and other surrounding circumstances, were similar to plaintiff's use.

Application of several of these principles is found in *Brake v. Beech Aircraft Corp.*,[41] a wrongful death action brought by the survivors of two persons killed when their twin-engine aircraft crashed in circumstances suggesting a stall-spin. On a verdict for the manufacturer, plaintiffs appealed two evidentiary rulings at trial. On the first, the trial court's exclusion of plaintiff's evidence of other, similar stall-spin accidents involving the same aircraft, the appellate court upheld exclusion, stating that plaintiffs had "failed to lay a foundation of similarity between the accidents discussed therein and the accident in this case." Likewise the court upheld the rejection at trial of five other accident memoranda involving defendant's plane, and three other National Transportation Safety Board investigative memoranda, because plaintiff had laid no foundation of similarity.

Should the manufacturer be able to introduce evidence that it has received no reports of, or complaints concerning, the alleged defect? In some circumstances, the answer is yes. Evidence of the absence of complaints must be accompanied by a foundation similar to that needed for affirmative evidence of complaints. As stated by one court, "The offering party must establish, as a necessary foundation, that the absence of claims occurred

[40] 351 S.E.2d 897 (S.C. Ct. App. 1986).

[41] 184 Cal. App. 3d 930, 229 Cal. Rptr. 336 (1986). *See also* Nakajima v. General Motors Corp., 857 F. Supp. 100 (D.D.C. 1994) (dissimilarity of prior bus rear door opening incidents).

while the same product was used under substantially the same conditions as those encountered by the plaintiff in the pending litigation."[42]

[3] Subsequent Product Changes

The majority of jurisdictions have adopted the rule of evidence that subsequent product changes, or other post-incident remedial measures, cannot be used by plaintiff to prove that a defendant manufacturer's conduct before the change was negligent.

This approach, stated in Fed. R. Evid. 407, is binding upon federal courts, and has been greatly influential in the developing state law. Rule 407 provides that evidence of subsequent measures "is not admissible to prove negligence or culpable conduct," but may be admitted where probative of other issues, such as "ownership, control, or feasibility of precautionary measures, if controverted."

Where, as is normally the case, plaintiff's products liability cause of action sounds in both negligence and strict liability, the issue arises whether Rule 407 or a similar state evidence rule should operate to exclude evidence or remedial measures on the strict liability claim, even though the strict liability cause of action does not sound in "negligence or culpable conduct." Authority is split on the question, with some courts finding that the policies for excluding the evidence on plaintiff's negligence count should apply with equal force to prevent introduction of remedial evidence on plaintiff's strict liability count.[43] Other courts have concluded that Fed. R. Evid. 407 should be narrowly construed, permitting remedial measures evidence to be introduced for any reason other than to prove defendant's negligence.[44]

[4] Violation of a Statute, Ordinance or Regulation

Defendant's violation of a statute, ordinance or regulation pertaining to the design, manufacture or marketing of a product may, depending upon the relationship of the rule to the product risk and the harm plaintiff suffers, be considered negligence per se, create a permissible inference of negligence, or be considered merely evidence of negligence. The governing decisional law is discussed above at §§ 6.01-.07.

[5] Res Ipsa Loquitur

In an action grounded in negligence, the doctrine of res ipsa loquitur permits the plaintiff to shift to the defendant the burden of proof on the issue of negligence upon the showing that the injury-causing product was one over which the defendant had complete control, and that the accident resulting in injury was of such a nature that it ordinarily would not occur in the absence of negligence by the defendant.

---

[42] Salvi v. Montgomery Ward & Co., 489 N.E.2d 394 (Ill. Ct. App. 1986).

[43] *E.g.*, Nasios v. Pennwalt Corp., Prod. Liab. Rep. (CCH) ¶ 12,479 (D. Md. 1990).

[44] McFarland v. Bruno Machinery Corp., 626 N.E.2d 659 (Ohio 1994).

The doctrine received early expression in the celebrated English case of *Byrne v. Boadle*,[45] which involved a pedestrian's injury from a falling barrel of flour as he passed beneath a jugger-hoist and other lifting and lowering mechanisms in use at the premises of the defendant. In a time long before effective pretrial discovery of a party opponent, and cognizant of the futility of plaintiff's efforts to learn from defendant's servants the cause of the mishap, the court of appeals noted that the circumstances of the accident were such as to be "prima facie evidence of negligence." Blending pragmatic considerations with a desire to provide a remedy to the innocent plaintiff dispossessed of the means of proving his case, the court held that the accident itself may "itself raise a presumption of negligence."

In modern commerce, the product claimed to have caused an injury has long since left the control of defendant. How have court's treated the common law requirement that the injury-causing instrumentality be under defendant's control? Restatement § 328 comment g provides one answer, and reads: "It may be enough that the defendant was formerly in control, at the time of the probable negligence as in the case of the beverage bottler whose product poisons the consumer, when there is sufficient evidence to eliminate the responsibility of intermediate others."

§ 17.03 WARRANTIES

[A] *Introduction*

In products liability, warranty represents the merging of contract and tort, providing, within its rules, remedies for persons who have purchased, or perhaps have only been exposed to, products that do not satisfy ordinary expectations, or are dangerous, or both.

Superseding the Uniform Sales Act, the UCC is in effect, in whole or in substantial part, in every state except Louisiana. Importantly, the UCC creates or codifies implied warranties covering every transaction it covers. There are broad areas of congruence between a user's or consumer's remedies in tort and those in warranty, a practical consequence of which is that plaintiff's breach of warranty are today almost the invariable component, together with claims in negligence and strict liability, of a plaintiff's products liability cause of action.

[B] *Express Warranties*

Express warranties are seller representations to the buyer of the quality, performance, construction, or durability of a product. The express warranty is an undertaking, of a piece with the terms of the sale itself, that the chattel sold has certain characteristics or qualities. Such warranties may be oral, or written, and they must precede or accompany the sale. A nonverbal,

---

[45] 2 H. & C. 722 (Ex. 1866). *See generally* David E. Seidelson, *Res Ipsa Loquitur: The Big Umbrella*, 25 Duq. L. Rev. 387 (1987).

express warranty need not be in words, for a description of the article may be pictorial, or by blueprint, technical specifications, samples, models, or even by past deliveries that have set a standard that may be fairly considered a description of what the article is represented to be.

[1] Representations of Fact

To be an express warranty, a seller's affirmation must be one of fact, which is to say that such oral or written statement must be more than simply the seller's opinion of the product. The latter representations, frequently involving the seller's encomium upon the product and nothing more, are for convenience often described as "puffing." An express warranty, on the other hand, arises where the seller "factually describes an important aspect of the product,"[46] as to which one would expect the seller, but not the buyer, to be familiar.

Illustrative of a statement that represents only the seller's opinion of the product, and consequently would be considered only "puffing," arose in one court's express warranty evaluation where plaintiff had suffered an adverse skin reaction from use of hair dye. Evidence showed that the selling clerk had assured the buyer that she, the clerk, had used the same product and that her own hair came out "very nice" and "very natural."[47] The court concluded that the clerk's statement was puffing, and not a representation of fact creating an express warranty, explaining that such puffing occurs when the seller "merely states an opinion or judgment upon a matter of which the seller has no special knowledge, and on which the buyer may be expected also to have an opinion and to exercise his judgment."

Accordingly, a seller's statement that his product was "as good or better" than that of a competitor would not create an express warranty; neither would the seller's characterization of the product as a "good quality ladder," the statement that a diamond being sold was worth twice the purchase price, an assertion that, by use of the product, the buyer would reap a substantial profit, or an assurance that the product sold may be legally used.

Where the representation of safety or harmlessness is both specific and unambiguous, it will be found to create an express warranty reaching to the full extent of the representation. Thus, express warranties have been found to be conveyed by a tire manufacturer's advertisement, "If it saves your life once, it's a bargain" where plaintiff's decedent was injured fatally following a blowout;[48] or a booklet accompanying a steam vaporizer stating that it was safe to be used all night, and featuring a picture of the appliance in use near a baby's crib, where a toddler was badly burned when the

---

[46] Hauter v. Zogarts, 120 Cal. Rptr. 681, 534 P.2d 377 (1975).

[47] Carpenter v. Alberto-Culver Co., 184 N.W.2d 547 (Mich. Ct. App. 1970) (held: comments constituted "puffing," and not an express warranty).

[48] Collins v. Uniroyal, Inc., 64 N.J. 260, 315 A.2d 16 (1974).

vaporizer overturned;[49] or a shipping carton and instruction book statement that a golf training device was "completely safe — ball will not hit player" where the plaintiff, of negligible golf experience, hit beneath the ball, catching the attached cord and causing the ball to fly back, hitting him in the head and causing severe injury.[50]

There is no determinate number of means by which an express warranty can be imparted. Representative of the range of settings in which an express warranty can be made include a sales lady's comment that a pressure cooker would not explode, or a label on a can of chicken stating "Boned Chicken" read in conjunction with advertisements stating "No Bones." In addition to the express warranties commonly found in advertisements, circulars, or package inserts, express warranties have been found to be created by language on tags, pamphlets, and specification sheets.

[2] Basis of the Bargain

Under UCC § 2-313(1), a seller's affirmation of fact can become an express warranty if it "becomes a basis of the bargain." As a general rule, to be considered part of the basis of the bargain of the sale, the seller's statement must, in terms of timing, precede or accompany the sale. This is to say, the affirmation must be communicated to the buyer while the sale is hot, or at least warm.

As to interpretation of this matter the comments to UCC § 2-313(1) are only modestly helpful, stating that the "precise time when words of description or affirmation are made . . . is not material," but that instead the sole pertinent question is whether the language can be "fairly . . . regarded as part of the contract."[51] Where the seller elects, in writing or orally, to adopt the manufacturer's warranty, the seller will be liable for breach of that warranty.

The authority is divided as to the buyer's burden of proof concerning reliance upon the seller's representations. There is approval for the conclusion that comment 3 to UCC § 2-313[52] shifts the burden of proving nonreliance to the seller.[53] Other authority suggests that UCC § 2-313 eliminates the need to show reliance altogether.[54]

---

[49] McCormack v. Hankscraft Co., 154 N.W.2d 488 (Minn. 1967).

[50] Hauter v. Zogarts, 534 P.2d 377 (Cal. 1975).

[51] UCC § 2-313(1), cmt. 7.

[52] UCC § 2-313 cmt. 3 reads, in pertinent part:

> In actual practice affirmations of fact made by the seller about the goods during a bargain are regarded as part of the description of those goods; hence no particular reliance on such statements needbe shown to weave them into the fabric of the agreement. Rather, any fact which is to take such affirmations, once made, out of the agreement requires clear affirmative proof.

[53] *See* Boyd, *Representing Consumers — The Uniform Commercial Code and Beyond*, 9 Ariz. L. Rev. 372, 385 (1968).

[54] *See* White and Summers, UNIFORM COMMERCIAL CODE (2d) § 9-4 (1980).

[C] *Implied Warranties*

[1] Merchantability

In its essence, the implied warranty of merchantability means that a seller of a product warrants that goods sold pass within the ordinary description of like goods, and are fit and may be safely used for their intended purpose. UCC § 2-314 lists in the conjunctive six standards with which a product must conform to be merchantable. As set out in that provision, to be merchantable, goods must be *at least* such as: "(a) pass without objection in the trade under the contract description; and (b) in the case of fungible goods, are of fair average quality within the description; and (c) are fit for the ordinary purposes for which such goods are used; and (d) run, within the variations permitted by the agreement, of even kind, quality and quantity within each unit and among all units involved; and (e) are adequately contained, packaged, and labeled as the agreement may require; and (f) conform to the promises or affirmations of fact made on the container or label if any." The section concludes by stating that, absent exclusion or modification, "other implied warranties may arise from course of dealing or usage of trade."

"Merchantability" to many courts has simply meant reasonable fitness for the general purposes for which the article is sold and used. It does not imply absolute perfection; it does not impose on the seller a duty to provide an article that will not wear out; it does not necessarily imply even high quality. Thus, the fitness need not be absolute, and the warranty is met when the article conforms to ordinary standards and is of the average grade, quality, and value of similar goods sold in commerce.

This warranty does not depend on the seller's knowledge of the particular purpose for which the buyer requires the goods; it is enough if he knows the general purpose for which such products are commonly used. As a merchant in such goods, he is presumed to have that knowledge.

The moment in time at which an implied warranty of merchantability takes effect has been actively litigated in the context of shopper injuries occurring after the shopper takes the product from the shelf, but prior to technical sale. Among this genre of cases are those involving beverage bottles that explode or fragment in the shopper's hands. Noting comment 1 to § 2-314, which states that "The seller's obligation applies to present sales as well as to contracts to sell . . .," most of the decisions have concluded that (1) the merchant's placement of the product on the shelf constitutes an offer of sale, and (2) the buyer's removal of the product from the shelf constitutes an acceptance, creating a contract sufficient for application of UCC § 2-314.

Not only the product in the bottle or container, but the bottle, container, or packaging itself is subject to the standards of UCC § 2-314. Thus there is no literal impediment to vindication of liability against a restaurateur-purveyor of wine by the glass, should the glass break in use, by characterizing the glass as packaging for the sale of the wine.

The implied warranty of merchantability runs with all such goods sold, without regard to the presence or absence of any other warranty. As with all warranties, the breach of this warranty does not require that the manufacturer or seller have been negligent, or have failed in any duty of care. This is illustrated by an action involving the sale of chickens later determined to be infected with a communicable illness requiring their destruction. The seller argued that at the then current state of animal medicine avian leukosis made incidence of the disease unavoidable even with the exercise of the utmost care. The court rejected this argument, stating that the seller's diligence or lack thereof, concededly relevant to negligence, was not relevant in an action for breach of the implied warranty of merchantability.[55]

[a] Requirement That the Seller Be a Merchant

In an action for breach of implied warranty of merchantability under UCC § 2-314, it is necessary that the seller be a "merchant" of such products in the ordinary course of trade. Consistent with this, it has been held that volunteer parent organizations providing food at school functions are not merchants as that term is used in the code, nor would persons engaged in isolated sales or "garage" sales be merchants within the meaning of UCC § 2-314.

[b] Fit for the Ordinary Purpose

What is or is not "fit for [its] ordinary purpose" within the meaning of UCC § 2-314(2)(a), (c) has proved, in the main, to be an issue of ordinary understanding. For example, shoes will be expected to have their heels firmly attached so as not to disengage in normal use, and hair lotion should not burn the user's scalp. On the other hand, insignificant flaws or irregularities should not render the product unmerchantable. It follows, therefore, that the presence of one small bone in a fish filet will not breach an implied warranty of merchantability, nor will minor damage to a new car that does not affect the vehicle's "usefulness or drivability."

To create an actionable breach of implied warranty of merchantability, it is necessary that the product failure or mishap have occurred in an "ordinary" use of the product. Some seemingly extreme uses of products have been found to create a jury question as to "ordinary" use, such as where

[55] Vlases v. Montgomery Ward & Co., 377 F.2d 846 (3d Cir. 1967). *See also* Bowler v. Stewart-Warner Corp., 563 A.2d 344, 345-346 (D.C. Ct. App. 1989) (in implied warranty suit, plaintiff not required to show negligence).

a child sprayed flammable hair spray on her dress and hair because of the pleasant fragrance.[56]

A distinct issue in warranty is raised by the unusual or idiosyncratic reaction of a purchaser to an over-the-counter pharmaceutical. In one illustrative action, the court evaluated the plaintiff's claim that the use of defendant manufacturer's topical anaesthetic triggered a systemic allergic illness. There was no evidence of any comparable reaction by other users. The court concluded that the plaintiff's cause of action must fail, for "a product must adversely affect at least some significant number of persons before the question of 'merchantability' arises."[57]

[2] Fitness for a Particular Purpose

Uniform Commercial Code § 2-315 states:

> Where the seller at the time of contracting has reason to know any particular purpose for which the goods are required and that the buyer is relying on the seller's skill or judgment to select or furnish suitable goods, there is unless excluded or modified under the next section an implied warranty that the goods shall be fit for such purpose.

Two requirements must be met for the creation of an implied warranty of fitness for a particular purpose under UCC § 2-315. First, the buyer must rely on the seller's skill or judgment to select or furnish suitable goods. Second, at the time of the sale or contracting to sell, the seller must have reason to know of the buyer's purpose and that the buyer is relying on the seller's skill or judgment. The existence or absence of an implied warranty of fitness for a particular purpose is ordinarily a question of fact.

Unlike UCC § 2-314 remedies which require the seller to be a merchant of such goods in the ordinary course, UCC § 2-315 states only that the person be a seller. The authors of this section, while observing that the former warranty operates only where the seller is a merchant with consequent "skill and judgment," provide that a warranty under UCC § 2-315 can arise "as to non-merchants where this is justified by the particular circumstances."

The Code's use of the phrase "particular purpose" is deliberate, and intended to distinguish UCC § 2-314. Comment 2 to UCC § 2-315 makes this clear in stating that "particular purpose envisages a specific use by the buyer which is peculiar to the nature of his business. . . ." The warranty

---

[56] Hardman v. Helene Curtis Indus., Inc., 198 N.E.2d 681, 691 (Ill. Ct. App. 1964), the court commenting: "The essential question presented by a claim of breach of implied warranty of merchantability is whether the product failed to safely and adequately satisfy the uses to which such products are ordinarily put." *Cf.* Toney v. Kawasaki Heavy Industries, Ltd., 975 F.2d 162 (5th Cir. 1992) (open and obvious lack of leg protection on a motorcycle supported conclusion that absence of protection did not render vehicle unfit for its ordinary purpose.).

[57] Griggs v. Combe, Inc., 456 So. 2d 790, 792 (Ala. 1984).

of fitness for a particular purpose may be breached even though the goods sold are not "defective" in the usual sense. It may be breached when a product properly made and merchantable is simply the wrong one for the buyer's particular use.

The ordinary purpose-particular purpose conundrum may be explored further, using as a premise the statement that the warranty of fitness for a particular purpose is more narrow, specific, and precise than its implied warranty of merchantability counterpart. As the authors of Comment 2 to UCC § 2-315 state, a particular purpose differs from an ordinary purpose "in that it envisages a specific use by the buyer which is particular to the nature of his business." It follows that when goods are purchased for the ordinary purposes for which such goods are used, there arises no implied warranty of fitness for a particular purpose. Thus, in reviewing an action brought by an individual who purchased a yacht for pleasure cruising, only to discover dry rot and fuel tank problems, one court determined that the purchaser's use of the craft as a pleasure craft on inland lakes constituted usage "well within the ordinary usage of such goods," obviating recovery under a cause of action in implied warranty of fitness for a particular purpose.[58]

[D] *To Whom Warranties Run*

In its most elementary form, privity connotes a direct contractual relationship between the buyer and the seller. Today, the privity defense lacks the persuasiveness it enjoyed in an earlier day. Starting with the 1960 New Jersey decision in *Henningsen*,[59] and continuing through to the present, the defense of lack of privity is in a continuing retreat, and is becoming less of an obstacle for the injured claimant.

In the analysis of any privity problem, a distinction must be drawn between vertical and horizontal privity. "Vertical privity" is concerned with the relationship between parties in the chain of distribution of goods: manufacturers, distributors, wholesalers, retail dealers, and purchasers. "Horizontal privity," in contrast, refers to those parties outside of the chain of distribution most often family members, guests, and employees of the retail purchaser, innocent bystanders, and other injured third parties.

The privity defense in products liability is now subject to the provisions of the UCC as implemented in a majority of jurisdictions.[60] UCC § 2-318, entitled Third Party Beneficiaries of Warranties Express or Implied, offers three alternatives from which each state may elect to whom a warranty runs, and provides:

---

[58] Smith v. Stewart, 667 P.2d 358 (Kan. 1983).

[59] 32 N.J. 358, 161 A.2d 69 (1960).

[60] *See also* discussion *supra* at § 17.01[A][2][a].

Alternative A

A seller's warranty whether express or implied extends to any natural person who is in the family or household of his buyer or who is a guest in his home if it is reasonable to expect that such person may use, consume or be affected by the goods and who is injured in person by breach of the warranty. A seller may not exclude or limit the operation of this section.

Alternative B

A seller's warranty whether express or implied extends to any natural person who may reasonably be expected to use, consume or be affected by the goods and who is injured in person by breach of the warranty. A seller may not exclude or limit the operation of this section.

Alternative C

A seller's warranty whether express or implied extends to any person who may reasonably be expected to use, consume, or be affected by the goods and who is injured by the breach of the warranty. A seller may not exclude or limit the operation of this section with respect to injury to the person of an individual to whom the warranty extends.

Section 2-318 is primarily concerned with the question of horizontal privity — to whom the warranty runs, or who is a proper plaintiff in the action, and leaves the issue of vertical privity unanswered. The last sentence of all three alternatives to UCC § 2-318 provides that, "A seller may not exclude or limit the operation of this section." This language does not prohibit a seller from excluding or disclaiming a warranty as permitted by UCC § 2-316, nor does it preclude the limiting of remedies via UCC §§ 2-718 and 719. Comment 1 to § 2-318 clearly states: "What this last sentence forbids is exclusion of liability by the seller to the persons to whom the warranties which he has made to his buyer would extend under this section." Accordingly, for example, in a state using Alternative C, the seller cannot exclude from its warranty those third parties who could reasonably be expected to be affected by the goods.

Transactions other than outright sale may raise privity issues. For example, in automobile lease-purchase arrangements, the leasing company may function in much the way as would a finance company in a conventional sale. In such a setting, where the product has been put under the control of the consumer rather as it would have been in a sale, a court may find the lessee to be the equivalent of a buyer, and in privity with the seller, reasoning that any different conclusion would "exalt form over substance."[61] Whether a class of third-party beneficiaries is protected largely depends on which Alternative the state in question has chosen.

Alternative A. Alternative A to UCC § 2-318 is the most widely-adopted of the three alternatives, with twenty-eight states following its language. It is the most restrictive regarding the class of beneficiaries protected, for in order to fall within the protected class (those outside the chain of distribution entitled to bring a warranty action), a party must be (1) a "natural" person (not a corporation or partnership) who is (2) a family or household member, or a guest of the purchaser, who (3) could foreseeably be injured by a breach of warranty. Finally, only personal injury is compensable.

In decisions adopting a restrictive interpretation of Alternative A, courts have denied a cause of action in warranty to the wife of a person struck and killed by a vehicle leased by the defendant automobile leasing corporation,[62] to a school girl injured when a stone thrown by a rotary lawnmower came through an opening in the classroom window and struck her in the eye,[63] to the employee of a transport company engaged in moving products contained in cartons manufactured by the defendant,[64] or to a person sustaining neck injuries from diving into a shallow pool purchased from a woman who had purchased it from the original purchaser.[65]

The reference in UCC § 2-318 Alternative A to the third-party beneficiary status of a "guest" of the purchaser requires, by its express terms, that it be a "guest in (the) home" of the buyer. There is, therefore, authority that a guest in the buyer's automobile will not be considered an third-party beneficiary under this provision.

Alternative B. Alternative B to UCC § 2-318 is less restrictive than A in that it extends the class of third-party beneficiaries beyond the "family or household of (the) buyer or who is a guest . . ." This Alternative, while retaining the requirement that the plaintiff be a "natural" person, extends protection to "any natural person who may reasonably be expected to use, consume or be affected by the goods . . ." Included in this class would be employees and bystanders — those not ultimate purchasers. Alternative B, however, also requires personal injury.

Alternative C. Alternative C is the most expansive version of UCC § 2-318 in terms of the class of persons and entities to which it extends third-party protection in the warranty action. Adopted by at least eleven

[61] Werber v. Mercedes Benz of North America, Inc., 152 Cal. App. 2d 1039, 199 Cal. Rptr. 205 (1985).

[62] Hoffman v. A.B. Chance, 346 F. Supp. 991 (M.D. Pa. 1972).

[63] Stovall & Co. v. Tate, 184 S.E.2d 834 (Ga. Ct. App. 1971).

[64] Maynard v. General Electric Co., 350 F. Supp. 949 (S.D. W. Va. 1972), *aff'd* 486 F.2d 538 (4th Cir. 1973).

[65] Corbin v. Coleco Industries, Inc., 748 F.2d 411 (7th Cir. 1984).

jurisdictions, it extends warranty protection to any entity, not limited to natural persons, who could foreseeably be injured by a breach of warranty. Alternative C also permits recovery for losses other than personal injury, a position conforming to that taken in Restatement § 402A. Several states have either enacted legislation quite similar to Alternative C, or taken the additional step of expressly removing vertical or horizontal privity defenses altogether.

[E] *Warranty Limitations and Disclaimers*

Article 2 of the Code permits the seller to disclaim warranties and limit the remedies available to the buyer. The seller's ability to disclaim warranties is defined in UCC § 2-316, while the provisions for seller's ability to limit remedies available to the buyer may be found at UCC § 2-719.

From the outset, it is important to distinguish between disclaimers and limits on remedies for breach of warranty. A disclaimer is an attempt to avoid or eliminate a warranty altogether. If effective, a disclaimer leaves the aggrieved buyer totally without a warranty remedy under the Code. This includes not just the loss of any right to return the goods, but also the right to seek money damages. By contrast, rather than precluding all remedies, the remedy limitation of UCC § 2-719 operates in a different fashion. A warranty limitation operates to restrict the remedy available to an aggrieved buyer. A common limitation might, for example, provide that the buyer's remedy will be confined to repair or replacement, with no seller liability for incidental or consequential damages. Where a seller attempts to limit the buyer's remedies under § 2-719, any extant warranties given, express or implied, remain in effect.

As a general rule, under UCC § 2-316(1), once an express warranty has been made it cannot be disclaimed. This is particularly true when the express warranty is in writing. The rationale for this is readily apparent, as it is facially inconsistent for a seller to give an express warranty at first and then take it away with a blanket disclaimer. Therefore, under UCC § 2-316(1) any language of disclaimer which is inconsistent with the language of express warranty will not be given effect.

[1] Disclaimer of Implied Warranties

Unlike express warranties, implied warranties of merchantability or fitness for a particular purpose can generally be disclaimed, provided that the seller carefully follows the disclosure and conspicuousness protocols established in UCC §§ 2-316(2) and (3). As the seller's ability to disclaim a warranty is strictly construed, failure to comply with the requirements of these two subdivisions will result in an ineffective disclaimer.

Section 2-316(2) sets forth the guidelines on disclaimers of implied warranties of quality, and provides that any language purporting to exclude or modify the implied warranty of merchantability "must mention merchantability and in case of a writing must be conspicuous." The language of subsection (2) continues by stating that for the seller to exclude or modify any implied warranty of fitness the exclusion must be by a writing and conspicuous. Lastly, UCC § 2-316(2) suggests that the seller wishing to exclude all implied warranties of fitness use language that states, for example, that "there are no warranties which extend beyond the description on the face hereof."

The requirement of § 2-316(2) that "merchantability" be specifically mentioned to effect the disclaimer of the implied warranty of merchantability has received the approval of an overwhelming majority of decisions. With few exceptions the courts have held that the seller's use of words that are only similar to "merchantability" will fail to disclaim the implied warranty.

There are, on the other hand, no particular words that must be used to disclaim the implied warranty of fitness for a particular purpose. Absent a suggestion from the Code or from the comments, the rules of ordinary meaning and conspicuousness necessarily suffice, and therefore a statement in writing that there are no warranties is sufficient to disclaim this implied warranty. The comment authors suggest specifically this statement: "There are no warranties which extend beyond the description on the face hereof."

[a] Conspicuousness

Subsection (2) to UCC § 2-316 requires that disclaimers of any implied warranties be conspicuous. "Conspicuous," as defined by UCC § 2-201(10), connotes language "so written that a reasonable person against whom it is to operate ought to have noticed it." That language goes on to state that "A printed heading in capitals . . . is conspicuous" and that "Language in the body of a form is 'conspicuous' if it is in larger or other contrasting type or color." The issue of conspicuousness, the provision states, is for resolution by the court. That determination contemplates an objective test — is attention reasonably called to the disclaimer? If the language of the disclaimer fails this test, the courts will refuse to give it effect.

The goal for the seller wishing to disclaim a warranty is to make the disclaimer as clear and as conspicuous as possible, while at the same time to avoid making the entire warranty too conspicuous, thus detracting from, and making less conspicuous, the disclaimer language. A distinct, but related issue has arisen where the disclaimer was, arguably, insufficiently conspicuous, but the buyer had actual knowledge of it. Some courts have disregarded the Code's objective standard and have looked instead at the subjective traits of the buyer, such as, for example, the buyer's actual knowledge, expertise, or experience. As the paramount objective of UCC § 2-316 is to avoid surprise to the buyer, his knowledge of the disclaimer should be sufficient, by this rationale, to give it effect, insofar as his knowledge effectively obviates any unbargained-for surprises. However, as a general rule, where the disclaimer fails the objective standard of UCC § 2-316, most courts will nullify it regardless of the buyer's knowledge.

As a general rule, post-sale disclaimers are held invalid by the courts. For example, the disclaimer may be found on an invoice that reaches the buyer after the deal is closed or it may be found in sales literature or an operator's manual not received by the buyer until after the sale. One reason for holding that post-contract disclaimers are not binding is on the contract theory that no meeting of the minds has taken place, and thus the post-sale disclaimer should not properly be considered part of the basis of the bargain between the buyer and the seller.

[b] "As Is" Disclaimers

A seller may also effectively disclaim implied warranties of quality by communicating to the buyer that the product must be accepted "as is," or with all faults. This option is described in UCC § 2-316(3)(a), and operates as an alternative to § 2-316(2), for application of § 2-316(3)(a) does not require that the seller follow the guidelines of § 2-316(2), and a disclaimer, therefore, does not need to mention "merchantability." All that is required by § 2-316(3)(a) is "language which in common understanding calls the buyer's attention to the exclusion of warranties and makes plain that there is no implied warranty." While § 2-316(2) gives guidelines for disclaiming both implied warranties of quality, albeit through application of different recommended language, an "as is" disclaimer under UCC § 2-316(3)(a) properly used permits the seller effectively to disclaim both warranties of merchantability and fitness simultaneously. The seller may effectively disclaim all warranties using the terms set forth explicitly in UCC § 2-316(3)(a), including "as is," "with all faults," or, as is added by comment 7, "as they stand." Use of language other than that endorsed by the authors of the provision invites an adverse determination.

[2] Warranty Limitations

The Code provides at UCC § 2-719 for the seller's limiting of the buyer's remedies. As with warranty disclaimers, the seller's prerogative in limiting warranties is not unfettered. In the absence of language disclaiming one or more of the implied warranties under UCC § 2-316, limiting language under UCC § 2-316 is properly considered to add limited warranty coverage to implied warranties, rather than excluding any such implied warranties. Thus, an express warranty limiting remedies to, for example, a period of one year and the buyer's return of the product for repair should be interpreted as providing warranty coverage in addition to any implied warranty of merchantability or implied warranty of fitness for a particular purpose.

Comment 1 to UCC § 2-719 states that if, due to circumstances, a facially fair warranty limitation fails in its essential purpose, the limitation will be avoided and the parties' rights will be determined in accordance with general warranty principles. Thus, where under a warranty limitation confining the buyer's remedies to replacement or repairs of defective parts the seller's repeated efforts to remedy the problem fail, the seller will not be relieved of liability.

The most prominent restriction upon the seller's ability to limit warran ty remedies is set forth in UCC § 2-719(3), which states plainly that limitations on consequential damages will not be given ef fect where they are unconscionable. That subsection continues by stating that w here the consequential damages sought are associated with injury to a person, any purported warranty limitation on consequential damages will be considered p rima facie unconscionable. A leading decision involving the interpretation of t his Code provision is the New Jersey Supreme Court's *Collins v. Uniroyal, Inc.*,[66] in which the plaintiffs' decedent had been killed in an automobile accident caused by tire blowout, five months after equipping his automobile with new tires. The seller's warranty disclaimed consequential damages, and purported to limit the seller's liability to repair or replacement. In agreement with the lower court's conclusion that the manufacturer had not overcome the presumption of unconscionability provided in the Code, the Court noted that particularly where, as in the case before it, the manufacturer made express representations as to the safety of the product, the ordinary buyer was more likely to be purchasing the tire in reliance upon the safety assurances than out of attraction to the repair or replacement remedy, making the attempted warranty limitation on damages and liability a fortiori unconscionable.

§ 17.04 STRICT LIABILITY IN TORT

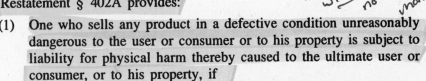

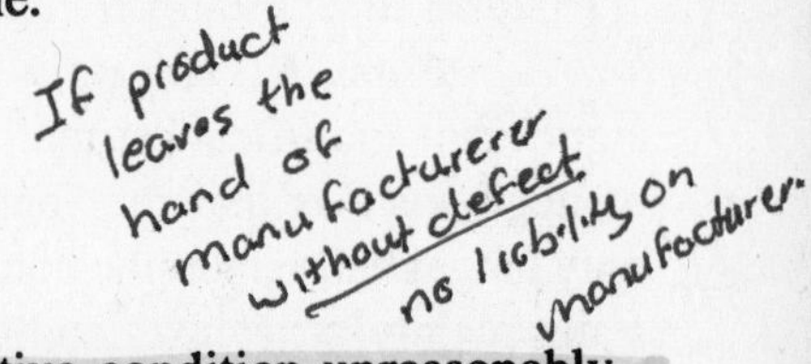

If product
leaves the
hand of
manufacturer
without defect
no liability on
manufacturer.

[A] *The Restatement View*

Restatement § 402A provides:

(1) One who sells any product in a defective condition unreasonably dangerous to the user or consumer or to his property is subject to liability for physical harm thereby caused to the ultimate user or consumer, or to his property, if

- (a) the seller is engaged in the business of selling such a product, and
- (b) it is expected to and does reach the user or consumer without substantial change in the condition in which it is sold.

(2) The rule stated in Subsection (1) applies although

- (a) the seller has exercised all possible care in the preparation and sale of his product, and

---

[66] 64 N.J. 260, 315 A.2d 16 (1974). *See also* Herrick v. Monsanto Co., 874 F.2d 594 (8th Cir. 1989) (limitation unconscionable where it would leave plaintiff without a remedy for crop loss caused by ineffective herbicide).

(b) the user or consumer has not bought the product from or entered into any contractual relation with the seller.

The rationale for strict liability given by courts construing Restatement § 402A tracks closely the reasoning of Justice Traynor in *Escola*,[67] and includes reference to the manufacturer's ability to foresee some hazards and to guard against their occurrence, the ability of the manufacturer to insure against the risk of injury and thereby to spread the cost of risk avoidance among its customers, and the difficulty, born of the complexities of modern manufacture, of the consumer in identifying and proving negligent conduct on the part of the manufacturer or others in the chain of distribution.

[1] Necessity of Showing a Sale

The plaintiff in strict liability must identify the supplier of the allegedly defective product and establish a causal relationship between the product and plaintiff's injury. In some jurisdictions, strict liability in tort has been expanded to certain services, bailments, and leases.

In strict liability as in warranty, the defendant supplier must be a seller in the ordinary course. Therefore, the remedy of strict liability in tort will fail where the transaction is fairly described as an "occasional sale," or one in which the supplier is not engaged in the regular activity of a manufacturer, distributor, or retailer as a part of his business as required by § 402A(1).

[2] Necessity of Showing a Defect

Plaintiff must establish that the product was defective, and that the defect was a substantial factor in bringing about plaintiff's harm. The most significant modification that strict liability in tort worked upon the rules of negligence is that the focus is upon the condition of the product, and only tangentially upon the conduct of the manufacturer or seller. As § 402A states plainly, strict tort liability will apply "although the seller has exercised all possible care in the preparation and sale of his product." Nonetheless, even under strict tort liability principles, a manufacturer or seller is not an insurer of the safety of the products he makes or sells. The fact that injury results from the use of the product is not itself sufficient to impose liability upon the seller. It must also be shown that the product was defective and that such defect was a cause of the injury.

Defendant's violation of a safety statute or regulation may, without more, support a finding that the product is defective. For example, in *Stanton by Brooks v. Astra Pharmaceutical Products, Inc.*,[68] an action brought on behalf of a child who suffered a massive adverse reaction to the administration of the local anesthetic Xylocaine, the evidence at trial showed that defendant had failed to file adverse reaction reports as required by federal

[67] Discussed *supra* at § 17.01[C].

[68] 718 F.2d 553 (3d Cir. 1983).

law. In the court's words, where the fact finder could conclude "that the FDA would have, if the missing data had been disclosed, required dissemination to the medical community of the now disclosed fact," a finding of defect would be warranted because the product "left the seller's hands . . . 'in a condition not contemplated by the ultimate consumer, which would be unreasonably dangerous to him.' "[69]

By statute in some jurisdictions a product implicated in an injury will be conclusively presumed to be nondefective where the accident occurs more than a certain number of years following initial sale, or following manufacture. Such statutes are called statutes of repose.

[3] The Meaning of Defect

[a] The Consumer Expectations Test

The authors of § 402A comment g explain that the rule applies "only where the product is, at the time it leaves the seller's hands, in a condition not contemplated by the ultimate consumer, which will be unreasonably dangerous to him." This "consumer expectations" test of defectiveness focuses on the reasonable expectations of the user and the surprise element of the danger involved, and has been adopted by many courts.

It is often difficult to determine in particular instances the reasonable expectation of the consumer. No consumer can reasonably be held to expect defective brakes in a new automobile, or beetles in beverages, and thus a car that cannot brake to a complete stop, or a beverage containing deteriorated fauna, is obviously defective. But what about a cherry pit in a cherry pie, or a fish bone in a bowl of fish chowder, or an olive pit in a martini olive? In such cases some courts have applied the "foreign-natural" test to determine defectiveness, and have held that cherry pits are "natural" to cherry pie, and fish bones are "natural" to fish chowder.

The consumer envisioned by the "consumer expectations" test is the ordinary adult consumer. Consider for example, the injuries suffered by a five-year-old child while playing with matches, which ignited his pajamas. In the ensuing flammability action against the pajama seller, the court identified the applicable standard as whether the pajamas were dangerously flammable to an extent beyond that which would be contemplated by the parent purchasing them for a child.

The Section 402A comment i test imputes to this hypothetical adult consumer "ordinary knowledge common to the community as to [the product's] characteristics." The special background and experience of an individual plaintiff is of no moment, as the proper evaluation is that of the *community* familiarity with the risk. If the individual plaintiff does have a particularized knowledge of the hazard, defendant may use such proof

[69] *Id.*, 718 F.2d at 570; Restatement § 402A cmt. i.

in a defense based upon plaintiff's assumption of the risk, but not on the issue whether the product creates an unreasonable hazard. Accordingly, the sometimes specialized knowledge of a class of consumers, such as, for example, the particular knowledge members of the farming community might have of agricultural equipment, takes on importance in the evaluation of the seller's duty to warn. It is generally agreed that the seller may defend the claim that a product was defective and unreasonably dangerous due to absence of adequate warnings or instructions for safe use, with proof that the user was a member of a presumptively sophisticated class of consumers who could be fairly expected to be aware of the risks of the particular product and the means of using the product safely.

[b] The Risk/Utility Test

There are probably very few cases in which a plaintiff would be entitled to recover on strict tort liability principles in which he would not also have been able to recover on negligence principles, particularly if he is aided by the doctrine of res ipsa loquitur. It would seem therefore that the same test for defectiveness that is applied in a negligence case could therefore be applied in a strict tort liability case, omitting only the duty of reasonable care. Seen in this light, the function of strict tort liability is to impute to the seller what amounts to constructive knowledge of the condition of the product.

Under the risk/utility test, the product is defective as designed only where the magnitude of the hazards outweigh the individual utility or broader societal benefits of the product. The risk/utility test posits, in effect, that only reasonably safe products should be marketed, and defines reasonably safe products as those whose utility outweighs the inherent risk, "provided that risk has been reduced to the greatest extent possible consistent with the product's continued utility."[70]

A seven-factor evaluation proposed for a risk/utility analysis in determining the defective condition of a product was advanced initially by Dean John Wade, and has been followed, as adapted, by courts in most jurisdictions. As stated by one court: "In balancing the risks inherent in a product, as designed, against its utility and cost, the jury may consider several factors.. . . Those factors may include the following: (1) the utility of the product to the public as a whole and to the individual user; (2) the nature of the product that is, the likelihood that it will cause injury; (3) the availability of a safer design; (4) the potential for designing and manufacturing the product so that it is safer but remains functional and reasonably priced; (5) the ability of the plaintiff to have avoided injury by careful use of the product; (6) the degree of awareness of the potential danger of the product which reasonably can be attributed to the plaintiff; and (7) the

[70] Beshada v. Johns-Manville Products Corp., 90 N.J. 191, 199, 447 A.2d 539, 544 (1982).

manufacturer's ability to spread any cost related to improving the safety of the design."[71]

[c] The Hybrid Barker v. Lull Engineering Test

In *Barker v. Lull Engineering Co.*[72] the California Supreme Court synthesized the most workable features of the consumer expectation test and the risk/utility test into a hybrid test that, its adherents argue, preserves the attributes of both. In *Barker*, the court commends a process whereby the:

> trial judge instruct [s] the jury that a product is defective in design (1) if the plaintiff demonstrates that the product failed to perform as safely as an ordinary consumer would expect when used in an intended or reasonably foreseeable manner, or (2) if the plaintiff proves that the product's design proximately caused his injury and the defendant fails to prove . . . that on balance the benefits of the challenged design outweighed the risk of danger inherent in such a design.[73]

It is immediately apparent that the first prong of the *Barker* analysis derives from the implied warranty of merchantability and comments g and i to Restatement § 402A. The *Barker* definition departs from a common application of the warranty rule, however, by relieving the plaintiff of the burden of showing the actual defect alleged. Under *Barker*, the plaintiff would only be required to show that he or she used the product in the way intended or in another reasonably foreseeable way, and that the product failed to perform safely.

The second prong of the *Barker* test comes into play where the product performance is apparently commensurate with ordinary consumer expectations of safety, but the product still exposes persons to "excessive preventable danger." Under the *Barker* test, in such circumstances plaintiff may undertake to prove that the product's design proximately caused plaintiff's injury or loss. Upon such proof, the burden of proof shifts to the defendant to show that "on balance the benefits of the challenged design outweighed the risk of danger inherent in such design."

The *Barker* court concludes by suggesting a succinct set of factors the trier of fact might consider in measuring the benefits of the challenged

---

[71] Voss v. Black & Decker Mfg. Co., 59 N.Y.2d 102, 450 N.E.2d 204 (1983).

[72] 143 Cal. Rptr. 225, 235, 573 P.2d 443, 453 (1978).

[73] In Soule v. General Motors Corp., 34 Cal. Rptr. 2d 607, 882 P.2d 298 (1994), the California Supreme Court reinterpreted the alternative tests of *Barker*, *i.e.*, the consumer expectations test and the risk/utility test. In an automobile crashworthiness test involving complex engineering issues, the California court concluded that juries should only be permitted to place exclusive reliance upon the consumer expectations standard where "everyday experience of the product's users permits a conclusion that the product's design violated minimum safety assumption." *Id.* at 617. Where complex technical or design issues "g[o] beyond the common experience of the product's users," the court continued, "the jury must engage in the balancing of risks and benefits" under *Barker*'s second prong.

design against the risk of danger. Comparable to, if shorter than, the Wade formulation, the risk/utility considerations suggested by the California court authorize the finder of fact to consider the following competing factors: "the gravity of the danger posed by the challenged design, the likelihood that such danger would occur, the mechanical feasibility of a safer alternative design, the financial cost of an improved design, and the adverse consequences to the product and to the consumer that would result from an alternative design."[74]

[4] Necessity of Showing Unreasonable Danger

Restatement § 402A comments g and i together establish that for strict liability to attach, the product must be "dangerous to an extent beyond that which would be contemplated by the ordinary consumer who purchases it, with the ordinary knowledge common to the community as to its characteristics."

The requirement of unreasonable danger has been interpreted to mean that the product must be more dangerous than an ordinary consumer would expect when the product is used in its intended or reasonably foreseeable manner. Illumination on this point is found in decisions holding it to be foreseeable that a motor vehicle may be involved in a collision, and foreseeable that a load may drop on the operator of a front end loader unprotected by overhead protection, or that an automobile owner might place his hand inside a wheel cover with sharp edges to determine the source of an unexplained noise. Conversely, it has been held to be unforeseeable that a child will kick over a burning smudge pot, or that a person bent upon suicide will lock herself inside the trunk of an automobile.

Whether a product is unreasonably dangerous cannot be measured in absolute terms. It necessarily involves a balancing of equities; a weighing of the likelihood and gravity of harm against the utility of the product and the burden of taking precautions which would be effective to eliminate the danger. It is for this reason that some courts have rejected "unreasonable danger" as an element of strict tort liability, and have held that all the plaintiff must establish is the defect, the damage, and a causal connection between the two.

A failure to provide adequate warnings or instructions may leave a product unreasonably dangerous to the user or to others.[75] A manufacturer or seller is not required to warn of every conceivable danger that may result from a use or misuse of his product, however. The comments to the Restatement state that the seller may reasonably assume that those with common allergies, will be aware of them, and the seller is not required to warn against them. So also a seller is not required to warn with respect

[74] *Id.*, 143 Cal. Rptr. at 237, 573 P.2d at 455.

[75] *See* discussion *infra* at § 17.05.

to products or ingredients which are only dangerous when consumed in excessive quantity, or over a long period of time, or when the danger or potentiality of danger is obvious, or generally known and recognized.

Thus, it is clear that the product that is defective because it contains inadequate directions or warnings is similar to the product that is defective because of its design, in that the defect can only be defined in terms of the *unreasonable* danger it presents to the user or consumer.

[a] Showing Alternative Feasible Design

Except in circumstances in which defendant's product is so frivolous or dangerous or both as to be lacking altogether in utility, a plaintiff's proof of defect must show that there was at the time of the original manufacture of the product some technologically feasible, safer alternative for it. In the words of the court in *McCormack v. Hankscraft Co.*, "To urge that a [product] is not a dangerous instrumentality is not persuasive to a reviewing court where the evidence reasonably permits a finding that a simple, practical, inexpensive, alternative design . . . would have substantially reduced or eliminated the danger[.]"[76]

The requirement of showing an alternative practical design can be seen as an element of the risk-utility analysis, in which one factor to be weighed is "the manufacturer's ability to eliminate the unsafe character of the product without impairing its usefulness or making it too expensive to maintain its utility."[77]

The failure of the plaintiff to satisfy the burden of demonstrating a technically more safe and feasible design as an alternative to the challenged design of defendant required the reversal of plaintiff's judgment below in *Garst v. General Motors Corp.*,[78] an action for death and injuries caused by operation of a 40-ton earth moving machine, where plaintiff was unable to prove that it was feasible, by even the most current technology, to manufacture braking systems that were either impervious to mud, or if sealed, not susceptible to overheating. In contrast, *Dawson v. Chrysler Corp.*,[79] demonstrates fulfillment of the requisite showing of alternative feasible design. In *Dawson* a policeman on duty was severely injured, after

[76] 278 Minn. 322, 154 N.W.2d 488 (1967). *E.g.*, Ackley v. Wyeth Laboratories, Inc., 919 F.2d 397 (6th Cir. 1990) (in action brought on behalf of child allegedly injured by DPT vaccination, parents required to show effective, safer alternative vaccination).

[77] Wilson v. Piper Aircraft Corp., 282 Or. 61, 577 P.2d 1322 (1978), *rehearing denied*, 282 Or. 411, 579 P.2d 1287 (1978), *citing* Phillips v. Kimwood Machine Co., 269 Or. 485, 525 P.2d 1033 (1974).

See Huddell v. Levin, 537 F.2d 726, 737 (3d Cir. 1976) (plaintiff's burden in a design defect case includes a showing that there was available an "alternative, safer design, practicable under the circumstances.").

[78] 207 Kan. 2, 484 P.2d 47 (1971).

[79] 630 F.2d 950 (3d Cir. 1981), *cert. denied*, 450 U.S. 959 (1981).

his vehicle skidded into a utility pole, by the second collision of his body with the unreinforced interior area of the vehicle that was most vulnerable to the stationary force of the pole. Plaintiff introduced expert testimony to prove that the manufacturer's frame could not withstand even low speed impacts. To further prove the feasibility of an alternative design, plaintiff's experts produced a substitute design calling for a continuous frame with an additional cross member running between the two B-posts, and showed further that such a design was both known to the industry before the accident, and had been extensively and successfully tested.

[5] The Unavoidably Unsafe Product

There are some products which, in the present state of human knowledge, are incapable of being made completely safe for their intended and ordinary use. This is especially common in the field of drugs, and the Reporters' Notes to § 402A cite the example of the Pasteur vaccine for the treatment of rabies, the injection of which occasionally results in very serious and damaging consequences, continuing: "Since the disease itself invariably leads to a dreadful death, both the marketing and the use of the vaccine are fully justified, notwithstanding the unavoidable high degree of risk which they involve. Such a product, properly prepared, and accompanied by proper directions and warnings, is not defective, nor is it *unreasonably* dangerous."

Designation of a product as "unavoidably unsafe" is not a complete defense, for it only permits the manufacturer to avoid strict liability. Plaintiff may still prove liability in negligence upon showing that the product — usually a pharmaceutical — was marketed without due care in preparation, or in its warnings or instructions.

Courts have generally followed the Restatement view, and have held that if it is shown that the product is unavoidably unsafe, there is no liability, provided the product has an extraordinarily high utility that outweighs the dangers incident to the use, and provided appropriate directions or warnings of the danger are given to the consumer. Comment k has described it as essentially applying negligence principles, with the rationale that application of strict liability to pharmaceuticals "would chill, if not smother, the research, development, productions, and marketing of new or experimental drugs necessary to alleviate or kill the ills to which we are all subject."

Consistent with such considerations, in *Davila v. Bodelson*,[80] where plaintiff, a mother, alleged that administration of a drug to her during the delivery of her baby resulted in the seizure disorder and cerebral palsy of the infant, the court approved the giving of the unavoidably unsafe instruction upon its review of the testimony of defendant's experts that the drug could cause hypertonic contractions "even with proper administration,"

[80] 704 P.2d 1119 (N.M. App. 1985), *cert. denied*, App. 704 P.2d 431 (N.M. 1985).

but that despite the risk attending the use of the product during delivery, the drug remained "a valuable and beneficial drug for the induction of labor."

[6] Effect of Changes After Leaving Control of Defect

In strict products liability, the defect must be proved to have existed at the time the product left defendant's control, as§ 402A contemplates that the product is "expected to, and does reach the user or consumer without substantial change in the condition in which it is sold." Where the product is substantially altered after manufacture, the change may defeat a claim based upon strict tort liability. The change must be of such a nature that it appears that it is the change that is responsible for the injury, rather than the original design, manufacturing, or marketing processes. Here the requirement of § 402A introduces no new element in a products liability case, but rather simply requires evidence that the original defect, not the change, was the proximate cause of the injury.

As the burden is upon the plaintiff to establish that the defect existed at the time the product left the control of the defendant, courts have held that the plaintiff must show that the defect did not arise from improper intermediate handling.[81] It has been held that evidence of reasonable and proper handling of a product after it left the control of the defendant manufacturer or seller and the time of the occurrence of the injury creates an inference that the defect did not come into being in that interim, but existed prior thereto.

The plaintiff is not required to eliminate all possible causes of the accident other than a defect existing at the time the product left the control of the defendant. Rather, he has sustained his burden if the evidence indicates that, more probably than not, the defect did not arise from subsequent improper handling or misuse of the product.

[7] Strict Liability for Miscellaneous Transactions

[a] Leased Property and Bailments

By its terms, § 402A imposes liability only upon one who sells a product in a defective condition. However, many courts have held that a sale, in the technical sense of passing legal title, is not essential to the application of strict tort liability, and that the rule can be invoked in the case of leased

---

[81] Samansky v. Rush-Presbyterian-St. Luke's Medical Center, 567 N.E.2d 386 (Ill. Ct. App. 1990), *appeal denied*, 575 N.E.2d 923 (Ill. 1991) (plaintiff made sufficient showing that central venous pressure catheter was in defective condition at the time it left the manufacturer). *Cf.* Landrine v. Mego Corp., 95 A.D.2d 759, 464 N.Y.S.2d 516 (1983) (balloon manufacturer would not be held liable where, unknown to it, its balloons were incorporated into a doll that simulated the blowing of bubble gum bubbles, and a child died after ingesting a balloon while playing with the doll).

or bailed goods, provided the defendant is in the business of such transactions.

The growing use of leasing, both as a substitute for purchasing and as a matter of temporary convenience, has bolstered the rationale for applying strict tort liability to the lease as to the sales transaction. In *Crowe v. Public Bldg. Comm'n of Chicago*,[82] the Illinois Supreme Court held a lessor strictly liable, reasoning that public policy imposed strict liability "upon sellers . . . as well as manufacturers, arising from their integral role in the overall producing and marketing procedure . . . . The public policy which justifies the use of strict liability as a means of shifting the burden of initial loss from the injured user applies with equal force whether the product is placed in the stream of commerce by a seller or by a lessor."

Bailors and licensors have also been held strictly liable, although the decisions have not been uniform. Strict products liability has been applied to a defendant engaged in the business of operating a self-service laundry, and who was thereby a licensor of a laundry machine to the user, who was injured due to a defect in the machine.[83] In the suit brought by a plaintiff who claimed injury due to a defect in the machine, the court held that licensors, like manufacturers, sellers, or lessors, were an integral part of the overall marketing process that should bear the cost of injuries resulting from defective products. Because the licensor provided the product for use by the public, the court added, it consequently played more than an incidental role in the overall marketing program of the product. However, in *Shaw v. Fairyland at Harvey's, Inc.*,[84] where the plaintiff sought recovery on warranty grounds for death caused by a dangerously defective gondola on a Ferris wheel, the court denied recovery on any strict liability theory. The court held that as strict liability was limited to manufacturers and other suppliers of "objects," users of amusement devices must prove negligence in order to recover.

[b] Services

As a general rule, courts have not extended the reach of strict liability to persons providing services. The accepted rationale for not extending strict liability to the ordinary provision of services is that services do not involve "mass production and distribution, nor are there any consumers needing protection from an unknown manufacturer or seller."[85]

Those cases that have extended strict tort liability or warranty recovery to services have thus far limited recovery to transactions that were commercial in character, rather than professional, and to cases in which the injury

---

[82] 74 Ill. 2d 10, 383 N.E.2d 951 (1978). *See also* Wilson v. Dover Skating Center, Ltd., 566 A.2d 1020 (Del. 1989).

[83] Garcia v. Halsett, 3 Cal. App. 3d 319, 82 Cal. Rptr. 420 (1970).

[84] 26 A.D.2d 576, 271 N.Y.S.2d 70 (1966).

[85] Kaplan v. C Lazy U Ranch, 615 F. Supp. 234, 238 n.3 (D. Colo. 1985).

was caused by a defective product, rather than from a defect in the service itself. Thus, in *Newmark v. Gimbels, Inc.*,[86] the court imposed strict liability on a beauty parlor operator for injuries to a customer's hair and scalp resulting from use of a permanent wave solution. The fact that the solution was applied to the customer from the original container, thus giving the operator no meaningful opportunity to discover its defective qualities, was held not to relieve the operator of liability. In the court's view, the operator occupied the status of a retailer and was part of the overall producing and marketing enterprise, with the responsibility to bear the costs of injuries resulting from defective products. This approach was adopted in the Reporters' Notes to § 402A, which state that "consumption includes all ultimate uses for which the product is intended, and [thus] the customer in a beauty shop to whose hair a permanent wave solution is applied by the shop is a consumer" who can recover under strict tort liability principles, provided that the injury resulted from such defect, rather than from a misapplication of the product by the operator.

The court in *Newmark* was careful to limit its holding to commercial transactions, however, and specifically distinguished the services of dentists and physicians in that those professional services "bear such a necessary and intimate relationship to public health and welfare that their obligations ought to be grounded and expressed in a duty to exercise reasonable competence and care toward their patients."[87] The *Newmark* court distinguished that action from the earlier decision in *Magrine v. Krasnica*,[88] in which it refused to impose strict liability upon a dentist when a defective hypodermic needle broke in plaintiff's jaw, noting that the dentist did not put the needle into the stream of commerce, nor did he promote its purchase by the public. The *Magrine* court found that strict liability principles were not applicable to a professional person of this or a similar type because the essence of his relationship with his patient was not selling products, but rather the furnishing of professional skills.

[c] Blood Shield Statutes

Practically all states have enacted statutes that make warranty or strict tort liability principles inapplicable to blood transfusions. The ordinary operation of such statutes is to render a hospital, blood bank or medical personnel liable for damages sustained due to contaminated blood only on a negligence basis.[89] The result is to relieve the administering agency from

[86] 258 A.2d 697 (N.J. 1969).

[87] 258 A.2d 703. The court continued, "In our judgment, the nature of the services, the utility and the need for them, involving as they do the health and even the survival of many people, are so important to the general welfare as to outweigh in the policy scale any need for the imposition on dentists and doctors of the rules of strict liability in tort."

[88] 94 N.J. Super. 228, 227 A.2d 539 (1967), *aff'd*, 53 N.J. 259, 250 A.2d 129 (1969).

[89] New York Public Health Law § 580 is fairly typical of the type of statute that has been enacted relative to the use of blood, and provides:

liability if it can be shown that the defect in the blood could not have been discovered in the exercise of reasonable care, unless it appears that such agency was negligent in some other aspect of the transaction, such as in failing to exercise reasonable care in the selection of donors, in the handling or processing of the blood, or in incorrectly matching the blood to the blood type of the recipient.

In the absence of a statute defining the basis of liability, the majority of courts have likewise refused to apply strict liability principles, either in warranty or in tort, to blood transfusions. A leading case in this area is *Perlmutter v. Beth David Hospital,*[90] decided by the New York Court of Appeals prior to the enactment of the statute defining a hospital's liability, in which the plaintiff, who had contracted homologous serum jaundice following a blood transfusion, alleged that the administration of defective blood, for which a separate charge was made, constituted a sale of goods by the hospital. The court denied recovery, holding that the transaction was primarily for services, that the implied warranties were inapplicable, and that the plaintiff was not entitled to split the transaction in order to treat the supplying of blood as a sale for purposes of warranty while treating as services the other care received at the hospital.

While nearly all states have adopted statutes providing a negligence standard for blood transmitted disease, most significantly HIV and hepatitis, representative of the diverse approaches taken by the individual states is the form endorsed in Illinois. That statute, after identifying the importance of blood and blood component transfusions to the general health and welfare, states that a strict liability rule "inhibits the exercise of sound medical judgment and restricts the availability of important scientific knowledge and materials." The statute thereafter states that a provider need only "warrant" that he has "exercised due care and followed professional standards of care in providing the service according to the current state of the medical arts."[91] In contrast, Idaho prescribes a standard of negligence, except for the classes of paid blood donors or for-profit blood banks, to which the rule of strict liability is to apply.[92]

[d] Real Estate

Under rules of common law there were no warranties of quality in the sale of real property. The rule was *caveat emptor*. Even under negligence

The collection, processing, storage, distribution or use of blood or a blood derivative for the purpose of diagnosis, prevention of disease or the assessment of medical condition is hereby declared to be a public health service and shall not be construed to be, and is declared not to be, a sale of such blood or blood derivative, for any purpose or purposes whatsoever.

[90] 308 N.Y. 100, 123 N.E.2d 792 (1954).

[91] Ill. Rev. Stat. 1981, ch. 111 1/2, §§ 5101-03.

[92] Idaho Code § 39-3702 (1977).

principles the circumstances under which a purchaser could recover for physical harm caused by a dangerous condition of the premises were strictly limited. The sale of real estate was considered to be governed by different considerations than those normally accompanying the sale of a chattel, and great importance was attached to the deed of conveyance, which was taken to represent the full agreement of the parties, and to exclude all other terms. It was assumed that the vendee would exercise greater care in the inspection of land or improvements than he might be expected to exercise in the purchase of personal property, and would thereby draw his own conclusions as to the condition of the premises.

Rejecting this logic, in 1964 the Colorado Supreme Court held that the builder of a new house was liable to the initial purchaser on implied warranties that the dwelling conformed to statutory requirements, and that it was built in a workmanlike manner, and fit for habitation.[93] This was soon followed by a number of similar decisions, holding the vendor liable on warranty principles.[94] With the rapid acceptance of strict tort liability, its application to real property was to be expected. Privity of contract has been held an essential requirement in an action seeking economic damages against a homebuilder based upon a breach of an implied warranty of habitability. In *Brown v. Fowler*, the South Dakota Supreme Court concluded this was a reasonable requirement for an implied warranty of realty because, in contrast to personalty, often the builder is the vendor of the home and the purchaser is the ultimate consumer. To eliminate privity would be to make the vendor-builder an insurer of the habitability of the house to future buyers, since the buyer would have to prove only that the builder-vendor did not transfer a reasonably habitable house. Thus, a subsequent purchaser of a settling house could not sue the builder-vendor for economic damages. The court held, however, that privity is not a requirement in an action against the builder-vendor for negligent construction.[95]

Nothing in the language of Restatement § 402A would preclude the doctrine from being applied to real estate, as § 402A simply provides that one who sells any product in a defective condition unreasonably dangerous to the user or consumer is subject to liability for physical harm. The question presented is whether land, or improvements placed thereon, can be considered a "product." The courts in recent decisions have found little difficulty

---

[93] Carpenter v. Donohoe, 154 Colo. 78, 388 P.2d 399 (1964).

[94] *E.g.*, Fenton Area Public Schools v. Sorensen-Gross Const. Co., 124 Mich. App. 631, 335 N.W.2d 221 (1983) (a roof is considered a product and can be subject to a products liability cause of action); Bethlahmy v. Bechtel, 91 Idaho 55, 415 P.2d 698(1966); Waggoner v. Midwestern Development, Inc., 83S.D. 57, 154 N.W.2d 803 (1967); Humber v. Morton, 426S.W.2d 554 (Tex. 1968); House v. Thornton, 76 Wash. 2d 428, 457 P.2d 199 (1969); Crawley v. Terhune, 437S.W.2d 743 (Ky. 1969); Rothberg v. Olenik, 128 Vt. 295, 262 A.2d 461 (1970); Wawak v. Stewart, 247 Ark. 1093, 449 S.W.2d 922 (1970); Rogowicz v. Taylor & Gray, Inc., 498 S.W.2d 352 (Tex. Ct. Civ. App. 1973).

[95] 279 N.W.2d 907 (S.D. 1979).

in answering that question in the affirmative. One rationale for so doing was suggested by a court that pointed out that:

> When in our modern society a person purchases a tract house from an advertised model, he relies upon the skill of the developer and the implied representation that the house will be erected in a reasonably workmanlike manner and reasonably fit for habitation, that the purchaser ordinarily does not have the means to protect himself either by hiring the experts to supervise and inspect or by provision in the deed, and that the public interest dictates that the cost of injury from defects should be borne by the developer who created the danger and who is in a better economic position to bear the loss rather than the injured party who relied upon the developer's skill and relied representation.[96]

[e] Used Products

The language of Restatement § 402A does not, by its terms, preclude its application to the sale of defective used products. As the reasonable expectations of a consumer, an orthodox measure of a product's defectiveness or nondefectiveness, are generally measured in terms of an expected level of acceptable performance over a range of contemplated, including secondary, uses, the difference between the standard as applied to new and used products would seem to be the difference in reasonable consumer expectations. Used products generally bring lower prices because the consumer expects that the quality and durability will be lower than in a new product. As the ordinary consumer should reasonably expect that a product will have a finite life, strict liability will not be imposed where the defect arises simply because the product has worn out.

Although the language of § 402A is broad enough to include used products, the decisions are divided as to whether the rule should be applied to a retail seller. Public policy arguments abide on both sides of the issue. On the one hand, as in sales of defective new products, significant concern must be given to the protection of public health and safety from the dangers of returning a defective product to the market. Further, it is the retailer who profits from the transaction, can better absorb the cost of injury than can the consumer, and is, in any event, often easier to locate and serve with process than is the manufacturer. Accordingly, some courts have held that the seller of a used product has a duty to make safe any product he returns to the stream of commerce.

On the other hand, the argument against strict liability for the retail seller of used products is that it plays a significant role in our economy, providing consumers with access to goods which might, if new, be available only at higher prices. Because the nature of the used product business entails the

---

[96] Becker v. IRM Corp., 698 P.2d 116, 119-120 (Cal. 1985) (*citing with approval* Schipper v. Levitt & Sons, Inc., 207 A.2d 314, 325-326 (N.J. 1965)).

sale of worn and often damaged products, it could be a severe economic burden to require dealers to inspect and repair worn products, or to warn against particular dangers.

Although most courts have ruled that the seller of used goods is not to be held strictly liable for injuries caused by defects, even when the defect exists at the time of sale, even in these jurisdictions the seller may face liability if his contact with the product is more than simply that of a trader or a conduit. If the dealer rebuilds the product or represents that it is new, he may be held strictly liable.[97]

§ 17.05 THE DUTY TO WARN

[A] *Generally*

Although a product is unerringly designed, manufactured and assembled, a seller may be liable if the product has a potential for injury that is not readily apparent to the user and carries no warnings of the risk or, where appropriate, instructions as to how to use the product safely. The duty to warn is perhaps the most widely-employed claim in modern products liability litigation.

A seller's responsibility for providing adequate warnings may be found under principles of strict liability, negligence, and warranty. In the aggregate, these duties are well described as a seller's informational obligation. Under strict liability, a seller's failure to warn may result in liability if the warning deficiency renders the product "unreasonably dangerous." Under negligence principles, a supplier may be liable for injury or damage incident to a failure to warn adequately when it knows or should know that the product is likely to pose an unreasonable risk without warnings. In warranty, an inadequate warning may render a product unsuited for the ordinary purpose for which it is used, constituting a breach of the implied warranty of merchantability.

To be adequate under any theory of liability, a warning, by its size, location and intensity of language or symbol, must be calculated to impress upon a reasonably prudent user of the product the nature and extent of the hazard. The language used must be direct and should, where appropriate, describe methods of safe use. An adequate warning should also advise of significant hazards from reasonably foreseeable misuse of the product and, where appropriate, antidotes for misuse.

It is valuable at the outset to distinguish warnings from instructions. Warnings call attention to a danger, while instructions are intended to describe procedures for effective and reasonably safe product use. Thus, a product's warning may be adequate, while its instructions are deficient.

---

[97] *See* Zavala-Pizano v. Industrial Handling Equipment Co., 847 F. Supp. 621 (C.D. Ill. 1994) (quoting 1 M. Stuart Madden, PRODUCTS LIABILITY § 3.26 (2d ed. 1988)).

Conversely, instructions may not alert the consumer of the danger to be avoided, or a warning may highlight the danger but not state how the consumer may avoid it.

[B] *Failure to Warn as Negligence*

In common law negligence, a seller or supplier has a duty to give adequate warnings of any risk involved in the use of a product when the seller "knows of or has reason to know" that in the absence of such warnings the product is likely to be dangerous for its intended or reasonably foreseeable use. This duty to warn under negligence principles is triggered where the potential for harm from the use of the product without warnings or instructions is significant or unreasonable.

Determining whether the risk is unreasonable requires a balancing of the seriousness of harm, and the probability that the harm will occur if appropriate steps are not taken, against the cost or burden of taking precautions. The manufacturer's duty to warn under negligence principles attaches when it knows or "should know" of a product's hazards. Significantly, of all of the members in the chain of distribution, only the manufacturer is charged with the should know standard. In contrast, the seller or the distributor of a product manufactured by another must, under negligence principles, give a warning only when it knows or *has reason to know* of hazards. This lesser obligation has been construed to mean that the nonmanufacturing seller should warn when it has actual knowledge of a hazard or when it has been given "information from which a person of reasonable intelligence . . . would infer that the (risk) exists . . . ."[98]

The duty to warn under conventional negligence principles turns upon the reasonable foreseeability of harm by use of or exposure to the product in the absence of warnings. It is not necessary that the manufacturer appreciate the specific nature of the hazard posed by the product to create the duty to warn. This issue is tied to the question of the foreseeability of the harm. In the end, probably no standard provides any better guidance than that of one court that observed: "If there is some probability of harm sufficiently serious that ordinary men would take precautions to avoid it, then failure to do so is negligence."[99]

---

[98] Comment a to Restatement § 401 elaborates upon the distinction between the "reason to know" and the "should know" standards of §§ 388 and 401 respectively. The comment states:

> The words "reason to know" . . . are used to denote the fact that the actor has information from which a person of reasonable intelligence or of the superior intelligence of the actor would infer that the fact in question exists or that such person would govern his conduct upon the assumption that such fact exists. The words "reason to know" do not impose any duty to ascertain unknown facts, and are to be distinguished from the words "should know" . . .

[99] Bean v. Ross Mf'g Co., 344 S.W.2d 18, 25 (Mo. 1961), *cited with approval* in Moran v. Faberge, Inc., 273 Md. App. 538, 332 A.2d 11 (1975).

Coequal with foreseeability as part of the evaluation of the manufacturer's duty to warn under negligence principles is the familiar weighing of costs against benefits. There are two questions for resolution. First, what is the likelihood of harm if warnings are not used, and what will be the seriousness of that harm? Second, what is the cost or burden of taking appropriate precautions?[100]

Illustrative is *Dougherty v. Hooker Chem. Corp.*,[101] a wrongful death action brought by the widow of an employee of an aircraft manufacturer who purchased the chemical solvent trichloroethylene, which caused the employee's death. The court therein cast the seller's duty of care concerning warnings in this way:

> The care to be exercised in discharging the duty to warn is . . . measured by the dangerous potentialities of the commodity as well as the foreseeable use to which it might be put . . . The determination of whether the method or means utilized to warn is sufficient will depend upon a balancing of considerations involving among other factors, the dangerous nature of the product, the form in which the product is used, the intensity and form of the warnings given, the burdens to be imposed by requiring warnings, and the likelihood that the particular warning will be adequately communicated to those who will foreseeably use the product.

[C] *Failure to Warn as Strict Liability*

A generally accepted standard is that a dangerously defective article is one "which a reasonable man would not put into the stream of commerce if he had knowledge of its harmful character."[102] Thus in the context of failure to warn jurisprudence, the duties to warn strict liability and negligence theories are almost indistinguishable.

---

[100] Restatement § 291 provides the general risk-utility standard that may be applied to the supplier's duty to warn under negligence principles. That section states:

> Where an act is one which a reasonable man would recognize as involving a risk of harm to another, the risk is unreasonable and the act is negligent if the risk is of such magnitude as to outweigh what the law regards as the utility of the act or the particular manner in which it is done.

This cost-benefit analysis is of particular relevance to circumstances in which the product is not to be handled by the manufacturer's immediate vendee, but is instead to be used by a third party, such as the vendee's employee. Restatement § 388 cmt. n states:

> [T]he magnitude of the risk involved must be compared with the burden which would be imposed by requiring them . . ., and the magnitude of the risk is determined not only by the chance that some harm may result but also the serious or trivial character of the harm which is likely to result.

See Boyle v. California Chem. Co., 221 F. Supp. 669 (D. Or. 1963) (liquid weed killer "Triox", targeted to home gardener, found to have warnings that were inadequate to convey extreme toxicity of dermal contact, and consequential need for cautious disposal of waste).

[101] 540 F.2d 174 (3d Cir. 1976).

[102] Phillips v. Kimwood Mach. Co., 525 P.2d 1033 (Or. 1974).

The comments to Restatement § 402A provide guidance both as to the distinctions and similarities between negligence and strict liability. Comment a states that in general "[t]he rule of strict liability subjects the seller to liability to the user or consumer even though he has exercised all possible care in the preparation of the product." Comment j, in turn, states the seller's obligation to inform the consumer or user of hazards of which the seller either knew or should have known at the time of initial sale. Even in strict liability, therefore, "a seller is under a duty to warn of only those dangers that are reasonably foreseeable," a standard which by its grounding in foreseeability "coincides with the standard of due care in negligence cases."[103]

The now conventional inquiry in duty to warn claims brought in strict liability is "(1) whether the manufacturer knew or should have known of the danger, and (2) whether the manufacturer was negligent in failing to communicate this superior knowledge to the user or consumer of its product."[104] The decisional law by now establishes that where there is a hazard and a feasible means of its abatement by dissemination of warnings or instructions, the seller will be strictly liable for failing to do so.

In strict liability and negligence alike, the absence or inadequacy of warnings or instructions must be of such a nature as to render the product unreasonably dangerous. Comment i emphasizes that the evaluation of what is unreasonably dangerous is the focal point of the strict liability inquiry, be the product hazard attributable to mismanufacture, a design or formulation defect, or a failure to provide adequate warnings. A prevalent means for evaluation of when an alleged warning inadequacy renders a product unreasonably dangerous in strict liability requires reference to the "ordinary consumer," posited in comment i, and the consumer expectation test. Under the consumer expectation test, a product will be considered to have been sold in a defective condition and to be unreasonably dangerous where it is "dangerous to an extent beyond that which would be contemplated by the ordinary consumer" purchasing it.

One helpful analysis places the claims of unreasonable danger and inadequate warning in strict liability in the context of two tests as to whether a product is safe: (1) whether the product's utility outweighs the risk to its user, and (2) if the utility outweighs the risk, whether the risk has been reduced to a reasonable level without a material diminution of the product's utility. Even when a product succeeds in passing the first standard, it must also pass the second. Many warnings cases in strict liability reflect clearly the second standard, for they advance the proposition that "regardless of the overall cost benefit calculation the product is unsafe because a warning

---

[103] Borel v. Fibreboard Paper Products Corp., 493 F.2d 1076, 1088 (5th Cir. 1973), *cert. denied*, 419 U.S. 869 (1974).

[104] *Borel*, 493 F.2d at 1089.

could have made it safer at virtually no added cost and without limiting its utility."[105]

While in strict liability the manufacturer will be presumed to have a knowledge of any hazardous propensities of the product sold, the general rule is that this imputed knowledge extends only to what is scientifically knowable at the time of manufacture. This conclusion is reached with both explicit and implicit reference to the language of comment k, and the suggestion therein that limitations imposed by "the present state of human knowledge" may be properly considered in determining what degree of safety was or is possible to achieve in a particular product, and comment j, which describes the seller's obligation to warn "if he has knowledge, or by the application of reasonable, developed human skill and foresight should have knowledge, of the presence of . . . the danger."

In *Beshada v. Johns-Manville Products Corp.*,[106] the New Jersey Supreme Court decision held that a manufacturer might still be strictly liable for failure to warn even if the risk was scientifically unknowable at the time of manufacture. Such a conclusion, according to the court, is consistent with the strict liability goals of risk spreading, accident avoidance, and maintenance of a manageable judicial fact-finding process. The court provocatively adds that the holding could fairly be viewed as creating "an incentive for [manufacturers] to invest more actively in safety research." *Beshada*'s rule of imputing to the manufacturer knowledge of risks that were not scientifically knowable at the time of manufacture has not been followed in other jurisdictions, and was later confined to its facts by the New Jersey high court in *Feldman v. Lederle Laboratories.*[107]

[D] *Failure to Warn as a Breach of Warranty*

The absence of adequate warnings or instructions on a product may in some circumstances support a finding that the product marketed in this condition is not merchantable, and is in breach of UCC § 2-314. The Fifth Circuit Court of Appeals so concluded in the influential decision of *Borel v. Fibreboard Paper Products Corp.*,[108] in which the plaintiff, an industrial insulation worker who contracted mesothelioma and asbestosis as a result of thirty-three years of exposure to asbestos, brought an action against certain manufacturers of insulation products containing asbestos. The warranty count of the complaint alleged that the defendant's products were unreasonably dangerous and unmerchantable, because of defendant's "failure to provide adequate warnings of the foreseeable danger associated with them." The court held that the manufacturer's failure to provide

105 Beshada v. Johns-Manville Prods. Corp., 447 A.2d 539, 545 (N.J. 1982).

106 447 A.2d 539 (N.J. 1982).

107 479 A.2d 374 (N.J. 1984).

108 493 F.2d 1076 (5th Cir. 1973), *cert. denied*, 419 U.S. 869 (1974).

adequate warnings rendered the insulation products unreasonably dangerous, sufficient to support the allegations both of breach of implied warranty of merchantability and strict liability in tort. One important distinction between warranty and tort as applied to allegations of failure to warn is that the manufacturer's duty to warn under a tort theory is "continuous," in that it is not interrupted by the manufacture or the sale of the product.[109] In contrast, under warranty theory, on the other hand, the seller's obligation is that the product be merchantable, or not unreasonably dangerous, at the time of initial sale.

[E] *The Effect of Obviousness of Danger*

In many situations the risk associated with use of, or exposure to, a product is of such a nature that it is known to the buyer or consumer, or is readily apparent to the casual observer. The majority rule is that there exists no duty to warn of certain obviously hazardous conditions. Authority consistent with this conclusion has involved slingshots, BB guns, darts, chairs on casters for invalids, kerosene used by industrial workers, and the activity of diving from a roof into a four-foot-deep swimming pool. The position taken in the decisions comprising this body of law is stated by one court in this language: "A manufacturer cannot manufacture a knife that will not cut or a hammer that will not mash a thumb or a stove that will not burn a finger. The law does not require him to warn of such common dangers."[110]

The doctrine denying recovery for injuries caused by product hazards that are obvious or known to the user or consumer has been applied even where the injured parties are children, embracing a logic that prompted one court in an action caused by slingshot to state: "Ever since David slew Goliath young and old alike have known that slingshots can be dangerous and deadly."[111]

Importantly, under the known danger doctrine, the user's generalized awareness of some peril will not defeat recovery unless the user knows of the specific risk involved and of its magnitude.[112] Illustrative is one action in which the court found that the plaintiff, severely injured by diving into a shallow pool, raised sufficient issue of material fact to avoid summary

---

109 Bly v. Otis Elevator Co., 713 F.2d 1040, 1046 (4th Cir. 1983), *on rehearing*, 754 F.2d 1111 (4th Cir.1985).

110 Jamieson v. Woodward & Lothrop, 247 F.2d 23, 26 (D.C. Cir. 1957). *Jamieson* involved the plaintiff's purchase of an elastic exerciser that was essentially "an ordinary rubber rope, about the thickness of a large lead pencil, about forty inches long, with loops on the ends." Plaintiff was injured when the extended exerciser slipped and struck her in the eye. *See also* Glittenberg v. Doughboy Recreational Industries, Inc., 491 N.W.2d 208 (Mich. 1992) (risk of diving into above-ground pool is open and obvious).

111 Bojorquez v. House of Toys, Inc., 62 Cal. App. 3d 930, 931, 133 Cal. Rptr. 483, 484 (Cal. Ct. App. 1976).

112 *See, e.g.*, Hopkins v. E. I. Du Pont de Nemours & Co., 199 F.2d 930 (3d Cir. 1952).

judgment since the evidence suggested that the plaintiff had some knowledge of some risk, but no appreciation of the entirety of the peril, including death, paralysis or other serious injury.[113] It has been suggested that the obviousness of the danger should not be an absolute defense, but rather should constitute but one of the factors in determining whether a product poses an unreasonable danger.[114]

[F] *The Effect of Unintended or Unforeseeable Use*

Generally stated, a manufacturer is required only to produce a product that is reasonably safe for its intended use. Where misuse of the product may create an unreasonable risk of injury or damage, the manufacturer must provide warnings adequate to permit the user to avert the hazard. This duty to warn extends to all risk-creating misuse that is reasonably foreseeable and is not limited by whether the foreseeable misuse is likely or unlikely; it need only be reasonably foreseeable.

A galvanizing influence in this development has been comment k to Restatement § 395, which states that "[t]he manufacturer may . . . reasonably anticipate other uses than the one for which the chattel is primarily intended." The issue has been stated by one court is "whether the plaintiff was acting within a commonly known area of conduct."[115] By such a common conduct standard, therefore, a kitchen chair used by a consumer to reach a high shelf was found to be in foreseeable use when the backrest failed to support her weight, causing injury.

Moran v. Faberge, Inc. involved an injury from ignition of women's cologne and corroborated the court's observation that "[t]he idle mind knows not what it is it wants."[116] In that suit, two teen-aged girls were passing casual time in one family's recreation room when one decided to scent a lighted candle by pouring some of defendant's cologne on the bottom of the taper. The immediate ignition severely burned one of the two girls. The cologne carried no warning as to its alcohol content; about it's low flash point, described by an expert witness as approximately room temperature; or about the hazards associated with its use around open flame.

In the personal injury suit that followed, the manufacturer claimed no duty to warn existed for a hazard that was so obvious and was, moreover, occasioned by the injured girl's unusual, even bizarre use of the cologne. In finding for plaintiff, the Maryland Court of Appeals first described the duty to warn most broadly, stating that "a duty to warn is imposed on a manufacturer if the item it produces has an inherent and hidden danger about

---

[113] Corbin v. Coleco Indus. Inc., 748 F.2d 411 (7th Cir. 1984).

[114] Olson v. A.W. Chesterton Co., 256 N.W.2d 530, 537-38 (N.D. 1977).

[115] Note, *Foreseeability in Product Design and Duty to Warn Cases Distinctions and Misconceptions*, 1968 Wis. L. Rev. 228, 233.

[116] Moran v. Faberge, Inc., 332 A.2d 11, 13 (Md. Ct. App. 1975).

which the producer knows, or should know, could be a substantial factor in bringing injury to an individual or his property." To the Maryland court, the issue was not that the manufacturer should have foreseen the injured girl's improvident behavior, but instead, whether a cologne with a substantial alcohol content and a low flash point might reasonably be used near an open flame. In the household environment, the court concluded, it was reasonably foreseeable, giving rise to the manufacturer's duty to warn.

By requiring that a manufacturer anticipate the environment in which a product will be used, and the risks of misuse, however unorthodox, that may inhere in such an environment, the court in *Moran* did no more than follow a line of authority that antedates strict liability in tort and which found a most succinct expression in *Spruill v. Boyle-Midway, Inc.*[117] The court in *Spruill* held that, in addition to foreseeing the literal intended uses of the product, the seller "must also be expected to anticipate the environment which is normal for the use of his product, and where . . . that environment is the home, he must anticipate the reasonable foreseeable risks of the use of his product in such an environment . . . [even] though such risks may be incidental to the use for which the product was intended." Consistent with the doctrine expressed in *Moran* and *Spruill*, it is today well settled that the manufacturer must design for, and impart warnings about, foreseeable involvement of its product in mishaps that may be unrelated to the product's intended use. Thus, to use one example, the manufacturer of clothes must foresee that the wearer may, unwittingly, bring the garment into contact with cigarettes, stove burners, or other sources of ignition. The manufacturer will be liable for any injury occasioned by the garment's unreasonable flammability in such a setting, notwithstanding the fact that bringing the fabric into contact with an ignition source is surely not an intended use of the product. It is, nevertheless, a foreseeable misuse.

In a duty to warn action, a third party's negligence is not a defense unless that negligence is the sole proximate cause of the plaintiff's injuries. Instructive is the holding in one action brought by a patient who, while being x-rayed on a tilted table, was dropped to the floor when the foot rest on the mechanical examination platform disengaged.[118] The evidence showed that the foot rest could disengage by the same method used to determine positive engagement, posing, in the view of the court, an "unreasonable and foreseeable" hazard. That a hospital technician might have misused the product by not understanding that subtle distinction should not, resolved the court, prevent a jury from concluding that the manufacturer's conduct was the proximate cause of the plaintiff's injuries.

[117] 308 F.2d 79 (4th Cir. 1962).

[118] Ontai v. Straub Clinic and Hospital, Inc., 659 P.2d 734 (Haw. 1983).

[G] *Causation and Disregard of Warnings*

In the failure to warn claim, as in other products liability causes of action, the plaintiff's proof must establish causation. In its most elementary form, such proof will show that, had the seller supplied an adequate warning, the injured claimant would have altered his or her behavior so as to avoid injury.

Pivotal to the successful maintenance of plaintiff's claim of actionable failure to warn is the demonstration that the seller's failure to warn adequately of the hazard was the cause-in-fact and the proximate cause of the injury. As expressed by one court, "the evidence must be such as to support a reasonable inference, rather than a guess, that the existence of an adequate warning may have prevented the accident[.]"[119] An illustrative jury instruction on the requirement of plaintiff's proof of proximate cause in a duty to warn claim as expressed by one court states:

> [T]he words proximate cause . . . mean first, that there must have been a connection between the conduct of the defendants, . . . which the plaintiff claims was negligent and the injury complained of by the plaintiff, and second, that the occurrence which is claimed to have produced that injury was a natural and probable result of such conduct of the defendant. . .[120]

Two presumptions, both bearing on causation, have gained widespread approval in duty to warn litigation. The first, applicable where some warning is, in fact, given, is stated in comment j to Restatement § 402A. It provides that "[w]here a warning is given, the seller may reasonably assume that it will be read and heeded . . . ." The reciprocal presumption adopted by many courts is that when no warning has been given, a plaintiff may benefit from the presumption that had a warning been given, it would have been read and heeded.[121]

The manufacturer may also attempt to overcome the plaintiff's proof of causation by showing that the act of a third party, often the employer, or in the case of pharmaceuticals, the physician, operated as the "efficient" intervening cause of the injury, breaking the causal chain. Where the intervening conduct of a third party is implicated in the defense of an allegation of failure to warn, the defendant is required to show that the act or omission to act was not foreseeable. It is generally agreed, therefore, that even when the product's original defect, by warning, design or otherwise, is not the sole cause of the accident, but remains a substantial cause of the injury along with the subsequent conduct of the purchaser, the manufacturer will be liable. Thus, convincing authority holds that, absent the manufacturer's showing of an intervening superseding cause, the simple

---

[119] Conti v. Ford Motor Co., 743 F.2d 195, 198 (3d Cir. 1984).

[120] Warner v. General Motors Corp., 357 N.W.2d 689, 692-93 (Mich. Ct. App. 1984).

[121] *See* Theer v. Philip Carey Co., 628 A.2d 724 (N.J. 1993) (decedent's estate in asbestos action entitled to heeding presumption).

showing that the purchaser "failed to take reasonable steps" to protect against the risk created by the manufacturer should not permit a jury finding that the purchaser's conduct was the proximate cause of the injury.[122] In contrast, consider *Bennison v. Stillpass Transit Co.*,[123] where the employee of the purchaser was injured while cleaning out a tank which still smelled of gasoline and which was purchased from the defendant. The court held there that the authorization by the employer to use these cleaning procedures when gasoline vapors were still present in the tank constituted a break in causation sufficient to relieve the seller of liability.

Related but distinct policies affect the evaluation of whether the acts or omissions to act of a prescribing physician should exculpate a pharmaceutical manufacturer's failure to provide adequate warnings. As a general proposition, the manufacturer of a prescription drug has the legal duty to warn the medical profession, and not the individual patient, of any risk associated with the use of its products. The physician assumes the role of learned intermediary between the drug manufacturer and the patient and conveys to the patient, as appropriate, the information, warnings and instructions provided by the manufacturer. The troubling issue of causation often arises when the physician is alleged to have failed to do so. Illustrative is an action in which an ophthalmologist prescribed for a patient ethambutol hydrochloride, the use of which carried the risk of causing optic neuritis and attendant permanent loss of vision. The plaintiff's complaint alleged that the manufacturers of this ophthalmic drug issued warnings that were "ambiguous, incomplete, inadequate, [and] watered down." The defendants countered that the injury was probably caused by the physician's admitted departure from the eye testing procedures and dosage recommendations of the manufacturer. The court concluded that the issue of whether the physician's actions were not foreseeable and were the independent intervening cause was proper for jury resolution.[124]

One insightful treatment holding that a manufacturer's warnings to a physician may be inadequate to prevent liability arose from an action brought by a woman who alleged that she suffered a stroke caused by her use of oral contraceptives. In *MacDonald v. Ortho Pharmaceuticals*, the court recognized that in most circumstances involving prescription drugs the manufacturer satisfies its duty to warn by conveying the necessary and appropriate information to the treating physician.[125] It also examined the

[122] Butler v. PPG Industries, Inc., 2 Prod. Liab. Rep. (CCH) ¶ 10,595 at 28,252 (N.J. App. Div. 1985), to which discussion the court added:

> The public interest in assuring that defective products are not placed into the channels of trade imposes a duty on the manufacturer to take feasible steps to render his product safe; the manufacturer may not rely on "the haphazard conduct of the ultimate purchaser" to remedy or protect against defects for which he is responsible.

[123] 214 N.E.2d 213 (Ohio 1966).

[124] Ross v. Jacobs, 684 P.2d 1211 (Okl. Ct. App. 1984).

[125] MacDonald v. Ortho Pharmaceutical Corp., 394 Mass. 131, 475 N.E.2d 65, 69 (Mass. 1985), *cert. denied* 474 U.S. 920 (1985) ("[t]he duty of the ethical drug manufacturer is

patient-physician relationship in the administration of oral contraceptives in light of Restatement § 388 comment n, and concluded that in matters of the duty to warn, the manufacturer's reliance on an intermediary must be reasonable. The court discovered that unlike the ordinary circumstances of patient-physician consultation common to the authorization of most prescriptions, with oral contraceptives there existed (1) "heightened participation of patients relating to use," (2) "substantial risks," (3) the ease and practicability of direct warnings from the manufacturer to the user, and (4) the limited prescribing ("annual") and oral ("insufficient or . . . scanty . . .") contact with the physician, rendering it inadvisable to rely upon manufacturer communication to the medical community alone.

It is, however, by no means automatic that a manufacturer's showing of a health provider's negligent failure to heed a warning will exonerate the manufacturer when the warning is proved to be inadequate. The manufacturer may avoid liability in a failure to warn action only if it can establish affirmatively that the prescribing physician would not have heeded and followed an adequate warning.

[H] *The Duty of the Non-Manufacturing Seller*

Liability for failure to provide adequate warnings may be imposed upon all entities within the chain of distribution, including not only manufacturers, but suppliers, wholesalers, distributors and retailers as well. There are, however, recognized distinctions in nature and degree between the duty to warn of the manufacturer and that of the distributor or the retailer. The general rule is that the retailer or distributor has a duty to warn only in situations in which the defect or hazard is known, visible, or readily ascertainable. Ordinarily, therefore, the seller has no duty to warn of hidden or unknown defects.

The factors pertinent to whether to impose such a duty on the non-manufacturing seller involve weighing whether the distributor's "integral [role in] the overall producing and marketing enterprise [justifies its] bear[ing] the cost of injuries resulting from defective products."[126] The court in *Hall v. E.I. Dupont De Nemours & Co.* has followed this reasoning, suggesting that relevant factors include:

Factors

> (1) [T]he standard of care — itself a function of the foreseeability and gravity of risk and the capacity of avoiding it; (2) the participants' capabilities of promoting the requisite safety in the risk-creating process; (3) the need to protect the consumer, both in terms of ascertaining responsible parties and providing compensation; and (4) the participants'

to warn the doctor, rather than the patient, [although] the manufacturer is directly liable to the patient for a breach of such duty.")

[126] Vandermark v. Ford Motor Co., 391 P.2d 168, 171 (Cal. 1964).

ability to adjust the costs of liability among themselves in a continuing business relationship.[127]

Commercial lessors have also been found to be within the class of businesses owing a duty to warn of dangerous conditions in the use of their products, by reason of their regular dealing with the product, and superior position to analyze potential hazards. Illustrative of such policies, a commercial lessor of a motor home was, together with the motor home manufacturer, found strictly liable for failing to warn the lessee of the home about the inadequacy of the tires offered as original equipment for use on the home.[128] Reversing and remanding, the lower court's finding for defendant, an Ohio appeals court found that the plaintiff should have been allowed at trial to offer proof that the lessor "was aware that the tires supplied with the motor home were inadequate for its load as a basis for liability, and that [the lessor] failed to warn plaintiff of that defect . . . ."

Regarding pharmacists, the prevailing authority holds that in the absence of any evidence that the pharmacist altered the product by compounding, adding to, or deleting from the pharmaceutical prescribed, the pharmacist has no duty to warn. One court so holding relied substantially on its observation that, particularly with drugs, the manufacturer alone may have the practical opportunity to detect defects in a pharmaceutical.

The repairer or servicer of a product will not generally be found responsible for failure to warn of risks associated with the use of a product, particularly if the risk is not attributable to any act of the repairer.

[I] *Persons to be Warned*

Where the seller can reasonably foresee that the warning conveyed to the immediate vendee will not be adequate to reduce the risk of harm to the likely users of the product, the duty to warn has been interpreted to extend beyond the purchaser to persons who foreseeably will be endangered by use of or exposure to the product. Included are members of the public who might be injured as a result of lack of adequate warning.

The leading expression of the weighing process that should accompany a manufacturer's determination of whether additional warnings should be given beyond those available to the immediate purchaser is stated by the court in *Dougherty v. Hooker Chemical Co.*[129] That court called for the balancing of the following considerations: "the dangerous nature of the product, the form in which the product is used, the intensity and form of the warnings given, the burdens to be imposed by requiring warnings, and the likelihood that the particular warning will be adequately communicated to those who will foreseeably use the product . . . ."

---

[127] 345 F. Supp. 353, 375 (E.D.N.Y. 1972).

[128] Miles v. General Tire and Rubber Co., 460 N.E.2d 1377, 1379, 1380-82 (Ohio Ct. App. 1983).

[129] 540 F.2d 174 (3d Cir. 1976).

In some circumstances the class to which the duty is owed and that to which the warning should go are not coextensive. The professional user and the learned intermediary doctrines represent two such types of situations. The bystander doctrine represents another. The court in *Sills v. Massey-Ferguson, Inc.*[130] framed the bystander issue well in its disposition of an action brought against the manufacturer of a lawnmower for an injury suffered by a bystander struck in the jaw by a bolt picked up and thrown by the lawnmower. Identifying the duty of a manufacturer of a product that creates a hazard to give effective warnings to those who may foreseeably be affected by it, the court recognized that such a warning need not necessarily go to the person injured. It also recognized that, on the facts before it, "it would be admittedly difficult for a manufacturer to warn the general public" of the lawnmower projectile phenomenon. The appropriate warning in such a setting, the court concluded, would be one "adequate and sufficient . . . [to] apprise the reasonable person of the dangers at hand." This would probably be one as to safety precautions "given to the user of the mower . . . ."

Putting aside products for household use or consumption, the majority of the circumstances in which the seller's product will be used by those other than the immediate vendee are sales to commercial or industrial buyers whose employees will actually use or be exposed to the products. Interpretation of the seller's duty to warn in this commercial and industrial environment is guided by Restatement § 388 which provides that the seller owes a duty to communicate effective cautionary information to these employees or other ultimate users, unless it has reason to believe that those persons exposed to the product will realize its dangerous condition. Comment n offers the most particularized guidance for the supplier whose goods are to be used or consumed by persons other than the immediate buyer. One prominent example involves the manufacturer's sale to a business or a contractor of a product that will be used by the latter party's employees. Should a warning or other cautionary information be made to the immediate buyer, the issue posed is whether such method "gives a reasonable assurance that the information will reach those whose safety depends upon their having it." Comment n suggests that this evaluation comprehends (1) a weighing of the relative seriousness of the harm that may occur if the information is not conveyed effectively to the remote user, and (2) an assessment of the confidence the seller may reasonably repose in the immediate vendee to share the information with its servants.

When the manufacturer sells in bulk by means of conveyancing that do not involve packages or containers that may readily be labeled, the majority rule is that the bulk seller fulfills its duty to warn if it conveys to the immediate purchaser sufficient information concerning any pertinent product risks. The manufacturer must also be reasonably satisfied that the

[130] 296 F. Supp. 776 (N.D. Ind. 1969).

intermediary possesses the ability to impart such information to subsequent purchasers.

[1] The Allergic or Idiosyncratic User

Where a manufacturer's product is safe for use by most persons likely to come into contact with it, but is likely to create an allergic or highly unusual reaction in only a small proportion of the population, special issues arise as to the manufacturer's duty to warn the allergic or idiosyncratic individual.

One potential guideline is Restatement § 402A comment j, which provides that the manufacturer should provide a warning where "the product contains an ingredient to which a *substantial number* of the population are allergic, and the ingredient is one whose danger is not generally known . . . ."[131] For example, in *Kaempfe v. Lehn and Fink Products Corp.*,[132] the court held that there exists no manufacturer duty to warn unless the consumer is one of a "substantial number or of an identifiable class of persons who were allergic to the defendant's products." The court there found that there should be no recovery where the evidence showed only four complaints out of approximately 600,000 units of spray deodorant sold, an outcome required not only by "the weight of authority but also by common sense application of the negligence doctrine."

Particularly when only a very small proportion of the population is put at risk, the severity of the illness or injury to which the warning would be directed is properly a factor in determining whether the manufacturer has a duty to warn. Such was the logic of the court in *Davis v. Wyeth Laboratories, Inc.*,[133] an action involving the risk to participants in a mass polio immunization program of contracting the disease inoculated against, a risk argued to be only one in a million. Expressly rejecting the quantitative approach to determining the manufacturer's duty to warn, the court stated the test as being applicable to the law of informed consent as well as to products liability: "When, in a particular case, the risk qualitatively (*e.g.*, of death or major disability) as well as quantitatively, on balance with the end sought to be achieved, is such as to call for a true choice judgment, medical or personal, the warning must be given." The analysis in *Davis* is congruent with the emphasis given in *Wright v. Carter Products, Inc.*[134] that even if the risk is very slight, when the consequences of an injury are very grave, the manufacturer may in some circumstances have a duty to

[131] Emphasis added. Morris v. Pathmark Corp., 592 A.2d 331 (1991) (no warning liability absent evidence that the product contained an ingredient to which a significant number of persons were allergic).

[132] 21 A.D.2d 197, 249 N.Y.S.2d 840 (1964), *aff'd* 20 N.Y.2d 818, 231 N.E.2d 294 (1967).

[133] 399 F.2d 121 (9th Cir. 1968).

[134] 244 F.2d 53 (2d Cir. 1957).

warn "those few persons who it knows cannot apply its product without serious injury."

[2] The Professional User

As a general rule, there is no duty to give a warning to members of a trade or profession against dangers generally known to that group. For example, courts have held that there is no duty to warn about the dangers of high exposure to benzene when the individual exposed to the benzene is a professional tank stripper whose job required contact with comparably hazardous cargo, and that there is no duty to warn an experienced stuntman about the hazards of jumping from a height of 323 feet into an air cushion rated for 200 feet.

One obvious rationale for the professional user doctrine is that the product sold to or coming into contact with the professional may frequently be sold only to members of that trade. One can plausibly maintain that the producer of bulk quantities of rodenticide, sold only to seed and feed stores in bags not smaller than 100 pounds, can expect that the product will see only agricultural use, and that the users would have at least a rudimentary acquaintance with the safe use of rodenticide. A like supposition can be said to have led one court to conclude that a manufacturer should not have to warn a farmer about the dangers of drinking concentrated herbicide.

One early expression of this approach was offered in *Helene Curtis Industries, Inc. v. Pruitt,*[135] in which the injured party claimed, among other things, that the instructions accompanying the defendant's hair preparation inadequately described precautions that could have been taken and which would have lessened the likelihood or severity of the plaintiff's scalp burns. The manufacturer countered that its product was plainly marked "For Professional Use Only," that its warnings and other cautionary information was sufficient for the safe administration of the product by beauticians, and that it should not be required also to have prepared information for the audience of the plaintiff and her friend who assisted in the casual home administration of the product. With this latter proposition the court agreed, stating: "When these products were marketed, the makers could only foresee that they would be applied by a trained beautician. Therefore, the directions had to be adequate only for the professional's use."

Subsection (b) of Restatement § 388 has been interpreted as supporting the conclusion that no duty to warn exists if the user knows or should know of the hazard, especially when the user is a professional who should be aware of the characteristics of the product. Illustrative is the case of *Strong v. E.I. Du Pont De Nemours & Co.*[136] In *Strong*, the widow of the decedent,

---

[135] 385 F.2d 841 (5th Cir. 1967), *cert. denied*, 391 U.S. 913 (1968). *See* Werkenthein v. Bucher Petrochemical Co., 618 N.E.2d 902 (Ill. Ct. App. 1993) (no bulk chemical supplier duty to provide specific precaution against "sniff" testing by purchaser's chemist).

[136] 667 F.2d 682, 687 (8th Cir. 1981).

a construction supervisor for the public gas company, brought an action for the death of her husband who was killed by a gas explosion while investigating a report of gas odor. The explosion was attributed to a two-inch plastic pipe, containing a metal insert stiffener, which pulled from a compression coupling because of shrinkage in the plastic pipe due to cold. The plaintiff alleged, among other things, that the manufacturer failed to warn that such plastic pipe, when connected to steel pipe by means of compression coupling, would not maintain its integrity as the plastic pipe contracted with a drop in temperature. The court found for defendant, on the basis of evidence that the coupling in question had been installed under the direction of the decedent, and that the decedent was, prior to the explosion, aware of at least two other incidents involving similar pullouts.

Courts have not, however, reflexively denied recovery to experienced workers on the basis of a presumptive familiarity with any hazards associated with their trade or craft. Thus, in *Jackson v. Coast Paint & Lacquer Co.*,[137] an action was brought by a painter severely burned when the epoxy paint with which he was painting the inside of a railway tank car ignited. The evidence showed that while the plaintiff's employer may have been familiar with the risk that vapors accumulating in a confined area could create the risk of explosion when coming into contact with a spark, the plaintiff himself was not. Reversing, the Ninth Circuit held that the trial court had erred in giving an instruction that knowledge of the hazard on the part of the plaintiff's employer would obviate any need for a warning to the plaintiff. The court stated that "[t]he adequacy of warnings must be measured according to whatever knowledge and understanding may be common to painters who will actually open the containers and use the paints; the possibly superior knowledge and understanding of painting contractors is irrelevant."

The professional user exception is best reserved for factual settings involving an expert buyer of a product that is not available for general consumption. The product is to be used or handled either by the buyer exclusively or by those who work under the supervision of the buyer and who are already either experienced in the use or handling of the product or have been effectively informed concerning safe use and handling. A good example of the limited and appropriate application of the professional user rule is offered in *Martinez v. Dixie Carriers, Inc.*,[138] a suit brought by the widow of a shore-based worker who was overcome by noxious fumes while stripping a barge empty of all liquids. The barge in question had been used most recently to transport a petrochemical mixture containing a substantial concentration of benzene. Reversing the trial court's conclusion that the seller's cautionary information had been inadequate, the appeals court determined that the warnings were adequate, "[a]t least for the limited class

137 499 F.2d 809 (9th Cir. 1974).

138 529 F.2d 457 (5th Cir. 1976).

of professionals to which . . . employees belonged," because (1) there was "limited marketing" of the product, only to "industrial user[s]"; (2) the crew on which the decedent worked "was conversant with the hazards and precautions necessary for the safe handling of a chemical mixture with a high benzene content . . ."; and (3) the barge and its cargo displayed large permanent signs about "Dangerous Cargo," a benzene warning card pursuant to Coast Guard requirements, and a product identification card promulgated by a national trade group.

[J] *Adequacy of a Warning*

Once there is determined to be a duty to warn, the task of the finder of fact often is to evaluate whether any warnings or instructions that were provided were adequate. To be sufficient in the legal sense, the warning or instruction must be adequate, if followed, to render the product safe for its intended and foreseeable uses. Naturally, the publication of a warning or instructions must be timely, providing the opportunity for the user or consumer to understand and act upon the message.

Evaluation of the adequacy of a warning requires a balancing of considerations that include at least: (1) the dangerousness of the product; (2) the form in which the product is used; (3) the intensity and form of the warnings given; (4) the burdens to be imposed by requiring warnings; and (5) the likelihood that the particular warning will be adequately communicated to those who will foreseeably use the product.

Thus, measuring the adequacy of a warning requires consideration of both form and content. The form of the warning label, be it rendered in a separate tag or integrated into the printed material on the product's container, must first be such that it could reasonably be expected to catch the attention of the reasonably prudent man in the circumstances of its use. The content of the warning, in turn, then must be of such a nature as to be "comprehensible to the average user and to convey a fair indication of the nature and extent of the danger to the mind of a reasonably prudent person."[139] A warning may be inadequate if: (1) its physical characteristics, including its size and placement, are so small or obscure that the reasonable consumer would not read it; or (2) it fails to inform the reasonable consumer of the pertinent hazard and the means for its avoidance.[140]

The warning's conspicuousness, prominence, and size of print, in comparison to the print size employed for other parts of the manufacturer's

139 Harless v. Boyle-Midway Div., American Home Prods., 594 F.2d 1051, 1054 (5th Cir. 1979) (action brought in products liability following death of fourteen-year-old boy who attempted to use pressurized propellant as an intoxicant); *see* Garcia v. Dependable Shell Core Mach. Co., 783 S.W.2d 246, 249 n.2 (Tex. Ct. App. 1989).

140 *See* Brown v. Gulf Oil Co., Prod. Liab. Rep. (CCH) ¶ 10,474 (Tenn. Ct. App. 1985); *see also* Mark A. deTurck, Gerald M. Goldhober, Gary M. Richetto, *Effectiveness of Alcohol Beverage Warning Labels: Effects of Consumer Information Processing Objections and Color of Signal Word*, 17 J. Prod. & Tox. Liab. 187 (1995).

message, must be "adequate to alert the reasonably prudent person."[141] Thus, for example, a manufacturer's notice, printed on the label of bottles of its furniture polish in print of size and color identical to that used for the balance of the manufacturer's message, was held insufficient to avoid liability for the death of an infant who died of chemical pneumonia after ingesting only a small quantity of the product.[142]

A leading decision finding manufacturer liability for failure to warn of the "extent" and "gravity" of the risks posed by exposure to the manufacturer's product is *Borel v. Fibreboard Paper Products Co.*[143] *Borel* was an action by an insulation worker against manufacturers of insulation materials containing asbestos to recover for alleged breach of duty to warn adequately of the risks of asbestos-related disease. Reviewing warnings that cautioned, in part, that protracted inhalation of respirable asbestos "may" be harmful, and advised workers to "avoid breathing [asbestos] dust," the court responded sharply: "[N]one of these so-called 'cautions' intimated the gravity of the risk: the danger of fatal illness caused by asbestosis and mesothelioma or other cancers. The mild suggestion that inhalation of asbestos . . . 'may be harmful' conveys no idea of the extent of the danger."

Warning language that is ambiguous will be found to be inadequate to communicate the extent and the seriousness of the harm. In one action implicating a prescription drug in a patient's loss of vision with the potential for permanent blindness due to optic neuritis, the warning under review stated only that administration of the drug "may produce decreases in visual acuity which appear to be due to optic neuritis." That statement, in light of information available to the manufacturer indicating a "permanent loss of vision [to patients] in a significant number of instances," impressed the appellate court as being "highly ambiguous."[144]

First aid instructions that are "internally incongruous" may be found to be inadequate, as were the instructions for washing off an industrial strength acid coming into contact with the user's eyes or skin in *Stone v. Sterling Drug, Inc.*[145] This action followed injury to a worker who sustained burns to the back of her hand when the cleanser splashed during use. The court there reviewed the first aid instructions on the product's label, which advised one coming into contact with the product to "[w]ipe off the acid gently, immediately flood the surface with water, using soap freely, then cover with moist magnesia or baking soda." On the basis of expert testimony, the court

[141] First Nat'l Bank in Albuquerque v. Nor-Am Agric. Prods., Inc., 537 P.2d 682, 692 (N.M. Ct. App. 1975).

[142] Spruill v. Boyle-Midway, Inc., 308 F.2d 79 (4th Cir. 1972) (the warning had nothing to attract special attention to it except the words "safety note" and the language advising that the product "may be harmful, especially if swallowed by children.").

[143] 493 F.2d 1076 (5th Cir. 1973).

[144] Ross v. Jacobs, 684 P.2d 1211 (Okl. Ct. App. 1984).

[145] 111 A.D.2d 1017, 490 N.Y.S.2d 468, Prod. Liab. Rep. (CCH) ¶ 10,580 (1985).

found the instructions to be "woefully inadequate" in that they neglected to state that the irrigation with water should be sustained for at least fifteen minutes. The instructions were further found to be "internally incongruous" in that they advised fifteen minutes irrigation if the cleanser came into contact with a person's eyes, but no minimum amount of time, established as necessary by the evidence, for washing with water when the cleanser came into contact with the user's skin. This inadequacy, the court found, had in fact aggravated the plaintiff's injury. In addition to the responsibility for providing instructions for the safe use of a product when misuse, such as failure to follow instructions, would subject the consumer to serious hazards, the manufacturer must provide "adequate warnings of dangers that might be encountered if the instructions given are not followed."

Actions taken by the manufacturer or by persons working on its behalf can erode the efficacy of an otherwise adequate warning. In *Incollingo v. Ewing*,[146] the court held that the plaintiff should be able to adduce evidence that "detail men" working on behalf of a pharmaceutical manufacturer "overpromoted" the attributes of the drug in their presentations to the medical community at large and to such an extent as to obscure the import of cautionary written material accompanying sale of the pharmaceutical.

A container may carry an arguably sufficient warning and a comprehensive description of the uses to which the product may be put, but still be found to be in breach of the seller's duty to warn if the information fails to instruct the user as to how the product may be used safely. Such was the gist of the holding in an action brought by a laborer whose duties included the care of a golf course and who was sickened by exposure to an insecticide containing arsenic. Liability was found against the manufacturer who, while providing a warning employing the skull and crossbones and setting forth with "extreme particularity how, where, and for what purpose to use the product as an insecticide," nevertheless, failed to tell the user how to use the product in safety. The warning specifically failed to state that in applying the insecticide a respirator and protective clothing must be used.[147]

[K] *The Continuing Duty to Warn*

A post-sale duty to warn may attach even if the product was, at the time of manufacture and sale, reasonably safe for use (or arguably so), but through use or operation, has betrayed hazards not earlier known to the seller, or to other sellers of like products.

The leading and innovative decision of *Comstock v. General Motors Corp.*[148] involved the alleged failure of the automobile manufacturer to take

146 444 Pa. 263, 282 A.2d 206 (1971).

147 Edwards v. California Chemical Co., 245 So. 2d 259, 264-65 (Fla. Ct. App. 1971).

148 358 Mich. 163, 99 N.W.2d 627 (1959).

remedial measures after learning, soon after the model was put on the market, of its propensity to lose its brakes. A personal injury claim was brought by a mechanic at an automobile dealership who suffered severe injuries when a car rolled unimpeded into him in a service bay. The court, after first describing the manufacturer's general duty to warn at the point of sale, stated that "a like duty to give prompt warning exists when a latent defect which makes the product hazardous becomes known to the manufacturer shortly after the product has been put on the market."

Particularly with regard to manufacturers of ethical pharmaceuticals, the courts have interpreted the duty to warn as extending to a "continuous duty" to remain apprised of new scientific and medical developments and to inform the medical profession of pertinent developments related to treatment and side effects.[149] This continuing informational obligation imposed upon the manufacturer even after the marketing of the product is not confined to the passive interpretation of scientific, medical, or technical advances or revelations explored by third parties. Under certain circumstances, such as the manufacture and sale of pharmaceuticals as to which advancing medical inquiry may reveal risks not previously known, the manufacturer's continuing post-sale duties have been found to include the initiation of further investigations, studies or tests of its own.[150]

§ 17.06 STRICT PRODUCTS LIABILITY FOR MISREPRESENTATION

[A] *Restatement § 402B*

The modern rule for liability without fault for misrepresentation is stated at Restatement § 402B:

> "One engaged in the business of selling chattels who by advertising, labels, or otherwise, makes to the public a misrepresentation of material fact concerning the character or quality of a chattel sold by him is subject to liability for physical harm to a consumer of the chattel caused by justifiable reliance upon the misrepresentation, even though
>
> (a) it is not made fraudulently or negligently, and
>
> (b) the consumer has not bought the chattel from or entered into any contractual relation with the seller."

Review of two decisions having an enormous influence upon the formulation of the Restatement rule of strict liability for misrepresentation provides a valuable backdrop. The earlier of these two cases is *Baxter v.*

[149] Schenebeck v. Sterling Drug, Inc., 423 F.2d 919 (8th Cir. 1970) (applying Arkansas law) (identifying a "continuous duty . . . to warn physicians of the dangers incident to prescribing the drug, [and] to keep abreast of scientific developments touching upon the manufacturer's product and to notify the medical profession of any additional side effects discovered . . .").

[150] *See* Barson v. E.R. Squibb & Sons, Inc., 682 P.2d 832 (Utah 1984).

Ford Motor Co.,[151] and involved an automobile owner's injury when a pebble struck the windshield of his car, shattering it and sending a particle of glass into his eye. The catalogues for the automobile model for that year described the windshield glass as "TRIPLEX SHATTER-PROOF GLASS WINDSHIELD," and stated that the windshield "will not fly or shatter under the hardest impact."

The Washington Supreme Court noted that for a defect such as this "[a]n ordinary person would be unable to discover by the usual and customary examination of the automobile whether glass which would not fly or shatter was used in the windshield." Observing the recent and profound changes in commercial relations,[152] the court held that a seller misrepresenting a material fact, upon which the buyer relied in purchasing the product, would be strictly liable for injuries caused by the failure of the product to conform with the representation. Affirming on second appeal, the court confirmed that the innocence of the seller's misrepresentation should not affect the application of strict liability, stating: "If a person states as true material facts susceptible of knowledge to one who relies and acts thereon to his injury, if the representations are false, it is immaterial that he did not know they were false, or that he believed them to be true."

A second and influential decision is that entered in *Rogers v. Toni Home Permanent Co.*[153] In that action, plaintiff had suffered hair loss and severe scalp irritation after use of defendant's product, which had been labeled "safe" and "harmless." Imposing strict liability on the basis of defendant's misrepresentations, the court stated that "[t]he warranties made by the manufacturer in his advertisements and by the labels on his products are inducements to the ultimate consumers, and the manufacturer ought to be held to strict accountability to any consumer who buys the product in reliance upon such representations. . . ."

Not merely one more potential foundation for a products liability case, § 402B permits a tort recovery when injury is caused to the consumer of a *nondefective* product. The 1000-pound-test wire rope contains no defect; advertised as able to support 2000 pounds, it may well cause injury to one using it for that purpose. Under § 402B the action is perfectly straightforward: The plaintiff proves the representation; his reliance on it; its falsity;

[151] 168 Wash. 456, 12 P.2d 409 (1932).

[152] *Id.* ("Methods of doing business have undergone a great transition. Radio, billboards, and the products of the printing press have become the means of creating a large part of the demand that causes goods to depart from factories to the ultimate consumer. It would be unjust to recognize a rule that would permit manufacturers to create a demand for their products by representing that they possess qualities which they, in fact, do not possess, and then, because there is no privity of contract existing between the consumer and the manufacturer, deny the consumer the right to recover if damages result from the absence of those qualities, when such absence is not readily noticeable.").

[153] 167 Ohio St. 244, 147 N.E.2d 612 (1958).

and his resulting injury. The seller is liable because whatever he sold was not as he represented it to be. If a product is publicly advertised to be "safe" for use, its seller will be liable even to one whose injury from its use was the result of a rare adverse reaction, the injured consumer being as much entitled as anyone else to rely on the advertised assurance.

Comment j to § 402B states a requirement that plaintiff's reliance upon the representation be reasonable and justified.[154] The comment adds that, as with other common law misrepresentation, the rule "does not apply where the misrepresentation is not known, or there is indifference to it, and it does not influence the purchase or subsequent conduct."

Importantly, the injured party himself does not have to be the person who justifiably relied upon the representations of the seller, such as, for example, where the purchaser of an automobile has reasonably relied upon the misrepresentations of the seller and gives the vehicle to a family member as a gift. Should there be injury to the other family member attributable to the seller's misrepresentation, the requisite reliance for the injured person's cause of action would be supplied by the purchaser.

Restatement § 402B limits recovery for mislabeled goods to damages for "physical harm" to the user, in obvious contrast to § 402A which provides a remedy for injury to person or to the property of the user or others.

[B] *Section 402B and Advertising*

The reach of § 402B extends to the seller who "by advertising, labels, or otherwise, makes to the public a misrepresentation." The authors' comments accompanying the section establish that the rule is intended to apply only to those sellers who make and disseminate, in any form, representations to the public. Conversely, it is clear that a seller's individual representation to the individual buyer cannot create liability under § 402B. Comment h states a conforming interpretation of the rule in this way: "The rule stated in this section is limited to misrepresentations which are made by the seller to the public at large, in order to induce the purchase of the chattels sold, or are intended by the seller to, and do, reach the public."

Significantly, it has been held that the representations made by a pharmaceutical company to a physician to encourage use or prescription of a prescription drug should be considered a representation within the intendment of § 402B even where a regular forum for such representations

[154] Restatement § 402B cmt. j ("Since the liability here is for misrepresentation, the rules as to what will constitute justifiable reliance stated in Restatement §§ 537-545A are applicable to this section, so far as they are pertinent.").

is a person-to-person conversation between the representative and the physician.[155]

Advertising in all of its forms was the focus of the judicial concern expressed in *Rogers v. Toni Home Permanent Co.*,[156] which is immortalized in Illustration 3 to the comments to § 402B, and states that the manufacturer of a permanent wave preparation who places a label on the product stating that the product may be safely used in a particular manner, and that when so used will not injure hair, will be strictly liable to a consumer who, having read the label, purchases and uses the product in reliance upon the statements on the label and suffers damage to her hair and scalp.

It is axiomatic that no user can base an action for his product-caused injury on an advertisement that he never knew about when he used the product. Section 402B merely preserves what has long been the requirement of reliance. But it is equally clear that the advertisement need not be shown to have been the only inducement for the product's use. Indeed, the opinions which have detailed the evidence adduced to prove reliance demonstrate that little is generally required beyond the plaintiff's credible statement that he saw an advertisement and believed it to be true when he used the product.

Liability under § 402B requires a misrepresentation of a material fact, and the drafters of the section emphasize in the comments that the material facts must pertain to the quality or the character of the product; which is to say that the reliance must be "justifiable" and on a representation of "material fact." These requirements together operate to eliminate mere "puffing" or "sales talk" as the basis for an action under the section. An expression of the seller's opinion of his product is not a representation of a material fact.[157] Courts have become sensitive to claims for the safety of products, and thus, almost any assertion which directly or by reasonable inference represents a chattel as safe for use may be held to be a representation of material fact rather than a mere expression of opinion.

An illustrative application of § 402B is the California Supreme Court decision in *Hauter v. Zogarts*,[158] the "Golfing Gizmo" case in which plaintiff, a thirteen-year-old beginning golfer, was severely injured when he used a golfing toy represented to permit the user to "drive the ball with full power," and which stated further that it was "COMPLETELY SAFE

[155] *See* Crocker v. Winthrop Laboratories, 514 S.W.2d 429 (Tex. 1974) ("There is a heading of a paragraph in the product information of the 1967 edition of Physician's Desk Reference Book which reads: 'Absence of addiction liability.' This might be considered misleading, but in view of the evidence of verbal assurances as to the properties of Talwin by the drug company's representative, there is no need to deal further with printed materials."

[156] 167 Ohio St. 244, 147 N.E.2d 612 (1958).

[157] *E.g.*, Consolidated Papers, Inc. v. Dorr-Oliver, Inc., 451 N.W.2d 456 (Wis. Ct. App. 1989), *review denied*, 457 N.W.2d 323 (Wis. 1990) (representation that clarifier would have "long shelf life" was mere puffing).

[158] 120 Cal. Rptr. 681, 534 P.2d 377 (1975).

— BALL WILL NOT HIT PLAYER." Despite careful preparation and use in conformity with the seller's instructions, the boy was hit by a ball that did not return to the tee as the manufacturer intended.

Turning first to the requirement under § 402B that the seller's challenged representation must be one of a material fact, the court referred to repeated conclusions of other courts that similar promises of safety were representations of fact and not puffing.[159] The materiality of the representation could not be seriously questioned, the court continued, as "anyone learning to play golf naturally searches for a product that enables him to learn safely." The court then found that plaintiff's reliance upon defendant's assurances of safety was justifiable. Even conceding defendant's argument that experienced golfers were at some risk in playing the sport, the court concluded that "even though certain dangers are inherent in playing golf, the risk that a golfer's own ball will wrap itself around his club and strike the golfer on the follow through is not among those dangers. [Plaintiff's] injury stemmed from a risk inherent in defendant's product, not a risk inherent in the game of golf."

Comment h to § 402B states in part that the public representation required by the rule "may be made by public advertising in newspapers or television, by literature distributed to the public through dealers, by labels on the product sold, or leaflets accompanying it, or in any other manner, whether it be oral or written." By whatever means of communication defendant's representations were made, upon the commencement of litigation, plaintiff must demonstrate that the challenged statements or advertisements involved the same product, operated under conditions the same or similar to the conditions involved in plaintiff's use.

§ 17.07 THE RESTATEMENT (THIRD) OF TORTS: PRODUCTS LIABILITY

[A] *Introduction*

As this text is being published, the American Law Institute is pursuing a multi-year project that will result in a Restatement (Third) of Torts. The first project within the larger Restatement (Third) is a Products Liability Restatement, now in its second Tentative Draft.[160] The Reporters are Professors Aaron D. Twerski of Brooklyn Law School, and James A. Henderson, Jr. of Cornell Law School. The subject of Tentative Draft No. 2 is "Liability for the Sale or Distribution of Defective Products."

---

[159] *See* McCormack v. Hankscraft Co., 278 Minn. 322, 154 N.W.2d 488 (1967) (vaporizer described as "safe" and "practically foolproof").

[160] Restatement of the Law — Torts: Products Liability, Tentative Draft No. 2 (March 13, 1995) (American Law Institute) [hereinafter Tentative Draft No. 2 or Draft].

Restatement 3d

[B] *Manufacturing, Design and Informational Defects*

Draft § 2 sets out standards for product defectiveness. The Reporters state that "[r]ather than perpetuating confusion spawned by existing doctrinal categories [*i.e.*, strict liability, warranty, or negligence], §§ 1 and 2 define the liability for each form of defect in terms directly addressing the kinds of defects."[161] The "terms" employed by the Draft are familiar: manufacturing defect, design defect, and failure to warn. Draft § 2, entitled "Categories of Product Defect," states:

(a) a product contains a manufacturing defect when the product departs from its intended design even though all possible care was exercised in the preparation and marketing of the product;

(b) a product is defective in design when the foreseeable risks of harm posed by the product could have been reduced or avoided by the adoption of a reasonable alternative design by the seller or other distributor, or a predecessor in the commercial chain of distribution, and the omission of the alternative design renders the product not reasonably safe;

(c) a product is defective because of inadequate instructions or warnings when the foreseeable risks of harm posed by the product could have been reduced or avoided by the provision of reasonable instructions or warnings by the seller or other distributor, or a predecessor in the commercial chain of distrubution, and the omission of the instructions or warnings renders the product not reasonably safe.

---

[161] Tentative Draft No. 2, Reporters' comments at 4.

CHAPTER 18

NUISANCE AND TRESPASS

SYNOPSIS

§ 18.01 NUISANCE

[A] *Overview*

Although governed by its own set of rules that reflect its close relationship to the law of property, the law of nuisance is a subcategory of tort law in that the gravaman of the complaint in nuisance is the allegation of injury to person or property. As in other areas of tort, the injury need not be physical, and can include injury to rights or property enjoyment. Indeed, public nuisance redresses interests not necessarily tied to any particular piece of property, such as the public health, safety and welfare.

The law of nuisance recognizes two distinct categories of claims: private nuisance and public nuisance. Defendant's conduct may create an actionable public nuisance where it either interferes with a public right or convenience, or the public health or safety. It may constitute a private nuisance when it interferes with another's current possessory or beneficial interest in the use or quiet enjoyment of land.[1]

The complainant in private nuisance seeks to protect his own, current interest in the undisturbed enjoyment of or benefit from property. The plaintiff needn't own the property — he need only be a lawful occupant, or the holder of one or more other use rights. In contrast, for a suit in public nuisance, the complainant needn't have a property or use interest in any property affected by defendant's conduct.

An actor's conduct may incur liability in *both* private and public nuisance. For example, in *Wood v. Picollo*,[2] the defendants had maintained a hazardous chemical waste dump. The plaintiffs introduced expert testimony to establish that the chemicals could cause anemia and liver disease, and that the soil was permeable enough to allow seepage of the chemicals or airborne contamination from the defendant's trench onto plaintiffs' land and into public waters.

Finding both a private and public nuisance, the Rhode Island Supreme Court explained: "[t]he essential element of an actionable nuisance is that persons have suffered harm or are threatened with injuries that they ought not have to bear." The Court found the harm to individual plaintiffs' use of their property unquestionably to be of the type that a nuisance claim contemplates, and found further that continuation of the defendants' operation would "threaten to cause incalculable damage to the general public."

---

[1] For helpful general treatments of public and private nuisance, see William H. Rodgers, Jr., ENVIRONMENTAL LAW: AIR and WATER § 1.1 (1986); M. Stuart Madden, TOXIC TORTS DESK BOOK 34-41 (1992); William Prosser, *Private Actions for Public Nuisance*, 52 Va. L. Rev. 997 (1966).

[2] 443 A.2d 1244 (R.I. 1982).

[B] *Nuisance and Trespass Distinguished*

A claim in trespass ordinarily seeks damages for a physical intrusion onto a property, *i.e.*, the pollution or contamination of plaintiff's property by a substance, article or object. Where the intrusion is permanent — or if not permanent, serious or persistent — the suit sounds in trespass. As the gravamen of trespass is the interference with plaintiff's current possessory interest in property,[3] it stands to reason that intrusion onto plaintiff's land of stones, asphalt or phosphate slime impinges on that possessory interest.

To be distinguished, claims that a defendant's conduct creates conditions of noise, lights, odor or vibration that interferes with plaintiff's quiet enjoyment of the property ordinarily sound in nuisance.[4] These arguably lesser interferences, while vexing and an interference with plaintiff's use, enjoyment, or exploitation of her property, are generally not considered to dispossess plaintiff of her current possessory interest.

Consistent with this general rule, one court distinguished nuisance from trespass on the basis of the duration of the interference. A fleeting or temporary interference with plaintiff's right to enjoy his property might be categorized as nuisance, while invasion of the property by the same substance or matter, if chronic, or where the contamination was more difficult to eliminate, could be trespass. On this rationale, the court stated that "airborne particles [that are] transitory and quickly dissipate, [and therefore] do not interfere with a property owner's possessory rights [are] properly denominated nuisances."[5]

[1] Continuing Nuisance and Trespass; Permanent Nuisance and Trespass

The common law of nuisance and trespass has retained a distinction between so-called "continuing" and "permanent" nuisance and trespass. In general terms, a nuisance or trespass is "continuing" (or "temporary") if it could be discontinued or abated at any time, such as, for example, airborne particulate matter coming from an industrial smokestack, which could be abated by cessation of the industrial activity. A "permanent" nuisance or trespass, on the other hand, is an interference or an intrusion that has no ready means of elimination, such as the longstanding and perhaps ineradicable mercury contamination of a marshland.

---

[3] Restatement § 157, discussed below at § 18.02 of this Chapter.

[4] James A. Henderson, Jr. and Richard N. Pearson, THE TORTS PROCESS 929 (3d ed. 1988) ("When the interference is limited to light, noise, odor, or vibrations . . . courts generally hold that such intangible intrusions, in the absence of intent, are dealt with as nuisance cases, not trespass.").

[5] Bradley v. American Smelting and Refining Co., 709 P.2d 782, 791 (Wash. 1985). In that suit, involving intentional deposit of microscopic particles of arsenic and cadmium, the court added: "When, however, the particles or substance accumulat[e] on the land and d[o] not pass away, then a trespass has occurred."

The primary significance of the "continuing"-"permanent" distinction is that where a nuisance or a trespass is permanent, plaintiff must bring his cause of action within the applicable state statute of limitations, and must seek all damages in one suit. Where the nuisance or trespass is continuing, the continuing nature of the wrong permits plaintiff to "bring successive actions as damages accrue until abatement takes place."[6]

In *Mel Foster Co. Properties v. American Oil Co.*,[7] a nuisance action involving gasoline leakage from defendants' properties onto plaintiff's land, the Iowa Supreme Court identified the artificiality of the "continuing" (temporary)-"permanent" distinction, noting that "[s]cientific knowledge enables society to successfully clean up pollution once thought to be permanent; it also reveals hidden dangers in chemicals once thought to be safe." Observing further that successive actions to recover temporary damages "were contrary to the goal of efficient legal remedies," the court refashioned the common law meaning of "permanent" to mean "indefinite," and held that permanent damages should be recovered even where the pollution has been abated and the interference might be termed temporary "[w]hen a nuisance results in contamination of property for an indefinite period of time[.]"

[C] *Private Nuisance*

[1] Elements

[a] Unreasonable Interference

Private nuisance has been described as an "unreasonable interference with the use or enjoyment of a property interest [held by] an owner or possessor of land."[8] An unreasonable intrusion upon the land of a property owner, be it hyper-amplified music or toxic contamination, will, therefore, constitute nuisance if it unreasonably interferes with the occupant's capacity to use, or quietly enjoy, the property.

The distinction between "use" and "enjoyment" is not semantic, as some low-level airborne pollution may not altogether prevent an occupant from using his property, but may, nevertheless, interfere with his enjoyment of it, as might a variety of intrusions by odor.[9] At common law, it is accepted

[6] Capogeannis v. Superior Court, 15 Cal. Rptr. 2d 796, 800 (Cal. 1993) (trespass); Restatement § 899 cmt. d (A continuing trespass "confers upon the possessor of the land an option to maintain a succession of actions based on a theory of continuing trespass, or to treat the thing on the land as an aggravation of the original trespass.").

[7] 427 N.W.2d 171, 174 (Iowa 1988).

[8] William Prosser, John W. Wade and Victor E. Schwartz, TORTS — CASES AND MATERIALS 811 (9th ed. 1993). Restatement § 821D, defines "private nuisance" as "a nontrespassory invasion of another's interest in the private use and enjoyment of land."

[9] James A. Henderson, Jr. and Richard N. Pearson, THE TORTS PROCESS 929 (3d ed. 1988).

generally that "smoke, offensive odors, noise or vibrations" that "materially interfere" with the possessor's "ordinary comfort" may constitute a nuisance.[10]

Illustrative is the action in *Crushed Stone Co. v. Moore*,[11] a suit to enjoin the operation of a rock quarry. Plaintiffs, adjacent homeowners, alleged that the earth vibrated due to defendant's blasts, that limestone dust spewing from defendant's operations covered their vegetation, homes, furniture and clothing. The trial court found defendant's operations to constitute a public and private nuisance, and permanently enjoined their operations. Affirming, the Oklahoma Supreme Court held that the explosions and the limestone dust blowing from defendant's operations, given the proximity of the plaintiffs' premises to the quarry site, amounted to a nuisance, and that it was within the court's equitable powers to permanently enjoin defendant's operations.

An unreasonable interference might take a wide range of forms. The pollution of a residence's well water would interfere both with a resident's use *and* enjoyment of a property. In one suit alleging tri-chloroethylene contamination, a North Carolina district court found plaintiffs' claim in nuisance deficient for want of evidence that the presence of the chemical in the water had prevented them from indulging in such activities as fishing and swimming.[12] A sulphurous smell emanating from a business in a city's downtown financial district might constitute a nuisance if emitted every morning for several hours, but might not if it were discernable each day only in the two hours before dawn, when the affected office buildings and sidewalks alike were largely empty.

[b] Current Possessory Interest

A private nuisance claim can only be brought by one with a current possessory or beneficial interest in the property. For example, in *Arnoldt v. Ashland Oil, Inc.*,[13] plaintiffs, private individuals residing within close proximity to an oil refinery, brought an action for private nuisance. In reversing the trial court, the Supreme Court of Appeals of West Virginia held, *inter alia*, that the plaintiffs who were merely residing in homes, but who were neither owners nor named tenants, did not have standing to bring the private nuisance action.

The plaintiffs had contended that they exercised a "common right" in the residences and therefore were entitled to be a party to a private nuisance action against the refinery. The trial court relied on this "common right"

---

[10] Baldwin v. McClendon, 288 So. 2d 761 (Ala. 1976) (hog parlor proximate to plaintiff's land) (collecting authority).

[11] 369 P.2d 811 (Okl. 1962).

[12] Carroll v. Litton Systems, Inc., 1990 WL 312969, *34 (W.D.N.C. 1990).

[13] 412 S.E. 2d 795 (W. Va. 1991).

to permit plaintiffs' standing, *i.e.*, they had a common right to breathe pollution-free air and therefore had standing. Reversing, the West Virginia court held that this would be the case in a public nuisance action — "the existence of a common right to breathe air free from air pollution" would grant plaintiffs standing — however, this is not the case in a private nuisance action. It stated: "A possessory interest in land exists in a person who has a physical relation to the land of a kind which gives a certain degree of physical control over the land, and an intent so to exercise such control as to exclude other members of society in general from any present occupation of the land[.]"

As the claim of an individual whose possessory or beneficial use interest has lapsed will not support a claim in private nuisance, so too a beneficial use interest that is terminable will not support a private nuisance claim for future damages extending beyond the conclusion of the beneficial use. By way of example, in *Davey Compressor Co. v. City of Delray Beach*,[14] a town brought a nuisance action against a company that contaminated the town's water supply by dumping toxic solvents. The town's property right in the subterranean water was pursuant to a "water consumptive use permit" issued by the state water management district. Finding for the town that it should be awarded damages, the court nonetheless affirmed future damages only up to the Dec. 10, 1997 date the town's extant use permit would expire. No nuisance damages could be awarded for prospective harm beyond that date, the court held, as "appellee failed to establish its right to the use of the groundwater" beyond the expiration of the permit.

[c] Intentional or Unintentional Conduct

Restatement § 822 establishes liability in private nuisance for an "invasion of another's interest in the private use and enjoyment of land" where the invasion is "(a) intentional and unreasonable, or (b) unintentional and otherwise actionable under the rules controlling liability for negligent or reckless conduct, or for abnormally dangerous conditions or activities." This approach reduces plaintiff's burden where defendant's conduct is intentional, *i.e.*, plaintiff need not show in addition that defendant's conduct was negligent, reckless, or that it constituted an abnormally dangerous activity.

For example, in *Wood v. Picollo*, discussed above,[15] the court rejected defendant's contention that to be found liable in private or public nuisance, it must be found to have acted negligently. In the court's words: "liability in nuisance is predicated upon unreasonable injury rather than on unreasonable conduct." Thus, while a claim grounded in negligence requires proof that defendant's conduct was somehow substandard, the claim of intentional private nuisance does not require evidence that defendant acted without due

[14] 613 So. 2d 60 (Fla. Ct. App. 1993).

[15] *Supra* note 2.

care under the circumstances. Accordingly, in *Morgan v. High Penn Oil Co.*,[16] an adjoining landowner claimed that defendant's oil refining operation "emitted nauseating gases and odors in great quantities, which invaded plaintiff's land and other tracts of land within a distance of two miles, in such density as to render persons of ordinary sensitiveness uncomfortable and sick." Liability in intentional nuisance could be found, the North Carolina Supreme Court stated, "regardless of the degree of care or skill exercised by him to avoid such injury."[17]

For plaintiff's claim in nuisance "without fault," *i.e.*, without the need to show defendant's negligence, recklessness, or the existence of an abnormally dangerous activity, the threshold issue is: What constitutes "intentional" conduct? With respect to private and public nuisance alike, Restatement § 825 provides that an invasion is "intentional" if the actor "(a) acts for the purpose of causing it, or (b) knows that it is resulting or substantially certain to result from it." Thus for her conduct to be "intentional," a defendant does not have to act for the purpose of causing the invasion or the harm. Rather, it is sufficient that she know it is "substantially certain to result[.]"[18]

In nuisance actions as well as claims brought in trespass, the intentional character of a defendant's conduct may be proved circumstantially. For example, *Bradley v. American Smelting and Refining Co.*[19] involved a nuisance and trespass suit brought by landowners against the operator of a copper smelter, alleging that the smelter deposited "microscopic, airborne particles of heavy metals" on their property. The court permitted itself the inference that defendant "intended" the interference on the basis of its assumptions that defendant "had to know that the solids propelled into the air by the warm gasses would settle back to earth somewhere. It had to know that a purpose of the tall [smoke]stack was to disperse the gas, smoke and minute solids over as large an area as possible[,] . . . but that . . . contamination, though slight, would follow. . . ."

[2] Nature of the Interest Interfered With

The particular use to which a property is put, and the sensitivities of the persons using the property, are proper factors in evaluating if defendant's conduct constitutes an *unreasonable* interference that rises to the level of a nuisance. Using the example introduced earlier, if the morning sulphurous smell enveloped the premises of a nursery school playground or a retirement residence, the proprietors of either could argue plausibly that the odor interfered substantially with their use of the properties for those purposes. If, on the other hand, the odor affected only adjoining properties engaged

---

16 77 S.E.2d 682 (N.C. 1953).

17 *Id.*, citing Restatement § 825.

18 *See generally* § 1.01[B], [C], *supra.*

19 709 P.2d 782 (Wash. 1985).

in automobile wrecking and salvage operations, any interference with either use or enjoyment might be too insubstantial to warrant a remedy in private nuisance.

Some decisions distinguish nuisance *per se* from nuisance *per accidens.* A nuisance *per se* would be any act that constitutes a nuisance "at all times and under any circumstances,"[20] such as, for example, the permanent or chronic contamination of plaintiff's property. Nuisance *per accidens*, on the other hand, requires the fact finder's evaluation of whether, "under all the surrounding circumstances . . . [defendant's action] substantially interferes with [plaintiff's] comfortable enjoyment[.]"[21]

Illustrative is *Vickridge 1st and 2nd Addition Homeowners Ass'n v. Catholic Diocese,*[22] which involved an appeal from an order permanently enjoining defendant from constructing a football field and baseball diamond. Defendants, owners of two private parochial high schools, decided to merge the two schools at a single site and construct a football field, a baseball diamond and a running track. Plaintiffs brought a private nuisance action alleging that the planned facilities would result in drainage and on-street parking problems, as well as area property devaluation.

Reversing the trial court's injunction, the Kansas Supreme Court observed that

> a court of equity may enjoin a threatened or anticipated nuisance [if the] proposed structure will be a nuisance per se, but a mere prospect, possibility or threat of future annoyance or injury from a structure or instrumentality which is not a nuisance per se is not grounds for an injunction and equity will not interfere where the apprehended injury or annoyance is doubtful, uncertain, speculative or contingent.

Resolution of the issue necessarily, the court found, depended upon several factors, such as the type of neighborhood, proximity of the proposed structure, frequency of its use, and the nature of the resulting harm. The court found that the evidence submitted at trial was scant on these points, as "there was no evidence before the court that any such changes [such as night games with floodlights and a public address system] would be made[.]"

An owner or occupier's departure from a premises will not preclude a subsequent action in nuisance where the interference with another's rights of enjoyment of the property is of a continuing nature. A landowner who

---

20 Vickridge 1st and 2nd Addition Homeowners Ass'n v. Catholic Diocese, 510 P.2d 1296 (Kan. 1976).

21 *Id.* Successful nuisance claims *per accidens* have resulted in orders in abatement or damages for invasions by particulate matter such as limestone dust. *E.g.*, Crushed Stone Co. v. Moore, 369 P.2d 811 (Okla. 1962) (the injury claimed by plaintiff included, inter alia, aggravation of allergies and worsening of one resident's nervous condition).

22 510 P.2d 1296 (Kan. 1973).

has polluted or contaminated a property and then sold or leased it to another may remain liable "for the continuation of the nuisance" after the transfer, until the transferee "discovers the condition and has reasonable opportunity to abate it."[23] Significantly, however, although the vendor may be liable in nuisance to holders of rights to other property, the vendee cannot himself sue the vendor in nuisance. The federal appeals court in *Philadelphia Electric Company v. Hercules, Inc.*[24] so concluded, reasoning that a landholder's duty not to unreasonably interfere with use and enjoyment of land is owed to the landholder's *neighbors*, and not to the transferee of the land.[25] Thus unless the vendee can show that the seller fraudulently concealed a contamination nuisance, the buyer of a property may be assumed to have realized that a property's purchase price "reflect[ed] the possibility of environmental risks, even if the exact condition . . . was not discovered."[26]

The interference must be real and substantial, and not merely imagined. For example, in *Adkins v. Thomas Solvent Company*,[27] defendant Thomas Solvent Company owned and operated a chemical company. Twenty-two plaintiffs alleged that the company and other defendants contaminated the ground water near their property by improperly handling and storing wastes. The evidence showed conclusively that the alleged discharge by the defendants never reached, and never would reach, the plaintiffs' property.

Reinstating the trial court's dismissal, the Michigan Supreme Court concluded that the trial court had properly found that the plaintiffs failed to trace any significant interference with the use and enjoyment of land to an action of the defendants. Noting that the basis of the plaintiffs' complaint was the negative publicity surrounding the contamination of ground water in the area causing diminution in their property values, the Michigan court held that unfounded fears about dangers in the vicinity of property stemming from negative publicity did not constitute a significant interference with the use and enjoyment of land.

[3] Corrective Justice and Utilitarianism

Nowhere in tort law are the policies of corrective justice and utilitarianism in sharper conflict than in the law of nuisance. Corrective justice posits that when a defendant's conduct substantially interferes with the current

---

[23] Restatement § 840A ("Continuing Liability After Transfer of Land.").

[24] 762 F.2d 303 (3d Cir. 1985).

[25] The appeals court stated: "We believe that this result is consonant with the historical role of private nuisance law as a means of efficiently resolving conflicts between *neighboring* contemporaneous land uses. . . . Neighbors, unlike purchasers of the land upon which the nuisance exists, have no opportunity to protect themselves through inspection and negotiation." *Id.*, 762 F.2d at 314.

[26] *Id.*

[27] 487 N.W.2d 715 (Mich. 1992).

possessory or use interest of another in land, the complainant should be permitted to receive not only damages for the interference but also an injunction against its continuation. The right to an injunction, or to an order of abatement, the corrective justice approach urges, holds true no matter how great the economic interest of defendant's conduct, and without regard to how much one defendant's economic interest or investment may outweigh the plaintiff's economic interest. As expressed by an early 20th Century New York decision,[28] which involved the pollution by defendant's paper mill of water passing the property of a downstream riparian owner, "Although the damage to the plaintiff may be slight as compared with the defendant's expense in abating the condition, that is not a good reason for refusing an injunction. Neither courts of equity nor law can be guided by such a rule, for if followed to its logical conclusion it would deprive the poor litigant of his little property by giving it to those already rich. . . ."[29]

To be distinguished, a utilitarian approach affords great solicitude to the benefits a defendant's activities confer upon a community, and the investment defendant has made, in relationship to the magnitude of the economic harm suffered by the plaintiff. An early utilitarian holding was *Madison v. Ducktown Sulphur, Copper & Iron Co.*,[30] in which the court, refusing an injunction to farmers whose property suffered from sulphurous smoke emanating from defendant's copper mining open air "roasting" process, explained:

> In order to protect by the injunction several small tracts of land, aggregating in value less than $1000, we are asked to destroy other property worth nearly $2,000,000[.] . . . [An injunction] would be practically confiscation of the property of the defendants for the benefit of the complainants — an appropriation without compensation. . . .

---

[28] Whalen v. Union Bag and Paper Co., 101 N.E. 805 (N.Y. 1913).

[29] *See also* the seminal decision in Bamford v. Turnley, Court of Exchequer Chamber, 3 B. & S. 66 (1886). *Bamford* involved a large estate that was divided into lots which were later sold as building sites for houses. The defendant later began to construct his house by placing a brick kiln on one of his lots and firing bricks. Plaintiff brought a nuisance action for damages complaining of smoke and fumes from the defendant's kiln.

Reversing the judgment for the defendant, the Exchequer Chamber stated:

"those acts necessary for common and ordinary use and occupation of land and houses may be done without subjecting those who do them to an action. However, this principle would not accommodate those situations where what has been done was not the using of land in a common and ordinary way, but in an exceptional manner — not unnatural nor unusual, but not the common and ordinary use of land. . . . It is as much to the advantage of one owner as to the other owner; for the nuisance complained of, as a result of ordinary use of his neighbor's land, he himself will create in using his own, and the reciprocal nuisances are of a comparatively trifling character.

The court went on to say that even conceding that defendant's activity was for the public good, other demonstrably beneficial activities, such as railroads, are nonetheless required to bear the cost of losses occasioned by their activities.

[30] 83 S.W. 658 (Tenn. 1904).

Where the harm to plaintiff's land is substantial, many modern decisions have taken the corrective justice approach and have declined to permit defendant to exculpate itself by showing that the value of its conduct outweighed the gravity of any harm to plaintiff.[31] *Crushed Stone Co. v. Moore*[32] provides an illustrative corrective justice rationale for its holding, including its refusal to consider the utility of defendant's activities. In that action, operations at defendant's limestone quarry produced large amounts of rock dust as well as noise and vibrations from blasting. Defendants showed that their operations were planned to minimize dust, noise and vibrations; that they had recently invested some $13,000 to control the ill effects complained of; and that the value of the quarry was "well over $300,000."

The trial court found that the quarry amounted to a nuisance and ordered that all quarrying operations cease. On appeal, the Oklahoma Supreme Court held that the injunction was proper despite the contention that its issuance will cause defendants "grossly disproportionate hardship . . . in comparison with the . . . lesser injuries plaintiffs will suffer" from continued quarrying. Recognizing that in some cases considerations of the public's interest in the continuation of a business might require a "comparative injury" analysis that could result in permitting the business to continue upon payment of money damages to plaintiffs, the Oklahoma court decided that this was not such a case:

> [T]his court is among those holding that where damages in an action at law will not give plaintiffs an adequate remedy against a business operated in such a way that it has become a nuisance, and such operation causes plaintiffs substantial and irremediable injury, they are entitled, as a matter of right, to have same abated, by injunction . . . notwithstanding the comparative benefits conferred thereby or the comparative injury resulting therefrom.

Similarly, in *Berg v. Reaction Motors Division*,[33] the court rejected utilitarian considerations. For over a year, defendant regularly test-fired

---

[31] For example, in Jost v. Dairyland Power Coop., 172 N.W.2d 647, 653-54 (Wis. 1969), plaintiffs, crop growers with land proximate to defendant's coal-burning electric generating plant, claimed that the plant's daily discharge of approximately 90 tons of sulfur dioxide gas into the atmosphere whitened alfalfa leaves, killed or damaged pine and other trees, and generally lessened land values as a consequence of continuing crop loss. Rejecting appellee's argument that it should have been permitted to introduce evidence of the social and economic utility of its generating plant, the Wisconsin Supreme Court stated: "Whether its economic or social importance dwarfed the claim of a small farmer is of no consequence in this lawsuit. It will not be said that, because a great and socially useful enterprise will be liable in damages, an injury small by comparison will go unredressed. . . . To contend that a public utility, in pursuit of its praiseworthy and legitimate enterprise, can, in effect, deprive others of the full use of their property without compensation, poses a theory unknown to the law of Wisconsin, and in our opinion would constitute the taking of property without due process of law. . . ."

[32] 369 P.2d 811 (Okla. 1962).

[33] 181 A.2d 487 (N.J. 1962).

rocket engines pursuant to its contract with the Air Force to produce supersonic aircraft. Property owners and residents near the test site repeatedly complained about resultant noise, vibrations, and air blasts. The New Jersey Supreme Court held for plaintiffs, even though no negligence was found, placing considerable importance on the fact that damages were sought, rather than an injunction:

> . . . It may be assumed, for present purposes, that the defendant's activities were conducted with great care and had great public utility and that a court would hesitate to enjoin them notwithstanding the resulting structural damage to the neighboring property. But the issue before us is not whether there should be an injunction but whether the defendant may reasonably be expected to make monetary payment. On that issue there would appear to be little room for difference of opinion — every consideration of fairness and justness dictates that the defendant at least make its neighbors whole for the structural damage it caused.

The Restatement attempts to reconcile the corrective justice approach with the utilitarian one. Restatement § 826 provides that an intentional invasion of another's use of land is unreasonable if "the gravity of the harm outweighs the utility of the conduct[.]"[34] Where, in contrast, the utility of defendant's conduct outweighs the burden on plaintiff, and money damages can compensate for plaintiff's harm without causing financial ruin to defendant, money damages, and not an injunction, are an appropriate response.

While not expressly relying upon Restatement § 826, in *Boomer v. Atlantic Cement Co., Inc.*[35] the New York Court of Appeals effectively accepted the Restatement's invitation to permit nuisance-creating but beneficial activities to continue their operations upon the condition that they compensate neighboring landowners for their hardship. *Boomer* involved the wide-scale and conceded nuisance and trespass committed by a large cement plant. In proceedings below, a nuisance was found, and temporary damages were awarded, but plaintiffs' application for an injunction was denied. Writing for New York's highest court, Judge Bergan's opinion noted that the resolution of air quality issues "is likely to require massive public expenditure and to demand more than any local community can accomplish and to depend on regional and interstate controls."

It ultimately adopted a utilitarian approach that weighed the hardships imposed upon plaintiffs against the economic consequences of the requested injunction, stating: "The ground for denial of injunction, notwithstanding the finding both that there is a nuisance and that plaintiffs have been damaged substantially, is the large disparity in economic consequences of the nuisance and of the injunction."

---

[34] Restatement § 826(a).

[35] 257 N.E.2d 870 (N.Y. 1970).

Boomer recognized that to deny the injunction was to depart from *Whalen*'s corrective justice-no balancing approach discussed above. After discussing authority in which conditions properly considered continuing nuisances are nevertheless resolve by awards of permanent damages, "past, present and future," the court concluded:

> Thus it seems fair to both sides to grant permanent damages to plaintiffs which will terminate this private litigation. The theory of damage is the "servitude on land" of plaintiffs imposed by defendant's nuisance. . . . The judgment, by allowance of permanent damages imposing a servitude on land, which is the basis of the actions, would preclude future recovery by plaintiffs or their grantees.

In contrast, in *Carpenter v. The Double R Cattle Company, Inc.*,[36] the Idaho Supreme Court rejected the intermediate approach of *Boomer* and Restatement § 826(b) and declined to entertain a petition for nuisance damages against an economically significant regional industry. In *Carpenter*, the plaintiffs were homeowners who lived near the Double R Cattle feed lot operated and owned by the defendants. The plaintiffs contended that the spread and accumulation of manure, pollution of river and ground water, odor, insect infestation, increase in birds, dust, and noise at the feedlot constituted a nuisance. At trial, no nuisance was found. A court of appeals reversed, on the basis that the trial court did not give a jury instruction based upon Restatement § 826(b), which allows a finding of a nuisance even though the gravity of harm is outweighed by the utility of the conduct if the harm is "serious" and the payment of damages is "feasible" without forcing the business to discontinue.

The Idaho Supreme Court vacated, refusing to recognize Restatement § 826(b) as the law in Idaho. In so doing, the court noted Idaho's economic dependence upon agriculture, lumber, mining and industrial development, and reasoned that if the utility of the conduct and other criteria considered by the trial court were eliminated, an unreasonable burden would be placed upon industry.[37]

[D] *Public Nuisance*

[1] Generally

Public nuisance is defined widely as "an unreasonable interference with a right common to the general public."[38] Restatement § 821B states that "circumstances" that might give rise to the conclusion that defendant's

---

[36] 701 P.2d 222 (Idaho 1985).

[37] In a sharply worded dissent, Judge Bistline charged the majority with being a prisoner of a visualization of Idaho that had passed with the end of the cattle drives, criticizing the majority's refusal to make the important cattle industry at least pay for the hardship it causes to contiguous property owners.

[38] Restatement § 821B.

activity creates an *unreasonable* interference with a public right include evaluation of: "(a) whether the conduct involves a substantial interference with the public health, the public safety, the public peace, the public comfort or the public convenience, or (b) whether the conduct is of a continuing nature or has produced a permanent or long-lasting effect and, to the actor's knowledge, has a substantial detrimental effect upon the public right."

[2] Proper Complainants

Who may bring a suit in public nuisance? The answer to this question is affected by whether the suit is for damages, or for equitable relief, such as an injunction or an order in abatement. A public nuisance suit for damages may be brought by a public official or a public agency, or it may be brought by a private individual or business that has "suffered harm of a kind different from that suffered by other members of the public[.]"[39] For private party public nuisance claimants, this predicate showing of injury "different in kind" from that suffered by the public generally is known as the "special injury" rule.

For a public nuisance suit seeking an injunction or an order of abatement, plaintiffs may be: (1) a public body or agency bringing suit on behalf of the public; (2) a private party that, as above, has suffered "special injury," *i.e.*, injury "different in kind" from that suffered by other members of the public; or (3) the class representative(s) of a class action; or (4) one with standing to bring a "citizen" suit under state or federal law.

For the most part, the public nuisance remedy is enforced by a government body, such as a town, on behalf of the public. For example, depending upon the common law of a particular jurisdiction, a municipality might lodge a claim in public nuisance against a manufacturing facility discharging chemical effluent that is contaminating a nearby lake, killing aquatic life and precluding recreational sports and swimming. If the contamination is substantial, and the effect would take measurable time and expense to eliminate, the claim in public nuisance would state that the manufacturer's conduct has created an unreasonable interference with rights common to the public. The rights interfered with would be the public health, public safety, and the public convenience associated with fishing and aquatic sports.

Defendant's conduct may create a cause of action in public nuisance even where "neither the plaintiff nor the defendant acts in the exercise of private property rights."[40] For example, in *Burgess v. M/V Tomano*,[41] commercial clam diggers and fishermen were permitted to pursue a public nuisance claim, premised on an off coast oil spill, even though it was "uncontroverted" that "the right to fish or to harvest clams in Maine's coastal waters

---

[39] Restatement § 821C ("Who Can Recover For Public Nuisance").

[40] Philadelphia Electric Co. v. Hercules, Inc., 762 F.2d 303 (3d Cir. 1985).

[41] 370 F. Supp. 247 (D. Me. 1973).

is not the private right of any individual, but is a public right held by the State 'in trust for the common benefit of the people.'"[42]

[3] Special Injury Rule

While suits in public nuisance are usually brought by public bodies, such as a state or a political subdivision, under certain circumstances a private individual may sue in public nuisance. An individual may sue another in public nuisance where he proves that there is a substantial interference with a right common to the public, and additionally, that he has suffered special harm that is different from that burdening the public.

To illustrate, it would not suffice for the individual claimant in the lake contamination example above to bring an action in public nuisance claiming only that as a recreational fisherman and a swimmer, defendant's conduct interfered with his ability to pursue those activities safely. To so claim, he would merely be stating the harm the community suffered, without any specific, individual, and *different* harm he himself suffered.

On the other hand, what if our potential plaintiff owned the fishery with the contract to stock the lake with trout fingerlings on a periodic basis? If his contract with the town was canceled because the water became polluted, he would suffer the economic loss of that contract. He thereby would suffer an injury that was quite different from that suffered by the community at large. In this latter setting, our fishery owner might lodge a claim in public nuisance against the manufacturer even though the manufacturer's conduct encroached in no way upon fishery property or the owner's right to enjoy his property. Similarly, as one court has stated, "in substantially all of those cases in which commercial fishermen using public waters have sought [nuisance] damages for the pollution or other tortious invasion of those waters, they have been permitted to recover[,]"[43] in that each can show "he has suffered a damage particular to him — that is, damage different in kind, rather than simply in degree, from that sustained by the public generally."[44]

Personal physical injury is ordinarily held to be "special injury" under public nuisance doctrine. The rational for so holding was stated by the court in *Anderson v. W.R. Grace & Co.*,[45] a claim by residents that defendant's introduction of toxic chemicals into groundwater caused severe personal injuries, including childhood leukemia. Finding plaintiffs could, as individuals, bring a claim in public nuisance, the court explained: "[W]hen a plaintiff has sustained 'special or peculiar damage,' he or she may maintain an individual action . . . Injuries to a person's health are by their nature

[42] *Id.* at 249-250.

[43] *Id.* 370 F. Supp. at 250.

[44] *Id.*, 370 F. Supp. at 250.

[45] 628 F. Supp. 1219, 1233 (D. Mass. 1986).

'special and particular,' and cannot properly be said to be common or public . . . . As plaintiffs allege that they have suffered a variety of illnesses as a result of exposure to the contaminated water, they have standing to maintain this nuisance action."[46]

In *Anderson*, where plaintiff claimed personal physical injury as well as property damage arising from defendant's contamination of groundwater, the court stated that plaintiffs claiming in public nuisance "may only seek to obtain damages for their special injuries."[47] Thus, the court added, if public nuisance was proved, plaintiffs would be able to recover for "(1) the loss in rental value of their property, if any, (2) compensation for physical injuries, and (3) upon a showing of independent personal injury, damages for emotional distress."[48]

[4] Environmental Harm

A key aspect of the cause of action in public nuisance is that it provides another arrow in the quiver of state and local government in their efforts to reach generators and disposers of hazardous waste. Representative is a New York appellate court's decision in *New York v. Schenectady Chemicals, Inc.*[49] Since 1906, Schenectady had manufactured paints and other chemical products. To dispose of its wastes, Schenectady contracted with an independent contractor, one Mr. Loeffel. From the 1950's to the mid-1960's, Loeffel simply dumped raw wastes into lagoons directly above a major aquifer serving thousands of residents.

Bringing suit, New York set forth eight causes of action, the last five relying upon a nuisance theory. The State asserted that Schenectady created a public nuisance by the manner in which the wastes were disposed; that the generation and disposal of the wastes constituted an ultra-hazardous activity; and that Schenectady negligently permitted the creation and maintenance of a public nuisance by hiring an incompetent contractor.

In holding for the State, the court reasoned that Schenectady had created and was responsible for a public nuisance. Further concluding that Schenectady was vicariously liable under agency principles of law for Loeffel's conduct of disposing of the wastes, the court wrote: "everyone who creates a nuisance or participates in the creation or maintenance of a nuisance are liable jointly and severally for the wrong and injury done thereby [.]" *Schenectady* confirms the general principle that a generator of

---

[46] *Id.* at 1233.

[47] *Id.* at 1233.

[48] *Id.*

[49] 459 N.Y.S.2d 971 (App. 1983), *aff'd as modified* 479 N.Y.S.2d 1010 (App. 1984).

environmentally harmful material cannot immunize itself from liability by the simple expedient of retaining another for the disposal of the waste.[50]

[5] Economic Loss

What of an otherwise actionable nuisance from which plaintiff suffers economic loss, such as lost use or business down time, but no personal physical injury or property damage? The leading decision in *Louisiana ex rel. Guste v. M/V Testbank*,[51] involved a collision of the M/V Sea Daniel, an inbound bulk carrier, with the outbound M/V Testbank in the Gulf outlet of the Mississippi River. Containers on the Testbank containing PCP's were lost overboard.

Approximately forty-one lawsuits were brought by local fisherman, owners of seafood restaurants, marina and boat rentals, tackle and bait shops and the like, claiming loss of business. The defendant moved for summary judgment for all claims based on economic loss unaccompanied by physical damage to property. The trial court granted the defendant's motion as to most of the shore-based businesses, but preserved the claims asserted by commercial oystermen, shrimpers, crabbers and fishermen who had made commercial use of the waters. The court found that the commercial fishing interests deserved special protection.

Relying on *Robins Dry Dock & Repair Co. v. Flint*,[52] which denied recovery to a plaintiff for negligently inflicted interference with economic relations, the court of appeals affirmed the doctrine that claims for economic loss unaccompanied by physical damage to a proprietary interest were not recoverable. The *Robins* plaintiff was a time charterer of a steamship, who sued the defendant, a dry dock repair yard, for negligently damaging the plaintiff's propeller thus extending the length of time the plaintiff's ship was out of commission. That the *Testbank* plaintiffs' claims were alternatively styled in public nuisance should not alter this conclusion, the appeals court found, noting "we see no jurisprudential advantage in permitting the use of nuisance theory to skirt the *Robins* rule."

In another noteworthy waterway contamination case, *Pruitt v. Allied Chemical Corp.*,[53] the plaintiffs brought an action for negligence and nuisance, claiming the defendant polluted the James River and Chesapeake Bay. The plaintiffs claimed that defendants discharged the chemical

---

[50] The trial court had found five bases for holding Schenectady liable:

Moreover, defendant could be found liable for Loeffel's acts if: (1) it was negligent in retaining an incompetent contractor; (2) it failed, with knowledge thereof, to remedy or prevent an unlawful act; (3) the work itself was illegal; (4) the work itself was inherently dangerous; or (5) the work involved the creation of a nuisance.

See Restatement § 427B (liability for actions of independent contractor).

[51] 752 F.2d 1019 (5th Cir. 1985), *cert. denied*, 477 U.S. 903 (1986).

[52] 275 U.S. 303 (1927). *See* Chapter 19 *supra*.

[53] 523 F. Supp. 975 (E.D. Va. 1981).

"Kepone" into the waters, thereby contaminating the marine life. The class of plaintiffs included a variety of businesses which derived their incomes from enterprises related to either the harvesting or sale of marine life within the waters, and comprised regional "commercial fishermen; seafood wholesalers, retailers, distributors and processors; restaurateurs; marina, boat tackle and baitshop owners; and employees of all the above groups."

The district court found the defendants liable on a "constructive property" theory, *i.e.*, some of the plaintiffs had "a constructive property interest in the Bay's harvestable species." Having found liability, the court was presented with the question of who maintains a sufficient property interest in the contaminated waters so as to entitle them to receive lost profits from the defendant. Although every user of the Bay, either direct, as in the case of fishermen, or indirect, as in the case of restauranteurs, had suffered some degree of economic harm, they all cannot be entitled to recover from the defendant. In an effort to "tailor justice," the court held that plaintiffs who "suffered legally cognizable damages" were those whose damages were sufficiently direct, such as fishermen, boat, tackle and bait shop owners. Those whose damages existed, but were insufficiently direct so as to be legally cognizable, included seafood wholesalers, retailers, distributors and processors and restauranteurs.

[6] Prospective Nuisance

A court may grant an injunction or an order of abatement to turn away the risk of future harm where the risk of harm is substantial and the harm is imminent. For example, in *Village of Wilsonville v. SCA Services, Inc.,*[54] the defendant, SCA Services Inc., had operated a chemical-waste landfill site since 1977 within and adjacent to the village of Wilsonville. The plaintiff filed a complaint alleging that the operation of the defendant's chemical-waste-disposal site presented a public nuisance and a hazard to the health of the citizens of the village, county and state. The site was located above an abandoned coal mine, and expert testimony indicated that there was a possibility that pillar support failure could occur with added stress.

In substantiating their theory of nuisance, the plaintiffs presented expert testimony at trial that the site constituted a nuisance, alleging that the subsidence (diminished support) of the earth underneath the site made it unsafe. The plaintiff's expert went on to say that if ruptures in the earth occurred, artesian water could reach the trenches, thereby contaminating the water. The plaintiffs also argued through expert testimony that if sufficient oxygen reached the chemicals in the trenches, an explosive interaction could occur. Residents of the village testified that they had experienced symptoms such as headaches, runny noses, burning in the eyes, nausea and shortness of breath from the odors.

---

[54] 426 N.E.2d 824 (Ill. 1981).

The Illinois Supreme Court concluded that the plaintiffs had sufficiently established by a preponderance of the evidence that the chemical-waste-disposal site was a nuisance both presently and prospectively. Finding it to be highly probable that the chemical-waste-disposal site would bring about substantial injury, the court held that injunctive relief was appropriate, and quoted Dean Prosser's observation that "[o]ne distinguishing feature of equitable relief is that it may granted upon the threat of harm which has not yet occurred[.]"

§ 18.02 TRESPASS

[A] *Overview*

Trespass protects plaintiff's interest in the surface land itself, the earth or other material beneath the surface, and "the air space above it."[55] For this reason, depending upon the seriousness of the contamination of plaintiff's land or environment, defendant may be liable in trespass where the pollution or contamination interferes with plaintiff's possessory rights in the land, the land beneath it, or the ambient air.

Restatement § 158 provides:

> One is subject to liability to another for trespass, irrespective of whether he thereby causes harm to any legally protected interest of the other, if he intentionally
>
> (a) enters land in the possession of the other, or causes a thing or a third person to do so, or
>
> (b) remains on the land, or
>
> (c) fails to remove from the land a thing which he is under a duty to remove.

Who is a proper party plaintiff to a claim in trespass? In trespass, the interest protected is the right of "exclusive possession and physical condition of land."[56] Accordingly, a plaintiff pursuing a cause of action based on trespass must satisfy the court that he has a "possessory interest" in the property.[57]

[55] Restatement § 158 cmt. i. General discussions of the trespass cause of action include Putt and Bolla, *Invasion of Radioactive Particles as a Common Law Trespass: An Overview*, 3 Urb. L. Rev. 206 (1980); Comment, *Remedies for Intangible Intrusions: The Distinction Between Trespass and Nuisance Actions Against Lawfully Zoned Businesses in California*, 17 U.C. Davis L. Rev. 389 (1986).

[56] Restatement § 157 et seq. (Scope Note to Chapter 7, "Invasions of the Interest in the Exclusive Possession of Land and Its Physical Condition (Trespass on Land)" at 275). *See* discussion at § 18.01[B], *supra*.

[57] Carroll v. Litton Systems, Inc., 1990 WL 312969, 56 (W.D.N.C. 1990) (In a trichloroethylene case where plaintiffs claimed that they were exposed to defendant's chemical through groundwater, the court found that several of the plaintiffs' did not have a possessory interest in the wells claimed to be contaminated and therefore could not pursue an action based on trespass.).

Unlike claims in nuisance that can only be pursued by one with a current possessory or beneficial use interest in a property, a claimant in a trespass suit does not have to be the property's current or immediately prospective occupant. Restatement § 157 defines "possession" in the trespass context in such a way as to include one with a reversionary interest, such as a landlord or other owner not in current possession of the land or premises, if no other person is in current possession.

The claim in trespass is sometimes confused with that for private nuisance. As explained by a leading authority, "[t]he distinction which is now accepted is that trespass is an invasion of the plaintiff's interest in the exclusive possession of his land, while nuisance is an interference with his use and enjoyment of it."[58]

[B] *The Requirement of Intent*

Trespass is an intentional tort, and plaintiff must prove that an alleged trespasser had the requisite mental state to commit the tort. As discussed earlier in reference to intentional nuisance, Restatement § 8A states that the word "intent" is used in tort law ". . . to denote that the actor desires to cause the consequences of his act, or that he believes that the consequences are substantially certain to result from it."[59] An actor's awareness of the high degree of likelihood that a trespass will result from his activities may be proved circumstantially, as it was in *Bradley v. American Smelting,*[60] discussed above, where the smelter's tall smokestack alone evidenced its knowledge that trespassory particulate matter could be dispersed, but not eliminated, through release high above ground.

Accordingly, plaintiff need not prove that the defendant subjectively desired to trespass on the property. Rather, plaintiff must only prove that defendant intended the act that resulted in the trespass, *i.e.*, that defendant's act was volitional, and done with knowledge to a substantial certainty that the act would result in introduction of the substance onto plaintiff's property.[61] For this reason defendant may not defend an action in trespass by proving that he acted with even a reasonably mistaken belief that his actions, and the consequent material invasion, were authorized by plaintiff, or that the property was owned by another who had given apparent consent to the intrusion.[62] For example, in one suit involving a fuel-oil distributor's mistaken fuel delivery to a residence and accidental spillage resulting

---

[58] PROSSER AND KEETON ON THE LAW OF TORTS 622 (5th ed. 1984).

[59] *See generally* § 1.01[B], [C], *supra.*

[60] 709 Wash. 2d 782 (Wash. 1985).

[61] See Restatement § 158 cmt. i: "It is enough that an act is done with knowledge that it will to a substantial certainty result in the entry of a foreign matter."

[62] *See* Restatement § 164 ("Intrusions Under Mistake").

therefrom, the court rejected as a defense defendant's claim that it acted in a reasonable belief that the fuel had been ordered.[63]

[C] *The Requisite Physical Invasion and Harm*

In most jurisdictions, invasions of plaintiff's property that amount to trespass may also, if they interfere with plaintiff's use and enjoyment of the property, be actionable in nuisance. In such circumstances, "plaintiff may have his choice" of a claim in trespass or in nuisance, "or may proceed upon both."[64] It does not follow, however, that a claim in nuisance ordinarily imports facts sufficient for a claim in trespass.[65]

At common law, an actionable trespass was complete upon the tangible invasion of another's property. Nuisance, in contrast, requires a showing that defendant's conduct, invasory or otherwise, constitutes a "substantial and unreasonable" interference with plaintiff's use and enjoyment. As explained by Professor William H. Rodgers, "The distinction between [trespass and nuisance] was the difference between the old action of trespass and the action on the case: if there was a direct and immediate physical invasion of plaintiff's property, as by casting stones or water on it, it was a trespass; if the invasion was indirect, as by seepage of water, it was a nuisance. . . . [Today,] in trespass cases defendant's conduct typically results in an encroachment by 'something' upon plaintiff's exclusive right of possession."[66]

The requirement that a trespass involve invasion by a "thing" was considered and rejected by the Oregon Supreme Court in *Martin v. Reynolds Metals Co.*,[67] a claim involving the settling upon plaintiff's property of gaseous and particulate fluorides from defendant's aluminum smelter. Rejecting defendant's claim that plaintiff's claim should fail for want of any tangible trespassory "object" or "thing," the court answered:

> It is quite possible that in an earlier day when science had not yet peered into the molecular and atomic world of small particles, the courts could not fit an invasion through unseen physical instrumentalities into the requirement that a trespass can result only form a direct invasion. But

---

[63] Serota v. M. & M. Utilities, Inc., 55 Misc. 2d 286, 285 N.Y.S.2d 121, 124 (1967) ("Obviously, the defendant intended to come upon plaintiff's land and make an oil delivery and did not intend to commit a trespass or intentionally to cast oil upon plaintiff's land. His innocence and his mistaken belief that his visit was authorized is of no moment since his intent is clearly shown to have been to deliver oil. This unauthorized act, resulting in whatever damages which may have occurred, rendered him liable.")

[64] Mangini v. Aerojet-General Corp., 281 Cal. Rptr. 827, 230 Cal. App. 3d 1125 (Cal. Ct. App. 1991) (quoting Restatement § 821D cmt. e) (plaintiff's land contamination claim in nuisance, trespass, and other common law causes of action).

[65] *See* discussion at § 18.01[B], *supra*.

[66] William H. Rodgers, Jr., ENVIRONMENTAL LAW § 2.13 at 154 (1977).

[67] 342 P.2d 790 (1959), *cert. denied*, 362 U.S. 918 (1960).

in this atomic age even the uneducated know the great and awful force contained in the atom and what it can do to a man's property if it is released. In fact, the now famous equation $E = MC^2$ has taught us that mass and energy are equivalents and that our concept of "things" must be reframed.

The *Martin* holding that entry of invisible gases or microscopic particles may alone constitute a trespass has gained only scattered acceptance. In Dean Prosser's words, "the historical requirement of an intrusion by a person or some tangible thing seems a sounder way to go about protecting the exclusive right to the use of property."[68]

A defendant may be liable in trespass even where the trespassory invasion causes no compensable harm to plaintiff's property or interest in the property.[69] The invasion of plaintiff's property need not be direct, if plaintiff can prove that an intentional act of defendant resulted in the harm. Thus the causal intervention of natural conditions, such as deterioration, wind, or rain, in initiating or exacerbating the trespass will not absolve defendant of liability.[70] Illustratively, this approach was applied by the Oklahoma Supreme Court in one action where plaintiff claimed that defendant's dumping of asphalt waste on land contiguous to plaintiff's fish pond eventually resulted in the pollution of the pond.[71]

As in the doctrine of continuing nuisance, a polluter's failure to remove a pollutant or a contaminant from plaintiff's land may represent a "continuing" tort. The significance of the designation "continuing trespass" is primarily that of relieving some of the strictures of limitations periods within which the possessor would have to bring a toxic tort claim.[72]

That the plaintiff may be entitled to an injunction or to nominal damages for a technical or minimal trespass does not resolve the question of what level of harm plaintiff must show to receive compensatory damages. The leading Alabama decision of *Borland v. Sanders Lead Co.*[73] phrased the requirement in terms of "substantial" harm. *Borland* involved asphalt piled

---

[68] PROSSER AND KEETON ON TORTS 72 (5th. ed. 1984).

[69] One may be "subject to another for trespass, irrespective of whether he thereby causes harm to any legally protected interest of the other [.]" Restatement § 158.

[70] Comment i to Restatement § 158 gives these examples: "[O]ne who piles sand so close to his boundary that by force of gravity alone it slides down on to his neighbor's land, or who builds an embankment so that during ordinary rainfalls the dirt is washed from it upon adjacent lands, becomes a trespasser on the other's land."

[71] Rushing v. Hooper-McDonald, Inc., 300 So. 2d 94 (Ala. 1974) ("This court holds that it is not necessary that the asphalt or foreign matter be thrown or dumped directly and immediately upon the plaintiff's land but that it is sufficient if the act is done so that it will to a substantial certainty result in the entry of the asphalt or foreign matter onto the real property that the plaintiff possesses.")

[72] Restatement § 161 cmt. b.

[73] 369 So. 2d 523, 529 (Ala. 1979).

in a manner that permitted it to spill onto plaintiff's property. The Alabama court stated:

> a plaintiff must show (1) an invasion affecting an interest in the exclusive possession of his property; (2) and intentional doing of the act which results in the invasion; (3) reasonable foreseeability that the act done could result in an invasion of plaintiff's possessory interest; and (4) substantial damage to the res.

Consistent with a requirement that to receive compensatory damages plaintiff must show a substantial intrusion, in a suit involving trichloroethylene contamination of well water, a North Carolina federal district court held that a "de minimis [chemical] encroachments" are not enough to sustain an action in either trespass or nuisance.[74] Requiring a showing of "actual and substantial damages," the court held that the presence of the chemical, trichloroethylene, in the plaintiffs' wells was "trivial" because the chemical was present in the general atmosphere in even greater quantities than those found in the plaintiffs' wells. Also, the plaintiffs had neither shown any current physical harm nor that they were "reasonably certain" to suffer any harm in the future.[75]

---

[74] Carroll v. Litton Systems, Inc., 1990 WL 312969 (W.D.N.C. 1990).

[75] *Id.* at *58–*59.

CHAPTER 19

ECONOMIC TORTS

SYNOPSIS

§ 19.01 FRAUDULENT MISREPRESENTATION

[A] *Overview*

The tort of fraudulent misrepresentation or deceit provides for recovery for pure economic loss, unassociated with other injury.[1] Punitive damages,[2] can also be recovered where malice is proven. The essence of the tort is an intentional or reckless misrepresentation which induces a victim's reliance and causes economic damages. Fraudulent misrepresentation should be distinguished from potential liability for negligent or innocent misrepresentations.[3]

Misrepresentations can exist in the context of numerous other torts. For example, defendants who intentionally misrepresent that poison is candy, inducing the victim to eat it, or advise a photographer that it is safe to step back, intentionally causing his fall into the Grand Canyon, have committed batteries through misrepresentation.

The tort of fraudulent misrepresentation is designed to address economic (pecuniary) loss. The elements of this tort represent an attempt to balance the benefits of redressing fraudulent deception, with the recognition that ramifications of such deception in a purely economic, rather than physical, context can be overwhelming.

[B] *Definition*

The tort of fraudulent misrepresentation consists of five elements: (1) a material misrepresentation; (2) the defendant acted with the requisite scienter: she knew the statement was false or made it with reckless disregard as to its truth or falsity; (3) the defendant intended to induce reliance; (4) the misrepresentation caused plaintiff's justifiable reliance; (5) pecuniary damages resulted to the plaintiff.

[1] Material Misrepresentation By Defendant

As a general rule the misrepresentation by the defendant must be of a past or present material fact. For example, if A tells B that a painting he is selling was painted by Picasso, when it was not, a factual misrepresentation has been made. Even a statement that is technically accurate can constitute a misrepresentation if it intended to convey a factual misimpression. For example, if A tells B that his business's income has stabilized when the income is zero, A's statement can still be characterized as a

---

[1] *See generally* Leon Green, *Deceit*, 16 Va. L. Rev. 749 (1930); Page Keeton, *Fraud: The Necessity for an Intent to Deceive*, 5 UCLA L. Rev. 583 (1958); Fleming James, Jr. and Oscar S. Gray, *Misrepresentation (Pt. II)*, 37 Md. L. Rev. 488 (1978).

[2] *See supra* § 14.05.

[3] *See supra* § 10.04, for discussion of negligent misrepresentation; *see supra* § 17.06, for misrepresentation in context of products liability.

misrepresentation.[4] Nor must the misrepresentation necessarily be in words. Physically disguising a defect can suffice.[5]

Misrepresentation of a present intention is generally accepted as a misrepresentation of a "present" fact.[6] Consequently, a fraudulent promise, where the defendant at the time of the promise has no intention of keeping it, satisfies this requirement. On the other hand, a broken promise is not a misrepresentation if it was made in good faith.[7]

A corollary to the general rule that the misrepresentation must be a fact is that misrepresentations of opinion are usually not actionable.[8] Exceptions do exist. Opinions by experts to a nonexpert,[9] fiduciaries,[10] and defendants who mislead a victim as to their objectivity are actionable.[11] Furthermore, some statements, while phrased as opinions, may sufficiently imply underlying facts to make the speaker liable for the implied misrepresentation. This is particularly likely when the speaker's opinion is apparently based on access to information not available to the recipient of the statement.[12] For example, if A tells B that, in his opinion, the room he inspected is well suited for storing books, when A but not B has seen that the room is under water, A's opinion implies facts about the room which can constitute misrepresentation.[13]

Courts have historically struggled with defining when a misrepresentation of law could be actionable. A misrepresentation as to a matter of law can be actionable when it wrongly conveys asserted facts such as the existence

---

4 *See* Cahill v. Readon, 273 P. 653 (Colo. 1928).

5 *See* Herzog v. Capital Co., 164 P.2d 8 (Cal. 1945), where a defendant's painting over a leaky surface to hide its character was held to constitute misrepresentation. *See* Restatement § 550.

6 *See* Restatement § 530 cmt. a, reading "The statement of a man's mind is as much a fact as the state of his digestion." *See also* Restatement § 530 cmt. d, reading "The intention that is necessary to make this rule . . . applicable is the intention of the promisor where the agreement as entered into."

7 *See* California Conserving Co. v. D'Ananzo, 62 F.2d 528, 530 (2d Cir. 1933), where the court noted, "Promises like other utterances, must be read with their usual implications."

8 *See* W. Page Keeton, *Fraud: Misrepresentations of Opinion*, 21 Minn. L. Rev. 643 (1937).

9 *See, e.g.*, Ultramares Corp. v. Touche, 174 N.E. 441 (N.Y. 1931), where accountants' certification as to the financial condition of a company "made as true to their own knowledge," when they had no knowledge on the subject, may justify a finding of fraud. *See* Restatement § 542(a) noting maker of statement who "purports to have special knowledge of the matter that the recipient does not have can be liable for his opinion."

10 *See* Restatement § 542(b).

11 *See* Oltmer v. Zamora, 418 N.E.2d 506 (Ill. 1981). *See* Restatement § 543. *See also* §§ 542 (c) and 542 (d) also extending liability when speaker has successfully secured confidence of recipient or has some other special reason to believe recipient will rely on the opinion.

12 *See* Restatement § 539.

13 *See* Restatement § 539 cmt. a, illus. 1.

of a statute or court decision.[14] Opinions concerning legal consequences are treated like other opinions.[15] Consequently, if A claims to be an expert with special knowledge of the law, he can be liable for misrepresenting his legal opinion to B, who does not have special knowledge.[16]

Misrepresentations must also be material to be actionable. The Restatement defines an assertion as material if either a reasonable person would attach importance to it in determining his action in the relevant transaction or the maker of the statement either knows or should know the person to whom the misrepresentation is addressed is likely to regard it as important.[17]

Traditionally, a failure to disclose was not a basis for liability under misrepresentation. There are, however, exceptions where there is a duty to disclose,[18] and the tendency of courts has been to expand such duties. For example, fiduciaries have a duty to disclose material facts.[19] If an actor initially misleads a victim, even innocently, or conceals information, there also is a duty to disclose and correct the misimpression.[20] Furthermore, several courts have held that sellers in a transaction must disclose fundamental defects that the potential purchaser would not be likely to discover.[21]

---

[14] *See* Restatement § 545(1).

[15] *See* Restatement § 545(2). *See* Sorenson v. Gardner, 334 P.2d 471 (Or. 1959).

[16] *See* Restatement § 542(a) cmt. f.

[17] *See* Restatement § 538. *See also* Reed v. King, 193 Cal. Rptr. 130 (1983), where the court held that information regarding murders which occurred in a house for sale were material to the value of the house, and thus a duty to disclose existed. The court held that such a decrease in value would have affected the sales transaction.

[18] "One who fails to disclose to another a fact that he knows may justifiably induce the other to act or refrain from acting in a business transaction is subject to the same liability to the other as though he had represented the nonexistence of the matter that he has failed to disclose if, but only if, he is under a duty to the other to exercise reasonable care to disclose the matter in question." Restatement § 551(1).

[19] *See* Restatement § 551(2)(a), for the liability of fiduciaries for nondisclosure of known information.

[20] *See* Remeikis v. Boss & Phelps, Inc., 419 A.2d 986 (D.C. App. 1980), where it was held that a defendant who had undertaken to disclose partial information cannot stop short of full disclosure.

See also Restatement § 529, regarding the fraudulent character of a misrepresentation, which reads "A representation stating the truth so far as it goes but which the maker knows or believes to be materially misleading because of his failure to state additional or qualifying matter is a fraudulent misrepresentation."

See also Restatement § 551(2)(a), regarding liability for nondisclosure, which allows liability to be imposed upon a person in a business transaction if he fails to take reasonable care to disclose "matters known to him that he knows to be necessary to prevent his partial or ambiguous statement of the facts from being misleading." Subsequently acquired information also requires that the actor correct a previous representation. *See* Restatement § 551(2)(c).

[21] *See, e.g.*, Ollerman v. O'Rourke Co., 288 N.W.2d 95 (Wis. 1980), where the seller was held to have a duty to disclose to the buyer that an underground well existed that would prevent construction upon the real estate.

These decisions suggest an increasing trend to impose obligations of disclosure to avoid liability for misrepresentation in a transaction. The Restatement, for example, concludes that there is an obligation to disclose "facts basic to the transaction, if he knows that the other is about to enter it under a mistake as to them, and that the other, because of the relationship between them, the customs of the trade or other objective circumstances, would reasonably expect a disclosure of those facts."[22]

[2] Scienter

Fraudulent misrepresentation requires that the defendant knew the misrepresentation was false or acted with reckless disregard as to its truth or falsity.[23] Recklessness requires that the defendant made the representation consciously aware of his lack of knowledge about the representation's truth or falsity.[24] In either instance, the defendant is subjectively lying, either by stating what he knows to be a falsehood or asserting something as truthful without any subjective belief in its truth.[25] This indicates the defendant is acting with intentional culpability. Such conduct can constitute criminal theft under the common law crime of false pretenses and should be distinguished from mere inadvertence or negligent misrepresentation.

[3] Intent to Induce Reliance

The defendant must have intended the misrepresentation to have been relied upon as truthful by the victim. A joke which is not intended to be taken seriously is not actionable under this tort.[26] A victim who relies on a misrepresentation must be the intended recipient or one to whom the defendant had reason to expect the misrepresentation would be communicated and would be relied on in the same type of transaction.[27]

---

[22] *See* Restatement § 551(2)(e). *See also* Johnson v. Davis, 480 So. 2d 625 (Fla. 1985). *See also* Anthony T. Kronman, *Mistake, Disclosure, Information and the Law of Contracts*, 7 J. Legal Stud. 1 (1978), arguing there is less of a tendency to require disclosure of information that the possessor obtained through costly research which would otherwise deter such information gathering.

[23] *See generally* Henry T. Terry, *Intent to Defraud*, 25 Yale L.J. 87 (1915); Page Keeton, *Fraud: The Necessity for an Intent to Deceive*, 5 UCLA L. Rev. 583 (1958); Restatement § 526. For a discussion of negligent misrepresentation, see § 10.04, *supra*. For a discussion of misrepresentation in the context of products liability, see § 17.06, *supra*.

[24] The recklessness standard is similar to that established in the *New York Times v. Sullivan* standard of actual or constitutional malice for certain defamation actions. *See infra* § 21.03[D].

[25] *See* Restatement § 526.

[26] If the actor subsequently learns a victim will rely on a misrepresentation, he is obligated to correct the misimpression. *See* Restatement § 551(2)(d).

[27] *See* Restatement § 533, which provides: "The maker of a fraudulent misrepresentation is subject to liability for pecuniary loss to another who acts in justifiable reliance upon it if the misrepresentation, although not made directly to the other, is made to a third person and the maker intends or has reason to expect that its terms will be repeated or its substance

The potential for unanticipated victims abounds since misrepresentation can be endlessly repeated to others. Given a greater culpability of the defendant, the intentional tort generally allows a wider ambit of foreseeable plaintiffs than the negligent tort.[28] Nevertheless, even in the intentional context, courts are hesitant to include accidental, unforeseen victims among those who should be compensated.

[4] Causation

The misrepresentation must have caused reliance.[29] If the victim is not deceived, the tort is not actionable. In *Nader v. Allegheny Airlines,*[30] Ralph Nader, the prominent consumer advocate, was denied recovery for his claim based upon the failure of the airline to disclose its "overbooking" policy for confirmed airline reservations.[31] The federal appeals court ultimately rejected Nader's recovery, as he had been "bumped" previously and was aware of the airline's practice. What of the victim who investigates despite the misrepresentation, but is not successful in recognizing its falsity? The defendant's misrepresentation need not be the sole cause of the victim's deception. If the misrepresentation is a substantial factor in misleading the victim, he is not precluded from recovering losses.[32]

The maker of the misrepresentation is, however, only liable for damages that would be foreseeably caused by the deceit.[33] If the victim's reliance on the misrepresentation caused unforeseeable losses, those damages are not recoverable. This limitation is consistent with proximate cause principles.[34]

[5] Justifiable Reliance

It is traditionally stated that the victim's reliance must be "justifiable." Reliance is not justified when the misrepresentation is immaterial to the transaction. Nor is it usually justified when the misrepresentation is mere opinion, although, as discussed above, exceptions exist.[35] If this were the

communicated to the other, and that it will influence his conduct in the transaction or type of transaction involved."

But see Restatement § 533, caveat, where the American Law Institute expresses no opinion on whether liability can be extended beyond that which falls within the ambit of this section.

[28] *See supra* § 10.04.

[29] *See* Restatement § 546.

[30] 626 F.2d 1031 (D.C. Cir. 1980).

[31] This was prior to current FAA regulations, under which such overbooking is disclosed and regulated.

[32] *See, e.g.,* Fausett & Co. v. Bullard, 229 S.W.2d 490 (N.J. 1950). *See* Restatement § 546 cmt. b, and § 547. Note, however, that the reliance caused must be justifiable. *See* discussion § 19.01[B][5], *infra.*

[33] *See* Restatement § 548A.

[34] *See* § 12.03, *supra.*

[35] *See* Restatement §§ 537-545. *See* § 19.01 [B][1], *supra.*

complete meaning of the requirement that the victim's reliance be justified, one could simply focus on the nature of the specific misrepresentation. Courts, as noted by the Restatement, also look to "the qualities and characteristics of the particular plaintiff, and the circumstances of the particular case"[36] in determining when the plaintiff's reliance may be unjustified even when the misrepresentation is a material fact. The knowledgeable victim who relies on an obvious falsity, despite his ability to easily recognize the falsity, is unjustified in his reliance.[37]

The requirement of justifiable reliance should not be equated with contributory negligence which would require the plaintiff to exercise the caution of a reasonable person. Fraudulent misrepresentation is an intentional tort; thus, contributory negligence is no more a defense to intentional misrepresentation than it would be to battery for a victim who fails to duck as quickly as a reasonable person should.[38] Just as a weakling deserves to be protected from battery, even a fool deserves to be protected from intentional fraud.[39] Consequently, the fool who buys the Brooklyn Bridge is generally protected by the tort. Courts are less forgiving, however, as indicated above, to those whose capacity should have clearly prevented reliance. This is particularly likely where the court may question the authenticity of the reliance.

[6] Damages

There is disagreement over how damages should be measured in the tort of misrepresentation. A substantial majority of courts award pecuniary damages based on the "benefit of the bargain" if the misrepresentation had been true.[40] This approach is more typical of breach of contract actions. Courts argue that the similarity between contract warranty actions and the tort of misrepresentation justifies this approach. A minority of courts award only for the victim's "out of pocket" losses which is more typical of tort recoveries which generally try to restore the victim to his position prior to the tort.[41] Some jurisdictions combine the two approaches and will often allow the plaintiff the option of either measure of damage provided the benefit of bargain rule is sufficiently certain.[42]

---

[36] Restatement § 545A cmt. b.

[37] Restatement § 541.

[38] This is in contrast with negligent misrepresentation where contributory or comparative negligence are defenses. *See* Restatement § 552A and *supra* §§ 15.02, 15.03.

[39] "No rogue should enjoy his ill-gotten plunder for the simple reason that his victim is by chance a fool." Chamberlin v. Fuller, 9 A. 832, 836 (Vt. 1887).

[40] *See e.g.*, Dempsey v. Marshall, 344 S.W.2d 606 (Ky. 1961).

[41] *See e.g.*, Beardmore v. T.D. Burgess Co., 226 A.2d 329 (Md. 1967).

[42] *See* Hinkle v. Rockville Motor Co., 278 A.2d 42 (Md. 1971). The Restatement allows this option when the victim was in a business transaction with the maker of the fraudulent misrepresenter and not simply a third party who relied on the misrepresentation. Third-party victims are limited to out-of-pocket loss. *See* Restatement § 549.

Often the benefit-of-the-bargain measure results in higher damages since the victim presumably expected to gain financially in the transaction. For example, assume A pays $10,000 for land misrepresented to have mature timber valuable to the victim.[43] A may argue the land as represented was worth $15,000. In fact the land does not have this timber and is worth only $3,000. Under the benefit-of-the-bargain test, A would receive $15,000 (the bargained value) minus $3,000 (actual value of the land) or $12,000. Under the out-of-pocket approach, A would receive $10,000 paid minus the actual value, $3,000, or $7,000. Most courts, under either approach, generally allow additional consequential damages, such as physical injuries caused by the misrepresentation and where malice is proven, punitive damages. Since misrepresentation is primarily a pecuniary tort, damages for mental distress are ordinarily not awarded.[44]

§ 19.02 INTENTIONAL INTERFERENCE WITH CONTRACT AND INTENTIONAL INTERFERENCE WITH PROSPECTIVE ECONOMIC RELATIONS

[A] *Overview*

The two torts of intentional interference with contract and intentional interference with prospective economic relations protect parties from intentional disruptions in economic relationships.[45] While the two torts have similar basic elements, the tort of intentional interference with prospective economic relations recognizes more circumstances under which the defendant's interference is not deemed improper.

The tort of intentional interference with contract allows recovery when the defendant intentionally interferes with a valid contract between *other* parties.[46] In an historic English case, *Lumley v. Gye,*[47] an opera singer was induced to breach her contract with one theater company by a competing theater company which offered her more compensation. While the opera singer was liable for breaching the contract, the intermeddling theater company was liable for tortious interference with the contract between the opera singer and her original theater company.[48] Damages in such cases can be awarded for economic losses, mental distress, and punitive damages, if malice is proven.[49]

---

43 The example is derived from Restatement § 549, illus. 4.

44 *See* Cornell v. Wunschel, 408 N.W.2d 369 (Iowa 1987); Dan B. Dobbs, LAW OF REMEDIES: DAMAGES, EQUITY, RESTITUTION (2d ed. 1993) at 89.2(4).

45 For negligent interference with economic expectation, *see supra* § 10.04.

46 *See* Note, *Tortious Interference with Contractual Relations in the Nineteenth Century: The Transformation of Property, Contract, and Tort,* 93 Harv. L. Rev. 1510 (1980), for an examination of the tort's early stages.

47 118 Eng. Rep. 749 (Q.B. 1853).

48 *See* David F. Partlett, *From Victorian Opera to Rock and Rap: Inducement to Breach of Contract in the Music Industry,* 66 Tul. L. Rev. 771 (1992), for modern parallels.

49 Restatement § 774A.

With strong precedent dating from the English common law and unequivocal endorsement by the Restatement,[50] actions alleging intentional interference with contract have become increasingly numerous. The tort has gained widespread notoriety, underscored by Texaco's near bankruptcy after being found liable for interfering with the contract for the purchase of Getty Oil shares by Pennzoil.[51]

Justifications do exist for interference with non-terminable at-will contracts,[52] but they are quite limited. For example, there is no liability if the defendant interfered with a contract that was illegal or against public policy.[53]

The parallel tort of intentional interference with prospective economic relations, or prospective contractual relations, allows recovery when the defendant intentionally and unjustifiably disrupts the victim's economic expectations not embodied in an actual contract.[54] The historic origin for this tort is illustrated by the classic case brought against a trading post which had sought to discourage visits to its competitors by slinging stones and arrows towards its competitors' potential customers.[55] Such behavior would constitute assault and battery against prospective customers, but the tort of intentional interference with prospective economic relations also allowed the competitor an action for lost business.

The circumstances that justify interfering with non-terminable contracts also justify interfering with prospective economic relations. However, additional justifications exist for intentional interference with prospective economic relations, most notably fair competition.[56] These additional justifications also apply, generally, to "at-will" contracts. Terminable "at-will" contracts appear more analogous to non-enforceable economic relations than to non-terminable contracts. Consequently, the justifications for interference with prosective economic relations are also applicable to terminable "at-will" contracts.

[B] *Definitions*

The elements of the two torts are parallel. Interference with contract requires a valid contract[57] while interference with prospective economic

---

[50] *See* Restatement § 766 cmt. c.

[51] Texaco, Inc. v. Pennzoil, 729 S.W.2d 768 (Tx. Ct. App. 1987), *reversed and remanded*, 485 U.S. 994 (1988). *See infra* § 19.02[B][2].

[52] Such contracts are distinguished from contracts where the parties are free to terminate the contract at any time with reasonable notice.

[53] Restatement § 774.

[54] Restatement § 766B. The Restatement refers to the tort as intentional interference with prospective contractual relation. The tort is also referred to as intentional interference with prospective advantage or prospective economic or business advantage.

[55] Tarleton v. McGawley, Peake N.P., 170 Eng. Rep. 153 (1793).

[56] *See* Restatement § 768. *See* § 19.02[C], *infra*.

[57] *See* Restatement § 766, § 766A, § 766B.

relations requires a legitimate economic expectancy. The elements of the two torts are, respectively:

(1) A valid contract or economic expectancy between the plaintiff and a third party.

(2) Knowledge of the valid contract or economic expectancy by the defendant.[58]

(3) Intent by the defendant to interfere with the contract or economic expectancy.

(4) Interference caused by the defendant.

(5) Damages to plaintiff.[59]

This tort is applicable only to the intermeddler who disrupts a contract or other economic relationship between other parties and is not applicable to parties who may breach or disrupt their own contracts or economic relationships.

[1] Valid Contract or Economic Expectancy

Interference with contract requires proof of a valid contract.[60] Interference with prospective economic relations requires proof of a valid economic expectation. Mere hope for customers or economic profit is insufficient. For example, competitors in sporting events ordinarily do not have a sufficient expectancy to establish the tort since the outcome in most events is too speculative.[61]

---

[58] *See, e.g.*, Mid-Continent Tel. Corp. v. Home Tel. Co., 319 F. Supp. 1176 (N.D. Miss. 1970), where the difference between the market value and merger price of the corporation the plaintiff sought to acquire, but was tortiously interfered with, was found an economic expectation.

[59] *See, e.g.*, Buckaloo v. Johnson, 537 P.2d 865 (Cal. 1975).

[60] In Texaco, Inc. v. Pennzoil, 729 S.W.2d 768 (Tex. Ct. App. 1987), *reversed and remanded*, 485 U.S. 994 (1988), the unsigned oral agreement was held to be valid contract under applicable state law.

[61] Restatement § 774B special note. *See also* Youst v. Longo, 729 P.2d 728 (Cal. 1987), where the court went beyond the Restatement view and announced that public policy precludes such interference claims when connected to any sporting event. But the California Supreme Court let stand a previous ruling pertaining to political contests, Gold v. Los Angeles Democratic League, 122 Cal. Rptr. 732 (Cal. Ct. App. 1975). In *Gold*, a candidate for Los Angeles city office claimed he was the victim of a false and misleading mailing sent to voters by his opponent, purportedly costing him the election. The *Youst* court found *Gold* distinguishable based on the "public's right to accurate information regarding candidates." 729 P.2d at 734. The California Supreme Court endorsed the *Gold* decision despite the fact that there was no certainty that Gold would have won the election; he had lost the election by a four to one margin.

[2] Knowledge of Valid Contract or an Economic Expectancy by the Defendant

The defendant must know of the valid contract for interference with contract. However, this is generally understood to mean the defendant must know facts from which she should have concluded that a valid contract existed. In *Texaco, Inc. v. Pennzoil*, it was irrelevant whether Texaco actually concluded Pennzoil had a contract to buy Getty Oil stock based in part on an unsigned agreement. The relevant analysis was whether Texaco should have known, by the facts available to it, that the unsigned written agreement was nevertheless a valid oral contract.[62] Likewise, for interference with prospective economic relations, the defendant must know of a valid economic expectancy.

[3] Intent by the Defendant to Interfere With the Contract or Economic Expectancy

The interference must be intentional.[63] The Restatement interprets intent to mean either purposeful interference or a substantial certainty that interference will occur.[64] Some courts, however, have held that the intent must be purposeful.[65]

[4] Interference Caused by the Defendant

The defendant must actually cause the interference. Merely hiring an employee who has already breached a contract with a different employer does not establish that the defendant caused the employee to breach the contract.[66]

[5] Damages

The plaintiff must suffer damages. In addition to economic damages, compensation for mental distress[67] and punitive damages, where malice is established, may be awarded.

---

[62] Texaco, Inc. v. Pennzoil, 729 S.W.2d 768 (Tex. Ct. App. 1987), *reversed and remanded*, 485 U.S. 994 (1988). *See also* Restatement § 766 cmt. i.

[63] For negligent interference with economic expectation, see *supra* § 10.04.

[64] Restatement § 766 cmt. j.

[65] *See, e.g.*, Seaman's Direct Buying Service, Inc. v. Standard Oil Co., 686 P.2d 1158 (Cal. 1984), where the court found that "it is not enough that the actor perform the acts which caused the result — he or she must have intended to cause the result itself." *Id.* at 1164. Because there was no evidence that Standard acted with "purpose or design" to cause Seaman's to break its contract with the City of Eureka, there was no liability imposed regarding this contract. *Id.* at 1165.

[66] *Cf.* Middleton v. Wallichs Music and Entertainment Co., 536 P.2d 1072 (Ariz. Ct. App. 1975), involving a suit against a defendant who had allegedly induced the breaching of a lease.

[67] Restatement § 774A. *See also* Mooney v. Johnson Cattle Co., 634 P.2d 1333 (Or. 1981) for discussion of when mental distress may be compensated.

[C] *Justifications for Interference*

There is disagreement over whether the plaintiff or the defendant should bear the burden of proving whether the defendant's conduct in interfering with a contract or prospective economic relations is justified or improper. The Restatement takes no position on the issue.[68] An increasing number of courts are requiring the plaintiff to prove the defendant's interference is improper.[69]

There are recognized sets of circumstances which justify both interference with a valid contract and interference with prospective economic relations. These include statements of truthful information or honest advice within the scope of a request,[70] interference by a person responsible for the welfare of another while acting to protect that person's welfare,[71] interference with a contract which is illegal or violates public policy,[72] and interference by someone when protecting his or her own legally protected interests in good faith and by appropriate means.[73]

For example, A may truthfully inform B that his surgeon is incompetent, to induce B to breach the contract. Similarly, if B requests A's advice with regard to the surgery, then A may respond honestly even if such a response is inaccurate.[74] Furthermore, a person may also induce the breach of a contract which unlawfully interferes with a legally protected interest or right

---

[68] *See* Restatement § 767 cmt. b.

[69] *See* Della Penna v. Toyota Motor Sales, U.S.A., Inc., 902 P.2d 740 (Cal. 1995).

[70] Restatement § 772.

[71] Examples of this privilege include parent-child and attorney-client relations. *See* Restatement § 770. *See also* Brown Mackie College v. Graham, 768 F. Supp 1457 (D. Kan. 1991), where the defendant, an attorney, contacted dissatisfied students of the plaintiff's college and gave them the advice to both withdraw from the school and file actions against it. Because he was justified in contacting the students and had the right to give them advice as their attorney (and was therefore responsible for their welfare), his actions were found to be privileged. *But see* Caruso v. Local Union No. 690, 670 P.2d 240 (Wash. 1983), where a union was found liable for publishing articles in its newspaper encouraging members to not patronize the plaintiff's business. The union claimed to be acting in the best interests of its members, but the plaintiff was able to show the union's wrongful desire to interfere with his business.

[72] Restatement § 774.

[73] Restatement § 773.

[74] *Cf.* Pacific Gas & Electric Co. v. Bear Stearns & Co., 791 P.2d 587 (Cal. 1990), where the defendants advised one of their clients to sue the plaintiff in order to terminate its contract with the plaintiff. The court denied Pacific Gas & Electric's claim by concluding that "Our legal system is based on the idea that it is better for citizens to resolve their differences in court than to resort to self-help or force. It is repugnant to this basic philosophy to make it a tort to induce potentially meritorious litigation. To permit a cause of action for interference with contract or prospective economic advantage to be based on inducing potentially meritorious litigation on the contract would threaten free access to the courts by providing an end run around the limitations on the tort of malicious prosecution." *Id.* at 598.

of their own, such as A's inducing the breach of a contract for the sale of property to which A has title and control.

Additional circumstances will justify only interference with prospective economic relations or contracts which are terminable at will. These justifications include fair and ethical competition or ethical action to protect one's financial interest. For example, A may encourage customers to buy her hamburgers rather than B's, provided the customers do not have a non-terminable contract with B.[75] However, it would be unethical and consequently tortious to wrongly accuse B of selling hamburgers with spider eggs in order to induce B's customers to buy A's hamburgers. Such competition would be unfair and therefore not privileged.[76]

Restatement § 767 provides seven factors, including the defendant's alleged motive, to help determine other instances when interference with prospective economic relations or contract are not improper:

(a) the nature of the actor's conduct,

(b) the actor's motive,

(c) the interests of the other with which the actor's conduct interferes,

(d) the interests sought to be advanced by the actor,

(e) the social interests in protecting the freedom of action of the actor and the contractual interests of the other,

(f) the proximity or remoteness of the actor's conduct to the interference, and

(g) the relations between the parties.

This approach underscores the uncertainty that can exist as to what constitutes improper interference, particularly in the context of prospective economic relations. Interference with prospective economic relations is not, by itself, an inherent wrong, unlike interference with a non-terminable at-will contract. Instead, in many ways intentional interference with prospective economic relations can be seen as fair competition and a cornerstone of an efficient capitalist market system.

Broad judicial use of factors which define justified interference are a questionable substitute for more specific notice of what constitutes a wrong. It has consequently been argued by some scholars and courts that the tort of intentional interference of prospective economic relations ought to be restricted to imposing liability when there is a definable wrong committed

---

[75] *See* Restatement § 768 illus. 1.

[76] Such statements have been variously described as economic forms of libel or slander, trade libel, or "injurious falsehood [s]." *See* Restatement §§ 623A and 633. *See generally* William L. Prosser, *Injurious Falsehood: The Basis of Liability*, 59 Colum. L. Rev. 425 (1959); Arlen W. Langvardt, *Free Speech Versus Economic Harm: Accommodating Defamation, Commercial Speech, and Unfair Competition Considerations in the Law of Injurious Falsehood*, 62 Temp. L. Rev. 903 (1989). *See also infra* § 21.02[B][2].

by the defendant.[77] Otherwise, if no definable wrong has been committed, the defendant, and other potential defendants, will have limited notice of potential liability. This may, in turn, discourage economically efficient competition.[78]

§ 19.03 TORTIOUS BREACH OF THE COVENANT OF GOOD FAITH AND FAIR DEALING

In each contract, there is an implied covenant of good faith and fair dealing.[79] The purpose of the implied covenant is to allow for the terms of contracts to be interpreted fairly.[80] Consequently, what constitutes a breach of the covenant depends on the particular terms of the contract. If A contracts with B to perform when the clock strikes at noon, the implied covenant of good faith would impose liability if A destroyed the clock to avoid having to meet the precise terms of the contract.

While the covenant is in essence an implied contract term, occasionally courts have held that the breach of the implied covenant of good faith and fair dealing can also constitute a tort.[81] This allows for tort damages as

[77] *See* Dan B. Dobbs, *Tortious Interference with Contractual Relationships*, 34 Ark. L. Rev. 335 (1980); Harvey S. Perlman, *Interference with Contract and Other Economic Expectancies: A Case of Tort and Contract Doctrine*, 49 U. Chi. L. Rev. 61 (1982). *See also* Della Penna v. Toyota Motor Sales, U.S.A., Inc., 902 P.2d 740 (Cal. 1995), holding that interference for economic expectancy tort must be "wrongful by some legal measure other than the fact of interference itself."

Yet, it can be argued that wrongs in one tort context should not define appropriate wrongs to establish liability in a different context.

[78] Broad factors for defining justified and unjustified interferences heighten the costs of determining whether an activity will result in liability. Clearly definable wrongs would minimize such information costs and allow efficient market allocation. However, if these wrongs are not clearly definable, information as to liability may be imperfect or unattainable. If such is the case deterrence of wrongful activity either will not be achieved or will be achieved only at the loss of some activities which may not be wrongful. Thus, not only could some prices be pushed higher, but also some services could be completely lost because the probability of liability considered with the potential size of such liability may exceed any profit expected. *See generally* Harvey S. Perlman, *Interference with Contract and Other Economic Expectancies: A Clash of Tort and Contract Doctrine*, 49 U. Chi. L. Rev. 61 (1982).

[79] "Every contract imposes upon each party a duty of good faith and fair dealing in its performance and enforcement." Restatement (Second) of Contracts § 205.

[80] *See generally* Alfred Hill, *Breach of Contract as a Tort*, 74 Colum. L. Rev. 40 (1974).

[81] One of the earliest cases is Crisci v. Security Ins. Co., 426 P.2d 173 (Cal. 1967), where the court allowed an insured to recover for emotional damages suffered as a result of the insurer's refusal to settle a claim. The refusal was deemed a breach of the covenant of good faith and fair dealing. *See also* Gruenberg v. Aetna Ins. Co., 510 P.2d 1032 (Cal. 1973); Egan v. Mutual of Omaha Ins. Co., 620 P.2d 141 (Cal. 1979). *But see* A.A.A. Pool Service & Supply Co. v. Aetna Casualty & Surety Co., 395 A.2d 724 (R.I. 1978), where the court did not allow a bad faith refusal to settle an insurance claim to comprise an independent tort action.

well as contract damages. Tort damages can include, in addition to consequential economic loss, mental distress and punitive damages, where malice is proven. Such tort damages can far exceed ordinary contract damages. While contract remedies recognize that a breach may in fact be economically efficient and are therefore not intended to be punitive, the extensive potential tort damages are a response to what is viewed, at the least, as a serious private wrong.

The tortious breach of the covenant of good faith and fair dealing is generally limited to breaches by insurance companies in particular contexts. An insurance company's bad faith refusal to pay the insured can exist when an insured has suffered a loss and the insurer, as a result, has greater leverage over its claimant. In these situations, the tort of breach of the covenant of good faith and fair dealing provides an appropriate countermeasure against intentional efforts to deny or wrongfully reduce indemnification for a legitimate claim.[82] Without the threat of mental distress and punitive damages available in the tort action, an insurance company could potentially intentionally stonewall a valid claim from its client, recognizing that litigation, if pursued by the claimant, could at worse compel the company to pay only what it had refused to pay initially under the insurance contract.[83] However, there are concerns that the tort will subsume contract law's delicate effort to enforce contract expectations[84] by excessively punishing defendants, deterring economically efficient contract breakers, or recklessly creating high stakes litigation.

As noted above, courts ordinarily apply tortious breach of the covenant of good faith and fair dealing only in the context of insurance contracts.[85] For example, in *Foley v. Interactive Data Corp.*[86] the California Supreme

[82] "The relationship of insurer and insured is inherently unbalanced: the adhesive nature of insurance contracts places the insurer in a superior bargaining position." Egan v. Mutual of Omaha Ins. Co., 620 P.2d 141, 146 (Cal. 1979).

[83] *See, e.g.*, Egan v. Mutual of Omaha Ins. Co., 620 P.2d 141 (Cal. 1979), where the plaintiff "received his first payment from Mutual on the claim in issue . . . only after a long delay and a personal visit to the claims office . . . . Testimony was introduced that McEachen [Mutual's agent], although aware of plaintiff's good faith efforts to work, called plaintiff a fraud and told him that he sought benefits only because he did not want to return to work. . . . When plaintiff expressed his concern regarding the need for money during the approaching Christmas season and offered to submit to examination by a physician of Mutual's choice, McEachen only laughed, reducing plaintiff to tears in the presence of his wife and child." *Id.* at 147.

[84] Tort application "has the potential for distorting well-established principles of contract law." Beck v. Farmers Ins. Exchange, 701 P.2d 795, 799 (Utah 1985).

[85] *See, e.g.*, Nichols v. State Farm Mutual Auto. Ins. Co., 306 S.E.2d 616 (S.C. 1983) (bad faith refusal to pay benefits of automobile policy to insured); Green v. State Farm Fire & Casualty Co., 667 F.2d 22 (9th Cir. 1982) (bad faith refusal to pay fire policy; the defendant maintained that the cause of the fire was arson, but did not sufficiently support this argument).

[86] 765 P.2d 373 (Cal. 1988).

Court refused to extend the tortious breach of the covenant of good faith and fair dealing to employment contracts by concluding that employers have economic incentives to treat employees fairly. Therefore, any bargaining disparity is not comparable to the insurance context.[87]

Prior to its decision in *Foley*, the California Supreme Court in *Seaman's Direct Buying Service, Inc. v. Standard Oil Co.*,[88] held that a bad faith *denial* of the existence of a commercial contract could constitute a tort. The decision received national prominence for its implications for the ultimate expansion of the bad faith tort to all contracts. *Seaman's* was generally criticized and rarely followed.[89] In 1995, the California Supreme Court overruled *Seaman's* and joined with other states in limiting the bad faith tort to the insurance context.[90]

---

[87] *See, e.g.*, Thompson v. St. Regis Paper Co., 685 P.2d 1081 (Wash. 1984).

[88] 686 P.2d 1158 (Cal. 1984). *See also* Eileen A. Scallen, Comment, *Sailing the Unchartered Seas of Bad Faith: Seaman's Direct Buying Service Inc. v. Standard Oil Co.*, 69 Minn. L. Rev. 1161 (1985); Steven B. Katz, Note, *The California Tort of Bad Faith Breach, the Dissent in Seaman's v. Standard Oil, and the Role of Punitive Damages in Contract Doctrine*, 60 S. Cal. L. Rev. 509 (1987); James H. Cook, Comment, *Seaman's Direct Buying Service Inc. v. Standard Oil Co.: Tortious Breach of the Covenant of Good Faith and Fair Dealing in a Noninsurance Commercial Contract Case*, 71 Iowa L. Rev. 893 (1986).

[89] The subtle distinction between disputing the existence of a contract in good faith and denying it in bad faith has concerned courts. Witness Judge Kozinski's concurring opinion in Oki America, Inc. v. Microtech Int'l Inc., 872 F.2d 312, 314–315 (9th Cir. 1989):

> "Nowhere but in the Cloud Cuckooland of modern tort theory could a case like this have been concocted. One large corporation is complaining that another obstinately refused to acknowledge they had a contract. For this shocking misconduct it is demanding millions of dollars in punitive damages. I suppose we will next be seeing lawsuits seeking punitive damages for maliciously refusing to return telephone calls or adopting a condescending tone in interoffice memos . . . . The intrusion of the courts into every aspect of life . . . trivializes the law, and denies individuals and businesses the autonomy of adjusting mutual rights and responsibilities through voluntary contractual agreement."

[90] *See* Freeman & Mills, Inc. v. Belcher Oil Co., 900 P.2d 669 (Cal. 1995). *But see* Story v. Bozeman, 791 P.2d 767, 776 (Mont. 1990), extending bad faith tort to contracts where parties have special relationship.

CHAPTER 20

MISUSE OF LEGAL PROCESSES

SYNOPSIS

§ 20.01 OVERVIEW

Three torts, malicious prosecution,[1] the parallel tort of malicious institution of civil proceedings,[2] and abuse of process,[3] address misuse of the legal system. Malicious prosecution addresses wrongful criminal prosecution of an innocent defendant in bad faith. Malicious institution of civil proceedings addresses wrongful institution of a civil proceeding against a

[1] *See generally* Dan B. Dobbs, *Belief and Doubt in Malicious Prosecution and Libel*, 21 Ariz. L. Rev. 607 (1979).

[2] The Restatement refers to this tort as "wrongful civil proceedings." Restatement § 674.

[3] *See generally* Tobi Goldoftas, *Abuse of Process*, 13 Clev.-Mar. L. Rev. 163 (1964).

non-liable defendant in bad faith. Abuse of process addresses the misuse of legal processes such as depositions, subpoenas and property attachments.

It is abundantly clear that either a criminal prosecution or a civil suit can extract enormous economic costs and emotional pain from defendants. Malicious prosecution and malicious institution of civil proceedings, in very limited instances, allow the innocent defendant of a prosecution or civil suit to seek compensation for economic and emotional damages. In most cases, however, if A is acquitted after two years of criminal prosecution, the legal defense expenses, lost wages, and emotional turmoil are not recoverable. Abuse of process addresses the narrow issue of a misuse of particular legal processes within the litigation process, as opposed to the misuse of an entire cause of action. Such misuse can result in liability if, and only if, the plaintiff can prove the misuse was motivated by an improper purpose.

The judiciary has been very reluctant to hamper access to the courts by imposing costs on a wrongful litigant. American, unlike English, courts have traditionally not wanted to deter people from seeking legal redress with the fear that if they lost their case in court, they would have to compensate the vindicated defendants for their expenses. In addition, there is a hesitancy to address excessive litigation by imposing new litigation as a remedy. Malicious prosecution and the related torts reflect this reluctance by making recovery under these torts very difficult. Nevertheless, the increased perception of abusive litigation and the uncompensated toll it places on its victims raises questions concerning the adequacy of current remedies.[4]

§ 20.02 MALICIOUS PROSECUTION AND MALICIOUS INSTITUTION OF CIVIL PROCEEDINGS: DEFINITION

Malicious prosecution[5] addresses wrongful criminal prosecutions while malicious institution of civil proceedings addresses wrongful civil proceedings.[6] Otherwise, the elements of the two torts are similar and generally require:[7] (1) institution or continuation of a criminal or civil proceeding against the accused; (2) termination of the proceeding in favor of the accused; (3) absence of probable cause for prosecution or civil proceedings; (4) improper purpose of the accuser; and (5) damages suffered by the accused.

---

[4] Federal Rules of Civil Procedure provide federal courts with the power to sanction wrongful litigation by punishing the transgressing attorneys. *See* Fed. R. Civ. P. 11, 26.

[5] *See* Restatement § 653.

[6] *See generally* Restatement §§ 677-679. *See also* Sheila L. Birnbaum, *Physicians Counterattack: Liability of Lawyers for Instituting Unjustified Medical Malpractice Actions*, 45 Fordham L. Rev. 1003 (1977), for a review of the use of the tort by physicians in response to increased malpractice claims.

[7] *See, e.g.*, Shoemaker v. Selnes, 349 P.2d 473 (Or. 1960); Texas Skaggs, Inc. v. Graves, 582 S.W.2d 863 (Tex. Ct. App. 1979).

[A] *Institution or Continuation of Criminal or Civil Proceedings Against the Plaintiff*

The defendant must be responsible for initiating or in some way supporting the continuation of the legal proceedings against the plaintiff.[8] This may be accomplished by asking another to bring[9] or maintain the suit.[10] However, the mere fact that an individual testified falsely against the plaintiff in court is not sufficient, by itself, to maintain an action for malicious prosecution or malicious institution of civil proceedings, although it may be used as evidence that the defendant engaged in other instigating activity with the requisite improper purpose.[11]

[B] *Termination of the Proceeding in Favor of the Plaintiff*

Suits based on malicious prosecution or, in most instances, malicious institution of civil proceedings cannot be filed until after the initial criminal or civil proceedings have been *terminated* in favor of the individual wanting to institute such an action.[12] With the exception of an ex parte proceeding,[13] neither tort can be brought until the alleged wrongful litigation is fully completed. Furthermore, the proceedings complained of must have resulted in exoneration.[14] The mere failure to continue to prosecute a criminal case or to proceed in a civil case does not necessarily connote clear exoneration.[15] The potential to evade accountability under these torts by dropping

---

[8] *See* Schleicher v. Western State Bank, 314 N.W.2d 293 (N.D. 1982), where the bank was not found liable for malicious prosecution because there was no evidence that the bank initiated the criminal fraud investigation regarding the plaintiff's alleged fraud.

[9] *See, e.g.*, Gilbert v. Emmons, 42 Ill. 143 (1866).

[10] *See* Lampos v. Bazar, 527 P.2d 376 (Or. 1974), where the defendant continued the initial action against the plaintiff despite learning of information which would have exculpated the plaintiff. *See also* Restatement § 662 cmt. f.

[11] Historically, courts have precluded civil liability for a witness's testimony to preclude pressures that might intimidate a witness. False statements to a prosecutor which stimulate her to initiate a proceeding are not immune. *See, e.g.*, Fusario v. Cavallaro, 142 A. 391 (Conn. 1928). *See also* Restatement § 655 cmt. c.

[12] "Otherwise he might recover in the action and yet be convicted in the original prosecution." Fisher v. Bristow, 99 Eng. Rep. 140 (1779).

[13] An exception exists for ex parte proceedings, such as a proceeding to attach property. In ex parte proceeding, the defendant is not accorded an opportunity to contest the action. In that instance, although remedies exist for the defendant whose property has been attached to reverse the attachment, the entire litigation need not be terminated to allow the tort of malicious institution of civil proceeding. *See* Restatement § 674(b) and cmt. k.

[14] *See, e.g.*, Lackner v. LaCroix, 602 P.2d 393 (Cal. 1979), where the statute of limitations terminated the original suit, the defendant in that suit was not allowed to institute an action for malicious institution of civil proceedings, since termination did not imply exoneration.

[15] "A termination of criminal proceedings in favor of the accused other than by acquittal is not a sufficient termination to meet the requirements of a cause of action for malicious prosecution if (a) the charge is withdrawn or the prosecution abandoned pursuant to an agreement of compromise with the accused; or (b) the charge is withdrawn or the prosecution abandoned because of misconduct on the part of the accused or in his behalf for the purpose

the proceeding just prior to an anticipated finding for the defendant has encouraged some modern movement to a less technical approach to discerning exoneration.[16]

[C] *Absence of Probable Cause*

Furthermore, there must be no probable cause for the criminal prosecution or civil proceedings.[17] Even if there is vindication in the previous litigation, the plaintiff in these torts must prove there was no reasonable basis for the defendant to believe them guilty of the criminal charge or potentially liable in the civil proceedings.[18] The Restatement also interprets probable cause to require that the accuser must have a subjective belief in the guilt or liability of the accused in addition to a reasonable basis for that belief.[19] The Restatement position has gained increasing acceptance.[20]

[D] *Improper Purpose or Malice of the Accuser*

Historically, the plaintiff was required to prove that the accuser acted with "malice" in bringing the prosecution or civil suit. The potentially misleading ambiguity of the term malice prompted the Restatement to replace the element of malice with the requirement that the accuser acted with an improper purpose.[21] Whether courts use the Restatement terminology or retain the requirement of malice, courts generally do require proof of an improper purpose. An improper purpose is clearly established if the

---

of preventing proper trial; or (c) the charge is withdrawn or the proceeding abandoned out of mercy requested by or accepted by the accused; or (d) new proceedings for the same offense have been properly instituted and have not been terminated in favor of the accused." Restatement § 660.

[16] *See, e.g.*, Davis v. City of San Antonio, 752 S.W.2d 518, 519 (Tex. 1988), where a city employee was discharged after "numerous items of city-owned property were discovered at his residence." The employee was indicted by a grand jury on the charge of official misconduct, but eighteen months later the prosecutor dropped the charges. The employee then sued the city for malicious prosecution, and the jury found in his favor. In a vague ruling, the court upheld the jury's verdict, noting that "there was *some evidence* supporting the jury's findings that the criminal proceedings were terminated in favor of [the employee]." *Id.* at 523 (emphasis added). *See also* Restatement § 660 cmt. d, which states that "[t]he abandonment of proceedings because the accuser believes that the accused is innocent or that a conviction has, in the natural course of events, become impossible or improbable, is a sufficient termination in favor of the accused."

[17] *See generally* Restatement § 662, pertaining to actions for malicious prosection, and Restatement § 675, pertaining to actions for malicious institution of civil proceedings.

[18] While mere possibility that the accused is guilty does not justify criminal proceedings, a possibility of liability can justify civil litigation. *See* Restatement § 674 cmt. e.

[19] *See* Restatement § 662(c).

[20] *See, e.g.*, Texas Skaggs, Inc. v. Graves, 582 S.W.2d 863 (Texas Ct. Civ. App. 1979). Since the tort also requires malice or an improper purpose, the addition of a requirement that the accuser have a subjective belief in the guilt or liability of the accused appears to be of limited significance.

[21] *See* Restatement §§ 668, 676.

accuser brought or maintained a criminal proceeding against an individual he did not think was guilty or a civil proceeding against someone he did not think was potentially liable. Simply disliking the accused should not satisfy the requirement of malice in this context since it may be quite appropriate to have ill feelings toward a wrongdoer.

The Restatement also indicates that an accuser acts with an improper motive when he brings an action to harass the accused or gain some extraneous advantage unrelated to the merits of the litigation, even when the accuser in fact believes the accused is guilty or liable of the charge. Nevertheless, even when such behavior is characterized as an improper purpose, the accuser cannot be found liable for malicious prosecution or malicious institution of a civil proceeding without also acting without probable cause as discussed above.[22] Consequently, so long as he reasonably and sincerely believes the accused is guilty or liable, the accused cannot be found to have committed the tort whatever his primary purpose was in initiating or maintaining the legal proceedings. Improper purpose is only critical when the accuser has not acted reasonably in presuming the accused guilty or liable.

[E] *Damages*

Damages must be established, which, given the burden of defending a lawsuit, is hardly a difficult hurdle. Damages include the economic consequences of the wrongful litigation as well as emotional distress,[23] reputational injury, and, where malice is established, punitive damages.[24]

A significant minority of states adhere to the so-called "English rule." The rule allows the tort of malicious institution of a civil proceeding to be brought only when the civil proceeding resulted in some special damage, such as the seizure of the person, the attachment of property, or an injunction.[25] The majority of American courts reject the English rule and allow actions based solely on damage to reputation, emotional injury, and the cost of litigation.[26] The English rule can be justified in this country

[22] *See* Restatement § 668 cmt. g.; § 676 cmt. c. *See e.g.*, Kitchens v. Barlow, 164 So. 2d 745 (Miss. 1964), where the accuser brought the initial suit primarily as leverage to collect debt unrelated to the litigation.

[23] *See, e.g.*, Piper v. Scher, 533 A.2d 974, 976 (N.J. Super. Ct. 1987), where the court noted that the plaintiff had been subject to "arrest, fingerprinting, photographing, adverse publicity, the hiring of counsel, preparation for trial and the like, with their attendant stresses."

[24] *See* Restatement §§ 670 and 671, pertaining to damages in actions for malicious prosecution, and Restatement § 681, pertaining to damages in actions for malicious institution of civil proceedings.

[25] *See* Friedman v. Dozorc, 312 N.W.2d 585 (Mich. 1981), adopting the English rule. The rule does not impact on malicious prosecution for criminal proceedings.

[26] *See* Restatement § 681 authorizing recovery for legal expenses, emotional and reputational injury.

as limiting additional litigation as a remedy to excessive litigation except in the case of extraordinary damage. On the other hand, it should be recognized that the English rule may reflect that winning litigants in England, unlike in the United States, are already awarded legal fees without the need to allege malicious institution of civil proceedings.

§ 20.03 IMMUNITY OF PUBLIC OFFICIALS

Prosecutors, judges, other public officials,[27] and the government which employs them are generally immune from discretionary decisions to prosecute.[28] Consequently, they are not potential defendants in a suit for malicious prosecution. This does not, however, preclude malicious prosecution claims against others who fabricate evidence with the intent to stimulate wrongful prosecutions. The immunity underscores the limited remedies available under the tort to alleged victims of wrongful prosecutions.

§ 20.04 INTERACTION BETWEEN FALSE IMPRISONMENT AND MALICIOUS PROSECUTION AND MALICIOUS INSTITUTION OF CIVIL PROCEEDINGS

As discussed under false imprisonment,[29] imprisonment under criminal process or civil commitment does not constitute false imprisonment as long as proper legal procedures are followed. Malicious prosecutions and malicious institution of civil proceedings must address such abuses. If imprisonment is outside of proper legal procedures, including unprivileged arrests by law enforcement agents, false imprisonment, including the more specific variant of that tort, false arrest, may be applicable.

§ 20.05 ABUSE OF PROCESS

Abuse of process constitutes the intentional misuse of either a civil or criminal legal process for an ulterior purpose resulting in damage to the plaintiff.[30] Unlike malicious prosecution or malicious institution of civil

[27] *See generally* Richard A. Epstein, *Private-Law Models for Official Immunity*, 42 Law & Contemp. Probs. 53 (1978); Ronald A. Cass, *Damage Suits Against Public Officers*, 129 U. Pa. L. Rev. 1110 (1981). *See, e.g.*, Blake v. Rupe, 651 P.2d 1096 (Wyo. 1982). Note that public defenders are, in general, denied any immunity because of the public policy view that public defenders should represent their clients as vigorously as possible. *See, e.g.*, Reese v. Danforth, 406 A.2d 735, 739 (Pa. 1979), where the court analogized the public defender-defendant relationship to a "private attorney-client relationship" and therefore found that a public defender "ought to be subject to liability for tortious conduct."

[28] *See supra* § 15.05[E]. *See, e.g.*, Stump v. Sparkman, 435 U.S. 349 (1978), *rehearing denied*, 436 U.S. 951 (1978), where a judge was not held liable when he did not give an adolescent girl a hearing before ordering that she be sterilized. *See also* J. Randolph Block, *Stump v. Sparkman and the History of Judicial Immunity*, 1980 Duke L.J. 879. Generally, however, the immunity does not exist when a judge is not acting in a judicial capacity. *See* Butz v. Economou, 438 U.S. 478 (1978).

[29] *See supra* § 1.04[D].

[30] Restatement § 682.

proceedings, there is no need to await the outcome of a criminal prosecution or civil suit.[31] Abuse of process addresses the wrongful use of a legal process within such litigation.[32] The use can be wrongful regardless of who ultimately wins the litigation within which the particular legal process has been improperly used.[33]

For example, if A subpoenas B to be in Chicago for a deposition in a civil suit for the ulterior purpose of keeping B away from an important meeting in San Francisco, A has abused the subpoena process.[34] Similarly, if A attaches real property, ostensibly to preserve the assets for judgment if A is successful against B in a lawsuit, but actually only does so to sabotage B's real estate sale by clouding the land's title, A can be liable for abuse of process.[35] The plaintiff in an abuse of process action has the difficult onus of proving an ulterior purpose.[36]

---

[31] *See* Restatement § 682.

[32] *See* Restatement § 682 cmt. a, which reads "The gravamen of the misconduct for which the liability stated in this Section is imposed is not the wrongful procurement of legal process or the wrongful initiation of criminal or civil proceeding; it is the misuse of process, no matter how properly obtained, for any purpose other than that which it is designed to accomplish."

[33] *See* Brownsell v. Klawitter, 306 N.W.2d 41 (Wis. 1981), where the court noted that a suit based upon a claim of abuse of process could proceed without termination of the previous action in favor of the plaintiff. *See also* Ash v. Cohn, 194 A. 174, 176 (N.J. 1937), where the court noted "an abuse of process may occur in the course of a prosecution which has been malicious and wrongful throughout."

[34] *See, e.g.*, Board of Ed. of Farmingdale Union Free Sch. Dist. v. Farmingdale Classroom Teachers Ass'n, 343 N.E.2d 278 (N.Y. 1975), where the court held that issuing subpoenas for 87 teachers all to appear in court at the same time, with refusal to accommodate them through staggering their appearances, presented a prima facie case for abuse of process. The school had been forced to hire 71 substitute teachers to deal with the lack of teachers on that day.

[35] *But see* Restatement § 682 cmt. b, which notes that "there is no action for abuse of process when the process is used for the purpose for which it is intended, but there is an incidental motive."

[36] *See, e.g.*, Maniaci v. Marquette University, 184 N.W.2d 168 (Wis. 1971) (plaintiff had to prove the ulterior purpose of detention to ostensibly determine mental competency was actually for the purposes of confining student until parents could be reached); Ginsberg v. Ginsberg, 84 A.D.2d 573 (N.Y. 2d Dep't 1981) (plaintiff had to prove the use of subpoenas for harassment purposes).

CHAPTER 21

DEFAMATION

SYNOPSIS

[D] *Actual Malice*
[E] *Falsity*
[F] *Conclusion*

§ 21.01 OVERVIEW

The law of defamation is particularly intricate due to its unique blend of common law and First Amendment principles. For historical reasons, common law defamation has developed its own set of complex rules. Reputational harm was considered a grave injury in socially stratified England and the legal system treated it accordingly. Over time, a number of common law privileges have been recognized, making a plaintiff's defamation case more challenging, however. These privileges continue to play an important role in defamation litigation today.

Starting in 1964, the U.S. Supreme Court recognized constitutional limitations on defamation claims. Since then, courts have been struggling to find an accommodation between a plaintiff's right to be compensated for reputational harm and a defendant's right to free speech. These judicial efforts, rather than clarifying the law of defamation, have added even greater complexity. In addition, the constitutional overlay continues to be reworked. In general, there has been a move away from constitutional protection in the defamation arena during the last two decades, a development that has added renewed importance to the common law rules.

This Chapter begins with an examination of common law defamation, looking at pleading requirements, damages and privileges. The Chapter then provides an overview of the constitutional dimensions of defamation law.[1]

§ 21.02 COMMON LAW DEFAMATION

At common law, defamation was a strict liability tort. As such, a plaintiff could recover without proving any fault on the part of the defendant. Furthermore, the falsity of the allegedly defamatory statement was presumed. Finally, in most instances, damages were presumed. Thus, in most common law defamation actions the plaintiff only had to prove 1) a defamatory statement 2) about the plaintiff 3) that was "published." The defendant then had the opportunity to try to assert a defense, such as the truth of the statement.

Thus, at common law, a defendant could quite unwittingly defame another and be responsible for significant damages. For example, D's photographer takes a picture of X and the woman accompanying him. X tells the photographer that he and the woman are engaged to marry. D

[1] Entire treatises have been dedicated to the topic of defamation law. *See, e.g.*, Robert D. Sack and Sandra S. Baron, LIBEL, SLANDER, AND RELATED PROBLEMS (2d ed. 1994); Rodney A. Smolla, LAW OF DEFAMATION (1994).

publishes a caption saying the photo is of X and his fiancee. X is in fact married to P, who sues D for defamation, claiming that the caption harms her reputation by suggesting that P is not married to the man with whom she is living. Under common law defamation rules, P would prevail.[2]

[A] *Defamatory Statement*

The plaintiff must persuade a jury that the statement at issue is defamatory. To be defamatory under the general common law rule, a statement must hold the plaintiff up to scorn, ridicule, or contempt. The Restatement provides that a communication is defamatory if it "tends so to harm the reputation of another as to lower him in the estimation of the community or to deter third persons from associating or dealing with him."[3] Usually, a communication would be construed as defamatory under either the common law or the Restatement definition. There are situations where the test used could yield different results, however.

A defamatory statement, then, is one that harms reputation by injuring a person's general character or causing personal disgrace. Typically, such communications accuse a person of immoral or criminal conduct. Mere insults, hyperbole, or obvious jokes cannot be the basis for a defamation action.

A court determines as a matter of law whether any interpretation of the communication could be construed as defamatory, while it is for a jury to decide whether the statement in the case before it is actually defamatory.[4] The court and jury give that language its "fair and natural meaning" as understood by reasonable persons, rejecting tortured and extreme interpretations.[5] The context in which the language is used and even the punctuation, as where words are placed in quotation marks,[6] may affect the determination of whether it is defamatory.

[1] Defamatory To Whom?

For the plaintiff to prevail in a defamation action, it is not necessary that she show that most people to whom the statement was communicated would

---

[2] Cassidy v. Daily Mirror Newspapers, Ltd., [1929] 2 K.B. 331.

[3] Restatement § 559.

[4] Similarly, where the statement is clearly defamatory, the judge may decide that it is defamatory per se. As one court explained: "If a published statement is susceptible of one meaning only, and that meaning is defamatory, the statement is libelous as a matter of law. Conversely, if the statement is susceptible of only a non-defamatory meaning, it cannot be considered libelous, justifying dismissal of the action. However, in cases where the statement is capable of being assigned more than one meaning, one of which is defamatory and another not, the question of whether its content is defamatory is one that must be resolved by the trier of fact. (citations omitted)" Romaine v. Kallinger, 537 A.2d 284, 288 (N.J. 1988).

[5] *See id.* (jury could not find statement that the plaintiff knew a junkie to be defamatory).

[6] *See, e.g.*, Wildstein v. New York Post Corp., 243 N.Y.S.2d 386 (1965) (defendant's use of quotation marks around "associated" could have created defamatory meaning).

have interpreted it in a defamatory fashion. Rather, it is enough for the plaintiff to show that a "substantial and respectable minority"[7] or a "right-thinking minority" would comprehend the defamatory nature of the communication. And this group can be quite small. For example, an expert on Palestinian art and culture was defamed by an article incorrectly bearing her name because errors in the article made the plaintiff appear incompetent to other experts in the field. Although the overwhelming majority of the readers did not have the expertise to discern these errors, it was enough that a very small number of highly trained experts in the field did.[8]

If the group that could interpret the communication in a way that injures the plaintiff's reputation is of a blatantly anti-social nature, courts may deny the plaintiff a defamation action. Thus, a neo-Nazi wrongly accused of marrying someone Jewish will have no defamation action. Similarly, where the communication wrongly states that the plaintiff has cooperated with law enforcement, thus lowering his reputation in the eyes of his criminal compatriots, no defamation action will follow.

Hard cases arise where the communication at issue should not be defamatory to "right-thinking" people, but could create potential reputational harm in a significant segment of society nonetheless. In one case, the plaintiff brought a defamation action because he was alleged to be a communist sympathizer. The court permitted the plaintiff's action, while acknowledging that the statement should not cause reputational harm when read by "right-thinking people."[9] Similarly, courts have confronted this issue in the context of whether the imputation of homosexuality should be the basis for a defamation action.[10]

---

[7] Restatement § 559 cmt. e.

[8] Ben-Oliel v. Press Pub. Co., 167 N.E. 432 (N.Y. 1929).

[9] Grant v. Reader's Digest Ass'n, 151 F.2d 733 (2d Cir. 1945). Judge Hand explained for the court: "A man may value his reputation even among those who do not embrace the prevailing moral standards; and it would seem that the jury should be allowed to appraise how far he should be indemnified for the disesteem of such persons. That is the usual rule. . . . We do not believe, therefore, that we need say whether 'right-thinking' people would harbor similar feelings. . . It is enough if there be some, as there certainly are, who would feel so, even though they would be 'wrong-thinking' people if they did." Id. at 734-735.

[10] *See, e.g.*, Matherson v. Marchello, 473 N.Y.S.2d 998, 1005 (N.Y. App. Div. 1984) ("In short, despite the fact that an increasing number of homosexuals are publicly expressing satisfaction and even pride in their status, the potential and probable harm of a false charge of homosexuality, in terms of social and economic impact, cannot be ignored."). *See also* Nazeri v. Missouri Valley College, 860 S.W. 2d 303 (Mo. 1993) ("Despite the efforts of many homosexual groups to foster greater acceptance, homosexuality is still viewed with disfavor, if not outright contempt, by a sizeable proportion of our population.").

Know difference.

[2] Statements Not Facially Defamatory: Inducement and Innuendo

Some statements are facially defamatory. For example, the statement — "Fred Rexmurth of 1344 Floride Lane embezzled millions of dollars from his employer." — is defamatory on its face; nothing needs to be added for a reader to fully understand the defamatory nature of the statement.

Sometimes the defamatory impact can only be understood by the addition of extrinsic information. In such situations the plaintiff is obligated to plead the extra facts needed to make the statement defamatory ("inducement") or to explain the defamatory impact ("innuendo") if it is not obvious. For example, assume a law school newspaper prints "Professor X, a professor of torts, spends several evenings a week doing 'pro bono' work at 5050 Main Street." This statement is not defamatory on its face, so Professor X in a defamation action would have to plead the additional facts that make the statement defamatory, such as the fact that 5050 Main Street is the location of a brothel. With this inducement, Professor X would then plead that the defamatory innuendo is that he frequents a bordello.

[B] *Of and Concerning the Plaintiff*

The plaintiff must show that the defamatory communication was understood as referring to her.[11] If the plaintiff can show this, it is irrelevant that the defendant did not intend for the statement to refer to the plaintiff.[12] Similarly, even if the defendant intended to create a fictional character, a defamation action will lie where recipients of the communication reasonably believe that the character is really the plaintiff.

Where the plaintiff is not expressly named in the communication, the plaintiff must plead "colloquium" to connect herself to the defamatory statement. Thus, if the article in the "pro bono" hypothetical discussed above had stated — "The youngest torts professor on the Acme Law School faculty spends several evenings a week doing 'pro bono' work at 5050 Main Street." — Professor X would have to allege colloquium, that he is the youngest torts professor on the Acme law faculty.

[1] Group Defamation

Sometimes defamatory communications do not specifically name individuals but ascribe discrediting behavior to unnamed members of a group. If the group is small and the defamatory sting may attach to each group

[11] Under common law, the defamation plaintiff must be alive both at the time of the alleged defamation and at the time of trial because the interest is the vindication of reputational harm. A few jurisdictions have enacted statutes permitting the survival of a defamation action so that the death of the defamation plaintiff prior to trial does not terminate the lawsuit.

[12] Restatement § 564 ("A defamatory communication is made concerning the person to whom its recipient correctly, or mistakenly but reasonably, understands it was intended to refer.").

member, each member of the group may bring a defamation action. Again, returning to the "pro bono" hypothetical, if the statement had read — "An Acme Law School torts professor spends several evenings a week doing 'pro bono' work at 5050 Main Street." — each of the four torts professors at Acme Law School could bring a defamation action if a reasonable reader could believe the statement referred to that professor. The larger the group, the less likely it is that a court will permit a defamation action by all the affected group members. Where the line is to be drawn, however, is far from clear.[13]

[2] Corporate Plaintiffs

Corporations and other business entities may be defamation plaintiffs where the communication tends to cast aspersions on their business character, such as trustworthiness, or deters third parties from dealing with them.[14] Where the attack is on a product, the action is typically for product disparagement.[15]

[C] *Publication*

A plaintiff must establish that the defamatory communication was published, as that term of art is defined in the defamation context. For a communication to be published it must simply reach one person other than the defamation plaintiff.[16] The number of recipients may be relevant to the damages the plaintiff suffered, but for this element to be established only a single third party need receive the communication and understand its defamatory thrust.

Typically, publication is not a hurdle for the plaintiff because the defendant intended to disseminate the defamatory statement. In cases where the defendant asserts that she did not intend for anyone other than the plaintiff to receive the communication, the question becomes whether the defendant was negligent in not realizing the message could be discovered by a third party. If the statement is enclosed in a sealed letter mailed to

---

[13] In one famous case the defendant authors stated that "some" of the models at Dallas' Neiman-Marcus Department Store were "callgirls," the saleswomen "were good too," and that most of the salesmen were "fairies." All nine models sued, 30 of 382 saleswomen sued and 15 of 25 salesmen sued. The action by the saleswomen was dismissed, while the other two proceeded. Neiman-Marcus v. Lait, 13 F.R.D. 311 (S.D.N.Y. 1952). See also Arcand v. Evening Call Pub. Co., 567 F.2d 1163 (1st Cir. 1977), where the court refused to permit all 21 members of the police force to sue the defendant for suggesting that one unidentified member of the force had locked himself in the back of a cruiser with a female passenger.

[14] Restatement § 561.

[15] For an action for disparagement (sometimes called trade libel or injurious falsehood), the plaintiff typically must show that a defendant intentionally or recklessly published a false assertion of fact about the plaintiff's goods or property that caused the plaintiff to suffer actual pecuniary loss.

[16] Restatement § 577 ("Publication of a defamatory matter is its communication intentionally or by a negligent act to one other than the person defamed.").

the plaintiff, there is no publication, provided the defendant had no reason to believe another person would read the plaintiff's mail. Sending the same statement on a postcard, however, could lead to liability even if the defendant did not desire a third person to read the communication. If the postcard was written in Greek because the defendant mistakenly believed no one other than the plaintiff would understand it, a jury question would be created.

[1] Republication Rule

Any repetition of a defamation is considered publication, even if the republisher attributes the statement to the initial source. Initially, following this notion literally, each copy of a book or newspaper constituted a new publication. Most jurisdictions today have adopted by statute or court decision a single publication rule by which an entire edition of a book or periodical constitutes a single publication. This places a clearer and shorter statute of limitations on any defamation action arising from the initial publication.

[D] *Damages*

In most defamation cases, a plaintiff's reputational injury may be presumed, permitting the plaintiff to recover compensation without any proof beyond the defamatory nature of the communication. In the defamation context, such damages are called "general damages." General damages provide compensation for the emotional trauma and harm suffered by the plaintiff whose reputation was besmirched. There are situations, however, where the plaintiff must plead and prove a specific type of loss, called "special damages," in order to prevail. Special damages are specific economic losses flowing from the defamation, such as lost profits. They must be pled with specificity. If the plaintiff proves these special damages, she may then recover general damages.

The damages recoverable to a defamation plaintiff depend on whether the defamatory communication is considered libel or slander and, if slander, whether the defamation falls into a category denominated "slander per se." The early common law treated libel as more harmful than slander and set up damage rules accordingly. The different treatement was due largely to libel's more permanent form. Slander's destructive power was seen as more fleeting.[17] The distinction remains important today.

[17] There is debate about whether the distinction between libel and slander makes sense. Is a letter read by one person that much more harmful than a speech heard by a thousand? Matherson v. Marchello, 473 N.Y.S.2d 998, 1001 (N.Y. App. Div. 1984) ("As a result of historical accident which, though not sensibly defensible today, is so well settled as to be beyond our ability to uproot it, there is a schism between the law governing slander and the law governing libel (citations omitted).").

[1] The Libel/Slander Distinction

It is usually easy to distinguish between libel and slander. Slander is an oral utterance while libel is a more permanent expression, such as a writing, photo, statue or sculpture.[18] Generally, where the defamation is communicated by sight it is libel, where via sound it is slander.

Modern forms of technology have challenged the libel/slander distinction. For example, while movies have been considered libel, courts have struggled with how to treat radio and television broadcasts. Some courts have gone so far as to adopt a fractured result that if a broadcast is read from a script it is libel, while if it is not, it is slander.[19] Because of the permanence and reach of modern broadcasts, it is likely most courts would find them to constitute libel.[20]

[2] Slander and Slander Per Se

Where the defamation is characterized as slander, the plaintiff generally must meet the substantial burden of pleading and proving special damages. Since early common law, however, certain slanderous statements were deemed so horrible that reputational injury to plaintiffs could be presumed even without any proof of special damages. These special "slander per se" categories are widely followed today and, although theoretically other categories can be envisioned, courts have typically stayed close to the four well-established slander per se categories.

The four traditional slander per se categories permit presumed reputational damages absent special damage. The first situation involves slanderous communications that directly call into question the plaintiff's competence to perform adequately in her trade or profession. Thus, suggesting cowardice in a soldier or illiteracy in a lawyer could constitute slander per se, though the converse, lack of bravery in a lawyer and illiteracy of a soldier might not. The second slander per se category involves statements claiming the plaintiff has a current, loathsome disease, such as syphilis or AIDS. The third category involves allegations of serious criminal misbehavior by the plaintiff, typically criminal activity involving moral turpitude. The final category is the most controversial. It traditionally arose where the defendant

---

[18] The Restatement provides a broad definition of libel which includes any communication "that has the potentially harmful qualities characteristic of written or printed words." Slander constitutes "spoken words, transitory gestures" and communications that are not libel. Restatement § 568.

[19] *See, e.g.*, Brueggemeyer v. American Broadcasting Companies, Inc., 684 F. Supp. 452 (N.D. Texas 1988) (applying Texas law).

[20] *See, e.g.*, Brown v. Hearst Corporation, 862 F. Supp. 622 (D. Mass. 1994) (applying Massachusetts law). This is the Restatement view as well. See Restatement § 568A. Some jurisdictions, in order to provide greater legal protection to the media, have statutes labeling broadcasts as slander. *See, e.g.*, Cal. Civ. Code § 46 (communications "by radio or any mechanical or other means" are slander).

suggested a lack of chastity in a woman. While it may be that this category has outlived any usefulness, the Restatement proposes that this slander per se category encompass any serious sexual misconduct regardless of gender.[21]

[3] Libel and Libel Per Quod

Under the traditional view, which remains the position of most jurisdictions and of the Restatement, any libel plaintiff may recover general (presumed) damages. Some states have narrowed this approach, however, and have distinguished libel per se (libel on its face) from libel per quod (libel that requires extrinsic evidence such as inducement or innuendo). In these states, the plaintiff may recover general damages for libel per se. For libel per quod, however, the plaintiff must show special damages (as in the slander context) unless the libel falls into one of the slander per se categories. Thus, in the earlier "pro bono" hypothetical about an unnamed professor frequenting a certain address,[22] in jurisdictions that draw this distinction the plaintiff would have to prove special damages unless he could show that that statement falls into one of the "per se" categories (which it might since it suggests engaging in a crime of moral turpitude).

[E] *Common Law Defenses*

Because at common law a plaintiff could often establish a prima facie case of defamation quite easily, the defendant often had to look to the available defenses in order to avoid liability. Although the constitutionalization of the tort of defamation has profoundly affected some of the traditional common law defenses, most remain extremely important. This section looks at the most important common law defense — that of truth — before exploring most of the absolute and qualified privileges available to a defamation defendant.

[1] Substantial Truth

The defamation cause of action was intended to permit plaintiffs to vindicate reputational harm caused by false communications about the plaintiff. Thus, if the communication in issue was true, there was no basis for a defamation action. At common law, however, the defamatory communication was presumed false, and it was incumbent upon the defendant to establish truth as a defense.[23] Proving the truth of a statement can be difficult and expensive, as any serious dispute necessitates a full-blown trial.

A defendant does not establish truth by showing the literal truth of the communication, as where the defendant writes "X stated that P was an

---

[21] Restatement § 574.

[22] *See supra* § 21.02[A][2].

[23] Now, because of constitutional developments, the plaintiff has the burden of proving falsity in most defamation cases. *See infra* § 21.03[E].

embezzler." Even if X made that statement, as a republisher of the defamation, D would have to show that P was in fact an embezzler to prevail in a libel action brought by P. The defendant needs to show the truth of the underlying allegation, not just the accuracy of the attribution.

While the defendant had to show the accuracy and truth of the statement in issue, she did not have to show the literal truth of every aspect—substantial truth is the test. Of course, there is debate about what constitutes substantial truth. If the D newspaper reported that P killed 12 people over five years, when in fact P killed 11, there would be no doubt that D could establish substantial truth. But if the paper had reported that P had killed 12 people when he in fact had *robbed* 11 people, it is unlikely that substantial truth could be found. A report that P robbed dozens poses a debatable issue.[24]

[2] Absolute Privileges

Of significant continuing importance are absolute privileges under which a defendant may escape liability even if she knew that the statement was false or published it in order to hurt the plaintiff's reputation. There are a few contexts that rely so heavily on unfettered discourse that the law provides immunity from defamation liability. These absolute privileges typically arise in governmental proceedings involving judicial, legislative and executive communications. In the judicial context, statements made in court or in official court papers are absolutely privileged as long as relevant to the court proceeding.[25] Thus, if witness D, knowing the statement is false and in order to harm P, states on the witness stand in a criminal battery case, that D saw P beat X, P could not recover against D for defamation.[26] Comments made outside the courtroom are similarly privileged if they are closely related to the litigation, as would be an attorney's interview of a prospective witness. On the other hand, an attorney's comments about a case to the media would likely be too far removed from the litigation to enable the attorney to assert an absolute privilege.[27]

---

[24] A related concept is that of the libel-proof plaintiff whose reputation is so low that the additional information can have no real impact. Conversely, a plaintiff's reputation can be so impeccable that no one would believe the allegedly defamatory statement.

[25] As one court explained: "The socially important interests promoted by the absolute privilege in this area include the fearless prosecution and defense of claims which leads to complete exposure of pertinent information for a tribunal's disposition. The privilege protects judges, parties, lawyers, witnesses and jurors. The defense is absolute in that the speaker's motive, purpose or reasonableness in uttering a false statement do not affect the defense." Green Acres Trust v. London, 688 P.2d 617, 621 (Ariz. 1984).

[26] A criminal prosecution of D for perjury, however, would be a possibility.

[27] *See, e.g.*, Green Acres Trust v. London, 688 P.2d 617 (Ariz. 1984) (attorney's statement to reporter about class-action lawsuit filed the next day not absolutely privileged because extra-judicial comments to reporters not necessary to the conduct of the lawsuit).

A similar absolute privilege applies to legislators and high-level executive officers. Thus, a legislator could not be liable for defamation even though she makes a knowingly false statement during debate on the floor of the legislature.[28]

In addition, communications made privately by one spouse to another are absolutely privileged, as are television or radio stations' obligatory broadcasts of a candidate's response to another candidate pursuant to laws mandating equal access in the electoral process.

[3] Qualified Privileges

Qualified (or conditional) privileges play an important role in defamation litigation. These privileges have developed due to the recognition that there are certain interests which could be seriously impaired by the common law's strict liability approach to defamation. Qualified privileges are based on the social utility of protecting communications made in connection with the speaker's moral, legal or social obligations. Thus, a person has a qualified privilege to protect her own interest, as where she is wrongly accused of a crime and, to exculpate herself, implicates P. Similarly, where a person responds to a perceived duty to convey information that is of interest to a third party, a qualified privilege attaches. Thus, if a prospective employer asks D about P, D's former employee, D has a qualified privilege to provide information. The third party must need the information and be able to act on it, and it must be relevant. Additionally, where the defendant and the recipient of the information share a common interest, such as a group affiliation or a common employer, there is a qualified privilege to convey relevant information. Thus, if employee D informs his employer that P, whom the employer is about to hire, was fired from his last job due to incompetence, a qualified privilege applies.

As the name suggests, these privileges can be lost. Once a judge decides that a qualified privilege applies, a jury considers whether the defendant has lost the privilege. A defendant may lose a qualified privilege in several ways: by failing to have an honest belief that the statement was true;[29] by failing to have an objectively reasonable belief that the statement was true; or by disclosing the information to more people than necessary (that is, excessive publication). Thus, in the example where D, the employee accused of theft who implicated P, there would be no qualified privilege if D did not honestly believe P was the thief, had no reasonable basis to believe

---

[28] This absolute privilege does not apply, however, to legislators' statements at press conferences, in newsletters, or in phone calls because they are not part of the "deliberative process." Hutchinson v. Proxmire, 443 U.S. 111 (1979).

[29] In many jurisdictions, the defendant must be reckless, rather than merely negligent, to lose the privilege. Where Constitutional protections protect defendants from liability without fault (*see infa* § 21.03[C]), requiring recklessness to lose the privilege provides elevated protection to the defendant. *See* Marchesi v. Franchino, 387 A.2d 1129 (N.J. 1978).

so, or if she shared her suspicions with co-workers who were in no position to take any appropriate disciplinary action against P.

Another important qualified privilege in many jurisdictions is the "fair and accurate report" privilege. Without this privilege, a newspaper reporting — "At last night's City Council meeting, X accused Mayor P of embezzling city funds." — would find itself liable for defamation as a republisher of X's defamation. This privilege permits a report of public meetings, and probably information in public records, provided that the report is an accurate and unbiased account.[30]

§ 21.03 CONSTITUTIONAL CONSTRAINTS

Because defamatory speech is false speech, courts had repeatedly determined that the First Amendment played no role in the defamation context. Thus, defamation law was entirely defined by the law of the states without any constraints imposed by the United States Constitution.

Things changed dramatically in 1964, however, when the United States Supreme Court determined that the Constitution affected the contours of defamation law in certain contexts.[31] Thus began the "constitutionalization" of defamation law, and, with it, an additional layer of complexity. The constitutional developments have affected both proof of fault and falsity in defamation cases. As the Court's constitutional defamation jurisprudence has developed, an analysis of a defamation case typically requires a consideration of the status of the plaintiff (whether she is a public official, public figure or private person) and of the subject matter of the defamation (whether it is of public or private concern).[32] While the common law defamation rules have remained important because they determine pleading requirements and provide various defenses, the constitutional overlay has had a profound impact on many defamation cases.

[A] *Public Officials*

The constitutionalization of defamation law began with the Court's 1964 decision of *New York Times v. Sullivan.* The factual context of the case

---

[30] *See, e.g.*, Medico v. Time, Inc., 643 F.2d 134 (3d Cir. 1981).

[31] It has been said that the Court's decision in 1964 to inject First Amendment concerns into defamation law was an occasion for "dancing in the streets." *See* Harry Kalven, Jr., *The New York Times Case: A Note on "the Central Meaning of the First Amendment,"* 1964 Sup. Ct. Rev. 191, 221 n.125 (crediting Alexander Meiklejohn with the statement, with which Kalven agreed). While there may have been expressions of joy by jounalists, surely all did not share in the revelry as there was no cause for celebration by defamation *plaintiffs*.

[32] Some judges and commentators have suggested that the status of the defendant—media or nonmedia—should be another consideration. This position has not garnered wide support. While the United States Supreme Court has expressly left undecided whether nonmedia defendants are entitled to the same constitutional protections as media defendants (*see* Milkovich v. Lorain Journal Co., 497 U.S. 1, 19 n.6 (1990)), most courts and commentators appear ready to apply the same protections to all defamation defendants regardless of status.

is critical as it explains what moved the Court to inject First Amendment concerns into the law of defamation.[33] In 1960, the *New York Times* ran a paid full-page advertisement signed by a number of prominent religious, entertainment and community leaders asking for donations to defend Martin Luther King, Jr. against a perjury indictment, and to assist in various ways with the civil rights struggle in which African-Americans were then engaged. The text of the advertisement contained several inaccuracies such as claims that the Montgomery, Alabama police department ringed the campus of Alabama State College when in fact they were stationed near the campus; that the police padlocked the dining facilities when they did not do so; and that Dr. King had been arrested seven times when he had in fact been arrested four times. The Montgomery City Commissioner charged with overseeing the police, L.B. Sullivan, filed a defamation action against the *New York Times* and several of the persons who signed the advertisement. Under Alabama's defamation law, which was generally similar to that of much of the country, to state a prima facie case for libel, Sullivan only had to show that the statement was defamatory, of and concerning him, and published. No fault was required on the part of the defendants, and the falsity of the statements was presumed.[34] A jury awarded Sullivan the exact amount he sought in the libel action, $500,000.[35]

The Supreme Court recognized the grave harm that could be inflicted on unpopular viewpoints under common law defamation. Focusing heavily on the importance of permitting criticism of government officers, the majority of the Court held that a public official could only prevail in a defamation action where the public official shows that the defendant either knew that the statement was false or recklessly disregarded whether the communication was false, a fault standard known as "actual malice."[36] The Court also required that this actual malice standard be proven by "convincing clarity," which has been interpreted as requiring the plaintiff to establish

[33] Indeed, at least one commentator has criticized the *Sullivan* decision, contending that "[t]he source of many of the modern problems with the law of defamation is that the *New York Times* decision was influenced too heavily by the dramatic facts of the underlying dispute. . . ." Richard A. Epstein, *Was New York Times v. Sullivan Wrong*?, 53 U. Chi. L. Rev. 782, 787 (1986) (arguing against the constitutionalization of defamation law and contending that the common law approach to defamation was a better way of handling defamation cases).

[34] The jury rejected the defendants' effort to assert the substantial truth of the statements. Further, the jury found the statements to be "of and concerning" Sullivan even though he was nowhere named in the advertisement.

[35] Sullivan's action was only one of 11 defamation actions that had been filed against the New York Times, putting the newspaper at risk of judgments exceeding $5 million. Anthony Lewis has written an excellent book about the *Sullivan* case that chronicles the interesting background that gave rise to the litigation. *See* Anthony Lewis, MAKE NO LAW: THE SULLIVAN CASE AND THE FIRST AMENDMENT (Random House 1991).

[36] *See infra* § 21.03[D].

actual malice by the heightened burden of proof of "clear and convincing evidence."[37]

Although providing significant First Amendment protection to the defendants, the majority did not provide an absolute privilege to defame public officials.[38] Instead, the Court created a *qualified* privilege, a privilege that could be lost by clear and convincing evidence of actual malice.

The *Sullivan* decision only affects defamation actions against public officials. Thus, a challenge is to identify those who fit into the public official category. Not everyone who is paid by the government is classified as a public official. Rather, it is those individuals who are positioned to affect policy — those "who have, or appear to the public to have, substantial responsibility for or control over the conduct of governmental affairs"[39] — who must show actual malice in order to recover for defamation.[40] As one moves away from those at the top of the decision-making structure, the issue becomes cloudier. There is debate, for example, about whether functionaries in government-run services, such as police officers, public school teachers and, government lawyers, should be characterized as public officials for defamation purposes.[41]

---

[37] This heightened burden of proof can be particularly important in the context of a defendant's effort to dispose of a defamation action before trial by use of a motion for summary judgment. The court in determining the motion is to keep in mind the higher burden the plaintiff has at trial, making it easier for the court to grant the defendant's motion for summary judgment in many cases where actual malice is in dispute. Anderson v. Liberty Lobby, Inc., 477 U.S. 242 (1986).

[38] This was the position of the three concurring justices. They called for an absolute privilege to criticize government officials out of concern that permitting a jury to make the call on whether there was actual malice might still lead to the punishment of unpopular viewpoints. Aware of the risk of remanding the case to an Alabama jury, the majority ultimately determined that no jury could reasonably find either clear and convincing evidence of actual malice or that the statements in issue were "of and concerning" the plaintiff Sullivan. The high court's review of the record was quite extraordinary, and has led to a constitutional standard requiring appellate courts to engage in an independent review of the lower court record in determining the existence of a jury question on actual malice. *See* Bose Corp. v. Consumers Union, 466 U.S. 485 (1984).

[39] Rosenblatt, v. Baer, 383 U.S. 75, 85 (1966).

[40] The court extended the reach of *Sullivan* to candidates for public office, noting anything that "might touch on an official's fitness for office" fell within the privilege. Monitor Patriot Co. v. Roy, 401 U.S. 265 (1971).

[41] Most courts have determined that police officers are public officials while public school teachers are not. One court posited a three-factor inquiry for determining whether a person is a public official for defamation purposes, asking whether the person 1) occupies a position of apparent importance so that the public is interested in that person's qualifications or performance; 2) has access to the media in order to counter the defamation; and 3) assumes the risk of criticism because of her public position. Kassel v. Gannett Co., 875 F.2d 935 (1st Cir. 1989) (staff psychologist of the Veteran's Administration is not a public official).

[B] *Public Figures*

The constitutionalization of defamation law continued in earnest when a few years after *Sullivan* the Court determined that "public figures," like public officials, should have to prove actual malice in order to prevail in defamation actions. Noting that the "differentiation between 'public figures' and 'public officials' and the adoption of separate standards of proof for each have no basis in law, logic, or First Amendment policy," Chief Justice Warren explained:

> [I]t is plain that although they are not subject to the restraints of the political process, "public figures," like "public officials," often play an influential role in ordering society. And surely as a class these "public figures" have as ready access as "public officials" to mass media of communication, both to influence policy and to counter criticism of their views and activities."[42]

The Court in expanding the *Sullivan* doctrine to public figures, further noted that public figures assume the risk of some reputational harm by involving themselves in issues of importance.

Substantial litigation has involved who constitutes a public figure for defamation purposes. The Court has recognized two general categories of public figures: an all-purpose public figure, who is someone widely known (like William F. Buckley, Michael Jordan or Madonna) and a limited public figure, who is a person who either "voluntarily injects himself or is drawn into a particular public controversy and thereby becomes a public figure for a limited range of issues" related to that person's public figure status.[43] Sometimes a plaintiff's status is evident; other times, however, it is quite debatable.

The Supreme Court has narrowly circumscribed the public figure category. The Court has been aware that classifying a person as a public figure has a profound impact on that individual's ability to receive compensation for reputational harm, as she must show actual malice in order to recover any damages. Regarding all-purpose public figure status, the Court has made clear that it "would not lightly assume that a citizen's participation in community and professional affairs rendered him a public figure for all purposes."[44] Similarly, in four decisions during the last twenty-two years

---

[42] Curtis Publishing Co. v. Butts, 388 U.S. 130, 163-164 (1967).

[43] Gertz v. Robert Welch, Inc., 418 U.S. 323, 351 (1974). Thus, the chief executive officer for a large supermarket chain may be a limited public figure for matters dealing with the supermarket industry, although she lacks any general fame or notoriety. *See* Waldbaum v. Fairchild Publications, Inc., 627 F.2d 1287 (D.C. Cir. 1980).

[44] Gertz v. Robert Welch, Inc., 418 U.S. 323, 352 (1974). The Court added: "Absent clear evidence of general fame or notoriety in the community, and pervasive involvement in the affairs of society, an individual should not be deemed a public personality for all aspects of his life." *Id.*

the Court has made clear its intention to define narrowly the limited public figure category as well. Thus, the Court found each of the following to be private figure plaintiffs: a prominent attorney involved in a high-profile case and various community affairs;[45] a socialite who, while involved in a highly publicized divorce from the heir to the Firestone tire fortune, called press conferences to discuss the proceedings;[46] a man who 15 years earlier had pleaded guilty to contempt charges for refusing to appear before a grand jury investigating Soviet espionage;[47] and a research scientist who was singled out by a U.S. Senator for engaging in frivolous research at public expense.[48] One court, after examining these cases, has posited a three-prong test for a court's determination of whether a plaintiff is a limited public figure: 1) Was there a legitimate public controversy that had ramifications beyond the parties in the defamation suit?; 2) Did the plaintiffs thrust themselves into the forefront of the dispute?; 3) Was the defamation related to the plaintiff's participation in the dispute?[49]

[C] *Private Persons*

The constitutional law of defamation has become particularly complex when it deals with plaintiffs who are neither public officials nor public figures. The current state of the law in the private plaintiff context requires that the subject matter of the defamation be analyzed to discern whether it deals with matters of public concern or matters of private concern. Lower courts have had to grapple with this issue because the United States Supreme Court has provided little guidance about how this determination is made beyond advising that one should look at the "content, form, and context" of the communication.[50] Thus, the more widely distributed the communication, the more likely that it is of public concern. Further, even though the status of the defendant is not a determinative factor in defamation law, if there is a media defendant, it is probable that the subject matter is of public concern.

[1] Public Concern

The Supreme Court has created an elaborate scheme when a defamation action is brought by a private plaintiff and involves a matter of public concern. The proof requirements depend in large measure on the kind of damages the plaintiff is seeking, and are affected by the state's own law of defamation.

---

[45] Gertz v. Robert Welch, Inc., 418 U.S. 323 (1974).

[46] Time, Inc. v. Firestone, 424 U.S. 448 (1976).

[47] Wolston v. Reader's Digest Assn., Inc., 443 U.S. 157 (1979).

[48] Hutchinson v. Proxmire, 443 U.S. 111 (1979).

[49] Waldbaum v. Fairchild Publications, Inc., 627 F.2d 1287 (D.C. Cir. 1980) (CEO of nation's second largest consumer cooperative market is a limited public figure for issues related to supermarket industry).

[50] Dun & Bradstreet, Inc. v. Greenmoss Builders, Inc., 472 U.S. 749, 761 (1985).

The Supreme Court's decision of *Gertz v. Robert Welch, Inc.* lays out the applicable rules in the private person/public concern context.[51] In *Gertz*, the Court acknowledged that private plaintiffs should be able to recover more readily than public plaintiffs for defamation. The Court determined that states could permit private plaintiffs to recover damages for "actual injury," defined as proven "impairment of reputation and standing in the community, personal humiliation, and mental anguish and suffering,"[52] under any standard other than strict liability.[53] The Court held that the tougher fault standard of actual malice was appropriate when the plaintiff sought either presumed damages or punitive damages.[54]

[2] Private Concern

The constitutional interest is highly limited (or possibly absent) in a case involving a private plaintiff and a private matter. The exact standard remains uncertain because the Court has yet to clarify its *Dun & Bradstreet v. Greenmoss, Inc.*[55] decision.

In *Dun & Bradstreet*, the plurality held that the Constitution does not require that a private plaintiff suing in a case involving a matter of private concern prove actual malice to recover presumed and punitive damages, as is required of private plaintiffs suing in cases involving matters of public concern. It is unclear whether the decision would permit a state to return to the common law strict liability approach in these cases or whether some low level of fault, such as negligence, might be constitutionally required. It is clear that the First Amendment interests are greatly reduced in the private concern context.

---

[51] Nowhere in *Gertz* does the Court discuss the kind of subject matter involved. The Court spends its time determining that the plaintiff is not a public figure and outlines the standard to be used for private plaintiffs. Only after more than a decade, do we learn in *Dun & Bradstreet* that *Gertz* was intended to apply only to matters of public concern. And this interpretation is nothing short of surprising. Much of the Court's impetus for deciding the *Gertz* case was to overrule its decision of Rosenbloom v. Metromedia, Inc., 403 U.S. 29 (1971), in which the plurality determined that the actual malice standard should apply to any case involving matters of public concern, regardless of the plaintiff's status. Thus, many interpreted *Gertz* as rejecting any focus on the subject matter involved in the defamation.

[52] Gertz v. Robert Welch, Inc., 418 U.S. 323, 350 (1974).

[53] Thus, it is up to the states to define the standard of fault to be required of private plaintiffs seeking to prove actual injury in cases involving matters of public concern, so long as the state does not revert to common law strict liability. Most states have employed a negligence standard, although a state wishing to provide greater protection to defendants in defamation cases is free to use an actual malice standard.

[54] For punitive damages, the plaintiff must also satisfy the state's punitive damage standard, such as by showing maliciousness, wilfulness or deliberate wrongdoing. See *supra* § 14.05.

[55] 472 U.S. 749 (1985).

[D] *Actual Malice*

As defamation law now stands, public officials, public figures and private plaintiffs seeking presumed or punitive damages must show clear and convincing evidence of actual malice. The fault standard of actual malice requires the plaintiff to prove that either the defendant knew of the falsity or was reckless as to truth or falsity. This is an exacting standard, requiring that the plaintiff show more than a defendant's failure to investigate or unreasonable conduct. Instead, a plaintiff must prove that the defendant was at least reckless, a standard compelling proof that the defendant had "in fact entertained serious doubts as to the truth of his publication."[56]

While the Court has not yet backed away from this actual malice standard, the Court has noted that a defendant's "deliberate decision not to acquire knowledge of facts that might confirm the probable falsity" of a communication, "the purposeful avoidance of the truth," could constitute actual malice.[57] The Court may be moving slowly toward redefining actual malice slightly so that it can be satisfied with a lower level of fault on the part of the defendant.

[E] *Falsity*

At common law, the falsity of the defamatory statement was presumed and truth was a defense. The Supreme Court has determined that in cases involving public officials, public figures, or private figures and public concern, the Constitution mandates that the plaintiff prove falsity as part of her prima facie case.[58] The Court has decided neither whether an elevated burden of proof is required on the falsity element nor whether a state may return to the common law rules regarding falsity where the subject matter is private.

[F] *Conclusion*

Defamation law remains in flux. During the 1960s, the Court took dramatic steps to inject constitutional concerns into defamation law. Beginning in the 1970s, however, the Court has retreated, and it remains unlikely that there will be an expansion of First Amendment protections in defamation law. Indeed, some members of the Court have expressed hostility toward the constitutionalization of defamation law, a few going so far as to suggest a reconsideration of the soundness of *Sullivan*.[59] It is

---

[56] St. Amant v. Thompson, 390 U.S. 727, 731 (1968). More recently, the Supreme Court held that deliberate alteration of quotations does not itself establish actual malice in Masson v. New Yorker Magazine, 501 U.S. 496 (1991).

[57] Harte-Hanks Communications, Inc. v. Connaughton, 491 U.S. 657, 692 (1989).

[58] Philadelphia Newspapers, Inc. v. Hepps, 475 U.S. 767 (1986).

[59] *See, e.g.*, Dun & Bradstreet, Inc. v. Greenmoss Builders, Inc., 472 U.S. 749 (1985) (White, J., concurring) ("I have also become convinced that the Court struck an improvident balance in the New York Times case between the public's interest in being fully informed about public officials and public affairs and the competing interest of those who have been defamed in vindicating their reputation.").

unlikely, however, that the Court will take the dramatic steps needed to permit a return to pre-1964 defamation law, but it will probably permit states to move in that direction as it retracts some of the constitutional protections it has given to the defamation area.

CHAPTER 22

INVASION OF PRIVACY

SYNOPSIS

§ 22.01 OVERVIEW

While several historic torts, such as trespass to land, act to protect privacy interests, it was not until this century that courts began to recognize actions based specifically on a right of privacy.[1] Indeed, a single law review article by Louis D. Brandeis and Samuel D. Warren, "The Right of Privacy,"[2] is generally credited with significant influence in prompting ultimate judicial acceptance of the tort. The Restatement has defined four separate torts for invasion of privacy: intrusion upon seclusion, appropriation of plaintiff's name or picture, placing the plaintiff in a false light before the public, and public disclosure of private facts.[3] All four privacy torts enjoy general judicial acceptance today. Each of the four privacy torts poses substantial, but distinct, policy concerns.

---

[1] *See* Pavesich v. New England Life Ins. Co., 50 S.E. 68 (Ga. 1905). *See generally* Randall P. Bezanson, *The Right to Privacy Revisited: Privacy, News, and Social Change, 1890-1990*, 80 Cal. L. Rev. 1133 (1992); Ken Gormley, *One Hundred Years of Privacy*, 1992 Wis. L. Rev. 1335 (1992).

[2] 4 Harv. L. Rev. 193 (1890). The article was prompted by Warren's distress over newspaper coverage of a family wedding.

[3] *See generally* Restatement § 652A, which introduces the torts.

§ 22.02 INTRUSION UPON SECLUSION

One of the four generally recognized privacy torts is intrusion upon seclusion. The Restatement definition of the tort is: "One who intentionally intrudes, physically or otherwise, upon the solitude or seclusion of another or his private affairs or concerns, is subject to liability to the other for invasion of his privacy, if the intrusion would be highly offensive to a reasonable person."[4]

The tort addresses acts of intrusion and other interferences with a victim's "zone of privacy."[5] A classic instance of such intrusion is the placing of a microphone under the matrimonial mattress.[6] There is no requirement that information be obtained or communicated; it is the intrusion itself that constitutes the interference. While such interference may also constitute trespass, there is no requirement that trespass be committed.[7] For example, the intrusion may be spying through high powered binoculars into an area the victim rightly could expect to be private.[8] There is also no requirement that the victim be aware of the intrusion, although constant disturbance, such as the incessant following and photographing of a celebrity, can lead to liability based on interfering with the victim's tranquility.[9]

Liability for intrusion upon seclusion can be imposed even if the information obtained proves to be in the public interest by, for example, revealing illegality or public corruption.[10] In *Pearson v. Dodd*,[11] a columnist escaped liability for searches of a U.S. Senator's private office file only because it could not be proven that the columnist had instigated the search, despite evidence of official corruption.[12] In another notable case,

---

[4] Restatement § 652B.

[5] *See* Restatement § 652B cmts. a and b.

[6] Hamberger v. Eastman, 206 A.2d 239 (N.H. 1964).

[7] *See* Pearson v. Dodd, 410 F.2d 701, 704 (D.C. Cir. 1969), *cert. denied*, 395 U.S. 947 (1969), where the court noted that intrusion could occur "by physical trespass or not." *See infra* text.

[8] *See* Alabama Electronic Co-Op, Inc. v. Partridge, 225 So. 2d 848 (Ala. 1969). *Cf.* Souder v. Pendleton Detectives, Inc., 88 So. 2d 716 (La. Ct. App. 1956), where the defendants were found liable for watching the plaintiff through the plaintiff's home windows.

[9] *See* Galella v. Onassis, 487 F.2d 986 (2d Cir. 1973), involving a "paparazzo" who continued to photograph the plaintiff despite temporary restraining orders.

[10] This is despite the Restatement (Second) of Agency § 395 cmt. f, which states, in part, that "an agent is privileged to reveal information confidentially acquired by him in the course of his agency in the protection of a superior interest of himself or of a third person. Thus, if the confidential information is to the effect that the principal is committing or is about to commit a crime, the agent is under no duty not to reveal it."

[11] *See supra* note 7.

[12] Two former employees of Senator Dodd, with the assistance of two of his current staff, removed, copied, and replaced documents from his files. The copies were then given to columnist Jack Anderson, who was aware of the manner in which the documents were obtained. Pearson v. Dodd, 410 F.2d 701, 703 (D.C. Cir. 1969), *cert. denied*, 395 U.S. 947 (1969).

Life magazine was held liable because its reporter used a hidden microphone while posing as a patient for an alleged faith healer in the healer's living room.[13] Such cases illustrate the potential application of the tort to investigative journalism without reference to the value of the information obtained.[14]

§ 22.03 APPROPRIATION OF NAME OR PICTURE AND THE RIGHT OF PUBLICITY

The Restatement has defined appropriation of an individual's name or picture as one of the four privacy torts.[15] The Restatement defines the tort simply as: "One who appropriates to his own use or benefit the name or likeness of another is subject to liability to the other for invasion of his privacy."[16]

Clearly, the dimensions of the tort are difficult to delineate. The tort applies to an unauthorized endorsement of a product, for example.[17] It does not, however, apply to journalistic articles or books about a person. Consequently, while it is tortious to, without authorization, indicate an individual has endorsed a product,[18] it is not tortious, and indeed protected by the First Amendment, to place a person's picture on the cover of a magazine and write a feature article about her.[19] Accordingly, an unauthorized book length biography with pictures does not constitute appropriation.[20] A gray area exists where courts must struggle with the limits of the tort. A calendar with unauthorized pictures would probably be held to constitute appropriation, but it is less clear whether a calendar of covers from a sports magazine with pictures of individuals would be protected.[21]

---

[13] Dietemann v. Time, Inc., 449 F.2d 245 (9th Cir. 1971).

[14] *See generally* John W. Wade, *The Tort Liability of Investigative Reporters*, 37 Vand. L. Rev. 301 (1984); Note, Lyrissa C. Barnett, *Intrusion and the Investigative Reporter*, 71 Tex. L. Rev. 433 (1992).

[15] *See generally* Sheldon W. Halpern, *The Right of Publicity: Commercial Exploitation of the Associative Value of Personality*, 39 Vand. L. Rev. 1199 (1986).

[16] Restatement § 652C.

[17] *See, e.g.*, Flake v. Greensboro News Co., 195 S.E. 55 (N.C. 1938).

[18] *See* Pavesich v. New England Life Ins. Co., 50 S.E. 68 (Ga. 1905), where the plaintiff's name and photo, as well as a falsified testimonial, were used by his insurance company for advertising purposes.

[19] *See, e.g.*, Cher v. Forum International, Ltd., 692 F.2d 634 (9th Cir. 1982), *cert. denied*, 462 U.S. 1120 (1983), where *Star* magazine was found not liable for publishing a story and interview with plaintiff Cher which had been obtained from another source, but *Forum* magazine was found liable based upon misrepresentations made about the plaintiff's endorsement (or lack thereof).

[20] However, truly intimate details might constitute another form of invasion of privacy. *See infra* § 22.05.

[21] *Cf.* Namath v. Sports Illustrated, 352 N.E.2d 584 (N.Y. 1976), where the defendant used a photograph of the plaintiff from its magazine in its advertising. The court allowed the use of the photograph based on the magazine's need to demonstrate its content and noted

In the context of celebrities, a separate but parallel tort, the right of publicity, generally exists.[22] The tort is virtually identical to the privacy-appropriation tort, but in many states may be inheritable so that heirs of a celebrity may sue for the unauthorized exploitation of the celebrity's identity.[23] In contrast, the privacy torts, including appropriation, are generally not inheritable. The right of publicity tort also recognizes that the interest being protected involves economic rather than privacy interests, although actions based on appropriation undoubtedly are, in many instances, concerned with economic interests as well.

Courts have struggled with what beyond a victim's name or picture should constitute appropriation, particularly in the context of the right of publicity. For example, one court found a defendant liable for the unauthorized imitation of Bette Midler's voice in an automobile commercial,[24] and another held that a product line of portable toilets named "Here's Johnny"[25] was tortious. Nevertheless, satirical imitations of an individual should not be tortious so long as it is clear that the victim is not performing or endorsing the product.[26]

Another issue of controversy includes a news depiction of an acrobatic stunt. In *Zacchini v. Scripps-Howard Broadcasting Co.*,[27] the United States Supreme Court held that broadcasting the entire act was not legitimate news coverage but rather an appropriation of the stuntman's exhibition rights. *Zacchini* illustrates the potential subtle line between news coverage of individuals and events and wrongful appropriation of a performance.[28]

---

that nothing in the advertisement implied that the plaintiff endorsed the defendant's magazine.

[22] *See* Haelan Laboratories v. Topps Chewing Gum, 202 F.2d 866 (2d Cir. 1953), where an exclusive licensee was found to have a "right of publicity" which entitled the licensee to enjoin and prevent other parties from using the licensed name.

[23] *See* Martin Luther King, Jr., Center for Social Change, Inc. v. American Heritage Products, Inc., 296 S.E.2d 697 (Ga. 1982), where the plaintiff prevented the defendant from making busts of King.

[24] Midler v. Ford Motor Co., 849 F.2d 460 (9th Cir. 1988), *cert. denied*, 503 U.S. 951 (1992). The court found against the defendant based on the distinctiveness of Midler's voice. Midler had also recently declined the defendant's offer to have her version air in exchange for payment.

[25] Carson v. Here's Johnny Portable Toilets, Inc., 698 F.2d 831 (6th Cir. 1983).

[26] *See* Waits v. Frito-Lay, Inc., 978 F.2d 1093 (9th Cir. 1992), where the court indicated that in order to be held liable for the imitation, the defendant's representation would have to be so realistic that individuals familiar with the plaintiff's voice would believe that the plaintiff performed it.

[27] 433 U.S. 562 (1977).

[28] "The broadcast of a film of petitioner's entire act poses a substantial threat to the economic value of that performance. . . . Petitioner does not seek to enjoin the broadcast of his performance; he simply wants to be paid for it." *Id.* at 575, 578.

§ 22.04 FALSE LIGHT

The privacy tort of false light has gained general acceptance through its inclusion in the Restatement.[29] The tort overlaps in large measure with defamation,[30] and one could question whether the differences that do exist warrant the independent tort of false light or whether the tort could have been extrapolated into defamation.[31]

The elements of false light which must be established by all plaintiffs include the defendant's (1) publicizing (2) false facts (3) that a reasonable person would object to. In the case of a matter of public interest, all plaintiffs (public or private) must in addition establish that the defendant acted with *New York Times* malice (knowledge of falsity or reckless disregard toward the truth).[32]

The element of publicizing requires that the defendant communicate the false facts to a substantial number of people. Publicizing constitutes a greater requirement than the comparable element in defamation, "publication," which only requires communication to one person other than the defined victim.

False facts that a reasonable person[33] would object to encompasses a broad category that includes, but is not limited to, defamatory statements actionable under defamation.[34] Defamatory statements must be seriously damaging to the reputation. For example, a Democrat may find it reasonably offensive to be publicized as a Republican, but the false statement would rarely be characterized as seriously damaging to the reputation.[35]

---

[29] The tort is said to have it beginnings in Lord Byron v. Johnston, 35 Eng. Rep. 851 (1816), where Byron was successful in stopping the circulation of a poem he considered poor and others claimed he wrote.

[30] Prosser noted that permitting a plaintiff's damage in an action for false light is "clearly that of reputation, with the same overtones of mental distress in defamation." William L. Prosser, *Privacy*, 48 Cal. L. Rev. 383, 400 (1960). See § 21.02, *supra*.

[31] "In many if not most cases . . . the false light is defamatory and an action for libel or slander will also lie." Renwick v. The News and Observer Publishing Co., 312 S.E.2d 405 (N.C. 1984), *cert. denied*, 469 U.S. 858 (1984). North Carolina has rejected the false light tort on the grounds that it is duplicative, along with Massachusetts, Minnesota, Ohio, and Wisconsin. *See generally* Diane L. Zimmerman, *False Light Invasion of Privacy: The Light that Failed*, 64 N.Y.U. L. Rev. 364 (1989).

[32] New York Times v. Sullivan, 376 U.S. 254 (1964). *See also* Anthony Lewis, MAKE NO LAW: THE SULLIVAN CASE AND THE FIRST AMENDMENT (1991). *See* Restatement § 652E. *See* Chapter 21.

[33] Particularly sensitive individuals receive no special consideration. Carlisle v. Fawcett Publications, Inc., 20 Cal. Rptr. 405 (Cal. Ct. App. 1962).

[34] *See supra* § 21.02 [A].

[35] *See* Schwartz v. Edrington, 62 So. 660 (La. 1913), where the plaintiff, a Democrat, signed a nominating petition. After finding out that the person whom he had signed to nominate was a Republican, the plaintiff desired to have his name removed from the petition. The circulator refused to do so and continued circulating the petition bearing the plaintiff's name. The defendant was found liable.

Docudrama embellishments or fabrications in magazine features are often best addressed by false light.[36] For example, an alleged true account of a pilot preventing a hijacking might include a fabricated, though perfectly innocent, romance between an unmarried pilot and unmarried passenger. While not defamatory, the falsehood may be offensive to either or both of the parties depicted. In *Cantrell v. Forest City Publishing Co.*,[37] the U.S. Supreme Court upheld a false light claim where the defendant authored a magazine article which described how the widow of one of several people killed when a bridge collapsed was devoid of emotion. In fact, she had not been interviewed and was not even present during the time the reporters were at her family's residence.[38]

The *New York Times* actual malice standard is required, based on the United States Supreme Court's decision in *Time v. Hill*,[39] for both public and private plaintiffs in a matter involving the public interest. This exceeds the constitutional requirement in defamation for private plaintiffs under *Gertz v. Robert Welch, Inc.*,[40] where only fault (generally interpreted to mean negligence toward the truth) is required. Instead, *New York Times* actual malice (knowledge of the falsity or recklessness toward the truth), which is only required for public figures in defamation,[41] is required of all plaintiffs suing for being portrayed in a false light. Some courts and commentators suggest *Time v. Hill* is obsolete because its imposition of the *New York Times* actual malice requirement for private plaintiffs preceded the lower threshold established for private figures in *Gertz v. Robert Welch, Inc.*[42] On the other hand, because only offensive and not defamatory falsity is required, perhaps the higher culpability should be required.[43]

---

[36] *See* Peay v. Curtis Publishing Co., 78 F. Supp. 305 (D. D.C. 1948), where a photograph of the plaintiff, a taxi driver, was used in a story about the dishonest practices of taxi drivers. *See also* Time v. Hill, 385 U.S. 374 (1967), note 39, *infra*.

[37] 419 U.S. 245 (1974).

[38] Despite her absence, the reporter wrote that "Margaret Cantrell will talk neither about what happened nor how they are doing. She wears the same mask of non-expression she wore at the funeral. She is a proud woman. Her world has changed. She says that after it happened, the people in town offered to help them out with money and they refused to take it." *Id.* at 248.

[39] 385 U.S. 374 (1967). In Time v. Hill, a family held hostage complained that a *Life* magazine account of a forthcoming play and movie described as "inspired" by the incident inaccurately portrayed the violence perpetrated against them.

[40] 418 U.S. 323 (1974).

[41] *See* defamation discussion, *supra* § 21.03.

[42] *See* Jones v. Palmer Communications, Inc., 440 N.W.2d 884 (Iowa 1989), where the court held that false light cases are subject to the same constitutional standards as defamation cases.

[43] *See, e.g.*, Lovgren v. Citizens First National Bank, 534 N.E.2d 987 (Ill. 1989), requiring the plaintiff prove at least reckless falsification in order to maintain a false light action.

Since the tort of false light overlaps with defamation to so large an extent,[44] some plaintiffs have attempted to characterize claims as false light rather than defamation to evade special damage requirements for slander or retraction statutes specific to the defamation tort. The trend is for courts to reject the use of false light to evade such defamation rules by labeling the action a false light claim.

§ 22.05 PUBLIC DISCLOSURE OF PRIVATE FACTS

Public disclosure of private facts constitutes the privacy tort most associated with the concept of privacy. The tort elements include (1) publicity of (2) private facts (3) highly offensive to a reasonable person which are (4) not of a legitimate public interest.[45]

The requirement of publicity requires, as with false light,[46] that the defendant communicate the private facts to a significant group of people.[47] This, as indicated previously, contrasts with the publication element in defamation which only requires communication to one person other than the defamed.

The requirement that the facts be private has been rigorously enforced by courts. For example, in *Sipple v. Chronicle Publishing Co.*,[48] the California court held that the public revelation in a newspaper column that a bystander who had grabbed the arm of an individual attempting to shoot President Ford was gay was not disclosing a private fact. The court reasoned that the individual's sexual orientation was known by many in the San Francisco gay community, despite the fact the man's midwestern parents were unaware of their son's sexual orientation until the columnist's report was distributed by the national media.[49]

Indeed, the United States Supreme Court has held in two cases that information in the public record and thus subject to inspection cannot be

[44] "The interest protected by this Section is the interest of the individual in not being made to appear before the public in an objectionable false light or false position, or in other words, otherwise than as he is. In many cases to which the rule stated here applies, the publicity given to the plaintiff is defamatory, so that he would have an action for libel or slander . . .. In such a case the action for invasion of privacy will afford an alternative or additional remedy, and the plaintiff can proceed upon either theory, or both, although he can have but one recovery for a single instance for publicity." Restatement § 652E cmt. b. *See supra* Chapter 21.

[45] Restatement § 652D.

[46] *See supra* § 22.04.

[47] " 'Publicity' . . . means that the matter is made public, by communicating it to the public at large, or to so many persons that the matter must be regarded as substantially certain to become one of public knowledge." Restatement § 652D cmt. a.

[48] 201 Cal. Rptr. 665 (Cal. Ct. App. 1984).

[49] The court also held it was of legitimate public interest to know the sexual orientation of the plaintiff and thereby negate stereotypes of gays. *See also* David H. Pollack, *Forced Out of the Closet: Sexual Orientation and the Legal Dilemma of "Outing,"* 46 U. Miami. L. Rev. 711 (1992).

actionable under the First Amendment.[50] In both cases, the identity of a rape victim was published based on police files, public records subject to inspection. The Supreme Court's decisions raise the question whether a prominent California Supreme Court decision, *Briscoe v. Reader's Digest Ass'n, Inc.*,[51] which held it tortious to reveal a citizen was convicted of a crime 11 years earlier, was correct because the information in that case was also public and available for inspection. On its face, this raises the unsettling but no doubt anomalous situation of former felons being afforded more privacy than recent rape victims. Probably *Briscoe* is now no longer valid, although it has been argued that publicizing old public records as in *Briscoe* could lead to liability while publication of newer records would not.

The private facts must also be highly offensive to a reasonable person. Consequently, a janitor's suit against the publisher of a college English textbook which reprinted a periodical article revealing that he had returned money that fell from an armored truck, causing him contempt and ridicule among his associates, was rejected because the information was not offensive.[52]

Furthermore, the tort is not actionable when revelation of the private facts is of legitimate public interest. In one case, for example, a magazine's revelation that a prominent child prodigy was living years later in squalid conditions and had a menial job was of legitimate interest in evaluating how society's child prodigies perform in life.[53]

Such cases illustrate the difficulty plaintiffs have in establishing the disclosure of private fact privacy tort. It must be emphasized that the tort, unlike defamation, makes communication of true facts subject to liability. Clearly the courts are concerned with limiting the scope of liability for truthful information. Within such limits, however, courts appear to accept invasion of protected privacy as a valid basis for liability even when the information disclosed is accurate.

---

[50] Cox Broadcasting Corp. v. Cohn, 420 U.S. 469 (1975); The Florida Star v. B.J.F., 491 U.S. 524 (1989).

[51] 483 P.2d 34 (Cal. 1971).

[52] Johnson v. Harcourt, Brace, Jovanovich, Inc., 118 Cal. Rptr. 370 (Cal. Ct. App. 1974).

[53] Sidis v. F-R Publishing Corp., 113 F.2d 806 (2d Cir. 1940). The case also illustrates how a former public figure may still be of legitimate public interest years later.

TABLE OF CASES

[References are to page numbers.]

[References are to page numbers.]

C

[References are to page numbers.]

D

E

F

[References are to page numbers.]

G

H

[References are to page numbers.]

I

J

K

[References are to page numbers.]

[References are to page numbers.]

N

O

P

[References are to page numbers.]

R

S

[References are to page numbers.]

T

[References are to page numbers.]

[References are to page numbers.]

INDEX

[References are to page numbers.]

A

[References are to page numbers.]

[References are to page numbers.]

[References are to page numbers.]

D

[References are to page numbers.]

[References are to page numbers.]

E

[References are to page numbers.]

[References are to page numbers.]

F

[References are to page numbers.]

G

H

I

[References are to page numbers.]

[References are to page numbers.]

L

M

[References are to page numbers.]

[References are to page numbers.]

[References are to page numbers.]

[References are to page numbers.]

[References are to page numbers.]

[References are to page numbers.]

[References are to page numbers.]

[References are to page numbers.]

S

[References are to page numbers.]

[References are to page numbers.]

[References are to page numbers.]

[References are to page numbers.]